° BARROW

ALASKA

° NOME

° DAWSON

CANADA
Journey

SITKA °

° EDMONTON

ALEUTIANS

N O R T H

SEATTLE °

A M E R I C A

Bertha Elliott
The Hickman
210

HAWAII

P A C I F I C   O C E A N

THE SOUTH PACIFIC
Tales of the South Pacific
Rascals in Paradise
Return to Paradise

JADALCANAL

SAMOA

NEW HEBRIDES
FIJI

TONTOUTA
° **NOUMEA**

TAHITI

NORFOLK

THE WRITER'S WORLD

KOREA Subject of a complete book   **BALI** Subject of a book segment

NEW ZEALAND

To Bertha~
From Joan
Christmas 1991

BOOKS BY
JAMES A. MICHENER

Tales of the South Pacific
The Fires of Spring
Return to Paradise
The Voice of Asia
The Bridges at Toko-Ri
Sayonara
The Floating World
The Bridges at Andau
Hawaii
Report of the County Chairman
Caravans
The Source
Iberia
Presidential Lottery
The Quality of Life
Kent State: What Happened and Why
The Drifters
A Michener Miscellany: 1950–1970
Centennial
Sports in America
Chesapeake
The Covenant
Space
Poland
Texas
Legacy
Alaska
Journey
Caribbean
The Eagle and the Raven
Pilgrimage
The Novel
The World Is My Home: A Memoir

with A. Grove Day
Rascals in Paradise

with John Kings
Six Days in Havana

The World Is My Home: A Memoir

AMERICA SEPTENTRION.

Anian R.

Grande Riuer

Nova Francia

Norombega

Terra Nova

C Rezo

Forest

MAR DEL

Comie

Tiguex

C Blanco

California

Totonna

Hispan nova

Virginea Florida

C S Romana

Hunds

Cuba I.

Spagnola

Anttilhas I.

I. Solis

MAR DEL

NORT I.

Aequinochialis

Quito

Cardinas

Manoa

ZUR

Hispanis

A Maximiana E

RI

Brasi

Formetabu

Pedro

Lima

Perou

L A

lia

Tropicus Capricornis

MERI DIO:

Margalas

R Lanetri

Mare Pacificum

Chili

NAL

Patagonum

Regio

AUSTRALIS

RA

Terra del Fago

Fr. Magellani

INCOGNITA

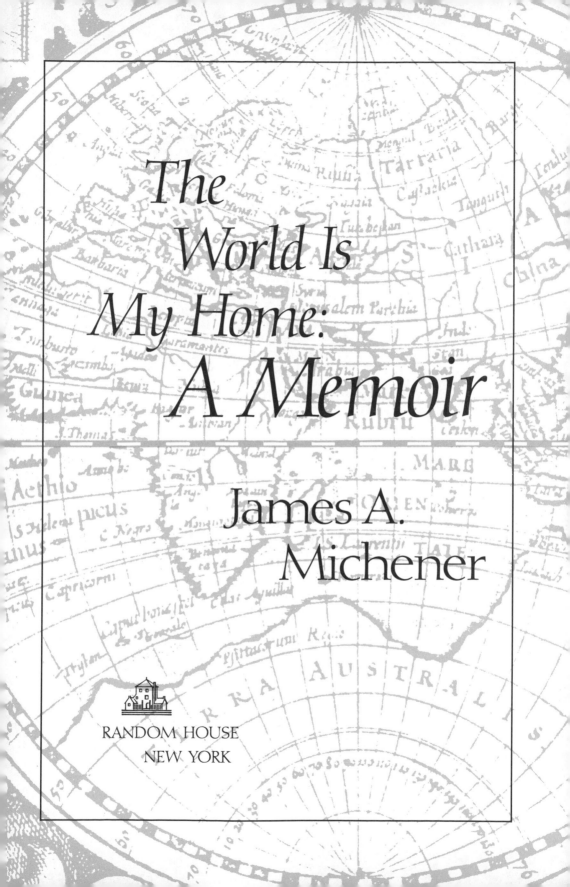

The World Is My Home: A Memoir

James A. Michener

RANDOM HOUSE
NEW YORK

The names and identifying details of a few individuals
and some place names have been changed to protect
the privacy of those involved.

Copyright © 1992 by James A. Michener
Maps copyright © 1992 by Jean Paul Tremblay

All rights reserved under International and Pan-American
Copyright Conventions. Published in the United States
by Random House, Inc., New York and simultaneously
in Canada by Random House of Canada Limited,
Toronto.

Grateful acknowledgment is made to
Sterling Lord Literistic, Inc.,
for permission to reprint excerpts from *Ross and Tom,*
by John Leggett (Simon and Schuster, 1974.)
Copyright © 1974 by John Leggett. Reprinted by
permission of Sterling Lord Literistic, Inc.

Library of Congress Cataloging-in-Publication Data

Michener, James A. (James Albert).
The world is my home : a memoir / James A.
Michener.—1st ed.
p.   cm.
ISBN 0-679-40134-2
1. Michener, James A. (James Albert), 1907–
—Biography.
2. Authors, American—20th century—Biography.
I. Title.
PS3525.I19Z476   1992
813'.54—dc20
[B]   91-18447

Manufactured in the United States of America

24689753

FIRST EDITION

This book was set in 10.5/13 Times Roman.

Book design by Carole Lowenstein

Contents

The World Is My Home: A Memoir

I

Mutiny

_T_HIS WILL BE a strange kind of autobiography because I shall offer the first seven chapters as if I had never written a book, the last seven as if that were all I had done.

I segregate the material in this way for two reasons: I want the reader to see in careful detail the kind of ordinary human being who becomes a writer and then to see the complex and contradictory motivations that enable him to remain one.

I have been impelled to attempt this project because of an experience that occurred eighty years ago when I was a country lad of five, and was of such powerful import that the memory of it has never left me. The farmer living at the end of our lane had an aging apple tree that had once been abundantly productive but had now lost its energy and ability to bear any fruit at all. The farmer, on an early spring day I still remember, hammered eight nails, long and rusty, into the trunk of the tree. Four were knocked in close to the ground on four different sides of the trunk, four higher up and well spaced about the circumference.

That autumn a miracle happened. The tired old tree, having been goaded back to life, produced a bumper crop of juicy red apples, bigger and better than we had seen before. When I asked how this had happened, the farmer explained: 'Hammerin' in the rusty nails gave it a shock to remind it that its job is to produce apples.'

'Was it important that the nails were rusty?'

'Maybe it made the mineral in the nail easier to digest.'

'Was eight important?'

'If you're goin' to send a message, be sure it's heard.'

'Could you do the same next year?'

'A substantial jolt lasts about ten years.'

'Will you knock in more nails then?'

'By that time we both may be finished,' he said, but I was unable to verify this prediction, for by that time our family had moved away from the lane.

In the 1980s, when I was nearly eighty years old, I had some fairly large rusty nails hammered into my trunk—a quintuple bypass heart surgery, a new left hip, a dental rebuilding, an attack of permanent vertigo—and, like a sensible apple tree, I resolved to resume bearing fruit. But before I started my concentrated effort I needed both a rationalization and a guide for the arduous work I planned to do.

As had happened so frequently in my lifetime, I found the intellectual and emotional guidance I needed not in the Bible, into which I dipped regularly, but rather in the great English poems on which I had been reared and many of which I had memorized. I was particularly impressed by the relevancy of the opening lines of that splendid sonnet which young John Keats had penned when he feared, with good cause as events proved, that he might die prematurely, which he did, at age twenty-six:

> When I have fears that I may cease to be
> Before my pen has gleaned my teeming brain,
> Before high-pilèd books, in charactery,
> Hold like rich garners the full-ripened grain . . .

How apt those words seemed because there was such a wealth of enticing subjects about which I wanted to write that my brain, too, could justly be termed teeming. But I was almost eighty years old; much of what I would like to do would have to be left unfinished. Since it took me about three years to write a long work, if I had thirty viable subjects the task would require ninety years. That would make me one hundred and seventy when I finished, and I could not recall any writers who continued working so long, not even the doughty ancients in the Old Testament.

I knew what my ambitions were, but I was doubtful about my capacity to fulfill them. Fortunately, I had in my teens memorized those powerful lines composed by John Milton when, in midlife, he was struck blind. I had recited them to myself a thousand times, and now they rushed back to give me the kind of strength that he had found:

> When I consider how my light is spent,
> Ere half my days, in this dark world and wide,
> And that one Talent which is death to hide,
> Lodged with me useless, though my Soul more bent
> To serve therewith my Maker, and present,
> My true account, lest he returning chide . . .

That ringing challenge, that determination to 'present my true account,' had defined the goal of my writing, so firmly grounded that it had become a permanent ambition. At Kent State I endeavored to render an unbiased account of the tragic killings, in South Africa an honest report of the racial injustices, in Israel the deadly duel between religions, in Hungary the unembellished facts about the revolution, and in Poland a factual account of that nation's long struggle.

Any explanation for my prolific output these last four years thus relies upon the precept of Keats, whom I think of as a gifted friend pondering his future, and upon the stern admonition of Milton, whom I regard as a mentor, encouraging me to give 'a true account.' Much of what I am about to say will sound improbable or even preposterous, but it is true. It can best be considered a hesitant *apologia pro vita mea,* and I hope it will be so received.

Between the years 1986 and 1991 I would write eleven books, publish seven of them, including two very long ones, and have the other three completed in their third revisions and awaiting publication. It was an almost indecent display of frenzied industry, but it was carried out slowly, carefully, each morning at the typewriter and each afternoon at research or quiet reflection.

This piling up of manuscripts was not entirely my fault and certainly was not engineered by me. My longtime and trusted editor in New York faced health problems that necessitated postponing work on one of my long books; uncertainties in the publishing business caused other delays; and my own confusion as to what I ought to do next added to the problems. But that I did this prodigious amount of work, keeping all things in order, there can be no doubt. There the manuscripts are, and this one was the most persistent. I wrote it in three different offices in three different states, on three different typewriters assisted by three different secretaries with their word processors, and three new editors with keen skills. This is a book that almost forced itself to be written.

One nagging question remains. Did the old tree get back to work producing apples only because the shock of the rusty nails reminded it of death? By analogy, did I labor so diligently because of my age and the approach of a time when I could work no more? Was I, like Keats at twenty-six, apprehensive of work-ending death?

I think not. I write at eighty-five for the same reasons that impelled me to write at forty-five: I was born with a passionate desire to communicate, to organize experience, to tell tales that dramatize the adventures which readers might have had. I have been that ancient man who sat by the campfire at night and regaled the hunters with imaginative recitations about their prowess. The job of an apple tree is to bear apples. The job of a storyteller is to tell stories, and I have concentrated on that obligation.

Because the Pacific Ocean would play such a dominant role in both my life and my writing, I will feel most at ease if I explain how I became intimately involved with that part of the world. I discovered it late, never venturing on it until the middle stages of World War II, when I was sent as a Navy lieutenant to the battle zone in the Solomon Islands northwest of Guadalcanal. As a Quaker I was exempt from actual military service but had declined to use my religion as an excuse to avoid the conflict because as a college professor of history I knew all too well that Hitler and Japan posed major threats to world civilization. I volunteered for the Navy.

But I must not cloak myself in glory. My draft board had decided to grab me for the Army, as one of the oldest men to be so taken, because the unsavory chairman of my local board despised me and saw a chance to do me in. I outsmarted him. Two days before he ordered me to report to Fort Dix I took refuge in the Navy on the principle that I would rather sail to war than march. Actually, I had served for some years in Europe as an ordinary seaman (honorary) in the English merchant fleet in the Mediterranean, a sea I knew intimately, and the Navy was glad to get me for that theater of war, but by the time I was in uniform it was obvious that we had our war in the Mediterranean well in hand, so I was shipped out to the Pacific.

A large group of us civilians who happened to be in Navy uniforms were placed aboard a battered troop transport of the Cape class, and since it was one of the sorriest ships in service it had been given one of the sorriest names, *Cape Horn,* that bleak and forbidding rocky tip at the far end of South America that terrifies mariners.

As a lieutenant who had been an enlisted man not long ago, I was berthed in an improvised cubbyhole on deck with two fellow would-be officers also fresh from civilian life. Bill Collins was a tall, rangy, relaxed bond salesman from Merrill Lynch's Los Angeles office who joined us with an openly stated objective of getting through the war as painlessly as possible. He had smuggled aboard six bottles of Southern Comfort, which he shared with his friends as if he were a Mississippi riverboat gambler softening them up for a scam. He was witty with an easygoing drawl, irreverent as to military custom, and delightful to be with, for his stories were never tedious or needlessly prolonged.

Our third member was a businessman from Detroit, Jay Hammen, a small, nervous fellow marked by an exceptional desire to please and a willingness always to do more than his share of any unpleasant task. His experience in the Michigan area had been wide and he had acquired a commonsense approach to life that was more serious and subdued than that of Collins. I liked both my mates, but what they thought of me I would never know.

Because the ships (such as destroyers and cruisers) that would normally protect a troop transport were in short supply, the *Cape Horn* was being dispatched to the far end of the Pacific totally alone, in a condition known with remarkable accuracy as bare-ass. We were very slow, an awkward ship that would be unable to adopt evasive tactics, and we had as our protection only one small, poorly manned and generally ineffective gun forward. Any determined Japanese submarine that latched onto our tail as we moved slowly westward could have had us for the picking.

We defended ourselves with two tactics. At unpredictable moments we would suddenly turn in some totally random direction, run a short distance, then turn again, and maybe even repeat the performance in less than half an hour. As Collins said in approving the tactics: 'We're still ducks but not sitting ducks.' And each evening, as soon as mere darkness had turned into total blackness, we threw overboard in one gigantic lump sum all the garbage collected during the previous twenty-four hours. A ship's officer on the bullhorn explained: 'We do this in a lump so that if a Jap submarine finds it tomorrow morning, it will not be able to deduce as it would from a strung-out trail the direction we were heading in. And we do it at sunset so we'll be as far away as possible by morning.'

He peppered us with instructions on his bullhorn, so that the most common sound on our long, dreary trip west was his stern command: 'Now hear this!' blasting at us ten or fifteen times each day. I remember vividly two of his early directives: 'In order not to leave a detectable trail floating on the sea for a Jap submarine to latch onto and track us down, you will throw nothing, I repeat nothing, overboard, night or day. If you are caught doing so, it's into the brig on bread and water. And if it looks to us as if you had been doing it on purpose to leave such a trail, you will be shot.' He also warned: 'Most of you have never before been on a ship. Do not, I repeat do not, sit on the protective railing that goes around the ship or act up when in its vicinity. Because I promise you that if you fall overboard our captain has orders to continue on course and not stop dead in the water so that a Jap submarine could pop us. I repeat, we will not stop or double back to pick you up.'

Well, a clown whom the three of us in our cubbyhole had spotted as a loudmouthed sailor did perch on the railing and did fall off. As warned, we sailed straight ahead, and as his anguished screams grew faint we felt that the war had overtaken us and was grappling for us with clammy hands.

The following descriptions of men aboard the *Cape Horn* are so preposterous that I hope someone who participated in the mutiny will step forward to substantiate what I am about to say; lacking that verification I can only affirm that what I state is sober truth, downplayed if anything, and with only the names invented.

Our ship was under the command of a Captain Bossard, an elderly man who so far as I knew had served many years in the merchant fleet. I have to be vague on the matter because during our entire trip of about a month, no one saw him, or heard him speak, or had any kind of communication with him. He remained in his cabin forward the whole time, and word passed, on what authority no one could say, that he was perpetually drunk. For this I cannot vouch.

It seems ridiculous for me to say that the Army colonel in charge of us was practically the same as the captain, but that is true. We saw him once and heard him only then, in a slurred series of seven or eight sentences warning us on how to behave aboard the *Cape Horn,* and then we never again saw him. The natural suspicion that he too was permanently drunk in companionship with the captain was easy to accept.

Gradually, in bits and pieces picked up from members of the disconsolate crew or from the four Marines manning the gun, we learned that the *Cape Horn,* always manned by these same two officers and staffed by the same crew, had made numerous trips like ours back and forth across the Pacific: 'A month out, a month back, that's six round trips a year, boring as hell.' Clearly the *Cape Horn* was not a happy ship, and Bill Collins who'd had broad experience in work conditions, predicted: 'In a mess like this, you can expect something bad to happen.'

The reader must remember that I had served happily in the British merchant fleet and had been an ipso facto member of the seamen's union. Also in my teaching I had always presented unionism in a favorable light, for I knew that in the early 1930s unions were necessary in America. But now I was to find myself facing one of its uglier aspects.

If we did not see anything of our two commanders, we saw more than enough of their unfriendly crew. They occupied a large, improvised deck cabin directly across from ours, and they were a surly lot, merchant mariners with many voyages under their belts before the war began, and bored beyond reason by having civilians like us in their way and asking stupid questions. I remember them as unkempt, dirty, mean-mouthed and slovenly in all they did; they were a difficult lot to like and I did not like them, nor did any of the other officers I knew or any of the enlisted men with whom we worked.

The reasons for our displeasure were palpable and ever-present. Four still rankle when I remember them. Because transport ships like the *Cape Horn* did sometimes have to sail into war zones where fighting was heavy, although most of them never came close, these civilian sailors received extremely large risk bonuses amounting, we were told, to something like $850 a month; in contrast our ordinary enlisted men, who took the same risks but had been sworn into military service, received only $21 a month. This outrageous discrepancy could never be ignored: 'If you volunteer to fight for your country, you get twenty-one dollars. If you dodge the draft and find a job on a ship you get eleven hundred fifty.' This last figure came from an authenticated case, and it became the standard comparison, but perhaps not a legitimate one, since unusual bonuses might have inflated it. But that the gross difference was a slap in the face of patriotism no one could deny.

The next two discrepancies were particularly blatant because they were thrown in our faces every day, especially in the faces of the three of us who lived opposite the civilians. They had their own mess with their own cooks and a larder of the best possible foodstuffs; this was their union's demand, which was strictly enforced by having one member aboard who reported on the meals, and he could create trouble if his men were not fed according to his demands. Our own food was an incredible swill such as Iowa farmers customarily feed their pigs. I have always been remarkably uncritical about my food; if there's enough of it I'm content and friends have described me as 'always a gourmand, never a gourmet.' But even I found the food that was being thrown at us totally unacceptable. At some meals not even the soggy bread was edible, and both Collins and Hammen, being more fastidious than I, refused even to report for meals; they would not go through that indignity. They preferred staying in our cubbyhole drinking Southern Comfort. Once when I asked Collins how he had been able to acquire so much of this drink when alcohol was so extremely scarce that it had to be jealously rationed, he explained: 'You must realize that the South won the Civil War. They're smarter than we are. They put so much sugar in the drink they succeeded in getting it classified as a dessert, not a whiskey.'

So there we were, underpaid volunteers and overpaid merchant sailors, sharing the same deck, our quarters not far apart, with us in uniform eating slops and them in civilian clothes eating steaks and chops and fresh vegetables. And not only did they eat such meals, they did so in quarters into which we could peek if we wished, and they cooked them in such a way that the aromas drifted over to us, whether we were peeking or not.

If Collins and Hammen were more or less indifferent to the food problem, they were even more outraged than I by another discrepancy. Because there were so many of us naval bodies aboard the *Cape Horn* and space for the storage of water was so limited, not only was the taking of showers prohibited, there being no way to pipe sea water into the system, but the available supply of drinking water was also restricted. We could actually go thirsty for a day at a time, and I could justify this because of the exigencies of wartime; besides, none of us was in any danger from prolonged thirst. If you were willing to stand in line long enough, you did get something to drink, and at meals there was coffee.

But here a new union rule came into play to protect the civilian sailor: he was guaranteed a certain number of showers a week and with fresh water. So a new indignity confronted us: while we thirsted for water we could not get, the men across the way were taking noisy showers, and lots of them. It was so infuriating that I still bristle when I think of it.

But what was most enraging was the fact that whereas we military personnel had to be extremely careful about showing any light in the darkness, not even the flash of a cigarette lighter, lest a prowling submarine spot us, the civilian sailors seemed not to be bound by this rule. They smoked as they wished, were careless about masking their portholes, and almost constantly provided illumination for any Japanese enemy to spot, even from a great distance. What was worse, the door of the big area across from us was often left wide open so that it was not a fragment of light that escaped but an immense shaft illuminating the entire deck.

'Ask them to close the door,' Collins called to me once when I was outside our quarters and he inside, so I crossed the deck and called in politely: 'Fellows, will you please watch the light?' It was the first time I had spoken to any of the civilians. It was an unpleasant experience because one of them snarled: 'Mind your own affairs, Boy Scout,' but he did slam the door shut.

Now I must digress briefly to explain why the light gave me such distress. When I was a student at a university in Scotland, I had shipped aboard a British merchant ship carrying coal to the Mediterranean and bringing oranges back to Scotland for the making of marmalade, and in long voyages, when I had what might be called honorary papers in the British merchant fleet—salary of one shilling for nine weeks' work—I learned a great deal about the sea. Because of the intense way I had studied my job I probably knew more about navigation than most of the civilian sailors on the *Cape Horn,* but what pertained directly to the present situation was that during the years when Great Britain was at war and the United States wasn't, several of my former shipmates had written to inform me of their adventures: 'The ship we sailed on together was lost to U-boats off Malta' and 'Our Captain Ried has had three ships sunk under him and survived every time. They're giving him a medal' and 'A lot of our boys have gone down. The German subs are dreadful.' Sea warfare had been painfully brought home to me in those letters.

Furthermore, among my duties prior to coming to the Pacific had been the task of being custodian of secret and highly restricted battle reports from various theaters of war—bombing runs by our planes based in Europe on targets like the Ploesti oil fields in Rumania and the heavy-water plants at Peenemünde in Germany and our naval battles at Coral Sea and Midway—so that I knew rather more about the horrors of war than most, and I took the conflict more seriously. I knew how many British and American ships had been lost to enemy submarines, German and Japanese alike, so I was not at all satisfied when the men across the way refused to darken their door immediately, and did so with ill grace when they finally did. My serious disaffection began at that point.

In the dark and gloomy dungeon that served as our mess deck, where hundreds of unwashed sailors collected three times a day to see what garbage would be served, I had for some reason I could not have explained taken notice of a Navy lieutenant somewhat younger than I—I was thirty-six, one of the oldest civilians drafted in World War II—a man who, in every action, seemed to command attention. He looked exactly like Lieutenant Colonel Oliver North, and as I came to know him, I fell completely under his spell.

I knew him only as Richmond, the city from which he came. He had been, I believe, the head of a construction company and, as such, was accustomed to giving orders and being obeyed. He had adapted easily to Navy life, which he seemed to enjoy, and he held himself and others to high standards of deportment. When, in the first days, there was crowding at the spots where drinking water was made available, he assumed command: 'All right, you men. Shape up. Form a line starting at that door. You, Lieutenant J. G., post yourself at the door and don't allow any more to crowd in until these men thin out.' I was impressed by the way Richmond handled himself and by his obvious desire to see anything with which he might be involved move forward in an orderly way.

The first words he ever spoke to me—I would not have intruded on him—were memorable: 'Lieutenant, who in hell is running this tub?' When I told him that rumor said there was a captain of the ship and a commander of troops, but that each stayed drunk in the captain's cabin, he growled: 'I can believe it.'

At a later meal he asked: 'Lieutenant, is this food as god-awful as I think it is?' and I said: 'Worse,' and together we made a quick verbal summary of the miserable swill we were being fed, with him designating certain abominations that he held to be indefensible: 'To serve what might be decent bacon, if handled properly, in big greasy chunks that look as if they had been cut into cubes by a bayonet is downright disgraceful. Coffee should be hot, no reason to serve it cold. Let me make the pancakes, I'll turn them out edible. And that slop they serve as stew with stuff you can't identify or chew, how in hell do they make it?'

On the evening after his first outburst, which covered many more complaints than those I now remember, he thanked Collins for the swig of Southern Comfort Bill allowed him, then joined us at supper, and by chance we were served that night some of the most dreadful stuff so far. No one could detect what it was, although some kind of meat scraps did surface through the rancid grease, and there were potatoes that were supposed to have been mashed, but beyond that it was anybody's guess. None of us could eat anything but the bread, which itself had been baked without salt and had no flavor.

We four left the table like all the others, hungry and outraged, but the ultimate insult hit when we reached the deck, for from the quarters of the civilian sailors came the infuriating odor of steak properly grilling and hot coffee properly brewed. In addition, the door to their quarters was wide open and casting a brilliant light out to sea.

Richmond was so infuriated that he whipped out his revolver, banged his way into the quarters where the steak was cooking and cried: 'Darken this door or I will shoot out that light!' And the civilians, seeing that he was the kind of loose cannon who would do exactly what he said, obeyed.

That spontaneous act launched the work that Richmond and I did together in our exploration of the ship. While Bill Collins and Jay Hammen started to collect, mentally, a list of grievances that our Navy men had to suffer, and they were real and numerous, the kind of offenses that any good captain would correct in a hurry or any commander of troops would insist be corrected, Richmond and I prowled all corners of the *Cape Horn* and satisfied ourselves on various points as he ticked them off: 'There is a captain in that cabin up there, but no one ever sees him. And there is an Army colonel in charge of us, but I've never seen him either. It's probable that they're both drunk all the time. And there is a set of four lockers below containing what has to be food supplies that can't be too putrid when they leave the refrigeration.' Then he had a sharp idea: 'Let's see what happens to the good food when it hits the galley,' and with his .45 moved into visible position and mine still well hidden, we went to where the cooks performed their indecencies. When we saw the disorder, the misuse of equipment and the visible uncleanliness, Richmond exploded: 'How can self-respecting Navy cooks tolerate this?'

It was a question that, in the phrase popular at the time 'opened up a whole new can of worms,' for the chief cook, or the fat, greasy man who claimed to fill that role, told us an amazing thing: 'We're not Navy. We belong to the ship. Have for years.'

Richmond dropped his voice and his challenging arrogance: 'Let's see if I have this straight. You're hired by the shipping company, not the Navy?'

'That's right.'

'But who selects the food in those lockers? Who pays for it?'

'What is this? Who in hell are you?'

Richmond's question seemed to me so appropriate that I thought the cooks might resist our inquiries, but Richmond had an effective answer: 'An officer of the United States Navy checking on what's been going on around here,' and he delivered these words in such a threatening way that the cooks snapped to attention.

'O.K. So who buys the food?'

'We do.'

'You mean the ship's officers?'

'I mean us. Him and me. We know the chandlers.'

'Just what I thought,' Richmond said, but since he'd given me no indication that he thought anything, he must have invented his conclusion at that moment. Then he added: 'I want to inspect those lockers. Now!'

'You can't do that, no matter who you are. Company property. Our property.'

Without raising his voice, Richmond placed his .45 on the meat-chopping block, keeping his right hand close: 'This says loud and clear: "Open those lockers!" ' and he said this with such an explicit threat that the cooks unlocked them, but Richmond prudently ordered me to stay outside with my gun: 'We don't want some clown closing the doors behind us.'

When he was finished with his inspection he took over my guard position and said: 'Prof, it's important that you see, too.' When I went inside I was shocked, for there hung fine cuts of meat while the smaller sections were filled with chickens and chops, and the shelves with firm vegetables.

When I came out I said: 'Enough in there to feed the whole ship the way we ought to be fed,' but the cooks, now obviously worried, protested: 'Hey, wait! That stuff's for the ship's crew. Union rules.'

'*All* that stuff?' Richmond asked and he accented the first word so heavily that that cooks knew he could no longer be lied to. So they offered the lame excuse that, yes, much of the food was for Navy passengers, but that it was being held back in case of an emergency. When Richmond asked: 'What emergency?' the head cook said: 'Just an emergency. Any kind.'

Looking at each of the cooks long and sharp, Richmond said: 'We'll be back,' and he left the strong impression that he meant what he said.

We went to a quiet corner of the *Cape Horn* and Richmond asked: 'What next?' We kicked this around for a while with my pointing out: 'From what I've read about ships at sea, let alone the formal Navy, it's pretty dangerous for anyone to start trouble. Mutiny and all that. The rules are quite stringent.'

'But isn't it obvious, Prof, that our government is paying this ship to transport us in reasonably decent style and that someone is taking that money and slipping it into his own pocket?'

'There are those union rules about feeding the civilian crew properly.'

This angered him: 'Damn it all, we saw enough food down there to feed an army. We could *all* be eating the way those others do.'

He suggested that I go back to my own quarters and write out the list of situations that proved the Navy was being shortchanged while he looked into the problem of why we didn't have enough drinking water. But when I went back to my tiny cabin I found that Collins and Hammen had decided they wanted no part of a formal protest—a prudent decision—because they could not foresee where it might lead. Collins in particular advised me not to go ahead.

I now faced a difficult situation, because I was well aware that for underlings aboard a ship of any kind to form a committee to compile complaints against the captain, no matter how inept he was, could be interpreted as mutinous, and for such an event to take place aboard a Navy vessel, and by juniors in uniform, would almost automatically warrant a court-martial with every likelihood of a guilty verdict with dire consequences. Of course, if a captain went berserk to the point of incapacity, his juniors were obliged to assume command, but even then, so dangerous was such a precedent that a board of inquiry would be convened and perhaps even a court-martial to verify that some intolerable condition existed that menaced the safety not of the sailors but of the ship.

Richmond and I were sailing in dangerous waters. For him the critical moment had been the drawing of his .45 in the cooks' area. For me it would be the actual drafting of the bill of complaint, and perhaps my danger was the greater, for in Richmond's case the only evidence against him would be the word of cooks who were probably stealing from the Navy, while in my case the piece of paper would exist as hard proof of my guilt.

Aware of the treacherous maelstrom into which I was navigating, I was about to withdraw when Richmond said: 'Prof, the only thing that makes sense in this crazy affair is that someone aboard this ship is stealing supplies and selling them ashore. And judging by what we aren't getting in the mess, that someone must be making a bundle.'

That did it. I felt strongly that if someone was defrauding not only our government and my Navy but also the civilians like me who were being dragged into the battlefields when assignment to the South Seas was abuse enough, I would blow the whistle. Moving to a quiet corner of the deck, I drafted a bill of some dozen particulars that Richmond and I could authenticate, but when I showed it to him he guffawed: 'Look at your Number seven. You complain that the food is inedible.'

'It is. You said so at the top of your voice.'

'But in your Number eleven you say: "And the servings are too small." '

When I took back my paper and studied it, I came up with what was for me a logical explanation: 'For the average sailor the food is inedible, you know that. But for the clowns who are so hungry they eat it anyway, there isn't enough.' I did not convince him, so with his help I redrafted my list, and when the war ended and I filed away my papers I saw that original list, with all my points. It still exists as an evidence of how close I came to an actionable military offense, especially since it could be proved that Richmond and I had backed it up with overt action, including his threatening the cooks with his .45.

It came to naught for a hilarious reason. When Richmond and I had our ducks in a row, the formal complaint neatly written out, we marched forward to where the ship's captain and the troop commander had their quarters to present our complaints, including one that Richmond had uncovered while I was doing my writing: 'Hell, Prof! They have enough water on this tub to give everyone all we need. What are they saving it for? To make just a little more cumshaw, I do believe.'

But when we reached our superiors' quarters they handled us in the most effective way possible: they simply refused to see us, or even open their doors to tell us to go away! We stood around for a while, looking silly, then backed off and never did confront the scoundrels.

But now we were angry, and although I cannot speak for Richmond, I know what I felt: 'Hell, if they want us to run the ship our way, we'll do it.' And marching behind Richmond I returned to the cooks' area and the big lockers, ordered the men to reopen the doors and again stood guard while Richmond went in and broke loose an ample supply of meats and vegetables and processed flour for the making of pancakes and biscuits. We then directed the cooks to prepare for the troops a supper as good as what the civilian sailors would be getting, and we also released several storage tanks of water. During the rest of our voyage we continued to feed the crew proper food, never making waves or doing anything conspicuously dramatic.

I have often wondered, in retrospect, why our two commanders allowed us to get away with this brazen behavior, and several explanations have come belatedly to mind. The two men had been on this run so many times before that they realized it was no big deal. Japan did not have enough submarines to waste them in these waters and against meaningless targets like our godforsaken bucket. Jittery civilians like Richmond and me might take battle-area rules against lights seriously, but old hands like the crew felt no urgency to follow them. The two commanders must have learned that Richmond had forced open the food lockers at gunpoint and that I had stood guard while he broke out the meat and vegetables, but if we kept things muted and refrained from making open trouble for them, they would make no trouble for us. Furthermore, if they were to arrest us and invoke a court-martial, they would be involved in months of unpleasantness that would have to reveal their mismanagement, so it was wiser to let things slide. Finally, the trip would soon be over and we two troublemakers would be gone, with our misbehavior forgotten and even dismissed. We had been no more than minor pests who would vanish with the breeze.

Eventually I reached the same forgiving assessment of the merchant marine sailors; they were toughened professionals required by the exigencies of the war to bother with a cargo of excited amateurs and their most important task was to protect their own turf: high wages, good meals, hot showers. Looking back, I realize they must have laughed at Richmond and me, but when I tell you later what military job Richmond would be performing on the landing beaches, you will realize that he was not the kind to take anything lightly; and when you learn of my brushes with death and the critical tasks I would be called upon to perform, and the evaluations of others I would be required to make, you will appreciate that I, too, was one who took obligations seriously. Richmond and I had found a ship in disarray, and had taken steps to rectify it, but I no longer have the intense animosity I originally felt toward the union men who saw life differently.

Toward the end of our zigzag journey, Richmond and I met one last time to discuss conditions aboard the *Cape Horn*. I asked: 'What are we going to do about the money that's being lost through fraud?' and he replied: 'No longer our worry. The food was important. The money? I used to think, when I was paid to check on clerks at the store, that money was made to be stolen—especially paper money in large amounts—by the bosses.'

He wanted to discuss more important matters: 'Prof, what kind of job can a man with your background do in the Navy?' and I explained: 'I'm to visit all the Navy air units to be sure they have the necessary manuals for the operation and maintenance of our airplanes, especially those on our carriers.'

'A paper pusher?'

'I've also been doing work on the secret reports that tell our pilots the structural limits of their planes. How fast and deep they can dive before their wings fall off.'

'Very useful to know, I should think.'

'And, very important, the capabilities of the Japanese airplane. My papers preach one doctrine over and over: "If you meet a Jap Zero one on one, turn around and scram like hell, because you're outnumbered. He can turn on a dime and shoot you down every time." In a dogfight those Jap planes are murder.'

'Then why are we doing so well?' he asked, and I told him about the other papers I had: 'If we put two of our planes up there against two of theirs we win every time. We interweave, I protect your tail, you protect mine. And oh boy! Our planes, because they are so big and heavy, can carry armor plate protecting pilot and fuel tanks. The light maneuverable Jap planes have no such protection, so sooner or later, with our superior strategies, down they go.'

He looked at me with respect: 'You mean you're sharp enough to conduct studies like that?' and I said: 'Hell no. Scientific geniuses make the studies. I just push the paper.'

He was extremely interested when I explained my three peripheral jobs: 'We spend a fortune trying to teach our airmen three things. Don't walk into propellers, which spin so fast you can't see them. Put your wheels down when landing. And if you lose your engine on takeoff, plow in straight ahead, no matter what lies there, because if you try to turn back to the airfield or the carrier, you'll crash everytime. Torque will spin you in to port.'

'You lose men that way?'

'Scores. Brightest men in America. They walk into propellers, mincemeat. They land with their wheels still up, burn to death. They try to get back to base with no power, they buy the farm.'

I'd talked enough, and when I asked him what duty he was headed for he told me of a military task about which I knew nothing: 'Beachmaster. Only a few of us. Terrific job, they station us carefully.'

'What is the job?'

'When there's an amphibious landing, the admiral in charge commands while the troops are aboard his ships, the general when they're on land. We've found at all the major landings that there's a fearfully critical period when things are piling up on the beach: men, mobile guns, supplies, the whole crap of modern warfare. If you leave it to chance there's total chaos. In those crucial minutes between the admiral letting go and the general taking over, the beachmaster takes charge. He understands the master plan, but he also knows that, in the crash of landing, things can go horribly wrong. Everything here, nothing over there. With a bullhorn and his nerve he sorts it out.'

When Richmond described the beach he would be controlling while

a barrage from the heavy guns of the offshore naval vessels flew overhead, sniper fire from the Japanese suicide squads smashed into Americans who had just waded in from the surf, and the incredible confusion
of a snafued amphibious landing imperiled everything, I could visualize
him at the center, .45 in hand, directing traffic and efficiently imposing
order upon the chaos.

'Sounds like a pretty dangerous job. If the Japs don't get you, our own
colonels will, if they think you're pushing them around.'

'No! Every officer has been warned: "In those first minutes the beachmaster is in control." '

'Will they believe it?'

'When I say it they will.' He said this without bravado, but I knew
he meant it, for he added: 'The beachmasters who lose their nerve don't
last long. They're accident-prone. The tough ones, who know what
they're doing, they never let control slip away.'

'But you can't train for a job like that. We don't have stateside areas
set aside for American battleships blazing away and Jap snipers gunning
at you, and the chaos.'

'Oh yes, we can train, Prof. We listen to reports from men who've
been there. We study photographs, even movies. And we imagine ourselves in the middle of it all.' He paused in the tropic night and concluded: 'No one is going to take my beach away from me. No one.'

I never saw Richmond after we landed at Guadalcanal, nor did I ever
hear from him or about him, but I have often wondered on what
congested tropical beach he led the American forces ashore and staked
out the vital areas and moved amid the chaos establishing order. I have
prayed that he was one of the beachmasters who survived, and I believe
he might have been, because he would have attacked the perilous job
with every intention of doing so.

The manner in which Bill Collins, Jay Hammen and I finished our trip
across the Pacific in the *Cape Horn* was so incredible that I hope one
of my former partners is still alive to verify what I am about to report,
for the events of that final night changed the rest of my life.

We finally dropped anchor off the southern end of Espiritu Santo, the
big, brutal island southeast of Guadalcanal, and by an odd chance I
spent my first night in the South Pacific on a ship anchored not far from
the dock that served the copra plantation of the Frenchman Aubert
Ratard, whom I would come to know so favorably in the long months
ahead. He had among his Tonkinese workers a tough, conniving woman

who bore the surprising name of Bloody Mary, and I would often surmise in years to come: 'She must have been in her hut that night, staring out at the *Cape Horn* while I was aboard staring through the night in her direction. If so, it was a spiritual meeting that would bear wondrous fruit.'

Our long trip was ended, but since none of us had yet seen either our captain or our troop commander, Collins, Hammen and I strolled toward their quarters to bid them an insolent farewell, because we did want to see what kind of men would allow a bunch of civilian draftees to take their ship away from them and make no complaint about it. But even this last visit was frustrated, becuase the officers did not show, nor could we ascertain where they might be.

Collins, as a major participant in a civilian business operation in Los Angeles, was so disgusted with this unprofessional behavior that he forced his way into the captain's office, and there the three of us lounged, recalling events of the tedious voyage. And as Bill listened to one of my reports on how Richmond had behaved with the cooks, his hands idly shuffled some papers on the captain's desk and he came upon a form on which orders sending naval personnel to their next assignments were written. Without giving it much thought he said: 'Michener, in our conversations you've often mentioned how you love to travel. I'm going to see to it that you get your chance.'

He then typed out a set of orders for me that gave me authorization to travel pretty much as I wished throughout the military zones of the South Pacific on what he designated as 'tours of inspection.' He then rummaged about some more, found a stamp that looked official, hammered it onto my new orders and signed them 'Admiral Collins.'

It was those orders, augmented later by a battery of more legitimate ones, that enabled me to get started on my exhaustive exploration of the South Pacific. I used Bill's authorization to get to exotic places like Norfolk Island, where remnants of the *Bounty* mutineers settled when they fled Pitcairn, and wild Pentecost, where daring black men dived from the tops of extremely tall trees, stout vines tied about their ankles to break their fall just as their heads were about to crash, and mysterious Malakula of the headhunters. But mostly I used it in the early days to travel those ominous islands of The Slot where the great night sea battles were fought between an aggressive Japanese force and a defensive American Navy striving to hold its own after the debacle at Pearl Harbor. Rarely has a forged document been put to livelier use.

Years later, during a visit to Los Angeles, I met Collins again. Once more he was at Merrill Lynch. Once more he was the free-and-easy gentleman noted for his relaxed manner and his fondness for Southern

Comfort. We laughed about the disgraceful *Cape Horn* and thought of Jay Hammen back in Detroit at his old stand. As we parted, Bill said: 'You certainly used those papers we fixed up for you that night,' and I thanked him again.

In my thirties I was a man of middle height, middle weight and so average in all respects that wherever I went through the years I would come upon other men who looked exactly like me. The confusion caused by such resemblance was sometimes embarrassing. Friends would say: 'I saw you the other day in Omaha. How come?' and I would not have been there in years. Occasionally I would come upon one of those doubles and would be astonished to see how identical his appearance was to mine. It was uncanny, but it also prevented me from ever thinking I was anything special.

Up to this time I had done nothing out of the ordinary. I'd held several jobs, had always retained the good opinion of my employers, had never so far as I could recall ever caused anyone any trouble. I paid my taxes regularly and always voted, Republican at first because everyone in my rural Pennsylvania hometown voted that way, then Democratic when I moved out to the more liberated political climate of Colorado. When I sailed on the *Cape Horn* I didn't realize that I was on my way to a divorce, my wife having joined the Army when I went into the Navy. The prolonged separation that followed as we served in vastly different parts of the world had altered us so radically that when peace finally arrived, reunion was impossible, for we scarcely knew each other.

I was in general soft-spoken but prone to get overexcited by any important social issue and as a result I'd had my nose broken three times by butting in where I was not wanted. As a friend explained: 'Jim sometimes gets caught speaking when he should be listening.' Although I participated in numerous fights, I cannot recall any that I won.

When a basic principle was involved, as in the case of the shameful conditions aboard the *Cape Horn,* I would dig in, and long after others had surrendered the fight I would still be there flailing away. At such times I could become rather irresponsible, unwilling to quit or even to see the damage I might be doing myself. I did not surrender easily, but that characteristic, which manifested itself on numerous occasions, was not a sign of my moral courage; it was more an innate desire to see the thing that someone else might have started brought to a sensible conclusion. I was never afraid to be humiliated or loath to bear the consequences of my stubbornness or stupidity.

Such behavior was not likely to produce many friends, nor did I ever have any close ones. Men chose me on their side when teams were being put together more for my stability than for any dazzling quality of leadership. I was content to work alone, study alone, travel alone, and think alone, but those choosing sides realized that I could also be a very strong team player. I did cherish the camaraderie that came with battles well fought or exciting adventures shared, and I think those who worked with me discovered early that I enjoyed talking about shared experiences and organizing in my oral reports what happened to whom and why. I did not make myself the hero of these narratives, but focused rather on the group experiences.

I realized that I had been allowed a much wider involvement in various forms of human activity than other men my age, having run the gamut from extreme poverty to the widest possible academic travel, and this had meant hard work in a variety of jobs, deep study of the arts, and intense involvement in education. I had attended eight universities and colleges and had successfully taught at almost every level, from first grade to postdoctorate classes at Harvard.

But I was far from a pedant and had enjoyed comparable positive results in American business to which, when my wartime duties ended, I fully expected to return. I also supposed that I would spend the rest of my life doing nothing spectacular both before and after my retirement at age sixty-five.

I was, in short, an average American male whose personality and intellectual assets and liabilities evened out, some favorable, some not. Had things gone wrong in our mutiny and had I been incarcerated for a long term, few would have noted or regretted the fact, and those who did would properly have said: 'It's a shame, but he was probably headed that way from the beginning, because he never really fitted in. Not much was lost.'

A note on financial assets and liabilities: at age forty I had accumulated savings of only eight hundred dollars, with little prospect of ever increasing that amount significantly. All the personal property I had accumulated prior to the war had been stolen from me by vultures who prowled New York City in the 1940s buying up the household goods of men and women who were being drafted, and then refusing to pay even one penny because they knew that the owners, now in uniform on far-off battlefields, would not be able to track them down or enforce payment. In this despicable way I had stolen from me a splendid set of plain oak furniture made by one of the finest firms in North Carolina, and my collection of eighteen treasured Baedeker guidebooks, two losses that rankle to this day. I was not at age forty what you would call an all-time winner, and I had revealed no aptitude for writing other than academic jargon.

II

Tour

WHEN I AM ASKED what I did during my stint in the Navy in World War II I have several options. If a gang of veterans is sitting around lying about their heroics, I can chip in a few real-life accounts of night missions or daytime flying through that incredible semipermanent front that hung between Guadalcanal and Espiritu Santo, surviving plane crashes and a few other goodies. But if I want to relate precisely what it was like, I prefer to tell of a duty tour I took during the later stages of the war.

Admiral William Halsey had been directed by Washington to look into a curious affair on the easternmost edge of his South Pacific command, and he, aware of my knowledge of the islands, had bucked the problem along to his much loved Uncle Billy Calhoun, admiral in charge of 'the train,' a military term referring to the vital supply line that ran from Detroit to San Francisco to Hawaii to Noumea to the battlefront. Those of us who worked for Uncle Billy believed that he had played a major role in smothering the Japanese with matériel, and the fighting admirals agreed.

When Calhoun summoned me he said: 'They tell me, Michener, that you know the islands. I want you to take a swing and find out what's happening on Bora Bora. We're having a lot of trouble with the enlisted men.'

Being somewhat familiar with problems like this, I said: 'When they've been on an island for a long time and think we've forgotten them, they get restless and want to get back home.'

'No,' Calhoun said. 'Trouble with this crowd is, they don't want to go home, and when we try to send them, they raise merry hell.'

'Never heard of such a thing.'

'Nor anybody. Now get out there and find out.'

I was then passed along to one of his aides, Commodore Richard Glass, nephew of Carter Glass, the distinguished Virginia senator, and one of the few commodores in our Navy. In this century the time-honored rank of commodore, equal to brigadier general in the Army, had fallen into disuse but had been revived so that a naval officer who had to share an island or command post with the Army, Marine or foreign brigadier could have rank equal to that of his opposite number.

Glass was almost an archetype of the ideal Navy man: tall, thin, handsome, with an easy manner and a strong reputation for getting things done. When he heard about my mission, he added one additional job before passing me along to his aides: 'We've had several reports from the queen of Tonga saying that things are getting a bit out of hand on her island. She wants our help in cleaning up. Drop by and see what's the matter.'

Commodore Glass's staff had three other jobs for me, and the executing of these would carry me pretty well around the eastern theater of the Pacific war, the part that was now quiescent. 'When there was danger of invasion, we had no problems,' the staff said. 'Now that everything's relaxed, there's hell all over the place.'

One aide said that on Samoa, which was then British, there was an American general who was giving a bit of trouble. It seemed that he was building a road across the island without permission from either the British government or our own authorities: 'Road doesn't seem to go anywhere. Cloudy picture. Tell us what's going on.'

There was also the problem of the American official in Papeete, the capital of Tahiti, about whom there had been negative reports: 'But these are so ridiculous we won't prejudice your own investigation by letting you see them. But do look into this matter of the top-secret code books.'

The final mission was a humanitarian one: 'On the remote atoll of Pukapuka, far from Tahiti, there's a beachcombing American writer, broken-down chap, married an island girl and all that—three kids, maybe five or six. Natives have reported by radio he's been using the needle and is dying. Fly up there and see what's to be done.'

'What's his name? Maybe I know him.'

'Robert Dean Frisbie. Those who know tell us his books are first class, but nobody's seen any of them. Anyway, we can't leave an American citizen dying on some atoll. Hurricane could sweep him away.'

As I left the last meeting I thought: This is a pretty full plate for a mere lieutenant, but the other officers know that what Halsey said was true. I do know these islands and maybe I can bring some sense to these matters. But the situation that intrigued me especially was the one on Bora Bora, where enlisted men were about to mutiny because they were being returned home as heroes. That really merited looking into.

But an even more interesting case presented itself when a legal officer of high rank took me aside for a briefing: 'Michener, I want you to read this court-martial record, take no notes and forget it when you're finished. Deals with a messy affair on Matareva,* and on your way back, depending on how you schedule your flights, we want you to visit the island and let us know, top secret, what you think happened.' He then handed me a rather thick file, which dealt with the court-martial held recently in Noumea, the capital of the French island of New Caledonia, which served as Halsey's headquarters even though he was usually stationed far to the north.

The case involved a hush-hush affair on a remote island about which I had heard only whispers: 'What in hell happened on Matareva?' we had asked one another, and the only sensible answer we got was: 'The whole damned place went ape.' Now I would find out, but as I read about the unbelievably sickening background, I felt dizzy, and was relieved when the account of the actual court-martial conjured up a more normal scene with the five officers behind a table with the crisp brigadier general of the Marines in charge, and the court reporters at their dictation machines. I could also visualize the two dozen accused, all young and trim in the laundered uniforms to which they were entitled when being tried, lest they give an unfairly poor impression in battle-worn gear. But I could not visualize any of them giving in open court the testimony they apparently had given.

I read transfixed, and when the file had narrowed to only a few pages I was bewildered: How can this disaster be cleaned up in the remaining six pages? A hundred loose ends cried out for testimony! And then I came to an ending for which no one could have been prepared: the young Marine general had taken it upon himself, without consultation

*Matareva is an imaginary island. It has been given a fictitious name to protect the privacy of those involved in the real-life military tragedy.

with his other judges, to halt the case with the bald announcement 'The trial is over. The twenty-two accused will be dismissed from the service and shipped out this night on any available transport. And no one will speak abroad of what has happened in this courtroom.'

When I asked my briefing officer what had happened next he said: 'As you learned from the file, it was one of the worst cases the Marines have ever faced, maybe *the* worst. So their young general acted prudently when he halted the trial to keep even worse testimony from getting onto the record.'

'How did his superiors who ordered the trial feel about that?'

'Bull Halsey had wanted those Marines scorched, and when the young general let them off the hook, he really blew his stack. I was there: "Get me that son-of-a-bitch, now!" and when the general stood before him, Halsey raved: "I'll have you busted! You'll leave this area in disgrace." Young fellow never flinched, stood straight and said: "I knew you'd be furious, so I typed out what the next line of testimony would have paraded before the world. Would you really want this displayed in the record?" Halsey read it, said not a word, passed the paper along to me. When I looked up, Bull had his right arm on the general's shoulder and was walking him slowly toward the door, where he said: "Anderson, if you had permitted that trial to proceed I'd have chewed your ass for having allowed that sewage to get into the Navy record," and we've never heard another word about Matareva. But rumors have filtered back to Washington and they want a coded report, just to complete court records. Stop by the island and give me something that I can forward . . . but clean it up.'

With that handful of commissions I was driven out to the airfield at Tontouta, where I hooked up with a tough crew of four who had flown their miracle DC-3 to all parts of the southeastern war zone: New Caledonia to Tahiti. I had ridden with them often and had complete faith in their skill to find and land upon the most remote islands. I also had more than adequate reason to rely upon the great DC-3, workhorse of the world. I had little confidence in some of the other planes I had flown in, especially the tricky B-26s, which tended to go down on takeoff if improperly balanced, but the DC-3s I could depend on to fly me anywhere and get me safely back.

I was aware as I flew eastward that I was heading away from the war zone, but recently I had seen a lot of war and flown as a passenger on various bombing missions, so I was entitled to a respite. Also, I had fallen victim to what my managing officer in BuPers, the Bureau of Personnel that assigned officers to jobs, called 'the menace of the card punch.' The records and abilities of all officers had been entered on IBM cards containing many little boxes into which operators working clever machines punched holes, showing what the officer in question could do; mine apparently showed among a good many other things that I had a master's degree in history, so when an electric beam probed its way through my card and ten thousand others it alerted BuPers to the fact that they had a trained historian way out on a tropical island, precisely where he was needed. Result? After I had completed one full tour of duty, some of it quite demanding, I was approached by a courteous rear admiral who said: 'Michener, without question you have enough points to get out of this war zone and pick up a good assignment stateside. But we have an important job for which you seem ideally qualified. Your aviation duty has made you familiar with most of the islands, more than anyone else we can find. We need a historian, someone with brains and a sense of military movement, to start compiling a history of the Navy in these waters. Samuel Eliot Morison of Harvard will be your boss, and you'll be asked to fly to every corner of our theater. It means another full tour of duty out here, but we'd be grateful—Halsey, Morison, the crowd—if you'd consent.'

No one then, or up to now, knew why I was prepared to accept so rapidly, but I had two good reasons: I had recently had a refulgent experience on the airstrip at Tontouta in New Caledonia which I will describe later, and this made me eager to revisit as much of the South Pacific as possible; secondly, I had reason to suppose that my marriage might be dissolved, so that I really had no burning desire to get back home. I was prepared to accept another tour of duty, but fortunately I did not reveal that fact immediately.

In order to sweeten the invitation, which the admiral admitted was just a bit out of line, he uttered words of purest gold: 'Now, Lieutenant, if you take this job you realize that I will issue you permanent orders authorizing you to travel to whatever parts of our command you judge you must visit in order to complete your work,' and then he added the words that caused a Navy man's heart to skip a beat: 'Fagtrans and Per Diem.' The first meant First Available Government Transportation; the second that I would be able to present my travel orders and documentation to any pay officer, no matter where I was, and receive immediate cash payment for my living expenses. An imaginative young man with a yen for travel who had a Fagtrans and Per Diem in his pocket could see a good deal of the world.

I accepted the additional assignment, which was why Admiral Halsey could say that he had heard I knew a good deal about the South Pacific.

I would spend two full tours of duty, nearly four years, in the tropics, the first two often in battle areas, the last two in paradise.

At dusk on the day my trip began we reached the Fiji island of Viti Levu, which I had more or less made my headquarters during long spells, and as we rode into town from the airport I saw again those sights that had inspired me years earlier. There were the green fields; there among the mountains rose the peak shaped exactly like a human finger—Joske's Thumb, it was called—guardian to the capital town of Suva.

How enchanting that town was to those of us who had been fighting on islands like Guadalcanal and Bougainville with never an amenity. Here were streets with lights, crossroads where black traffic officers stood six feet four inches high topped by gigantic erect headdresses that made them tower even more. Dressed in khaki kilts, they directed traffic with the grace of ballerinas. Here were streets filled with Indian shops and Fijian shoppers, with now and then a group of colonial Englishmen who were managing the supplies of war from little offices in the center of town, as well as British military officers from warships lying in the harbor for refitting. At what I took to be the south end of town and somewhat beyond the city limits were sights that still charmed me. First, there was the great flat field where rugby matches were played, originally between a local Fijian team and one from any visiting ship, but they had to be stopped because the Fijians were so enormous and played with such abandon that they not only defeated the visitors but dismembered them. Now cricket was played instead, and with the same wild delight.

On the hill and beyond the field rose Government House, occupied in those years by a rising official who would later be the distinguished governor-general of Hong Kong. He had an American wife, who proved helpful in that period when many American officers like me either passed through on government business or holed up in the local hotel for weeks on end. They were a gracious couple who served the Allies well, and I used to see them riding in state as they came down from Government House and into town. They reminded everyone that Great Britain still ruled Fiji and all similar islands and would continue to do so for the next hundred years. At least I thought so, for when the G-G rode past in his Rolls-Royce I felt curiously secure.

And then came the target of any trip I would ever make to Fiji: one of the memorable hotels of the world, not majestic and not particularly spacious, but a haven to all who crossed the Pacific on tourist ships or who now came in by airplane. It was the Grand Pacific Hotel, famed

G.P.H. of the travel books, a big, squarish building of several floors, with a huge central dining area filled with small tables, each meticulously fitted with fine silver and china, bud vases, and a facing porch leading out to the lawn that went down to the sea. It was grand, and it certainly was pacific, and the barefoot Indians who served the meals had a grace that few hotels in the world could offer and none surpass.

G.P.H. was my home away from home, the place where I would hear a hundred stories that would serve me well in later years, the place where I got to know the silly foibles and the tremendous internal strength of Englishmen who served overseas, the place that was the setting of one of the great love stories of my life. How glad I was to be back in this grand place at the start of my travels.

During the war years the American government must have subsidized the G.P.H. in some secret way, because any American officer on travel duty was allowed to reside there for as long as he liked for one pound a day, three excellent meals included. Since that was less than $4.85 a day, the management must have shuddered when they saw a free-loader like me sign the register saying that I'd be around for a week or two. However, my official position enabled me to do the hotel a good turn now and then, like finding cargo space on our planes for things they needed, and in time I was greeted by the hotel personnel as an old friend.

On this night when I checked in I found myself facing a cheery young woman of about thirty whom I had not seen before, and when I asked who she was she said with no hesitation: 'Laura Henslow, from Christchurch in New Zealand.' Since she had never heard of me, I had to present my travel orders before I could get the special rate, and she checked their authenticity with a manager who, when he saw my name, came out to greet me. He assured her that I was legitimate, and since I had nothing better to do and she was so congenial, I remained by the desk talking with her for some time.

She had worked in two different New Zealand hotels, one on the cold South Island, one on the warm North, and had been urgently sent for to bring some order into the G.P.H. business systems, which had been overtaxed by war traffic. She was obviously a clever woman and so attractive that I was surprised when I learned she was not married. 'You'll not remain single long,' I prophesied and she replied: 'I've had my chances, but I do prize my freedom.'

Since it would be some time before my plane would be free to carry me out to Bora Bora, I had four or five days in Suva, which meant three great meals a day, fine gin and tonics at night and good conversation. In the daytime, starting at two, I would go to see my good friend Pandit

Karmasingh, who owned the local movie theater, where those wonderful Indian films that ran four and a half hours played. I had once done him a small favor and he adopted me, introducing me to Indian life in the islands and to Indian drama in his theater, which he allowed me to enter free whenever I wished.

An Indian film was an art form as bizarre and rigid in structure as a Forty-second Street burlesque: it had a dramatic line involving terrible conflicts, fights, betrayals and tearful reconciliations, but at some point in the film it was obligatory to insert either a very long classical dance or a scene from one of the ancient epics with gods and demons all over the place.

One of Karmasingh's favorite films, which I liked so much I saw it three times in the course of my various visits, focused upon the first woman in India to become a lawyer; and in her maiden case she is called upon to defend the very handsome man who wooed her and left her at the altar while he ran off with another woman, a slut if I ever saw one. When this other woman is found dead under suspicious circumstances he is brought to trial as the killer. It took one hour for the fledgling lawyer to decide whether or not to take the case, and you could see that she went through hell as she tried to make up her mind. The trial itself required two hours, one of which was taken up by her impassioned address to the jury, in which she said 'Gentlemen of the jury' in English at least fifty times. The rest of the dialogue was in Hindi, of course, but Mr. Karmasingh had placed a boy beside me who spoke English and kept me informed as to what was going on, although much of the time he was as bewildered as I. I started wondering: How are they going to get the gods in this one? The solution was this: as she searches for the one plea to the jury that will save her faithless lover, she falls asleep and in a dream sequence in which the gods participate they help resolve her problem; she gives a marvelous peroration, saves her man, and at the conclusion walks off into the Indian sunset with him. She was an excellent actress, looked fine in a lawyer's wig, and convinced me of her lover's innocence.

On this trip I saw only one Indian film, because the next day I was invited to an affair in the center of town. For the first time in Fijian history, a locally born Fijian young man, tall and broad and handsome with a massive head of hair and very white teeth, was being ordained as a Catholic priest. As a schoolboy he had been a star athlete, a first-class scholar at the seminary, and a devout young man in the final studies that entitled him to enter the priesthood. His accomplishments were the pride of not only the Catholics but also the Protestants of Fiji,

for it reminded the young black men of their churches that they too
could enter the Church of England priesthoods and Methodist minis-
tries. Robert Derrick, my friend in Fiji who had once been a Protestant
missionary there, took me to the ordination, where I saw a boy carrying
a sign which read CONGRATULATIONS FATHER BEGA. When I read it
I received a lesson from Derrick in the damage that very bright people
can often inflict: 'The name's pronounced Mbenga. One of the earliest
London missionaries fancied himself an amateur philologist who decided to give the world its only sensible system of spelling. Since in
Fijian *b* was always preceded by *m,* he said: "Let *b* stand for *mb,* and
since *g* is always preceded by *n,* let *g* be read *ng."* So what you see on
that sign is really Mbenga.' He told me that the all-wise one had also
decided that since Fijian did not use the letter *c,* it would be used to
stand for *th,* which meant that Fiji's great black leader who pronounced
his name Thakambau, had to spell it Cakabau, to the utter confusion
of all who followed.

The service was memorable, for flowers flooded the altar and a marvelous Fijian choir with voices like bass drums and tubas sang majestically. Father Bega seemed to me the ideal young man to have broken
the tabu against black clergymen, for he had all the outward attributes
to recommend him, and if, in addition he possessed an inner devotion,
he was going to provide Fiji with an admirable priest. Robert Derrick
said he felt sure he would.

The service ended with a homily by a bishop with a name like Cald-
well or Dawson, an elderly man who announced that his see was the
entire South Pacific and that he was going from here to visit his churches
in Samoa; he spoke movingly of how overjoyed he was personally to be
in attendance when a Fijian young man was taken as a priest into the
church he governed: 'May he be the first of many, for he symbolizes the
fact that the Holy Church is increasingly a part of our island life.' I liked
the bishop intuitively and understood why his fatherly approach had
won the hearts and support of people throughout his scattered see.
When I met him after his brief comment, I told him that I too was flying
east to Samoa and invited him to ride with me, but he said: 'Alas, I go
to British Samoa, you to American, so I cannot fly with you. However,
the two islands are only a few miles apart, so perhaps we shall meet after
all.'

As I was speaking to the bishop I saw that Laura, the New Zealand
woman from the hotel, had also attended the induction of Father Bega
and now wanted to congratulate him. But since thirty or forty huge
Fijian women wished to do the same, she was quietly leaving the line,

when he saw her and raised his left fist with his thumb extended to acknowledge that he had seen her; when he did this his hand looked exactly like Joske's Thumb, the guardian rock of Suva, and I judged this to be a very good omen.

The flight to Samoa was so storm-tossed that I was relieved when we dropped very low, almost touching the waves, where we found stable air for a turn to the north and a fishhook back to the important American base at Pago Pago (pronounced Fijian style, Pango Pango). I had of course read Somerset Maugham's finest short story, 'Rain,' which depicted the tropical village to perfection, and I believed I understood both Sadie Thompson and Reverend Davidson; certainly I felt at home in Pago and I started early on the first morning trying to find some clue as to what had been happening at the American base in British Samoa. When not much information was forthcoming I realized that the brass was not going to confide much to a mere lieutenant, so I decided to wait till I reached British Samoa, a New Zealand mandate, to make my inquiries.

On any trip to a new island I scheduled two or three days for an exploration. And this allowed me to attend in a village near Pago Pago a meeting of the high chiefs—nine or ten in a total island population of about twenty thousand—and while listening to the chiefs' orators, men who would report with great fury what their superiors were thinking, since the chiefs themselves did not orate, I had my first taste of the extremely bland island liquor, kava, a whitish drink of some thickness ladled out from a huge carved bowl into individual halves of coconut shell, also carved and polished into cups that were works of art. I was most eager to taste this liquor that was famous in island stories. It was supposed to have a mildly narcotic effect, and I found it cool and pleasingly prickly to the tongue and gums. But I lost my enthusiasm when I saw how it was made: older women chewed the root of a shrub, *Piper methysticum,* of the pepper family, until their mouths were filled with saliva, which they then spat into a big bowl from whose accumulation our drinks were ladled out. I did not imbibe much beyond that first tasting.

I was in some strange way disappointed by American Samoa. It lacked size, both geographically and in the behavior of its islanders, who seemed cramped and almost afraid of themselves. I found none of the spaciousness of spirit that was supposed to mark the natives of Polynesia, and since this was the first island with such people that I was seeing outside Hawaii, which I had been able to visit only briefly and in wartime, I was not much impressed. I remember telling my bunkmate in Navy quarters: 'If this is the famed Polynesia that Stevenson and the Frenchmen wrote about, someone's been lying.' I saw few memorable characters, no beautiful women, and certainly no way of life that would have allured me; but I must hasten to add that this was wartime, the hand of the U.S. Navy was heavy upon the land, and the islanders were not a happy lot. I judged that in peacetime, when they were living under their own rules, the atmosphere might have been a lot more congenial. But I certainly did not 'go Asiatic,' as the enlisted men phrased it, over the Samoa I was allowed to see. I remember it mostly as a dark, cold, rainy place.

At the end of a brief stay I was assigned a small plane that would fly me westward over the Pacific on the short flight to British Samoa, each of whose two islands, Upolu and Savaii, was much bigger and supposedly more beautiful than the American one. I was not aware when I climbed into that plane that I was about to fly into paradise, but when, a short time later, I was deposited at the far western end of Upolu, the island nearest Pago Pago and the one on which the American troops were stationed, I found myself set down amid tall palm trees that edged a handsome shoreline stretching east and west on the great Pacific Ocean. It was a magnificent setting, but represented only a small portion of the glory into which I was about to be initiated.

When my gear was out of the plane, the American island commander, a Navy man who had been alerted to my coming, greeted me. He assured me that every courtesy would be extended, and indicated a smiling Samoan driver with a jeep: 'Samosila will see that you get wherever you have to go,' and with that he saluted after instructing Samosila: 'See that he gets what he needs.' I felt certain that the island commander and I would get along without either causing the other any trouble, and during my extended stay I had no cause to modify or retract that early conclusion.

'Where am I to bunk down?' I asked Samosila as I climbed into his jeep, and he said: 'We got Navy quarters on base but ever'body think mo' betta' you stay in Apia.' I recognized this as the name of the capital town of Samoa, some two dozen miles to the east. I liked the idea, for I wanted to give the Samoan Islands a chance to redeem their reputation after my dismal introduction at Pago Pago.

The next hour was one of the most wonderful of my life, for as we headed eastward on a coral-topped road as smooth as Navy engineers could make it with their huge scrapers, we had on our left that flawless

beach with small white-sand coves appearing here and there, lined by
the tallest palm trees I had ever seen. There was no monotony to the
road, for we were in the hour before sunset, and a golden light suffused
everything, edging the palms with iridescent fronds against the deep
blue sky. Even the waves that reached the shore not twenty feet from
us as we drove seemed kindly, with no hint of the way storms could lash
them into a fury.

But even if nature had not conspired to make the shoreline incomparably lovely, views inland would have made this journey to Apia unforgettable, because perched in the midst of huge coconut plantations stood
tiny villages, or more typically, collections of two or three of the most
exquisite human habitations I had ever seen. On moderately high stone
platforms generous in size and built of coral rock perfectly fitted to
produce a firm level foundation, stood the famous Samoan fales whose
name was so reminiscent of the character of Polynesian life. *Fale* in
Samoa, *hale* in Hawaii, *whare* in New Zealand, the word is always the
same and pronounced pretty much the same, for the *f* isn't sounded like
f, the *h* isn't really an *h,* and the *wh* sounds nothing like an ordinary
wh, while the *l* and *r* represent only one independent sound much like
a sigh. But if a Samoan fale is beautiful to hear pronounced—fah-lay—it
is even more so to the eye, because it is roofed by palm fronds woven
into exquisite patterns and supported by seven or eight huge upright
coconut trunks that show golden when the sun strikes them. The fale
is thus a kind of huge altar set upon a handsome platform, and its salient
characteristic is that it has no walls; the upright coconut trunks stand
like pillars or a committee of ancient gods convened to oversee the
behavior of the mortals who occupy that platform.

Privacy is obtained at night by pulling cords that drop wide curtains
made from woven fibers taken from the coconut palms, and when one
sees those curtains fall gracefully at night, one has the feeling that peace
and benediction have descended upon that house. An unbroken chain
of Samoan fales at dusk, strung out under the palms and not concentrated in villages, is a sight of humanity at its aesthetic best and a
warming reassurance that not all humans are either ugly or stupid, for
the ancient people who devised that pattern of living were artists of the
highest order.

But I am not being completely accurate. What really made the first
drive along the Samoan lagoons so unforgettable was not the domestic
architecture on the right but the human spectacle on the left. As night
approached, men and women from the fales came down to the beach to
bathe and, throwing off their sarongs, waded out into the soft white

breakers to splash themselves with water and frolic aimlessly in the ocean for a while before settling down for the night. Many others before me had said that the men and women of Samoa were among the physically perfect specimens of humanity: very tall, robust of limb, elegant in posture, with golden skin, luxuriant hair, dazzlingly white teeth, expressive eyes, and a serenity of movement, they were truly gods from some happy earlier age.

My duties in the South Pacific had given me the rare and almost unequaled opportunity of knowing intimately the three great human types of the far-flung area. I would ultimately serve on forty-nine different islands, covering each of the major groups of inhabitants. To the northwest lay the islands of Micronesia (from the Greek words *micro,* small, and *nesia,* islands), bearing historic names like Guam, Saipan, Palau and Truk. Its people, descended from a very mixed stock containing Spanish elements, tend to be medium-sized and light brown in color, and have long been capable of self-government.

The next sizable area to the southwest is Melanesia (*mela,* black) containing the larger islands like Guadalcanal, Bougainville and New Caledonia that became known in wartime. Its people tend to be small, very black, widely scattered on tiny islands and late in developing any forms of self-government. However, the big islands of Fiji at the extreme eastern border of Melanesia have produced people who are gigantic in size, most handsome in appearance, and long capable of self-government.

The third major grouping, Polynesia (*poly,* many), occupies the eastern portion of the South Pacific; it contains glorious islands like Tahiti, Rarotonga, Samoa and Hawaii, and is populated by the attractive people made famous by Paul Gauguin, Pierre Loti and Robert Louis Stevenson. The line separating Melanesia from Polynesia is delineated by a remarkable pair of coincidences: one an arbitrary, geographical coincidence, the other an inherent, genetic one. World geographers, acting in rare harmony, decreed in 1884 that the International Date Line would create the least confusion if it ran down the middle of the Pacific Ocean, between Samoa on the east and Fiji on the west. Thus, when it is 11:59 P.M. on Tuesday in Samoa, the passage of two minutes makes it 12:01 A.M. in Fiji, but not Wednesday as might be expected, but Thursday. The world's day begins in Fiji and ends in Samoa, so that Thursday in Melanesia is always Wednesday in Polynesia.

The other aspect of this arbitrary line is the more dramatic: Polynesians, regardless of the island group on which they live, are relatively light-skinned, tallish and historically have been well able to govern themselves, while everyone west of the line—except the Fijian—is dark-skinned, shortish and up to now not well trained in self-government. Polynesia has been favorably treated by writers and artists, Melanesia has been largely ignored, and to a lesser extent the same can be said of Micronesia. When European writers exclaim about the beauty of South Pacific maidens, they invariably mean those of Polynesia.

I would in time become familiar with all the different peoples of Polynesia, including the very handsome Hawaiians and Tahitians, as well as the powerful Maori of New Zealand,* but none surpassed or even equaled those majestic people I saw bathing in the ocean that first night in Samoa; and years of travel and comparison merely confirmed that early evaluation. To see a group of Samoans, men and women, walking serenely along the road from the airport to Apia was to see a procession on Olympus or in Asgard of the gods moving in stately procession to some meeting of importance.

Of course, much of the charm of that panorama unfolding beside the sea lay in the fact that half the people rising from the waves clothed in nothing but golden sunlight were young women of remarkable beauty and grace of movement. Each emerged and shook off the salt water, then deftly wrapped herself in a many-patterned sarong with a swaying movement so lovely that I was enraptured. Often in the past I had laughed at Hollywood's overuse of sarongs, especially on actresses who knew very little about how to use them effectively. Now I saw that for a Samoan, man or woman, to rise from the sea and swing a length of cloth about the body was truly an act of control and grace and beauty.

It was well after sunset that first night when Samosila deposited me at a kind of hotel that in the years ahead I would come to know intimately and with growing affection. It was a modest place in those first years, but it had already achieved well-deserved fame throughout the Pacific,

*Although New Zealand lies well west of the date line and is not therefore technically in Polynesia, at some very early date its islands were settled by adventurous people who had left India and Malaysia, hopped eastward, island by island, all the way to Tahiti, and from there, much later, *doubled back* to New Zealand and northward to Hawaii. Those in New Zealand are called Maoris, but they were and are Polynesians.

especially wherever American troops who had served on Samoa went. It was run by a magnificent woman in her late forties who would become known as the queen of the South Seas, honored by writers of several nations and by her own government, which used her portrait on its most popular postage stamp. She was Aggie Grey, daughter of a Scottish adventurer and a Samoan maiden, and even before the war she was well known for the comfortable and relaxed manner in which she ran her boardinghouse in Apia. The influx of people caused by the war led her to expand her operations tremendously, building one small shack after another near her house and transforming the whole into a rambling tropical hotel that would have delighted Somerset Maugham or Joseph Conrad.

If I made no impression on her that first night, and she could never remember how we first met, she certainly had a deep impact on me; I recall staying up with her and her musicians and singing girls until two in the morning. Tall and fine of feature, she had great skill in dancing to her own deep-voiced singing. The prototypical Samoan dance was called the siva-siva and consisted of solo dancing by a man or a woman—others could join in as separate participants—the graceful movements accentuated by a kind of hauteur that seemed to ignore the physical surroundings. No one did the siva better than Aggie, and as the evenings wore on she would be called upon many times to join some admiral or general as he tried in his inept way to copy her movements.

Aggie Grey's featured three prized assets in this haven from the shooting war: cold beer, great island music and a bevy of the most delectable young Samoan women, who seemed to have come from all parts of the island. At that time I didn't have the rank, the money or the courage to participate in the nightly activities, but I came to know the island girls and to marvel at the easy manner in which they bandied with the numerous American officers who came to woo them. Years later, I gave an interview to a New Zealand newspaper during a visit to Auckland in which I said that I could still remember the names of these young goddesses and I rattled off a few. Some half dozen of them were then living in New Zealand and they phoned one another and came as a group to my hotel, where Aggie, lively as ever, joined us. We held siva-siva and the women told me about the men they had married and how life had been: 'We remember you so well. The American who sat mostly in the corner, watching everything, until finally Aggie would go over and make you join her in siva-siva and you sang "Tofa, My Felengi," "Goodbye my Friend," and were very strong on "You Are My Sunshine." Those were wonderful nights, and the war ended, and in

Samoa nobody was dead and life continued.' They were handsome women, still tall and slim and vivacious.

I think that half the good stories I heard about the war reached me at Aggie Grey's, where I laid over whenever I got the chance. I liked staying with her much more than being in my quarters out at the American airfield, and I met there a host of American military people who found one excuse or another for stopping over in British Samoa. And no matter how many came or how elevated their rank was, Aggie made them all feel at home, and in time, in return for her courtesies, acquired American refrigerators and generators and tires for her car and books and canned goods and bottles brought in secretly from far places. She was extremely openhanded and shared her treasures generously. At the close of one stay I figured that I owed her more than a hundred dollars, but she told me to keep my wallet closed. I said: 'No other choice. There's nothing in it,' and she said: 'No matter. You ate only the food you brought me from the PX.'

I had the greatest admiration for Aggie, for she was a woman who could adapt to anything. If some other event of magnitude instead of a war had disrupted her life, she would have adjusted to it just as easily as she did to consequences of the Japanese attack in the Pacific. One enemy submarine on a suicide mission did lob two shells into Samoa, but they caused no damage, and each year Aggie's hotel increased in size and importance.

Halfway through my first stay with her I was distressed to learn that the Samoan woman I was supposed to report upon, the one to whose fale on the far side of the island the lovesick general had built the road at enormous expense to the American taxpayer, was Aggie's younger and very beautiful sister. When I asked in Apia about the matter, I was met only with silence, and since I was afraid to tackle Aggie on the subject, I left Apia after my stay with only meager information. Yes, it was Aggie's sister. Yes, the road had been built. Yes, the general who built it had left the island for frontline duty farther north. Yes, they were fine people and everyone regarded both her and him with the deepest affection. My investigation of this very costly road was diverted by one of the strangest episodes of the war. I shall endeavor to be absolutely precise in what I am about to relate, for as you will guess when I am through, I deemed it improper to report any of this during wartime.

When I returned to the west end of the island to occupy military quarters at the informal air base, I found that whereas there were some five or six dozen young American men on duty during the daylight hours, after sunset there were only six, and it occurred to me that if a

Japanese submarine surfaced off that end of the island at any time after six in the evening, a handful of its commandos could capture not only the air base but the entire island. As a quasi-representative of Admiral Halsey I had to do something about that.

The commanding officer was a middle-aged lieutenant colonel, proud of the fact that he ran a well-organized base with an absolute minimum of trouble: 'No drunkenness, no brawling, no scuffles with natives.' Before I could interrogate him about his men, or their absence, he said: 'Come with me to the fence gates at seven tomorrow morning and you'll see what I mean.'

At six-thirty he roused me and at seven we were at the gates, throwing salutes to three different open-sided trucks as they rolled in from different parts of the island, each carrying some twenty happy enlisted men, a few of whom bothered to toss salutes back at us. For the next eleven hours, 7:00 A.M. till 6:00 P.M., that base was as well run as any I had visited, but at dusk those same three trucks went back through the gates, each with its twenty-odd enlisted men while six remained behind to guard the fort.

On my second day at the base I said: 'I'd like to ride out with one of the trucks tomorrow night and see what's happening,' and since no objection was made I climbed up front to find to my surprise and pleasure that the driver was my own Samosila, and I wondered what kind of trip I was embarking on. It took me only a short time to learn, for when our truck came to a collection of three fales, their sidewalls up and the stark coconut poles bright in the sunset glow, four men jumped off and hurried to the fales, where lovely young women, barefoot and wearing sarongs, came out to greet them and welcome them to the quarters the men had made their own.

At the next stop, farther along, we lost four more enlisted men, and at the third stop a young second lieutenant bade us farewell and gave his Samoan girl a big hello. Out to the far end of his run Samosila drove his truck, depositing young swains along the way. At the last stop we dropped only one. Samosila parked his truck there and said: 'We stay here tonight. Johnson friend to my sister,' and for the first time I slept in one of the gracious Samoan fales, spotlessly clean with neat woven walls to be rolled down when the time came to sleep.

Samosila's sister was a delightful girl, about nineteen I would guess or maybe younger, and she had met her man, Johnson, when her brother brought him home for a Samoan dinner of fish and coconut milk. She and the American had become close friends, with Johnson bringing many things from the PX for her family, and he, like all the others, was making her fale his home, with the approval of her parents and certainly of Samosila. In the morning, refreshed and happy, Johnson climbed into the truck and Samosila took the wheel with me a trifle bewildered beside him. This time when we stopped sleepy-eyed Americans climbed down from the fale platforms and headed for the truck. At seven sharp our truck and the other two were at the gates and the day's work began.

Samosila informed me that a family whose father was an official of some standing on the island had taken note of me on my various trips and had concluded that I was a responsible officer, since I was a full Navy lieutenant; he wondered if Samosila would bring me around to his fale to meet his daughter, Matua. When I agreed I found that his fale was one of the best and neatest and that Matua was one of the most attractive girls on the island, about eighteen and as stately as a young queen, which in essence she was.

Samosila gave me a remarkable message from Matua's father that I can only repeat in the words in which it was delivered to me: 'Matua not happy. All girls have good American boys. Many girls gonna have babies, strong American babies. Good for Samoa, good for Matua. But Matua all alone. Why you not stop by our fale till time you go?'

That was the proposal delivered with the aplomb and dignity used in inviting a guest to a formal dinner, and I was flabbergasted. Since an invitation like that was indeed a rare thing, it merited a response that was totally candid; 'As a boy I had mumps—lumps in my neck. As a result I have reason to believe that I can't have babies.' They understood what I was saying and there was a profound silence, but then the father spoke: 'Samosila your friend. He say you fine man. No matter about baby. We like to have American here, like all others. You stay.' And that was how I happily learned the rules of life within a Samoan fale, with its latticework and woven ceilings and the majestic coconut palm pillars that held it up. If I speak well of Samoa and its people, it is because I lived for a while in one of the fales beside that glorious, ocean-swept coral road leading from the little airstrip to Apia.

It should be obvious that I had now compromised myself so completely that I had sacrificed any right to criticize a lovelorn general who had used government funds to build a first-class highway from the north side, where he was stationed, to the south side, where Aggie Grey's sister lived. So I approached the problem of the road with apprehension and a good deal of confusion. But with Samosila's help I started my investigation.

We drove east from the airfield toward Apia as if heading back to Aggie Grey's, but at a point somewhere near the halfway mark we turned sharply to the right—that is, toward the southern shore of the island—and we were soon on a fine road among low hills cut by shallow ravines. It was obvious that the American engineers who had built the road had spent on it a good deal of study, ingenuity and money, for it climbed easily through rather difficult terrain until it reached a height from which I could look down upon one of the most serene sights I would see in the islands. It was a half-moon bay protected by a small reef and lined with palm trees, almost an artist's vision of a haven from storms, and around its perimeter stood some half dozen fales of better than average construction, one of which had attached to it a kind of Western addition. That, I was told, was the house of Aggie's sister, the one to whom the general came on his visits. He was remembered in the other fales as a fine man who had brought many good things to this side of the island, which had previously been ignored by the British government. Why Aggie's sister had settled in this once remote hiding place I never fathomed, and after my inspection of the area and the road leading to it I decided what I would say in my report: 'If the Japanese *had* invaded the north side of Upolu and *had* tried to attack the south side, this road would have been quite valuable to the American defenses.'

As I made this note I thought of the great story Alexander King had circulated in Greenwich Village about the impecunious student from India who cadged one free meal after another from him, always paying for them by reciting as he left, well fed, a short blessing in Hindi. One night, irritated by the fact that his Indian guest never offered anything other than the mumbled prayer, King demanded to know what the words meant. Which was: 'May this house be safe from tigers.' When King remonstrated that that was a silly statement to make in Greenwich Village in return for all the good food the young man had eaten, the Indian asked: 'Well, have you been bothered by tigers lately?' If the Japanese *had* invaded, that road *would* have been of great value.

Meanwhile the Catholic bishop was holding vast prayer services in Apia, so that when I returned to Aggie's rooming house I found all rooms taken by the visiting faithful from other islands. But Aggie found me quarters in a fale occupied by the family of one of her ablest singers, a young woman of great beauty whose younger sister was in a state of depression. The great Catholic conclave was to end with the laymen giving a huge ball supervised by Aggie and her musicians, and if there was anything on earth the young girls and ladies of Samoa loved more than a gala I never discovered it.

But so many longed to attend that the dancing area would have exploded with saronged and swaying bodies if Aggie and the bishop, working together, hadn't devised one of the most effective weeding-out procedures I had ever heard of. They announced throughout Upolu and Savaii: 'Only those girls will be admitted to the ball who are known to live in the European style.' The question then became: 'Who's a European?' Englishmen were, of course, and Frenchmen too; so also were white Americans. But trouble came with the numerous Samoans, where distinctions were more difficult to make. The girls who sang and danced at Aggie's were obviously European, and so were the typists at the stores and those who worked indoors at the American base and at the PX. But then definitions fell into a gray area until the bishop solved the problem with a judgment Solomonic in its fairness and ease of enforcement: 'Any girl will be considered European if she wears shoes.' Small wonder the bishop was so highly regarded throughout his island see.

It was fortunate that I had stopped first in Samoa among the Polynesian islands because it was there that I not only formed a friendship with Aggie Grey, a friendship that would last throughout our lives, but also was inducted into the joys of Polynesian life. And what were they? Singing, enjoying the wonders of nature, sitting around at night swapping yarns, lovemaking, organizing a feast or a gala at the merest pretense, accepting one's fellows pretty much as they are, and exhibiting a warmth that nourished the heart. Nowhere were all these more in evidence than the place to which I traveled next, Bora Bora, a magical island belonging to France and situated some hundred and fifty miles northwest of Tahiti.

To put it quite simply, Bora Bora is the most beautiful island in the world. Geologically it consists of a series of concentric circles: first an almost perfect coral reef about ten miles in diameter, with deep blue tempestuous ocean waves on the outside, lime-green placid water on the inside; then the island itself, a masterpiece of dark green, almost circular in form but broken by deeply indented bays defined by tall palm trees swaying in the breeze, which seems to be constant; and in what might be called the center of the island a gigantic, dark pillar of rock, the basalt plug of an ancient volcano whose more fragile sides have broken and eroded away. The three components—reef, island, volcano—are so perfectly placed and so harmonious in their relationship that they seem to have been designed by some master artist. To come back to Bora Bora at the close of day after a long trip in a small boat and to see the setting sun illuminate the volcanic tower, massive and brooding in gold, is to see the South Pacific at its unforgettable best.

The people in those war years were as attractive as their island, the most natural and uninhibited Polynesians of all, the ones who regularly won the wild dancing competition held in Tahiti to celebrate Bastille Day on July 14. One event at that riotous celebration summarizes the Bora Bora attitude. In the boxing tournament I helped the Bora Bora men, for I was a Bora Boran at heart, and we had a powerful young fighter who had a good chance of winning if we could keep him under control and prevent him from flailing his arms about to no purpose. Explained our coach: 'Our problem is to get him drunk enough so he's brave but keep him sober enough so he has a rough idea of what he's doing.' I would often think of that dilemma in the weeks I worked on the island.

For I was working. I was writing an account of the amazing events that had transpired since that day in 1942 when a small American troop transport had slipped through the lone opening in the reef to land an armed contingent. Its job was to defend the island should the Japanese, whose fleet had unfettered sway over the Pacific as a result of the Pearl Harbor disaster, decide to occupy the island. Should the Japanese succeed in invading, the situation could become serious, especially since many of the leading citizens in Papeete (on Tahiti), the capital of French Polynesia, had openly proclaimed their allegiance to Vichy France, under the shameful leadership of the pro-Nazi general Pétain. In the early days of America's war against Japan the planning had been quite open: 'We'll let the Vichy men hold Tahiti. We'll hold Bora Bora and neutralize them.'

But others were writing of the delicate negotiations that prevented the Vichy forces from holding Tahiti; I was not privy to those records and had no justification in even voicing an opinion; my job was to summarize what had happened on our island of Bora Bora then and now, when our troops were on the verge of rioting if they were forced to go home.

The airstrip for the island was unique: a long, beautiful coral pathway, wide enough to accept a DC-3, built of shimmering white coral that almost blinded the eye. It was located not on the island itself, which was too hilly to permit a strip, but far out on the fringing reef. Landing at Bora Bora was the best possible introduction to the island; when I first came, as we flew in low over the dark Pacific, I saw to my left the towering basaltic pillar from the old volcano and the lime-green beauty of the lagoon, then there was a sudden drop and the crunch of tires on the packed coral. I was in the heartland of Polynesia.

No sooner had the plane come to a halt than I was greeted by two men for whom I would always feel a deep affection and about whom I would write not a favorable report but a glowing one. The first was a

United States Navy lieutenant, whom I shall call Hazzard because I once promised him that I would never use his real name in view of the unusual facts he knew I would have to relate. He was about thirty-five, tall, nice-looking but not handsome, a bit overweight from good living on the island without much to do, slightly balding, with a big round face showing almost bovine contentment. Lieutenant Hazzard was a happy man and he wanted those serving under him to be the same.

He was accompanied by a slim, handsome French official a few years older than himself, M. Francis Sanford—his real name—one of the sharpest, most trustworthy and congenial colonial administrators I would ever meet. At that stage he was merely a former schoolteacher who, because he spoke English, had been appointed to serve as liaison with the Americans on this remote island. He was not well regarded, I would learn, by the Vichy partisans in Papeete, but he trod such a meticulous line between keeping both the Americans and the French happy that he was embraced by both sides. Since I shall have a good many complimentary things to say about Sanford and the reader may suspect, understandably, that I had been bedazzled by a sharp political manipulator, I must reveal that in later years this clever schoolteacher became the political leader of all French Polynesia, a task in which he proved so effective that he was elected to the Parliament in Paris as an honored member of the Senate, where he fought for a sensible colonial policy. Upon his return to the Pacific, he became governor of French Polynesia. Sanford was a born winner, and I am proud to say that I detected this at first sight.

Before the week was out I think I understood both his immediate tactic and his long-range strategy: to maintain friendship with the Americans now, but to persuade them in the future to leave behind as much heavy equipment as possible so that when peace came and the Americans were gone, they would abandon the infrastructure for a new way of life on the island; to accomplish this he would resort to imaginative strategies—mere theft was routine.

Perched in the rear of a small boat between these two superior men, I sped over the glassy waters of the lagoon and late in the afternoon stepped ashore to meet for the first time the rebellious enlisted men of Bora Bora. At first sight they seemed a decent lot, under thirty, reasonably trim, courteous in their attitude toward me, even though they knew I might do them damage if I didn't like what I saw, and about as typical a group of young fellows as one could have found. I detected no sign of tension, no untoward fear of their commanding officer, and not a thing about which I might be suspicious. Unpacking my gear in the quarters to which I had been assigned and testing the typewriter they had been ordered to provide me with, I thought: This is going to be just a little more complex than I'd suspected. But when the yeoman assigned to help me with my paperwork while I was there came to lead me to the mess, I saw nothing unusual in his attitude nor anything suspicious in the dining area, where the food was good but not spectacular and the deportment pretty much in accordance with Navy routine. But if I was surveying the men critically, they were doing the same with me; I doubt, however, that I was revealing anything other than my general bewilderment.

When my yeoman suggested that I might like to attend the seven o'clock movie, the big event on the island, he betrayed his eagerness to see it; so as not to disappoint him, I assented. We walked to a nearby structure, part tent, part Quonset, in which nearly ninety chairs had been placed in orderly rows, and there the forty or fifty sailors who made up the cadre had gathered, each sitting primly beside an empty chair, which meant that no two sailors were seated side by side. I could not guess the reason for this. I also noticed that the first two rows contained no one.

At seven a bugle blew, all stood, and down the sloping center aisle marched Lieutenant Hazzard in a freshly pressed uniform with eyes majestically fixed straight ahead. When he was about to take his seat, he spread his arms outward and we sat down too. Then the bugle blew again and here came the miracle of Bora Bora. Into the hall marched in stately procession a group of people, including a handsome young woman, about twenty-three I judged, and rather large, who followed the path that Hazzard had taken, but she did not sit beside him. Deferentially she sat in the middle of the row behind him, while her entourage, consisting of her mother, an aunt, an uncle and her younger sister, took seats on either side of her. When that was done, the gates were thrown open, as it were, and into the hall came a flood of the liveliest young girls I had seen in a long time, who joyously took seats beside their chosen sailors, after which several dozen young men, brothers of the girls perhaps, filed in to take the rest of the empty seats. Now the Bora Bora movie could begin.

I shall never forget that show, and as you shall see, I would have good reason to remember it. *Flying Down to Rio* was a Dolores Del Rio fluff movie, with a story line that no one could follow, but it was saved for the islanders by a comedy trio called The Three Greeks, whose childish antics were keyed exactly to their tastes. They also cheered when hundreds of chorus girls were shown dancing on the wings of a score of airplanes that were supposed to be in flight. For the American sailors there was the thrill of seeing Fred Astaire and Ginger Rogers dancing together for the first time; they were not yet stars in that early film, but even in their brief appearance they were showstoppers, floating on air and making the big hall throb with their vitality.

The effect of the show was somewhat spoiled by the tendency of the audience to anticipate comedy bits by starting to laugh, and this became so annoying that I asked my yeoman: 'Have they seen this picture before?' and he said: 'About a dozen times.' I was to see it six times, and always with the greatest delight, for there was really nothing else to do in the early part of the evening, and like the sailors I came to relish the scenes with which I was becoming familiar because I could now appreciate the clever ways in which the actors set them up. The Three Greeks knew how to use to humorous effect the old vaudeville shticks to make us all laugh as heartily on the sixth repetition as on the first. If I were asked today to list my all-time favorite movies, the test for inclusion would be this: Did I enjoy this movie as much as I did *Flying Down to Rio*?

We had two other films on the island, Westerns, which the islanders loved, and each played four or five times while I was in residence, but to me no horse, however handsome, could be as compelling as the new stars, Fred and Ginger, displaying their magic.

At the end of the film, the bugle blew again; Lieutenant Hazzard rose, strode up the ramp, looking sternly ahead, with the stately young woman walking behind him, and her family behind her. When they were outside, the bugle blew again and the rest of us were free to leave. It was about nine o'clock when we returned to the soft night air that made Bora Bora so delightful, and I noticed that the situation was like that at the air base in Samoa: Here almost all the enlisted men left the base accompanied by their laughing and chattering vahines.

The word *vahine* (meaning woman) surfaced in almost everything I learned about Bora Bora. Lieutenant Hazzard's regal vahine was named Malama, daughter of a man who could be called a chief, and she was a powerful influence in keeping the lesser vahines under control, for they feared a rebuke from her or even a stern glance. My yeoman's vahine had been disturbed that he had wanted to sit with me on that first night and not with her, but she was probably mollified when he accompanied her home to their palm-lined hut after the show ended.

I cannot now recall what name the Tahitians used—Bora Borans were Tahitians, of course—for their fales; the sailors called them huts, and it seemed as if each man stationed on Bora Bora had his own hut.

In many cases it was built for him by the men of the girl's family because they approved of her association with the Americans who could bring food and other necessary items to the place. I inspected several of the huts, always with older members of the girls' family in attendance, to ensure that I gained a good impression of how their daughters lived. I found the little houses both clean and practical: a bed of coconut matting, a table, a chair, nails to hang the sailors' clothes so they would be neat, and not much else, for living took place out of doors or at the naval base; the hut was for night affairs only, including sleeping.

As at Samoa, some six or eight men remained on duty at the base overnight, and the officers had quarters for their vahines on base too, with Lieutenant Hazzard's Malama supervising everything in exactly the same way that I had seen superior Navy wives taking charge of the private careers of their Annapolis-trained husbands. It was a well-run base marked by an unusual degree of happiness.

When I got to know Francis Sanford and his tall, elegant wife, Lysa, who had a sharp eye for human folly, I found him to be like every good local administrator who worked with our Navy: amiable and conciliatory, performing wonders in helping to keep things moving forward without friction, but ruthless in protecting the interests of his homeland.

The prototype of this kind of superintelligent operator I came to admire—the kind of official I would want to be if any foreign country ever invaded America—was a gangling, delightful Oxford graduate on a Micronesian island with whom I worked at one time. There was an English base on a small island a short distance from where I was stationed, and it was his habit to have himself rowed over to my base by four black men. Coming casually ashore, he would be all rumpled with hair awry and elbows sticking out so awkwardly that our men called him Sprocket, after the toothed wheel used on bicycles.

'Here comes Sprocket!' they would shout as he ambled ashore, picking his way through stacks of expensive gear. 'I say, chaps!' he would cry in a rather high voice. 'D'jew happen to have a spanner?'

Our boys would ask what a spanner was and he would explain that it was what they called a monkey wrench, and they would collapse with laughter: 'He calls this a spanner!' and after they quieted down he would ask: 'D'jew happen to have one a mite bigger?' and at the end of his visit he would traipse back to his waiting boat with a handful of our most expensive wrenches.

In that subtle way, with our Americans laughing at his ungainly manner, his shyness and his Oxford accent, Sprocket transferred from our big island to his little one such a treasure of goods that when I rowed over to see for myself what he was doing I found him living amid a wealth of goods rarely seen in one place even in peacetime. The rascal had one of everything: stove, refrigerator, generator, compressor—plus piles of canned goods. 'You're living like a king,' I complained, 'and I'm living like a pauper.' And he said: 'You have to know how to work the system.' Next day when I went to our big island I watched him sailing over from his small one and coming ashore with that boyish smile, that unkempt hair, those awkward elbows and that Oxford accent, and I thought: How damned unfair to let that genial manipulator loose among a gang of decent farm boys from Iowa. That day he wondered if they happened to have any spare petrol, and after they roared with laughter at his word for gasoline he took back two barrels.

I admired Sprocket, for his island was a bleak spot, which his ingenuity had converted into a habitable place; but I liked Francis Sanford even more for the orderly way in which he managed the Vichy men in Papeete, and the Americans in Bora Bora. He did not connive, so far as I could see, at having his island girls captivate the American sailors, but when they did he wanted to be sure that the girls were treated decently. I think it was he who introduced a Sears Roebuck catalog, which the girls combed for things that the sailors could order for them, and pretty soon Sears was doing an impressive business with Bora Bora. I was present several times when planes flew in with sizable cargoes, all of which seemed to have come from Sears.

Sanford and his wife kept watch to see that the girls were not abused or taken advantage of. Men who behaved poorly or with gross indifference to the girls' rights were noted by Sanford, reported to the island command and quietly shipped back to Texas or Minnesota, a punishment that the others tried to avoid. Sanford ran a clean island, one of the best occupied areas I would inspect in the entire Pacific, and I saluted him for his efficiency and wisdom.

I felt that I had a fairly good grasp of the situation by the time I reached the twentieth page of my report, but it was through the case of Ordinary Seaman Gosford that I got down to basics. He was from Alabama, a farm boy from the peanut belt and the recipient of a desultory education that had stopped well before the eighth grade. He was about twenty when I interviewed him concerning the problem that was causing him such distress that he was no longer able to do his work. Lieutenant Hazzard had asked me to see if I could help and now Gosford sat before me, twisting his fingers.

'What's the problem?'

'I'm being sent home.'

'You do something wrong?'

'Oh, no!' He looked like the kind of sailor who would never do anything wrong.

'So what is it? Trouble with a girl?'

'Oh, no! Terua and I get along fine.'

'And you don't want to go home?'

'Nobody on this rock wants to go home.'

'What's happening, then?'

'I may have to go.'

'Lieutenant Hazzard told me nothing specific about your case.'

'It's Mom. She insists I come home.'

'She sick, or something?'

'No. She hears about other men from the war front, they come home after eighteen months.'

'How long have you been here?'

'Two years. No bad marks. Nothing against me, nothing at all.'

'Then what's the bind?'

'Mom knows our senator . . . in Washington . . . and she has him all steamed up . . . and he says it's a disgrace . . . to keep a boy overseas in enemy territory for two years.'

'Has he done anything about it?'

'He's told the Navy he wants me off this rock toot sweet. I expect an order any day.'

When I inquired I learned that the order had already arrived. Seaman Judson Gosford of Dothan, Alabama, was to be shipped out immediately, so that he could join his family for the kind of extended leave to which overseas heroes were entitled. When Hazzard showed me the dispatch he pointed to the order: 'Because the senator is personally interested in the case, release Gosford soonest.' Since his ejection from Bora Bora was irreversible I took special interest in his case, and when I accompanied him to the hut in which he and the island girl Terua had lived for the past two years I found the main cause of his grief. Terua was pregnant, so that not only had he the normal desire of all Americans not to be sent home from this paradise, but he also had the complication of impending fatherhood.

And complication it was, for when I assured Gosford that I might be able to arrange for the Navy to take into account what it called 'compassionate understanding,' which would mean a delay of orders till the baby was born, Gosford almost went into a spasm: 'Oh, Lieutenant Michener! No! No! It would kill my mother if she ever got to know, Navy messages and all that.'

'Why?'

'She would have to find out sooner or later that Terua was a nigger.'

When I tried to assure him that this could be kept secret—I myself would draft the messages and dream up some other excuse—he balked: 'The senator would be sure to find out the real reason. After the trouble he's taken, how would it look for him to see that I didn't want to come because I was having a nigger baby?'

This was a dilemma I could not solve. Everyone in the muddle seemed to have right on his or her side. Mrs. Gosford back in Dothan was right in wanting her son back home. The senator from Alabama was right in thinking that any one of his young constituents who had spent two years in the battle zone was a certified hero entitled to leave. And it was understandable that Terua would want her lover to stay until their child was born. But Gosford himself had the strongest reason of all: he did not want to go home and leave an island paradise, the likes of which he might never see again.

I noted the various points of view and finally consulted with Francis Sanford and Base Commander Hazzard, who agreed that Seaman Gosford was both an ideal enlisted man and the quasi-husband of the vahine Terua, who was herself an exemplary island girl from a good family. A sad injustice was being committed, but we could see no escape. Hazzard said: 'If his mother hadn't involved the senator we might brazen this out, but if he starts firing rockets at Halsey, and Gosford is still here, it's my ass, and I cannot allow that.' He felt, with some justification I thought, that if high brass in the Navy started looking into the Bora Bora situation, more than his ass might be in jeopardy.

So, in a decision that was going to have unforeseen ramifications for me, we decided that Seaman Gosford would have to leave Bora Bora by the next plane, which was what that word *soonest* meant, and no appeal would be entertained: the young hero had to leave the war zone for the safety of southern Alabama. Commander Hazzard, Terua and I accompanied him out to the airstrip, and there he made his tearful farewells. From the shack that served as the strip office Francis Sanford appeared to check on whether Gosford was leaving Terua an adequate departure present; he learned that like most of the sailors when they left the island, the Alabamian had provided his girl with more than a hundred dollars. The plane came in, wheeled about, and Gosford was on his way home.

On our return from the reef to the island I noticed Terua carefully for the first time and realized what an ingratiating girl she was and how readily her smile at some kind word drove away her tears. I was eager that she not waste the money Gosford had left, and when I deposited her at the Bora Bora landing I saw with pleasure that her father and two brothers were awaiting her, so I told them: 'She has money. See that she buys the things she needs,' and they nodded.

Two days later as I was working with my yeoman I was visited by Terua's father and he had an astonishing proposal: 'Michener Officer, we see you. We know you good man. Not right you live alone. You very kind to Terua. We see. We like you live with us, many fine girls know you, see you. They do not want you live alone.'

I had no idea why this invitation was being extended, but it was reinforced the next day by the return of the father with two older friends: 'Michener Officer, you kind man. You help everybody. No good you live alone,' and they said that if I was sensitive about being an officer and living with an island girl, they would build me a small hut next to the one Gosford and Terua had used, and it was now made clear that she was in no way involved in this proposal; she was concerned solely with the impending birth of her child.

I refused the offer of the hut and the accompanying housekeeper but I did keep in touch with Terua's father, who had made this generous and sympathetic offer. I agreed with him that it was not good to live alone, and had I been stationed permanently on Bora Bora I am sure I would not have done so, but as a visiting officer writing the history of America's unusual occupation of the island I felt that I had better remain unattached, lest I later be accused of the very improprieties I might have to be reporting.

And so my tour of duty on Bora Bora drew to a close. As time came to leave, at least a dozen sailors begged me not to use their names and not to let the rest of the world in on the secret of Bora Bora. 'It would be hard to explain to those outside. They might not understand.' I promised I would keep the secret, but I suppose that my yeoman, who had typed all my notes, must have told them that I had composed a fairly faithful account but that I had not used real names.

When the time came for me to leave, my report completed, I made a startling discovery: I had become a Gosford. I did not want to go, and felt that the necessity to do so was unfair. I wanted to remain with Terua and her family till the baby was born. I wanted to see *Flying Down to Rio* two or three times a week. I wanted to retain the friendship of Sanford and Hazzard. But most of all I had grown to love the island, its volcano and glorious lagoon, and I did not want to lose them.

In the long years ahead whenever anyone would ask: 'Michener, you've seen most of the world. What was the very best spot of all?' my answer would invariably be: 'Bora Bora.'

It was now time for me to head south to the capital town, Papeete, where I had to attend to the matter of the secret code books. I left, escorted by Sanford and his wife as passengers in the *Hiro*, a rickety old inter-island steamer owned by an extraordinary American beachcomber who had sailed north to meet us. Lew Hirshon, then in his mid-forties, had left a wealthy Long Island family in the early 1930s for a college boy's journey around the world, but he had gotten no farther than Tahiti, as he explained on our first night out: 'I climbed down out of the vessel which had brought me from San Francisco and when I saw that glorious waterfront in Papeete with yachts from all over the world backed in stern-to, I cried: "This is for me!" and I have never left. I run a big plantation, tend palms and ship out copra. I do some island trading in the *Hiro*, named after a Polynesian god of the sea, and I have a great time.

'I wasn't in the island long before I noticed the extreme beauty of the girls, but I had made friends with the wonderful old Chinese trader Tiong Ban, and whenever I found a girl I would walk her past his shop and he would wag his head "No, no! Not good for you." and I would drop her. But one day I met this gorgeous girl, French-Polynesian, and when I took her past he ran out of his shop and grabbed my hands and cried: "Yes, yes! This one for you!" and I married her.'

While Lew went to his quarters to wash up, Sanford told me that Lew's wife had been the most beautiful woman in the islands, a true .goddess, but that she had died. He had then fallen in love with two sisters: Elianne, the lovely singer, and her even more beautiful younger sister, whose name I now forget. It had been touch and go which one he would marry, but when it seemed that he was going to delay making a decision, for he was often absent taking trips about the islands in the *Hiro*, the younger married a Frenchman, and when Lew came back, having decided to marry her, he found her taken, and so he grabbed Elianne. 'And when you see her you won't be able to imagine how the other could have been prettier.'

On the night before we landed I initiated discreet inquiries regarding the man whose errant behavior I was supposed to investigate unobtrusively, and my traveling companion told me that Ratchett Kimbrell, an older U.S. government type on an undefined mission, was one of the gentlest, best-loved Americans ever to come to the island. It seemed that his job was to keep an eye on the Vichy elements in Tahiti, and to accomplish this he operated what was less than an embassy but more than a mere consulate, and since it dealt with extremely sensitive inter-governmental relations, he had been given unusually restrictive orders. 'Neither fish nor fowl,' Lew said and Sanford added: 'But he's an asset beyond price.' And then Lew revealed the truth of the matter: 'A most difficult man to classify. I know Ratchett well, but I don't know him at all.'

In the morning all thoughts of rogue government men vanished when I saw for the first time that glorious Papeete waterfront along whose quay I would spend so many hours in the years ahead. There were the yachts, stern-to side by side, debouching almost into the very center of the city. From the rear of one's boat one stepped almost directly into Quinn's Bar, where the legendary American pianist Eddie Lund held sway, or into the grubby hotels that had once entertained many of the world's most adventurous writers and artists. The Papeete waterfront at dawn on a windswept day with the sun about to appear was a sight to gladden the heart, for here came scores of people on their way to the market carrying the rich produce of the islands: fish from Moorea, bananas from Raiatea, breadfruit from the Presqu'île, that oval penin-sula on the eastern side of the island, and chickens and pigs from everywhere. Here too came the young girls to scout the incoming ships and to greet sailors from old arrivals like the *Hiro.* It was a parade of never flagging interest, of perpetual newness and delight.

It was said with some accuracy that when an American yacht arrived on that waterfront with nine sailors, eight beautiful girls appeared mys-teriously within fifteen minutes. When a small ship dropped anchor with forty sailors, thirty-eight girls appeared. And when a French warship with two thousand men hove to, nineteen hundred eager girls showed up. Tahiti was a sailors' paradise, but it was also a staid, well-governed French colony with good restaurants, cable services and numerous branches of the Banc d'Indochine. It was unique—half Polynesian, half Chinese, a mix that produced some of the most handsome Polynesian types.

From this waterfront small boats set out for little islands with glorious names: Les Îles Sous le Vent, The Islands Under the Wind; Fakarava, Rangiroa, Pukarua, Mangareva, Pitcairn and Melville's Marquesas. A wandering man with imagination could spend five years on this water-front, drifting off to one island after another but returning always to the wonder of Tahiti.

I had trustworthy guides on my first trip, Sanford and Hirshon, and

they introduced me to the local luminaries, including the minor diplomat Ratchett Kimbrell, who had rented a big wooden house in the
center of Papeete from which he conducted such casual U.S. government business as came his way. Kimbrell gave me a lot of trouble,
because I could never pin down exactly who he was, and when I tried
to sort things out I became even more confused, for both Hirshorn and
Sanford warned me: 'In Tahiti you don't try to unravel every situation.
The United States has four representatives here, their duties not clearly
defined.' When I asked who they were, he startled me: 'First there's the
Honorable Richard M. de Lambert, official consul and a State Department gentleman of distinction. Then there's the man you're interested
in, Ratchett Kimbrell, who seems to be a self-motivated operative. Then
there's this mysterious young naval officer McClintock, and now we
have you, and no one knows what your interest is in Tahitian affairs.'
When I studied Kimbrell I concluded that his quasi-government post
was a cover. But to hide what I did not know. From my briefing at
headquarters I knew he was in disfavor with Washington for having
rather airily assured a Norwegian skipper that he didn't really need
papers from him to clear for Honolulu, and his issuance of passports had
been a disgrace.

Kimbrell confused me, because my only knowledge of quasi-diplo-
mats had come from the movies, where they all looked like Lewis Stone
with chiseled features, neat white hair and aloof manners. Kimbrell, by
contrast, was a slob. He was in his fifties, overweight, with an undistinguished round face that always looked as if it needed a shave, and a
fringe of unkempt white hair. He had a bit of a stoop, a round belly and
a habit of wearing bedroom slippers during the daytime, even when
conducting business in his office.

He was assisted in his labors by a secretary, a local young woman,
and therein lay the beginning of his troubles, for in choosing his secretary he had passed over several older women who handled English well
and one who had actually served as secretary to one of his predecessors.
Instead he picked one of the all-time beauties of Polynesia, and if I use
this description with obvious enthusiasm I do it also with strict adher-
ence to the truth, for Reri, her professional name, had been the glowing
star of Robert Flaherty's 1931 motion picture classic, *Tabu,* and had also
acted in the Laughton-Gable 1935 blockbuster, *Mutiny on the Bounty.*
During a publicity tour of France she was reputed to have been the
constant companion of Maurice Chevalier and the toast of the boule-
vards because of her joyous, uninhibited behavior. In 1944, when I knew
her, she had put on a little weight, was somewhat younger than I and

possessed one of the most radiant faces I had ever seen. She was a glorious woman, Anna Chevalier in real life, member of the immense Chevalier family with seven or eight young girls almost as pretty as she, and a major feature of island life. Tahiti was proud of Reri.

We liked each other from the start, but I knew she was spoken for by at least two strong-minded men and maybe more, and she suspected that I might be in Tahiti to check on her rather unconventional behavior. I let her know in one unspoken way or another that she had nothing to fear from me, and she let me know that I was more than welcome to make my headquarters in one of the big houses her family occupied: 'You'll hardly be noticed,' she said, and that turned out to be true, for when I was given a bunk in the big wooden house I was one of fifteen or sixteen and no one noticed my comings and goings.

Because some of the things I have to report concerning Tahiti in those days may seem unusual or even outrageous, I had better relate two incidents that established the pattern for me. Once while I was hanging out in Quinn's Bar listening to Eddie Lund pound out his rhythms, the gang received a cable from a London free-lance writer informing us that he would be arriving in Tahiti shortly on an exciting assignment and he required a young woman who could drive a Renault, swim under water and develop Kodak film. We spent several days endeavoring to find a young woman who had the rather specific qualifications and who would also be his attractive hostess. For a time it looked as if we were going to fail, because the requirement for the ability to develop film eliminated several otherwise eligible beauties.

Filling the request became a challenge, as if failing to do so would somehow be a blot not only on Tahiti but also on the Quinn's Bar gang. However, some ingenious fellow concluded that he could teach the most likely of the applicants to handle the Kodak, so when the young man arrived from London all was in readiness. He was met at the airport by a fine-looking young woman driving a Renault and fully prepared to help him on his article on reef life in Polynesia with some excellent underwater color photographs. After doing the article he stayed on for some months, for as he told us: 'It would be crazy to go back to London in February.' Later I saw that the beautiful girl who had done much of the underwater work for him was driving a rather smart Renault, which he had left behind in appreciation for her services.

More to the point, I think, was the incident that occurred during my first trip when a ne'er-do-well from Austria, a fascinating chap, arrived with the announcement that he was a baron. Now, we all knew he wasn't a baron, couldn't possibly be, and had probably left Vienna just ahead of the sheriff, but as someone at Quinn's pointed out: 'We've never had a baron in Papeete and it would be rather nice.' So he was accepted on his own terms, and when I saw him years later I discovered that he had made himself into a baron, and he was a lot more convincing in his role than some true barons I had known in Austria.

In Tahiti one could be whatever one desired to be, and several times I saw someone who had been a man the day before suddenly appear as a woman, with the implied announcement that henceforth that was his gender, and she was accepted as such without further comment.

With that sort of attitude the people of Papeete were not especially concerned when mystery-man Robert Kimbrell fell in love with his secretary, Reri (there was some question among the gang at Quinn's as to whether Reri knew how to type; giving her the benefit of the doubt, we said 'Maybe'). Our real discussion centered on the fact that Reri was also being avidly courted by a stranger whom none of us could properly place. Lieutenant Commander Paul McClintock was obviously an American naval officer, and he appeared to be on temporary duty from our naval headquarters in Honolulu. We took an instant dislike to each other, for I spotted him as a pompous snob, an Annapolis man, no doubt, and he dismissed me as a mere lieutenant scarcely worthy of his attention. I had to admit, however, that he was taller, trimmer, better-looking, more military in appearance and more secretive in whatever he was doing than I was. At one point I began to wonder if he had been sent down to check on me.

What really sickened me was that McClintock was behaving like such an ass, bringing scorn on the rest of us in uniform. He was in love with Reri, whom he had seen in *Tabu* when it came to Amherst when he was a junior there, and he was now overcome by the wonder of his romantic situation: being on one of the most famous islands in the South Seas and being the swain of a Polynesian movie celebrity. Of course, I felt pretty much the same, but I was not making a fool of myself about it.

So here was this tropical quadrangle: the radiant Polynesian movie star is loved by the moonstruck U.S. Navy lieutenant commander, who does not know that she is sleeping with the older diplomat, all of whom are being watched with envy by a somewhat junior officer on Halsey's staff. I envied Reri the exciting life she had known in Paris; I envied Ratchett Kimbrell the fact that he had Reri as his love and I did not; and I envied McClintock for his handsome bearing, his important assignment in Honolulu and his willingness to pay open court to a beautiful woman. I would not admit to myself that in this affair I was a sorry mess, but in fact I was not far from it.

I took evil delight in watching from my own safe hiding places Lieutenant Commander McClintock come marching home at eleven each evening with Reri on his arm, he having treated her to the best dinner available in Papeete with a helping of French champagne, and now bidding her a chaste good night as if he were an actor in a scene from Dumas or Victor Hugo: kissing her hand, looking at her longingly and then marching off, his heart on fire. It was too much.

In the meantime Ratchett Kimbrell would have been waiting among some flowering bushes across from the hotel where McClintock had been led to believe Reri was staying, and when the consul was satisfied that the lovesick officer was safely gone, out he came in his bedroom slippers, shuffled across the open area, took the waiting Reri by the arm and led her off to bed in the consulate.

My problem with Ratchett and Reri had nothing to do with who was sleeping with whom or that an important naval officer was being made to look ridiculous; it involved something more serious. Ratchett, fed up with the dull routine of his duties in Tahiti, had turned over his top-secret code books to Reri. She kept them in the unlocked drawer of her desk and not only found pleasure in unraveling the messages that came to the office but also invited any girlfriends who happened to be dropping by to experience the fun of deciphering top-secret material. This had been going on for some time before I reached Papeete and the facts in the cables were widely known, not because Reri had talked but because some of her friends had circulated stories of what had come in via code.

I found it impossible to believe that either Washington or Allied headquarters in Noumea (in New Caledonia) knew anything specific about the code books, because if they did they surely would have taken steps to halt the practice. Their information dealt only with Ratchett's failure to certify ships properly and the general carelessness of his operation; there was probably also something about allowing native women to have the run of his offices, but I supposed that this had happened at other posts without disrupting things.

I did not know what to do about the code books, for I was obviously not the 'senior United States officer present,' a phrase that carried considerable weight in the military; Lieutenant Commander McClintock outranked me by a considerable margin, and it was quite possible that he too was in Tahiti to look into the Kimbrell business. At any rate I decided to leave the matter to others for the time being; my assignment had been merely to find out what was happening.

In the meantime, through the good offices of Lew Hirshorn, I was meeting an exciting array of Tahitian residents. There were English remittance men living well on allowances that would have been niggardly had their recipients fled to southern France, sons of important American industrial families who had gone native and Europeans of all sorts. But the man I had been most eager to meet was not in Tahiti during the war. On later trips I would get to know James Norman Hall, famous co-author of the *Bounty* trilogy, and his delightful English-Polynesian wife, Lala Winchester, daughter of an English sea captain and a Tahitian princess. They were a grand couple, he stately and reserved, she a bubbling fount of funny stories and outrageous rumors about the ridiculous behavior of island couples.

Hall was famous for his novels and the superb movies that had been made from them. Most strangers who made a pilgrimage from their cruise ships to see him praised *Mutiny on the Bounty,* but I had been especially taken by both the book and the movie of *Hurricane,* and he was amused to find that I could recall one admirable scene after another of that grand picture: 'I liked *Bounty* of course. Everyone did. But I must say I preferred *Hurricane* because it dealt with island life, island characters and settings.' He made no comment, but when I began to show that I could recall most of the scenes in the picture, he became interested.

'Why did it strike you so favorably?' he asked, and I said: 'From that opening scene when the island doctor played by Thomas Mitchell stands at the railing of his ship and speaks mournfully of the lost island of Manakoora to the final scene, when Raymond Massey, looking through his telescope, sees clearly that the escaping criminal, Jon Hall, and his wife, Dorothy Lamour, are in the canoe, but tells his wife, Mary Astor: "You're right. . . . It's only a floating log," it was all so Tahiti, so right.'

'You really studied the picture, didn't you?'

'I memorized it—saw it twice in the States—and then we had it at our base at Espiritu Santo.'

Of course, everyone who visited Tahiti heard the rumor that Hall's collaborator, Charles Nordhoff, had supplied the poetic passages in their books and had created the characters, while Hall merely worked out the plot devices and the long narrative portions, but having met Hall and seen the poetry in his eyes when I mentioned specific scenes, I gave no credence to that rumor. I did ask him how the partners had decided whose name should come first, and he gave an instructive answer: 'It's always effective to end a sentence or anything else with a short, crisp word. Hall and Nordhoff doesn't sound half as effective.'

I never met Nordoff and am not sure he was living in Tahiti during my various trips, and, except for that terse comment about name order, I never heard Hall speak about him; I judged that he was fed up with visitors who wanted to discuss aspects of their collaboration, one of the most famous in history.

But to get back to my wartime stay in Tahiti: I was sorry to have missed Hall for a specific reason. I had been told he was a friend of Robert Dean Frisbie, the writer, and I regretted not learning what Hall might know about him. But Lew Hirshorn was able to fill that gap: 'Everyone in Tahiti knows the Frisbie story. Young American of great promise, came out here penniless and went native. Could write like an angel, even Hall says that: "Great talent. Knows far more about the islands than I ever will, but self-destructive. Doomed." The Americans in Tahiti often discuss what we can do to help Frisbie. He has four or five children, you know, and even though we feel sorry for the way he has to live, we do admire him for refusing to abandon the kids. Where he goes, they go. But he's a cantankerous son-of-a-bitch. Won't let you help him, so we've pretty much written him off.'

'His wife?'

'Dead.'

'If I am able to help him, then what?'

'He'll go on dragging his kids from one lonely atoll to another, pitiful case. Hall told me once: "Because I've found a steady life I've known the paradise that the South Pacific can be. Frisbie knows the hell." '

'What's he doing on Pukapuka?'

'Dying.'

I had never met Frisbie, but I had read one of his books that had been recommended to me by an Australian who had given it the same high praise as Hall. It was a lovely, relaxed account of life in the area I was coming to know so well, and it was obvious to me, having once been a book editor, that if Frisbie got hold of himself he could write a fine novel about the kind of adventures he'd had. To learn that he was dying was a shock.

But I would wait till I reached Pukapuka to grapple with that sad problem. Now I was immersed in the Ratchett Kimbrell matter and the more I saw of Ratchett, this relaxed Pickwick of a man, the more I liked him, for he was a person of wit but no guile. If he allowed Reri to handle his secret code books it was because he felt that she would gain pleasure from an exercise that bored him, and if he was willing to allow Lieutenant Commander McClintock to woo Reri during the early hours of the evening it was probably because it gave her a feeling of the old days in Paris to have such a young and gallant admirer. And, of course, Ratchett knew that when the young man had gone back to his hotel afire with the dreams of the South Pacific, Reri would be coming home with him. Me? I was now enraptured with one of Reri's younger sisters or cousins, but I was as forlorn as McClintock because she was in love with someone else.

Still, I was enjoying myself in Papeete, for in the early part of the evening we all went to the movie house, which was a lively scene with young people all over the place and a level of noisy involvement that I had not seen elsewhere. The island had only one film, a colossal disaster called *South of Pago Pago*.

Victor McLaglen was the chief hero, Jon Hall of *Hurricane* the secondary hero, but we did not go to cheer them; we went to participate in one of the funniest scenes ever filmed. It hadn't been meant to be funny when shot or when shown in a typical theater—in fact, it wasn't even amusing in any normal situation—but in Papeete in that crowded theater it caused riots three nights a week.

The hilarity involved a local fellow, Bill Bambridge, who, after holding many jobs in Tahiti, wound up in Hollywood, where he was offered a series of minor roles, one of which was that of the native chieftain in *South of Pago Pago*. Bambridge was known in Tahiti to enjoy a beer now and then.

In his big scene, the one we waited for with mouths watering, Bambridge plays the part of an island chieftain striving to protect his people from the villains, who are endeavoring to neutralize him by getting him drunk. When the chief villain offers him a big glass of whiskey, he says in high moral dudgeon: 'No! I never touch the stuff!' whereupon the house went wild. I saw this movie four times, and at each screening the big self-denial scene got an increasingly rousing hand; the rest of the movie I have forgotten, but Bambridge's big scene ranks in my memory with Clark Gable carrying Vivien Leigh up those stairs in *Gone With the Wind*.

Ratchett Kimbrell's story came to an anticlimactic end, for when stars-in-his-eyes Lieutenant Commander McClintock was called back to Honolulu, he bade Reri a tearful farewell, kissed both her hands and was ferried to the airstrip at Bora Bora. Then, of course, Ratchett had Reri completely to himself. He eyed me suspiciously for a while as a possible rival in the McClintock vein, but my ambitions did not fly so high, and things were going along rather peacefully, with Reri and the other girls handling the secret dispatches and me sampling island life in the sprawling home of Reri's family.

Then one day as I was lounging in Quinn's, listening to Eddie Lund, two girls ran in from the American consulate with a message for me. It had arrived in code, of course, but they had decoded it and passed it around for others to see. It advised me that there had been trouble with the young Catholic priest in Fiji and that I should stop by the island on my way from Pukapuka.

The cable gave me much to think about, but the problems of the priest were not foremost. I wondered what might have happened if that cable had warned me about some possible misbehavior of the Vichy French supporters on the island, with the girls decoding it and passing it among their friends in the bars. The possible consequences were not pretty, so with my cable in my hand I went to confront Ratchett.

He was at home, unshaved, dressed in old clothes and in his customary bedroom slippers. He had apparently been drinking rather heavily the night before, for his eyes were not focusing sharply and it took him some moments to realize who I was. When he did, he asked: 'What is it, Michener?' and when I complained about how my cable had been mishandled by Reri's friends and warned him for the first time that things would have to be changed in Papeete, he produced a cable of his own, which informed him that his duties in Tahiti were being terminated and that he was being transferred to a post in Australia. I asked him somewhat acidly if Reri and her friends had decoded that one too, and he replied: 'They decode them all. Nothing important ever comes this way,' and since he was now being moved out of Tahiti, I saw no reason to file any report on his highly personal interpretations of government duty.

I left Papeete on the *Hiro,* but it was a lonely trip north, for neither Lew Hirshon nor Francis Sanford sailed with me, and as the old ship edged its way out of the lovely harbor, with the mountains of Moorea in the distance, I thought how painfully anticlimactic my trip to Tahiti had been. I began to form towering visions of how it ought to have been, if one were writing a book about it. The island would have been more beautiful, the grubby little interisland boats along the quay luxurious yachts. Ratchett Kimbrell would have been a distinguished diplomat, a former American ambassador who looked like Lewis Stone on a top-secret mission on which the fate of America in the Pacific depended, Reri fifteen years younger and the star not only of *Tabu* but also of *Mutiny on the Bounty;* she would also have been a Japanese spy, although how that could be I hadn't quite worked out. Lieutenant Commander McClintock would have been even better-looking than he was, more like Clark Gable, and he would have been an American operative, a real do-or-die type, who had been sent there disguised as a foppish

officer from Hawaii, but was actually a hero of the deadly Pacific war
with hidden medals he had won in his aerial battles with Zeros, six of
which he had shot down. And I would have been the disciplined observer with the golden pen of a Somerset Maugham or the silvery
resonance of a Joseph Conrad.

What a romance I might have fashioned, with a proper literary climax: James Norman Hall and I take a secret flight north to rescue the
dying Robert Dean Frisbie, whom we would find writing the final
perfect pages of his last novel, which would ensure his immortality.

My sojourn in Tahiti might have happened the way I wished it had,
and it ought to have, but it didn't.

If Bora Bora from the air presented concentric circles with a majestic
dead volcano in the center, Pukapuka showed only a circular lagoon
completely empty but subtended by one of the most miserable reefs in
the Pacific. At places only a few yards wide and a few feet above sea
level, the land of the island turned endlessly until it completed the circle,
providing here and there widened-out areas where clusters of mean huts
clung perilously to what solid land there was. It was a place of utter
loneliness, the end of the world, and all who saw it for the first time in
those years had the same thought: Come a major hurricane, such as the
one in the movie, this place is a goner.

As Hall had told me, there were two Pukapukas in the vicinity of
Tahiti, one well to the northeast, the other somewhat farther to the
northwest. We were headed for the latter, and when we dropped low
over the ocean to line up for the narrow runway, it seemed as if there
was no land available, only the dark ocean to the south, gray lagoon to
the north. Then suddenly and with a touch of mystery the coral reef
loomed up and we were throwing dust.

There was no airport building. Since we were in a hurry, we dropped
the ramp quickly and ran down the metal stairs. There, standing with
no shade to protect him, stood Frisbie, whose writings about the Pacific
were some of the finest on the subject. He seemed old and frail. A man
with an immense lantern jaw, as much of it as could be seen under his
greasy pandanus hat, he wore torn clothes that had not been mended
in years and a pair of soiled sneakers. What a pitiful contrast he was to
James Norman Hall, whom I would meet later, a man of comparable
talent but infinitely greater discipline. Was this the end of the writer, to
be dying alone and ill and penniless on a remote atoll? It was fearful to
see, this wreck of a man once great with promise, the ultimate beachcomber.

And then my attention was diverted from the mournful figure of Frisbie to one of the most touching tableaux I would ever see. To the airplane to bid their father farewell had come four of the Frisbie children, all clean and bright-faced and smiling. The oldest daughter, Johnnie, about fourteen, had risen early, we learned, and had scrubbed her brother and two sisters, dressing them in their best so that they would look proper when they went to say good-bye for what might be the last time. The boy was a lively lad, quite handsome, with mixed Caucasian-Polynesian features, while the other two sisters, twelve and ten, in island smocks and with flowers in their hair, could have been characters in an island fairy tale: They were handsome girls—Johnnie sober and responsible, Elaine round-faced and rowdy, Nga already a great beauty with luminous eyes and finely formed facial bones, the kind that most women long for.

If their father represented the prototypical fate of the beachcomber, his four children symbolized the splendid results of the Caucasian-Polynesian mix, as if to justify the great adventure of white men coming into the tropics. The juxtaposition was so painful that I had to look away as waves of emotion swept over me. In a few minutes we were going to load Frisbie onto our plane and whisk him away to a hospital in Samoa while his four children, only one even in her teens, stood bravely on the edge of the runway to watch him depart. How many children does one know, their mother dead, who are abandoned in such a predicament? How many children could survive on such a bleak atoll?

Deeply moved, I collected a handful of bills from our crew, and after we had taken aboard their father on a kind of stretcher, I ran down the steps and gave the oldest girl the money. Embracing her, I whispered: 'We'll save your father and we'll come back to rescue you,' and we were off, but as long as Pukapuka remained in sight I stared down to see those children standing on the coral strand.

I cannot leave them there, not even in memory. Some years later, when I was working in Hawaii, I received a cryptic letter from Rarotonga, capital of the Cook Islands. It came from a couple I did not know, but they must have been a wonderful pair, for they wrote:

> We cannot guess by what terrible routes they reached here, but the three daughters of Robert Dean Frisbie are in Rarotonga. Their father died, as one might have expected, from a rusty hypodermic and no one knows what to do with the girls. We have learned that American law requires them to get onto

American soil within the next two weeks if they hope to establish their claims to citizenship. Otherwise they must remain
Polynesian islanders the rest of their lives.

We have collected enough money to ship them by air to
Honolulu in time to save them. For the love of God, do something to help these wonderful children.

In the last few days of their eligibility, by utilizing the airplane tickets
the good samaritans in Rarotonga had supplied, Johnnie, Elaine and
Nga slipped into the United States, where we found homes for them.
Lovely girls and well trained by their father, they fitted easily into
American schools and later into American life. Johnnie published a
book about her growing up and married Carl Hebenstreit, a television
producer. Elaine married Don Over, a millionaire magazine publisher.
And cool beautiful Nga went to Hollywood, where she married Adam
West, star of the television series *Batman.* I saw them often, and thought
of them as the magical fruit of the beachcomber syndrome. Even now
I have a vision of them as they stood together on the coral strand of that
isolated atoll. Had they not been the kind of children who would rise
early on that morning and dress in their best to greet us and coura-
geously bid their dying father farewell they would never have made it
to the States. The boy had elected not to join them; he wanted to become
a jockey in New Zealand, which he did.

During the flight from Pukapuka to the U.S. naval hospital in American
Samoa I tended Frisbie, holding his head occasionally in my lap, and
in moments when he felt strong enough to talk he told me of how he
had reached the South Seas and of how he had wandered among the
little islands, always preferring them to the big ones, and of how he had
met his island wife. I think he said that he had lived on both the
Pukapukas, but that his preference had been for the one on which I had
found him. He had for a brief spell been an agent for the famous Burns
Philp line of island stores, a task at which he said he was not very good,
and he chuckled when he recalled his inept storekeeping. It was clear
to me that his vital energies were failing and I hoped we could get him
to the hospital while he was still conscious.

As soon as I entertained that painful thought I realized that what
really bothered me was a much more selfish concern: I hoped he did not
die on the airplane because if he did it would be a considerable inconve-

nience to us—it was imperative that we press on to my duties in Fiji, whatever they turned out to be.

When we had him in the Navy ambulance I told the doctor in charge: 'Remind the authorities that he left four kids behind on Pukapuka,' but the doctor replied, quite properly: 'Let's do first things first. Let's see if we can keep him alive.' I went to the rear door of the ambulance, and, using his Polynesian name, said to him: 'Ropati, the doctors are quite hopeful, and I'll start things moving to rescue your kids when I get back to Noumea.' And I saw Frisbie no more.

When I arrived late that afternoon in Fiji and went to the G.P.H. in Suva, I found the hotel abuzz with gossip of one sort or another, but two substantiated facts stood out: Bishop Dawson had flown in from his convocation in Samoa and seemed to be in charge of urgent discussions on some crisis, no doubt the one for which I had been recalled; and the New Zealand girl, Laura Henslow, was still in charge of the registration desk, although somewhat flustered to see me when I stopped to sign her ledger. 'Have you heard?' she asked as I handed back the pen, and I replied: 'Nobody tells me anything.' Visibly wincing, she said: 'This time there's a lot to tell.'

In Fiji in those days the U.S. Navy maintained a one-man liaison office and I telephoned the officer in charge, asking him to have dinner with me in my hotel, and shortly he was sitting at my regular table while the barefoot and beturbaned Indian waiter who served me so well hovered over us. It was under his care that I learned to eat lamb curry, a dish of which I became excessively fond, especially when it was accompanied by Major Grey's chutney, a remarkable concoction for which the major, whoever he was, deserved full marks.

'What's happening?' I asked, placing before my guest the cable I had received in Tahiti; he did not even look at it, for Noumea had sent him a copy. Pushing it back, he said: 'All hell's broken loose, but maybe that isn't the phrase to use, because it's a Church matter.'

'Involving what?'

Jerking his right thumb back over his shoulder toward the direction of the reception desk, he said softly: 'The New Zealand girl. The young priest we just ordained, he's fallen in love with her.'

'Are you Catholic?'

'No, but I helped Bishop Dawson at the ordination ceremony. Remember?'

'Is that why the bishop hurried back from the big do in Samoa?'

'It is.'

'And what can I do to help?'

'Stand by. This thing could develop in a lot of different ways.'

'That's not very helpful,' and since the chair in which I was sitting provided a clear view of Laura's desk, I could see she was still as agitated as she was when she greeted me. When she caught me staring at her, she waved her hands back and forth across her face as if she wished to make herself invisible. I could see that she was in trouble, and as our liaison officer continued his explanation I understood why.

'We think it started shortly after Laura's arrival from New Zealand. That would be well before his formal ordination, but well after he had been assured that he would be accepted as the first Fijian to ascend to the priesthood.' He stopped, looked down at his lap and smoothed the crisp linen napkin. 'The ugly part about this to me—as I said, I'm not a Catholic—is that he must have known about this long before he accepted ordination, and we're positive he knew what he might be about to do that day of the big celebration. He was already teetering when he accepted entry into the priesthood. I call that dirty pool, damned dirty.'

'What precisely is he thinking of?'

'Resigning from the priesthood. Resigning from Catholicism, probably. Eloping with her and getting the hell off the island.' With obvious bitterness he revealed the surprising cause of his anger: 'What eats me about this is that it's so unfair to Bishop Dawson. After all, he sponsored Bega, put his neck on the line to promote the young fool, first of his kind, and then to have it blow up in his face. Rotten. Rotten.'

'How's he taking it?' and with my eyes I indicated the table at which the bishop was dining alone, looking morose.

'He's a living saint. No wonder they love him in the islands. Never raises his voice. Never threatens anyone. Seems to have only two ambitions. Protect the Church and save the young fellow for the priesthood. He seems willing to make any concession—move him to another island—send him back to the seminary. Dawson is my kind of churchman, and I'm in his corner all the way.'

'And Laura?'

He was less than enthusiastic: 'They tell me she's proving very stubborn. Insists that since she and Bega really love one another, she will allow nothing to part them.'

'What does he say?'

'He doesn't know what hit him. Everything coming down on him at once. Priesthood, sex, people shouting at him, but as I said, Bishop Dawson never shouts. Just argues persuasively, pointing out the inevitables. He must despise the mess—Dawson, that is—coming so late in his life and so damned disappointing.'

When I asked why the Navy was involved, and what I was supposed to report, he gave a good answer: 'We can't afford to have any disturbance in Fiji that might disrupt our supply routes, and a lot of military shipping refuels in this harbor. Also, if things deteriorate we may be calling for a planc to get these people out of here in one hell of a hurry.'

I responded: 'I like your use of the military word *deteriorate*. You see this as a logistical problem, don't you?'

He laughed: 'In a way I do. In a well-ordered world where you live by the book, young priests do not fall in love with desk clerks,' and his last words that evening were a warning: 'Stand by for whatever happens. This thing can go either way—up, down or kerplooie,' and he threw his two hands apart, fingers extended, as if a bomb had exploded.

When he returned for some late-night work at his office, I went up to the desk and asked Laura: 'What goes on, Lady Macbeth?' and she jerked her right thumb back toward the management office, well hidden from the big dining room: 'They're firing me tomorrow morning. Government House is getting into the act, too.' Bringing her fingertips to her lips, she smiled ruefully and said: 'Michener, I could have used you these last three weeks.'

'Tough?'

'Very.'

'How did you meet him?'

She moved away from me as if uncertain of my reliability and apparently decided that the less she said the less anyone could use against her in case the enemy had sent me to spy on her: 'We met. Suva isn't a jail, you know. People do move about.'

'He's ready to leave the Church, isn't he?' When she refused to reply I asked: 'You a Catholic?'

'Church of England, but I take all religions seriously.'

'Your parents living?'

'Yes, but in this they don't figure.'

'What's Bishop Dawson been saying?'

'Drip, drip, drip. He thinks that in time water will wear away stone. But not this stone.'

'So you're determined?' I asked and she replied with a phrase she must have acquired from some schoolbook: 'I have been forged in fire.'

Her actions the next day showed this was not a careless use of words. Laura was discharged and told to get off the premises by nightfall; her continued presence jeopardized the good reputation of the hotel. That morning Bishop Dawson and several other high dignitaries were to meet with Father Bega in a last-ditch effort to persuade him to change his mind, put this sickness away from his heart and return full-fledged to the Church. Someone warned Laura of this meeting and with her jaw set she asked me to take her into the center of Suva to where the meeting was to be held, and on the way she told me with fierce determination: 'If he meets with them alone, he'll change his mind. I've got to stand with him or he'll crumble.' When I asked: 'Might it not be better if he did?' she said: 'No! They're using him, not as a man but as a symbol. A priest. The first Fijian to make that grade. I want him as a man.' She moved away from me in the taxi and said from her corner: 'The next half hour will determine everything. I will not allow him to meet those men alone. I will stand with him and they will be powerless to budge us.'

I was not allowed to attend the meeting, but it must have been a hectic one, with voices raised, and we heard later that only Bishop Dawson, that sage and kindly man, tried to cool tempers and keep the discussion focused on things that mattered. Apparently he was defeated by the rocklike insistence of Laura Henslow, a white woman fighting to defend her right to love a black man. The meeting lasted far more than the half hour Laura had predicted, and it was more heated than she had anticipated, but sometime after twelve, with tempers frayed, men broke from the meeting and informed me and the officer serving as acting American consul in Fiji: 'They'll be leaving. Advise Noumea to have the plane from Hawaii stop over at Nadi.'

That was the end of the storm over the heroic love affair that shook Fiji to its roots; Bishop Dawson had not been able to muster enough ecclesiastical power to defeat the stubborn New Zealand woman who by the sheerest accident and to her own amazement had fallen in love with the towering black priest for whom the Church had had such high hopes.

We traveled from Suva to Nadi, pronounced 'Nandi,' in separate cars: Laura and her priest in one, the bishop and two of his junior officials in theirs, the acting consul and I in ours, and since the ride was a long one, through some of the most rugged terrain of the South Pacific— coconut groves, winding trails up small hills and long runs beside the sea—it was dark before we pulled into the big military base at Nadi. Since the plane had not yet arrived from Honolulu, we waited in three separate groups, but American officers moved among us holding clipboards containing the documents we would have to sign to complete authorization for this extraordinary flight. The plane was not a commercial airliner but a B-17, a heavy bomber, which proposed, after refueling, to fly direct to Brisbane in Australia, where hurried plans were even then being made for Catholic officials to receive the fugitives and make such dispositions as they deemed best. What they would be no one in Fiji knew, least of all the fleeing lovers, who seemed more composed than any of us.

At last the huge plane came in and a ground officer told me: 'It would be more sensible if it laid over tonight and flew out in the morning, but our orders were strict: "Get them out of here tonight!" and we're doing it.'

It was something like one-thirty in the morning when the bomber completed its refueling and the ramp was ready to receive the exiles-to-be. Now all groups moved toward the plane, Laura striding defiantly and holding hands with the priest, who was still dressed in clerical garb; Bishop Dawson followed close behind—a sad and defeated cleric—along with officers from the base, with the consul and me bringing up the rear.

At the foot of the ramp Bishop Dawson moved forward to embrace Father Bega and give him his blessing; Laura he ignored. Other clergymen did the same, and I believe it was to restore a kind of balance that Laura signaled for me to come and bid her farewell. I kissed her warmly, and then came an embarrassing moment, for I had never met Father Bega face-to-face, and I did not know how to address him. But Laura saved the day by saying easily: 'Thomas, this is an American officer who has been very kind to me,' and we shook hands.

As they climbed the ramp I was attacked by an inadvertent thought: She looks so white and he so black. And I wondered if they had any concept of the fearful troubles they would have in Australia, which I had recently found to be one of the most race-conscious nations on earth, and an unworthy idea flashed: I wonder if Dawson and the Noumea authorities are sending them to Australia to teach them a lesson?

Then they were gone, vanishing into the cavernous belly of the bomber, and since it contained no windows from which they could wave to us, we saw them no more. All doors closed, the big plane moved out to the far end of the runway, lights seemed to spring up from everywhere, propellers whirred, and the giant creature sped down the runway at us and then rose majestically into the dark sky.

While helping to arrange the expulsion of Father Bega from Fiji, I received instructions from headquarters in Noumea: 'British Foreign

Office raising hell about behavior our men at Navy Base in Tonga. Foul-up involving little red truck. Fly down and send us fullest details.' I was pleased with the assignment because I had never visited Tonga but did know that it was a fairy-tale kingdom comprising a group of islands some five hundred miles southeast of Fiji. After the couple left for Australia, I flew direct from Nadi to Nuku'alofa, capital of the kingdom. There I fell immediately under the spell of the gigantic Queen of Tonga, six feet eight inches tall and about three hundred pounds, who would cause such a sensation in London some years later when she attended both the burial of King George VI and the coronation of Queen Elizabeth II. That her towering bulk and warm gracious smile made her the prime favorite of those processions came as no surprise to those of us who had known her during the war.

Queen Salote kept on her palace grounds a gigantic sea turtle reputed to be at least two hundred years old—some claimed three. Among other unusual sights in her kingdom was the mystic holy place consisting of two massive upright stones across whose tops rested an enormous platform—who erected them, when and for what purpose no one could say—and the nightly flight of thousands upon thousands of big bats, so many that they darkened the sky. It was our pleasure to go out at dusk with shotguns and knock a score or so out of the sky as they flew overhead, and we did not do this for sport; Tongans dived for the fallen bats, whose flesh they cooked into an excellent stew.

If I have given the impression that my extended tour of duty through the islands of my domain was somewhat free and easy, the reader should remember that on Bora Bora I worked diligently to compile the record of our military occupation of that island and now on Tonga I was similarly engaged with hour upon hour of research, interviews, calculating the number of our troops involved, and trying to solve the mystery of the little red truck.

I spent about three weeks assembling the easy answers and another week dictating my guess as to what had happened, but while doing so I broke down so often in uncontrollable laughter that I am not sure I provided a coherent account, and I see no point in trying to recall the specifics of my report, which ran to many hilarious pages. But a brief summary of what could happen to a group of military men in a tropical paradise when no one was looking might prove instructive.

In the early days of the war the kingdom of Tonga played a role of some importance, because it was feared that the Japanese attack, which could strike at any moment, might bypass Fiji, which was better protected, and capture Tonga, whose numerous islands could provide many fine anchorages for Japanese warships. Hurried steps were taken to defend against this danger, and in a corner of the town of Nuku'alofa a very large warehouse, which in peacetime had belonged to the trading firm of Burns Philp, was converted into a Navy warehouse. Crammed with valuable fighting gear and supplies to help withstand a siege, that warehouse became the focal point of my report, for everything that happened on Tonga in the period for which I was responsible revolved around that warehouse and its precious contents.

Since the anchorages of Tonga were the targets of importance, the U.S. Navy was naturally placed in control, and I would suppose that in the early days someone like a rear admiral had been in command. But as the battlefronts moved farther and farther north—to Guadalcanal, Bougainville and islands like Tarawa and Saipan—it was clear that the Japanese fleet could no longer risk the long run to Tonga to do minor damage. The danger was over. Experienced admirals and captains were required in the forward areas, and Tonga was left to fend for itself, which was when I came into the picture.

Only Gilbert and Sullivan could have done justice to what happened next. The principal comedian was a weak-chinned, inept, frightened naval officer of moderate rank who found himself commanding officer of the island and whom I shall call simply The Commander. From seeing too many movies he had come to believe that Navy captains should bluster and rasp out commands, but at the same time he was terrified of any emergency and handled it simply by disappearing. In one incident after another, when I tried to find out how The Commander handled it, I was told: 'He disappeared. We didn't see him for three days. Couldn't find him,' and when I asked: 'Where did he disappear to?' my informants would say: 'He just vanished. Maybe hiding in bed.' In not one crisis did The Commander ever participate.

He was a totally average man, indistinguishable in any way from the multitude of overweight forty-year-olds with thinning hair found in any populated area. He did have one peculiarity, which many of his men commented upon: from any group of women he had a penchant for picking out the prostitute and moving her into his quarters—on the Navy base. With such a commanding officer it was clear that our operation on Tonga was going to have problems.

But all was not lost. Assigned to Tonga was an extraordinary medical doctor, a Navy lieutenant commander whom I shall call merely The Doctor, a brisk, capable fellow who had all his life wanted to see military action and who, when he saw that his superior, The Commander, had abandoned even the pretext of running the base, leaped into the breach.

A staff officer who in no way was entitled to command, The Doctor, everyone agreed, proved himself to be an almost ideal Navy line officer. He was not afraid to issue orders, and they were usually the right ones. Nor was he loath to keep his men in line, for when necessary he could be stern.

He looked the part he liked to play: trim, with a firm jaw, eyes that missed little, a crisp voice suited to command and a handsome bearing. After spending a few days observing the pitiful performance of The Commander, he moved in and took control.

Like even the best men, he did have one weakness: he simply loved to discharge his heavy .45 revolver, for its powerful snap made him feel as if he were commanding not a backwater naval base on a peaceful island but a four-master fighting pirates on the open seas. Men who had enjoyed serving under him told me: 'Doc just loved to fire that cannon of his.' He'd hear a noise at night and come out blazing. In the afternoon a bird of some kind would fly near his quarters, and out would come the .45. At other times, we would see him standing on the sick-bay porch just firing away at a coconut palm as if he were determined to cut it down with bullets, just for the hell of it. He was one gun-happy man, and we used to say: 'Stay around him long enough and you'll lose a leg.'

But the base on Tonga might easily have operated without trouble, for The Commander never made waves and the captain was basically a responsible man, but they had the misfortune to operate in the midst of an unusual population, described in the official history in this blunt way: 'No native people in the South Pacific have such a bad reputation for petty thieving as do those of Tonga.' That judgment is mild, because the Tongans who lived around the naval base in Nuku'alofa carried theft to a degree of proficiency that would have awed Fagin or even an Al Capone, and the presence of what they saw as wealthy American troops in their midst made their mouths water.

Chief of the thieves in my time was a sly young fellow named Tipi, in his mid-twenties, wiry, light tan in coloring with jet-black hair, very white teeth, which he flashed at me whenever I interrogated him, and an awesome capacity for lying and covering his tracks. Had he continued with school, which he quit after the third grade, he would almost certainly have had a brilliant career in business or as a salesman for some reputable firm. As it was, all his aptitude for wheeling and dealing went into thieving, and when he came up against the gun-toting doctor, he surpassed himself in his acts of cunning.

It started, so far as I could reconstruct the episode, shortly after The Commander surrendered control and allowed The Doctor to assume command. Thirsting to taste the fruits of power, the belligerent doctor issued a battery of orders calculated to ensure discipline on the island, but this action caused irritation among both the sailors and the Tongan work force: 'Lieutenant Michener, he treated us natives same as cattle. We handled valuable equipment for Navy, never lose nothin'. Natives drive Navy cars, trucks, take better care your people do. Girl typists mo bettah than yeomen, everyone say that. Goin' movies at night part of our pay. Now all changed, we don't like.'

As soon as Tipi heard the first rumbles of discontent, he swung into action with his master plan, and the first step he took was to immobilize The Commander completely, with the enthusiastic aid of a prostitute with the unlikely name of Meredith. When I asked how she had acquired it, a Tongan girl who worked as a secretary on the base told me: 'She has a Tongan name, but one of her friends saw Meredith in a book and said: "This sound pretty, just like you," and the name stuck.' As to the productive meeting with The Commander, several eager gossipmongers informed me: 'Tipi arrange, and pretty soon Meredith sleeping on base and fixing for Navy equipment all kinds—refrigerators, stoves— to go to her little house next to Tipi's, and things she got extra, it goes to Tipi.'

Men on the base rarely saw The Commander after Meredith moved in, but now Tipi had to neutralize The Doctor, and he did this in an ingenious way. He had Tongan workmen build a small pistol range far removed from the big warehouse, and there The Doctor conducted target practice for hours at a time. The drill on the base became: 'Commander in bed with Meredith, Doctor busy at the range, nobody guardin' the store.'

It was here that the little red truck became a major part of the story of Tonga because it was involved in an outrageous series of events that came to a violent head on August 14, 1944, before I reached the island. A native enabled me after considerable questioning to piece together a reasonable account of what happened: 'I work with Tipi like you already know. My job, watch The Commander's shack be sure he in bed with Meredith, watch the pistol range be sure The Doctor over there. I give signal "All O.K." then Tipi drive little red truck down that lane way over there, nobody see from here, he go around back.' Another of Tipi's cohorts enlightened me: 'We get wire cutters, three men, me, two others. We go back the big warehouse nobody can see, we cut snip, snip, snip'—his hands opened and closed rapidly as if holding wire cutters— 'and we cut two panels out of warehouse, big enough red truck drive right in.'

'For what purpose?'

'First time Tipi drive his truck in, he take only cigarettes, canned food, things native people like, all what you call PX stuff.'

'How could he sell it? We have military police, you know.'

'Not sell! Give away!'

'Surely somebody must have discovered the big hole in the back of the warehouse?'

'Commander asleep, Captain firing gun. Navy chiefs all home their Tongan girls.'

'So what happened next?'

'Tipi never take enough make police catch on. Next trip radios, washing machines, fine set of tools.'

That was how things stood on the evening before the fourteenth of August.

In the morning The Doctor found that a gasoline can had been stolen from his jeep, so he went to an official of the Tongan government to lodge a formal complaint. While he was inside the office, thieves jacked up his jeep to steal all four tires, and when everyone ran out to inspect the cannibalized car, a different set of thieves sneaked in through the back of the office and stole most of the furniture, plus The Doctor's briefcase.

That did it. In a rage The Doctor returned to his own quarters, and then, without actually issuing orders, he more or less let the men know that he would not interfere if they stormed through the Tongan community repossessing whatever they identified as goods stolen from the Navy. The news was received in the barracks with wild enthusiasm, and with The Doctor in the van with two loaded revolvers, what became known in Navy records as The Great Cigarette Raid began.

The rampage lasted all of the fourteenth to midnight, and all the next day till sunset, and the cataloging of brutalities, forcible recovery of goods and indignities visited on peaceful civilians would fill many pages. In reports provided me, three incidents especially caught my eye and I included them in my official account. One group of sailors, outraged by the way in which the prostitute Meredith had lorded it over them while serving as the The Commander's mistress, raided the house she maintained in the village and from which she plied her trade when not sleeping on the base, but found nothing. The place was bare, as was the normally well-furnished house next door belonging to Tipi; that clever lad, forewarned that a riot might be brewing, had moved all valuable items out of the two houses and hidden them amid distant trees.

Another group of commandos stormed into the house of a notorious thief and finding no Navy property on the premises, although they knew he must have a hoard stashed somewhere, were so frustrated that one sailor, to scare the man, whipped out his revolver and fired into the roof above the thief's head, whereupon the other sailors commenced firing their guns through the roof until sunlight streamed in. Neighbors told me later: 'We afraid that many in community being executed.'

The culminating episode occurred when another gang came upon a house whose prosperous look seemed to prove it had been furnished with Navy goods. The sailors rushed in, manhandled the elderly man they found in a room furnished like a study, then assembled all the women in the place and terrorized them, threatening to shoot them and the old man unless they relinquished the stolen goods. Belatedly, Tongan police rushed in to inform the raiders that they had wrecked the residence of the Prime Minister. During all this fury, no one had seen or heard from The Commander, and where he was hiding I never found out.

When the two-day rampage ended, The Doctor blew down the barrels of his revolvers to clear them of smoke, and returned to his quarters firmly convinced that the Tongans had been taught a lesson. But when I interrogated islanders about the aftermath, I found this was hardly the case: 'Pretty soon all quiet, The Commander asleep again with Meredith. Doctor shooting at the range. All nice. So Tipi bring his red truck again, we back it into big hole where no one see us and we start to haul out real big things—generators—like that.'

'What did Tipi do with such things?'

'Nobody lookin', he takes them to ships in harbor, they go to islands in the Ha'apa Group, maybe Vava'u Group, far away, they need things same like us.'

'But why did you always go in the afternoon? You might have been seen.'

'Night time they very careful. Guards. Big dogs too, we not try.'

'And you were never caught?'

'Nobody see us. Look, you sit here same Commander, you not see back of warehouse, specially you sleep in bed, very happy.'

In order to give my report verisimilitude, I knew I had to inspect the big warehouse myself. So, along with a Tongan policeman, a guard from the nearly disabled base and my two informants, I went to the big front doors, unlocked the double bolts and stepped into the gloomy grayness of the huge building. To my astonishment it was completely empty. There was only a big gaping hole in the rear.

'Where's the gear?' I asked, and the Navy guard said: 'I told you—he stole it all.'

I was aghast, for to empty a building that size Tipi must have made scores of trips in his truck, and his fellow thieves confirmed what he said.

'First time easy, small stuff. Then bigger, still easy. Everything easy, he just keep goin' till all gone.'

'Where did it go?'

'Like before. Small things, PX food, like that to people here. Big things take four men to carry, always on little ships to other islands.'

'You mean, *everything* that was in here—you shipped it all out?'

'Yep. All go.'

'What happened to the little red truck?'

'Shore police gettin' suspicious. Him, me, we paint it white.'

'And then?'

'Maybe ship to Ha'apa Group, maybe Vava'u, maybe Tipi go fetch when he get out of jail.'

I felt a keen desire to see this mastermind and persuaded the Tongan officer to let me visit the rude jail. I happened to be entering just as an attractive young woman was on her way in to see the prisoner. It was Meredith, Tipi's friend, who had proved so helpful in Tipi's plans. We talked for about an hour, and I deduced that Tipi had propelled Meredith into The Commander's bed not primarily to provide cover while he emptied the warehouse but rather to enable each of them to cadge a newly built house from the Navy. Everything in Meredith's house and his, including walls, ceilings and roofs, had been either stolen from the Navy by Tipi or given to Meredith by The Commander, and I could believe the report that the citizens of Tonga, especially the young women, had profited to the extent of at least one million dollars from the occupation, not counting lawful salaries.

'Did you really like The Commander, Meredith?'

'Oh, yes. Kind man, he help me fix my house.'

'He gave you many things?'

'Yes. He one good man, got two babies Oklahoma.'

I asked Tipi what he would do when his prison term ended and he said brightly: 'I think maybe go back work Navy. Old commander go, new man maybe need help.'

'Where did you get the little red truck?'

He considered this for some moments, then said: 'It belong Commander. Navy blue. Two men, me, we paint it red one night, he never guess.'

'Where is it now?'

'Vava'u.'

'You bring it back when you get out?'

'Yes. My brother have it, he give it back when I ask.' As I was about to leave the pair he asked: 'You speak me good, police? Tell them I needed at naval base?'

Our base was much reduced when I berthed there during the writing of my report, but as the Marines say in their famous poster, 'We're looking for a few good men,' and I made the recommendation to Queen Salote, who towered over me as I spoke. She told me how gratified everyone on her islands was that the American occupation had gone so smoothly, and that without sensible and understanding men like The Commander this would not have been possible. She asked: 'If we pardon this Tipi fellow, would you reemploy him at your base? and I said a firm 'Yes.' I needed what only he could tell me.

Halfway through the writing of my report, when I was distressed by the ravages The Commander and The Doctor had visited upon our friendly ally Tonga, I drafted a paragraph that was intended as an evaluation of this gross miscarriage of military deportment:

> If the Tongan experience proves anything constructive, it is that incompetent base commanders must be identified early and moved out quickly. But they should not be replaced by medical doctors just out of civilian life who love revolvers and have dreams of military glory, especially if there are attractive girls about who have larcenous friends.

But later my attitude was somewhat softened:

> When these two lovable clowns were finally removed from Tonga, their place was taken by a fine young lieutenant in the Naval Reserve named P.G. Polowniak whose wise administration had the place back on track within three weeks. They should have sent him two years earlier.

My last stop was Matareva. Just as with Tonga, Matareva had been vitally important in the early days of the war. When the threat of Japanese invasion waned, the real fighting men were moved north. A cadre was left behind to guard the place, and an officer not qualified for the job was left in charge, a mirror image of The Commander at Tonga.

But there the similarities end: Tonga was manned by happy-go-lucky sailors, Matareva by a company of sharply trained Marines; and where events on a bypassed and forgotten tropical base at Tonga led to comedy, on Matareva they would end in tragedy.

When I first landed on Matareva and was driven from the airstrip to the Marine base, I was struck by the vast difference between this reef-lined island and Samoa. Here there was no coral road edging the sea and lined with palms and handsome fales; the road was mean and provided no vistas. Certainly there were no smiling maidens rising from the sea to wrap sarongs around their handsome brown bodies. This was Melanesia, and a general gloominess seemed to prevail. The base was defended around its entire perimeter by three strands of barbed wire, inside which stood a row of unpainted barracks, now three-fourths empty; no flowers and only a few trees relieved the starkness. As soon as the Marines landed in early 1942 the site had been bulldozed to prevent any Japanese infiltrators from finding cover. In those days the danger had been real and a Major General Tompkins had run a taut ship, but by 1943 men of his stamp were long gone.

My pressing desire upon entering the base was to learn as much about Captain Mark Dorn as I could, but after the total housecleaning prior to the big court-martial there were no Americans stationed here now who had known him. There was just hearsay, residual memories: 'We know that he came from an FFV . . .' When I looked puzzled, a junior officer explained the initials: 'First Family of Virginia—going way back. He'd been chairman of the Honor Board at the University of Virginia—very strict outfit—one peek at someone else's examination booklet and you were out on your ass, no appeal if Mark Dorn's board decided you were guilty.'

'He'd been in R.O.T.C.,' another man volunteered, 'either on campus if they had a company or in summer training of some kind and had elected to join the Marines—Quantico—gung-ho all the way—Jack Armstrong, the All-American boy. I've heard from men who were in training with him that he was moderately well liked, but that real tough guys thought he took the book of rules too seriously. He didn't smoke or drink, and poker games would have been quite beyond him.'

'He had a normal experience in the Corps, I guess,' the first officer said, 'but I can't say what it consisted of. Next you hear of him after Quantico, he's on this rock.'

And there the discussion ended, because no Marine, especially no officer, was willing to speak in even the most guarded language about Dorn's experience on Matareva. I went to my bunk that first night aware that I was not going to learn much from the present gang occupying the island. Just as I was about to fall asleep I saw through the open window by my bunk—there was no glass anywhere in the barracks—the three strands of barbed wire surrounding the base and they loomed so ominously in the starlight that I thought: They wired themselves in and

prevented the therapy of nature from helping. And the longer I remained on Matareva the more constricting that barbed wire became.

From my study of the court-martial summaries in the files at Noumea
I had learned that the other Marine I had to get information on was Staff
Sergeant Mike Hazen, but when I tried to probe his case with my new
bunkmates, I got absolutely nowhere. No one knew anything about him
or about his service on Matareva or on any prior duty station, and no
one cared to know; he was a man who never existed, and my queries
about him were not welcomed.

However, outside the gates of the base there were many who had
known both Dorn and Hazen, Matarevan men and women who had
worked inside the wire during the first hectic days and also in the quieter
days when Dorn was in command, and one old fellow had a photograph
of the two, which was helpful. As he handed it to me he said: 'Habit
our island, kids see white man have camera shout "Poto me! Poto me!"
same word you call take photo. I standin' here Dorn this side, Hazen
that I shout like a kid: "Hey, you poto me!" and the one guy do . . .
fine picture I think—this me, this Hazen—this Captain Dorn.'

Flanking the dark man, who looked younger then, stood Captain
Dorn in work clothes with head uncovered, showing hair, parted neatly
down the right side and not Marine crew-cut-short but more like the cut
of a young businessman. His shirt was open at the neck and betrayed
signs that he had been working hard and sweating, but he was apparently in excellent shape, for he showed no fat, and his eyes were bright.
Except for his slightly long hair, he seemed the typical Marine junior
officer, able, well trained and ready for anything.

Staff Sergeant Hazen was quite different: barrel-chested, jutting jaw,
hair clipped tight almost to the scalp so that he looked like a skinhead,
mean eyes and hamlike hands—a fighting Marine, who could have been
used on a recruiting poster. But one thing bothered me: he was a staff
sergeant, not a drill sergeant, and when I asked about this the old fellow
explained: 'Hazen he type, keep papers in office. He check my work slip,
sign his name, other man pay me.' Mike Hazen was not your typical
yeoman, the name we used for his position in the Navy.

From the native I picked up only desultory information about the two
men: Dorn was a competent commander, but no fiery leader like his
predecessor, and Hazen was far above average as an office-bound sergeant—his men liked him and some of his Matarevan workmen considered him the best ever. However, from odd bits of information I got the
feeling that Hazen had played favorites and that it was not always merit
that had led to promotions among the native work force; but I was really

getting nowhere until one of his former workmen told me: 'Mo bettah you talk Ropati, Burns Philp store—he knows all.'

When I walked the short distance to the island store, one of the chain operated by the historic firm in Sydney, Australia, I found behind the counter a young Matarevan whose father or grandfather must have been an English sailor who took up beachcombing on this or some other island, for I was later to learn that his legal name was Robert Weed, known locally as Ropati, a fine-looking chap probably in his late twenties, with a light-tan complexion, very black hair, white even teeth and fluent English: 'I'm not employed here. Just helping out. I heard you'd flown in from Nadi.'

'Yes. I suppose it's already known that I came here to check a few points about the Dorn-Hazen affair.'

'You're about the fifth American officer who's come here to ask me about that. Who sent you to see me?'

'The old fellow who used to run the motor pool at the Marine base.'

'Yes. Now, anything he told you is apt to be true. Excellent man, very loyal to the Marines. They ought to give him a uniform.'

'He was vague about what job you had held.'

'Jobs,' Ropati corrected. 'Why don't we sit on the porch?' In any island town the center of life tended to be the Burns Philp store—a combination of grocery, dry goods store, automotive repair shop, bank and a place for gossip—and as we sat there in the warm morning air several customers stopped by, all greeting Ropati and nodding when he said: 'The boy inside will help you' while he remained with me.

He sat, I remember, with his right foot resting on the bench we shared, his arms clasped about his knee, a position that would have been impossible for me and I commented on this: 'You must be double-jointed?' and he laughed: 'Exercise. Tennis on the court over there.' I told him that I was an avid tennis player and he said: 'We must have a try one morning. Early, before it gets too hot.' Then he added: 'Captain Dorn built the court. Enlisted the help of scores of people like me. Said he must not use any Marine money for such a project and was careful to provide his personal money for net and wire for the backstop.'

'An honorable man?'

'A gentleman. To him everything had to be done honestly—"up front" he called it.'

'Why did he get into trouble?'

Ropati drew his knee tighter against his chest, and, weighing his words very carefully, said: 'If he had whipped out his revolver and shot Hazen that first day— You're not going to write about this, are you?'

In the few minutes we had talked I had gained considerable respect for this young man and was eager to have him talk freely, so I leveled with him in the manner I hoped he would with me: 'I read the full court-martial report up to the point where they broke it off—they didn't want material like that in the record where someone might uncover it later.'

'We heard they ended it abruptly. They were going to fly me to Noumea to testify, and I was at the airfield, ready to go, but then they called it off. Best for all, maybe.'

'Best for all. But since you now know what I know, I'd really like to zero in.'

'Now, that's strange. Coincidental you might say. For some time I've been wanting to clear my mind about this affair.' He paused, as if ashamed or embarrassed about what he was going to say next: 'I've thought that some years down the line I might want to write about this. Brett Hilder, the Burns Philp ship captain, told me I ought to think about writing. You know that Louis Becke and Robert Dean Frisbie both worked for this company accumulating ideas about the South Seas before they started writing books.'

When I told him that only a few weeks ago I had rescued Frisbie from Pukapuka, he became intensely interested: 'One of the best writers we've had. A poet of the lonely reefs.' And the knowledge that I had recently helped Frisbie and conversed with Hall's friends encouraged him to trust me. Now he wanted to talk.

I debriefed him—the military phrase covers nicely such interrogation—over a period of about a week, long talks interspersed with good tennis, and in that time I learned the main details of what Ropati described accurately as 'the long downward slide of Captain Dorn.'

'It must have started in his boyhood. He showed me pictures one Christmas of his family in Virginia. Prussian Germans who had crossed the ocean to fight in the American Revolution, stayed on to buy a plantation. Fought in the Civil War, too, with Lee. His mother seems to have been hewn out of rock, raised him to see situations as black or white whenever moral decisions had to be made.'

Recalling things Dorn had told him about his family, Ropati asked: 'Did his record show that at the University of Virginia he was chairman of the committee that administered the honor system? Real big at Virginia, drum flourishes and all that.'

'What job did you have that allowed you to be so close that he would tell you such details?'

'Liaison. I had been appointed by the Colonial Office in London to see that relations between the Marines and the Matarevan natives were conducted honorably—fair pay and all that.'

'Was it a productive relationship?'

'The best. Never met a finer man than Dorn. A bit tense, but sane and sober and, above all, a man of the most severe attention to honor in all details.'

'Too rigid for his own good?' I asked.

'Not at all. He understood and appreciated Marine traditions to an admirable degree. In the beginning his men understood this and respected him.'

'What went wrong?'

'Staff Sergeant Hazen. If I were writing about this, and someday I might—'

'Where did you get your education? You use proper words, as in "If I *were* writing." '

'University of Auckland. Those New Zealand schools, if you get the right professors, can be excellent.'

'So if you do write, what will you say about Hazen?'

'I would place before my reader the problem that Shakespeare posed when he wrote about Iago: "Can there be pure, unmotivated evil in the world?" and more important: "Can a good man remain blind to the fact that an evil one is out to destroy him?" '

'Hazen was that kind of evil?'

'He was. I detected it fairly early. Dorn never did, until it was far too late.'

'What did you see that Dorn didn't?'

'That from the first day Hazen arrived on base—Dorn was here first by a good margin—Hazen was determined to destroy him. He hated him. He envied his Virginian upbringing, the fact that Dorn had gone to university and he hadn't. The fact that Dorn was proud of his family, while he had none that he knew of. But what really galled him was that the Marines respected Dorn for being a gung-ho type, the kind of man the Corps wanted, while he, Hazen, was just a staff sergeant shuffling papers.' Ropati stopped because he suspected that what he had to say next might be too revealing: 'He hated me, too, because I had the ear of the British government and a limited kind of power over the islanders employed at the base.'

'So how did Hazen start his moves?'

'He tried to sabotage every order that Dorn issued. In subtle ways. Not getting the word passed. Letting the men know they really didn't have to bother about that one. Snide comments. Telling me that Dorn's treatment of the Matarevans was unjust, not realizing that it was I who'd set the wage scales.'

'But if you saw, why didn't Dorn see?'

'He was what you call a Boy Scout. A true believer. To him Hazen was a Marine who had been promoted to staff sergeant by his superiors, so he was in Dorn's eyes a good one.'

When I asked a more probing question he evaded in a curious way: 'I think at this point you'd better talk with Tetua. Parts of the story she knows better than I do,' and he led me to the grass-roofed hut of an island girl whose movements were like palm trees swaying in the wind. She was lovely, with long black hair falling to her waist, a radiant smile and a serenity that seemed impervious to any storm, any disappointment. She had the kind of natural unaffected beauty that Gauguin loved to paint, and it was evident that she represented the best of half a dozen different nationalities—English, German, Chinese, Australian, French, Polynesian. Her English was soft and perfect, showing that she too had been to school in New Zealand.

During our long talks she told a story that could have happened only in the islands: 'Before I met Dorn I knew he was married. That's the first thing island women learn about a newcomer and my friends warned me: "You can set your cap for him, but it won't do you much good." But they were pleased—our women are like that—when we fell in love, and I made no secret of it. Anyway, who can keep a secret on Matareva?'

'What went wrong?'

'Hazen. For reasons I did not know at the time, he despised me. Did everything he could to humiliate me. To break me away from Mark, or Mark from me, he didn't care which.'

'But why?'

'Ropati tells me that you've read the court-martial report. Have you?'

'Yes.'

'Then it won't surprise you if I tell you that I realized early on that Hazen was a confirmed homosexual.'

I was not surprised because that was what the court-martial record was all about, but those were the days when people, especially young women, did not use that word casually, and its sudden explosion in the air startled me. The reason the court-martial had been such a fierce jolt to the Navy was that because of the crowding of young men in cramped quarters aboard destroyers and submarines, our service had developed an almost mortal fear of homosexuality. When a sailor was convicted of it he was thrown into a brig where supertough Marine guards were not only allowed but encouraged to brutalize him. In 1944 naval officers were taught to be terrified of homosexuality.

Tetua, seeing my uneasiness, said quietly: 'Hazen's dislike of me stemmed from that fact. But he also felt it necessary to oppose me because I was Mark's friend. He saw that so long as I remained faithful, Mark could not be isolated.' Now her placid face became clouded, and after a long pause during which she was obviously trying to decide which of many ugly paths through the dark jungle she wished to go, she said: 'It quickly became quite deadly, Lieutenant Michener. Hazen was inside the wire fence with all the Marines. Mark was outside with only me.'

'What about Ropati? Wasn't he on your side?'

Silence. 'I don't know how to answer that, not in a way you'd understand. I think you'd better ask Ropati about that.'

So I went back to my tennis partner, who was more than willing to explain what Tetua had preferred not to discuss: 'When Hazen had Dorn isolated, as Tetua properly described it, he began a systematic campaign to entice the younger Marines into his net.'

'What do you mean by that?'

He persuaded one after another of those young men to engage in sexual acts with him, and when they were indoctrinated he passed them along to others like himself. It was incredible, his malignant power.'

'The testimony, before it was silenced, said that some twenty of the young Marines joined what Hazen called The Club, and that's not easy to imagine. Nearly two dozen typical Marines—'

'More like three dozen. The whole area behind the fence went ape.'

This was shocking even though in Noumea I had known the general facts. Three dozen Marines, like the ones I had known on various bases and with whom I had flown on bombing missions out of Emirau, behaving in this way—it was difficult to believe. Controlling my emotions, I asked quietly: 'What role did you play?'

'From the first Hazen had taken a special interest in me. He put his arm around me and confided: "Ropati, I appreciate your skill in handling the Matarevans—" '

I lost my temper: 'Goddammit! He was just a staff sergeant! What was he doing, giving you his benediction, and what were you doing accepting it.'

'Lieutenant, he was running the base. He was in charge.' Ropati's voice rose perceptibly, for he was as contemptuous of my blindness as I had been of what I had thought was his. 'And how did he prove to me that he was in charge? When he failed three times to get me into bed

with him, he calmly drafted a report to my superiors in London charg-
ing me with incompetence and theft of funds that should have gone to
the islanders.' His voice rose to a shout: 'And—I—was—fired!'

Humbled by his passion that had obviously been long pent up I
suggested quietly that we walk over to Tetua's shack and clarify matters.
We sat together with a pitcher of lemonade that she provided, and I
asked a series of short questions.

'So inside the fence was a homosexual riot?' Yes.

'At least thirty Marines cooperating?' Maybe more.

'U.S. Marines! What in hell came over them?' Loneliness, the feeling
that they had been forgotten, betrayed by the high command. Month
after month no women, no mail, the same movie night after night, no
newspapers. The slow erosion of character through self-pity.

'Did any refuse to participate?' Obviously there were quite a few.

'How did Hazen handle them?'

'Ostracism. He was in control, remember.'

'Where in hell was Captain Dorn?' This required a long, involved
explanation, with Ropati speaking as one who had worked inside the
fence and seen the Machiavellian maneuvers that had rendered Dorn
powerless, even though he was a senior captain and Hazen not even a
commissioned officer; and Tetua describing the pitiful manner in which
Dorn had been emotionally and psychologically destroyed by Hazen's
campaign: 'After Ropati was fired and ordered by Hazen to stay off the
base, it was Dorn, Ropati and me outside trying to combat the horror
inside.' And once more I asked the question that had perplexed Marine
headquarters in Noumea: 'Why didn't somebody do something to stop
this?'

The explanation, simple yet heartbreaking, was offered by Ropati:
'Sometimes we wait till the vital moment has passed, and when we do
shout, nobody hears.'

'But you told me that you had spotted Hazen as a troublemaker right
off the bat. And you, Terua, you knew that he had strong homosexual
tendencies.' Their joint explanation stunned me: 'We both thought that
Dorn knew, but that he was biding his time. We waited, and since he
was the commander, we assumed he knew what he was doing.' Then
came Terua's sad voice: 'Too late he discovered he was powerless to do
anything.' Her voice broke and for some moments she wept quietly, then
said with great pain: 'In the end—maybe you know—Hazen wouldn't
even allow him to come onto the base. Locked the gate against him and
jeered when he tried to break in.'

Realizing that she could say no more because of her weeping, I turned to Ropati: 'You mean that a captain of the United States Marines stood by powerless while a staff sergeant took his detachment away from him?'

'Yes.'

'How in hell did it happen? Tell me, for God's sake. How did it happen?'

'Slowly.'

'But how did you two let it happen?'

'Do two Materava islanders move in to discipline a detachment of United States Marines?'

Since no one could provide an answer to that question, I turned to the final subject on which I and the men in Noumea required instruction: 'What about the murder of the Matarevan?'

'You read the record.'

'Yes, but the trial ended before that testimony could be entered. All we had was the prosecutor's opening promise that he would also bring witnesses to prove that a murder had been committed.'

'I was to have been that witness,' Ropati said. 'But as I told you, I was left on the airstrip here. Never testified.'

'Not to anyone?'

'Questions were asked. My answers must be on file somewhere.'

'None that I could find.'

'What I would have said—been able to say, that is—wouldn't have resulted in formal charges of murder, so maybe it's just as well I didn't go. The facts as I was able to put them together were like this. There was a handsome Matareva man working on the base, and two of Hazen's men became his lovers. A violent argument took place, some of the Marines not involved in Hazen's Club heard loud voices, and next morning the Matareva man was found dead—some distance from where the argument had occurred.' He held his palms up: 'Was it, wasn't it? Who knows, and as to who did it no one even offered a guess.'

'But it was murder?'

'Well, it's not easy to commit suicide by stabbing yourself in the middle of your back and bashing in the back of your skull.'

Like Admiral Halsey when he finished with the court-martial record, I had heard far more about the Matareva incident than I really cared to know; I was satisfied that a first-class Marine captain from a fine family in Virginia had allowed a vicious enlisted man on a remote tropical island to steal his command, corrupt it totally, and lead it into the swamp of a hideous court-martial. Something like that should never have been allowed to happen, but happen it did.

When I walked out to the airstrip to catch the plane that would take me back to Noumea, Robert Weed and Tetua Stanton walked with me to the ramp. 'It's been a lively stay,' I said. 'I listened to a lot I really didn't want to hear.' But when I asked specifically, 'What's your final judgment on Captain Dorn?' Tetua said: 'I was damned unhappy that he was already married,' and Ropati added: 'One of the best men I'll ever meet. Had he kept off this island I believe he'd have had a brilliant Marine Corps record. At the front, facing a known enemy like the Japanese he'd have charged right to the top of the hill and won medals. In the rear, facing an unknown enemy like Mike Hazen, he never knew the battle was under way till he was forced to surrender his sword, his epaulets, his honor.' As I climbed the ramp I told Ropati: 'You sound as if maybe you could be a writer.'

But Tetua brought the tragic story back to the young officer she had loved: 'What happened to Mark?'

'The Navy officers who detested homosexuals wanted to crucify him—throw him into one of their infamous jails, where he would be beaten and battered. But others warned: "You can't do that without a formal court-martial—a justified military order." '

'So what happened?'

'It took a lot of questioning to find out, because people had been ordered not to talk. But I learned from an enlisted man who typed the orders that Dorn, Hazen and the three dozen others were spirited out of the war zone, slipped back into the States, and quietly dismissed from the service.'

As I look back from the vantage point of 1991 at the mixed-up events and emotions of that tour taken almost half a century ago, I find great consolation in the fact that somewhere in the dark and dusty files of the Navy my two field reports on Bora Bora and Tonga lie safely hidden. Each was carefully written and properly typed and each ran to about eighty very full pages, and I suppose that sometime around the year A.D. 2050 some mole, sorting through the junk, will stumble upon them and cry: 'Hey, these must have been written by that guy who wrote the books.'

That they got safely into the files I know, because I placed them there, and confirmation came when the official histories of the two islands were compiled. I have copies of those histories and note that they quote copiously from my work, the Bora Bora one identifying me repeatedly in footnotes that verify the many interviews I conducted on various islands of French Polynesia.*

*History of the United States Naval Station Bora Bora, Society Islands of French Oceania. Bora Bora, 9 July 1945. Submitted by John J. Allen [no rank shown] carbon

The Tonga history uses much of my work verbatim but does not mention my name, referring to me only as 'one naval observer' or 'a visiting historical officer from ComSoPac,' and I regret that most of my more amusing episodes were censored.* I imagine that some Annapolis-trained superior officer read about the little red truck on Tonga, or the sailor who burst into tears when he had to leave Bora Bora, and growled: 'We can't have stuff like that in here! Creates a disgraceful portrait of the Navy!' and the scissors went to work.

I do hope my reports will be found in their uncensored form. If published, together with a few notes, they will make an interesting book showing not naval strategy but how a young officer reacted to Polynesia in the turbulent days while he was learning how to tell interesting stories about the islands. Many of the ideas that would direct the rest of my working life were first expressed in those reports.

I did not submit formal reports on five of the most interesting situations I helped handle on this tour. I told headquarters nothing about the two wonderful Grey sisters in Samoa; I judged their relations with the U.S. government to have been as profitable to us as to them and two finer women I never investigated. Nor was there anything I cared to say about Ratchett Kimbrell and his individualistic interpretation of State Department regulations on Tahiti; I liked him, respected Lieutenant Commander McClintock and loved Reri; and the island girls who decoded the top-secret transmissions didn't do a great deal of harm, I felt sure.

Two of the other events were so personal that I could not see them as Navy business. The rescue of Robert Dean Frisbie from the reef at Pukapuka and his three daughters from Rarotonga was an act of grace to a fellow writer, and the echoes of that adventure still reverberate in my heart. Someone should write a coherent account of that remarkable family.

The Catholic priest and the New Zealand girl stand apart. I regarded her as one of those enviable young women with a warm heart and a steel backbone. She was worth knowing and cherishing as a friend, and to see

---

copy to Lieut. J.A. Michener, ComSoPac Historical Officer. An excellent summary of the early days of the American occupation of code name Bobcat, with running account of feud between Vichy and DeGaullist factions, plus comment on the abortive movement to have Tahiti become part of the United States. [My material, of course, covers only the latter stages of the occupation.]

*History of the United States Naval Advanced Base Togatabu. Noumea, no date but internal evidence indicates early 1946. Submitted by Lieut. Cmdr. John Burke. Early part from records, latter part based heavily upon my report but not attributed to me.

her leaving that night for unknown worlds was a page from the drama
of war. Their affair moved me deeply and perplexed me even more, and
I still have no explanation of the matter. It seemed to me then, and still
does, that the three principals—the priest, the young woman and Bishop
Dawson—acted in conformity to his or her convictions and moral beliefs, and I could fault no one, and certainly not the ultimate resolution
of the impasse.

And of course there was no written report from me on the sad affair
of the Marine detachment on the little island of Matareva. There was
at one time the official court-martial record that ended so dramatically
with the young general proroguing it and facing the wrath of Admiral
Halsey. I read it in breathless detail, adding here and there my own
confirming notes in black ink, but some months later when I wanted to
consult the record for a note I was making I was told that all copies had
been destroyed, under orders from Halsey.

I have often reflected on the incidents at Matareva and Bora Bora.
The similarities between the two were striking: two remote islands far
from the war; two groups of men isolated there and left pretty much to
their own devices. But the Bora Bora group, under the guidance of a
wise and gentle officer and the cooperation of several score of joyous
young women, created a little paradise in which, so far as I could detect,
there had never been a criminal or an evil act, if one discounted the
natives' theft of gasoline for their stolen cars, in which they carried
goods taken from the warehouses. What was important was that there
were no stabbings, no wild drunkenness, no aiding the enemy after
nightfall. On Matareva almost the identical type of young men, Marines
this time, fell under the command of a junior officer unequal to the task,
and then under the domination of a malevolent staff sergeant who
corrupted the place, instituted a reign of terror that alienated the natives
and led to murder and the total dissolution of a military unit.

What was the difference between the two groups? It was certainly not
in the training or the traditions of the two services, Navy and Marine,
nor, so far as I could ascertain, the basic character of the two commanding officers. The crucial difference was that Bora Bora was Polynesian,
while Matareva was Melanesian. Over the past three centuries many
European and American explorers and travelers have testified that the
young women of Polynesia—Tahitian, Samoan, Cook Islander, Hawaiian—were some of the most gracious and delightful in the world, and
I believe that they would not have *allowed* the American military on
their islands to turn to evil. There would have been too much laughter.
If the mad staff sergeant of Matareva had started his operations on

Samoa, Aggie Grey would have asked: 'What you doin', son?' And had he tried his machinations on Tahiti, Reri or one of her nineteen cousins would have said: 'We havin' a party our place, you come,' and the poison would have been neutralized.

Years after the war ended, Chinn Ho, the Hawaiian entrepreneur, and I flew down to Bora Bora and met three of the young women who had lived with the sailors. They remembered me as the man who asked questions and I remembered them as the girls who gave answers no one could have believed: 'I paid for this stove.' 'I ordered this dress from Papeete.' 'My uncle gave me this, he works on Raiatea.'

On this visit we recalled old times, and they introduced me to young girls and boys of fourteen and fifteen who'd had American fathers, and there was none of the hatred that confronted such wartime children in countries like Japan, Korea, Vietnam and Thailand. Here they were living in sunshine beside the lagoon; and they showed only mild interest to hear that I had known their fathers. When they had gone back to their games, some of the island women told Chinn and me: 'Those were days of laughter and nights of love and we often talk about them.'

'Are you married?' I asked and they all said: 'Sure.'

This was a real tour involving real islands, people and incidents, and even though some identities have had to be masked, it has been as faithfully reported as the passage of nearly half a century will permit. It was exceptional in that it dealt only with the backwaters of war, and I was always mindful of the fact that while I was exploring the joyous wonders of Polynesia many of my friends were landing on quite different islands: Tarawa, Saipan, Okinawa. I never forgot that difference.

But I make no apologies for having traveled to that quiet theater of war, because on many earlier tours I had prowled up and down that deadly chain of islands guarding the Slot, where the destinies of the United States and Japan were determined in fearful night battles between warships that could not see one another: Savo, Guadalcanal, Tulagi, Bougainville, Vella Lavella and distant Emirau, from which I flew as passenger on bombing missions over Rabaul and Kavieng. How ardently we supported General MacArthur's command decision to bypass those impregnable fortresses and allow the Japanese holding them to wither. Had we attempted head-on invasions, we would have lost thousands of young men. I had seen enough war, so I was not eager for such duty.

During one trip to the Treasury Islands I accompanied a heavily

armed patrol seeking a gun fight with troublesome Japanese remnants
on lonely Mono island. We did not find the Japanese, but as we panted
to the top of a steep hill, dripping with sweat in the humid jungle, we
came upon one of the most miserable Melanesian villages I would ever
see, a truly pitiful place with scrawny residents and only one pig. On
a rude signboard attached to a tree, someone had affixed a cardboard
giving the settlement's name, and it was so completely different from
ordinary names, so musical to my ear that I borrowed a pencil and in
a soggy notebook jotted the name against the day when I might want
to use it for some purpose I could not then envisage: Bali-ha'i.

III

Vice

WHEN I WAS SEVEN YEARS OLD I fell prey to a vice that modified the remainder of my life, and although after a while I discovered its pernicious tendency I was by then so deeply infected that I could not free myself of its influence. I made several efforts to purge myself, and always failed, because the pull toward old habits was too great for me to resist.

I was introduced to this vice by a singular man, my Uncle Arthur, whose life had both noble and tragic overtones. He was grotesquely fat and suffered all the disabilities that accompanied that condition. He puffed and wheezed and sought the shade; he made jokes about himself; and occasionally he would embark on fierce diets in which he would starve himself, then break out of his routine with a quart of peach ice cream.

My first memory of this interesting man is of the time he brought our impoverished family an impressive ice-cream freezer, complete with crank, wooden bucket, steel cylinder and bags of salt. On Sunday mornings, whenever he was visiting, which was not often enough, Uncle Arthur would supervise the making of an ice cream that in my experience has rarely been surpassed. He would bring ripe peaches, a peck of them, and fresh cream. My mother would use milk, sugar, vanilla and a very light, high-quality corn starch to make a custard, into which Uncle Arthur would pour the cream and the peeled and finely chopped peaches, throwing in at the end some three or four that had been sliced into large chunks: 'So you'll know it's peach and not something else.'

This custard, cooled to room temperature, which could be rather high in our hot summers, was then poured into the steel cylinder, inserted into the wooden bucket, covered carefully by the mechanism that revolved it, and surrounded by ice packed tight with liberal amounts of rock salt. Then the crank was attached, and the turning by hand began. Uncle Arthur always got the mechanism started, grinding away for about fifteen minutes. Then, while the mixture was still soft enough to permit a child of five to turn it, I was allowed to spin the handle.

We never started making the ice cream until after church, so that I did not begin my stint until about one o'clock, by which time I was ravenously hungry, and the longer I worked the hungrier I became. Our custom was that we held off our noonday meal, called dinner, until the ice cream had been frozen, for then it could be packed in more ice and, as Uncle Arthur explained, 'ripen' while we ate.

I would crank till my arms ached, feeling the custard growing thicker inside its steel container. In later years I have seen electrical freezers in which a motor did all the work, and I have wondered if the resulting ice cream could possibly taste as good as ours did, which we painfully worked on, minute after minute.

When my little hands could no longer make the steel container rotate within its bed of ice, Uncle Arthur would grandiosely move me aside, sit before the freezer, bring it back between his chubby knees and announce in a loud voice: 'Let a man take over.' He would then crank until he got blue in the face. Sweat would pour down his brow, but on he would go, putting the finishing touches to what was invariably a masterpiece. As I watched admiringly he would say: 'It's these last hard minutes that keep the ice cream from forming into crystals.' This had happened once, and the family was so ashamed of itself, with Mom blaming it on the poor custard she had made, and me claiming there hadn't been enough salt. But Uncle Arthur knew the reason: 'We quit turning the crank too soon, and all because someone thought the work was too hard.' He stared at me balefully.

When not even big Uncle Arthur could move the crank, my mother would take over while he lay back, exhausted. She unhooked the contraption that rotated the container, pulled out the four revolving blades that had enabled the custard to freeze so smoothly, the wooden paddles dripping with the finest ice cream ever made, rich and flecked with peaches, and smooth and cold.

At this wonderful moment, when it was ensured that we had made another fine batch, I always hoped that she would hand the four paddles to me. This never happened. Always they went to Uncle Arthur, who must have been much hungrier than I, for he literally wolfed down the ice cream, his large round face beaming in ecstasy. He was a severe judge of ice cream; he had always lived within the empire of the Philadelphia ice-cream makers, incontestably the best in the world, and he had standards. When he pronounced 'Pretty good,' as he licked off the blades, we could be satisfied that in about two hours we would once more taste a perfect dessert.

As soon as he had cleaned the wooden paddles, he asked me to fetch the burlap, and when a tight steel lid was placed over the opening in the container, he forced it to the bottom of the wooden keg, heaped ice and salt around it, and covered everything with this heavy, wet burlap. The mixer was then wheeled into deep shade, and the ice cream was allowed to ripen and freeze even harder than it had before we finished the churning.

Now everyone was ready for dinner, and we ate with special joy, for we knew that an hour or so after we finished, the freezer would be opened. Then Mom would dip her spoon into the frozen delicacy and give her judgment, and this was the one that mattered. Never was the ice cream flawless: 'I think we skimped on the cream,' or 'The peaches were not quite ripe.' But she always gave it passing marks, save the time Uncle Arthur and I had allowed it to form into crystals, when she wept.

When Mom had approved the day's work, Uncle Arthur took a special spoon, very large and square in the bowl, very stout of handle, and with it he scooped out huge portions of ice cream. When I saw the gargantuan portion he gave me for helping, and felt the cold dish against my hands and saw the flecks and even lumps of peach, I knew that this was a very good Sunday.

I said that Uncle Arthur was both noble and tragic. His nobility lay in sharing his modest income with my mother, his sister Mabel, insofar as he could, and there were many times when our poor family would have been infinitely poorer had he not arrived on the scene with relief. He offered his aid with a willingness that always astounded me, for we really had no claim on him.

He was tragic because his was an unfulfilled life. A brilliant man in some respects, he had been unable to gain an education that would have allowed him to use his talents, and he had been unable to educate himself. He was forced, therefore, to work in jobs that did not allow him to utilize his potential, and gradually life slipped away from him. I never knew when he made the great surrender, but I was aware that it had been made. I always loved Uncle Arthur for his open-handed generosity, and I pitied him as his shoulders began to sag.

What vice did this big, amiable man bring into our home that affected me so deeply? About two years after he had given us the ice cream freezer he appeared on the trolley car from Philadelphia bearing a large and heavy package, accompanied by a smaller square one, which he kept trapped under his right arm. As soon as he saw me he sighed with relief and handed me the square package, warning: 'Guard that with your life. Drop it and I'll kill you.'

Like an acolyte performing some sacred rite, I carried the smaller package home while Uncle Arthur struggled with the larger one. I can be certain that I was seven at the time, because he told me twice during the journey: 'Be careful with that package! It's a present for your seventh birthday.' My birthday was long since past, and I remembered with some sadness that it had gone largely unnoticed, and certainly with no present from Uncle Arthur. But three months late, here I was, bringing home my own present.

At the house no one could guess what the packages contained, and this pleased Uncle Arthur, for with a dramatic flair he uncovered his treasure. It was a Victrola, and not the cheapest model. It had a crank, a lid, a turntable, an arm for the voice box, and a grille, which hid the speaker. The motor whirred almost silently, and the effect was one of beautiful simplicity.

'It works this way,' Uncle Arthur explained, and with minute repitition of detail, he explained the mysterious mechanism, announcing all the warnings that would govern the use of this precious gift. Over and over he repeated the instructions, until I at last understood them thoroughly. He even explained the governor that controlled the speed of the turntable and why we must never touch it lest the voices sound too low or too high, and only when he felt that we understood the rules did he ask for my package.

Opening it tenderly, as if he felt that he had brought something truly special, something that would remake the lives of everyone in the family, he brought forth three records, each in its own heavy brown-paper cover. They were, and I can see them now as clearly as on that first magical day, two records with black labels—*Cohen on the Telephone*, and *The Stars and Stripes Forever*—and one with a handsome red label, the sextette from *Lucia di Lammermoor*, backed by the quartet from

Rigoletto. The last record had cost Uncle Arthur an appalling sum; it was the famous Victor 10000, originally issued at $7.00 but now selling for $3.50, and he assured us it was the finest record ever made.

The first piece of music I ever heard on a Victrola was the quartet from *Rigoletto,* sung by Enrico Caruso, Amelita Galli-Curci, Flora Perini and Guiseppe de Luca. With Uncle Arthur standing protectively over the machine, and the family gathered reverently, the faraway, thin and reedy voice of Caruso burst into the song of love, after which the other voices came in, one by one, until a grand ensemble resulted. It was a long selection, and we stood entranced; as the voices rose to a climax and broke off, leaving the orchestra to sound a few concluding notes, we knew that we had entered a new world.

It might sound apocryphal, perhaps, if I were to state that I appreciated at this first hearing the grandeur of Caruso's voice and the wonderful intricacy of the quartet but the incontrovertible fact is that from that moment on I began to collect operatic records; I memorized the *Victor Records* catalog; I engraved on my mind the brief stories of the operas and the tiny illustrations that accompanied them; I knew the biographies of all the great singers and in time had vocal samples of each. And I have kept that first wonderful record with me for the past seventy-five years, playing it and its golden companions until I memorized every note and understood every nuance.

And I have been a slave to opera ever since. I believe I have seen almost every major one presented in my lifetime except Umberto Giordano's *Andrea Chenier,* whose concluding passages, as I shall explain later, have become one of my great favorites. I have seen opera in China, in Japan, in all the countries of Europe, in Australia, in South America; in Tashkent in farthest Russia I saw one tremendous performance, in which the individual singers performed in four different languages. I have heard every great singer of this century.

With the aid of the scores I memorized the operas, to the point at which I possibly could have conducted them, *Aida, La Traviata, Rigoletto, Otello, Lohengrin, Carmen, La Bohème, Cavalleria Rusticana, Pagliacci, Norma, Madama Butterfly* and *Faust,* and learned where each instrument in the orchestra was supposed to come in. And at one time or another I have owned better than 75 percent of those stunning first records issued by Victor: Caruso, Martinelli, Galli-Curci, Bori, Tetrazzini, Destinn, and the thundering men's voices, De Luca, Amato, Ruffo, Scotti and Journet. I knew by heart some thousand arias, duets, trios and other ensembles, and from the first I treasured especially the operatic choruses, which I have chanted to myself around the world. I think it is fair to say that with Uncle Arthur's auspicious launching, I became an opera addict.

But the constant musical companion of my early youth, when I had not the money to indulge my passion—I acquired my records painfully and one by one—was the Victor catalog. Seven and one-quarter inches high by five inches wide, it was paperbound in a different color each year, and I waited avidly for each new issue, bringing it home like the treasure it was. I could tell at a glance which artists had issued new operatic selections, and I watched for any change in the illustrations of either the operas or the singers. Faust embraced Marguerite while Mephistopheles diverted the attention of Dame Marthe. I found the illustrations for *La Bohème* disappointing, just as later I would find the actual stagings far too bleak. *Aida* was a disaster; the minute photograph showed not less than a hundred singers and no one could decipher who was doing what. The most satisfying depiction in the first catalog I owned, the 1914 version, came with *Rigoletto:* the young duke stood to the left, and Maddalena to the right behind the wall, with Gilda being drawn away from the shameful scene by her father, the hunchback. Sometimes in later years at public performances of *Rigoletto* I would see four singers disposed precisely as they had been in that first photograph, and the memories of my childhood would come flooding back.

I studied carefully the postage-stamp-size portraits of the singers, and Caruso became more real to me than the man next door; I saw him in a dozen different roles, commanding the stage, and I was beginning to have enough of his records to hear him in many of these parts. For reasons I cannot explain, I was particularly enchanted by Luisa Tetrazzini, whose voice I preferred over those of all other sopranos. I was fascinated, years later when I knew most of her records by heart, to follow in *The New York Times* the sad account of her family's hauling her into court in an attempt to deprive her of the right to supervise her fortune; the family members claimed that she was senile and dissipating money that would one day come to them if it was properly managed. At the height of the trial Madame Tetrazzini stood up and tossed off a couple of arias with such superb mastery that the judge had to conclude that she was still in possession of her faculties. I was delighted with the verdict.

I pored over the catalog, not only the red pages that listed operatic records, but also the pages for nonclassical music, which I sometimes liked but did not respect, and occasionally I came upon some arcane note that perplexed me. I remember especially the one that appeared in the Victor catalog until well into the 1920s:

Note—by "coon songs" are meant up-to-date comic songs in
negro dialect. The humor of many of these coon songs cannot
be called refined, and for that reason we have distinguished
them from old-fashioned dark humor, these songs being listed
under "Fisk Jubilee Quartet" and "Tuskegee."

Coon songs derived their humor from ridiculing Negroes, while the
Cohen records featured a ridiculous Jewish man's linguistic misadven-
tures on the telephone, in the restaurant or while trying to purchase a
train ticket. Several families on our street had such records, and I can
recall our neighbors gathering about our Victrola and slapping their legs
with delight as Negroes and Jews made fools of themselves. The record
our family contributed to the gaiety, *Cohen on the Telephone,* was the
favorite, but for some reason I would find difficult to explain, I considered it offensive. Even at age seven I preferred *Rigoletto* to coon songs
or the ridiculing of Jewish immigrants.

Another Red Seal record that Uncle Arthur brought us was the true
beginning of my love for what might be called standard operatic singing;
after all, the famous quartet and sextet of the first record can be appreciated by anyone, for those numbers are spectacular pyrotechnics.
This new record offered Caruso and a baritone singing two of the most
magical duets ever composed for men's voices: the 'Solenne in quest'
ora' from Verdi's *La Forza del Destino* and perhaps an even finer number, the duet from *Les Pêcheurs des Perles.* For some ten years I knew
the latter only as sung in Italian, 'Dal tempio al limitar,' and I was
convinced that it had originally been offered in that form; I was disturbed to find that it was from a French opera and that the real words
were 'Au fond du temple,' translated into English as 'From the depths
of the temple.'

These two duets opened my ears and mind to the amazing powers of
the human voice: the way the artists alternately displayed their individual vocal glory and then joined each other in the most delicate harmony
was a revelation. As a very young boy I had discovered that style in art
sometimes consists of pushing something forward into a conspicuous
position, then drawing it back so that it is lost in an ensemble. I found
these duets infinitely more instructive than the more showy quartet and
sextet; I memorized every nuance and believed that I could even hear
the baritone taking a deep breath before launching into a difficult passage. Again and again I played the duet, listening to how Caruso used
his voice and identifying the manner in which he infused passion into
his singing. Today, if I hear even a few notes at the beginning of either

of these duets, I am thrown headlong into the full range of the music, and I have sometimes played my recent recordings of these numbers ten or fifteen times in a row, so hungry have I been to relive the joy I found in them seventy years ago. In these days I find that I prefer the Bizet, and by a large margin. The *Forza* duet speaks of the love two brave men can have for each other; the *Pearl Fishers* duet recalls the love two men had for a beautiful girl. Each is good; but I find the latter the more affecting.

In the final days of college an event occurred that intensified my addiction to opera: I came upon three different music stores whose owners were liquidating their stocks of Red Seal records on the credible grounds that with the advent of radio there would no longer be much interest in the old records. The first store, in Philadelphia, was selling its stock at $1.00 per record. The second, in New York, was selling at $.69 a record. And the third store in Pottstown, Pennsylvania, with a gigantic collection, was getting rid of them at $.50 each.

I spent several hundred dollars of my first regular salary on these precious records, untouched by any needle, and started a collection that would be unmatched among my acquaintances. Now great new voices sang for me: Gigli, Pertile, Bjoerling, Castagna, Pons, Sayao, Ponselle, Warren, Rethberg, Pinza and one whose name few now remember except those who truly cherish the beauty of the human voice, Toti dal Monte. She did not sing much in America, nor did she make an abundance of records, but I acquired almost every one she did make.

I had always had the habit, which I adhered to in my response to the arts, of trying to look or listen with an unprejudiced intellect. For example, whenever I entered a museum I would walk to the center of each room, from where I could see no labels, and ask myself: What is worth noting here? By taking this approach I not only discovered some excellent art but also gained confidence in my artistic judgment so that I have never had any hesitancy in relying upon my own taste. I have consistently fortified it with the opinions of others—I read a great deal of criticism—but I have never allowed critics to dissuade me from making my own evaluations. As a result my appreciation of the arts has been nothing but positive, and it has been one of the best parts of my life. I doubt that I would have felt this way had I been overawed by the opinions of others.

The record that lives in my memory as perhaps the finest I ever owned was sung by Gigli, Rethberg and Pinza; it offered two trios I had never heard of, from two Verdi operas I would never see. From *I Lombardi* came the 'Qual voluttà trascorrere,' a passionate outcry in which the three voices blend superbly. From *Ernani* came the inspired 'Ernani, involami,' of which the accompanying notes said:

> With the words 'Ernani, involami' (Ernani, fly with me) Elvira, sung by Miss Rethberg, begins a coloratura of great brilliance, whereupon Don Carlos, King of Castile, sung by Mr. Pinza, breaks into the room and begins to make violent love to her. She is about to be dragged off by force when Ernani, sung by Mr. Gigli, steps forth to save her.

I have never met anyone else who prized this record, nor have I ever talked with anyone who even knew of the *I Lombardi* trio, but to me it remains an almost perfect example of what ensemble singing can be, and I vastly prefer it to other more famous trios, such as the one in the concluding scene in *Faust*.

But it was Toti dal Monte who totally captivated me. She sang one or two seasons at the Metropolitan, but she was short and dumpy— 'Little Toti,' they called her—so her appeal was limited. But she had a voice of crystalline beauty that she handled superbly. She seems to have been one of those singers who sound better on records than they do live, and she won the hearts of listeners all over the world. She gave me great joy, and I am proud to be the honorary and perpetual president of the Toti dal Monte Admirers Club.

Among the bargain records I acquired by chance I discovered marvels I would otherwise have missed: Martial Singher intoning the malevolent 'Scintille, diamant,' from Offenbach's *Tales of Hoffmann;* Eleanor Steber's dark lament for Euridice, lost in Hades, from Gluck's opera; or the impassioned contralto aria from *Don Carlos,* 'O, mio regina,' in which the one-eyed Princess Eboli acknowledges the harm she has done her queen.

Another record from *Don Carlos* would play a curious role in my life. I would like to claim that at first hearing I recognized this for the fine composition it was, and for the extraordinary singing it represented, but I did not. It was the 'Dormiro sol nel manto,' in which King Philip of Spain says that he will sleep one day in his kingly shroud in the depths of the Escorial; it is a terrifying song of despair sung by a bass or a bass baritone. Here the singer was Ezio Pinza, a name I had learned only a few weeks earlier as the powerful voice in the *Lombardi* trio. When I first heard his great aria from *Don Carlos,* I thought little of it. Indeed, I preferred another unknown selection, which appeared on the reverse side: 'O tu Palermo,' from *I Vespri Siciliani.* But the more I heard the *Don Carlos* aria, the more I came to love it both as a piece of music and as an exhibition of what a dynamic singer like Pinza can do, and I sought out his other recordings, paying full price for them when I could not find them in the bargain basements. My response to Pinza must have been prophetic, for twenty years later he would sing in the musical play *South Pacific,* based on my book *Tales of the South Pacific,* and in this role so ideally suited to his remarkable talents he would find the popular recognition that had eluded him even though he had been one of the finest Mephistopheles and Don Giovannis ever to sing at the Metropolitan Opera House.

At our first meeting, when I was nervous about facing a man whose work I treasured, and he was nervous about his ability to speak in English—he memorized lines that were phonetically written at first—the atmosphere was eased when I told him how much I admired 'Dormiro sol nel manto.' And in an apartment high above New York, where we were conducting an audition, we sang the great aria together. It was a disaster, of course; not only can I not carry a tune, but the aria begins with a tremendous, rumbling recitative, 'Ella giammai m'amo' (She never loved me), which had not been on my record because it would have made the cutting too long. So Pinza sang the complete aria, while I kept trying to butt in with the popular last half. He smiled and, continuing to sing, reached the overpowering moment when the king foresees his death: 'I shall sleep in my kingly shroud beneath the black vault, here in the Escorial.' I knew all the words—many dozens of times I had sung them with Pinza—and now we were really singing them together.

During *South Pacific*'s long run on Broadway, I became good friends with Pinza and often we sang 'Dormiro sol nel manto' together; and the rumbling tones issuing from his deep chest would drown out the ineffectual noises I was able to muster.

Among the discards I found a delightful thing put together by two famous American singers, the soprano Alma Gluck and the contralto Louise Homer. They joined in making 'Whispering Hope,' a sentimental old hymn with harmony so close as to be breathtaking. From the moment I played the record, which had come to me as part of a huge bundle, I was enslaved by it. The two voices blended with such delicious precision that an air of sanctity pervaded my room; this was religious singing of the most heartwarming kind. I should think that if the record was reissued with stereophonic background orchestra it might once more enjoy the enormous popularity it had in the 1920s.*

*When I wrote *Centennial* forty years after first hearing 'Whispering Hope,' it served as an amusing leitmotif for a long section of the novel, and served well.

While listening to my new records I discovered that I had a pronounced fondness for operatic choruses, and one day I stumbled upon
what is generally considered to be the most effective chorus ever presented in an opera, the simple plainsong of the exiled Jews in Verdi's
Nabucco. In Babylon the exiles remember Jerusalem, and in their home-
sickness they sing: 'Va, pensiero, sull' ali dorate' (Go, my thought, on
golden wings. . . .) This four-verse chorus, sung in unison against a
simple accompaniment, swept Italy and all the other opera-loving nations. It was played at memorials, and when Verdi was buried in 1901
his mourners automatically began singing his best-loved composition.
At his state funeral sometime later, Arturo Toscanini led a chorus of
eight hundred in the number that had been Verdi's favorite. Considering
all this, it is remarkable that I did not even hear the music until I was
past fifty.

I am not sure that much else in opera escaped me, and yet one day
in a pile of records sent to me by a now-defunct dealer in New York I
came upon that staggering chorus from *Fidelio*. Its position in Beethoven's opera is not unlike that of 'Va, pensiero' in Verdi's *Nabucco*: a
gang of prisoners is released for a few moments from their dark cells,
and as they see the light for the first time in months they sing softly 'O
welche Lust' (O, what delight!). This may have been the most powerfully
operatic record I ever acquired, for the music spoke to me with overwhelming force. Through it I saw all prisoners, and the great dungeons
of Piranesi, along with the cruel injustices of the world. Whenever I am
confronted by civil tragedy I tend to recall this chorus; its steady beat
throbs in my heart, and through it I suffer with those who are suffering.
If I am an avowed liberal, and if I have been willing to spend time and
effort in supporting worthy causes, it is partly because my attitudes were
formed by the deeply humanistic qualities of the great operas. None had
a stronger influence on me than *Fidelio;* if at some future time, someone
should want to name a theme song that would exemplify what I hoped
to have stood for in life, it could only be 'O welche Lust.'

In the area of human emotions, as opposed to the intellectualism of
Fidelio, the record that superseded all others was another that I stumbled upon. It was a ten-inch record, and I avoided these because they
seemed to give an inadequate return for the money spent acquiring them
and the time spent in playing them. But this one appeared in a pile that
a store wanted to get rid of, and I suppose I got it for next to nothing.
It was a duet I had never heard before from an opera about which I knew
nothing, Arrigo Boito's *Mefistofele.* Margherita and Faust are singing
in prison of remembered days: 'Lontano, lontano,' ('Far away, far

away,' or as always given in the catalog and on the record, 'Far away from all strife.') This time, from the moment the turntable started revolving, I appreciated the duet at its full value; it is a remarkable composition, very brief, and totally tragic. For me it subsumes all human experience where men and women are involved with love. It is a statement of human passion that echoes forever—the lost glories, the futile hopes, the remembered passions, the burning desire to reach some other place where love will be everlasting. Occasionally in my travels I have come upon someone who knew this duet; such admirers are not numerous, but they have made it immortal. It is not an important piece of music; it just happened to impress me when I was forming my values, and in a thousand instances when I have been far removed from record players or operas or singers this duet has echoed through my mind. I know of only one version, an extremely old one sung in French by Geraldine Farrar and Edmond Clément. No finer recording was ever made, for on this one they become all star-crossed lovers. How they could have expressed so much in such a brief time span is truly a marvel.

If opera has had the moral effect on me that I have just stated, as in the case of 'O welche Lust,' how dare I say, as I did earlier, that it was a destructive vice?

From that moment when I first heard the quartet from *Rigoletto,* I was enmeshed in a form of art which is inherently romantic, passionate, absurd and illogical. The stories upon which opera is founded are so preposterous that no rational man or woman should really bother with them. I have never met a person with a really first-class mind who wasted his or her time on opera; it is a make-believe world, reserved for us lesser types who can anesthetize our sense of reason, who can take the nonsense so seriously that we would memorize scores and texts— betraying an inability to separate common sense from the sheerest fantasy.

I have been damaged, in some ways, by my fixation on opera, for it has helped to delude me into seeing human experience in a more dramatic form than facts would warrant; it has edged me always closer to romanticism and away from reality; it has made me a confirmed liberal when saner men, pondering the objective record, tend to be pessimistic conservatives; and it has encouraged me toward artistic conventions that I might have done well to avoid. For example, my love of the operatic aria has encouraged me to allow my characters to declaim at length when a brief speech might be more effective, and my enormous respect for the great duets tempts me to have two characters speaking to each other just a bit longer than the literary scene would warrant. In almost every respect my dalliance with opera has influenced my understanding of the problems of art. That sunny afternoon when Uncle Arthur lugged his fateful Victrola into our home, he condemned me to some wrong values and set my small feet upon some improper roads.

And yet much of the mindset that has enabled me to enjoy a creative life was acquired through my intensive study of opera. I absorbed the verities expressed in the individual arias, taking seriously the lessons championed there, and I think it is fair to say that I have been guided in my moral decisions as much by the lessons I acquired from opera as by the preachings of either the Old or the New Testaments.

The first of the two scenes from opera that best illustrate this curious teaching power comes at the opening of the third act of *La Bohème,* where the two pairs of lovers meet in the snowy dawn at one of the gates of Paris. The days of rapturous lovemaking are over, and the time for harsh reassessment is at hand; the lovers see each other in a new light, and when I see or hear them singing their impassioned music, I see not operatic performers but real people who live down the street. Boy meets girl in the way Rodolfo met Mimi; they draw apart; they see new aspects of the one they loved; they experience anguish and soaring emotions; and the dream fades. As I have been allowed to observe the world's emotional life, I have often found it is six o'clock on a snowy morning and the gates are locked.

I recommend that young men listen with attention to the powerful solos, duets and trios of the third act of *Aida,* for they deal with loyalty and patriotism and love and temptation, and few human lives will be lived to their conclusion without having to confront one or another of these aspects of human behavior. When I hear this magnificent music, so perfectly attuned to the problems of the three characters, I become Radames and face the terrible decisions he must make: love versus duty, treason versus loyalty, a passionate moment versus a long life of service, personal gratification versus the advancement of one's career. These are the kinds of problems that confront not only Radames but many young men everywhere.

Several times I have had to deal with such problems and have reacted in accordance with the convictions about loyalty forged when I put myself in the place of Radames. Treason to my country, or even disloyalty, would be absolutely impossible for me, not because I am a strictly moral man but because as Radames I see what such behavior can lead to.

The tragedy of the young American politicians who were undone by the Watergate scandals was that they had not faced in their imaginations the conditions that were going to overtake them in real life. There are infinitely more practical ways of acquiring moral bases than going to see *Aida,* but that's how I found mine, and I would hope that others would find theirs in their own preferred areas of interest.

But the segment of opera that touches my wandering life most intimately comes at the conclusion of Wagner's *Das Rheingold,* a difficult work that many may not enjoy. The gods, assembled after a chain of hellish actions and betrayals, finally attain their goal: they are free to cross over the arched bridge from darkness into the sunny glories of Asgard and Valhalla. All the wanderings I have done are epitomized for me in their stately passage: their uncertainty as they are about to enter a new world with new complexities; the hopefulness of Wotan as he perceives possibilities; the inexorable fate that cuts us all down to unheroic size; and the mysterious forces released with the discovery of any new world. I have spent much of my life crossing golden bridges to new lands and new adventures and have always done so largely in terms of this towering scene. If grand opera had given me nothing more than this guideline to the travels and explorations I would make, it would have served me well.

My obsession with opera was well advanced before I learned what pure music was. While a sophomore in Swarthmore College I was stopped in the hallway by Professor Fritz Klees of the English department who had never had me in class. 'They tell me you're doing first-class work,' he said, 'I have a free ticket to the Philadelphia Symphony for Saturday night. Would you care to join me?' Eager for any new experience in learning, I accepted. I looked in the paper to see what the program would be and learned that the famous Boston conductor, Serge Koussevitzky, was conducting a program of only two works, Beethoven's Fifth and Third. Doing what any self-respecting young scholar would do when faced with an intellectual challenge, I hurried to the library and checked out books—Beethoven, symphony, orchestra and general musical history. By the time I climbed the stairs at the incomparable Academy of Music I was prepared to treat the forthcoming concert with respect based on some knowledge.

I remember that one of the books on which I had crammed had described the revolutionary way in which Beethoven had ended his third movement of the Fifth, with only heavy passages in the double bass making the transition, without pause, into the glorious final movement. 'This,' said the writer, 'is something powerful to listen for.' And I prepared to listen. The four opening chords of the first movement were also praised, but I was not prepared for the majesty with which they filled that hall.

It was music so grand, so inevitable that it swept me along, breathless; I was stunned by the brilliance that a strong conductor and a superb orchestra, working together, could produce, so that by the end of the third movement, I was limp from this earthshaking experience. And then the low rumble that my guide had spoken of began, and by the time the transition led to the explosion of the final movement, that song of triumph, I was literally out of my chair as I leaned forward to see which instruments were taking over from the rumbling double basses to create this heavenly sound. I had started my serious musical education with Beethoven's Fifth.

Of course, after the intermission, I listened carefully to hear in the Third the six crashing chords that indicated Beethoven's disenchantment with his erstwhile hero Napoleon. I left the Academy convinced that I must return again and again, and I did. In fact, with money saved from wherever possible, I purchased a season ticket for the Saturday night-concerts—top of the balcony—and grabbed a copy of the *Public Ledger* each week to see what the music critic, Samuel Laciar, would have to say about that Saturday's concert. In this way I underwent one of the finest musical educations a young man could have.

Week after week, for three years, I attended the Philadelphia concerts and agreed with the critics that our orchestra was rather better than any of the others that visited the city. I felt the same about Leopold Stokowski, the wild man of that period, and through his artistry I became an afficionado of composers like Bach and Brahms, De Falla and Ravel. But I was so eager to experience the full range of classical music that whenever I purchased three or four albums of the composers I liked, I would buy one example of the most difficult contemporary music available, and make myself like it. In this arbitrary manner I acquired Arnold Schoenberg's *Verklärte Nacht* and came to appreciate it enormously.

My unusual manner of learning music left me with an unbalanced musical education, as shown by the fact that I refused to have much to do with either Mozart or Chopin, since they did not fit into any of the neat categories I had set up. In later years, when I had more sense, these two great composers became permanent favorites, music to ease and reassure the soul.

As a young man I became a devotee of Heathkits. Neatly packaged components with which one could assemble in his own kitchen a radio, a record player, and later a television, they were a boy's delight, a grown man's recreation. For a minor percentage of the cost of a completed machine, the Heathkit buyer, if he had the brains to follow the directions, got his machine at a bargain. I developed a hobby of assembling two or three quite valuable sound systems each year and building handsome wooden cabinets to house them. I would try them out for a month or so to see if the improvements made the sound better, and then give them to schools or churches as my contribution to the appreciation of music. I suppose I must have disposed of some twenty-five systems in this manner, but when Heathkits turned to homemade television sets, the instructions became too complicated for me.

But music was so important to me that starting in 1934 I began to build reproductive systems with three sets of extremely heavy filtering devices monitoring the wires leading to three different loudspeakers. On the first wire my assistant, a high school junior, and I would filter out all the bass notes to provide a high tenor; on the third we would eliminate the high notes to give us a deep rumble, and on the middle wire we knocked off the excessive highs and lows so that the powerful middle tones that carried tunes could come forth most effectively. Placing the three speakers far apart, we had remarkably good stereo sound twenty years before commercial systems caught up with the idea.

Then, in my maturity, I discovered chamber music, and on my invented system I learned the wonders of the Beethoven quartets, the grandeur of Brahms, the artful simplicity of Mozart and the delight of pieces like Dvořák's *American Quartet,* Schumann's quintet for piano and strings and Schubert's wonderful octet. Two compositions led all others in my affection: Beethoven's mystical last quartet, No. 16 in F major, and the marvelous Brahms quintet for piano and strings. In my later years I played these last three numbers more frequently than any others, and I have come to feel that in Beethoven's last work the rapid pizzicato movement was a signal that he felt his end approaching and he must hurry.

What a benediction classical music is to those who have grown to know and love it. I will say only this about my own reactions: whenever I am alone and playing Beethoven's Fifth, I eagerly anticipate the third movement, and when the rumble comes in on the double basses and the great transition is made into sunlight, I stand in reverent remembrance of that magical night when I was introduced to music such as this.

In the same year that I first heard Uncle Arthur's records—that is, when I was seven—I found in an old magazine that some thoughtful person had given us a reproduction of a painting in color which quite changed my life in another direction. The picture was by the modest English painter of rural scenes, George Morland (1763–1804) and it depicted a farrier shoeing a horse in front of an open barn. It so caught my fancy that I tore out the page, trimmed its edges, and pasted it on a piece of cardboard. And with that simple action I embarked on another enthusiasm of lasting interest.

I had entered the world of painting, and art was to have an effect on me comparable to that of my exploration into opera. For with my Morland as a start, I began collecting reproductions of paintings, usually of postcard size, finding them wherever I could and keeping them in order so that I could thumb through at leisure what soon became my private art collection. Through all the years of my life, no matter where I went, I would take my collection of photographs of paintings or part of it with me, and it would be constantly refined by the addition of better cards of paintings by artists I already admired or new cards of paintings by artists I had only just discovered.

I would maintain this practice for more than seventy years, building in time a small collection of the cards, rigorously weeded, of some hundred and fifty of the greatest paintings of all time. But always I would keep in an honored position the George Morland whose magical charm never faded for me, even when it was surrounded by the work of much finer artists. His *Forge* was the key that unlocked for me the infinite riches of the visual arts.

The second reproduction to find a place in my collection exemplifies the kind of child I was, for in another magazine I saw a painting that quite bowled me over with the freshness of its color and the almost majestic disposition of its forms. It was a landscape painting by an American artist, Willard Metcalf (1858–1925), and I was so taken by the excellence of his work that I thought it only proper that I send him a letter to tell him so: 'I think your picture of the field and the tree is very fine. It is in a magazine I am not allowed to tear, so if you have a copy you can spare, I would like to have it.' I signed my name and age and almost by return mail I received a most encouraging letter from the artist, telling me that he agreed with me that it was a good painting and that I seemed to have a sharp eye, which he encouraged me to develop. The letter and the clipping showing the painting that accompanied it entered my collection.

Neither Morland nor Metcalf was what one might categorize as a world-class painter. They were excellent, and they certainly awakened my latent interest in art, and for that reason I permanently treasured them. But with my third reproduction, and a very fine one it was in standard postcard size, I entered the world of international art of the highest caliber. I can't recall how I got my hands on the postcard—perhaps a teacher gave it to me—but it showed one of the seminal paintings of world art, the one that opened the eyes of European painters to the realities of landscape painting. It bore a name that enchanted me, and from the first moment I saw it, it has been enshrined in my memory, to be recalled whenever I chance to see a row of fine trees leading down a country lane. The *Avenue at Middelharnis,* by the Dutch painter Meindert Hobbema (1638–1709), seems at first to be simplicity itself—it is a perfectly flat landscape with minute distant buildings showing, and down the dead middle of the canvas runs a dirt road flanked on either side by a row of very tall, scraggly trees of almost repugnant form, totally bare of limbs for 90 percent of their height but topped by mis-shapen crowns of small, heavy branches. It would seem as if almost anyone could paint a better picture than this, but if it commanded my attention and affection at age seven, so also did it captivate the artistic world; it proved that noble landscape painting could be achieved by using simple color, simple design and straightforward execution. People who love painting love *Avenue, Middelharnis,* and I am pleased to say that as a child I made that discovery on my own.

After a slow start, I began finding copies of great paintings wherever I looked, and in later years I haunted museums to find what cards they had for sale. In time I believe that I visited every important museum in the world, save only one of the best, the one in Dresden; and if I were able to fly there tomorrow, I am sure I would purchase twenty or thirty cards to fill the blank spaces in my little hand-carried museum.

Of course, in the early days I saw art as the domain of acknowledged masters like Raphael, Titian, Rembrandt and Rubens, whose paintings flourished in the reproduction trade. It was some time before I discovered other painters, such as Constable, whom I cherished, and Poussin, whose stateliness delighted me. In my youth I am ashamed to confess, I temporarily fell under the spell of a sentimental Englishwoman, Mrs. Jameson, who wrote extremely interesting and readable books based on the concept that great art could be identified by the degree to which it exemplified noble and moral ideals. I agreed with her that one could see that since Raphael specialized in paintings of the Madonna and Fra Angelico in those depicting saintly devotion, they had to be finer artists than ones who did not use such holy subjects. And even though Tintoretto did depict religious themes, he did so in such a violent manner that he could not be considered to be in the first rank.

Mrs. Jameson's sermonizing was ridiculous, but with no other art critic to read, I accepted her judgments—for about half a year. During that time I devoured her various writings, but somewhere toward the middle of her third book I suddenly realized that she had no place in her theory of art for paintings like Morland's *Forge* or Hobbema's *Middelharnis;* in fact, she would have summarily dismissed both paintings. Nevertheless, she was invaluable to my education, for she taught me what not to look for in art. If she liked it, I had to be suspicious.

With more sophisticated ciceroni I began to discover, still in postcard size, the great works of Masaccio, Piero della Francesca and Mantegna, but I was still obviously locked into the Italian school, as Mrs. Jameson had been. She would have had scant time for someone like Dürer and none at all for Holbein, whose works offered very little moral uplift.

My highly restricted art education was rudely disrupted by three dazzling discoveries that modified both my understanding of art and my approach to it. In some out-of-the-way source I found a postcard showing a goldfinch resting on a hanging perch of some kind, just that and nothing more, but it was so exquisitely painted and so perfect in all dimensions that I fell in love with it. No other painting, not even those first three lucky discoveries, would have the effect on me that *The Goldfinch,* by the Dutch painter Carel Fabritius (1622–1654), would. But when I looked into art books I could find no mention of Fabritius; he seemed to have cut no figure whatever in Dutch art. I was about to discard him from my collection when it occurred to me that to like his goldfinch, which I obviously did, required no formal approval from anyone. This was a notable painting for reasons I could not quite determine, and even if no one else appreciated it, I did,* and with that arrogant conclusion I began my steady progress toward a theory of art and its relationship to the individual.

But a third adventure awaited, one whose repercussions would uplift the later years of my life. In a glossy magazine I came upon a fine reproduction of a landscape like no other I had seen up to that time. It bore no relationship to either my Metcalf or my Hobbema, but it was compelling, for it showed in wispy, almost fragmentary detail, an Asian landscape that I took to be Chinese. It was such a pleasing work that

---

*Later I would find that scores of people, among them great experts, liked the painting as much as I did, and through the years I found many reproductions of it, and it was this experience that encouraged me to develop the concept of 'a minor classic,' which will appear later in this chapter as an idea of great importance to me. I also learned that Fabritius was the teacher of Vermeer.

I took careful note of the artist: 'Ando Hiroshige, Japanese woodblock artist (1797–1858).' That introduction started me on the way to meet some of the most congenial artists in world history, a collection of men who in the eighteenth and nineteenth centuries would produce a wealth of rather small woodblock prints that have never been excelled or even equaled: Masanobu, Harunobu, Kiyonaga, Utamaro, Sharaku, Hokusai in more or less chronological order. I became such a devotee that I would in time own one of the major private collections of their art, some six thousand prime examples. Finally I came to American contemporary painting. After spending two years reading almost everything in print about it, I made out a comprehensive list of the notable painters and began combing the galleries with my wife to locate paintings we could afford. We decided early to confine our purchases to paintings done in my lifetime, after 1907, which put us right at the great Armory show of 1912, which launched American modern painting. In time we would acquire some four hundred major canvases.

I cannot recall where I was when I came upon an art magazine that contained a magnificent reproduction of a painting by an Italian Renaissance artist named Benozzo Gozzoli. It showed a scene in the life of a young boy whose behavior was so exemplary that he became a saint. The colors were gold, red and blue, with an effect so stunning that I adopted the painting as my reigning favorite, a painting I had discovered by myself and liked because of its simple purity.

Sometime later, when I had read all I could about the artist—he was a Florentine (1420–1497), who had worked with both Ghiberti, on the great bronze doors of the baptistery of Santa Maria del Fiore in Florence, and Fra Angelico, on the frescoes in St. Mark's convent in Venice—*Life* published one of those extensive inserts in full color that helped the magazine establish its reputation; this particular series showed the famous frescoes in the chapel of the Palazzo Medici in Florence. Page after big page illustrated how the artist, Gozzoli, had converted the simple biblical tale of the three magi into a glorification of the Medici family, whose members were shown parading grandly against the backdrop of a typical Italian landscape.

I cherished those pages, for they proved that the artist I had discovered had been a man of importance who painted works of great beauty. I was additionally charmed by the fact that Benozzo Gozzoli of the Palazzo had six z's. His importance in my life would far exceed his role as one more gifted Italian painter with an interesting name.

. . .

Starting as a lad in primary school, I was required to memorize traditional poems selected by enthusiastic and patriotic teachers. Since I had a natural liking for poetry, I found the memorization easy and learned the verse with such tenacity that they reverberate in my memory: 'The breaking waves dashed high / On a stern and rock-bound coast . . .' (Felicia Hemans); 'Behind him lay the gray Azores, / Behind the Gates of Hercules . . .' (Joaquin Miller); 'Abou Ben Adhem (may his tribe increase!) / Awoke one night from a deep dream of peace . . .' (Leigh Hunt); 'Listen, my children, and you shall hear / Of the midnight ride of Paul Revere . . . (Henry Wadsworth Longfellow); 'For all sad words of tongue or pen, / The saddest are these: "It might have been!" . . .' (John Greenleaf Whittier); 'Not a drum was heard, not a funeral note, / As his corse to the rampart we hurried . . .' (Charles Wolfe); 'and what is so rare as a day in June? / Then, if ever, come perfect days . . .' (James Russell Lowell); 'The mind has a thousand eyes / And the heart but one; / Yet the light of a whole life dies / when its love is done. . . .' (Francis W. Bourdillon).

How many such poems was I required to memorize? Perhaps four a year for twelve years—that's almost fifty. How many did I memorize on my own? Perhaps six times that number, but I soon realized that nothing I had memorized was of much merit. However the verses were imprinted in my consciousness, and I have concluded: 'It's better to have something in there than nothing.'

It was not till I reached college that I began to understand poetry. It began when I had the good luck to act in two Shakespearean plays, one of which was *Twelfth Night*. Not only did I memorize my own lines, Duke Orsino's, but also those of most of the other members of the cast. Was there ever a gentler description of a mournful love song than the one Orsino gives when he asks the clown to sing?

> . . .; it is old and plain;
> The spinsters and the knitters in the sun,
> And the free maids that weave their thread with bones
> Do use to chant it; it is silly sooth,
> And dallies with the innocence of love,
> Like the old age.

Those lines, elfinlike and meaningless in part, have danced in my head and lived with me for sixty years among the most precious memories of my college years; they are worth, I estimate, the entire fall term in which I memorized them.

But with my more advanced studies I naturally selected more substantial lines to memorize, and now the facile jingles of childhood were replaced by some of the greatest lines in English poetry: 'Then felt I like some watcher of the skies / When a new planet swims into his ken . . . (John Keats); 'Not in entire forgetfulness, / And not in utter nakedness, / But trailing clouds of glory do we come . . .' (William Wordsworth); 'I waked, she fled, and day brought back my night . . .' (John Milton); 'Go, lovely rose— / Tell her that wastes her time and me . . .' (Edmund Waller); 'Nothing beside remains. Round the decay / Of that colossal wreck, boundless and bare, / The lone and level sands stretch far away . . .' (Percy Bysshe Shelley); 'Yonder a maid and her wight / Come whispering by; / War's annals will cloud into night / Ere their story die . . .' (Thomas Hardy).

But always, through the decades, I have gone back to the sonnets of Shakespeare, those impeccable masterworks of the English language. I once could recite half a dozen, and even today I can call up many single lines and couplets that illuminate my life:

> Not mine own fears, nor the prophetic soul
> Of the wide world dreaming on things to come . . .
>
> .
>
> But if the while I think on thee, dear friend,
> All losses are restored and sorrows end.
>
> .
>
> When in disgrace with fortune and men's eyes
> I all alone beweep my outcast state . . .
>
> .
>
> Bare ruined choirs, where late the sweet birds sang . . .
>
> .
>
> When to the sessions of sweet silent thought
> I summon up remembrance of things past . . .
>
> .
>
> And peace proclaims olives of endless age . . .

I think that anyone who lives a long life carries with him or her a heavy baggage of memory and rules of thumb and old wives' tales; mine was heavy indeed, and in some ways was perhaps a disadvantage, but it was composed of the creations of the best minds of past centuries, and the burden grew more treasured every year I bore it.

I spend almost no day without looking at some piece of art, and I am delighted at this moment to be at my typewriter with a handsome calendar on the wall before me showing a painting by my old friend Willard Metcalf—*Gloucester Harbor, 1895,* from the collection at Amherst College; it is as handsomely done as the first picture of his I saw back in 1914, and at my elbow hangs the Fabritius *Goldfinch,* which is increasingly recognized as a minor classic. On my record player I have 'Lontano, lontano,' and in the anthology beside my reading lamp a bookmark leads me to 'The Eve of St. Agnes.'

These riches never die. The great songs echo still, the colors of the paintings do not fade. They accompanied me as I trudged the lower heights of Nanga Parbat in the Himalayas and comforted me as I stood lashed to the wheel while our small boat wallowed through the tail end of a Pacific typhoon. They have echoed in my mind when I needed consolation and been at hand when I required dedication to some old task or inspiration in a new. As I child I probed for the secrets of art; as a young man I tried to winnow the good from the bad; and as an adult I remain totally committed. Perhaps I have loved art too much and allowed myself to be made a prisoner of it, but from the manner in which I began my exploration it could have ended no other way.

How simply it started: a freezer of peach ice cream, a Caruso record and a copy of a George Morland painting.

IV

Travel

ONE OF MY EARLIEST MEMORIES is of the road that ran before my house in the Pennsylvania village of Doylestown. It was remarkable, I thought, that whereas on the east it ended abruptly at a farm about a half mile from where I lived, giving it a wonderfully finite feeling, on the west it ran forever, leading to strange places and wondrous adventures that I could not even imagine.

It was a magical road, and often when I walked back home after finishing my work harvesting asparagus for the man who owned the farm at which the road ended, I would visualize myself continuing to walk westward, right past my house and on through the dusk toward the wonders that my geography books assured me existed out west. I always saw myself as traveling alone, moving into one great adventure after another, and never did my mind tire of that imaginary exercise. Back home in the light of the kerosene lamps that I had to clean and fill each evening before they were lit, I would pore over my maps and try to conjure from the little pictures of Iowa and Colorado visions of what those distant places must be like. Before I was nine or ten I could identify all the states on the blank maps we were given in school to test our knowledge, so that the distinctive shape of Nevada—our most beautiful state, geometrically speaking—was as familiar to me as our own Pennsylvania, which had classical rectangular dimensions. At that time, seeing the states purely as shapes, I remember wondering how anyone could take pride in states with shattered outlines like Michigan, Maryland or even Virginia.

There was in our town a delightful boy about my age who gave us much concern. His name was Ted Johnson, and like me he was an orphan, but unlike me some birth accident or unspecified defect had left him unable to do sums at school or read with any proficiency. He was a lovable fellow, everyone testified to that, and he fumbled his way along, never quite on target but constantly surprising us with his sudden bursts of keen understanding and ability to do things we couldn't, like hearing birds sing before we did or seeing in familiar objects aspects that we had overlooked. Since neither Ted nor I had parents, we were thrown together often, and I came to know him better than most people did. As buddies we did many things together.

It was Ted who got me my first salaried job, at age eleven or twelve, cultivating flowering plants at the big Burpee Seed Company's meadows west of town. But it was something else Ted proposed when we were thirteen that had a lasting influence on me. Although we were little more than children, we—Ted in particular—were sturdier than some of our classmates, so it would have been difficult for strangers to tell exactly how old we were. One summer day Ted astonished me by saying: 'Nothing much doing in Doylestown. Why don't we see what's happening in New York?' I deemed the idea sensible, so off we started on the first important journey of my life.

We started from Doylestown for the seventy-five mile trip to New York City with less than twenty-five cents each, and with not the slightest doubt in the world that we would make it. Later I would travel across much of the United States with even less financing, for these were years of innocence, for Ted, for me and for the nation.

The automobile had just fallen to a price range affordable by even ordinary families, and when they owned one they wanted to use it often. They enjoyed picking up adventurous young hitchhikers and talking with them and perhaps, if the boys proved interesting, even treating them to a meal. A boy with enterprise could, in those simpler years, travel where he wished without fear of criminals moving in on him or deviates molesting him.

At night a young hitchhiker had no trouble finding a place to sleep, for in most towns if he reported himself at the police station the officers would allow him to sleep in the jail and even perhaps give him breakfast before he started out in the morning. Or the car owners who had picked him up would invite him to sleep at their place, or he could always find a barn or an unused building. During most of the time I engaged in such travel I had not yet begun to shave, so morning preparations presented no problems, and by the time the sun was up I was on my way. They were years of wonder and enchantment, those early years of hitchhiking about the country, some of the best years I would know, and if I developed my basic attitude of accepting people pretty much as I found them, it was because I started my travels with a slow-witted lad of enormous courage, optimism and goodwill. And largely because of his genial way with strangers, I kept meeting American citizens of all levels who took me into their cars, their confidence and often their homes.

On that first trip we reached New York without trouble and without spending any of our capital, for a truck driver allowed us to ride free in his vehicle on the ferry that crossed from New Jersey into the city. And there we had a great time, cadging free food from the back doors of restaurants and seeing with wide-eyed wonder sights we did not understand and whose historical importance we did not appreciate. We had learned in school that Times Square was the center of the city, and we asked our way, marveling at the tall buildings as we walked. I wish I could report that on this first trip into the city I introduced myself to that most marvelous of American streets, Forty-second, which contained the three institutions which were to prove so crucial in my education: the New York Public Library, Gray's Pharmacy just off Forty-second on Broadway, and that endless chain of inexpensive motion picture theaters that at that time showed the current popular films, between Seventh and Eighth Avenues. If Forty-second Street were to have been excised from my education, I might have ended up an unfeeling clod.

On my first acquaintance with the street I did not appreciate its power; indeed I cannot recall that I was even aware that it was there. After two wonderful days in the city, subsisting on what I do not remember, Ted and I headed homeward, still with a few cents in our pockets and also with engaging smiles that encouraged the owners of new automobiles to pick us up from waiting corners and drive us homeward, often with a hot dog or a soda thrown in.

Ted and I were so exhilarated by our first success that after we were back home for a few boring weeks, we set out again, this time with a little more money, and headed for Florida. I remember that trip as the best he and I would take, for it led us into states with romantic names and histories, such as Virginia with its battlefields and Georgia with its cotton. Again we met with unfailing kindness and assistance, and we slept in some fine homes, whose owners gave a new definition to the phrase 'Southern hospitality.'

The roads we traveled this time were most often dirt, even between important cities, and we saw large expanses of the rural South, shuddering at some of the old-time slave shacks we passed and finding our sleeping places near cotton gins. Each of us carried a small cloth bag into which we crammed whatever gear we had collected for the trip; I had a toothbrush, a cake of soap, which I used for both hands and teeth, and some odd bits of clothing that I changed into when we washed our soiled laundry at night in some jail.

We gained a most favorable opinion of the South, especially certain stopping places in the Carolinas where our stays were almost story-book delightful. I can still remember one fine house we were invited into west of Charleston, whose row of trees leading from the road to the door were almost the epitome of the word *welcome*. If all this sounds somewhat incredible, you must remember that in those days—1920 it was or perhaps 1921—there were not many youths like us on the road, and people were enthralled to learn how young we were and how daring—they would keep us awake after supper so we could tell them of our adventures. In all the years I hitchhiked, usually alone, I never had an experience in which I felt menaced or even begrudged a favor. I corresponded with a few of the people I met when I returned home, for I remembered them as being gracious and the kind I would have liked to know better.

We did not get to Florida that first time. In a small Georgia town the police took a jaundiced view of us when we applied for an overnight stay in their jail: 'How old are you kids?' Ted said we were sixteen. 'Your folks know you're down here? Where did you say you was from?' When Ted said Philadelphia, the policeman snorted and asked: 'How much cash do you kids have? Spread it out, all of it.'

When he saw our pitiful treasury he summoned his superior, who was even gruffer: 'What do you kids think you're doing?' When Ted told them we were heading for Florida, the chief officer growled: 'Not through this state,' and he did not invite us to stay in his jail; he threw us into a cell and turned the key. It was a gloomy night.

In the morning the first policeman we had talked to unlocked our cell, gave us hot drinks and some pancakes and told us we were to turn right around and head back to Philadelphia. But before we were ready to leave the jail he arranged for a truck being driven north by one of his friends to take us on as passengers clear to the Virginia border, from which another truck would carry us into Richmond. As we thanked him for taking care of us, he gave the truck driver fifty cents, with instructions to feed us on the way. And in this manner we said farewell to Georgia.

I have often recalled those policemen, and have appreciated how sensibly they behaved toward us; they impressed upon us the dangers we might run into on the road and the concern policemen had for penniless young boys wandering aimlessly on the nation's highways. Also, one night in a locked cell had a salutary effect, for it made me swear I would never again give anyone cause to keep me locked up for even one day; and through the rest of my life I kept that boyhood pledge. I have seen a lot of jails and have successfully avoided being inside any of them.

Nevertheless, chastened though we were, later that year Ted and I decided that having almost seen Florida, we really ought to see Canada, so we set out again with finances similar to those before. When we went through New York City again, we greeted it as an old friend, and then got onto the exciting shore road along which even then was the uninterrupted city of New York-New Haven-Providence-Boston. It was a compelling experience, an introduction to a whole new concept of American life, and I was enthralled by the idea of an endless city. I did not see the ugliness, or the junkyards with discarded cars and sofas, or the areas in which the extremely poor lived; I saw only the boundless vitality of the region, the hundreds upon hundreds of little shops and factories, and the trucks hauling the products away to freight cars on the waiting railway line. I saw the power of America, the tremendous force of its efforts to make things and move them about. I saw wealth being created, and it shouted back a challenge: 'Be part of this. Make something important and move it across the whole United States.'

Very shortly I would be seeing the immense industrial installations at Detroit, but they would not generate in me the profound excitement that the small factories along the New York–Boston highway did. Perhaps it was because I saw the lesser ones when my mind and my perceptions were clearer, or more impressionable or simply more receptive, but as would occur so often in my life, experiences of the greatest potential significance seemed to reach me precisely when I required them most, or was most attentive to them. Certainly this would happen again and again until at the end I had been effectively exposed to a score of different fields. But recently I have begun to think, in retrospect, that the experiences must have always been there and available to me, except that I was too naive to recognize their importance until the proper time. A wise friend who knew me during the formative years—say, twelve through twenty-two—described me as 'dumb and happy,' and that might have been accurate, for I was a happy warrior moving unawares through a succession of minefields. I came through remarkably unscathed, delighted with the world as I had found it, and always prepared to face gladly the next encounter it offered.

Our failure to enter Florida was almost repeated with Canada. We found Maine so much bigger than we had expected and its new-car drivers so few and cautious that our progress north was painfully slow. However we did ultimately reach the border, stepped across and could boast: 'Well, we got to Canada!' But we turned about and headed home. I did not grieve at our failure, for that New York–Boston exploration had been strangely powerful.

In Detroit I had a maiden aunt of great wisdom, with a distinguished career in public school teaching; when black students started crowding the Detroit schools, many delicately balanced and frightened white teachers, especially the women, quit the system, but Aunt Laura sailed right into the heart of one of most troubled schools and became a champion of black students and their problems, winning national accolades for the superior quality of her work. Years later, when she retired from her nearly all-black school in Detroit, she was resting on our porch in Doylestown when a young boy who was a student at a military school in Maryland stopped by to tell her how through lack of strong faculty direction his school had become ungovernable, with students raising a constant ruckus. After hearing his mournful story she said: 'I could clear up a situation like that in one week.' Back at school the young fellow told the administration of Aunt Laura's boast and they sneered: 'We'd like to see her try.' The upshot was that at age seventy-one she became acting principal of the school, and she did tame the rebellious students within a week. You did not fool around with Aunt Laura.

When I was thirteen or fourteen she invited me to spend the summer with her in Detroit, and so with less than a dollar in my pocket and a big knapsack on my back, I hitchhiked out to Michigan. The journey was even better than it had been with Ted Johnson, for being alone I caught rides more easily than before. It was a marvelous trip along the beautiful roads and through the low mountains of Pennsylvania, but going through the cities of Cleveland and Toledo was equally interesting.

Detroit, especially as Aunt Laura showed it to me, was a fascination, for to my amazement Canada lay to the south of the city, not the north, and for the second time I edged my way into about six yards of our northern neighbor. I visited the big auto plants, rode out to Ann Arbor to inspect the campus of the University of Michigan, the first advanced educational institution I had ever seen, and explored the state rather thoroughly, hitchhiking here and there. But the big event of the summer was an extensive trip I took out to Iowa, again with less than a dollar to see me there and back.

I was headed to nowhere in particular, just drifting about to see what the West looked like. I skipped Chicago, but in the company of a family heading southwest I did come upon a highway that would be of considerable importance to me some sixteen years in the future in 1936. At that time our great national roads were not numbered, at least so far as I can remember, but in time this one would be U.S. 34, and I would spend many hours along it and five years at its terminal. I liked it when I first saw it, much of it still dirt, some of it paved in reddish brick. It climbed up and down small hills, darted through sleepy towns and revealed to me for the first time the open grandeur of the West, before the badlands and the Rocky Mountains intruded. It was a real voyage of discovery, an opening of grand vistas, never spectacular like those awesome parts of the Southwest where palisaded hills and deep canyons provide unique sights and sensations but quietly big and powerful. For many years, when I was more fully informed about the states, I would consider Iowa the most favorably, and it was a judgment I did not totally withdraw when later, after I had acquired more sophisticated data, Oregon preempted the apex.

Two questions naturally arise about such adventurous wandering by a young child. First, why did my elders, who loved me very much and who were most protective in all other aspects of childhood, allow me to take such trips? As I shall explain later, I came from an impoverished and in some respects a badly broken home, so there was no inclination on my part to stay there during vacation time, and indeed I never did after I landed my first summer job at Burpee's. Invariably, come the end of spring, I was away either working or hitting the road. My mother, as I will later explain, faced far graver problems than keeping me at home and, having given me a sound foundation in knowing the difference between right and wrong, between good friends and bad, and between constructive and destructive behavior, as well as a love of learning, she may have felt that she had done all she could and that I was henceforth on my own. She also knew that I was far older in many important respects than I looked, and that I was essentially a prudent, conservative boy who was not going to be easily led astray.

I am sure she was constantly worried during my absences, and I know she was distressed that she could not give me a pocketful of coins whenever I set out, but we both knew that that was impossible. Both she and Aunt Laura would have wanted to do everything for me they could, but their capacity was limited. Also, when I left either my mother or my aunt, I never said: 'I'm going to Canada' or 'I'm heading for Iowa.' I'm ashamed to say that I just went, although I did try to send postcards after I was safely started. And since, after those first three trips with Ted Johnson, I made every trip alone, I was my own pilot, my own counselor, and was able to do pretty much as I wished. I was a free agent.

Second, why did I feel driven to leave home or Aunt Laura's comfortable quarters in Detroit? My life at home in Doylestown could be rather bleak, for I had none of the clothes and games and equipment that boys my age would normally have had. All I really had was that music, the art I remember so well and the endless books from the library; the essential elements of those three I could take with me intellectually and without burdening my knapsack. When one hitchhikes, one spends long hours either waiting at a likely intersection or trudging down the road, and when I was so engaged I found comfort in singing Caruso's arias or in reciting the many poems I had memorized, or recalling the latest postcards I had added to my art collection. I was in many ways the poorest boy on the road, in others the richest, and I was always happy to be on the road meeting new people, hearing new stories and seeing new landscapes.

Was it some psychic maladjustment that drove me then and later to this incessant traveling? Was it some sickness of the spirit, some malaise of the kind that follows if the body is deprived of some essential vitamin, or the mere perversity of a restless young male? I have never been clever enough to analyze the impetus, but I doubt that it was related to any deep-seated psychic deficiency. I've said that home was not exciting enough to keep me tied to it, and I had no physical possessions of any kind to hold my interest for long periods of time. Yet I was not unhappy with my family, my school or my friends. The simple fact seems to have been that once I saw that mysterious road outside my house, the eastern part leading to a dead end, the western to worlds unknown, I was determined to explore the latter.

.   .   .

In high school and college I continued to hitchhike to all parts of the nation. I had had a treasured friend in high school, Lindsay Johnson, who was the son of a clergyman. I hitchhiked to see him when he was attending a small religious school in North Carolina, Elon College; one spring morning when he went to the college post office for his mail, there I was waiting for him. I had another friend, a young woman I liked very much, who went to school in Indiana, so I went out to see her. And I hitchhiked to certain places of great interest simply to see them. By then it was the late 1920s, when both the cars on the roads and the young people traveling them were more numerous, and I began to find myself with strangers older than myself and dangerous. One congenial gang persuaded me to go along on a railroad trip almost to the Rockies and, using empty boxcars and the structures under the cars, I went a fair distance. But a brush with railway police at a junction near Cheyenne terrified me, and I hitchhiked back, keeping to the highway system I knew, never again to mess around with the railroads.

In 1931, while teaching in a private school, it was as if some outside agency had been studying my behavior and concluded: 'That one is destined to travel!' I was awarded a small sum of money that would enable me, if I was frugal, which I had learned to be, to enjoy two years studying and traveling in Europe. In the month before I sailed out of New York I practically memorized train and ship schedules for the Europe of that time, and as soon as I landed in Scotland I began calculating how I could obtain the most for my stringently budgeted travel funds. With the help of knowledgeable Scottish university mates, I mastered the intricacies of budgeting so well that I was able to give myself the modern equivalent of the famous eighteenth-century Grand Tour, which all young gentlemen of respectable lineage were expected to take. For reasons I can't now recall, I missed the German cities, but I did visit Paris, Rome, Florence, Venice, Ferrara, Madrid, Brussels, Antwerp and Amsterdam. The Rome and Brussels visits were of vital political importance, as I shall later explain, but equally so, and in a radically different manner, were three less glamorous trips my Scottish friends made possible.

The first was a hiking trip clear across Scotland, which I did twice, first from St. Andrews to Oban, about a hundred and five miles, and the second from Inverness down that grand system of lochs to Fort William, about fifty-five miles. Seeing Scotland on foot in that plodding, patient way was to see in intimate detail the glory of the lochs set down amid brown hills, the beauty of the heather, the majestically unfolding landscapes, one after another as the path rose and fell. In those long hikes, broken by talks at night with men at the pubs or during the day with shepherds I met at the stiles, I learned what quiet, controlled people the Scots were, so admirably adjusted to their dour yet splendid land. They were warm in conversation and gracious in their hospitality, even though most of them had little more in their pockets than I.

While wandering aimlessly I became acquainted with a poem I had missed in college; I was caught by it on the first reading because it spoke to my condition. It was Matthew Arnold's 'The Scholar Gipsy,' and in its stately lines, so in harmony with my own view of the world, I came upon a passage in which I discerned a portrait of myself:

> Come, let me read the oft-read tale again:
>   The story of the Oxford scholar poor,
> Of pregnant parts and quick inventive brain,
>   Who, tired of knocking at Preferment's door,
>   One summer morn forsook
> His friends, and went to learn the Gipsy-lore,
>   And roam'd the world with that wild brotherhood,
>   And came, as most men deem'd, to little good,
> But came to Oxford and his friends no more.

The lines gripped me as if I could foresee the wild, fantastic time when I would travel with the gypsy-kuchi wanderers in Afghanistan and write a glowing book about them; as if I knew even then that I would never be able to dismiss my own longing to roam the world.

The second trip my Scottish friends suggested was one of the finest I would ever take: 'James, you should go out to Oban, catch a Mac-Brayne steamer, cross over the Minch, roughest body of water in Europe, and land on the wee island of Barra.'

'Why Barra?'

'When Knox's Protestants converted all the rest of Scotland to their dour faith, they were afraid to cross that stormy sea to Barra, so it remained Catholic, a braw singing place.'

The Minch was rougher than they had predicted; it always is. And Barra was such a grand 'singing place' that I spent three months there, and part of a summer later. It was such a fine adventure that I shall explain why later. Here it suffices to say that Barra is a small island of the Outer Hebrides, far out in the stormy Atlantic; its people, who were Catholic, were then among the poorest in Europe; and it contained right in the middle of the bay one of the most romantic castles in Great Britain, in my day almost a relic, today a fine memorial restored by a diligent chieftain of Barra who married an American girl and took American citizenship. To see Barra at any time was a privilege, to see it when it was still, to all outward appearances, in the Middle Ages, as it was when I knew it, was an exploration into the mists of history.

The third bit of advice my Scottish friends shared with me was one of those fortuitous strokes of fortune that can scarcely be believed after they happen, so exceedingly appropriate are they: 'Jim, you seem to enjoy getting about a bit. Have you looked into the program the shipping companies have out of Glasgow?'

'Like what?'

'Seems like it was made for you. They welcome young fellows, and you don't have to be a proper sailor or have papers or anything. You get in touch with their office and let them know you're in good health, and submit a paper from the police that you're responsible, and that's it.'

'But what do they do?'

'They check to see you're telling the truth, and if they like your letter and find that you are really responsible, they send you a note telling you to report to Glasgow, and when you get there— Jock's done this, he can tell you the details. But they sign you on as a kind of honorary member of the crew. You're a full-fledged member of the British Merchant Fleet and ten minutes later you're aboard a cargo ship heading out for the Mediterranean. Of course, if it's a shipping company located in Edinburgh, you sail out of Leith and hit the Baltic ports.'

'Do I have duties aboard ship?'

'The big thing is, you have shore leave as soon as your ship hits port, and you can leave ship at Leghorn for example and pick her back up at Messina in Sicily, ten days later. But when you're at sea, yes, you do have duties. You take the printed reports the ship receives from the government regarding changes in the time of flashing lights from lighthouses and warnings as to sunken ships and things like that, and you enter these changes on your ship's charts. And while you're doing this you learn a whale of a lot about the Mediterranean, if that's where your ship's going.'

'Do I pay them or do they pay me?'

'Standard rate for all assignments like this. You get one shilling a month and your board free.'

'Why do they do this? Sounds like a wonderful deal.'

'They want young Scots to know the sea.'

'But will they listen to an American?'

'You'll have to write and see.'

I did write, and the directors of the Bruce Line in Glasgow said they'd never had a Yank aboard one of their ships, and they'd be delighted to try their luck with me. Three days later I had my papers (Honorary) in the British Merchant Fleet and I was aboard a Bruce Line ship headed for the historic ports of the Mediterranean.

The line had seven or eight ships, each bearing a Spanish name that began and ended with the letter *a,* such as the *Almeria* or the *Almenada.* My ship was the smallest in the fleet, the *Alcira,* commanded by a tough little fighter, Captain Reid, whose first mate was a grizzled veteran nearing the end of his career named Mr. Macintosh. He was responsible for instructing me in my duties. I was twenty-four at the time, eager to learn the ways of the British fleet, and Macintosh must have felt that I was one of the last young men who would fall into his hands, for he took special pains with me, teaching me how to shoot the sun, how to mind the all-important chronometer, and how to study the documents with which I would work. Both he and Reid were happy to have an American aboard, and by the end of the second day we had settled down to one of the most delightful and instructive cruises I would ever encounter. For me there would be no Captain Bligh, no terror such as those from one of the Jack London books—there was just the companionship of two older men who were pleased to have with them a young foreigner who was eager to learn and pull his own weight on the voyage.

I would later learn that in World War II Captain Reid had the *Alcira* and two other Bruce Line ships sunk from under him and each time he swam clear to pick up another command. Toward the end of the war, my informant told me one night in Valencia, 'The little son-of-a-bitch was steering his ship right through a nest of Nazi submarines and daring them to hit him.' I believed every word of it, for he was a small dynamo who enjoyed responding to challenges.

The *Alcira* was a remarkably tough, well-built Dutch ship with a nose so blunt that the engines almost had to push her through the waves. We made about four knots, that's ninety-six miles a day, and when we battered our way into a heavy wind off Cape Finisterre on the Spanish coast we practically stood still for a whole day, making almost no headway. Never losing sight of that looming cliff proved that we were practically immobilized. But when the winds eased, we moved ahead and rounded Sagres, from where Prince Henry the Navigator had dispatched his Portuguese adventurers to probe the coast of Africa and the southern seas.

Now we approached Gibraltar, our little ship coming so close to shore that we could see the battlements and the vast water catchments, and then we were in the Mediterranean at last. Under sunny skies we headed across that noble sea, on whose shores were so many relics of European and African history.

When we left Glasgow, every available corner of our deck had been piled high with bituminous coal from Scottish mines, and so were our cargo holds. The tactic was to feed our engines during the early part of our trip with loose coal shoveled down from the decks, leaving as much as possible below for sale in Italy. Consequently, during the early days our decks and the rest of the ship were quite dirty, but now with the topside coal gone, sailors could hose down the *Alcira* and make her quite presentable preparatory to docking at one of the Italian seaports— which one we had not yet been advised. But the home office in Glasgow was monitoring markets carefully and would soon tell us where to go in order to sell our stored coal at maximum profit.

The wireless report that came was so exciting that I could almost believe it was intended solely to make me happy. We were to head directly into Civitavecchia, an ancient port for Rome. And why would that thrill me? Because one of my idols was the French writer Stendhal (whose real name was Marie Henri Beyle). And what had Stendhal to do with Civitavecchia?

He had been one of the most confused of all the great writers, a man of a thousand disasters. Everything he tried seemed to collapse about him, especially his attempts to get some attractive woman into either marriage or bed. He suffered in debacles so ridiculous that a lesser man might have committed suicide. Finally getting someone not attractive to cooperate, on his sole adventure with a woman he contracted a virulent venereal disease that remained with him for the rest of his tortured life.

But what he could do was write—he produced hard-grained, analytical novels, two of the best in world literature, *The Red and the Black* and *The Charterhouse of Parma.* But even with these masterpieces he could not attract popular acceptance or earn a living income, so it was fortunate that he succeeded in obtaining the sinecure of diplomatic representative at the now sleepy port of Civitavecchia. The first step I would take on the Continent would be in the town where he had labored for many years. What a way for a voyager with my interests to enter Europe!

Our ship coming in at dusk could not dock at a pier, so it anchored some distance offshore, but with two heavy hawsers attached to bollards on the dock. That left me with no way to land and see if I could find the house in which Stendhal had lived and worked. First Mate Mac-

intosh, seeing my grave disappointment, and perhaps remembering his
own first entry into Europe, told me quietly: 'If a man had the nerve,
he could work his way down those two hawsers, sort of like a monkey.
They won't give way, you know.' And with him helping me over the side
I grasped the two ropes, one in each hand, and planted my legs, one on
each rope, in such a manner that I was more or less supported, and in
that undignified posture I started to negotiate the fifteen precarious
yards to shore. I landed in Civatavecchia bottom first, but as I left the
hawsers swaying in the night breeze, I looked above and saw the top of
the stone fortress to which Baedeker had alerted me: this was the citadel
that Michelangelo had built to protect the treasure ships of Rome as
they disgorged their cargoes here. Michelangelo and Stendhal greeting
me in my first moments ashore! Throwing arms wide, and imitating
Edmond Dantes in *The Count of Monte Cristo,* who shouted when he
landed on his island of treasure: 'The world is mine!' I cried: 'Europe,
I salute you!'

I encountered a local gentleman who spoke English and was happy
to lead me to the Stendhal house, and I think he understood when I paid
my silent respects to the great Frenchman who has been called 'one of
the world's all-time losers.' Ten days later, when I rejoined the *Alcira*
in Palermo, I was satisfied that I had been allowed an exhilarating if
brief taste of Italy. It had been made possible by those friends at the
university who had told me about the generous Scottish shipping companies.

When I returned to the United States, I continued to hitchhike to all
parts of the country, except North Dakota, which in those years I could
never get to. I became moderately familiar with all regions of the country, but not with any thoroughness with the northwest, and certainly
neither Hawaii nor Alaska, two areas with which I would later be
involved rather intensely.

When peace came after World War II, I stumbled into one occupation
after another that took me to every continent. Later, when the government wanted to put me on a committee whose work had overseas
ramifications, material prepared for submission to the Senate prior to
my appearance for confirmation of the appointment showed that I had
worked substantially in some hundred and three different sovereign
nations, some of them extremely small and unimportant.

The travel in those years was fascinating. My work had made me
something of an expert on Asia, and in those exciting days when I was

active in all parts of that continent I used to keep a portable typewriter and a suitcase full of traveling clothes at one hotel in Tokyo and at others in Hong Kong, Singapore and Bangkok. When an urgent call came for me to fly to any part of Asia, I would simply go to the airport, fly to one of my cities, pick up my gear and be on my way. In those years I am certain that I gave away at least ten Olivetti typewriters that I had carried to places like Burma and Afghanistan with no chance of taking them out when I left in a hurry. Some of the machines had been provided by the agencies that had hired me, but an equal number had been my own purchases, whose loss I dismissed as the cost of doing business. In the United States I have lost another dozen, and as for suitcases filled with work clothes, I have had to abandon a score, never with much regret.

One of the joys of my life is that I have lived in the age of aviation, for I love to fly, did a great deal of it in the Navy and have subsequently flown in almost everything that had wings. Shortly after my seventy-fifth birthday, when I was working in California, some Air Force people asked me: 'But have you ever been up in a glider?' and when I said no, they cried: 'Well, here we go!' And they took me to one of those fields high in the hills near Edwards Air Force Base, at which we were working, and in minutes they had me up in the air behind the towplane. Something went wrong; the towplane broke off, and we spiraled swiftly down to earth, but straightened up at the last minute to make a fine, steady landing.

'You mustn't allow a mishap like that to sour you on gliding,' they told me, and in a few minutes we were aloft again, this time to high altitude, where we caught updrafts that kept us drifing there for about an hour of exquisite flight—silent, vibrationless and majestic.

Once when our government wanted to let our allies know that we really did have some secret weapons ready for their defense, I was chosen to write a revealing magazine article about the hitherto secret B-52 bomber squadron at Limestone Air Force Base in the extreme northern part of Maine, and to familiarize myself with the plane, I took a crash course as a bombardier in a group of B-52s secretly riding herd on the Soviet Union. I learned what the drill was if the United States was attacked and we had to counterattack. Having already studied details about Siberia, I understood our proposed strategy when some of the targets in Russia were revealed and exercises were mounted to simulate flights from Limestone to those targets.

Later I actually flew one of the powerful B-47 bombers two thirds of the way across the United States at an altitude of fifty thousand feet.

When I say I 'flew' it I mean just that, but with a qualification: at takeoff I occupied the rear copilot's seat, with the real pilot in control. However, when the plane was safely aloft, I took over the controls because the Air Force considered it important for me to experience the sensations of actually flying a plane of that size and speed if I was going to write a report about it. I accelerated, slowed, turned, banked, changed elevation and felt the entire operating system responding to my commands.

Because pilots know of my love for their profession, I have been asked to fly as their copilot on a score of different airlines, especially over the Pacific, and on five or six occasions I have actually been in the pilot's seat to work the iron mikes that operate the automatic systems. Always I have been aboard in some official capacity, but in the case of various foreign airlines that have allowed me to be in the cockpit my official role has not involved their nations.

It is somewhat surprising that I still love to fly, and that, not long ago, nearing my eighties, I flew as copilot to the most distant Aleutian Islands, for I have been involved in three major airplane accidents in which the three planes were totally destroyed. The crashes have had no effect on my love for planes; after each one I have promptly resumed flying.

The first crash was at Manus Island when our double-decker flying boat landed in the big anchorage and continued straight to the bottom in one smooth glide. Lives were lost, but those of us in the top deck escaped.

The second crash was memorable partly because of its aftermath. We were flying in to a landing on the perilous airstrip, as it then was, in American Samoa. Pilots who had to land here during the war will remember that they came in from the sea, flew straight down the short airstrip toward a mountain at the far end, turned abruptly to the right, banked and landed in the opposite direction from which they had approached—'a strict one-eighty,' I believe it was called, since the pilot had to make a turn of 180 degrees under the most demanding requirements of timing and altitude control.

I was strapped into a bucket seat molded in the middle of a long aluminum bench that ran the distance of the interior of the plane; this put me facing inward, and in the seat opposite me but somewhat to the rear sat an Air Force lieutenant colonel. As we turned to land I said to myself: 'Unh-uh! This field is hell. Too much moment on the port wheel.' I do not find this usage of *moment* in the dictionary, but it is accurate, I believe; in a situation like ours it means that sideways thrust exceeds the forward to such an extent that if the wheels touch before the accumulated moment is dispersed or relaxed, the lateral force would be so great that the landing gear would have to crumple inward.

I remember looking at the colonel questioningly but casually, as if nothing serious were afoot, and I raised my eyebrows as if to ask: 'Too much moment?' and he nodded back, completely composed, and revolved his right forefinger to indicate that 'Yep, we're going over.' And a moment later, as we both had known it would, our DC-3 landed with a thump, the port wheel crumpled inward, as predicted, and there was a fantastic mess with bodies and gear flying about. Since the motion threw me onto the colonel's body, we had trouble untangling ourselves before rescuing the others and then leaping from the wreckage in order to escape the gasoline fire that could be expected.

No lives were lost, and when the debris was cleared, the colonel and I retrieved some personal belongings and walked to the Pago Pago officers' club, quietly pleased with our coolness under stress and the fact that we had acted rather well in the emergency when some of the younger men had not—although neither of us said anything to that effect. After we washed up in the rooms assigned us we had a good dinner, after which he went about his duties and I lingered for a couple of Cokes, then started back to quarters in the dark.

A work crew digging a service-line ditch had left uncovered a hole, and I fell into it with a thud when I hit bottom. It happened so suddenly, in the dark, and on such unfamiliar terrain that the accumulated tension of the day's crash following a chain of close calls up north rendered me powerless even to call for help. There, stuck in a trench that I assumed was at least eight feet deep, I remained a helpless clod, until someone from the club happened by and summoned others to haul me out.

I was taken to the base infirmary, given a sedative and allowed to sleep till well into the next morning. Then I was taken by the medics who had rescued me to see the trench into which I had fallen. To my amazement, it could not have been more than eighteen inches deep: 'The captain who discovered you almost stepped on you, your butt was sticking up so high in the air.'

It was sobering, that inspection of my trench that was eight feet deep, for up to then I had considered myself impervious to afflictions like battle fatigue, nervous exhaustion and back-pain seizures, which I had classified as cowardly cop-outs. I was humbled to learn that although at a time of crisis I could be heroic, at another time I could be as helpless as a frightened child.

The third crash was totally different from the others. In 1957, while on a routine Army flight from Guam to Tokyo in that most reliable of all planes, the old DC-3, called alternatively the C-47 and the Dakota, our engines started to sputter and we found ourselves far out in the Pacific, with either no fuel or what we had contaminated by water condensation, so that we had no alternative but to crash-land in the sea. We had ample warning that we were going down, and I remember those last minutes vividly. I did not recall all my past life in an instant or begin saying prayers. I had only one thought: Those waves out there are so big there's going to be one hell of a bang. I'm flying my favorite way, backwards, with my head propped against the bulkhead to absorb the crash. I hope the pilot has read his manual on how to crash at sea. And as the oldest guy around, I hope I behave well.

By this time my work in aviation and my wide experience in planes of all kinds had convinced me that there was always a right way to do things, a way that gave you the greatest chance of survival, and how to land a plane in the middle of the ocean must have been analyzed to the last square inch of wave, the last configuration of plane. Wheels up or wheels down? Nose way up or slightly up? Straight in or at an angle to the waves? I knew none of the answers, but I knew they existed and hoped that our pilot had studied them.

He made a perfect gliding landing into a tremendously big wave that stopped our DC-3 instantly and totally, tearing out most of the bottom, and then a miracle occurred. The marvelous old plane, ripped almost to shreds, stayed afloat for three minutes. At a time like that, with so much to be done if lives are to be saved, it is astonishing how long three minutes can be. If a small group of men and women were properly drilled, they could carry out every piece of furniture in a small restaurant in three minutes; they could perform wonders. We were thirteen in the plane and at the moment of the crash, everyone knew what to do. One man threw open the big rear door. The sergeant threw out the rubber raft and activated the device that inflated it. Another man herded the eleven passengers in an orderly movement to the escape area. I checked the pilot's cabin to be sure the crew was getting out through a special exit, and the sergeant and I were the last to leave.

At the door I thought fleetingly of all my notes and papers that were about to go down, and then I was in the water. I was not far from the plane when it quietly sank. Buoyed up by my life vest, which worked perfectly, I thought how miraculous it was that we had all performed so admirably, and then I disgraced myself: when I finally succeeded in swimming to the rubber raft, which was now some distance away from me, I couldn't climb in. The raft had such big, slippery round sides that I simply could not hoist myself over the hump and slide in.

'For Christ's sake, old man, get in!' someone shouted, and I had to cry back: 'I can't get a hold anywhere!'

'Swing your ass up and over!' Since I have a notably plump rear end, that was an easy command to give but not easy to obey, so an exasperated Army man had to leap back into the water to help me; he gave me such a tremendous push from behind that I practically flew into the raft, landing in a heap on top of the others.

Our careful pilot, before we crashed, had sent out such a strong radio S.O.S: 'Mayday, Mayday!' (from the French *Venez m'aider,* Come help me) that stations in widely scattered points around the Pacific recorded it, and this enabled headquarters to triangulate the source of the call and locate us precisely as a tiny spot in the vast Pacific. A nearby Japanese fishing boat did not hear our call but it did receive instructions from land to hasten our rescue, and we were saved.

To passengers who fly over oceans I would give these assurances in case they are confronted by a crash landing at sea. If your pilot has studied the instructions his manual contains for such landings, there is a good chance you will survive. The little yellow life jackets your plane provides are amazingly effective. Take as much clothing as you can, especially a hat to prevent sunburn. It will be difficult getting into your life raft, and once safely aboard, you will probably be very seasick, for the rubber raft moves forward-backward, right-left, up-down, all at once, and so will your stomach. But quite important, perhaps fifty listening stations will have heard your distress signal, lines will intersect, and your probable position will be known.

Today, when I start a flight across an ocean, I listen attentively as the stewardess explains procedures for the life jackets and often think: I am probably the only person on this plane who ever had to use one in the middle of the ocean, and how grateful I was to have had one that day and to have it function properly, for I could not have made the raft without it. Half an hour after the rescue I was back aboard another DC-3 to resume my flight to Tokyo.

The closest I ever came to death was in a hotel in Saigon when I was trapped in my room on the top floor while there was a major riot on the floors below. Some Indians stationed in the area had been so outraged by political maltreatment that they stormed the hotel and started throwing guests out of the rooms, headfirst onto the concrete slabs outside. I watched with horror as they threw several to death from the rooms below me, then heard them storm onto my floor. From a room three doors down from me, they pitched out a fat Indian merchant who had been visiting Saigon, and he screamed to his death. Then they were at my door, kicking it open. For some reason I have never been able to explain, I grabbed my Olivetti portable, stood with it clasped protectively in front of my chest and shouted as they came at me: 'Press! Press!' They were so startled they simply nodded and withdrew.

Looking back on a lifetime of joyous travel, I have these answers to questions frequently asked.

'What was the most delightful place you ever visited?' Bora Bora. 'The most rewarding city?' A dead tie between Rome and London. 'The best ancient ruin?' Karnak and the temples along the Nile. 'The most romantic?' What used to be Angkor Wat in Cambodia. 'The most spiritual place?' Kyoto in Japan. 'The most overwhelming single building?' King Philip II's Escorial near Madrid. 'The best cuisine?' Chinese. 'The best special wine?' Asti Spumante. 'The best regular wine?' Châteauneuf-du-Pape. 'The best rosé wine?' Please, no comment, not in polite company. 'The best art museum?' Now, here the headaches begin, for each is superb in its own way: the Prado in Madrid, the Uffizi in Florence, the National Gallery in London, the National Gallery of Art in Washington. 'The best small museum?' The Frick in New York. 'The best musical auditorium?' The Philadelphia Academy of Music.

During a visit to Aruba with a touring group to which I was not attached, I saw a man who always sat alone. One day I asked: 'What brings you here?' and he said he made his living by arranging incentive tours for many big businesses in his area: 'You know, you sell eighteen more refrigerators than the next fellow and you earn a paid vacation. I handle arrangements for half a hundred different companies, no headache for them, a good living for me.'

He showed the answers he had received to a questionnaire he had circulated to ten thousand previous winners, answers to such questions as 'How did you like Egypt?' and 'Was the hotel food fine-good-fair-awful?' I was not much interested in the questions except for the last one, which he said he had just tucked in as an afterthought: 'Where would you like to go next?' The answer was overwhelming: 'Anywhere.' Ask me that same question tonight and you'll get the same answer.

Some questions require longer answers. 'The best ride you ever had?' On a bitterly cold winter's night we were trying to land our plane at Tromsø, Norway, far north of the Arctic Circle, but the field was closed in by a local blizzard. We landed instead at the small military emergency field at Bardu, some fifty miles away, and since we were in the land of perpetual night, time of day meant nothing. We climbed into the taxi of a driver who liked to sing and set out for Tromsø with him yodeling folk songs and us clinging like mad to whatever we could grab hold of in the backseat. The road had been cut through huge snowdrifts, which made it palisaded on both sides, and the driver's delight was to drive at breakneck speed directly at a turn in the road, crash into the solid wall of snow and ricochet off in the desired direction. When I asked what would happen if another madman like himself happened to be coming from the other direction, he said: 'With all this snow, I'd see his headlights reflected into the turn and slow down.' Later a waning moon appeared and we sang our way safely into Tromsø, a ride I would never want to forget or repeat.

'The finest dinner?' Unquestionably the eighteen-boy rijstafel at the old Hôtel des Indes in Java. In a garden under palm trees with an eleven-piece gamelan orchestra playing celestial music, a waiter places before you a large plate containing only one thing, a generous mound of white rice. But then from beyond the gamelan players come eighteen barefoot men wearing colorful Javanese turbans and carrying in each hand an exotic dish: fish, chicken, saté in a peanut sauce, pineapple, orange, six or seven unique fruits, curries, sauces, grated coconut, fried egg, crisp onion and various condiments I could never identify. Since each man brings two dishes, you have thirty-six in all, and during the leisurely meal the rice plate is refilled twice and the boys return with more delicacies, so one certainly does not lack for sustenance. The trick, of course, is to partake sparingly at first and allow the Lucullan meal to proceed as slowly as possible.

My second best meal was a late-night snack at the Ritz Hotel in Madrid. I had no breakfast (as is my custom), had to skip lunch in order to catch a plane from Rome, and missed dinner because the airline had forgotten the meals. When we reached the hotel it was so late that all the services were closed, so I prowled the nearby streets until I found a bottle of red wine, some excellent crusty bread, a slab of hard cheese and two small tins, one of Norwegian sardines, the other of salty anchovies. At midnight my wife and I had one of the most delectable meals we can remember, and the one we most often refer to when we recall the joyous surprises of travel.

'Any health problems?' I followed one invariable procedure: Do everything the doctor orders, take all my shots, then live as I've always lived and eat everything. In the old days we were required to have so many inoculations before we could fly overseas that one doctor said when recording my latest battery in the yellow book we were forced to carry: 'You're a human pincushion!' This regimen kept me free of all major diseases except a frightening case of malaria, which has dogged me for fifty years. Of course, in the first days of almost every major trip I become violently ill with a gastric upset, caused probably by unfamiliar water, but it lasts only a day and I welcome it as a benevolent purgative.

'With all the places you've been, is there any one place you'd not want to return to?' Calcutta. The poverty there, the death in the streets, the incredible living conditions were too much for even me to take—and I can tolerate almost anything. Once when I checked out of my hotel, no fewer than thirty men, most of whom I had never seen, had lined up for tips. Meticulously I looked into every face and tipped generously those eight or nine who had served me in some trivial way or another. When I climbed into the waiting bus, which would convey me to the plane that would take me away from that dreadful city, the men I had not tipped trailed the bus for the first block, screaming and cursing at me in a most hideous manner. When I asked an Englishman why the men were being so hostile, he asked: 'Didn't you tip them?' and I explained that I certainly had, and generously to those I remembered as having done something for me. He cried almost in pain: 'Oh, Mr. Michener, you've done a terribly wrong thing. You should have given everybody at least ten cents.' And then he added soberly: 'Because for them, ten American cents might truly be the difference between life and death.' I can still hear the screams of those anguished men of Calcutta who had received nothing from me.

'Which of your experiences best epitomizes the essence of traveling?' To be in a small boat at four in the morning in an ocean, any ocean, but particularly in the South Pacific, and to know that you are on a proper heading for a tropical island, and to watch as light from the still-hidden sun begins to filter into the eastern sky. And then, because you are in the part of the earth where, because of the bulge near the equator, the sun rises and sets with a tremendous crash, to see it suddenly explode into red brilliance, big enough to devour the world. And then to see ahead, its crest inflamed by the sun, the dim outline of the island you have been seeking, and to watch it slowly, magically rise from the sea until it becomes whole, a home for people, a resting place for birds.

One of the treasures of travel, one of the reasons we journey to distant places, is to intensify our appreciations of the familiar things we've known since childhood. Once when traveling on Lago di Garda, biggest of the lakes in northern Italy, a learned Englishman—a professor at Oxford, I believe—joined me at the railing and said: 'That lovely dot of land at the end of the spit is called Sirmione today. It's the famous

Sirmio of Catullus, who hurried here after his duties in distant Rome. He wrote a charming poem about his travels to that spot:

> Sweetest of sweets to me that pastime seems
> When the mind lays down its burden, when the pain
> Of travel o'er, our own cot we regain
> And nestle on the pillow of our dreams.

The poem expressed my own views on travel so precisely that I asked: 'Who translated it?' and the Englishman replied: 'From its archaic manner I'd say some undistinguished poet about 1840. The Latin original is compact and unrhymed, you know, but our fellow's stuck in a lot of extra words to achieve meter and rhyme.' Even so, I asked if he could write it down for me, and he did. I have recited the poem so constantly over the past sixty years that I almost think of it as my own.

'What is the most rewarding airplane flight you've taken?' A dead heat between two incomparables. Once on a clear, frosty day in winter when snow was everywhere in the high country, I flew with perfect visibility along the entire west–east rampart of the Himalayas, hour after hour above brutal Nanga Parbat, Annapurna, the lesser mountains of Kashmir, the ranges behind which Tibet lay hidden, mighty K-2 and then Everest itself, gigantic in snowy sunlight. There were the rivers, too, gracing the mountains like chains of glittering diamonds: ones with the magical names—Thelum, Chenab, Sutlej—connected with the Indus in Pakistan, the crowded Ganges; the incredible tangle of the world's least-known major river, the mighty Brahmaputra; and even a glimpse of the sprawling Mekong. That was a day of sheer grandeur, and never had Asia paraded itself with such a display of raw power: those gigantic mountains, those rivers whose floods could devastate large portions of a continent. But equally impressive in the way that one perfect pearl can excite more than a handful of diamonds was the Alaskan flight I often took from Anchorage to Juneau along the face of the great mountains there that rise directly out of the sea rather than from high tablelands as the Himalayas do. Here one sees the wildness of nature, the mysterious glaciers that emerge in darkness and die in silence, never reaching the ocean nor even seen by man except from a plane. I have cherished both these flights.

'Which country was the most memorable?' Without question, Afghanistan, and I believe that most foreigners who worked there in the postwar period of 1945–60 would say the same, for in those years the minute European and American communities living in Kabul or work-

ing on the building of the huge dam on the Helmand River experienced
a civilization that had no parallel at the time. In this major capital there
was no hotel, no public restaurant the Europeans could patronize or
would want to, no newspaper, no radio, no cinema and no social function in the indigenous community to which they would be welcomed.
It was the most primitive living any of us had ever experienced, and we
resolved the problem by resorting to certain stratagems. We entertained
one another seven days a week by taking turns hosting lunch and dinner.
One never ate alone and one never went out except to friends' houses.
On Friday nights we gathered to read plays from scripts that secretaries
in the various embassies had typed in multiple copies. We went on
picnics in the glorious mountains nearby. We took trips to see the
gigantic statues of Buddhist saints carved on the rocky walls of the Vale
of Bamian, one of the beauty spots of Asia. And I joined a caravan that
headed across the great desert Dasht-i-Margo to visit Herat, where I met
a rug merchant of whom I shall speak later. I organized another caravan
far to the north to visit the ruins of ancient Balkh, where Alexander the
Great in 328 B.C. met and married the beautiful Afghan girl Roxana,
making her queen of the known world. Afghanistan, primitive, murder-
ous, is a corner of the world loved by all who knew her then.

'What is most memorable?' I recall with greatest affection and longing
those days when I was a young man stepping off a plane after a difficult
work trip in some deprived Asian country and heading to one of the
hotels I frequented; the Peninsula in Hong Kong, the Raffles in Singapore, the Oriental in Bangkok or the sprawling Hôtel des Indes in
Djakarta, there to meet in the lounge my colleagues from around the
world. Strangers would gather to tell their stories or listen, excursions
would be arranged and I would once again feel the pulse of Asia and
the wonder at being able to lead such a life. We were careful never to
boast about what we had done. In the Foreign Correspondents Club in
Tokyo, where we headquartered, there were three helmets hanging on
the wall, and if anyone started boasting someone would quietly rise, put
on one of the helmets and say: 'Do tell us about the incoming enemy
fire,' and the bragging would stop. Once at the end of a long trip into
the very heart of Asia I said thoughtlessly: 'The other day as I was
coming out of the Khyber Pass,' and this time my listeners not only put
on their helmets, they groaned.

'Did any one trip exert an unexpected influence on you?' I was from
the start an impressionable person, and I think I traveled in order to be
changed from what I was, so it all led to alteration, whether for good
or ill it is not for me to judge. But I suppose those boyhood trips

established my lifelong pattern of wanting to be free and of seeking new vistas, experiences and friendships. There was one adventurous trip that had a more lasting influence than I realized at the time, and that was when I sailed across the Minch of Scotland to the Outer Hebrides and entered a Celtic fairyland.

The famous islands start at the north with the fairly big island of Lewis with Harris, where the highly regarded tweed is woven, and then a remarkable trio: North Uist, South Uist, with Benbecula in the middle. Then comes little Eriskay of the lovely music and finally Barra, with a string of uninhabited islets drifting down to the big lighthouse at the far tip.

Time having passed these remote islands by, the people lived in small stone cottages topped by thatched roofs, wore dark, heavy clothing made from cloth they wove themselves, talked mainly in Gaelic, a musical tongue, and subsisted on catches from the sea and grains imported from the mainland. Because their open fires burned peat instead of coal, everything about them had a clean, smoky odor as if just fumigated by some protective agent. They were a sturdy lot, not overly tall, not overly friendly, and fiendishly devious, which enabled them, when a stranger was in their midst, to joke about him in Gaelic while staring at him almost benevolently. If they accepted him, they did so with great warmth, inviting him to participate in the ceilidhs (pronounced key-lee) they held during the long winter nights. A ceilidh is an informal gathering of singers and storytellers who pass the night hours in someone's kitchen, seated about the peat fire while the storms from the North Atlantic howl outside. It can develop, as one inspired soloist after another introduces his or her favorite song of the islands, into a form of fellowship that has no equal. The folk songs of the Hebrides are chants of great emotional power and haunting beauty, and during the time I spent in the islands I learned most of them, an artistic treasure that has never tarnished.

But the special wonder of the Hebrides was the island of Benbecula, for it was linked to its two neighboring Uists in a unique way: at high tide it was a proper island with substantial waves cutting it off from the Uists, but at low tide it was connected to the Uists by broad exposed causeways, and carts or automobiles could move easily and safely from one island to the other, while many people walked to visit with friends on the neighboring islands. So on Benbecula the question always was 'When's the next tide?' and travelers were careful to gauge departures so that they were assured of enough time to reach the next island safely. Each year some careless or inebriated walker would start to cross too late and, caught by the implacable inrushing tides, be swept to his death.

In my travels I experienced two episodes of exquisite tension: one was walking from Quetta in Pakistan to Kandahar in Afghanistan without a visa for either country; the other, crossing in the dead of night from North Uist to Benbecula with a bright moon and the Atlantic Ocean waiting to reclaim the sandy road on which I walked—in the far distance a lone light shone to mark the way to safety on the middle island.

That winter in the Hebrides was tremendously important to me. On Barra I came to know everyone living on the island, and day after day I would walk to one corner of the island or another, halting whenever a low stone house hugging the ground seemed inviting and visiting with the occupants, taking tea with them or even stopping for the night and perhaps singing the old songs with them. Or I would go out with the peat gatherers and help as they cut soggy squares of that amazing fuel, a compact tangle of roots while still immersed in its swampy bog, an admirable slow-burning fuel when dried in the sun. And always, whatever I was doing, increasing my knowledge of island life in the midst of the turbulent Atlantic. Even while I was undergoing this splendid adventure I appreciated that it was something special, for I was sharing in a primitive way of life that forced me to reexamine all my values and cleanse my mind of fixed attitudes.

It was there in the Hebrides that I invented a new word to describe the change that had overtaken me, *nesomaniac,* one who is mad about islands—*neso,* in Greek, meaning island. I would become perhaps the only man in the world who had lived somewhat close to the inhabitants in both the old Hebrides in the Atlantic and the new Hebrides in the Pacific. I would also be probably the only one who ever spent an Easter on Christmas Island and a Christmas on Easter Island, and I would become so possessed by islands that I would do intensive work in the Hawaiian Islands and other parts of Polynesia, the islands of Melanesia, the Aleutian Islands near the Arctic Circle and the lovely islands of the Caribbean. I was attuned to islands; I knew at first hand what life was like on the lonely atolls and the storm-swept islands that Joseph Conrad, Pierre Loti, Somerset Maugham, Alec Waugh, Jack London and Robert Louis Stevenson had loved. At times, working in big cities far from nature, I have been sick with nesomania, and I think the reason is this: On the islands one has both the time and the inclination to communicate with the stars and the trees and the waves drifting ashore, one lives more intensely.

·   ·   ·

'Did any of your trips produce ugly or regrettable results?' When I studied at St. Andrews in Scotland I lived in one of the most delightful small towns in Europe. Perched on the edge of the North Sea, graced by a cathedral that had stood in dreamlike ruins for centuries, rich in narrow streets, ancient gateways, city walls and magnificent vistas over the sea to the east, rolling lands west and south, it merits the joyous cry Andrew Lang the Scottish scholar gave when he was a student there:

> St. Andrews by the Northern Sea,
> That is a haunted town to me.

As I surrendered to its spell I became aware that our university had a branch in the city of Dundee twelve miles away, across the Firth of Tay. It was a medical school, and Scottish lads who told me of it warned: 'It's a grubby industrial town, Dundee. You wouldn't like it, and its medical school should be abolished. Filled with American Jews,' This seemed so improbable that I journeyed to Dundee and sought out the medical school, thinking that I ought to know it if it formed part of my university, and I found that what the Scottish students had said was true: Dundee was a smaller version of Glasgow with all the latter's grubbiness but little of its charm.* It did have a medical school, and it was filled with American Jews, handsome, bright young men in their mid-twenties, who slaved at their medical books and rarely came across the Tay to the lovelier part of the university where I studied.

One of the rewards of travel to foreign lands for a young person is that she or he can sometimes catch an oblique view of the homeland, and in Dundee Medical School I caught a glimpse of an American scandal that shattered me and still makes me writhe. Let's call him Isidore Cohen, and let's say he came from Brooklyn. He speaks for the thousands of young men like him who crowded the four Scottish medical schools in those days—Edinburgh, Glasgow, St. Andrews, Aberdeen—and he told me: 'Yes, all the Americans on this hall are Jewish. We wanted to be doctors, had straight A averages in high school. Our fathers and uncles were doctors and we always supposed that we'd be, too, if we kept our grades high. But when it came time to enroll in a medical school in the States, we found that no university would have us. I mean no one, not even the ones with wretched medical schools. We

*Later in my books I would extol Dundee. It made the best orange marmalade, and its canny merchants owned many of the vast cattle ranches in the American West. When John Wayne fights to protect his ranch in Texas, his boss is giving orders from his office in Dundee.

were Jews and forbidden to study medicine. Oh, each medical school allowed two or three to enroll, especially if our parents had made big cash contributions to the school, but thousands of us could find no spot anywhere that would accept us. Sometime around 1925 word circulated that the Scottish medical schools, some of the most rigorous in the world, needed scholars, and would accept Jews. Of course, when the depression followed they begged us to come over, and here we are.' In 1931–32 I met scores of them, outcasts at home but welcomed in Scotland. Their parents had paid taxes for years and had been good citizens, but their sons were denied equality in education, one of the outrages of those days, one that sickened me.

In later years, when I traveled through the States I tried to follow the careers of these New York men who had sought refuge in Scotland, and I found they had become famous doctors and researchers, deans of medical schools, chief surgeons in major hospitals and professors who instructed the new generation of American doctors. If you subtracted from recent American medical history the contributions of those Jews trained in Scotland, our health-care system would be in worse condition than it is.

What did I learn in my travels? In whatever foreign country I visited I met dreamers who longed to reach America and its promise of an enriched life so I knew we had a country rich in opportunity, but I also met those brilliant Jews already in America who had been denied that promise. In the institutions of higher education in which I have worked I have labored to bring blacks and Hispanics, Orientals and the penniless into the system, because in Dundee I saw how terribly wrong it is to deprive those not in the mainstream of the education to which, in a country such as ours, they are entitled.

I had always supposed that as I grew older and more infirm my desire to travel would wane, but that has not happened. In my eighty-second year and beset by health problems that nearly crippled me, I found myself eager to take certain trips: a voyage in a small ship completely around South America to research a similar one made by a pirate in the 1660s; three tours of the complete Caribbean basin and its islands; an extended visit to the magical city of Cartagena to inspect its famous walls; a jaunt to London as an honorary mascot of the Miami Dolphins as the football team played an exhibition game against the San Francisco Forty-niners; an emotional trip to Warsaw to meet with writers I had known there twenty years earlier; a delightful visit to Japan to meet, decades later, the members of a girls' theatrical company about whom I had written a novel, *Sayonara,* which became a well-regarded motion picture; a nostalgic trip in a small sailboat back to Tahiti and the Marquesas of Gauguin; and a most moving trip to Rome to visit the Pope, whom I had known when he was a cardinal in Cracow.

There were tempting invitations from foreign governments that for one reason or another I had to decline. I was asked by China to take up residence and write about its recent history; by Russia to participate in a master symposium on space; by Korea to observe the changes in the country in whose mountains I had climbed during the war there; by Turkey to write about their Sephardic Jews. And there were equally tantalizing trips that various organizations wanted me to make: to New Zealand to help launch a production of *South Pacific;* to Australia to visit the outback; to Afghanistan to inspect the war camps; to Buenos Aires for a cultural session. And there were three meetings arranged by our government relating to commissions on which I had served in Munich, Portugal and Israel.

I do not cite these many offers of travel opportunities as a sign of my importance. What I wish to emphasize is that they do attest to one thing: if one displays an obvious sense of identification with the countries he visits, he will be welcomed back, and the older one grows the more treasured the friendships will become.

I have an urgent wish that I might respond 'I'll be there' to each invitation that comes my way, for I follow in the footsteps of Ulysses, whose call to action as sung by Tennyson I memorized long ago and often recited as I trudged down some glen:

> . . . Come, my friends,
> 'Tis not too late to seek a newer world.
> Push off, and sitting well in order smite
> The sounding furrows; for my purpose holds
> To sail beyond the sunset, and the baths
> Of all the western stars, until I die.
> It may be that the gulfs will wash us down;
> It may be we shall touch the Happy Isles,
> And see the great Achilles, whom we knew.

I have known the world, have loved it and would happily visit once more its farthest corners, but sooner or later the sands in the mariner's glass will run through and even Ulysses' ship must come to dock.

V

People

*I*ONCE MADE a long trip over the Dasht-i-Margo, the desert in Afghanistan, to the ancient city of Herat, where I lodged in a former mosque with earthen floors. I had been in my improvised quarters only a few minutes when a very thin, toothy man with longish black hair and a perpetual smile entered and started throwing onto the dirt floor twenty or thirty of the most enchantingly beautiful Persian rugs I had ever seen. Their designs were miraculous—intricate interweavings of Koranic symbols framed in geometric patterns that teased the eye—but their colors were also sheer delight: reds, yellows, greens and especially dark blues that were radiant.

They made my room a museum, one rug piled atop another, all peeking out at me, and when they were in place and the smiling man was satisfied with his handiwork—I supposed that this was a service of the so-called hotel—to my amazement he handed me a scrap of paper on which was written in pencil in English: MUHAMMAD ZAQIR, RUG MERCHANT, HERAT.

Aware at last of how I had been trapped, I protested: 'No! No! No rugs!' but without relaxing his smile the least bit he said in English: 'No necessity to buy. I leave here. You study, you learn to like,' and before I could protest further he was gone. I ran out to make him take back his rugs, for I wanted none of them, but he was already leading his laden camel away from the old mosque.

I assumed he had learned from the hotel manager that I was to be in Herat for five days, and it was obvious that he felt confident that within that period he could wear me down and persuade me to buy a rug. He started on the evening of that first day; he came back after supper to sit with me in the shadowy light cast by a flickering lamp. He said: 'Have you ever seen lovelier rugs? That one from my friend in Meshed. Those two from the dealer in Bukhara. This one from a place you know, maybe? Samarkand.'

When I asked him how he was able to trade with such towns in the Soviet Union he shrugged: 'Borders? Out here we don't bother,' and with a sweep of his hand that encompassed all the rugs he said: 'Not one woven in Afghanistan,' and I noted the compelling pronunciation he gave that name: Ahf-han-ee-stahn.

He sat for more than an hour with me that evening, and next day he was back before noon to start his serious bargaining: 'Michener-sahib, name German perhaps?' I told him it was more likely English, at which he laughed: 'English, Afghans, many battles, English always win but next day you march back to India, nothing change.' When I corrected him: 'I'm not English,' he said: 'I know. Pennsylvania. Three, four, maybe five of your rugs look great your place Pennsylvania.'

'But I don't need rugs there. I don't really want them.'

'Would they not look fine Pennsylvania?' and as if the rugs were of little value, he kicked the top ones aside to reveal the glowing wonders of those below.

When he returned that second night he got down to even more serious business: 'The big white and gold one you like, six hundred dollars.' On and on he went, and when it was clear that I had no interest whatever in the big ones, he subtly covered them over with the smaller six- by four-foot ones already in the room; then he ran out to his camel to fetch seven or eight of the size that I had in some unconscious way disclosed I might consider, and by the end of that session he knew that I was at least a possible purchaser of four or five of the handsome rugs.

'Ah, Michener-sahib, you have fine eye. That one from China, silk and wool, look at those tiny knots.' Then he gave me a lesson in rug making; he talked about the designs, the variation in knots, the wonderful compactness of the Chinese variety, the dazzling colors of the Samarkand. It was fascinating to hear him talk, and all the while he was wearing me down.

He was a persistent rascal, always watching till he saw me return to my mosque after work, then pouncing on me. On the third day, as he sat drinking tea with me while our chairs were perched on his treasury of rugs, four and five deep at some places and covering the entire floor, he knocked down one after another of my objections: 'You can't take them with you? No traveler can. I send them to you, camel here, ship Karachi, train New York, truck to your home Pennsylvania.' Pasted onto the pages of his notebook were addresses of buyers from all parts of the world to whom he had shipped his rugs, and I noticed that they had gone out from Meshed in Iran, Mazar-e-Sharif in Afghanistan and Bukhara in Russia; apparently he really moved about with his laden camel. But he also had, pasted close to the shipping address, letters from his customers proving that the rugs had finally reached their new owners. In our dealings he seemed to me an honest man.

On that third night, when it began to look as if I might escape without making a purchase even though I had shown an interest in six rugs, he hammered at me regarding payments: 'Now, Michener-sahib, I can take American dollars, you know.'

'I have no American dollars.' Rapidly he ran through the currencies that he would accept, British, Indian, Iranian, Pakistani, Afghani, in that descending order, until I had to stop him with a truthful statement: 'Muhammad, my friend, I have no money, none of any kind,' and before the last word had been uttered he cried: 'I take traveler's checks, American Express, Bank America in California,' and then I had to tell him the sad news: 'Muhammad, friend. I have no traveler's checks. Left them all locked up in the American embassy in Kabul. Because there are robbers on the road to Meshed.'

'I know. I know. But you are an honest man, Michener-sahib. I take your personal check.'

When I said truthfully that I had none, he asked simply: 'You like those six rugs?'

'Yes, you have made me appreciate them. I do.'

With a sweeping gesture he gathered the six beauties, rolled them deftly into a bundle and thrust them into my arms: 'You take them. Send me a check when you get to Pennsylvania.'

'You would trust me?'

'You look honest. Don't I look honest?' And he picked up one of his larger rugs, a real beauty, and showed me the fine knots: 'Bukhara. I got it there, could not pay. I send the money when I sell. Man in Bukhara trusts me. I trust you.'

I said I could not impose on him in that way. Something might happen to me or I might prove to be a crook, and the discussion ended, except that as he left me he asked: 'Michener, if you had the money, what rugs would you take with you?' and I said 'None, but if you could ship them, I'd take those four,' and he said: 'Those four you shall have. I'll find a way.'

Next day he was back in the mosque right after breakfast with an astonishing proposal: 'Michener-sahib, I can let you have those four rugs, special price, four hundred fifty dollars.' Before I could repeat my inability to pay, he said: 'Bargain like this you never see again. Tell you what to do. You write me a check.'

When I said, distressed at losing such a bargain: 'But I really have no blank checks,' he said: 'You told me yesterday. I believe you. But draw me one,' and from his folder he produced a sheet of ordinary paper and a pencil. He showed me how to draw a copy of a blank check, bearing the name of the bank, address, amount, etc.—and for the first time in my life I actually drew a blank check, filled in the amount and signed it, whereupon Muhammad Zaqir placed it in his file, folded the four rugs I had bought, tied them with string and attached my name and address. He piled the rugs onto his camel, and then mounted it to proceed on his way to Samarkand.

Back home in Pennsylvania I started to receive two different kinds of letters, perhaps fifteen of each. The following is a sample of the first category:

> I am a shipping agent in Istanbul and a freighter arrived here from Karachi bringing a large package, well wrapped, addressed to you in Pennsylvania. Upon receipt of your check for $19.50 American I will forward the package to you.

From Karachi, Istanbul, Trieste, Marseilles and heavens knows where else I received a steady flow of letters over a three-year period, and always the sum demanded was less than twenty dollars, so that I would say to myself: 'Well, I've invested so much in it already, I may as well risk a little more.' And off the check would go, with the rugs never getting any closer. Moreover, I was not at all sure that if they ever did reach me they would be my property, for my unusual check had never been submitted for payment, even though I had forewarned my local bank: 'If it ever does arrive, pay it immediately, because it's a debt of honor.'

The second group of letters explained the long delay:

> I am serving in Kabul as the Italian ambassador and was lately in Herat where a rug merchant showed me that remarkable check you gave him for something like five hundred dollars. He

asked me if I thought it would be paid if he forwarded it and I assured him that since you were a man of good reputation it would be. When I asked him why he had not submitted it sooner, he said: 'Michener-sahib a good name. I show his check everybody like you, sell many rugs.'

These letters came from French commercial travelers, English explorers, Indian merchants, almost anyone who might be expected to reach out-of-the-way Herat and take a room in that miserable old mosque.

In time the rugs arrived, just as Mohammed Zaqir had predicted they would, accompanied by so many shipping papers they were a museum in themselves. And after my improvised check had been used as an advertisement for nearly five years, it too came home to roost and was honored. Alas, shortly thereafter the rugs were stolen, but I remember them vividly and with longing. Especially do I remember the man who spent four days ingeniously persuading me to buy.

In my travels I have met many fascinating people like Zaqir, and while the escapades of some of the more exotic types might be amusing to recount, I have never treasured people simply for their peculiarities, and so the ones I will introduce briefly are those not only of interest in themselves but also of importance in developing my understanding of people. For example, my experience with the Afghan rug merchant and his ethical behavior led me to rethink my stereotypically negative attitudes toward Islam, and this reflection led me to compose a brief statement that circulated through the Muslim world as *Islam, the Misunderstood Religion.* This essay gained me entry to corners of Islam that would otherwise have been closed to me.

On the night when our dismal transport, the *Cape Horn,* anchored in Luganville Channel at Espiritu Santo in the New Hebrides, it stood not far from the copra plantation of the Frenchman Aubert Ratard. When I returned to work on that island, I met M. Ratard by chance and spent more than a score of days and nights with him and his family. He told me after my tenth or fifteenth visit that he was surprised by my intense interest in his Tonkinese plantation workers, and I remember telling him: 'Frenchmen I can meet anywhere, but Tonkinese are not so easy to come by.' And I made myself proficient in the problems of these handsome people.

It took me only a few days, despite the fact that my French was almost nonexistent, to learn that the Ratard Tonkinese were not happy, but this had nothing to do with either Ratard or the way he ran his plantation. The trouble was the war: 'We leave Tonkin three years. Sign paper, three years. Come here, work hard, save money, go home three years rich.' I told them that this was not a bad system and that it had proved useful in different countries, but they had a real complaint: 'War come. Three years finish. No go home. Four years, five years, no damn good.' Ratard, like his fellow Frenchmen, had been prepared to pay off his indentured Tonkinese and repatriate them, but the war made this absolutely impossible. So an ugly situation developed, for when the French colonial government extended the indentures to continue until the 'end of the war,' the planters received the benefit of keeping on their plantations Tonkinese men and women of long experience, workers of considerable increased value, but at the same old rates negotiated in some cases as long ago as six years. The situation was understandable, but it was not just.

The Tonkinese woman who explained this to me in her voluble French was about thirty-five, roundish in shape and outspoken in her advocacy of Tonkinese rights. I doubt that Ratard was pleased to have me talking with her, but he'd had proof of my respect for French positions and my willingness to help him procure from the Navy tools and other necessities he needed for his plantation. And he did admit, grudgingly perhaps, that this particular Tonkinese was one of the ablest of his work force. I never learned her real name, but because of her strong resistance to exploitation, she had come to be known as Bloody Mary, and that is how I still recall her.

She said that when the war ended, she would go to Tonkin, the area that would later be known as North Vietnam, and I got the strong impression that when she got there she intended to oppose French colonialism. She said further that in both New Hebrides and New Caledonia, the big French islands to the south, there would be trouble in the postwar years if the colonial governments tried to extend the indentures for another period: 'We go home. Plantation all finish.'

I would often think of her in later years when American troops were fighting their fruitless battles in Vietnam and I wondered if our leaders realized that the enemy they were fighting consisted of millions of determined people like Bloody Mary. But even I was deficient in my understanding, for when I wrote about her in *Tales of the South Pacific* I depicted her not as a potential revolutionary but as a Tonkinese woman with a pretty daughter to care for. The original Bloody Mary had no children—at least there were none in residence on Ratard's plantation.

. . .

On that stormy winter's day when I first crossed the Minch from Oban on the mainland of Scotland to the small island of Barra in the Outer Hebrides, I landed at dusk with no place to stay and no letters of introduction. A local man who met our ship said: 'Go see the Catholic priest. He pretty much runs things on this island,' and when I did I found a man in his forties, wise, congenial and understanding: 'It's a most unusual request. We've never had an American in my time here, and almost never a tourist in winter, no matter from what country. But I have in my church two fine women, sisters, who have a wee cottage near here, and sometimes in summer they take in hikers who come this way for a go at our heather hills. Maybe I can persuade them to take you.'

He left his manse, walked me along a rocky road that was almost in darkness, and led me, after about half a mile, to a low, stone-walled, thatch-roofed cottage with two windows and a stout door made of some heavy wood that must have been imported from the mainland, for Barra had no trees. It was a snug island dwelling of the kind used there for the past five centuries. Furthermore, it was exactly what I had hoped to find, so with enthusiasm I followed the priest to the door, which he banged on stoutly with his walking stick.

When the door opened, a woman in her sixties, somewhat unkempt, stared out at us. She was of average height, plump and with dancing eyes that greeted her much-loved priest warmly. When she spoke in Gaelic her voice was low and hoarse, so that she seemed a character such as the Brothers Grimm might have created.

'This is Morag Macneil,' the priest said, 'of the famous Macneils of Barra. But don't let the name awe you, because everyone hereabouts is a Macneil of Barra.' As the woman moved forward I saw with a shock that she had clubfeet, which were so deformed that she walked with an ugly clump.

When the priest explained who I was as well as the nature of my mission—to understand Hebridean life—she brushed him aside, surveyed me with a calculating eye and cried in English: 'Och! It'll be comfortin' to have a man about the house again, American and all.' Thus began one of the happiest spells of my wandering years. Leaving the priest standing at the door, she led me into her tiny two-room cottage, which had a small shack aft for storage, and showed me the bed I would have. As I tested it, she repeated her name, pronouncing it More-ock, and then she introduced her younger sister, Kiltag, pro-

nounced Kill-tock. I found them to be a talkative pair. Just before the
priest left, he asked me to join him at the door, where he said quietly:
'Apologies to a guest on our island, but I must be assured that you have
the money to pay these two good women. Strangers have been known—'
I showed him my wallet and he said: 'Would you be prepared to pay
in advance? Fruitless to think about lodging elsewhere if you don't like
it here, because there is no elsewhere.' I handed him the money for four
weeks, which he turned over to Morag.

The weeks went like this. On Sunday the three of us went to mass and
returned to a special meal consisting of wheaten cakes baked over a peat
fire, fish, jam from a big crock shipped in from Glasgow, and gallons
of hot tea made so dark that Kiltag said: 'We don't like it unless it's so
strong a mouse can walk on it.' On Sunday afternoon I took a stroll on
the hills, and at night we had a ceilidh, which two girls who interested
me very much attended. They were Campbells and suffered a degree of
ostracism because of an evil act perpetrated by their clansmen two and
a half centuries earlier in a glen far across the Minch. (Memories live
long in Barra.) They were a delightful pair. Each had left Barra from
time to time to work as maids on the mainland, and they had raffish
opinions of some of their mistresses. They were great fun to be with, and
on some nights when they and the Macneil sisters held ceilidh, the
stories flew.

The Campbell sisters had the naughty habit of hiding behind the
sheaves in the barn where the local swains did their courting, and they
found delight in chronicling the progress of each courtship, and since
few island girls married before they were pregnant, there were some
fascinating reports. Some natives took umbrage at this unseemly behavior of the Campbells, but Morag, the older of the Macneil sisters, was
more generous: 'They're young. They have to learn about these things.
Let them have fun.'

Morag was an extraordinary woman. She had been born in an era
before rural doctors knew how to correct clubfeet, but this deformity did
not keep her from enjoying life, although it had prevented her from
finding a husband. Somewhat overweight, decidedly blowsy and without
any teeth, natural or false, she did not look prepossessing, but her warm
heart, her desire to participate in whatever was happening on her island,
and her love of both storytelling and singing made her a special person
whose memory I cherish.

She was inordinately proud of being a member of the Macneil clan,
and she felt that the ruined castle perched on a rock in the middle of
the bay was in some strange way her domain. Walking with me to the

waterfront, she prevailed upon a fisherman to row us out to the castle. As we sat amid its ruins she told me of the great days in Barra. She knew English only imperfectly, but I had picked up enough Gaelic to manage the drift of her recitations as she shifted back and forth between the two languages.

Gaelic is incredibly difficult for an outlander to master. The lovely chorus of one of the great songs illustrates the problem—*cruidh mo chridh* is pronounced *crooch muh kree*—but when Morag told a tale, the words seemed to whisper their own meaning: 'In the time of troubles, when evil men roamed the glens, there was confusion over there,' and she indicated the mainland of Scotland, across the Minch. 'They forced good Catholics to become Protestant or lose their lives. All the fine Catholics in Oban and Mallaig and Glencoe had to deny the Pope and bow to John Knox. Then the evil ones crossed over to our Islands, and Skye turned color, The Lewis became Protestant and so did North Uist and Benbecula.'

At the end of this mournful recitation she keened: 'Ach me! the deadly wrong that was done in those days, with even stout members of the Clan Macdonald changing their religion, but then the evil ones came to the two islands they could never subdue, Eriskay and Barra, for under the leadership of our Macneil, none braver, these islands remained true Catholic. We are jewels in the Crown of the Pope.' And as we lingered amid the ruins of that castle in the safety of the bay, she told me of how the Macneils of Barra had resisted the full strength of the Protestants from both Scotland and England, remaining true to the ancient faith that had reached them many centuries ago from Ireland.

But the more I moved about with Morag—and she did not allow her crippled feet to keep her from stomping wherever she wanted to go—the more suspicious I became that her religion was more complicated than a mere Catholicism that had withstood Protestant pressure.

When we went together to the peat bogs not far from Castlebay, she told me: 'My father cut his peats from the bog. Dried them in piles over there. Kiltag and I hauled them to our cot, where they baked in the sun before we placed them in the fire in winter.' She showed me where men of the island still cut their small rectangles of dark, aromatic peat, which made a Scottish cottage such a warm and friendly place with its unique smell of burning roots.

However, it was not peat that was on her mind when she led me to the bogs: 'Here the wee folk live. In that glen my father saw them many times. Standing where you are now, James, I heard them sing like whispering angels. When men from my family had to leave Barra, no jobs here, we would walk with them to this bog for the last time to say good-bye to the hills and to the glens and ask blessings from the wee folk.' Then, for the first of several dramatic times during the next months, she lifted her face, turned to the low hills and cried: 'Uh to the hills, uh to the glens, uh to the folk who guard them, this is my friend James from America. Guard him while he is with us.' She did not cross herself, nor go through any ritual other than facing the hills, but her round face with its tousled hair was ecstatic and she was content that she had done her best to ingratiate me with the little people who had guarded that glen since the days of her father and those earlier peat cutters who had worked this bog for the past thousand years.

I am not happy with the way I have rendered the first words of her invocation. I have it as 'Uh to,' but it was more guttural and not separated into two words; perhaps 'Ugh-to the hills' would be closer, but the *g* does not look pretty. In any case the phrase was uttered as if it were special greetings to cherished friends and powers. That it was part of some ancient and valued relationship to the wee folk I have no doubt, for to her they were real. They had occupied the glens for generations. They had fought on the side of the Macneils when the family battled to hold off the Protestants, and in Barra life they were a force to be considered.

One night when the singing was strong and I sat with an arm around each of the saucy Campbell girls, Morag started a simple song that beguiled me until in the end it overwhelmed me. In her husky voice with her toothless mouth ill forming the words she sang a simple refrain:

> Vair me o-o rovano,
> Vair me o-o rovanee,
> Vair me o ru o ho,
> Sad am I without thee.

The Gaelic words, I learned later, meant nothing; they were just a chain of syllables wonderfully suited to the simple melody that suggested an aching heart. However, the song also had a verse in English, and its words were little short of magical:

> When I'm lonely, dear white heart,
> Black the night and wild the sea;

> By love's light my foot finds
> The old pathway to thee.

But it is in the second verse that the two lines occur which capture the essence of one of the greatest Hebridean songs:

> Thou'rt the music of my heart,
> Harp of joy, o cruidh mo chridh. . . .

With head thrown back and gazing upward as if lost in dreams of girlhood, Old Morag sang in a husky voice this storm-whipped love song, and when she finished, the Campbell girls cried: 'Let's sing it again.' And under the thatched roof with the Atlantic storm howling outside as it roared across the peat bog, we repeated this marvelous song until I had mastered the words.

'What's it called, this masterpiece?' I asked and the Campbells explained: ' "The Eriskay Love Lilt," named after the wee bit island east of our north tip.' I have often wondered why this simple statement of love has not caught on as a universally acclaimed folk song. But occasionally when I hum the melody absently someone overhears it and joins in, for he or she has learned it in a singing group, and once or twice I have heard it on the radio. It is a gift Morag gave me, which has been of inestimable value as much for its romantic aura as for its musical virtues.

When she saw that I had been captivated by the song, she told me about the island that was its source: 'Eriskay is a real island, you know. You could visit it. Just walk to the farthest end of Barra northward and find a fisherman eager to earn a few bob, and you're in Eriskay, a holy island it is, for it was from there that Flora Macdonald, may God rest her Catholic soul, took Bonnie Prince Charlie under her wing and sneaked him back to Skye past all his English enemies.'

Seeing that I was enthralled by her fantasies, that night she taught me the lyrical 'Skye Boat Song':

> Speed bonnie boat, like a bird on the wing,
> Over the sea to Skye.
> Carry the lad that's born to be king,
> Over the sea to Skye . . .
>   Flora will keep
>   Watch o'er thy sleep . . .

The drama of the dauntless crofters of Barra and Eriskay clinging to their Catholic religion in the face of tremendous pressures from the mainland had already gripped me, and to learn that an island maiden like one of the Campbell girls had succeeded in smuggling Bonnie Prince Charlie to safety in Skye made a visit to Eriskay obligatory. One morning, with the blessing of Old Morag and her wee folk, I set out to walk to the extreme northern end of Barra where, as predicted, I found a fisherman who would ferry me across to tiny Eriskay.

I carried with me the name of a family with whom I could stay, and the three days I spent on that exquisite little island with the fairy-tale name infected me forever with nesomania, the mad passion for islands. I walked every road in Eriskay, and this in midwinter with the Atlantic hammering the west coast. I listened to an account that was true but that sounded like some medieval French *roman* as an Eriskay fisherman spoke:

> 'There never was a future king more handsome and brave than our Bonnie Prince Charlie, heir to the thrones of Scotland and England. His loyal troops fought to the death, but at Culloden in 1746 they were overwhelmed, leaving him unprotected. With courage unbelievable and often alone in some pathetic disguise, he escaped the English army and fled in a small boat to our islands.
>
> 'Think of the temptations my ancestors faced! Twenty thousand English troops trying to find him and thirty thousand pounds promised the man who would betray him! Dressed as a peasant he roamed our isles, and we knew who he was but no one spoke. Slipping at last into Eriskay, he lay hidden in the croft of my ancestors, until the daughter of our family, Flora Macdonald, whose soul surely rests in heaven, dressed him in the clothes of her serving maid, Betty Burke, and in a small boat she and the Prince sailed over the sea to Skye, like the song says. When English soldiers stopped them as they landed and asked: "Who's this one?" she said: "My maid Betty Burke," and the Bonnie Prince was safely on his way to France.'*

To have visited Eriskay when I did was the kind of adventure that can set a young man's imagination galloping down paths he would never

*Some accounts claim that the prince and Flora sailed to Skye from Benbecula. In 1773 Flora emigrated to North Carolina; there her husband joined the British army during the American Revolution.

otherwise have known. To sleep in the croft of Flora Macdonald while the great ocean thunders outside is to know dreaming and the awesome power of old tales retold.

Some months before visiting Barra and Eriskay I had become acquainted with another folk song, more sophisticated in both words and music, the Russian ballad 'Stenka Razin.' It told of a Cossack revolutionary who swept the Volga regions in the 1670s, had a tempestuous love affair with a Persian princess and met his end by being drawn and quartered before a huge throng in Moscow. It was a happy coincidence that these two notable songs reached me simultaneously, for in a sense between them they encompassed my world at that time: 'Eriskay,' delicate and haunting, 'Razin,' bold and terrifying; 'Eriskay' whispering of love, 'Razin' shouting of battle; 'Eriskay' filled with the Gaelic tristesse that restrains Irishmen and Hebridean seamen; 'Razin' with the brute force that thrusts Russians forward.

I have sung these two songs in every corner of the world—'Eriskay' when I was feeling lonely or sentimental, 'Razin' when I was trying to visualize past empires and the vast movements of people. I have known many of the distinctive songs from all parts of the world, yet these two still represent for me the best in folk music. I have collected unusual songs and have been able to produce two highly professional records offering the best of Hawaiian and South Pacific music. But if I had known only 'Eriskay' and 'Razin' I would have sampled the very best, and that would have been sufficient.

The two songs had an effect upon me that I had not anticipated: they inspired me to compose a love song of my own. After devising a good simple melody, I wrestled with the lyrics:

> Soar, nightingale! soar to the stars above.
> Sing, nightingale! sing her my song of love.
> Fly, nightingale! fly through the silvery sea.
> Bring, nightingale! bring back her promise to me.

And then I decided to add an extra touch by rhyming the first words of alternating lines, and this produced the following:

> Fly, nightingale! fly to the blue above.
> Sing, nightingale! sing her my song of love.
> Sigh, nightingale! sigh for a love that's fled.
> Bring, nightingale, bring back her promise we'll wed.

Alas, my nightingale served me poorly, for while I was chanting my song through the glens of Scotland, my young lady, who I thought was waiting for me back in the States, married the other fellow. But the song remains and I sing it still.

Old Morag's other gift cut deep. For while living with her in that little thatched cottage whose stone walls were two feet thick—and well they had to be, considering the Atlantic gales—I began to understand all those women who struggled against incalculable odds, those sterling creatures who hold so much of the world together. In Morag I saw the essence of many valiant women I would later present in my works of fiction: Nyuk Tsin, Nellie Forbush, Ellie Zendt, the one-tusked mammoth of the Arctic, the South African aborigine herding her tribe across the barren desert. Old Morag would live in all of them, because her will, like theirs, was indomitable.

But most of all she revealed for me the heroism of my own mother, who also had to cope with handicaps of an even more disastrous kind. I had known the misery she suffered, had indeed participated in it, but I had never allowed it to traumatize me permanently; however, when I witnessed this island woman's struggles I appreciated more acutely the price my mother had paid for her survival—a story I shall save for the final chapter.

One day in the late winter it came time for me to leave Barra and get back to my university. Morag was sorry to see me go, as were the Campbell girls, and was appalled when it became clear that I was going to leave without saying good-bye to the little people in the peat bog. She led me back to that spot which had meant so much to me, and throwing back her tousled head she cried: 'Uh-to the hills, uh-to the glens, uh to the folk who mind the bog, James is leaving us. Make his passage across Minch a kindly one, and guard him wherever he goes.' After mumbling certain special instructions to the wee folk, she led me back to her cottage, where the Campbell sisters were waiting, and we walked together to the MacBrayne steamer, which was just coming past the castle ruins in the bay. Morag's prayers that the Minch crossing be gentle were futile, for that turbulent body of water is never calm. With great heaviness of heart I left Barra and Eriskay and the ocean ford at Benbecula and the endless ceilidhs of the Hebrides.

.   .   .

Shortly after I left Barra I became involved peripherally with a man who helped me understand myself better. I was in the Spanish city of Valencia on a Sunday afternoon when a bullfight was being held at the traditional time of *cinco de la tarde,* five in the afternoon. I had never seen a bullfight, nor had I read Ernest Hemingway's powerful *Death in the Afternoon* because it had not yet reached Europe, so I was not aware that my initiation was going to be with three of the finest matadors of their generation: the poetic Marcial Lalanda, oldest of the three; the tough, resilient Domingo Ortega, fighting in second place; and the flamboyant young star El Estudiante, the Student, as the beginner.

From the moment the fight began I was captivated by the pageantry, the color, the ritualism, the magnificence of the bull, the daring of the toreros and the life-and-death drama of the spectacle. Intuitively I became an aficionado, able to discriminate between the flowery display of Lalanda and the classical austerity of Ortega, which I found the more impressive. The arabesques of Lalanda I could do without, but the poignant dignity of Ortega moved me so deeply that for some weeks I followed him about the bullrings of Spain as he fought alongside most of the great matadors of that period. He eschewed bravura; he showed great respect for the bull both as an animal and as an adversary; and withal he displayed a mastery of style and substance that gave me intense pleasure.

I left Spain an Orteguista, for I had seen an artist who appeared to be in complete control both of himself and of his milieu. He seemed to have been about the same age as I. I now recall with enthusiasm the two times I had an opportunity to talk with him, for his squarish peasant face had gleamed with pleasure when in my halting Spanish I had let him know that I understood and appreciated what he was trying to do.

Through the years, in both Spain and Mexico, I followed his career and it pleased me to see that Ortega gradually became recognized as the epitome of the classical style. New fighters would become sensations, but their flame would quickly subside into ashes, while Ortega kept going on, his quiet skills improving year by year until as so often happens with men like him who move ever forward slowly but steadily, he became recognized universally as a man of gravity—that is, of a certain weightiness and seriousness of purpose.

I decided in those years of watching him and reading about him that in my own life I would like to resemble him, a man who sticks to his job, who conducts himself with a certain sobriety and serenity, and who stays at the task until he acquires a reputation for being a serious worker with a serious purpose. Four decades after that first bullfight in Valencia, when I was a guest of honor at a great bullfight in Madrid, Domingo Ortega, then a silver-haired old man, served as honorary president and I was taken to his box, high above the crowd, where I sat with him and spoke of old times when he was forging his reputation. He was covered with honors and revered as perhaps the purest artist of his generation. It was a privilege to see him in all his accumulated glory.

My early brush with bullfighters led to two of the happiest summers I would ever know, when I traveled through Mexico with two minor toreros—never matadors—who were grand figures in their own right. Rolleri, a taut, handsome man, was a master *peon de confianza,* trusted assistant, who had served most of the great matadors of his time. His friend Flaco Valencia was a gangling, awkward banderillero who by force of character had made himself a master of the art of running directly at the bull, pirouetting aside at the last minute and deftly planting the long barbed sticks in the shoulder muscles of the bull to make the bull drop his head and reveal the target spot when the matador takes over. Valencia deserved his nickname Flaco (Skinny), for he seemed to have no flesh on his body, and I often wondered as we traveled about how he generated the energy he displayed in the ring.

They were a splendid pair, the quiet, dignified Rolleri, beloved by matadors who were so often rescued from perilous situations by his bravery and skill, and Valencia the comic scarecrow, the amusing fellow with the delicate hands and wrists. We traveled together into many parts of Mexico, following the bulls, but on Sunday night at seven we tried always to be in a famous restaurant in Mexico City, El Tupinambo, where the bullfight fraternity assembled. There we listened to the gossip, exaggerated our escapades out in the country, and came to know the famous matadors of Mexico and those visiting from Spain. Rolleri and Valencia would have small glasses of the wine that toreros favored, while I would have a cup of the thick bitter chocolate with the smoky taste that I liked so much.

They were wonderful days, days when I learned about the art of bullfighting, for each morning during the week when we were not on the road I reported to the old red-walled bullring in the heart of Mexico City and there watched as bullfighters young and old went through their paces. I came to know a score of fighters, especially the young men on their way up. One of the most congenial was a young fellow whom we took out in the country twice for beginning fights. He called himself Cañito, Little Sugarcane, and he astounded me because he seemed totally without fear. In his earliest fights he displayed such enormous courage and more than adequate skill that I predicted he would one day be a luminary. He did not disappoint, for he became more than a star, but his lack of fear destroyed him; fighting a dangerous bull in 1960 with a recklessness that older matadors would have avoided, he was so badly gored that he lost a leg, and in later years I saw him hobbling about on crutches.

Quite different was another rising star, Luis Procuna. A polished fighter with a flair for the dramatic, he could be either very good or very bad. Long after I knew him briefly, he was caught by the camera in what is probably the finest bullfighting photograph of recent decades. Standing erect, with feet touching heel to toe and arms in perfect alignment, he brings an enormous bull right to his chest, but what makes the shot unforgettable is that his handsome face is twisted with an arrogant, triumphant sneer, tongue jammed into his right cheek, as if issuing a challenge to all watchers: 'O.K. layman. Try this one!' He went on to become one of the best.

Bullfighting introduced me to two men I will never forget. Curro Romero was a slim young man with one of those perfect faces that might have been carved from Grecian marble. In the ring he was a poet; sensible men went into ecstasy when he stood perilously close to some huge bull and unfurled a series of delicately linked passes. Orson Welles and Kenneth Tynan were great fans of his, and each told me that to see Curro on a good day was to see greatness in exquisite motion. Alas, I never saw him on a good day, even though I must have seen him fight forty times. Each time I saw him fight was a disaster, a calamity of such magnitude that had anyone but the gracious Curro suffered it, his career would have ended. With what looked like sheer cowardice he would refuse to give honest fight to even the mildest animal. Otherwise rational men would pay huge sums to see him fight in the vain hope that this time he might enact one of his masterpieces; but when he refused to try, they would riot, cursing him and throwing all sorts of objects at him. Long ago I wrote contemptuously of his misbehavior and in the decades that followed I received many letters saying simply: 'Yesterday I saw your Curro Romero in Seville and he was superb' or more often 'Yesterday I went to see your boy Curro and the riot became so bad they had to call out extra police. Everything you said was true.'

Just last year, when Curro must have been in his mid-sixties, at least eight correspondents airmailed me copies of full-page articles with striking photographs of what was termed 'Curro's grandest *bronca* [riot].' In a series of six or eight photographs it showed him running in craven fear from his bull and calling down upon himself a blizzard of seat cushions, which darkened the arena. Then police moved in, as always, to try to rush him out of the ring under a protective covering of their capes, but an enraged spectator who had paid good money to see this fraudulent affair, broke through the police, rushed up to Curro, and hit him with such a fearful blow that he fell into the dust as he appealed pitifully for help. The last photograph showed his undignified rump as he fled under the capes. Next year, I suppose, other tourists who remember what I wrote will send me new photographs of his latest disaster. How he can still lure people into the arena at those prices remains a mystery, but as Orson Welles said: 'Once you see him on a good day, you forget about all the others.'

It was my good fortune, in those years when I was following the bulls, to know rather well a gargantuan American who was an even more enthusiastic aficionado than I. He was Kenneth Vanderford, from some small town in Indiana. He had worked for many years with the Creole Oil Company in Venezuela, where he persuaded the management to pay him a good wage while he conducted what he called 'an intellectual study to prove to the Venezolanos that American big business was not heartless.' His study? 'With what names do Venezuelan parents most often christen their children?' His finding after two years of extensive and expensive travel: 'Maria for the girls, Juan for the boys.' I don't see how anyone could dislike a man so ingenious, and I prized him as a friend.

He was notorious in Spain because, with a full beard carefully trimmed, he looked exactly like Ernest Hemingway. In fact, even those of us who knew him well were sometimes either startled or confused because he *was* Hemingway. I think he enjoyed playing the role, for never did I hear him correct anyone who accosted him thinking that he was the famous writer, but he did make one attempt to limit the deception: He carried two sets of cards that he handed out to Hemingway admirers who asked for his autograph. One version was in Spanish, the other in English, and if he saw clearly that you were Spanish, you got the English card, and vice versa. The English version read:

> If I did not wear this beard, you
> would not think that I was

and while the lover of literature watched he would boldly sign 'Ernest Hemingway.' By the time the happy recipient found someone to translate the message into his own language, Vanderford would be far away.

He was a veritable encyclopedia of bullfighting, the confidant of many of the matadors who tolerated his crazy masquerade, and a fine scholar

of Spanish history. As he approached sixty with no foothold in America
and no Social Security, I helped him land a good job teaching Spanish
at Ripon University in Wisconsin, where he appeared on campus in a
flowing Spanish cape lined in red. I was told by one of his enthusiastic
students: 'He still looks like Hemingway and that perplexes a lot of
people who have vaguely heard that Ernest shot himself years ago.'

I have never been able to reconcile my love for animals and my
appreciation of the bullfight and have succeeded in keeping the conflicting emotions involving these contradictory attitudes compartmental-
ized. I am now prepared to believe avid hunters when they tell me: 'But
I cherish the animals I hunt,' and I have seen that such men often go
to great lengths to protect the very animals they chase and provide them
with breeding and ranging areas, often at considerable expense. I am
sure that Hemingway, who loved both bullfighting and the hunt for big
African animals, would have been among the first to provide money for
the welfare of animals. In my own case, I can only ascribe my conflicting
attitudes to the innate perversity of man and volunteer no other explanation.

My abiding interest in sports, which helped save me as a teenager, led
to one friendship that provided in American baseball the equivalent of
what I found in Spanish bullfighting in the controlled dignity of
Domingo Ortega, who became a role model for me.

Robin Roberts, of the hapless Philadelphia Phillies, was a big, uncom-
plicated chunk of All-American boy, witty, handsome, valiant through
the last out in the final inning. He was a fastball pitcher and one of the
best. Standing tall and robust on the mound, he delivered the ball with
such speed that it whizzed right past the luckless batters who faced him.
With a traditional last-place team he won an amazing number of games,
so that he was considered, for some years, one of the two or three best
pitchers in baseball.

It was not unusual for Robin with his superb speed to allow the
opposing team only one run, but his inept Phillies would get him no runs
whatever, so he would lose 1–0 or 2–1 or 3–2. Nevertheless, back he
would come in due rotation, only to lose once more. When he won
eighteen or twenty games a season, he really *won* them.

Robin had such a fastball, with not much curve, that opposing batters
learned: 'With Roberts, stand in there and swing. He's a gentleman.
He'll never dust you off. If you miss, you strike out. But if you're lucky
enough to connect, you have yourself a home run because when the ball
comes in so fast, it also goes out fast, right over the wall.'

He threw a shocking number of home-run balls, especially in the late innings, giving the other team the one or two runs they needed to defeat him. My lasting memory of Robin is of him standing out there on the mound, score tied 1–1 in the eighth, and him smoked in that high fast one, and wham! Out of the park and another 2–1 loss. I have often thought of my own behavior in metaphorical terms relating to Roberts's pitching experience. I stay in the game until the last possible moment. I do not try to mix up my pitches, but I am always willing to slam in that high, fastball, and if I do not get it past the batter, out of the park it goes. But I am still there, I am still throwing, always ready to try my luck on getting the next ball past that pesky batter. And if I fail this time, who gives a damn? We play again on Thursday.

When Roberts's honorable career ended—'He could of won thirty more games if he'd a thrown at the batter's head, but not Robin. He let them dig in and swing on that high fast one'—I became so outraged when he was passed over for entry into baseball's Hall of Fame that I started a one-man crusade to get him elected. I politicked as best I could; I wrote an ill-advised article for *The New York Times* in which I pointed out how unfair it was to have elected Whitey Ford and rejected Robin Roberts when Ford had far fewer victories, even though he had been backed up by one of the heaviest hitting teams in the majors, while Roberts had to struggle along with one of the weakest. The unfairness was palpable, and I expected Robin to be swept in by a huge margin that year. But I had overlooked the fact that Whitey Ford was a high-living cult hero, especially among the many powerful sportswriters in New York, while Roberts, as one man told me, 'was nothing but a big happy farm boy from the boonies.' Also, the writers did not like my intruding on their turf, and several told me so. Thus, instead of helping my friend gain election to the Hall of Fame, I was a principal cause of his being rejected, and I was disconsolate. But in the ensuing year several writers confided in me that my article had been unusually relevant and that Roberts had been unfairly denied. At the next vote, with me keeping my mouth shut, he was swept in, and I do believe I was happier about it than he was.

I also formed friendships with people in music whose tenacity I admired, most notably André Kostelanetz, an elfin Russian and a wizard with the baton, whom I met in the Pacific and with whom I often discussed music as we sat before the fire at his place or mine. One of the more hilarious evenings of my life resulted from his request for assistance: 'The technical situation is this, James. I want to cut a record of my favorite encores, but if I call an extra practice to rehearse them, the cost will be terrific. However, if we can play the seven encores after the concert on Saturday night, legitimately, then that practice time is paid for by the organization sponsoring the concert. Can you raise enough applause to keep us onstage for seven encores?' I said I'd try.

That night my wife and I had a front box overlooking not only the stage but also the audience. André kept the main concert just a mite short, which left the audience hungry for more, and they were so enthusiastic that for the first three encores there was no need for a claque. But the ending of Pachelbel's *Kanon* was so downbeat that some listeners began to leave; I started a rather loud clapping, which others picked up, and the exodus stopped.

Now André played his transcription of an admirable but short Chopin number, and I was able to keep the enthusiasm high. But when he tried as his fifth encore one of his and my great favorites, Samuel Barber's 'Adagio for Strings,' the critical moment came, for there was a substantial movement toward the exists. I halted this with a frenzied burst of clapping interspersed with shouts of 'More, more!' which others took up, and we were saved.

He played a real barn-burner for his sixth encore, but it must have been evident to any careful observer that the concert was over. However, at a signal from André I burst forth with my final effort, shouting at the top of my voice while I waved my arms: 'Bis! Bis!' This so surprised members of the audience that they stopped to stare at me and, thank heaven, some took up this French cry (meaning 'Again') and André was able to launch into his seventh encore. It was short, noisy and played by an orchestra that was nearly exhausted. When my wife and I joined André in the Green Room later, certain friends waiting there gushed: 'We've never heard such an ovation. Six encores!' and he said modestly: 'Seven.'

When *South Pacific* became the reigning hit on Broadway, tickets became so precious that I could not afford to see the musical after opening night, but this was no loss because I was free to enter the stage door of the Majestic Theater and watch the play from backstage, catching as much of the action as could be seen from the wings. It was thrilling to watch the actors, first as ordinary people backstage in costumes who were clearing their throats and blowing their noses, and then as make-believe characters onstage in the glare of thirty spotlights. The transformation was magical, and I never tired of seeing how personalities changed in that transition.

This opportunity to watch a theater at work allowed me to study two radically different approaches to art. I had assumed that when I was able, in the darkness, to talk with my friend Ezio Pinza we would resume our discussion of opera, but that did not happen ever again. Even though we spoke on many nights, when he learned that I was interested in sports he told me of the years when he was a professional bicyclist in Italy, and I could never hear enough of those rowdy experiences. As I listened I discovered in him an attitude toward art that not only amazed me but also gave me a model for my own later behavior.

While onstage he was involved in a dramatic situation: his role was that of a middle-aged French expatriate in love with an American nurse considerably younger than himself and, to complicate matters, he has two half-caste children by a Polynesian wife now dead. Well, prior to his going onstage he would be telling me, for example, about a bicycle race in Italy when the stage manager would warn: 'Three minutes, Mr. Pinza.' And he would go on talking. 'Two minutes, Mr. Pinza!' and we would be cycling somewhere near Verona. 'One minute, Mr. Pinza,' and I would watch him drop his bicycle, gear up his emotions, and stride onstage exactly on cue and totally prepared for the scene. But when he walked offstage he would resume his story with every bit of his original enthusiasm.

By contrast his co-star, Mary Martin—the young woman from Texas who had conquered Broadway in a series of small roles that by the force of her personality and artistry she had enlarged into starring parts— spent the moments before going onstage preparing herself emotionally to become the character she would be portraying. After a heartrending scene she would come off the stage so limp and with her eyes so filled with tears that she could not even see me or recognize me if she did. With her there was no quick resumption of her own life; even offstage she was still in the South Pacific and the nurse's sorrow was as real to her as if she herself were Nellie Forbush.

Two great artists, two radically different personalities, two attitudes toward art that were worlds apart, but each appropriate to the person in question. They behaved in characteristic fashion on the weekend when the musical had a full house on Friday night, at the Saturday matinee and on Saturday night, with a crucial national television show scheduled for Sunday. *South Pacific* was already a success in New Yo.., but the television presentation would determine how the nation at large was going to judge it, and, of course, both Pinza and Martin were tense with the prospect of being under the national spotlight.

Pinza, who had perhaps the more to lose, called in sick on Friday, allowing his understudy to sing the role. He did the same on Saturday afternoon and again on Saturday night, resting his voice and his vitality for the big test. Miss Martin, who never in the long run of the musical missed a performance, had to work extra hard at the three performances that lacked Pinza. The result? At the Sunday telecast she was visibly tired and vocally somewhat off, while Pinza, rested and strong as a lion, was so magnetic and magnificent in voice that he enchanted the nation. He was never confused about his priorities.

I tried to copy each of these artists. In my personal life I tried to keep myself low-key and detached like Pinza backstage, but in my artistic life I emulated the tremendous personal involvement of Mary Martin when she was onstage, and I found that this somewhat arbitrary and unnatural combination suited me perfectly.

Wherever I went in these exciting years of extended travel I studied people, listened to their stories, weighed the honesty of their statements and always judged myself in terms of their achievements. Could I have been as brave as the downed pilot who made his way by night from behind enemy lines in Korea? Could I ever lead a group of people the way the nomad chieftain did when he took his people across the wastelands of Afghanistan? Would I have sacrificed as much as the mother in Djakarta did to keep her five children with her? And suppose I had been born with two clubfeet like Old Morag and they had gone untreated?

In these self-assessments I often fell dismayingly short, but there were times when I felt I had done passably well. However, when I worked in the bleak refugee camps established in Thailand to house the boat people fleeing Vietnam, I came upon a group of young Frenchmen whose selflessness put me to shame, and never, not even in my imagination, could I ever have hoped to match them. They were doctors, members of Médecins Sans Frontières, a group organized in Paris, which believes that physicians should not move directly from university into big-city practices but that they must first volunteer to serve humanity in general, without significant pay, by working in the Third World. The ones I watched were young, bright, dedicated to their mission and in complete agreement with the philosophy of their group. I saw their unflagging devotion to the sick, and concluded that whereas I had worked, to the extent possible, at humanitarian tasks in many parts of the world, my contribution when compared with theirs ranked as nothing. In later years I saw their colleagues at work in other desperate locations, and my evaluation was always the same: I met no fellow Americans who equaled them for truly Christian service.

It was by accident that I met the two men who brought me unwavering pleasure throughout long years. I had been invited by some distinguished agency to report on happenings in Tahiti, and when I settled into my seat in the airplane in Los Angeles I saw across the aisle but somewhat ahead of me a face with which I, like most other Americans, was familiar. It was that of Walter Cronkite, the distinguished television commentator, a rather forbidding man with his wide knowledge and imposing manner of imparting it. I warned myself: Don't be boring in his presence!

Down the aisle, somewhat behind me, sat another gentleman whose round, cherubic face was also well known. It was the humorist Art Buchwald, who occasioned an even sterner self-admonition: Don't try to be funny on this trip! And I grew apprehensive lest this become a strained situation in which I would constantly have to watch myself.

When we landed at dawn we were met at the airport by a Tahitian princess laden with flowery leis for me. Beautiful of face, she weighed about three hundred pounds and had starred in a movie made from one of my novels, *Hawaii*, so when she saw me she rushed forward and embraced me so tightly that I was well nigh lost in her bosom. As she shoved me away she asked: 'And who are these two?' pointing to Cronkite and Buchwald. Art, fearing that he too was about to be smothered, shied away, but she caught him and gave him the same kind of embrace. Apparently Cronkite seemed too formidable, so all he got were flowers.

From then on, inhibitions were lost in the tumult of life on that enchanting island. When I first reached Tahiti during the war, natives had warned me: 'You should have seen it a dozen years ago. Then it was paradise.' And when I returned two or three times in later years I had been told: 'You should have been here a decade ago. Then it was great.' Now we heard the same thing, but Tahiti has an embrace like that of the princess who had welcomed us at the airport, and in the days that followed, Cronkite, Buchwald and I had the kind of vacation harried New Yorkers dream about. We toured the gorgeous islands, enjoyed native feasts, attended dances held in our honor, met longtime residents with their entertaining stories, paid our respects to the lively widow of James Norman Hall and climbed the colorful mountains that had been known to Captain Cook's men and Pierre Loti and Somerset Maugham.

The more we moved about, the more evident it became that Art Buchwald was even funnier in person than he was in print, for he kept up a fusillade of wit, the kind that grows naturally out of the immediate situation. At times he would be a brash New York wise guy reacting to a world he had never seen before and could not believe existed; next he was the bored and supersensitive Parisian boulevardier visiting the colo-

nies; at other times Cronkite and I would be the butt of his jokes, or he
would lampoon himself. He had one of the sharpest wits I had ever
known—all his remarks were improvised on the spot. And he sustained
his ad-libbing like machine-gun fire for nine days, and we all agreed that
he was one of the warmest traveling companions we had ever known.
In the years that followed, Art could make me laugh just by turning his
expressive face in my direction as if he were going to say something, and
when he did say something, I was never disappointed.

Cronkite was an amazement. He was always ready for an outing or
an interview with old settlers, or for a game. He and his son Chip and
I formed an exhibition team with a Frisbee. We had an unbroken
sequence of more than a hundred undropped tosses, at long distances,
and each of us developed an elegant throw that kept the Frisbee floating
upward in the air for an unbelievable length of time. I knew few more
enjoyable pastimes in the nonsense category, and our exhibitions were
applauded on all the islands.

Cronkite was an avid sailor, and wherever we went he wangled a
sailboat; in a sunset storm we covered that incomparable run from
Tahiti to nearby Moorea, surely one of the most spectacular cruises in
the world, and then, under my urging, because I wanted to see the
unspectacular low islands of the north, he finagled another boat and we
went sailing between those two islands, Raiatea and Huahine, that move
me so deeply because of my wartime experiences on them. What happened during our sail seems so improbable that I am almost embarrassed
to report it. As we pulled into the ancient quay at Raiatea we found
awaiting us at the tip end of the dock a very beautiful young American
woman in a native sarong, flowers in her dark hair and a violin at her
chin. As we approached the tie-up she played for us in the most exquisite
manner the solo parts of Brahms's violin concerto. She had been one of
the first violins of an important California orchestra and had fled to the
islands to find herself, and I have often wondered what she thought
when she found instead Cronkite, Buchwald and Michener coming at
her out of the island mists. An easier question is: What did we think?
We were staggered, complimented her on her playing, and offered her
a drink. I told her: 'You play that at concert level,' and she said: 'I
know.'

We spent most of our time on Bora Bora, still to me the finest island
in the world, where I renewed my friendship with those golden people
I had known during the war: 'Where is Francis Sanford?' Gone to Paris
as a big-shot politician. 'And where is Malama, the lieutenant's girl?'
Gone to live on Maupiti with her two American children. 'Do you ever

hear from any of the sailors who lived here during the war?' Many send us presents.

We were much taken with a blond-haired German who told me: 'One day in Germany after the war, horrible time, I read your book, Michener. And you made it sound so wonderful that my entire energy was to get to the South Pacific. And here I am on the finest island, and that glass-bottomed boat over there is mine and you will sail out with us.' We sat in the bottom of the boat, our arms cocked on a railing, and stared through glass at the bottom of the incomparable Bora Bora lagoon as he maneuvered his craft out into deep water. Using the central volcano and markers placed along the reef, he triangulated his boat over where he had learned the coral would be, and there an hour of enchantment began: while an island steersman who spoke a little English guided the boat, the German, clad in bathing trunks and armed only with a very long screwdriver tucked in his belt, put on his scuba gear, let himself down into the water and with his rubber fins propelled himself close to the bottom while his helper told us what would be happening.

'Everything is in order,' the islander in the boat said. 'Always same, every day. First the little fish, very colorful.' And myriads of blue and gold fish, each one about the length of a finger, crowded around the German, who dispersed them with a wave of his hand. 'Now he chum,' and from a pouch the German diver produced a handful of minced clam. As he scattered it the next group of fish moved in, much bigger and more varied in color: 'First light yellow, then blue come, then big black.' And as if the fish could hear the announcement they obeyed, a parade of dazzling beauty.

Adjusting the power in our boat to keep it locked in position, our guide then said: 'Now he dive deeper, get big clam,' and down he went, using his long screwdriver to pry a shellfish from coral at the bottom. After he had broken it open, he used the screwdriver to cut it into many parts, several of considerable size.

'Now we see for real!' the guide said, and as we watched the lovely coral formations over which the German hovered, we saw very large fish, maybe three feet long, begin to move in, and these he fed one at a time by hand. They did not crowd in on him, each fish apparently approaching on some kind of cue. At any rate the man steering the boat could foretell the order, for he called them out by color: 'Purple, green he come, maybe three blue, next one gold.

'We save this for last,' our guide said, and the German now recovered from his pouch the big pieces of clam he had sequestered there. And as he took his accustomed position among the coral heads, huge fish at least five feet long and two more almost six feet long came up to him slowly as if coming to meet an old friend. I was not prepared for what happened next. The German had placed between his teeth, with his lips holding it in position, a large chunk of clam, and as a huge fish approached slowly but steadily the German jutted out his face, whereupon the silvery fish deftly picked the clam from between his lips, brushed his face with its tail and swam on.

Six big fish in turn appeared to pick their snack from his lips, and when the parade ended, a tourist who had accompanied us gasped: 'My God! He's tamed an entire lagoon.' When we were back on shore the German told us: 'Mr. Michener made this life possible for me. I visualized it all when I read his books.'

The Cronkite-Buchwald-Michener excursion had an amusing conclusion, but it came years later. When it became known that we three musketeers knew one another and had gone on other explorations of Bali and Haiti and two of us to the Amazon, it became a habit for worthy charitable institutions in their fund-raising efforts to give a gala dinner in New York or Washington or Chicago to honor one of us. This enabled them to get a speech for free along with the possibility that we would invite the other two and get free speeches from them also. It became a racket, and since these were years when we were all in the limelight, more or less, we began to get two or three invitations a month. When Cronkite was honored, Buchwald and I were supposed to dance attendance upon him as if he were a Balkan prince, and when Buchwald received one of his dozen awards, Cronkite and I were to do the same. The unpleasant part of this fandango was that quite often the man being honored—say, Cronkite—was supposed to pay a thousand dollars for a table of eight, while Buchwald and I were also required to buy our own tables, 'since you will certainly want to honor your good friend.' Having taken vacations with these two clowns was turning out to be very expensive.

Two typical telephone calls illustrate how desperate charitable organizations are to find free speakers. 'Is this James Michener, the writer? We're giving a gala dinner on Friday night, Jewish Hospital on Long Island, and we want to award you the society's medal as one of America's greatest writers.' I explain that I'll be busy Friday. 'But'—petulantly—'Norman Mailer assured us you would be free.' Since Mailer and I had never spoken, I lied: 'I forgot to tell Norman of my previous obligation.' Long pause, then: 'Mr. Michener, do you happen to know any other famous American writer who might be free Friday night?' I said I knew that Gore Vidal would be free.

It was the next conversation that broke the camel's back: a demand from the brassy chairwoman handling a prize so distinguished that its award ceremony is covered by newspapers and television: 'Mr. Michener, you don't know me but I'm Gloria Nelson, and the committee that chose you for our big award puts the specific arrangements in my hands. Now, I suppose you know that it is customary for the recipient to take eight or nine tables—each seats ten, one thousand dollars per table. You invite your family, your college friends—a time for joyous reunion. Then we'd like to have you give us the names of eight or ten of your other friends, especially those you do business with. We hope you'll encourage each of them to take his own table. We've been told that you know Art Buchwald and Walter Cronkite. It would make the evening special if each of them would take a table and say a few words.'

Shocked by the size of the contribution—$16,000—I was supposed to make or con my friends into making, I asked: 'What date did you say the award was to be given?' When she replied, I said: 'What rotten luck I have to be in Belgium.'

'Cancel it.' she said. 'You have to attend our gala. The announcements saying you're coming have already been printed.' Very firmly I said: 'Use them for notes. Print new ones, because I can't be there.' Pleadingly: 'But, Mr. Michener, don't you have eight or ten friends who would take tables?' to which I replied: 'I don't even have eight or ten reliable enemies.' It was then that I decided there would have to be a Cronkite-Buchwald-Michener compact banning all such fund-raising scams, which, as soon as I proposed the idea, was approved by Buchwald, who organized it and laid down the ground rules. In the original agreement he had phrases like 'pain of death' and 'boiling oil,' but the essence was that from that day forward none of us would ever buy a ticket for a dinner honoring either of the other two. As Art phrased it with his customary tact: 'If that cheapie Walter Cronkite can't afford to pay for his own meals, let him not look to us to feed him.'

Resolutely we have kept to our original promises. I willingly broke the rule once to help honor Cronkite on his retirement; Art came out of retirement to honor me with one of the funniest speeches on record, a parody of my writing: 'Millions and millions of years ago there was a dinosaur in Bucks County. . . .' And recently Walter flew all the way to San Antonio to attend one of my dinners. On such occasions we enable our gracious hosts to collect thousands of dollars for good causes, and if we agreed to go out three or four nights a week we could collect millions. But we firmly refuse to buy tickets for the other guy's dinners.

I do not view this agreement as sacrosanct, and I am sure that Walter and Art don't either. We respect the people who want to honor us and certainly we respect the causes they support. If we were younger, had more time, and were trying to make our way in the world, we would go out more frequently and even joyously. I will let Cronkite speak for us. I told him I was about to sail on an extended trip around South America to gather material for a book and was afraid I was going to be pestered. 'I know just how you feel, Jim,' Cronkite said. 'Four years ago I took that trip and was scared to death I'd be pestered by everyone on board, but Cunard officials assured me: "We're accustomed to having passengers sail with us who want to be left alone. We know how to protect your privacy." On the third night after our departure from Miami, Betsy and I were sitting in a corner of the nearly empty bar, and I suddenly asked: "Betsy! When are they going to start pestering me?" " In that *cri de coeur* he spoke for all of us.

VI

Politics

My INTRODUCTION to politics was so shameful that I bore the scars for decades, but from it I learned a lesson of brotherhood that would dominate my adult life. In the autumn of 1917, when I was ten and in the grip of wartime hysteria focused against Germany and the Kaiser, I took a pair of old shoes to the elderly cobbler who had his shop a few doors from our home on North Main Street. This area had always been called Germany because many of the original settlers there had come from that country and their descendants still spoke that language at home rather than English. My shoemaker, of course, was German.

When I handed him my shoes I saw to my astonishment something I had not noticed before. On his wall, behind his lasts and knee-held anvils hung a large chromolithograph of the Kaiser. As as I stared at it over the old man's shoulder the glare from the hooded eyes was so menacing, the set of the jaw so cruel, that I was speechless, and fled the shop. I had seen the enemy about whom the orators ranted and he was lurking in my backyard.

Hurrying home, I brooded over the menace I had seen, and that night my worst fears were intensified, for our family went to the park before the courthouse where a fine-looking young officer from some

British regiment spoke eloquently about the horrors of fighting the Boche in Flanders and striving, with American aid, to keep the Kaiser out of Paris.

I did not sleep much that night, which I spent struggling against the Kaiser, dodging his submarines and holding him back in the trenches lest he storm Paris. I left my bed the next morning in such a blaze of patriotic fervor that I marched to the cobbler's, slammed my way into his workshop, and, ripping the traitorous portrait from the wall, carried it out into the street and tore it to bits before a small crowd that had gathered.

I heard for the first time the heady sound of applause, and there were admiring cries: 'He's a little hero, that one!' At the height of the celebration I looked past my aplauding neighbors to the doorway of the cobbler's shop, where the old man who had so often befriended me looked on in confusion and dismay.

Someone in the crowd reported my patriotic deed to the local newspaper, and I believe that the first time my name appeared in print was as the local hero, ten years old, who had struck a blow for the cause of the Allies and against the tyranny of the Hun. But the praise I received was dampened by the look I had seen on the old man's face as the poor cobbler watched his little world being torn apart by a child.

I was inducted into local politics in a manner almost as dramatic. Our elegant rural county of Bucks, tucked in between Philadelphia and New York, and one of the few counties in the nation known widely by name, was staunchly Republican and was ruled by a benevolent tyrant named Joe Grundy. He owned a profitable manufacturing plant at the lower end of the county and had but one ambition, to keep Bucks County totally Republican and the nation safely in the hands of the G.O.P. In later years he became president of the National Association of Manufacturers and a United States senator, and he fused the two positions so completely that no observer could discern whether he was acting as a senator or as a manufacturer.

He used to come up from his bastion in Bristol in a chauffeured car wearing high-buttoned shoes and a grim smile to dictate the governing of Doylestown, our county seat. He owned the local newspaper, the *Intelligencer*, and controlled its policies with an inflexible conservatism which ensured that not even a whisper of liberalism or pro-labor sentiment or salaciousness raise its ugly head. One issue of his paper has gone down in history as a notable example of his arch-Republicanism, for on the morning after a crucial national election in 1940 the front page consisted of a banner headline proclaiming that Bucks County had once more voted Republican, while in an obscure bottom right box appeared a small notice to the effect that some Democrat had won the presidency. Joe Grundy played hardball and was so able that he kept our town and county completely under his control.

I first became aware of his power in the fall of 1916, when I was nine years old and he was laboring desperately to keep Pennsylvania in the Republican column in the great presidential fight between the flabby Democratic incumbent, Woodrow Wilson, and the stalwart Republican challenger, Charles Evans Hughes. My family, obedient as always to the urgings of Joe Grundy, was ardently Republican on the solid grounds voiced by my mother: 'You can see that with that dignified beard Mr. Hughes *looks* like a president.' (In the next election she would tell me: 'James, you can see that Warren Harding with that handsome face and reserved manner *looks* like a president' but in the election after that she made no comment about her man Coolidge.)

The election was hard fought and Grundy marshaled his forces with wonderful skill so that on Tuesday night after heated balloting we were overjoyed to hear that Hughes had won and, following orders from Mr. Grundy's local henchmen, we traipsed into the middle of town to cheer an improvised Republican victory parade, and I went to bed that night satisfied that with Charles Evans Hughes in charge of the nation as a whole and Joe Grundy in command locally, the republic was on an even keel.

Of course, by midmorning on Wednesday we learned that a disgracefully wrong vote in California had delivered the presidency back into the hands of that pitiful man, Woodrow Wilson, and black despair settled over Bucks County. But the entire affair culminated for me on Friday night in a distasteful way, because a ragtag handful of Democrats gathered from various unsavory corners of the county convened in our town for a victory parade, and as my mother and I stood in the shadows in the alley beside the *Intelligencer* office, she delivered her contemptuous summary of the Democrats, a phrase that still rings in my ears: 'Look at them, James, not a Buick in the lot.'

My next incursion into politics was in the presidential election of 1928. I was then in college, and was so distressed by the virulent anti-Catholicism of the period that in a public rally attended by townspeople, I gave extemporaneously a rousing defense of freedom of religion. After the meeting the community's leading Republican, Frank Scheibley, was so impressed by my speech and its manner of delivery that he collared me, offered me a job, and later wanted to adopt me as his son. I was thus at an early age co-opted.

In rapid order, as I shall explain in more detail later, I was invited to sample socialism, fascism and communism, and learned a great deal about each. But I was not impressed with any of them and remained essentially one of Joe Grundy's boys, although the Great Depression did cause me to wonder why, if he and his buddies were so everlastingly smart, they had allowed this financial disaster to happen not only to me but also to themselves. But I remained a Republican.

At a critical point in my life I moved to Colorado, which was one of the best things I ever did, for the grand spaciousness of that setting and the freedom of political expression that was not only allowed but encouraged converted me from being a somewhat hidebound Eastern conservative into a free spirit. Colorado was an unusual state in that its voters rarely, and never in my time, awarded all three of its top political positions—governor and two senators—to the same party; the citizens preferred to have the power split among various factions, which meant that the political life there was wildly different from what I had known in Bucks County, where Joe Grundy told us how to vote and we obeyed. In Colorado a man or woman could be a member of any party or any faction within a party and still enjoy a serious chance of being elected to high office. In Pennsylvania I had learned to respect politics; in Colorado I learned to love it.

But most important was something there that helped me develop an intellectual strength I had not had before. There was in the town an informal but most congenial small restaurant named after the widow who ran it, a Mrs. Angell, and there in 1936 a group of like-minded men, two-thirds Republican, one-third Democrat, but all imbued with a love of argument and exploration of ideas, met twice a month for protracted debate on whatever problem was hottest at the moment. We had two clergymen—one liberal, one conservative—an admirable lawyer who had pleaded major cases before the U.S. Supreme Court, two scientists, one of the cantankerous leaders of the Colorado Senate, a wonderful school administrator, a fiery newspaper editor and a healthy scattering of businessmen, mostly on the conservative side. Because I had access to a gelatin duplicating pad, I was designated executive secretary in charge of finding speakers and convening the meetings. We paid, I remember, fifty-five cents a meeting in depression currency, and that covered a free meal for the invited guest. The meetings became so precious to all of us that we would go far out of our way to attend. Discussion was rigorous, informed and relevant, with ideas from the nation's frontier whipping about in grand style.

I think that any young person in his or her thirties who wants to build both character and a grasp of social reality would be well advised to either form or join a club like our Angell's, where hard ideas are discussed by hardheaded members, where ideas that the general public is not yet ready to embrace are dissected, and where decisions are hammered out for the welfare of the community. Sensible men have participated in such discussions from the beginning of time: in the wineshops of antiquity, the baths of ancient Rome, the coffeeshops of England, the town meetings of New England, the Friday-night meeting of the kibbutzim in Israel, the informal clubs of California and Texas and Vermont. Thoughtful people seek these meetings because they need them, and had I not stumbled into mine in Colorado I would have been a lesser man.

One summer a fiery evangelist, Harvey Springer, came into town and pitched his big tent near the college where I taught. There in nightly sessions of the most compelling nature, with frenzied speeches, haunting choral music and wild-eyed young women screaming while coming down the aisles to be saved, Reverend Springer launched a virulent attack on the two clergymen in our group and on me as a disruptive, liberal, atheistic professor. Like the many others under attack, I sneaked in to see how he operated and was awed by his ruthlessness and power. If I remember correctly, he divided his spiel into three parts: first, a most moving account of how in his early youth he was a lost soul because his teachers and his church had failed to give him proper guidance; second, a savage attack on Yale University, for reasons I never fully understood, but apparently he had applied to Yale for entrance to its divinity school, and been turned down; and last, to focus on concerns at the heart of the community, a withering blast at local churches, especially those of my two friends, and a condemnation of almost all college professors, especially me, for having stirred up trouble in the community by calling for fair treatment for Mexican field workers.

It was a solemn group at Angell's that week, because we met on Tuesday and Springer would be hurling his thunderbolts on the coming Sunday, and we knew that something had to be done to counteract his venom. Our two clergymen, who bore the brunt of his attack, were men of quiet demeanor and estimable probity, in no way prepared to equal him in diatribe, and I was a defenseless stripling in the face of his fiery denunciations, but all our members decided that we simply could not allow this poison to be injected into our community and we resolved to combat it in every way at our disposal. The editor would point out the danger in print; the clergymen would preach forcefully about the folly of replacing calm and rational analysis with lurid exhibitionism; and I would tell my students, many of whom were deeply impressed by Springer, that he was so ludicrous they should be able to see through him for the empty windbag that he was.

The next five days were hectic. At Wednesday and Thursday evening meetings in churches the local ministers quietly but with great force fought to expose and defuse Springer's nonsense; our businessmen warned their luncheon meetings of the dangers inherent in his rabble-rousing; our delightful insurance man, Montefiore Moses, was effective in pointing out that Springer was stealing great sums of money from our community in his nightly collections; and I counterattacked as vigor-ously as I could in defending Yale, our own college, its professors and myself against his insane charges.

Ultimately, Springer's evil was contained, and the evangelist with-drew from our community. He did surprisingly little damage to our local churches, and our newspaper grew in esteem because of the forth-right way it had stepped forward to protect our town. Some of my students were surprised to learn that a relatively quiet man like me had been willing to risk a frontal assault from a master mud-slinger.

Having seen Harvey Springer at close hand, having listened to his rantings and his foul misuse of facts, and having seen what damage he could do to a community while milking it of funds, I was intellectually and morally prepared in later life to assess at their true value such successors of his as Jim Bakker and Jimmy Swaggart. Springer brought his tent into our community to steal thousands of dollars that should have gone to local churches; his descendants invaded television signals and stole millions. Our Angell Club never looked to better advantage than during that week when it helped to hold the invading evangelist at bay.

During the curious presidential election of 1936, most of the national pundits were predicting that Alf Landon would by a comfortable margin deny Franklin Roosevelt a second term. I was teaching politics at the time and had recently returned to campus after a hitchhiking trip home from a meeting in Chicago. The newspapers all said that Landon was going to win big, but practically no one I met along the road—filling station men, truck drivers, automobile drivers who picked me up, and restaurant people—was for Landon. Almost universally they said: 'I'm voting for F.D.R. He got the nation back on keel.'

I had to be careful of what I said, for the powerful head of my department, a retired army colonel, was one of the most convinced Republicans I would ever meet, and using data like the *Literary Digest* poll, which showed Landon miles ahead, he was telling all his classes:

'Landon will win by a landslide. The nation has seen through Roosevelt and knows what a charlatan he is.' I had not, at that time, sufficient courage to contradict my boss, for he was a living terror where politics was concerned, but I did report to all my classes the results of my trip across the American heartland: 'Something is crazy here. Either those people all lied to me, or the *Digest* poll is spurious.' When my students asked who I thought would win, I said honestly: 'I don't know. I'm confused,' and when they pressed: 'Who do you want to win?' I replied: 'Teachers aren't supposed to influence their students on political mat- ters,' and the young people who had been bombarded daily by the head of their department burst into laughter.

On a fine autumn day most of the Angell's members went down to the Greeley railway station to watch as President Roosevelt's campaign train pulled in for a brief stop. Because we were early we saw the door to the rear platform swing open so that the president could come out to deliver his speech, and some of us gasped to see for the first time that he really was a cripple who had to be helped each step of the way. When he reached the railing that hemmed in the platform, he grasped it firmly, locked his leg braces into position and flashed that tremendous, cocky smile. 'My friends,' he began in the familiar voice, clear and strong, 'if I may call you my friends, and I think I may call you my friends . . .' It was campaign drama at its best, with the repetition of the popular phrase warming the hearts of his listeners. He said nothing of substance, waved, bade farewell to his friends and tootled off to Denver, where he was scheduled for the major speech of his Western swing.

When the president was gone, some of us Angell's members met for morning coffee to discuss the effect of his brief visit. Reports that morn- ing of Landon's continued superiority in the polls made even F.D.R.'s supporters afraid to predict victory, while the traditional Republicans in our group scorned Roosevelt's obvious attempt to play on the crowd's emotions. When I was asked for an opinion I said: 'I really don't know. He won no votes in that stop, and my boss insists that the polls are right and that Landon's going to win by a landslide.' I stopped, then added: 'But I can't get that trip out of my mind. I met nobody who was voting Republican, nobody, so maybe there's something we don't see.'

'You think Roosevelt has a chance?'

'I'm not making any predictions, but there's something screwy some- where.' I wish now that I had been able to read the signs more effectively and speak to my students and my Angell's colleagues more forcefully, because even before we went to bed that election night we knew that

Landon had carried only Maine and Vermont. Next day one of the newspapers had a big headline: WHA HOPPEN?

As a student of American political traditions I covered myself with shame in the 1948 presidential campaign. This is how it happened: I had recently moved to New York and thus was not eligible to vote, so I became a fairly popular impartial master of ceremonies at political rallies, where I did my best to ensure equal time to the Republicans, whose candidate was Thomas Dewey, and the rather disorganized Democrats, who tried to keep alive the myth that Harry Truman had an outside chance of winning. As one who had followed the campaign closely, I believed that the Republicans had a lead so comfortable that Truman had no chance, but I had to deal with a professor from New York University who appeared on my panel frequently and tried to convince the audience and me that the Democrats had a chance of carrying not only New York State but the entire nation. He was an able debater and one night when he had done his best without convincing any of us I told him rather condescendingly: 'You're very impressive, but your facts leave me cold. But I do admire the way you defend a doomed cause.'

'Mr. Michener! You don't seem to understand. Harry Truman's going to win.'

'Well, yes. He might carry New York.'

'I mean the whole country. He's going to be our next president.'

I was gracious in handling him, as an impartial chairman ought to be, but on the Monday night before the election, when we had a long debate on radio, I grew rather impatient with the ardent man, and when the time came for the final wrap-up I patronized him egregiously: 'I think we must all applaud Dr. Feinstein for his gallant attempt to defend the Democratic position, and as always, it is my great pleasure to turn the microphone over to him, for he is a real politician.'

He took it, glared at me, and said: 'Mr. Michener, tomorrow morning you're going to find that Harry S. Truman is still president for a full four-year term.' And he was right.

My personal introduction to the realities of political life began one afternoon when a stranger came up on our hill with an astonishing proposal. He was a fine-looking man, in his early thirties, clean-shaven, with an ingratiating smile, and wearing a dark suit and polished black shoes. He wanted to talk to me about a cultural organization of superb reputation (which I shall call Friends of Asia). He asked me what I knew of its work and I said: 'During my travels in Asia and in my conversations with scholars and experts of various kinds I've found its reputation to be the best. Does great work. Has first-class people on its staff.'

After a prolonged interrogation in the midst of which we went to Bob Brugger's bar in Pipersville for lunch, for which he insisted upon paying, we returned to my office and with the phone off the hook and no one around he told me: 'I'm from the federal government, authorized to talk with you directly. We suspect that this fine organization of which you speak so highly has been infiltrated by radicals, perhaps even Communists, and some of its representatives out in the field are doing real damage. The government has worked diligently with patriots inside that organization for them to take control and clean it up, to allow it to be what it ought to be.'

I said that sounded like a laudable aim, but what did it have to do with me? 'Simple, when they have their board meeting tomorrow, they want to elect you president of the outfit—new broom to sweep clean, a man with a good reputation in Asia and no blemishes we can find. You go in with full authority from the board, full backing from the government, and we're sure you can do the job.'

It was flattering to be considered for such a task, but I had been indoctrinated in my apprenticeship with newspapers and magazines with two immutable principles: The writer must never allow himself to become part of the story; and he must never, never be beholden to anyone other than the agency that is publicly paying him. Also, a writer must never serve as a secret agent for anything or anybody. Obedient to that strict code, I said: 'There's no way I could ally myself with you fellows in any secret operation,' and he said quickly: 'Nothing secret about this. Your election tomorrow will be made public, instantly, and when you travel in Asia you will be introduced everywhere as the president of Friends of Asia. You'll be performing a public service, and one of signal importance.'

I said that if all aspects were aboveboard I'd consider it, but he pressed: 'No, we've got to get this straightened out right now. Time is crucial,' and after more conversation I said: 'If it's as you say, I'll give you my answer at sunset tomorrow. You can wait one day.' Then he dropped his voice: 'There is, as you suspect, one catch I haven't explained. Because the government is so eager to get this mess cleared up, and because we think we can trust you, we're prepared to pump a considerable amount of money into the operation to rescue it, but you must stand ready to accept the money, and if trouble breaks as it might, to take on your shoulders alone public responsibility as to how the money was spent. In other words, you stand surety for the funds, and you simply cannot waffle if heat is applied.'

'And where will these funds come from?'

'The federal government. We're dead serious about restoring this organization to what it should be, and we're convinced that you're the man who can be trusted to do it.'

It was a heady offer and in a field in which I had slowly acquired a good deal of expertise. I no longer thought of it as the mysterious East, for I now knew Tokyo, Hong Kong, Kuala Lumpur, Rangoon and Jogjakarta rather better than I remembered Philadelphia and Boston, so the intellectual challenge was immense. But as I walked with my dogs at twilight and into the night, I formulated for the first time the end goal of my life. I had never dreamed of being a great writer, nor a college president, nor a political leader, nor a prominent businessman. My childhood, as the reader will see later, had been so unusual that such ambitions had had no time to mature; my job had always been to survive from Monday morning through Friday afternoon and the rest could take care of itself. But rather early in a precocious adulthood that was forced upon me I saw that one of the greatest boons on this earth was to be part of a well-organized society that provides safety, a free education and the opportunity to find one's optimum level. The only ambition I would ever have, the only one I would ever mention, even in my dreaming, was to be a good citizen. I had no higher aspiration, nor could I envisage one. I wanted to be known as a man who could be trusted to do honest work and relied upon to make those moves that would help hold society together, and as I struggled with the government's invitation well past midnight, I assessed it only in those simple terms. I could never be a flag-waving patriot, nor did I care to be a hero in any aspect of my life, but I did want to be a responsible citizen and this invitation to serve my society in an important sphere was tempting.

But then, as the night wore on, I came back to the code of the writer: I should be able to move into any situation with credentials that were clean and visible to all. I would come as a secret agent of no one, a supporter of no party, a proponent of no special interest or hidden agenda. This was not a trivial consideration, for those of us who worked in Asia in the tumultuous years of World War II and the Korean War knew several cases in which persons who were ostensibly newsmen had turned out to be secret agents and, in two instances, possibly double agents. Once such men were exposed, as they always seemed to be, their careers were ruined. I remember two who pleaded with me desperately to help them restore credentials that were irrecoverable. They may have been deluded by such books as Somerset Maugham's *Ashenden,* which is about a British agent, and the exploits of John Buchan (Lord Tweedsmuir) and Sir Compton Mackenzie, who were reputed to have combined writing and espionage. My two young men, each younger than I and in many ways more gifted, had destroyed themselves and there was no way I could help to save them.

The next day the government man was back with assurances that all would be up front and clearly stated if I would agree to be a moral custodian of the government funds, and on those terms I agreed to take on the assignment. It was a difficult one, requiring attention to tedious details in trying to save an organization that had begun to fall apart.

A good deal of government money came our way. We used it to clean up the difficult situation, and in due course I informed the government that because I had to be so constantly in Asia, I could no longer serve as head of the organization in the United States. Our board had done an excellent job. Scandal and theft of government funds had been prevented, and if the agency had had hard-core subversives they had either been expelled or driven to dig themselves even deeper underground. Most important to me, I had served my country without compromising my own integrity. It was in connection with this assignment that I underwent my first extensive F.B.I. check, a ritual that would be repeated numerous times in the future and right down to this day. I always knew when an investigation was under way because frightened neighbors would come whispering: 'Jim, the F.B.I. is on your trail. What have you done wrong?' and I was not allowed to tell them the real purpose of the questioning. In certain instances suspicious friends convinced themselves that because of the repeated checks—I would ultimately work in many branches of the government, each requiring its own check—I was a crypto-Communist, and they stopped associating with me, but even in such circumstances I had to keep my mouth shut.

In the election of 1960 Professor Arthur Meier Schlesinger, Sr., with whom I had studied at Harvard, suggested that I volunteer my services in John F. Kennedy's campaign for the presidency. So I worked as chairman in one of the critical suburban counties in the Philadelphia area.

Our strategy was well outlined by Johnny Welsh, the longtime Democratic leader in our area: 'We have no chance of winning our county.

Republicans are simply too strong. But we will win Philadelphia and Pittsburgh by big margins, so what we've got to do is fight like hell to keep the Republican margin as small as possible in our county so they can't eat away our big city totals.'

We were thus engaged in a holding action made more difficult by a local phenomenon that threatened to engulf us in a flood of hitherto unknown Republican votes. Our problem was this: Kennedy was known to be Catholic, and this would alienate our rural voters, who tended to be staunch Lutherans vigorously opposed to his religion, but we also had in our county a huge Pennsylvania Dutch population, plain-dressing Mennonites mostly, and their opposition to the Pope was deadly. They could be expected to vote unanimously against Kennedy, but even so we might have been able to win some of our other rural areas to vote for him had it not been for an unexpected turn of events.

Rural German families took politics seriously, but they never allowed their womenfolk to vote; it was unthinkable for a farm wife in the German area to go to the polls, and in all my years in Bucks County I had never seen one vote. But now with the threat of Catholicism hammering, the stolid Mennonite burghers ignored their custom and herded their women to the registration booths in numbers that appalled us. Johnny Welsh, watching this horde of confused women in black dresses marching in to make themselves eligible for the November voting, realized that something drastic must be done. For the first time we Democrats scoured the county to find Catholic convents, minor religious orders and individual nuns who had never registered before, and I spent much of September taking nuns to such places as garages and cigar stores to register them: 'It is,' said one Democratic helper, 'our women in black against their women in black.'

In the hottest days of the campaign, when all seemed to hang in the balance, a group of us received calls from Washington headquarters: 'In state after state we're not getting exposure in the newspapers and on television. Will you join a high-caliber barnstorming troupe and fly into those states to force them to give us space?'

When I received the call, I said I'd stop trying to find elusive nuns and join the team, but I wasn't sure what I could add, to which they said: 'We need you. We want to put together a classy mix they can't ignore. Arthur Schlesinger, Jr., and you for the people who read. Stan Musial for the men who love athletics. Jeff Chandler, Angie Dickinson, and Shelley Winters as our movie stars. En route five of the Kennedy family will join you, one by one in the various cities, and we'll see what we can accomplish.'

It was a three-week crusade, as I remember, in which each of us did whatever he or she could do best. Angie Dickinson was a treasure, a fragile-looking blonde with a ravishing smile and the ability to work endless hours. Jeff Chandler was as gracious a movie star as I would ever know. Schlesinger overpowered the newsmen who came to interview us, and Shelley Winters was her explosive self. But the star of our troupe was someone I had not expected to fill that role. I had always known of Stan Musial, the immortal baseball player with so many records to his name, but what I associated with him most was an unequaled feat: in one doubleheader he hit three home runs in the first game, two in the second. When men in the farmlands heard that we had Stan aboard, they drove out to the airfields in their pickups, waiting around in the dark till our plane landed, and I remember walking near a chain-link fence at some forlorn stop in Nebraska at one in the morning and hearing a father telling his son: 'You'll never forget this night, Claude. You saw Stan Musial.' But we lost Nebraska.

If our goal was to get media coverage for the party, we were a success, but if it was to win votes for Kennedy we were a flop. We went into eleven states where our ticket was weakest, and we used whatever tricks we could muster to get media attention not only for Jack Kennedy but for local candidates as well. We had some appalling disappointments, as when grass-level Republican leaders obstructed us at the airport or kept us from newspaper rooms or television cameras, but with Angie and Jeff and Stan the Man that was not easy to do. We were fighting tough local politics, and when someone like Ethel Kennedy flew in to join us, we gave as good as we got. In the course of that campaign, I would develop an enormous respect for Ethel, as tough a mind as I have known, as sharp an infighter.

On one emotional night in Denver when Byron "Whizzer" White, the football star and future Supreme Court justice did his futile best to bring Colorado into the Kennedy camp, I, as a kind of local boy well known in some quarters, gave what I thought was a rousing speech, but when I sat down, Ethel sitting behind me gave me a sharp cuff to the ear: 'Michener, damn it. There's a lot of Germans in this state. When you tell about Jack's older brother being shot down in an air battle, do not say that a German pilot did it. Just makes people angry.'

'What shall I say?'

'That he gave his life for his country over the North Sea.' We lost Colorado.

Our most amusing contretemps occurred in Boise, Idaho, a fine town, which in later years I grew to admire. Somehow or other the local

Democratic leadership had maneuvered a bid for us to address a luncheon in the local country club, but when the regular members heard that a gang of Democrats was going to invade their sanctuary, they—especially the women members—put their collective feet down. When we were met at the door and refused admission, it was decided that since I was the least political of the group and might be known for my books, I should do the negotiating, but I failed. I heard one woman say: 'It would contaminate the club.' We managed to find another venue, but that didn't accomplish much because almost no one came to hear us. We lost Idaho.

As a matter of doleful record, despite the fact that two other Kennedy girls flew out to help us, as well as Teddy and his beautiful wife, Joan—they were real campaigners—our fighting team lost every state into which we adventured, and Shelley Winters said afterward: 'If they'd sent us into more states, we'd have lost the whole election for them.' But there was a happy side to the story: minor candidates from several states assured us later that the media coverage we attained had helped in winning their local fights.

Our campaigning was a gallant effort, and it introduced me to some of the finest people I've ever known. I've traveled other times with Stan Musial, an American original. I have kept in touch with the Kennedys and have admired their dedication to public service. I consider Teddy Kennedy an admirable senator, and so will history. I mourned the death of Jeff Chandler, a solid citizen with both modesty and a sense of humor. And my heart skips a beat whenever I see Angie on the screen, younger year by year while the rest of us age. I never spent a better three weeks.

We spent election day in our home district, and when my wife, Mari, saw that extraordinary parade of German women in black dresses marching to the polls, followed by the Catholic nuns in their black habits, she cried: 'My God! They're coming out of the woodwork!' Our Dutch Republicans mustered far more of their first-time women voters than we Democrats did, but our nuns helped hold down the margin of the Republican victory in our county, and on that long, frenzied election night when the returns poured in, it was clear that whereas all the suburbs like Bucks County had been carried by the Republicans, our heroic efforts had kept the margin of their victory to a minimum, which meant that Democratic victories in Philadelphia and Pittsburgh were large enough to deliver Pennsylvania's electoral votes to Kennedy, who certainly needed them.

The experiences of this campaign, and the excellent politicians I met, Republican and Democrat alike, converted me to involvement in politics, a field of operation in which I would work for the rest of my life. I love politics and find it increasingly fascinating.

In 1962 I ran for Congress on the Democratic ticket in a district that was heavily Republican, and on the opening day of the campaign I was invited to address a Ukrainian church in Allentown. After a brief and what I considered inspiring series of comments, I asked if there were any questions and a dour man in the front row leaped to his feet: 'What is your attitude on House Bill 418-97?' I had never heard of it. Later I learned that it had something to do with granting political asylum to a high dignitary of the Ukrainian Church, which is totally different from the Russian Orthodox Church. Afraid to fake an answer, I said: 'I haven't studied that proposal yet,' and right there lost the entire Ukrainian vote in my district.

The district was unique in the United States in that it contained two massive steel mills, Bethlehem in the north, United States Steel in the south, and in those first months of campaigning I would learn that politics in this region consisted of reassuring one group after another, each in its own severely segregated church and club, that if the members voted for me they would have a man in Washington marvelously qualified to look after their separate interests. There were the big groups that you would expect in a steel area: Irish, German, Italian. But there were also small enclaves you had not been aware of before: Latvians, Slovaks, Czechs, Hungarians, Greeks and a dozen others. It is very sobering for a man to present himself to such an electorate.

My opponent was a capable little Napoleon who had served ten terms in office; he had never lost an election and did not propose to lose this one. Like a true master he fended off every advance I tried to make and was content to sit back and run a campaign exactly like all the previous ones that he had won with ease. I campaigned valiantly and did cut down his usual margin of victory, but he preserved his unbeaten record. I was disheartened by my loss and never made sour-grapes comments that it was just as well that I hadn't won because if I had I would probably not have been able to write certain books. I wanted to win; I gave it every ounce of energy I had; and I believe I would have been a good representative had I won. However, when my opponent retired from Congress, his place was taken by a younger Republican, who, I must admit, served the district rather better than I might have and progressed from a seat in the House to other positions of distinction.

When he retired, a vigorous young Democrat won the seat and I was elated.

Running for Congress was one of the best things I've done because campaigning in public knocks sense into a man. He begins to see his nation as a carefully assembled mosaic whose individual pieces require close attention. He also discovers that the timeless struggle between conservatives and liberals is good for the nation, for it ensures that procedures will be overhauled periodically under new managers. He develops an intense admiration for the men and women who keep the political process operating, and at the end of a campaign he finds that he has far more respect for an honest hardworking Republican opponent than for a wishy-washy Democrat who has never matched his energies with his hopes.

I do not want ever to be governed by men or women who have not subjected themselves to the election process and have thus learned humility. This conviction was strengthened in 1974, after President Nixon left office. A large poster showed sixty-four members of his team who had either landed in jail or been forced to resign under pressure, and not one of them had ever run for office, not any kind of office. They had all been called from private life to positions of great power without ever undergoing the sobering experience of asking voters for their support or the humbling experience of having lost. I am terrified of being governed by such men whose worth has not been tested. Let them undergo public scrutiny and prove themselves.

My lasting memory of my race for Congress is a joyous one. In the industrial southern end of my district a powerful political club existed, the Bensalem Loyal Democrats, and if a candidate wanted to win, it was obligatory that he enlist and keep the support of its members, because they did vote in sometimes surprising numbers, considering the relatively small registered population of the area. The club was run in heavy dictatorial fashion by the strangest ward politician in memory, a big, blowsy sixtyish woman with a brusque manner and no teeth. Josephine Morris was one of those clever gregarious people for whom politics was designed, and few played the game better than she. To encounter her loud, enthusiastic chatter for the first time invited laughter, but to watch her run her big district with an iron hand evoked awe.

Incredible as it now seems, the feature of any long campaign was the formal dinner Josephine threw on the Saturday night before the Tuesday election. Then her husky cohorts dressed in rented tuxedos, their wives appeared in new gowns, and Josephine, in a special dress acquired for each ball, reigned, assuring everyone that the vote she was going to turn in on Tuesday would be better than ever. She was one of the few leaders I would know who could deliver, a typical vote in her district being something like 816 to 7 in favor of the candidate she backed.

In 1962 she proclaimed loudly that this year she was backing me, and at the grand ball she presented me to her group as the savior of the Democratic party. It was a love feast, and I reveled in her friendliness and lively spirits. After the dinner and before the dancing to a nine-piece orchestra started, Josephine and her managers met with me and my people in a back room to discuss her demands, which were forthright: 'A seat for one of my people on the school board, the use of a pickup truck, a new traffic light at the corner near the Catholic Church, and three hundred fifty dollars for my workers on election day.' I agreed to everything and then drove north to attend a much larger meeting of my supporters in the Allentown end of my district, but as we passed through the sleeping villages whose votes we hoped for, I allowed myself a flush of enthusiasm: 'Well, we built our bridges in Bensalem,' but my cautious manager said: 'Don't count those chickens till the returns come in.'

On Tuesday night when the vote was announced I was appalled to hear that it was 816 for my opponent, 7 for me. When I stormed about to learn what had happened, my manager told me: 'It was those dirty Republicans. Their people got to Josephine late Monday night and promised her a seat on the school board, use of a truck, a new traffic light and three hundred fifty dollars for her workers.'

'But that's exactly what we promised her,' and he said: 'True, but they threw in four hundred feet of used sewer pipe.'

Not long thereafter I was felled by a major illness and as I lay in the hospital frightened and dispirited, my nurse said: 'Doctor told me you were to have no phone calls, but this woman insists and she made such a fuss . . .' It was Josephine Morris, of the Bensalem Loyal Democrats: 'Jim! We're all praying for you. You're one of the finest men we've ever worked with and we need you. The whole country needs you. Jim, our club is one thousand percent behind you, like always.'

When I hung up I started to laugh, recalling the night of that formal ball and the florid speeches and negotiating meetings afterward, and my laughter became so robust that the doctor came in to see what was the matter. I believe that my recovery started from that moment.

There was one final encounter with Josephine and her Loyals, one that I cherish. Later when I ran for an entirely different office, she called: 'Jim, we haven't seen you for too long, and we still love you. On Saturday afternoon next week we're throwing a gala picnic at the park, and our members agreed a hundred percent that they wanted you as

guest of honor, because in this coming vote we're behind you one
thousand percent, like always.'

Johnny Welsh, our acerbic county leader, drove me to the picnic, and
I think even he must have been impressed by the wellspring of good
wishes that engulfed me and the promises of undying support for my
campaign. Josephine delivered a stately oration about the good I had
done their party, and it was about as fine an accolade as any aspiring
politican could have, but when, on the drive home, I said: 'Johnny,
regardless of what she did to me in the past, an affair like that is damned
touching,' he growled: 'Don't be sentimental, Jim.'

'Why not? She wouldn't dare poleax me this time. Not after what she
just said.'

'Jim! Have you looked up a map of the new voting districts? Josephine
and I studied them last month. You're not running in her district
anymore, and she knows it.'

The position for which I was running in that race exemplifies a truth
about my political career. I ran five times for various jobs, lost two, won
three, but the rule was: 'Whenever the job had a salary, I lost. When
it was honorary, I won.' This time it was a nonpaying job, but it was
of supreme importance: we were going to try to revise the entire constitution of the Commonwealth of Pennsylvania in an effort to bring its
archaic components into the twentieth century and put the state in a
strong position to face the twenty-first. I was elected to serve as a
delegate, and when I met for the first time with the others I saw what
a sterling group of men and women had been chosen for this task:
Governor Scranton led the Republicans; two future governors were
among us—Dick Thornburgh the Republican, Bob Casey the Democrat—several federal judges who would have lifetime appointments and
numerous businessmen who would later manage large companies. It was
a strong contingent, some of the women being especially able, but we
were all well aware that every other major state that had tried to revise
its constitution had failed: New York, Texas, Michigan, and nearby
Maryland. We were determined not to fail.

The success of our effort stemmed largely, I believe, from the sagacious leadership given by Bill Scranton, as fine a politician as I would
ever know. He told his Republican cohorts: 'Yes, we do have a slight
majority, and we can bull this thing through pretty much as we wish,
but the Democrats have some of the feistiest infighters around, and
they'll be able to tie us in knots and ensure our defeat when we take our

results to the electorate for approval.' He prevailed upon his team to award us Democrats an absolutely fair share of all the administrative jobs in the convention, and as a consequence we worked as an unbreachable team, laboring through endless sessions to hammer out one of nation's best state constitutions.

As a result of Scranton's decision to share all important posts, I became secretary of the convention and in that official position worked diligently to find compromises between differing attitudes in the general debate, but as a private delegate I helped lead the fight for a more liberal, well-defined and strong government. I had come to Harrisburg, our state capital, hoping to help achieve five reforms: choose judges by merit selection rather than by chaotic elections in which voters knew none of the candidates; reduce the size of the legislature, which was preposterously large; abolish meaningless row offices, such as lay coroner and prothonotary; eliminate the ridiculous system whereby justices of the peace with no legal training were paid out of the fines they assessed; and tax property held by churches but not used for religious purposes.

I had studied the last problem as it had existed in Tudor England, in prerevolutionary France, in Rumania and especially in Mexico. In each of these countries the unceasing accumulation of property held in mortmain by churches had led to revolution and I wanted steps to be taken now to avoid that peril. One night, in a startling move, the convention voted to correct this impropriety. As we filed from the hall a small, wiry man with an agitated countenance stopped me and snarled: 'All right. You won tonight, but tomorrow morning the God-squad is going attack you so hard you'll never know what hit you,' and he must have been busy on the telephone all night, for at seven next morning my phone and those of the other delegates began ringing furiously, and by the time we convened at nine Harrisburg was filled with more church lobbyists than we had known existed.

With great force the God-squad moved in on us, swamping us with cajolery, protests and threats of excommunication if we did not immediately revoke the decision we had reached the night before. I, as secretary of the convention, was so heavily targeted that by eleven o'clock I saw that unless I signaled for retreat, I was going to be relentlessly persecuted. By noon the offending proposal had been killed, and I, among others, learned what could be altered in American life and what could not. In similar fashion I lost my other major battles: judges would be elected, the row offices would remain and the legislature would continue to be the largest in the nation by a wide margin. Only one of my proposed reforms was approved: we got rid of more than five hundred

untrained justices of the peace living on their fees, and replaced them
with salaried legal experts who have served the state well.

Despite my lost crusades, I consider the work I did in helping Pennsylvania move into the modern age the best single thing I have accomplished in my life. I attended every minute of every session, labored to
hold disparate elements together, and at dusk retired wearily to my
quarters, where my wife would have eight or ten of the delegates, a
different group each night, for those impassioned discussions that
seemed a mature continuation of my Angell Club meetings. Then, when
everyone else was in bed, I would sit at my typewriter putting down my
recollections of that day; the pages proliferated; they told a straightforward story of how a group of ordinary men and women struggled to
organize their society. I left them on file somewhere; perhaps in the next
century they can be recovered and edited by someone knowledgeable
about politics, for I should be proud to have them in print. Few readers
would be interested in them, but anyone who has ever labored in politics
would recognize the way events and procedures evolve.

Certain events at the convention loom large in my memory. When the
seating was arranged alphabetically so that Republicans and Democrats
could not cluster and be tempted to form party-line cliques, I was seated
next to a Mrs. Miller from Pittsburgh, who seemed not to know what
was going on. Democrats from her region came by now and then to tell
her how to vote, and she seemed always to listen and smile. Members
of my team whispered: 'Jim, keep an eye on Mrs. Miller, and when a
really important vote comes along and she isn't looking, reach over and
pull her toggle switch in favor of the vote we want.' I said that this
seemed improper, but they pointed out: 'If you don't tell her what to
do, someone else will.'

Only twice did I activate Mrs. Miller's toggle, and on both occasions
the vote was critical, but I was beginning to receive some very harsh
questionings about votes I was casting because they seemed contrary to
what my spoken positions had been. I said: 'Impossible! I never cast any
vote on that proposal! And certainly not a nay.' Then we found that
during a vote, when I was attending to my secretarial matters, Mrs.
Miller was pulling *my* toggle, and also the one to her left, whenever she
got the chance.

When the leatherette handbooks of the convention were distributed
I learned what a shrewd politician this Mrs. Miller, the frumpy housewife from Pittsburgh, really was, for whereas I simply accepted my copy
graciously, glad to get the permanent roster of the delegates, she sent
pages scurrying about picking up stray copies until she had about forty.

When I asked her what she was going to do with them, she explained: 'I've been getting reelected without opposition for thirty years. I understand politics. I'll mail one of these to each of my district helpers and word the letter so it sounds as if I had personally paid for them, just so they could have a record of what I've been doing.'

One of my defeats had tragic consequences. Throughout the convention I pleaded for our new constitution to contain a code of ethics, but the professional delegates pooh-poohed this condescendingly: 'Part-time amateurs don't really understand the workings of a full-time legislature. No code of ethics is necessary.' I then begged for at least a statement recommending that any legislator when proposing a bill or supporting it be encouraged to reveal any conflict of interest that might disqualify him: 'After he has stated his possible conflict, he can still vote for the bill, but the general body will know how to evaluate his vote.' This was rejected with hoots.

Within two years three delegates who had been the most outspoken in ridiculing my proposals fell into the precise traps against which I had been warning. One of the most distinguished Democrats suffered statewide humiliation when it was revealed that he had been vigorously supporting a proposal in which he had a strong but secret vested interest. A handsome, bright young Republican who was being heavily touted as a future governor was caught sponsoring legislation favoring a concern in which he too had a secret interest. Scandal ensued and there was no more talk of a governorship. Saddest of all was the case of the actual leader of the Democratic contingent to the legislature. He was caught in what amounted to selling favors and went to jail. I still believe that frank admission of personal interest prior to a vote is the way to handle such conflicts, and I am increasingly respectful of that unusual verb 'to recuse,' as in: 'He recused himself,' meaning that the official responsible for a decision, most often a judge, realized that in decency he ought to disqualify himself in this or that case because he has a personal interest and cannot render a just verdict.

If one reviews the printed minutes of our convention, one will see numerous instances in which I was opposed, rebuked and in one instance vilified. And, of course, I lost the major battles, so for me the sessions were hardly a success. But when the time came to appoint a small, powerful committee to supervise the implementation of the changes we had imposed, the leaders of both parties agreed that I should be the chairman, and I spent the better part of a year attending to those fascinating details. I thus spent about two full years discharging my civic duties and I doubt that I ever in my life was occupied with a more meaningful task, and when someone today chides me for my political naïveté I smile and think: Sonny, I wrestled with the God-squad and that's education enough.

In the 1970s Arthur Miller and I helped organize a small committee to protest the sorry abuses suffered by the United Nations Educational, Scientific and Cultural Organization (UNESCO) since it fell into the hands of a willful and destructive minority. Our complaints were three-fold: the organization was attacking the basis of free speech and a free press by demanding that reporters covering Third World nations be licensed by those nations in an effort to prevent adverse reporting; it had fallen captive to the Arab nations, who were using their voting strength to outlaw Israel and bar her from UNESCO operations; and it had allowed itself to become a platform for the most virulent and untruthful anti-American propaganda.

Miller and I had a long meeting in New York with the head of UNESCO, Amadou M'Bow of Senegal, who had shown a visceral anti-Americanism. Although he did listen with a bored expression as we outlined our anxieties, when we were finished he dismissed us as though we were a pair of schoolboys. It was frustrating that he had not attended seriously to any of our complaints and humiliating that we had been so abruptly rejected. As we left I said: 'Secretary M'Bow, if your organization persists in its present actions, you must realize that sooner or later if the United States is incessantly insulted we'll stop paying dues and even withdraw from UNESCO.' He replied that we were obligated by international law to pay the dues and that UNESCO formulated its own policies. In fairness I must also add that he said he could not see how anything done so far could justify the United States' even thinking of resigning.

I was now so deeply involved in this issue that when an international conference was convened in Paris, I flew over to join Isaac Stern and Arthur Rubenstein as members of the American delegation, but again we accomplished nothing, and after the sessions ended, UNESCO under the leadership of M'Bow continued its vigorous anti-American policies; it worked for suppression of freedom of the press; and its attitude toward Israel was disgusting.

Much later when our government developed the same distaste for UNESCO that I had experienced for a decade, a committee was appointed to advise the president on whether or not our country should resign from UNESCO and cease paying dues to an organization that continued to vilify us, and because of my long-term interest, I was invited to serve. This committee, headed by the able president of the University of South Carolina, James Holderman, started its sessions by reviewing every logical reason why we should remain in UNESCO, and the evidence was persuasive that we should. It did wonderful work in designating cultural treasures that should be protected. Its publications on out-of-the-way sites that enriched world art were handsome. Its work in education in Third World nations was commendable, and even the most jaundiced critic had to admit that its accomplishments in the field of art were not trivial.

But I was one of the delegates unable to ignore the evil done by looking at the good. Perhaps I had been unduly influenced by Secretary M'Bow's insolent behavior; perhaps I was overreacting to the insults heaped upon my country in the UNESCO debates; and perhaps I placed too much emphasis on the manner in which UNESCO fought to ostracize Israel; and perhaps I was culpable in other ways I did not recognize, but one thing was certain: I wanted the United States to withdraw from UNESCO and stop paying large annual fees to an agency that was abusing not only us but also the world's free press and Israel's just rights. I so testified, and persistently at every meeting of our commission, but several of the other members whom I admired most, such as Leonard Marks, the international specialist on broadcasting, argued that we remain members and pay our dues.

When I was again sent to Paris as a member of the presidential committee to monitor a plenary session of UNESCO I obtained a much more serious hearing than I had the first time I went there. This time I met a cadre of Secretary M'Bow's able young assistants from Third World nations who now had high-paying jobs in Paris with lavish expense accounts, and I found them as enjoyable companions as any I had known since my Navy days. They were bright, savvy, eager and completely aware that if my country stopped paying its dues, they might lose their cushy assignments. The reasons they gave me, over fine dinners, for the United States to overlook these past dissatisfactions were not only relevant but also persuasive, and had I remained under their influence for long I suspect I might have been dissuaded from my intentions. But when I studied the actual operation of UNESCO and saw how almost every aspect of its functioning was weighted unfairly against the United States, I became doubly offended. Secretary M'Bow, learning from his aides of my continued dissatisfaction, invited me through them to discuss whatever complaints I had, but remembering our earlier meetings, I had no desire to do so. I feared his primary interest would be to preserve his job and its luxurious amenities.

When I left Paris it was clear to me that our commission members who favored remaining in UNESCO outnumbered and outweighed in influence those of us who wished to withdraw, so as soon as I reached home I put aside all other work and drafted a carefully reasoned ten-page letter summarizing the reasons why we should leave. I marshaled a specific and devastating indictment of UNESCO as it was operating under M'Bow. The letter was widely distributed, and when the president finally announced our withdrawal, many who had been in the fight wrote to tell me that I had helped convince Washington that what they had wanted to do from the beginning had been correct.

From a succession of such experiences I was learning how a citizen can lose in an election but win the game. Although I had run in a district from which no Democrat could then have been sent to Congress, the vigor of my campaigning attracted such comment that I was appointed to a series of boards in Washington and found myself close to the heart of government. I must confess that all my appointments came from Republican presidents—the result of a salutary law governing the composition of committees. A board of five appointees, to be confirmed by the Senate, had to consist of no more than three members of the political party in power, the other two coming from either the party out of power or from independents. If the committee had seven members, there had to be three minority; if nine, four. Thus the president *had* to appoint somebody from the opposition, and I became known as the Democrat with whom Republicans could live. When a Democrat held the presidency his party put forward born-again fire-eaters, so that a moderate like me was no longer needed.

By a series of accidents I became a prototypical child of my century in that I was thrust into the middle of the struggle between democratic capitalism and Soviet Marxism. In a series of dramatic personal experiences Communism became a familiar opponent and one whose ruthless force I feared and respected.

· From 1950 through 1953 I reported on the Korean War, witnessing at close quarters the stubborn power of Chinese Communist land forces, the skill of Soviet airmen and the intransigence of the North Korean communists. I was especially concerned with the American soldiers who defected to the communist side and had many opportunities to observe European and Australian citizens who fought with the Chinese Communists and heaped insult upon the Americans.

· In 1956 I operated behind Russian lines during the Hungarian Revolution, led many freedom fighters to sanctuary in Austria, found homes for them in the United States and wrote an impassioned book about the uprising.

· In 1963 as a representative of the United States I participated in a remarkable semisecret conference in Leningrad at which I spoke forcefully for the liberation of the three former Baltic republics—Estonia, Latvia and Lithuania—much to the disgust of the Soviet conferees.

· In 1964 I traveled widely in the Russian provinces facing Afghanistan, and became aware that all was not well in the Soviet Union's many Asian republics. It was then that I first voiced a judgment whose validity became more apparent year by year: 'Russia is extremely vulnerable along her perimeters and in Siberia. If she launches any kind of outward aggression, she runs the risk of revolution in the non-Russian parts of her empire.'

· In the late 1960s I traveled four times along remote Russian flight lanes, catching glimpses of the distant frontiers, and my impression of fragile borders was intensified.

· In 1972 I accompanied President Nixon on his visit to Moscow, Iran and Poland, and I proved that I was never going to be a diplomat: At a huge public meeting in Moscow presided over by Ekaterina Furtseva, full-fledged member of the ruling Communist clique, and only female member of the Presidium, I became so outraged by the crude falsehoods she was peddling that I rose in the midst of her worst lies and stalked from the meeting, causing an uproar. Nixon would have been justified in sending me home for having caused a scandal, but a member of his staff confided: 'You served us well—made points we wanted to make but couldn't,' and I was allowed to stay. Not long thereafter, men in the Presidium fed up with Furtseva's tyrannical ways brought such grave charges against her—that she had expropriated government funds for the enhancement of her private dacha—that she was dismissed, and she died shortly thereafter in disgrace.

· From 1972 through 1981 I visited Poland nearly a dozen times, making myself familiar with all aspects of life under the Communist dictatorship imposed on that nation by the Soviet Union. At the conclusion of my studies I wrote a novel that depicted the heroism of the Polish people and the bleak harshness of life under Communist rule.

I thus acquired both a theoretical understanding of Communism and a practical experience of the system as it operated in Hungary, Russia, the non-Russian republics, Korea and Poland. I had combated the evil effects of Communism during my work with the Friends of Asia, had fought against it twice militarily in Hungary and in Korea, and had lived under its rule in Poland. But my intensive study of this twentieth-century phenomenon began when the United States government appointed me to a series of boards whose specific job it was to fight Communism. I would spend a quarter of a century at this task.

I was initially chosen for this kind of work by an exceptional man, one of those largely silent behind-the-scenes people who account for so much of what happens in government. Frank Shakespeare was a television executive whose personal politics made Genghis Khan and Bill Buckley seem like free-wheeling liberals. A graduate of Holy Cross, he was a medium-sized, onetime redhead with an ingratiating manner, a disarming Irish smile and a positive passion for aiming at the jugular. We would become trusted friends, a strange pair whose association began in the 1960s because the law required that he select some Democrat for an advisory board he controlled; I doubt if he was happy about taking me on, but he had learned that I was forthright in my Democratic allegiance and able to work at least as hard as he did. I found joy in watching him spin his webs and on several occasions have spoken strong words of endorsement in his behalf when he sought promotions, first to the ambassadorship in Portugal, later to the influential position as the president's personal representative at the Vatican.

I first met him when he was the pugnacious head of the United States Information Service, whose task it was to show foreign nations the constructive aspects of American life. Frank interpreted this as a directive to fight the Soviet Union, which, as a devout Catholic and confirmed supporter of capitalism he identified as the enemy. Had he been allowed by his advisory board, of which he made me a member, I do believe he would have invaded the three captive Baltic states in a rowboat.

The board that Shakespeare assembled was evaluated as 'unquestionably the most effective and best-run advisory board in the nation.' This was due not to any contribution I made, for I was very much the junior member, but to the rare skill demonstrated by its chairman, Frank Stanton, in running it. Of all the men I have known, Stanton utilized the highest percentage of whatever natural intelligence he was given at birth. I once calculated that he used about 96 percent of his abiliities, whereas I used no more than 56 percent of mine. He was soft-spoken, organized, incredibly swift in comprehending ideas and masterly in putting them into execution. To have known him was a privilege; to have worked with him for four or five years, an education.

His number two man when I came aboard was William F. Buckley, Jr., the right-wing ideologue and one of the funniest, most delightful and outrageous men in the nation. He and I were about as far apart politically as two men could be, but I held him in the warmest regard. Savagely brilliant and devastating in his witty dismissal of bores, he was one of the young men most influential in helping to swing the nation far to the right, a sinful performance for which I suppose God will forgive him, for he convinced me that God was of course both a Catholic and a conservative.

The third member was George Gallup, the pollster, an avuncular man with a wealth of accumulated wisdom and a gracious manner of presenting it. He surprised me by his extensive knowledge of nations other than the United States, information that he used when trying to determine American habits of thought. He spoke cautiously, but when some topic touched a deeply held opinion, he could be formidable, and he had a keen, practical sense of what radio broadcasting could accomplish in a cold war.

The fourth member was a longtime friend and delightful companion, Hobart Lewis, editor in chief of the *Reader's Digest*. Slow-spoken and conciliatory, Hobe always voiced the sensible conservative interpretation of a subject, but listened attentively if Stanton and I tried to knock it down. He was extremely knowledgeable and a stalwart supporter to have on one's side. When President Nixon visited in the Northeast, he often stayed with Lewis, who had been most active in Nixon's two campaigns for the presidency. In the bad summer of 1974 when Nixon was on the ropes, Hobe and I visited the White House with a bipartisan plan that might have enabled him to crawl out from under the mounting tragedy of Watergate. Hobe, understandably, wanted to help a friend; I sought to protect the office of the presidency, and I think we might have made some small contribution. But Rose Mary Woods, his personal secretary, told us: 'He's in terrible isolation. Sees no one but Bebe Rebozo. Not even Cabinet members can get in to see him. John Connally's been trying for days.' The solid counsel that Lewis wanted to give strengthened by my effort to line up Democrats who had the welfare of the nation at heart, was not allowed to be delivered, and when we retreated from the White House we knew that resignation had become inescapable.

Stanton's committee met each month in a suite at the Madison Hotel: on Sunday night we met with some important official of the government; at breakfast on Monday we were briefed by a major figure from the administration; and at luncheon we had as our guest a head of some major agency involved in work related to ours. Thus, in the years I served, I listened each year to some forty men such as David Packard of Defense, Elmo Zumwalt of the Navy, Pete Petersen of Commerce and Lawrence Eagleburger of State. The two lunches I remember best were the occasions when we listened to the strong and reassuring comments of John Ehrlichman of Mr. Nixon's staff, who would soon be in the headlines, and when I spoke warmly of Thomas Jefferson, only to be told by our guest Irving Kristol: 'I consider Jefferson to be one of the principal enemies of our nation and a man whose every idea ought to be combated.' I remember replying somewhat weakly: 'We seem to have a difference of opinion,' but he ignored me.

While on this board I visited as an informal inspector some nine different countries and covered myself with glory in a certain place where one of our young men was in considerable trouble and was about to be fired. I was known as a board member to whom staffers could apply for a second hearing, and after I had spent two days listening to this chap's lament about his mistreatment by an unfeeling superior and satisfying myself that he had indeed been abused, I wrote a strong report urging reconsideration, which was granted, saving the young man's career. Half a year later our inspector-general came to me and said without rancor: 'Michener, remember the staffer whose neck you saved? Against my recommendations? You might be interested in this follow-up,' and while he waited I read a harrowing statement. The young man, euphoric at having beaten the system with my assistance, had gone wild. He had cursed the head of the mission, slugged an assistant and been thrown out of a local disco bar, at whose exit door he tried to assault a policeman. 'Rather high spirits,' I said, but the inspector tapped the paper I was holding: 'Read the next part,' and I recall this is what it said: 'When we learned that he was spending far more money than his salary would warrant, we started an investigation and found that he was photographing his wife, Lucille, nude and in various interesting poses, developing the prints in our darkroom and selling them to local students.' Folding the papers neatly, I handed them back and said no more.

Under Stanton's guidance, our board did its best to give our agency good counsel in its fight against Communism. We suffered some disastrous mishandling of certain problems that we hastened to correct, but my worst memory is of our libraries abroad—those centers where local young people and university professors had access to the books about America that they needed—being severely bombed or blown to pieces. It astounded me that citizens of an undeveloped country, who need all the information and wisdom they could gather, would wantonly destroy the very agency that could help them. Often as the news reached headquarters concerning this or that library's destruction, I would visualize the carefully arranged reading room, the neat chairs, the rows of excellent books available to all who entered, and I would feel a deep sadness at the stupidity that had prompted such crimes. But never in my work for USIS did I doubt the value of what we were attempting abroad, because our enemies recognized the importance of keeping their own people in ignorance of our ideas based on freedom and democracy so that they could more easily enslave them. I was proud to be a soldier in such honorable warfare.

My next assignment brought me once again in conflict with the Soviet Union, for I was given an advisory job close to the high command of NASA (the National Aeronautics and Space Administration). I was the layman on this board of the world's foremost scientists and technical experts and I spent the years breathlessly trying to catch up, for almost every concept mentioned in our discussions was far more complex than anything I had ever dealt with before. I studied endlessly. I visited most of the NASA bases inspecting men and machines. I worked in the great laboratories. I tried out many of the training devices, watched launches, worked in control rooms, and came to know many of the second and third groups of astronauts who followed the first seven. At the end of my self-imposed training period, which lasted three full years, I understood our space program about as thoroughly as an average layman could, but far below the level of people like Walter Cronkite and Jules Bergman of television who had specialized in the field, and, of course, eons behind the great astronomers and astrophysicists who directed the program, but I did try to pull my weight.

In this work I was constantly reminded that in many areas of space exploration and utilization the Soviet Union was far ahead of us, a fact that most laymen did not appreciate. Russia had put the first satellite into orbit, *Sputnik;* the first man, Yuri Gagarin; and the first woman, Valentina Tereshkova. Its unmanned flights had been the first to bring samples back from the moon and first to photograph and name the features on the far side of that body. They had led, too, in explorations of Venus, had performed well with Mars, and had accomplished staggering feats of prolonged manned flight in space, far exceeding anything we did.

Mindful of our lagging in certain aspects of space exploration, I was exultant about our great triumphs: men walking on the surface of the moon, robotic landings on Mars, explorations of the far edges of our solar system, probes into the galaxy, and constant adventures into areas of space into which the Russians could not go because their technology was not sufficiently advanced. But, as in all our confrontations with the Russians, I had to be grudgingly admiring of their accomplishments and regretful that we seemed destined to be enemies instead of friends.

Periodically NASA assembled some thirty or forty of the best-qualified people in the nation to spend a couple of weeks together at some remote spot like Woods Hole and speculate on what space exploration might look like a quarter of a century down the line, and this was an exciting exercise. Nothing was too bizarre for us to speculate upon, but when our ideas were palpably absurd, they were either ignored or quickly disposed of. I worked in these sessions with some of the most scintillating minds I have ever known, men who lived constantly not on the frontier but infinitely beyond it, and I was awed by the power of their conceptions.

More than a decade before the idea of Star Wars surfaced in public, we studied available analyses of its basic principles and concluded that because of the magnitude of the space to be covered and the concentration of power required in each segment, the concept was not viable. I remember that several specific objections, some of which were too abstruse for me, were lodged against it, any one of which would disqualify it, but I am speaking only of the techniques and levels of information then available.

I gave my unflagging support to the idea of constructing a master computer, enormous in size and capacity, that would enable planners in all fields to attack a host of problems simultaneously. Its potential was best defined by an airplane designer who said: 'One of the greatest problems in designing an airplane is to determine how air will behave when it flows over the leading edge of the plane. Using a most intricate set of equations, we can analyze the problem for any specific point in the edge—wing tip, engine nacelle, cabin, Pitot tube area—but we obviously cannot afford to analyze all the points, for they are innumerable. So what we do is agree upon ten to twelve significant ones and extrapolate for the distances between. Now with the computer we're talking about we could analyze *all* the points simultaneously and produce an airplane completely suited to flying nose first through the air, no matter how violently its passage disturbs that air.'

We wanted that computer, but the scientists pointed out a major difficulty: 'To house the paperwork it would generate, or even the tapes on which the data were recorded, would require a set of buildings enormous in size.' When I asked how big the computer itself would have to be, they said: 'Not too big, of manageable size, but its capacity to generate data endlessly would be awesome. Especially if it were associated with the new space telescope.'

This gigantic telescope was to be inserted into a permanent orbit far above the atmosphere, whose elements disturb even the most powerful earthbound telescopes, which must waste much of their power simply penetrating the first score of miles. It would ride high in a region where nothing would impede its capacity to gather information from distances many times greater than those available to present telescopes. Even though I have been a galaxy connoisseur most of my adult life and know them as familiar neighbors, I cannot even guess what marvels await us when this great telescope starts to function. It will reveal wonders of which we have not dreamed, configurations which will bedazzle us and call for new theories of the universe, and it will bring even laymen pictures to tease and delight.*

One problem agitated NASA continuously: 'Should we specialize in manned space travel so heavily when unmanned exploration could be cheaper, less dangerous and more productive?' In something I wrote I postulated a debate between a scientist who plumped, as most do, for unmanned flight and a political leader, who had to pay the bills, who sponsored manned flight. I did my best to maintain an impartial position between them and shall do so here.

Briefly, most scientists know that unmanned vehicles projected far out into the solar system can do almost every important thing a manned flight can do at infinitely less cost and no danger to human life. It has been frustrating in recent years for knowing scientists to have to sit by and watch as time and equipment and money are dissipated in manned flights, when unmanned vehicles could have been speeding throughout the galaxy on missions almost guaranteed to deliver back to earth the data we seek. 'The present system,' such men argue, 'is wasteful and nonproductive, and it is scandalous that we persist in it.'

Proponents of manned flight counter the scientists' argument: 'Society will not agree to finance unmanned flights for an indefinite length of time, for the average taxpayer can see no return for his money. Such flights are monotonous, repetitive and largely unproductive of usable results. One tiny bit of additional knowledge about the moons of Saturn really does not justify its cost in effort and money. But once you put an

---

*After decades of analysis, preparation, checking and infuriating delays, the Hubble Space Telescope was launched in April 1990. By June 27 NASA realized that a trivial flaw in grinding the mirrors would make it impossible to send back to earth photographs of astronomical phenomena. Why had the mirrors not been tested? It would have cost too much.

American citizen inside that machine, you escalate the project to an entirely new level of excitement. You're back in the right-stuff arena that taxpayers can identify with—John Glenn, Neil Armstrong, Pete Conrad, they were men you could respect. Send an unmanned spaceship to Mars? People would lose interest at the end of the third day. Put two men in the same ship, people would watch breathlessly for the three years required. Two men and a woman? Even better. Two Americans, two Russians? For such an adventure we could find the money.'

My last concern, and my most persistent, was one about which I have not spoken before, but from my earliest days on the committee I was a strong advocate for allowing civilians to hitchhike a ride into space, and I furthered the applications of both Walter Cronkite and Jules Bergman. Had the program been given an earlier start, I too would have wanted to go with never a hint of hesitation. I urged such a program for three carefully evaluated reasons: (1) it could obviously be done, and safely, the work of John Young, Robert Crippen, Joe Engle and Richard Truly having proved the practicality of the shuttle; (2) Russia had carried many passengers into space, frequently citizens of other nations they wished to impress, and I felt we ought to catch up; and (3) I believed that the publicity to be garnered from such a flight would be advantageous to both NASA and the nation at large.

I served on the small committee that studied all aspects of the proposal and steadfastly defended the idea, although I remember that a woman member with experience in public relations did warn: 'You must also factor in the negative feedback if anything should go wrong with the mission. The presence of that civilian might do us great damage.' I was delighted when the government decided to forge ahead with the program, and again recommended that Cronkite and others be considered for selection as the first passenger. However, when someone, I never learned who, chose the lively New England science teacher Christa McAuliffe, I applauded: 'A stroke of genius.'

But I was even more pleased to see that a young woman I had worked with in those discussions about the future had been chosen. I had first met Judith Resnick in the astronaut offices in Houston and had talked with her several times about the possibility of her getting aboard one of the missions. At Woods Hole one summer we worked together for a couple of weeks, and in that time I found her to be a most solid young woman, skilled in her field and well qualified to defend her opinions in debate. Her constant cry was: 'Let's get more flights going and put me in one of them.' Sure enough, when Sally Ride broke the ice, Judith Resnick followed soon thereafter, with the delightful Dr. Anna Fisher not many months behind.

Judy Resnick was going to be the second woman to make two trips into space, Sally Ride having already done so, and I sent her a congratulatory note at having her dream come true so handsomely. As the *Challenger* prepared for that January takeoff with its civilian passenger I felt a sense of pride in being part of the team that had made this day possible, but I was not watching television at the crucial moment. A few moments after the launch my secretary called, her voice shaking: 'My God, Mr. Michener. Run to the television!' Despite the anguish in her voice I did not anticipate what I was going to see; that terrible bifurcated stream of debris signaling total disaster. I watched the horror as one branch slowly descended toward the sea and disappeared beneath the waves.

'Judy!' I cried as the ghostly trail vanished, and I could visualize the terrible scene in the cabin—I supposed that Judy had reached out to steady Christa McAuliffe—and then the darkness. It never occurred to me that the seven passengers might have died instantly in the blast, nor can I believe it now. They took the long plunge and it must have been terrifying.

The loss of that spaceship oppressed me. I had been with NASA when the prototype *Columbia* came on line and had interviewed its astronauts John Young and Robert Crippen, the latter in two extended visits. I was present for the first takeoff at Cape Kennedy and had watched with surging pride as Young, the Georgia wizard born without nerves, brought her safely down in California six days later. It was the greatest American triumph of the decade, and the subsequent flights had become almost routine. I remembered the meetings when our small committee argued so forcefully the pros and cons of civilian flight, and I recalled the quiet satisfaction I felt when the positions I had helped to defend were adopted. I felt as if I had personally sent Judy Resnik on the flight and had issued the invitation to Christa, and the sense of participatory guilt will never leave me.

Just as I finished my assignment with NASA I was asked to serve on what has probably been my most important job with the government, one that brought me in daily conflict with Communism in all its various manifestations. Always before, I had worked in an advisory capacity, but now I was placed on the board that actually managed the American stations fighting the propaganda battle of the airwaves with the Soviet Union. The Board for International Broadcasting in Washington manages two powerful stations that broadcast news originating from Munich, Germany: Radio Liberty to the constituent republics of the Soviet

Union; and Radio Free Europe to the captive nations behind the Iron Curtain. Although I was not the best candidate for the job, I had visited many of the Soviet republics, especially those in out-of-the-way areas, and I had worked in all the Iron Curtain countries except Bulgaria. I had also written a careful on-the-scene account of Hungary's anti-Communist revolution of 1956, and this had been translated into fifty-two languages. But I was not your classic cold war proponent, for although I saw clearly the menace of Communist Russia's expansionism and had inveighed against it, I lived for the day when the two great powers, the United States and Russia, could reach some kind of rapprochement. I never lost faith that this would one day occur, but in the meantime I was not only ready but eager to broadcast the truth about what was happening in the Soviet Union and in the nations it occupied.

The composition of the governing board gave me considerable pleasure, since its chairman was my old friend Frank Shakespeare, and this provided an opportunity to watch him once more in forceful action. He was as dedicated an anti-Soviet warrior as ever, prodding his radio stations to combat Russian propaganda and secrecy wherever and however possible. Because of my association with the Hungarian uprising in 1956, when the belligerence of the American broadcasts ignited false hopes among the freedom fighters, I was one of several who kept reminding Frank that our stations must never again raise hopes behind the Iron Curtain that we would be unable to support, and he was careful to broadcast truth, not incitement to rebellion. Nevertheless, many in our government wanted to silence our radios because of one unavoidable gaffe or another, and Shakespeare himself came under heavy fire because of his combative nature. I defended him, for I knew that although he saw Soviet-American relations as an eternal battleground he was far from being a damned fool, as his detractors sometimes called him.

Since his board consisted of nine members, he was entitled to have four loyal Republicans besides himself, and he chose with care. His right-hand man was Malcolm Forbes, Jr., a brilliant financial operative and a devout Republican who sometimes sounded as if he considered *The Wall Street Journal* a little left of center. He was a most rewarding man to work with, sagacious and a tough intellectual fighter against Communism. When strangers heard me speak favorably of him, they would ask: 'Is he that old Forbes billionaire who floats around in balloons?' and I would reply: 'No, he's the young Forbes millionaire who tends shop while his dad is out fooling with his toys.'

The other three Republican stalwarts were formidable veteran fighters for causes they believed in, especially our free society: Clair Burgener, the longtime congressman from Southern California; Ed Nye, head of one of the world's largest public relations firms and a Republican kingmaker; and Arch Madsen, soft-spoken powerhouse who ran the television and radio empire of the Mormon Church. They were good men to work with.

But it was in his selection of the four obligatory Democrats that Shakespeare showed his Machiavellian skill at its conniving best. After choosing me because I was an outspoken liberal and thus conspicuous as a non-Republican, he made a brilliant choice: Lane Kirkland, the feisty labor leader who bore a hundred battle scars that attested to his willingness to fight for workingmen. With Kirkland aboard, no one could charge us with being a rubber stamp for the administration. But now Shakespeare proved his wizardry, for he filled the remaining two Democratic slots with two extremely sharp men who were technically registered as Democrats but whose personal convictions and public behavior placed them at the extreme right of the Republican party: Ben Wattenberg, the wise and witty statistician and political columnist, and Michael Novak, the Catholic theologian, United Nations counselor and conservative commentator. These two were among the brightest of their generation, and they were so sharp-witted that I found it a delight to work with them, despite their extreme conservatism.

Shakespeare had converted the obligatory ratio of five Republicans to four Democrats into seven hard-core conservatives counterbalanced by two liberals, exactly the kind of mix he wanted. But Kirkland and I were not powerless, for we each had access to the public prints, and if the board misbehaved in any egregious way we could blow the whistle—and no one doubted that we would if we had to. That was never necessary.

Some of the most instructive days in my later years were the sessions of this board, either in Munich or in Washington. My fellow members were amazingly competent; we had first-class managers; and we did our best to give our stations both constructive leadership in the propaganda wars and full support when any scandal broke. Many problems arose when American citizens like us tried to supervise foreign nationals who broadcast in their own language to their own people. I sometimes felt that many of our European employees would like to start revolutions in their homelands tomorrow—they were tough characters who had been through the wars—but it was our job to disseminate accurate news, not to foment rebellion. Many critics cried: 'Close down the stations! They do more harm than good!' but having some sense of what life behind the curtain was like, I knew that sometimes we accomplished wonders by just keeping hope alive. I was proud to be part of that effort.*

My work in Washington on various committees and boards was both exciting and rewarding because I worked with some highly intelligent political leaders. Indeed, I saw our federal government at its best, for the elected officials in charge of matters in which I was interested were not only first-class intellects but also skilled political operatives. J. William Fulbright, the junior senator from Arkansas, was strongly opposed to one of the projects on which I was working, but he expressed his opinion so openly and sensibly that it was almost a pleasure to debate with him. Dante Fascell, a congressman from Florida, was a tower of strength in the foreign affairs committee he led; Claiborne Pell of Rhode Island, as a former employee of the State Department, was exceptionally perceptive in foreign affairs; and Alan Simpson of Wyoming talked sense.

I received a lesson in Washington maneuvering when I went before the Senate Foreign Relations Committee to be confirmed for an appointment to the governing board of the agency broadcasting into Russia. Jesse Helms of North Carolina tenaciously opposed everything I stood for, but he did so in such an ingratiating way, using exaggerated courtesy and never raising his voice or displaying anything but the warmest regard for me, and cut down my position with such elegant precision that I almost wanted to applaud when he finished. I did not mind being abused in high style, but was greatly pleased that he was prevented from placing his right-wing nominee on our board.

The exception to the graciousness with which we fought our battles, in which I had as many respected friends among the Republican opposition as among the Democratic majority, was a horrendous one that involved Wayne Hays, the venal congressman from Ohio, who had manipulated his chairmanship of a housekeeping committee into a czardom of power. 'Above all,' I was told upon joining the USIS board, 'be nice to Wayne Hays, because he has the power of life and death over

*In the August 1991 coup that tried to drag Russia back to strong-armed Communism, while Mikhail Gorbachev was under house arrest in the Crimea, his courage was sustained by foreign shortwave radio broadcasts, including those from the station our group had worked so diligently to preserve for just such an emergency. When the coup was defeated, Boris Yeltsin, mindful of the stout support our Radio Liberty had provided in recent years, invited us to open an office in Moscow—an amazing victory for truth, freedom and human decency.

us, as he does over congressmen, too.' My friend explained that Hays had quietly arrogated to himself the assignment of congressmen's offices, telephone services and parking slots: 'You oppose Wayne and you find yourself parking your car one mile from downtown Baltimore.'

I was always attentive to Hays and paid him due deference not because he could do anything to me personally but because I knew he had power over my board, which I had to protect. I learned how ugly his abuse of power could be when he sent us to hire immediately, for a sensitive post requiring background and judgment, one of his cronies who was appallingly inept. The officer to whose staff Hays's favorite was to be assigned said of him: 'The man's a Neanderthal. I doubt if he could rise to the Cro-Magnon stage in three hundred thousand years,' and we had to let Hays know: 'Wayne, your man is simply not capable. Sorry.' His response was simple and straightforward: 'I understand what you're saying. Now I hope you understand what I'm saying. Your agency will not receive five cents in funds until you appoint my man to the job I've selected for him.'

We junior members on the board almost laughed at such a blatant threat but the old-timers pointed out: 'He means what he says. Our hundred-million-dollar budget depends on our hiring his man—right now.' We refused, and that week Hays blocked all funds for our agency. When months passed without any money, and salaries of men and women in the field were being held ransom, it fell to Frank Stanton and me to see what kind of truce could be worked out, and a memorable meeting took place in the congressman's office. He respected Stanton as the head of a great television empire and he had read two of my books, so we assumed that we might have some leverage with him, but he did not even rise to greet us—he remained sitting with his feet on top of his cluttered desk. He wore a garish red-white-and-blue checkerboard sports jacket and kept a cigar stuck in his mouth while in the most vulgar and profane way he rejected every plea we made: 'You want your agency funds restored? Hire my man, and do it soon because my patience with you clowns is running out.'

Neither Stanton nor I was capable of wrestling with Hays in the snake pit he had built for himself; we were not that brutal, we did not express ourselves in his terms, which included blackmail as a strategy to solve any issue. We retreated from our session totally defeated, and said to our board: 'This fight is now in its eighteenth month and our people in the field are really suffering. We recommend that we hire his man.'

This was so repugnant to the other members of the board that they would have rejected our advice had Stanton not pointed out that if we did not hire Hays's man our budget would be held up for another eighteen months, which would drive us out of business. One member cried: 'No one congressman can do that!' and we replied: 'Oh yes, he can, if he's Wayne Hays.'

We hired the man, but kept him safely isolated. At the next public hearing before Hays's committee, Wayne eulogized Stanton and me from the podium as 'two of the finest public servants, men of the highest reputation,' and the budget went through.

Not long after this, Hays was trapped by congressmen he had bullied the way he abused Stanton and me. They disclosed to the Washington press that Hays had selected as an employee of Congress an attractive but unskilled young lady who served solely as his personal friend. She could not by her own confession type or file or perform any other normal secretarial functions. When a national scandal erupted, Hays was drummed out of office, his years of tyranny ended.

I relate this affair in detail because of the amusing aftermath. When word of the czar's fall from power circulated, few could have been more jubilant than the members of our board, for we had really suffered under his despotism—Stanton and I more personally than most. But not one of us telephoned the other to gloat over the autocrat's fall—we were afraid that Hays might have tapped our phones and we fully expected him to come roaring back to Congress, determined to wreak vengeance on any who had laughed at his disgrace.

In 1972, when President Nixon flew to his historic meeting with Chinese leaders in the capital, which was still called Peking, the big press plane that accompanied him had two extra seats after all the media people had been accommodated. These were assigned at the last moment to Bill Buckley and me, and we flew as interested citizens.

When people, after the scandal of Watergate, ask me: 'How can you speak well of Nixon? Why would you have tried to save his presidency?' I reply: 'You didn't see him in China at the apex of his career. He was sharp, daring and a shrewd negotiator.' As so often happens in political life, and as would happen again with President Ronald Reagan, it is the conservative famed for his right-wing policies who can best make a complete moral and political volte-face and strike a sensible deal with his adversaries. Had Democratic presidents made these complete reversals in their relationships with Communist China and Russia, they would have been impeached; when the conservative Republican leaders did the about-face, we hailed it as political genius, and in Nixon's case it was.

I had met the Chinese premier, Chou En-lai, for several conversations during the Bandung Conference of 1955, when twenty-nine nations dissatisfied with the leadership provided by the major industrial nations met in stormy sessions to protest and pass resolutions calling for a rearrangement of world power. I had been deeply impressed by Chou's conciliatory performance there and had told him so; now I was meeting him after he had become one of the most powerful leaders in the world, and again I congratulated him as we talked of the days in Bandung.

The Chinese had assigned as guide to me the head of what would be their equivalent of Associated Press, and he and his wife were examples of how thoroughly Mao Tse-tung's people worked, for the man knew all about me and used me to excellent purpose to learn about American politics. But I also used him by insisting that he take my complaints to his superiors, because the Chinese had been almost contemptuous of President Nixon and his party. I warned my guide: 'Your people must understand that if this chilly reception continues, the United States will play its Russian card, and when that happens China will be completely isolated.' Buckley was telling his guide the same, and what we said must have been fortified by others, for my guide became intensely interested in American-Russian-Chinese relations and, with the assistance of his wife, interrogated me intensively. He was well informed and in no way antagonistic, and he assured me that Mao and Chou were aware of our displeasure at the poor reception and would change that situation immediately. The close of the China visit was much more pleasant than the beginning.

Having started with Nixon on his 1972 mission, I stayed with him on his visits later that year to the Soviet Union, Iran and Poland, and although the results were less spectacular than in China, he himself appeared at better advantage. He was an admirable negotiator, a suave representative and a man of solid perceptions. He shone wherever he went and impressed all who met him with his obviously sincere desire for improved relations. People who would later have grounds to denigrate him would have difficulty ignoring these real triumphs of foreign policy.

In Iran I proved that I was unfit to be a secret agent, because these were the days when Mohammed Reza Shah Pahlavi was riding high and I was not clever enough to detect that his was a cardboard throne that would soon be toppled. But I was amused to see the leaders of our nation kowtowing to him because, as I kept reminding my fellow scribes: 'Remember that in 1919 his father was a peasant who got a job in the cavalry looking after the horses, a stable boy, if you please.'

'How did his son become Shah?'

'Revolts within the army, the old man becomes a general, revolts within the state, he becomes Shah. When he dies, his son inherits the job and awards himself the august title Shah-in-Shah.' But although I had known Iran moderately well prior to Nixon's visit, I was not perceptive enough to see how imperiled was the pompous King of Kings.

My perceptions were sharper when we stopped in Poland, my first visit to that country, for even in a whirlwind tour I became so convinced that events of great moment would have to erupt here that I would return time and again to study this unfortunate but heroic land with no defensible frontiers. In time I knew it so intimately that I would devote several years to exploring the meaning of Poland so that I could write about it in a coherent way.

In my travels with President Nixon I learned a limited amount about China, Russia, Iran and Poland, but a great deal about Nixon himself. I saw at close hand how his wife strove to support his missions and how she seemed always to be relegated to the background. I saw how Nixon maintained his uneasy relationship with the press, and I reached the conclusion that although he had a master touch in foreign relations, he was not at ease with his own people or his own country. Three times I would be his guest at the White House; once with the USIS board I would meet with him in the Oval Office as he wrestled with problems in Chile, and always I would see an extremely bright man, well informed on a wide variety of subjects, and one eager to please his constituency and leave a solid reputation behind.

When the Watergate scandals broke I told anyone who would listen: 'Eisenhower or Kennedy would handle this in one television broadcast: "We've made a wretched mistake, but the men principally responsible have been fired. I apologize for having let it happen and promise you it will never recur." And the American people would have bought it. Nixon can do the same.' But he never accepted the responsibility. I felt so grieved at seeing a powerful man go down that, as I said earlier, I volunteered to help stem the rot, and when this proved futile, I was one of the first to advise, in the pages of *The New York Times,* that he resign on the grounds that used to be used to get rid of faulty emperors in China: 'The mandate of heaven has been withdrawn.' He had lost the nation's confidence. I did not exult when he departed, for I had seen that he could have been a much better man than he proved to be in that dreadful year of 1974.

My other political service was a more rewarding experience in that it involved constructive counseling. In 1983, when American troops were slated to invade Grenada, our military leaders made a decision that seemed sensible to them at the time but perilously wrong in retrospect: 'We'll keep this operation entirely secret, both in planning and performance. Tell the news media nothing till it's neatly wrapped up.' The invasion took place within a total news blackout and all reporters, whether press or television, were kept totally uninformed till a decision had been reached and victory assured.

After the event all hell broke loose, because a principal tenet of warfare as conducted by a democracy—the electorate must be kept informed and involved—had been breached. Defenders of both the news media and the national welfare condemned this military arrogance so bitterly that the Pentagon realized, far too late, that it had run a fearful risk in conducting a secret war.

The criticism grew so strong that Defense Secretary Caspar Weinberger did a sensible thing: he consulted his Harvard classmate, Theodore White, the highly regarded political writer, and White recommended that Weinberger assemble a group of unexcitable older newsmen who had seen a lot of war to advise the military on how to avoid the pitfalls of the Grenada operation. This was done, and at the first Washington meeting of the small group Caspar and Teddy had selected, there were several who were veterans of a score of major battles in the field and policy struggles with their newspapers and television stations. Bob Sherrod, who had written some of the great on-the-scene reports of the Pacific war, was there, as were Walter Cronkite, who had covered the European theater; Eric Sevareid, with his wide knowledge of military affairs; and, of course, Teddy White, who had covered war in China. I was probably the oldest member, with extensive knowledge of both World War II and the Korean War. There was, of course, a public committee of experienced veterans meeting on this problem, too, and it included several of my friends, but we were the private clean-up crew whose discussions and findings would be kept private.

Our purpose was to help the military leaders avoid future actions that would alienate them from the general public, and although I played only a minor role in the discussions, it did fall to me to make the opening statement: 'For the military to argue that they kept the press out to protect reporters lest they get hurt is not only preposterous but degrading. In Korea the percentage of press people killed in action was higher than that of any of the armed services. We went everywhere, took all risks, and in a shocking number of cases saw our fellow reporters killed. Your generals must in decency not use that excuse again.'

Next I made my important point: 'The easiest way for an army to be defeated is for the home front to revolt against it. This happened to Russia in World War I and in a sense to Italy and Germany in World War II. A sequence of Grenadas, especially if a couple turn sour, could have a devastating effect on civilian morale and might erode support to a disastrous degree. Please, please take the whole society into your confidence if you start a military action.'

'Surely secrecy should be maintained in actual operations?' a general asked, and I said: 'Of course. Even far into the battle. But the general public must be allowed to know that a war is going on.'

At that point White and Cronkite assumed command of the discussion and their counsel was far more specific and relevant than mine. In the various meetings our informal committee held with Weinberger the harsh facts of military-civilian interrelationships were examined, and all of us older civilian men advised strenuously against secret military operations of any magnitude. At the same time we recognized and even appreciated the military's inherent distrust of newsmen, who seem so often to get military men into trouble.

Weinberger knew well what we were talking about and how relevant our recommendations were. I found him sharp, but left our final session suspecting that when another Grenada loomed, as it might at any moment in Central America, the inclination of the field commanders would still be: 'Keep the damned media away. They can only cause us trouble.' We were worried about the consequences if secrecy became the rule.

Shortly thereafter Teddy White died prematurely, and we met no more, but I believe we had said all we were entitled to say, and we had been heard.*

Why did I feel so strongly on such matters and what qualified me to speak so firmly? Two experiences.

Even though I could have been excused from service because of my religion, I had participated in World War II, a war that practically every American citizen had supported. No matter how deeply I penetrated into the recesses of the New Guinea jungle or how isolated I was on a remote coral atoll, I could feel the support of my countrymen and was reassured.

*Every principle that our committee recommended was ignored and violated in the Gulf crisis, where the military opted for the terribly dangerous strategy of fighting an overseas war without allowing on-the-spot press coverage. If our military persists in this arrogance, it will inevitably lose essential support.

In the Korean War I'd had an opposite experience: our democracy lacked the courage either to declare war against the Communists or to mobilize the civilian economy in support of the quasi-war we were fighting. Arbitrarily we told certain young men: 'You go to the icy ridges in Korea and protect us,' while telling other young men of similar age and background: 'You can remain home and earn a pile of money.' At the same time we assured the general public: 'Don't inconvenience yourself. Don't even pause in whatever you're doing. Make a bundle. There's no war.'

I was so disgusted with this unjust posture that I left my civilian work and, although approaching fifty, went to Korea. I accompanied the Marines on their retreat from the Hungnam reservoirs, flew combat missions with the Navy off their carriers, and served with a remarkable Marine division on the front farthest north in midwinter. The more I saw of the war, the more I realized how bitterly wrong it was for a democracy to engage in battle on foreign soil without enlisting the support of its entire civilian population. From the trenches and carriers I drafted an impassioned protest against the imposition of an unacceptable burden on the few who were called upon to fight. I knew then that if we got away with such immorality in Korea, and we did, we would be tempted to use the same strategy again, and we did—in Vietnam. When the troops of the Ohio National Guard murdered four student antiwar protesters at Kent State University in Ohio in 1970, I hurried out to investigate and found myself at the very heart of the danger I had foreseen so clearly in Korea. Surrounded by young men of draft age who did not want to go to Vietnam, I counseled many of them in long evening sessions after my day's work was done. They knew that the way the war was being conducted was militarily ridiculous, with no real drive to win, and disgraceful on a human level, with disadvantaged young men being called to overseas service while privileged young men had four escape hatches about which they were cynically informed: 'Mr. Michener, we face tough choices we have to make before our draft numbers come up. Safest and best is to hide in graduate school, law or medicine. Next best is to say we want to become teachers. Third best is to run off to Canada or Sweden. Fourth best is to wangle a spot in the National Guard, but if you do that you run a risk, though a very slight one, that your unit might be called up.'

Invariably I reminded them: 'There's a fifth way, the one I took in the other wars. Allow yourself to be drafted.'

When they said quite openly that they wanted none of that, I accepted their decision and then tried to analyze each of their options: 'Law and medicine are honorable careers and I see nothing wrong in pursuing them, but I think you would be better doctors and lawyers if you served your country first. I've been a teacher and know what dedication is required to work long hours for little pay. I don't think you ought to use that as a refuge, because we need good teachers, not runaways. Repugnant as it would be for me to kite out to either Canada or Sweden, I appreciate the reasons that might impel you to go, but I fear you'd have a heavy conscience later on, and undoubtedly even suffer legal penalties.'

'What about the National Guard?'

Here I faced an ugly dilemma, for although I was well aware that many young men looked on the National Guard as the most honorable way to avoid overseas service, I had had an experience that colored my views on the matter. For one long spell I served with a Marine division in the worst part of the Korean mountain front. Terrible weather, worse terrain. I lived in the tent next to General Selden, a tough old bird, and every night he invited me to attend the briefings for the next day, and they went like this: 'Tomorrow we attack at 0400. On our left flank we have those ROK's and we know they'll go forward with us. On our right flank we have that National Guard unit from''—and he mentioned the state from which it came—"so we have to be prepared for various contingencies. If they go forward with us and the ROK, fine, but of course they never do. If they stay in place but refuse to do their share, we must rush extra men to the right corner where their absence will make us vulnerable. If they start forward but then run back, we'll have to protect our whole right flank.' And that was the nature of each night's briefing.

When I asked why General Ridgway didn't remove the Guard unit from the line, Selden explained: 'Politics. If he did that, which he should, every National Guard general in the United States, and they're politicians you understand, not military men, would raise hell. Claim that we're downgrading the Guard.' He looked glum, then added: 'You know the problem with that unit over there: Mothers back in the home state'—he mentioned one of the wealthy, favored states—'protest to the papers: "Why should our sons have to go to Korea when the government could just as easily send units from the backward states like Mississippi or Arkansas?" When you have a Guard unit on your flank, you can count on having big trouble, political trouble.'

I told the young men at Kent State: 'I accompanied our Marines on several night patrols, and we could never depend on the National Guard unit to scout their terrain. They didn't like to go out at night. So don't ask me to recommend the Guard as a way out. It's available, but is it honorable?'

The Haddock Family

Robert

Arthur

aura

Hannah

Mabel

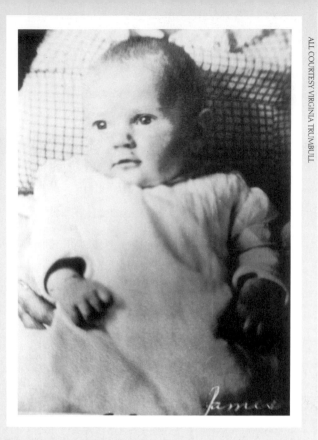

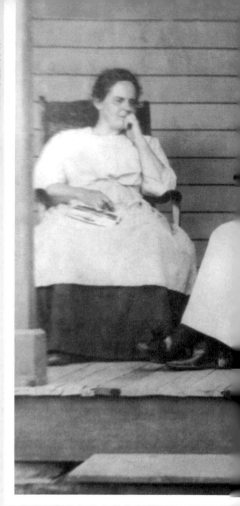

*Age two months,
and two years*

The house on Main Street

Left to right, top, Mabel, Laura, Hannah; bottom, Dorothy, Noel, James

Mabel

Mabel and Edwin Michener on their wedding day

Growing up

*Graduating from Doylestown High (left)
and Swarthmore College*

Young naval officer

Writing *Tales of the South Pacific* in a Quonset hut
on Espiritu Santo island, 4:00 A.M.

Aggie Grey

Josh Logan, Richard Rodgers, Oscar Hammerstein,
Mary Martin, James Michener

Mari Sabusawa Michener and husband

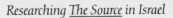

Researching <u>The Source</u> in Israel

© JOHN KINGS

*Researching on
the Mexican border
at El Paso (left),
and the law
in Marfa for
<u>Texas</u>*

© JOHN KINGS

Researching <u>Centennial</u> in Wyoming

*Researching
in Alaska
for the novel
<u>Alaska</u>*

*The writer standing very still
at the running of the bulls
in Pamplona*

*With the Cuban poet
Pablo Fernández
while researching
Six Days in Havana*

The Random House team in the 1970s: Bert Krantz, Albert Erskine, James Michener, Tony Wimpfheimer, Donald Klopfer

A visit in Rome with an old friend

*Receiving the nation's highest award for a civilian,
the Presidential Medal of Freedom, 1977*

Texas governor Ann Richards, Queen Elizabeth II, and Prince Philip

Keeping current

*Enjoying a Hans Hofmann painting in
the Michener Art Collection at the University of Texas*

With students

*Five Texas writers: (left to right) Liz Carpenter, Cactus Pryor,
Elizabeth Crook, James Michener, Stephen Harrigan*

At work

With those experiences modifying my attitudes toward the Vietnam war it is understandable that I did not want to become involved in what was a shameless adventure. Without doubt it was one of the most deplorable our nation has ever been involved in, not because the enlisted men in the field performed poorly, or because the young officers from West Point and Annapolis failed to do their jobs, but because as a nation we believed we could fight a war without our entire nation's being mobilized to prosecute the war, and because we adopted the hideous policy of sending the sons of poor families to do the fighting while the sons of the rich were offered a cheap escape. The conclusions I had drawn about the immoral aspects of the Korean War were reinforced by the injustices of our system in Vietnam.

My reaction to the efforts to avoid service was illogical: I understood when the young men who talked with me that winter at Kent State tried desperately to get into graduate school, and I turned my head when they enrolled to become teachers without any inclination for a career in education; I deplored their seeking asylum in some foreign country but knew why they were doing it; but I felt a kind of disgust for those who sneaked into the National Guard, for they were using a sly military trick to avoid an honorable commitment.

My work for the government ended in 1989, when, at the age of eighty-two, I retired voluntarily from the last of my assignments. Ironically, no sooner had I quit helping in the long battle against the Soviet Union than Europe began to enjoy the very freedoms for which I had struggled with pen and arms and personal resolve. Two nations that I had grown to love in the years of their distress—Hungary and Poland—attained liberties undreamed of when I worked there. Afghanistan saw the Russian retreat,* and victory seemed to be blossoming in all quarters.

As to my evaluation of Mikhail Gorbachev, I remember one of the last judgments volunteered at our Munich radio station prior to my departure: 'We are certain that *glasnost* and *perestroika* are real. All the information we receive from behind the Iron Curtain confirms that. The

---

*For a dozen years I served as chairman of a committee devoted to helping Afghan freedom fighters sustain their battle against the Russian invaders, and we collected substantial funds to help keep our men in the field. But when victory was achieved, I had a sad feeling that I had supported and helped to put in power the same kind of fanatical Muslim mullahs who were behaving so abominably in Iran, and I could visualize myself in the years ahead collecting new funds to oust the very fanatics I had helped place in command of this savage, wonderful nation, which I remember with such affection.

Baltic republics long for freedom. The Ukraine is hopeful. There are strong currents in Siberia. And all along the perimeter people strike for freedom. Incredible things are happening in Poland and Hungary, and the two Germanys are acting once more like brothers. So we know it's happening. But what it means, and how secure Gorbachev is in his leadership we cannot even guess.'

On a more relaxed note: One afternoon officials in Washington telephoned me with the surprising information I was to be appointed to the select committee that determines what postage stamps the government shall issue. If this sounds like a fairly routine or even dull task, one should listen in on the quarterly meetings of that group.

Few of the collateral operations of the government are more fraught with emotion, logrolling, pressure and even anger than this matter of what agencies and individuals should be honored on our postage stamps. By this device the popular heroes of the republic are identified and in a sense sanctified, so the competition is intense. If the state of Nebraska is honored, citizens of Alaska demand equal treatment. If farmers are glorified, engineers shout for attention. And the pressure becomes intense or even bitter when coonhounds are honored but collies are not. Hundreds and even thousands of groups clamor for deification, and to the committee falls the onerous and sometimes hilarious task of sorting out the unacceptables and then adjudicating among the eligibles.

Ridiculous as the competition sometimes becomes, the general process is not a trivial one, for if a nation keeps its issuing of stamps in reasonably good order, it will garner through the years an immense profit from merely selling those stamps to hungry collectors. This profit, for which no extra work need be done or services provided, can run into millions of dollars a year and can be lost if too many stamps or ones that are too ugly are issued, or if scandal touches their production. History is replete with sad tales of nations that destroyed their credibility and thus their lucrative sales by allowing or even supervising questionable practices. Today no serious collector would pay a penny for the stamps of such countries, while the wonderfully designed and chaste stamps of the British Empire, for example, grow each year in popularity and value.

Because the United States issued some really horrible stamps prior to the operations of our committee, our stamps internationally rank only in the second tier, but very high in that, and in the past three or four decades the improvement has been such that our reputation has soared. To be recognized as having philatelic merit a stamp must be issued for a legitimate postal use by a nation with a respectable reputation. It must be handsome in design and must depict some worthy or extremely interesting subject matter. While I hold my nose when looking at some of the junk that was forced upon our committee by political pressure, I glow with pride when I recall some of the best that I helped sponsor.

Two ironclad rules saved us from embarrassment: (1) We will issue no stamp honoring a specific religion; (2) We will authorize no stamp honoring an individual until he or she has been dead ten years, former presidents of the United States excepted. With that preamble, let me relate a handful of typical problems.

On the day in 1977 when Elvis Presley died prematurely, fat and dissolute at the age of forty-two, a frenzied movement was launched to have the event memorialized as a national holiday, with intense pressure applied on the stamp committee to honor him immediately. The movement spread, and not even our citation of the rule requiring the ten-year wait satisfied his grief-crazed fans: 'Elvis is not an ordinary man. He's bigger than presidents. He deserves his own rules.' When one group learned that I was on the committee, and this was some time after his death, they descended upon me with anguished pleas: 'Mr. Michener, Elvis must be honored. He's the most important American of this century.' When I asked, 'What about Franklin Roosevelt or General Eisenhower?' they said scornfully: 'Politicians, generals, who gives a damn about them? Elvis is something like a saint, bigger than life, bigger than anything.' I shocked the group by saying: 'I've never heard a Presley song. I've never seen a Presley movie.' Drawing back in horror, they asked: 'Where in hell have you been? The biggest thing of the century and you missed it?' I tried to explain that to the general public Elvis might be somewhat less important than they thought, and the reply of the leader was full of obscenities. The pressure never let up; there had never been anything like it in philatelic history. On the tenth anniversary of Presley's death it was reported that a stamp might be issued honoring the man whom his fans still believe to have been the greatest American of this century.

The second most intense campaign that I remember, and I used to receive a flood of mail promoting this cause or that well-known person, began when the huge family of the American woman who pioneered time-and-motion industrial studies in the early years of this century decided that she must be honored. Lillian Gilbreth had twelve children; they married and had their own numerous children, grandchildren and great-grandchildren, each of whom had at least twelve friends. Mrs. Gilbreth also belonged to several learned societies, and all their members had friends, so now the total number of people interested became astronomical, and it seemed as if each of them wrote to me and all the other members of the committee—profit to the government from the sale of ordinary stamps to the Gilbreths alone must have been sizable— and in the end we had to capitulate, or half the United States would have been alienated.

A campaign almost as volatile was launched by a large engineering society whose members demanded a stamp honoring their profession, and they went about their lobbying with a professionalism that was awesome. Since I had been inundated with mail, I assumed that we would again have to surrender, but to my surprise our feisty chairman withstood the onslaught with the most adroit letter of negative decision written during my tenure: 'I have received hundreds of letters imploring us to grant you a postage stamp honoring your society, but I don't think engineers respect stamps much or really need them, because every piece of mail I received had metered postage with not a stamp in the lot.'

This chairman, Belmont Faries, was an ideal man for his job, a tough bird who for many years had been stamp editor of the *Washington Star,* and who knew all aspects of philately, from both the producers' and the collectors' point of view. He knew all the scams, all the ingenious strategies by which enthusiasts tried to slip their favorite activity or person past our committee. Three examples of his leadership will illustrate how he operated.

Because I am often a coward, I shall call this European nation Splendovia, famous among other things for a large number of senators and representatives of Splendovian ancestry in the U.S. Congress. These legislators had formed a committee that hammered at us month after month to honor Splendovian accomplishments. By these tactics they were making our stamps look as if only Splendovians had ever been adventurous or run big businesses or been elected to office or written books. I thought we had pretty well exhausted the field when the congressional group insisted upon yet one more Splendovian memorial, but we simply could not think of anyone we had missed. Our committee included several excellent historians, men and women of the widest knowledge, but when a Splendovian name was finally proposed by the enthusiastic congressmen, our historians had to admit that they had never heard of the man. When they asked: 'Suppose we do issue the stamp. How do we justify it to collectors?' I suggested, in an attempt to be witty: 'Let's announce that he was the first man in history to breed Plymouth Rock chickens west of the 87th Meridian.' This occasioned some robust laughter, but not from Faries, who reminded us: 'This

matter is terribly important to the Splendovians. It's one of their legitimate ways to force themselves into the history of the nation. We'll
publish some rationalization for the stamp, but I doubt if anyone will
ever read it or buy the stamp.'

At our June meeting one year he was obviously grim as he rapped for
order: 'Ladies and gentlemen, I shall make an announcement and for
the first time in all our meetings I will entertain no comment or motions
when I am through. El Supremo insists that a stamp be issued honoring
a Hispanic, any Hispanic, and it is to be on sale by August fifteenth. The
national election will be held, as you know, in November.'

He was seen at his ecumenical best, I think, when a group of homosexual organizations petitioned for a stamp on the understandable grounds
that they represented a considerable segment of the population. He
presented their demand without any show of emotion and then sat back
as the expected storm broke. Because this petition arrived in the years
when there could be free discussion of such matters, when, as one might
say, 'the issue had come out of the closet,' there was no cry of moral
outrage and no snide bashing of unconventional life-styles. There was,
however, careful analysis of the request, with some members pointing
out that we had rejected groups much larger than this one and others
asking whether we really wanted to honor a group so far removed from
the historical norm. I gave the little speech the others probably expected,
pointing out that homosexuals were a part of the national fabric, and
that justice required equal treatment, etc., etc., but after having listened
to me with the greatest patience, Faries said quietly: 'I believe this
debate is meaningless, because we've already covered the problem.
We've honored a famous homosexual. Look at our issue Number 2010.'
When we rapidly shuffled our index of all U.S. stamps ever issued, we
found 2010, which was a benign scene from a novel by Horatio Alger,
whom we had honored with a delightful stamp in 1982.

'Yes,' Delmont said in his usual quiet voice, 'Alger was the son of a
respected Unitarian minister in New England. He attended Harvard
Divinity School and became a clergyman himself, gaining appointment
to an important church in Massachusetts. Unfortunately, he had such
an ungovernable fondness for choirboys that he was dismissed from his
church in disgrace and fled to New York, where, under a new name, he
gained fame by writing about older men who became attached to home-
less waifs, helping them gain fame and fortune. We printed 107,605,000
copies of his stamp. I think this shows we have solved this delicate
subject rather nicely, and I shall so inform the applicants.' We closed
our catalogs and moved to other business.

One continued battle confronted our committee. We did our best to obey the rule 'No religious stamps,' but the counterpressures were never-ending. The Catholics, who were both numerous and led by gifted persuaders, tried every imaginable trick to outsmart us, proposing stamps that clearly honored their religion but were disguised in various clever ways so as to slip into one of the acceptable categories. We were just as adroit in nullifying their campaigns, but in 1982 their quarterback swept right around our defensive backs. They proposed and won a stamp honoring Saint Francis of Assisi, not as a religious figure but as a nature lover who talked to birds. It was a beautiful maroon stamp depicting Saint Francis at his lovable best, and it raised a storm of protests from other religions.

In self-defense lest we get our heads broken, we honored Martin Luther as a philosopher and the famous old synagogue in Touro, Rhode Island, dating back to 1763, as a notable bit of architecture. I wanted to join the parade by honoring my old friend John Knox as the man who had disciplined Mary, Queen of Scots, but got nowhere. In the future I'm sure we can expect a score of imaginative suggestions for sneaking frankly religious stamps onto the roster under other categories, and I suspect little damage will be done.

The Catholics, however, carried home one tremendous victory. In 1943 Hungary issued the world's first Christmas stamp, an Adoration of the Magi, and it proved so popular that Australia copied the idea, and was followed by New Zealand, Canada and Great Britain. In the United States the idea lagged, primarily because our government was afraid to issue a stamp with religious overtones that might offend non-Christians, and when John F. Kennedy assumed the presidency he gave strict orders that no action be taken that might look as if his administration favored Catholics.

In 1962, in the face of a tremendous demand for a Christmas stamp, the problem was solved by issuing one that avoided the religious trap: a holly wreath against a white door, with two tall, slim candles and the designation four cents. As predicted, it proved immensely popular, with constant reruns in the hundreds of millions becoming necessary. As the holiday season ended, 861,970,000 stamps had been sold at a tremendous profit to the government.

The religious barrier still held, however, so we continued with a series of innocuous stamps showing Christmas trees and holly, but in 1966 the government issued a stamp with a frankly religious subject, a glorious Mother and Child by the Flemish painter Hans Memling. I will not detail the hell that broke loose with the appearance of that stamp, but

Jews and libertarians protested the religiosity and irate Protestants pointed out that the stamp depicted Mary not as the simple Virgin in a stable but as Mary, Queen of Heaven, with what seemed to them to be a Catholic missal in her left hand. What was worse, the baby Jesus had his left hand on the missal, as if he were approving Catholic theology. More than a billion copies were sold, and in a revised version another billion.

Protesters initiated lawsuits to halt distribution of the offending stamp, claiming that it breached laws separating church and state. A lower court approved the stamp, a higher ordered a retrial, and tempers flared, but finally it was decreed that the postal department was free to issue such stamps as it deemed desirable. But animosity remained, with one Protestant critic telling me in quiet fury: 'This is shameful propaganda, Michener, and it has to be halted.'

In 1970 the difficult problem was solved: 'In future there will be a choice: one stamp with a religious subject and the other reflecting the "secular joys" of the winter season.' That Solomonic decision has produced a series of Virgins, each more ravishingly beautiful than the last, accompanied by companion Christmas stamps that are clearly nonreligious, and a more dreary chain of snow scenes and holly berries and country farmhouses I have rarely seen, but in an attempt to maintain impartiality in the religious wars, this winterscape series continues. The score when I retired was Catholics 2, Committee 0, and I must say from the point of view of the artistic and historic aptness, I was with the Catholics all the way. After all, they had some fifty of the world's greatest artists to select from; the lay group had to rely on somebody in Brooklyn drawing sleigh bells.

Just as my running for Congress taught me the complexity of American political life, so my work with the stamp committee made me realize the passion with which Americans can defend the important symbols of their lives. It also boggled the mind that when we finally agree to honor someone like my good neighbor Pearl Buck that 185 million copies of her handsome sepia portrait done by the best artist available were going to be in circulation for the next decade and then repose in a million stamp collections throughout the world. As one of our members said one morning as we began our deliberations: 'Here we go again. Conferring immortality on a few lucky Americans.'

The intensity of partisanship with which spots in this hall of fame are contested accounted for my major disappointment when on the committee. On the first day I served, the postmaster general asked what subjects I might want to propose as I began my duties. I caused rude laughter among my companions when I replied: 'I'll want us to issue, in the most dignified outer frames available and with the finest engraved portraiture, a new series of our thirty-nine presidents.'

An old-timer in the stamp business explained why such a series would be impossible: 'We've tried it. Everyone wants it. Trouble is, in any series like that the problem arises: Which presidents get the popular stamps? The stamps that go on the letters and so on. Republicans or Democrats? The party in power insists that they get the popular denominations, maybe three billion copies of each stamp, leaving the party out of power with things like the thirty-nine-cent stamp, seven hundred fifty thousand copies.'

'I could live with that. As Senator Marcy warned: "To the victor belong the spoils." '

'But it's not so simple! It takes us a long time, several years at least, to crank up a full set of presidents, and if we're in a period in which party control might change, the party that's in will want to rush things and get their boys secure in the good spots, while the party that's out wants to delay so that the good ones will still be available when they take over.'

One day when I was wearied by the logrolling within the committee and the incessant pressures from without, I asked somewhat petulantly: 'Are we wasting our time on this nonsense?' and a high official of the postal service replied: 'No. Because your group has done its job so well in the past, our government picks up about a hundred and fifty million free dollars a year, so keep at it.'

The only time I campaigned strongly for a stamp, although I frequently tried to kill unworthy ones and often succeeded, was when decisions were being made for the popular 1984 issue depicting dogs that were typically or exclusively American. Our subcommittee on nature and wildlife included representative breeds like the malamute of Alaska and the black-and-tan coonhound of our Southern states but ignored my favorite, the Chesapeake Bay retriever, and also the American collie, the favorite of Dr. John C. Weaver, president emeritus of the University of Wisconsin system and professor of geography at the University of Southern California.

I was powerless to convince the committee that my dog, which few had seen, could stand with the best, and Dr. Weaver made no headway in championing his collie, so in fraternal outrage we formed an ad hoc committee, informing the others that we would vote for no dogs whatever unless we were assured that our two would be included. When I look at that handsome number 2099, showing my powerful Chesapeake Bay retriever in his dark red coat, I feel that my time on the committee was well spent, and I am sure Dr. Weaver feels the same way about his gold-white collie. Thus do grown men play boys' games.

My commitment to the total earth, and my love for it in all its manifestations, presented me with recurring dilemmas: where to live, and to what segment of the earth did I owe my allegiance?

The first problem was not academic, because American law at that time not only permitted American citizens to live abroad but also gave them a financial advantage for doing so. I knew nothing of this until one day when my accountant was making out my income tax: 'Jim! Haven't you been out of the country working in Asia for more than five hundred one consecutive days?' When I nodded, he exclaimed: 'Then you get all your income taxes for last year excused! You pay nothing!' I could not believe it, but it was true, and when I asked around I found that many men were finding it profitable to take up residence in Ireland, which offered additional inducements, or Switzerland, where life was exciting and abundant. I was often approached with interesting proposals: 'You can take a cottage here, do your writing and save a bundle.' Although I was tempted, I never succumbed, and I had two good reasons for my refusal, one rather high-minded and the other largely pragmatic.

I felt a powerful obligation to keep my legal residence within the United States because the nation had given me a free education from elementary school through postdoctorate work in the finest universities and I thought that in return it was entitled to a share of whatever I earned. I have never deviated from that decision.

The more practical reason was that as I watched the actors and writers who took advantage of the free life overseas, I was distressed by its effect upon their work. If the expatriate was an actor he received only junk parts in films made overseas: 'He's already over here. He'll have to take the role and we can get him for peanuts.' Such actors were never summoned home to take on a really important role or one that would enhance their reputation. They demeaned themselves in movies thrown together by marginal Italian or Spanish companies or by underfinanced American adventurers shooting in those countries. With each year they remained overseas their reputations declined.

Writers tended to suffer in their own way. They lost touch with America and American themes. They wrote trivially, or under pressure from distant agents, or in areas they would not have touched had they been back home under the eyes of publisher and counselor. In the worst instance, they became rootless expatriates, yearning for home but afraid to go back lest they lose a temporary tax advantage. They and the actors saved money, but they did so at terrible cost to themselves and their careers. They had made a bargain with the devil and he paid them with counterfeit.

The problem of allegiance is more complex. If a man becomes a citizen of the world, which many do, as he travels and works abroad and sees the merits of lands other than his own, he must, if he has any sensitivity at all, ask himself: 'To what entity do I owe my allegiance?' and it will not be preposterous for him to reply: 'I really owe my debt to the entire world, for I am as at home in London or Tokyo as I am in Sioux Falls, and I am just as obligated to the people of those areas as I am to those of South Dakota.'

With me this question surfaced constantly because I have been at ease in all lands. I was once extremely happy in the Indonesian city of Bandung in Java; I have rarely been more content than I have been while working in Seville; London is a constant lure and Tokyo is incomparable. I felt a deep affinity for Singapore, a positive identity with Cracow in Poland and have been able to do consistently worthwhile work in places as diverse as Teruel in Spain, Djakarta in Indonesia, Rangoon in Burma, Lahore in Pakistan and Nome in Alaska. Apparently I can work anywhere and in any climate, so it would be feasible for me to settle wherever my fancy dictates.

In ancient legend there was the mighty Antaeus, son of the god Poseidon and Ge (Mother Earth), who successfully challenged every stranger he met to a wrestling match. He derived his extraordinary power from keeping one foot in solid contact with his native earth; Hercules, learning of his secret, defeated him by lifting him high in the air and killed him. Many artists are like Antaeus: Deprive them of contact with the particular corner of the earth where they were born and they become aimless and in some instances powerless. I am one of those people. For better or for worse I was reared in a small rural town in eastern Pennsylvania near low mountains, a wonderful canal and the Delaware River, and when I am absent too long I begin to diminish. My terrain has been enlarged to include all the United States, especially places in which I've worked like Hawaii, Colorado, Texas, Alaska and Florida. My affinity is with the American soil: I need it, I am nourished by it, and I am faithful to it.

That I am a citizen of the world is quite clear, but I have never been willing to adopt an affiliation with something vague and amorphous. My home is only one nation within the greater entity, but I serve the whole much more effectively when I serve my homeland best. Like Antaeus, I lose power when I lose touch.

. . .

As I approached the age of eighty-two I was confronted by a savage
rejection of everything decent I had ever stood for. In the 1988 election
President Reagan announced that anyone who was a liberal—he used
the phrase 'the L word,' as if it were fatally contaminated—was outside
the mainstream of American life and intimated that the liberal's patriotism was suspect. Vice President George Bush went a lot further by
shouting that anyone who did not wish to recite the Pledge of Allegiance
was probably false to the honored traditions of our nation, while Senator
Quayle declared: 'Michael Dukakis is a member of the American Civil
Libertics Union, but George Bush is a member of the National Rifle
Association,' as if that made the former a loathsome traitor and the
latter a great patriot. I found all this denigration of liberals personally
offensive.

As I was being ejected from the mainstream of American life, I
stumbled into a situation that forced me to evaluate all aspects of my
political life. I was living in Florida so as to be near the Caribbean Sea,
about which I was doing extensive research. Because I wanted to catch
the flavor of the area, I not only read newspapers and watched television
but also listened for the first time in my life to what was accurately
termed 'talk radio,' keeping my set tuned permanently to Station
WNQS, which provided a running report on the topics that really
concerned the local citizens. What I learned from this listening was
invaluable.

Tuesday and Wednesday nights were assigned to a soft-spoken, congenial, well-informed man named Norman Neem in Juno Beach. He
conducted a call-in show that became a must for me, because in it he
abused, vilified and scorned every noble cause to which I had devoted
my entire life. It seemed to me that he was against any law that sought
to improve the lot of the poor, any tax that endeavored to improve the
quality of our national life, any act in Congress that hoped to better the
condition of the nation as a whole, any movement that tried to lessen
police brutality, any bill that struggled to maintain a fair balance between the contending forces in our society and any move to improve
education, protect public health, or strengthen the supervision of agencies running wild.

His scorn for all Democratic politicians was boundless, with
Kennedy, McGovern, Carter, Mondale and Dukakis bearing the brunt
of his vilification week after week. It seemed that he saw nothing wrong
with Nixon, Ford, Bush or Quayle, while his admiration for Reagan
verged on the worshipful. I could never quite determine what kind of

government he was for, but at various intervals I guessed that what he really wanted was some version of either Robert Welch's United States or Lyndon LaRouche's. It also seemed that if he had his way blacks, women, children and the poor would suffer even worse constraints than they do at present, and the millionaires, tycoons, big businessmen and generals would prosper as never before. Every man in our public life whom I distrusted I heard him enshrine as a hero; and every cause for which I had worked he denigrated with a scorn that was brilliant.

It was extremely fortunate that I had come upon Neem, because he possessed such a strong native intelligence that he made his positions almost palatable; sometimes after I heard him sign off on midweek nights I started my evening walk with considerable fear: God, I hope no one who listens to his show and agrees with him knows I'm a liberal, because if he did he could shoot me.

Neem's weekly diatribes were the best thing that happened to me in Florida, for they made me stop, take a long hard look at myself, and determine where I might possibly have gone wrong. As I engaged in this introspection, I learned one valuable trick: 'Listen carefully to Neem. Identify exactly what he's saying. And then adopt a position one hundred and eighty degrees in the opposite direction, as far from him as you can get, and you'll be on the right track.' This simple rule forced me to define my beliefs and renew my opposition to all the things I intuitively detested; had he been a lamebrain or a mere ranter I could have dismissed him, but because he was so able in his marshaling of facts, street rumors and inherited positions, such as reverence for the Pledge of Allegiance and maniacal hatred of the A.C.L.U., I had to clarify my own thinking, and thus confirmed who I was and what I believed.

I decided that I was both a humanist and a liberal, each of the most dangerous and vilified type, and so I shall be increasingly until I die.

I am a humanist because I think humanity can, with constant moral guidance, create reasonably decent societies. I think that young people who want to understand the world can profit from studying the works of Plato and Socrates, the behavior of the three Thomases—Aquinas, More and Jefferson—the austere analyses of Immanuel Kant and the political leadership of Abraham Lincoln and Franklin Roosevelt. I like the educational theories of John Dewey and the pragmatism of William James. I am terrified of restrictive religious doctrine, having learned from history that when men who adhere to any form of it are in control, common men like me are in peril. I do not believe that pure reason can solve the perpetual problems unless it is modified by poetry and art and social vision. In the later decades of my life I have learned to be suspi-

cious of those well-meaning men who were noisy liberals or even Communists in their youth, only to become hard-edged and even savage
right-wingers in their maturity, trampling upon the very flags under
which they had once marched so proudly. I find such men abhorrent,
never to be trusted; I do not wish to associate with those among my
acquaintances who have taken that craven course because they are
turncoats who will once again become liberals when the bankruptcy of
their present allegiances becomes evident.

I am, in other words, a humanist, and if you want to charge me with
being the most virulent kind, a secular humanist, I accept the accusation, but I do not want to be accused of atheism. No man who loves
Deuteronomy and that first chapter of James can be totally antireligious.

A charge that can be lodged against me is that I am a knee-jerk liberal,
for I confess to that sin. When I find that a widow has been left penniless
and alone with three children, my knee jerks. When I learn that funds
for a library have been diminished almost to the vanishing point, my
knee jerks. When I find that a playground for children is being closed
down while a bowling alley for grown men is being opened, my knee
jerks. When men of ill intent cut back on teachers' salaries and lunches
for children, my knee jerks. When the free flow of ideas is restricted,
when health services are denied whole segments of the population, when
universities double their fees, my knee jerks, and when I learn that all
the universities in Texas combined graduated two future teachers qualified to teach calculus but more than five hundred trained to coach
football, my knee jerks, and I hope never to grow so old or indifferent
that I can listen to wrong and immoral choices being made without my
knee flashing a warning.

Why does it jerk? To alert me that I have been passive and inattentive
too long, to remind me that one of the noblest purposes for which
human beings are put on earth is to strive to make their societies better,
to see to it that gross inequities are not perpetuated. And to halt them
requires both effort and financial contributions, usually in the form of
taxes. The best expenditure of money I have made in my life has not
been for what made me either happier or more comfortable, but for the
taxes I have paid to the various governments under which I have lived.
In general, governments have spent their share of my money more
wisely and with better results than I have spent my own funds, and one
aspect of my life about which I am most ashamed is that I spent most
of a decade living in three states that had no state income tax—Texas,
Florida, Alaska—and the deficiencies that the first two suffered because
of that lack were evident daily. I like states like New York, Massachu-

setts and California that do tax and try to spend their income wisely.

One of the sickest economic preachments has been 'the trickle-down theory': 'If you allow the very rich to make as much money as they can without governmental restraint, they will magnanimously allow some of their largess to trickle down to the peasants below.' Most advocates of the theory do not express it in those blunt terms, but I have found that that is what they mean. I am not for across-the-board redistribution of wealth, and I know that rich people invest their money in enterprises that create employment, and I can cite a dozen other constructive uses of great wealth; but I still believe that society prospers most when there are laws to bring that wealth back into circulation, when there are taxes to provide social services that otherwise might not be available, when there is governmental surveillance to ensure proper business practices and prevent manipulation of financial markets, and when profits are plowed into research and the education of new generations.

When I have been dead ten years and a family comes to tend the flowers on the grave next to mine, and they talk about the latest pitiful inequity plaguing their town, they will hear a rattling from my grave and can properly say: 'That's Jim again. His knee is still jerking.'

VII

Ideas

*D*URING A LIFETIME of study and speculation, I discovered solely on my own only three ideas, but two were of such universal applicability that they stamped my thinking life. The third applied to only me, but it determined how I would spend my productive years.

The speculating I did was not upon raw data, or new data that called for some new organizing principle or explanation; I was not challenged by frontier facts. What I speculated upon was data already in being, the great range of human experience. I was concerned with what man had known, not with what he was about to know, and I was not unhappy with my choice, for it placed me early and deeply within the great movements of man's history and thought.

The books I have carried with me wherever I have moved for any considerable working stay have been invariable. Among them is Karl Ploetz's great piece of German scholarship, his *Epitome of World History,* in its 1915 English version, which I have referred to constantly throughout my working life. I doubt that I could think constructively without it, because it summarizes what was happening simultaneously in various parts of the world during whatever period I may be studying.

I carry with me also a good atlas, preferably one of those admirable ones published through the years by the great Scottish cartographer John George Bartholomew and his successors. Because of some magic touch the mountains and elevations on these maps seem to spring up from the page. I have met many scholars who are not entirely happy with other maps, but from childhood days I have also respected the fine maps of America's National Geographic Society and have in my permanent study a collection of some sixty of them dating back to 1915.

And of course I carry a dictionary, the best available. Sometimes when I have to look up a word, I waste a great deal of time because I start to read the dictionary as if it were a novel that makes me eager to see what comes next. The words of English have been endlessly fascinating for me and I would judge that I have mastered not more than a sixth of them. If the total runs to something like 550,000, that would be 92,000, and that figure might be far too high. But my word chase goes on and the interest never flags.

Utilizing these tools and others, which out of the world's accumulation of ideas have been most important to me in building a life?

Concerning religion, about whose outward forms I have no deep conviction, I have revered the Book of Deuteronomy while rejecting the older codification of laws, Leviticus, for which I have no feeling of identification. I have liked Thomas Aquinas and his thoroughness, finding him in that regard much like Maimonides, whom I treasure. I have never been much moved by Saint Francis or any of the other Catholic saints except Sebastian, with whom I developed at an early age an intense identification. Whenever adverse forces seemed to combine against me, I would visualize myself as Sebastian, standing calmly against a pillar while my enemies' arrows pierced my extremities without ever striking a mortal spot or making me wince.

The New Testament has caused me great trouble, because by nature I ought to have identified with Saint Paul, and I have wrestled with him all my life, finding him in the end just another Aristotle. He is not my man, so I missed entirely the greatness of the Pauline letters, but I studied his words constantly and found two passages that affected me deeply but in contrary ways. In First Corinthians, Paul spoke tellingly of athletics, saying: 'Know ye not that they which run in a race run all, but one receiveth the prize? So run that ye may obtain.' I read this long before Vince Lombardi uttered his version of the same principle: 'Winning isn't the main thing, it's the only thing.' Early in life I decided that I would never battle to be first, or aspire to be first, or bend either my life or my attitudes in order to be first, and the older I got and the more

I watched other men strive inordinately to be first, the more satisfied I was to settle somewhere else. Saint Paul's and Lombardi's pronouncements made me decide on my priorities, and I am more at ease with my own doctrine now than when I first framed it.

On the other hand, at a formative period in my life I was involved with a fine boys' school which had as its motto a wonderful passage from Saint Paul that I must have either recited or heard others recite at least a hundred times:

> Finally, brethren, whatsoever things are true, whatsoever things are honest, whatsoever things are just, whatsoever things are pure, whatsoever things are lovely, whatsoever things are of good report; if there be any virtue, and if there be any praise, think on these things.

Only a man of experience, judgment and conviction could have summarized so well the task of a young man as he faces life, and for that passage alone I can forgive Paul the other extravagances, which I find objectionable, because those words have been a kind of lantern to me, especially when I was alone in distant places and in alien cultures. Of his famous dicta I took as my permanent touchstone *whatsoever things are pure.* I tried to live a pure life by not worshiping false gods, or satisfying myself with sham, or seeking cheap goals. I tried always to engage in tasks that had some significance and to associate with people who were trying to accomplish worthy ends.

To adopt a less lofty tone, substitute for *pure* the word *clean* or *simple.* I have taken major steps and sacrificed much to lead a simple life, cleansed of extravagances in either action or thought. It was inevitable, I suppose, that with the basic attitude derived from Paul's Epistle to the Philippians, I would become a Quaker.

Like many young men who have biblical names, I was interested in what my patron saint had to say about things, and even today it seems providential that in the first chapter of the General Epistle of James he seemed to speak specifically to me and provided me with all the moral instruction I would need:

> For if any be a hearer of the word, and not a doer, he is like unto a man beholding his natural face in a glass: For he beholdeth himself, and goeth his way, and straightway forgetteth what manner of man he was. But whoso looketh into the perfect law of liberty, and continueth therein, he being not a forgetful

hearer, but a doer of the work, this man shall be blessed in his deed. . . . Pure religion . . . is this, To visit the fatherless and widows in their affliction, and to keep himself unspotted from the world.

How passing strange that James should have spoken to me in a few sentences that summarized the philosophy of both the saint and the follower. I have never analyzed the Christian life beyond that simple passage and can, for that reason, be termed a man who tried to be a Christian pragmatist or, in present-day terms, a liberal humanist. The words of Paul and James, each a saint, were admirable beacons for a young man who was not.

In philosophy I responded to Plato's austere approach but failed to recognize the moral grandeur of Socrates. Aristotle repelled me, for I have watched his authoritarian dicta utilized to justify reactionary movements in life and art. In my analysis of society I relied upon Rousseau, Adam Smith and Karl Marx and found none wholly to my taste. For some reason I have never been able to explain fully, I fell under the spell of the English economist David Ricardo, offspring of Dutch Jews who emigrated to England and attained wide social acceptance. I was impressed by his quantity theory of money, which I misinterpreted as meaning that there was in the economic society at any given time a fixed quantity of circulating money, which had to be divided among owners of money, owners of land and workingmen, and that if one of the three gained an unfair advantage or proportion of the wealth, it could only be at the expense of the other two. As I looked about me at home, in England and on the Continent I saw only confirmation of this theory, overlooking the fact that Ricardo also dealt with the more serious problem of how a government could, by its monetary policy, actually increase the quantity of money so that all could share in a larger whole.

Finding evidence in the American depressions of 1873, 1893 and 1929 that Ricardo's supposed theories were correct, I realized that if any government operated on the quantity theory of money as I understood it, grave penalties would be placed on all workingmen and women. What was required, I clearly saw, was a more flexible system of monetary control, and I realized that I would have been an agrarian agitator in 1873 and a William Jennings Bryan supporter in the 1890s.

In the dark days of 1930 a college friend and I proceeded rather far in drafting a short book giving the college graduate's view of what changes might be advisable in the wake of the 1929 crash. Peter Nehemkis, my coauthor, was a brilliant fellow, far more sophisticated than I, and later he became a lawyer of distinction, but I was better grounded in the facts of American life at various levels than he.

We put together a strong outline, which was his work mostly, with much telling material to prove our contentions, which was my contribution. We believed that available wealth should be distributed more equitably (his idea) in order to make more money available to the working classes (our idea) so that they could buy more of the nation's goods (my idea). We also felt that quotas in American colleges, especially in law and medicine, were destructive of democracy and a brake on economic progress (his idea). We wrote two sample chapters, and when they were finished I arranged an appointment in New York with the one man we thought might understand what we were attempting. At that time I was a Republican and Peter a Democrat, but we saw no hope whatever in the two major parties, so my Saturday-morning meeting was with Norman Thomas, the perennial Socialist candidate for president. He was generous with his time and attentive to our summaries of the national situation. It must have sounded incredibly naive, but when he started asking me about specifics, and I could inform him about working and living conditions as I had seen them in various parts of the nation, he paid attention and said: 'You have a sharp eye. Go back and tell your colleague to go ahead with this. I think we could find you a publisher.'

Alas, Nehemkis had to attend principally to his law studies, and without his philosophical guidance I floundered around. When word came that I had won a traveling scholarship for Europe, I was left with the doleful task of informing Mr. Thomas that both Peter and I would be incommunicado for some years. I remember the great Socialist as a gentle, understanding man; I had met him for only about three hours, but he taught me much in that short span and I often wished in later years that I could have served as his amanuensis or political aide of some sort, for his ideas ignited fires in my mind and I would have profited from such an arrangement.

My going to Europe in the fall of 1931 had profound consequences, one negative, the other wildly productive. Because I was absent from the United States during the worst two years of the depression, its full force never quite hit me, although an aftermath, as I shall explain later, did allow me at least belatedly to appreciate its horror. I therefore missed the traumatic experiences that produced powerful writing by those who remained at home in the midst of the crisis, and I have always regretted that loss.

However, my political experiences in Europe came in a parallel context: I witnessed the hellish despair and hopelessness, which led to the dole, in industrial Scottish cities like Glasgow and Dundee, where dank nights and gray, rainy afternoons seemed perpetual. At a boardinghouse in London I met a brilliant Afrikaner student who assumed that because I had come from a former British colony I would be as strongly anti-British as he. Disgusted that I did not agree with all his charges against the English, he conducted for my benefit an advanced seminar on conditions in his country, about which I had previously known little. He was an ardent Dutch patriot and assured me that sooner or later his Afrikaners would kick the English out and take control of the country. In later years I observed that a great deal of what he predicted came true.

At about the same time I met in Amsterdam a group of Javanese students who told me in the same impassioned tones that they would one day evict their present Dutch landowners from the Netherlands East Indies, another part of the world about which I knew nothing. They told me I must read a certain book about their land. I supposed that it would be some fiery tract written in bad Dutch or worse English detailing the wrongs Europeans had done to corrupt an idyllic tropical paradise. It was nothing of the kind; *Max Havelaar* was a brilliant book by a perceptive Dutchman, Eduard Douwes Dekker, who wrote under the pseudonym Multatuli (Many Sorrows); it is the classic depiction of colonialism and a stunning portrait of Java, a land with which I immediately fell in love.

My Javanese friends were a brilliant lot, all being educated in the Netherlands, a nation they professed to hate, and their conversations with me were both revealing and exciting. Each of them spoke three or four languages, which put me at a sore disadvantage, but since all but one knew English, we conversed easily. I was impressed by the intensity of their political opposition to the Netherlands, but I was also pleased to note that they liked things Dutch, for they told me that if I wanted to understand the Dutch soul I should read a novel that had recently been translated into English, *Old People and the Things That Pass,* by Louis Couperus, and I profited just as much from this as I did from *Havelaar.*

But mostly I took away from these friends an appreciation of the deep passions that motivated young people of all colonial nations who were plotting to wrest their homelands away from European control. I saw that the Javanese-Dutch agitation in Java was going to be quite different from the Afrikaner-English struggle in South Africa because the latter was between two European-derived civilizations, whereas the former involved two civilizations that were vastly different—an Asiatic society of great antiquity and a modern industrial European state. My experience with these two anticolonial struggles in their incipient stages made me believe that continued confrontation was inescapable, and that neither the Afrikaners in South Africa nor the Javanese in the Netherlands Indies had any chance whatever of prevailing. And when I later met Indian students who told me that they would one day win their independence from Great Britain and young Filipinos who spoke of their determination to be free of the United States, I supposed that their aspirations too were chimerical.

But from taking part in such conversations in various cities in Europe I made myself into something of an expert on at least the discussion of colonialism, and as I grew older and better informed I began to understand the currents sweeping the modern world and was not surprised when colonialism collapsed worldwide.

But in those fateful years of 1931–33 I was being slowly exposed to darker and more ominous forces abroad in Europe and later the entire world: fascism and communism.

In an attempt to indoctrinate young men like me, Mussolini's government in Rome inaugurated a most clever tactic: it offered students throughout Europe railroad passes at unbelievably low rates from wherever they were studying to eight different Italian cities. With your ticket, however, came a printed cardboard form containing eight blank circles corresponding to the eight cities, each of which had to be stamped with a different official stamp, not merely in the cities but in cultural exhibits in each depicting the glories of Italian history and the accomplishments of the present fascist government. If you didn't visit the eight exhibitions and get your cardboard stamped, your return railroad ticket would not be valid.

It was a typical bit of Mussolini's self-aggrandizement, and on me, at least, it worked, for although I was interested mainly in Italian painting, I also found, somewhat against my will, that I was absorbing a good deal of fascist propaganda in the form of glorious exhibits showing the richness of Mussolini's accomplishments. That year Italy's principal foreign foe was neither France nor Ethiopia but Yugoslavia and the poster attacks against her were so virulent and so ably buttressed by historical exhibits proving her perfidy that to this day I can visualize brutal

Yugoslavia attacking guiltless Italy. This is the result of Mussolini's devilishly adroit propaganda campaign asserting that the contested city of Trieste was joined to Italy by the Adriatic Sea but separated from Yugoslavia by impenetrable mountains. I have never seen geography used more effectively as a political tool.

But the accidental fallout of this gift trip to Italy was a chance experience that not even Mussolini could have predicted or arranged. When I took one of the authorized side trips to Lago de Garda, one of my favorite spots in the world, I left the lake boat at Riva, the attractive town at the north end that serves as an entrance point to the mountains nearby, and as I started into the lower hills I joined a group of German students who had availed themselves of the same kind of travel pass I was using. We spent three days together that changed my life because even at that early date they were followers of Adolf Hitler, a leader I had not heard of before, and the passion they displayed when speaking of what Germany was going to achieve under his inspiration alerted me for the first time to the demonic force that was about to sweep over Europe. These six or seven students were young gods, handsome, intelligent, dedicated and strong—although I had always been a good walker, especially where endurance rather than speed was required, they outdistanced me so easily and so constantly that one or two had to lag behind out of mere decency to keep me company.

In those Italian hills that summer we had a continuing seminar, each hour of which enlightened me with new facts about Germany, Europe and the world. I had never thought much about Jews except that they were among the finest people in the world, an opinion I had acquired at Swarthmore College in Pennsylvania. A private Christian college of the highest academic standing, it observed, as was typical at the time, a quota system that allowed only one Jewish boy and one Jewish girl to enroll in each class. The competition for those two spots was so intense that each year we received only the very ablest high school seniors in America. Since my years in the school enabled me to know seven different classes, three ahead of me, three behind, I had known fourteen Jewish classmates and they were, like my coauthor Nehemkis, the brightest, handsomest, richest and best-dressed kids in the college. The Jewish girls were so attractive that scores of Gentile boys wanted to date them, nor did the Jewish boys have trouble getting dates, for they were far more sophisticated than us Pennsylvania farm yokels. There had been only one Jew in my hometown and he was liked by most of us.

I therefore had a completely favorable opinion of Jews, and it was startling to hear about the nefarious acts they were reported to be guilty of not only in Germany and Italy but in the rest of Europe. The young Germans spoke with fire about their plans to eliminate Jewish misbehavior 'once and for all.' They were so intense in their hatred of those they called 'enemies of the state' that I deemed it best not to inform them that my experiences with Jews had been quite different.

Curiously, I was not much interested at that time in the antics of their leader, Adolf Hitler, for with my limited knowledge I did not see him as either a long-term threat or even a politician who might attain temporary power, but it was obvious that my hiking companions had an entirely different interpretation of what he might become. They did not, so far as I can recall, ever use the title *Führer* (leader), but they obviously idolized him as such.

The Germans continued on into Austria, leaving me behind in Italy. I had immense respect for their hiking ability—they knew what physical discipline was—and for their broad intelligence; they were superior young men and the first of their breed that I had met. Was I intuitively afraid of them or their inflammatory message? Not at all. I considered them no more than German versions of Peter Nehemkis and me, young students trying to understand their society and the moves it should make in the future. As we parted I waved good-bye and thought no more about the subjects they had thrust upon me.

But in the next academic year in Scotland I met an exchange student from a university in Munich who had a much more serious interpretation of what was happening in Germany. Herr Ludenberg, as I shall call him, was entirely different from my godlike Alpine associates at Lago de Garda: he was short and fat and came from the lower middle class. Most important, he was quietly introspective while they had been arrogantly activist, and even today it seems a miracle to me that this quite ordinary German of twenty-two with no apparent intellectual brilliance should have seen so clearly in the winter of 1933 the major steps his country was about to take during the next six years.

As we began our talks, which covered a long period of time and never became concentrated into direct questions and answers, he told me that several events were inevitable: 'This man, Hitler, will attain supreme power. The army and the big industrialists will see to that. Very quickly he will achieve a union with Austria, because the Austrians will insist on it. Both the Polish border and the one with France will have to be adjusted in our favor, maybe with Czechoslovakia, too.'

'But won't that make the other powers unite against what he's doing?'

'I don't think they will, because he won't do it all at once. No big gulps, just little nips, here and there.'

'Do you see war in Europe?'

'No. France and England will never unite against us. Impossible.'

'Then you think Hitler will have his way? Pretty much as he pleases?'

'Yes. But I also think that when he gets his way and solidifies the German people and gives them their proper border, he'll be satisfied, and the new day can begin.' I remember that as he said these words for the first time his little eyes, sunk deep in his chubby face, glowed with excitement, but what he said next is what I remember best: 'He's put it all down in a book just now translated into English. It's called *My Struggle.* You ought to read it.'

I did not—that is, not until ten years later, when I was in uniform in the South Pacific and then it was too late to do me much good. Herr Ludenberg in his quiet way continued with his efforts to educate me, and he did a splendid job. He was not, of course, concentrating on me; his major efforts to explain the new Germany were directed at British students, with whom he was on the most congenial terms. He was a brilliant debater and his mild personal appearance allowed him to make subtle points without arousing antagonism. He was fiercely convinced that Great Britain's destiny lay with Germany and not with either France or the United States, but I got the impression that whereas he knew a great deal about France, having traveled there for several summers, he knew no more about my country than I knew about his. From several things I was told he said—he never said them openly to me—I judged that he had a rather poor opinion of the United States, and he believed that once his man Hitler got started, the numerous Germans in the States would rally to his support, especially if he had succeeded in making an alliance with England.

But Ludenberg was most impressive when he talked about the regeneration of Germany, its escape from the indignities of the Versailles Peace Treaty of 1919: 'Those wrongs will be corrected. Boundaries will be readjusted. Apologies will be demanded and received.' He may have spelled out precisely what he and Hitler meant by those phrases, but if so, I forget what he proposed; I do, however, know that he was serious.

He was extremely outspoken about the political changes that would have to take place in Germany: 'All vestiges of Versailles will be wiped clean. The German people are not disposed to take the outward forms of democracy seriously. We're not like the United States or Great Britain, a mix of many different peoples, some of them degenerate. We're one people, Nordic, strong, intellectually at the top of the heap, great philosophers, musicians, artists. We deserve our own kind of government and we'll get it.'

'What kind will it be?' I asked.

'Strong central leadership. Society properly disciplined rather than messing all over the place. And I think'—he paused—'probably restricting the right to vote, if we have voting, to proper Germans only.' Quickly he added: 'Of course, others will be free to live among us, and they'll be fully protected, but only on our terms.'

Never in our conversations did Herr Ludenberg mention the word 'Nazi' nor did he ever make any reference to the swastika. He did mention war as an agency of national policy but he foresaw none of Herr Hitler's triumphs as being attained through the use of arms. His whole message was that Hitler's ends would be achieved because they were inevitable; they represented the irresistible force of history, and persons of good sense, such as myself and my British friends, would see the propriety of allowing Germany to reassert her historical rights, and once that was done, the world could move forward in justice and harmony. In all the time I knew him, Ludenberg never rattled the sword, never issued threats.

When I recalled the disgust my other German friends in the Austrian mountains had vehemently expressed against Jews, I was surprised that Ludenberg had never once mentioned the problem, and I began to think that maybe this anti-Semitism was an aberration limited to Germany's upper classes. But when I asked him one day: 'How do your Jews fit into your new pattern?' his face darkened, as if he were displeased that I had broached this unpleasant topic, and he started once or twice to give an explanation but reconsidered. In the end he drew back, studied me to see whether I could be trusted and apparently decided not. 'They may have to be disciplined,' he said.

Now came one of the dangerous turning points in my life. I had formed the habit of crossing the English Channel on those remarkable ferries that plied regularly to ports like Calais, Dunkirk, Ostend, Antwerp and Amsterdam, and this gave me an opportunity not only to visit the famed art galleries in the big cities but also to meet young people who liked the same mode of travel and whose interest in the contemporary world was at least as deep as mine. In this way, and because I was consciously casting about for new acquaintances who could teach me something, I fell in with a group of Belgian students at one of the art galleries who were on their way to a big student gathering in Brussels, a short train ride to the south.

When we reached that city we were met by two young women with arm bands and were led to a large, bare meeting hall at a school of some kind, and there unwittingly I received my introduction to Europe's vibrant university Communist movement. I was surrounded by students from a dozen different nations, Spain, Italy and Greece north to Sweden, Norway and Denmark, with everything in between on both east and west. I was the only American and I was there by chance. They were Communists and they were serious about it.

Then followed two or three days of the most intense intellectual gymnastics, with older speakers from various countries explaining the relative conditions of their movement and the likelihood of their party's attaining power in the near future. Speakers from Russia, addressing all of us as if we were committed to the revolution, gave general encouragement insisting that time was on our side. Enthusiastic orators from Spain claimed that they might be able to take power at any moment, but those from Italy warned that whereas their long-term chances looked good, Mussolini was too powerful at the moment to be toppled easily. Speakers from Great Britain were not optimistic.

At this powerful Communist gathering I was in exactly the position I had been in when I was traveling with a fascist rail pass to the political exhibitions in the Italian cities, or when I was mountain climbing in the lower Alps with my National Socialist friends or holding long discussions with Herr Ludenberg, the philosophical supporter of Adolf Hitler: I was striving to understand the world; I wanted to know what Communism offered its young people to make it so alluring, and in those days in Brussels I found out.

But in the discussion groups, in which I took as active a part as my limited command of languages permitted, I discovered something significant. When the European delegates spoke of the downtrodden poor or the bitter hardships endured by the underprivileged, they were talking in bookish generalities lacking any foundation in personal experience, and I quickly learned that I knew far more about the real poverty of the world than any of the other participants. In America I had witnessed the worst of small-town economic deprivation, the worst of homelessness as men drifted across the nation without jobs or hope, and all the other dislocations in society for which Communism was supposed to be the only solution. In short, without being aware of the fact, I knew far more about social disparities than they did.

I did not feel confident in the midst of so many to argue that in the United States, at least, there were ways other than Communism of dealing with disaffections caused by dire poverty, but the more I heard of the analyses of European conditions and prospects, the more convinced I became that in America the solution did not lie in Communism.

The three days I spent in that powerful assembly in Brussels were three of the most rewarding I would spend anywhere. The session was in effect an intense seminar that filled in the gaps in my college curriculum, where Karl Marx was never mentioned and not one professor seemed to realize that an eruption of the most titanic kind was about to engulf Central Europe. I would have remained a lesser man had I not gone to Brussels.

In 1932 a British merchant ship took me to the east coast of Spain, and I traveled up to the remote mountain town of Teruel, which was to become the center of bitter fighting in the civil war. There and in Valencia I saw clearly that Spain's fragile democracy was in peril from both the right and the left, with the resolution capable of going either way. In Teruel I met men who were determined to see that the antidemocratic forces did not prevail, and when I asked if they thought they could hold off the military if it decided to take arms against the republic, they said: 'All Europe will jump to our defense. They will not allow our country to be stolen from us.' It was clear that when they referred to 'all Europe,' they meant 'all left-wing and Communist sympathizers,' for to save their newly won freedoms they would accept help from any source.

Such was my political education in Europe: I saw dreadful poverty and unemployment in Great Britain; triumphant fascism in Italy; nascent Nazism in Germany; Communism gaining ground in Europe; and the prologue to civil war in Spain. These were the great challenges of my age and I had been close to the heart of each.

The darkest day of my life came years later on a snowy street corner in Washington, D.C., when the infamous McCarthy era was at its height.

A former teacher friend of mine, Bill Vitarelli, had contemplated studying for the priesthood but had become instead an expert in woodworking, ceramics and puppet making. Since I had once spent a summer touring the eastern United States as a professional puppeteer of moderate skill, I fell in with Vitarelli and together we put together a puppet show that played the big department stores. He was unbelievably skilled with his hands, excited about the possibility of teaching young people, and interested in almost everything. He was an easy man to like, a difficult man to protect from his enthusiasms. And he had been, among other things, the man who got me started in 1953 on professional fortune-telling. I realized what a free spirit he was and that he might find himself in trouble in a straitlaced environment.

Bill was in trouble, but that was not news, for he was always in trouble of some kind. This time it was serious, so serious indeed that his entire career and even his livelihood were in jeopardy. I had helped him get a government job teaching school in Guam and Palau in my old South Pacific arena, and he was doing a spectacularly good job when news came from Washington that an unnamed accuser had formally charged him with being a Communist. He was brought back to Washington to stand before one of those infamous in-house investigative tribunals whose three members would determine the relevance of the indictment. If the three men, who were not lawyers, decided from the evidence they had that he had lied about not being a Communist his teaching career would be destroyed.

As in all such cases, Vitarelli was kept in ignorance of the specific charge against him. He was not allowed to know who had lodged it, what its gravamen was, what part of his varied career it pertained to, or what infamous thing he was supposed to have done. All he was permitted to know was that someone among our two hundred million citizens had told someone else: 'Bill Vitarelli is a Communist,' and faced with that meager, shadowy charge he was required to prove that he was not a Communist.

In such a desperate situation it was crucial for Bill to enlist in his defense the most reliable character witnesses he could, and after consultation with a magnificent old Quaker lawyer it was decided that I should go first to defend his character as solidly and unqualifiedly as possible.

Of course I was obligated to do so, but now excruciating anxiety gripped me: if I went before the committee and swore that I had never myself been involved in Communist activities, and if the people who were determined to hound Vitarelli out of public life took the trouble to look into my background in Europe, they could easily find out that I had twice intimately associated with German Nazis and, what was infinitely worse, I had also attended that big Communist meeting in Brussels and allowed my name to get on a roster somewhere (because for some time thereafter I received through the mail in Scotland materials from the Communist party in Scotland, where, during the depression, underground cells flourished).

For some weeks I had agonized over this and now on this bleak wintry day on a street corner in the shadow of a gray government building Bill Vitarelli, on the verge of having his life destroyed, was pleading with me to promise to be his first character witness. I could not confide my own vulnerability, nor could I give any other reasonable excuse for not stepping forward, so I hedged, and as I did so, looking like a vacillating coward, he suddenly screamed: 'My God, Jim! This is my life. What can

I do to persuade you?' His cry was so anguished that with no further thought as to my own safety, I said: 'I'll be there.'

The three men of the investigative committee, ordinary government employees from the same department as the accused—I believe it was Interior, since Guam and the Palau Islands came under that jurisdiction, but I could be wrong—sat behind a long desk on a dais in a large drab room. There were tipstaves and court reporters taking down every word I said, and the atmosphere was solemn.

When the meeting began, the chairman asked who the first witness was, and Vitarelli's gray-haired lawyer indicated that I would take the stand. The chairman asked me who my employers were, and I was able to say truthfully that I had last worked for the *Reader's Digest, The Saturday Evening Post* and the *New York Herald Tribune,* three of the most conservative publications in America. Here I was, far more suspect than Vitarelli because of my behavior in Europe, testifying in his behalf as a solid American patriot solely because of my association with agencies having impeccable credentials.

I was on the stand, I believe, for most of that first day. My defense of Bill proved so strong, covered so many different areas of his life and was so unwavering that the tribunal felt that it had to rebut some of my remarks. As they proceeded to do so I noticed for the first time in such hearings—I would participate in several other cases—that a moment would come when these three ordinary men would begin to see themselves as latter-day Solons and would imitate the mannerisms of the wise judges they had seen in their favorite movie. All of the judicial proceedings were a farce, of course: Bill had been indicted, so he must be guilty.

The mundane interrupted the high drama when during a recess we all went to the men's room and each of the judges asked me for my autograph, saying how much he had liked some of my work. I thought I was justified in concluding that I had saved the day for Vit. When my testimony resumed I stuck to my guns, assuring the investigators that Vitarelli could never have been a Communist for the good reason that he was such a lone wolf he had refused to join anything. But even as I was fervently defending him, I had the sickening thought: My God! I have no idea what I'm supposed to be defending him against.

My fears were realized: when the verdict was handed down some days later, Vitarelli was found to have been a Communist and was therefore fired forever from government service and left without a penny, but with a wife and five children to support.

Sometime later I met one of the officers of the trial and he astonished me by revealing that it was my testimony that had condemned Vit. I was so visibly staggered that the man said: 'Yes, more than three times the judges led you by easy steps to the point where, if you had been telling the whole truth, you would have explained what happened in the Georgia case. But you always shied away, so it was clear to all of us that you were either hiding something or lying.'

'Georgia case? I never heard the name Georgia mentioned till this minute. Not by anybody. What in hell was the Georgia case?'

'We couldn't tell you because then you'd know the nature of the evidence against him. It was your shifty silence that did him in.'

I was so enraged by this terrible miscarriage of justice, and so was the old Quaker lawyer and some of Vit's other friends, that we mounted a campaign that took this world's worst example of injustice all the way to the Supreme Court. In the meantime, in order to keep Vit and his family alive, I put him on my personal payroll. A titanic struggle began between a group of ordinary citizens and the full majesty of the government as represented by the awesome power of Senator McCarthy, but slowly, thanks to the devotion and brilliance of other defenders of a free society, the justices of the Supreme Court began to look at this miserable affair, and the Vitarelli case became the first victim of these infamous tribunals to have its judgment overturned.

Vit's name was cleared. His back pay was restored. He was able to return to the job he loved, teaching the natives on Palau, and an ugly footnote to American history in the 1950s was rectified to the extent that such hurtful damage can ever be mended.

In that dark period of national hysteria I was proud to testify in behalf of many friends accused of being disloyal to their country, and in the process it occurred to me that the type of life I had led had brought me into contact with an unusual number of men and women who were exploring the frontiers of knowledge. When I defended one of my former professors at Harvard I thought how revolting it was that although I was not qualified to substitute for him in the classroom, I had been put in the position of verifying his patriotism. I also defended a college classmate whose rather popular name was confused with another. And I defended a newspaperman who had written an article that someone had deemed criminally irreverent.

A young man in New York who at one time had badgered me for months to join him in the Communist party found himself in serious trouble and asked me to swear that he had never even considered Communism, but this I would not do. When he whined: 'Why not? I thought you were my friend?' I reminded him: 'You hammered me pretty hard, but you didn't even believe in it yourself,' and I would have nothing more to do with him.

Those were bad times, some of the most shameful we've gone through in my lifetime. As I paraded myself as witness beyond reproach because of my affiliation with those three stalwart pillars of conservatism, the *Digest, Post* and *Tribune,* I often reflected on what might have happened to me had I spent those two years not in Europe but in New York and Chicago and especially Hollywood, where I would have been susceptible to pressures from older men whom I respected to involve myself in certain meetings or protests. For doing infinitely far less than I did in Europe, I would have been blacklisted and perhaps even sent to jail, for the anger I showed in the Vitarelli case could easily have been directed against the House Un-American Activities Committee and I could have been charged with contempt.

Years later I finally solved the mystery about 'the Georgia case' that I had presumably handled so poorly that my friend Bill Vitarelli was found guilty of being a Communist. It seems there was a middle-aged woman teacher, who read subversion in every editorial and saw flame-throwing violence in every black face, who had attended a teachers' conference in Atlanta, where she heard a visiting professor from New York, name of Vitarelli, utter an appalling statement that others testified he had said: 'Sooner or later circumstances will force you to surrender your bourgeois attitudes,' and as soon as she heard that fatal word *bourgeois* she knew she was in the presence of a Communist. So she entered an official complaint against Vitarelli even though she did not know him and had never spoken to him. Hers was the only complaint ever lodged against Bill, but it nearly succeeded in ruining his life.

I not only participated in the fire storms of my generation but also tried to fathom what they meant. Under Mussolini's persuasive enticements in 1933 I saw the best of Italian fascism, and quickly detected its spurious grandeurs and essential emptiness. I was tardy in appreciating the brutality of Nazism because my young German instructors were careful to mask its hideous anti-Semitism; indeed, when they spoke of wanting to correct the injustices of the Versailles Treaty of 1919 I sympathized. But when the Nazis invaded Spain to help establish fascism there, then annexed Austria, and with Kristallnacht revealed their plans for destroying all Jews, I knew that one day we must go to war to stop Hitler's madness.

Communism affected me more profoundly than fascism because it has a formal intellectual base that can be analyzed, while fascism does not. I never knew exactly what view of world society fascism proposed, while I saw that Communism offered a pseudoscientific theory that had been developed by Marx, Engels and Lenin and was embraced by millions in Europe and hundreds of thousands in the Americas. But as I studied its operation I saw that not only did it promise more than it could deliver but it also crushed freedom. Communism made me a defender of liberalism and democracy.

Spain impressed me deeply, as it has the habit of doing with visitors from Anglo-Saxon backgrounds, and I made a careful study of Spanish life, including its politics. In the 1930s many idealists flocked there from various countries to combat Franco's fascist rebellion, but I had developed a belief that civil tranquility is essential to a decent society, and so, although I despised Franco, I never doubted that he was preferable to chaos.

My work took me to a score of former British colonies, where I had an opportunity to observe the condition in which England had left her possessions when freedom was either grasped or granted. I saw that of all the powers—and here I include the United States—England performed the best in preparing her erstwhile colonies to launch out on their own. Even in South Africa, where racism has a tenacious hold, she left a legacy of law and order, educational opportunities, financial stability and general honesty in civil life. Belgium behaved the poorest, while the United States won no laurels in her temporary management of the Philippines and her longer custodianship of Guam, Samoa, Puerto Rico and the Virgin Islands.

During the brief period when McCarthyism threatened freedom in the United States I reflected on Mussolini's prediction: 'Each nation will acquire the fascism to which it is entitled.' The shameful behavior of our government in those years confirmed a belief I'd had for some time: that it would be easy, if the United States turned sour, to establish Nazi-like concentration camps in almost any part of our nation and find eager recruits to staff them. It was clear that the eternal vigilance that Thomas Jefferson and other patriots had urged would always be required.

During World War II I was sent to Manus, in the Admiralty Islands, north of New Guinea, where we maintained a big naval base. After servicing the various aviation installations in the area and the carriers in the lagoon, and participating in the bombing of Rabaul and Kavieng, I grabbed some R&R in Wewak on the north coast of New Guinea and accompanied a group on a long canoe ride up the gloomy Sepik River, one of the least-known important rivers in the world.

We were soon in the grass-shack land of headhunting cannibals. But we had little fear, since we were a body of ten or twelve and well armed, and also we knew that under steady and compassionate Australian pressure the savages were relinquishing their ancient rituals. In fact, we camped with them in one of their villages for two nights, and as we sat with them around the fire before climbing into sleeping bags with mosquito nets, we listened to them telling stories in a language we, of course, could not understand. As I listened to one old fellow I admired the exquisitely carved shell he was wearing as a breastplate. Then the singing started and the mix of men's and women's voices, the high and the rumbling low, paralleled what one might have heard in a fine church choir in some English city. And it occurred to me that the old man telling his story and the person who had carved the breastplate and the singers who performed according to traditional rules of their tribe were artists as fine as any I had known elsewhere in the world. They had successfully preserved a culture that was in its own way and purposes as rich as mine. I felt a tremendous affinity with these people and I experienced an epiphany: 'We are all brothers. We all face the same problems and find the same satisfactions. We are united in one great band. I am one with all of them, in all lands, in all climates, in all conditions. Since we brothers occupy the entire earth, the world is our home.'

I was at the midpoint of my travels throughout the world. I had seen Europe and much of North America, including Canada and Mexico, and now I was familiar with the vast complexity of the Pacific, including New Zealand, Australia and some of the Dutch East Indies. I would soon begin my first tentative exploration of Asia. I would within a few years have seen all the world except three places only: the great Amazon River, China and the South Pole; Much later, in the most unexpected manner, I would see the first two; the South Pole I would never see, to my lasting regret.

I think that first visit to the Sepik occurred in early 1944.* Tonight, nearly half a century later on the opposite side of the world from that dark river, I feel the surge of brotherhood I experienced that night. No matter where in the world I have traveled, I have never felt that I was an alien, for I have tried to meet all men as though they were kin and have been able to share with them their hopes, their fears, their political uncertainties.

*Forty years later I took my wife on an exploration of the Sepik, and we returned to that same village, where they no longer headhunt but where they still tell stories and carve and sing. Now when I ask her: 'Of all the places we've been together, which one would you want to return to?' she invariably replies: 'The Sepik.'

This concept that the people of all geographical areas and civilizations are my brothers and sisters has created a never-ending problem for me: if I'm so closely bound to them, does it follow that I owe allegiance to all nations? Or do I owe a special debt of patriotism only to my homeland? I have never been able to answer such questions categorically, for obviously I have been a citizen of the world, at home everywhere, at ease in all cultures, with all religions, and with all kinds of people living under almost every conceivable form of government. I have been invited to take up residence in a dozen different countries and have evaluated the merits of every invitation.

But from my earliest days I have had an intense love for my native country and have never seriously considered living for any extended period anywhere but under the protection of its flag. For that reason I have never acquired a home overseas, or kept my money there, or expressed any allegiance to a foreign way of life.

This indissoluble affection for my homeland is based on a compelling reason: only the United States' system of free public education enabled me to escape from a severely disadvantaged childhood, and when asked about it I say: 'Had I been born in Yugoslavia under the conditions of my childhood, I would have spent my life counting gasoline drums.' In the American system I was able to attend eight different colleges and universities, always at government expense. The debt I owe my country is incalculable.

I have been so intensely associated with my homeland, and all corners of it, that I would be emasculated if I were forced to leave it. In fact, all the times I have worked abroad have only strengthened my ties to the country of my birth. To honor it, I have planted, I would judge, about three thousand trees, some fingerlings, some so large they had to be moved by gangs of men working with a truck. I have been driven to do this because I wanted to replenish the soil that in so many ways nourished me.

I knew instinctively that I required contact with my homeland—with my hillside, the rivulet at the bottom of my hill and the broad Delaware River, on which I had done so much of my early exploring when I rode north and south on the coal barges that drifted up and down the canal that fringed the river. Some of the most exciting families I knew in those days were the ones who lived on the huge barges that came down out of the Pennsylvania coal fields to deliver their cargo to the Philadelphia furnaces. For me to get back to those scenes after a long absence abroad was an emotional experience whose impact never diminished.

But if I was so responsive to the land to which I was umbilically tied, why did I work abroad so often and for such extended periods? More significantly, why did I write so repeatedly on foreign lands and foreign cultures? Was this not a schizophrenic act, which might in time produce serious emotional problems and which certainly produced intellectual contradictions? If I loved my country so profoundly, why did I seek my inspiration abroad? I was aware of the problem and often wondered how and why it had occurred.

When I analyzed the matter seriously I made a curious discovery. It seemed that many American writers, and among them some of our very best, had suffered this confusion. Born and educated in the United States, they had been able to do their best writing only when they fled the place, as if they needed distance from a familiar society if they wanted to comprehend the subtlety of life and find a pattern for writing about it. I studied in some detail the lives of six of our best American writers, choosing a varied group in order to ensure a wide coverage of types: two elegant stylists, Henry James and T. S. Eliot; one extraordinary mythmaker, Herman Melville; a powerful original, Ernest Hemingway; and two who gained enormous popularity, Pearl Buck and Jack London.

What I discovered was amazing. Each of these writers found his or her most effective subject matter outside the United States: James and Eliot in England; Hemingway in Spain and Cuba; Melville and London in the Pacific; and Buck in China. The three who won the Nobel Prize—Eliot, Buck and Hemingway—did so for work done outside the States; and all matured intellectually and artistically abroad. Two of the greatest, James and Eliot, actually relinquished American citizenship and became naturalized citizens of Great Britain, a country they found more congenial.

In other words, six extremely talented predecessors had, for remarkably similar causes, behaved much like me. I concluded that I need make no apologies for aping them, but, like Hemingway, I also tackled several American themes and problems. And if I was a citizen of the world, I was not cast in the Gary Davis mold, for he had felt that in order to embrace all cutlures he had to surrender his American passport. Instead, the more I grew to apprciate and love the world, the more firmly I rooted myself in America.

In later years my ambivalence regarding this abiding conflict between the claims of the entire earth and those of my native corner of it reached a head when the government nominated me to work on committees dealing with sensitive information. Appointment necessitated careful clearance by the F.B.I. and during one extended period I was investigated almost yearly. Old hands in Washington explained: 'The Bureau has found that if its investigators query sources without revealing the purpose of their inquiry—clearance for an appointment to an important job as opposed to investigation based on suspicion of criminal or treasonous activity—they get better results. If the person being questioned gets the idea that you may be subversive, they rack their brains to recall anything you may have done wrong.'

One such investigation proved memorable. At a White House meeting with President Nixon he informed me that another of the checks was being made regarding an appointment he had in mind, but in the weeks that followed friends flashed none of the warning signals. Later a Washington acquaintance told me why: 'Philadelphia headquarters received instructions: "Full field check on James A. Michener, Pipersville, Pennsylvania, for assignment to a committee dealing with foreign affairs." They looked in the phone book, got your address, and the investigation was under way. Very thorough.'

'Never heard of it. They didn't check me. What happened?'

'In due course, Philadelphia reported: "Have investigated Michener intensively. Clean as a hound's tooth. But we cannot guess what foreign affairs position he might be appointed to." Now let me ask you. What happened?'

'The early Micheners were a prolific lot, had kids all over the place. In my home county, Bucks, there used to be six James A. Micheners. Today I live in a village of about fifteen families, and two of us are James A. Michener.'

'The one they investigated? What does he do?'

'Works in a nearby stove factory. One of the nicest guys you could ever meet.'

The events in the lives of the other James A. Micheners caused both amusement and irritation. When one of them was hit by a truck, I was reported as being near death, and my wife was once startled to learn at her hairdresser's that she had filed for divorce. Such affairs caused me to contemplate what might happen if someone with my name committed a real crime, and this led me to a painful review of recent cases in which American men and women of some stature in their communities had engaged in treasonous activity by acting as agents of foreign powers.

Treason seems to me the ultimate crime, beyond which there is nothing worse; it is similar to patricide, but much more evil because there have been instances in which an irrationally abusive father has become such a threat to his children that they have had to kill him in self-defense. I can find no justification for treason; it is totally abhorrent.

An experienced operative for naval intelligence explained several factors that can operate to turn a man against his homeland: 'Why is the military so apprehensive when they see one of their officers accumulating big debts, especially gambling ones? Because they have learned that such debts often lead to treason. Foreign spies see that the officer needs money and would be susceptible to their approaches. Same with homosexuality. Very vulnerable to blackmail.'

He then told me about a fascinating counterintelligence tactic: 'By analyzing hundreds of cases and seeking the correlations between them, we discovered that if an officer subscribed to leftist magazines like *The Nation* and *The New Republic,* if he patronized foreign movies, especially the Russian ones, and if he allowed his wife to retain her maiden name, his loyalty had to be under suspicion.'

When I said that under those tests I could be convicted, he changed the subject: 'What gives us the greatest worry is that whenever the armed services terminate a lot of officers in a general retrenchment those men are so embittered by the arbitrary treatment that they decide to get back some of the money they've lost by selling secrets to the enemy. So the armed services save nothing. Why not? Because they have to hire an almost equal number of investigators for counterespionage duties, keeping track of the disgruntled men.'

I have not known personally any of the traitors in the categories he mentioned, but I have followed the trials of a dozen or more as the sordid details were revealed. I have also been dismayed by the appalling case of the Cambridge spy ring that included Maclean, Burgess, Philby and especially Blunt.

I am aware that millions of our citizens go through life without pondering the problem of treason and there's no reason why they should. But those of us who work abroad, or love foreign countries, or are attracted to the idea of world citizenship ought to contemplate these matters seriously and decide at some early stage that allegiance to one's country, whether citizenship was acquired by birth or naturalization, is not negotiable.

During World War II, I was caught up inadvertently in what officials thought was a case of international espionage.

On Sunday morning, May 5, 1940, before the United States entered the war, I was reading the front page of that day's *New York Times* when I saw an article that exploded in my mind like a flash of lightning.

Written by William L. Laurence, the *Times'* science writer, the story dealt in revealing detail with the inspired efforts of Hitler's scientists at a place called Peenemünde, on a remote island in the Baltic, to produce a significant supply of 'heavy water,' a phrase I had heard before but about which I had only a vague understanding. I hunched over the paper and read every word with extreme care, learning that 'heavy water' was water in which each molecule consists of deuterium (or two atoms of heavy hydrogen), which could be used to produce a system whereby the atom could be converted into a bomb. The article said that it thus appeared evident that German and Allied scientists were engaged in a race whose outcome might determine who would win the war.

I was shocked by these facts and surprised that so much had been revealed, for this information, coupled with what I had already deduced by myself, proved that momentous research was being done. Surprisingly, I met at that time, and later when I was in my Navy uniform, not one person who had read the article and certainly none who had appreciated its historic significance. I was additionally frustrated and perplexed when no newspaper carried any follow-up on the *Times* article, or even any oblique reference to it.

When I joined the Navy I carried with me the memory of that article about the inevitable race between America's scientists and Nazi Germany's for the creation of a bomb that would have the power to destroy cities. I therefore read with special interest secret aviation reports on the importance of an obscure German scientific research center on Peenemünde. From something I read, and it could have been the *Times* article, I deduced that it was at Peenemünde that the Germans were working on problems relating to heavy water, and the place became a fixation in my thinking.*

But I was in a quandary, for no one I knew had heard of either Peenemünde or heavy water; either I had miscalculated their importance or I had misunderstood what that disturbing article had said about them. Therefore, on my next visit to New York, in naval uniform, I went to my old friend the New York Public Library on Fifth Avenue at Forty-second and said to the grouchy man staffing the reference desk: 'About a month ago I read an article in *The New York Times,* front page, about some scientific experiments done by the Germans. I wonder if you could check your index and verify the article and the date so I can look it up.'

He did far more than consult the index. Glaring at me with eyes

---

*Years later I would read everything in English relating to Peenemünde and use it as a locale for a major portion of one of my novels.

popped wide open, he must have pressed a signal button, because I was quickly surrounded by two men who whisked me off to a private room for interrogation: 'Why did you ask for that particular story?' 'Are you entitled to wear that uniform?' 'But if your duty station is in Washington, why would you be in this library in New York?' And most pressing: 'What do you know about heavy water?'

It was a grueling session, because I was able to give only a garbled explanation of why I was there. I will not review the steps I had to take to establish my innocence of wrongdoing and deny any affiliation with a foreign government, especially German or Russian, but in time my interrogators accepted the fact that I was in naval aviation, I was entitled to my uniform, and I was simply a geography nut who had been able to put two and two together when exotic foreign places like Peenemünde were involved.

Later, I learned that the *Times* article and its reprint in *The Saturday Evening Post* had set alarm bells ringing throughout Washington, for it had revealed, as I saw immediately, data of the most sensitive nature on a problem of vital importance to the whole world: the possibility of producing an atomic bomb. I was convinced that such a bomb was going to be developed, by either our scientists or Hitler's, and it was a terrifying prospect.

I also learned that directives had been flashed to all agencies that no comment of any kind could be published about the articles, nor any editorial speculation, nor any follow-up of any kind. Libraries were alerted to detain any reader who might ask for those editions of the *Times* or the *Post,* and it was this precaution that had trapped me. My interrogation, even though guarded, revealed enough information to reinforce all that I had suspected, so during my tour of duty in the South Pacific I carried with me the heavy realization that my world might explode at any moment. When it did, over Hiroshima, I was not surprised.

In 1955 I was in India awaiting an appointment with Jawaharlal Nehru, then head of state, and his office suggested that since he would not be able to see me for a few days I might like to make the colorful trip from New Delhi up into the mountains where the British had maintained their summer capital at Simla. In the days of the Raj, in the middle of spring, each department of government would move all its people and important papers the hundred and eighty miles north to find refuge in the cool mountain air.

I enjoyed Simla, having come there with an old friend, Sohan Lal, an Indian publisher of sorts and a wonderful bon vivant who knew Paris and New York as well as he did Delhi and the mountains. When his son married, shortly after my departure, he hired four trains to take the entire wedding party from Delhi up to Simla, and the schedule of festivities covered an entire week.

Thanks to Sohan's hospitality, I caught a glimpse of what Simla must have been like in the past, in the time of Rudyard Kipling. One day I was walking with my wife far from Simla on a road that had led to the lower approaches to Tibet. As we neared the border, which was marked by a small wooden sign that said in several languages PROCEED NO FARTHER, I heard a clicking sound I thought must be coming from some animals or insects. But as we turned the corner we saw on a double lane leading to the frontier a huge number of women, perhaps a thousand, all on their knees banging small hammers against rocks to break them into fragments, which other women were placing by hand in the roadbed, with each little piece positioned to fit properly and then tapped gently to make it secure. I had never before seen such a concentration of manual labor, and I thought of the building of the pyramids or the great temples at Angkor Wat, which had been achieved in this painstaking way. The difference between those ancient structures and the roadway was that the latter did not require such labor-intensive methods of construction. One good bulldozer could have accomplished in an hour all the work on which these many women spent that entire day. It was an unacceptable waste of human effort, and I became so engrossed that when my wife decided to head back to our hotel I remained to analyze this mammoth project.

I saw how the larger stones were unloaded from trucks that brought them in from the distant rail terminal and how each stone had to be lifted down, since there were no dump trucks. The man who did the lifting dropped the stone at the most convenient point, from which another man lifted it, taking it closer to the roadbed, where still another and another carried it farther until finally it reached the women working with their hammers. I counted some eleven transfers of each stone until it reached the spot where its fragments were embedded in the roadbed.

'My God!' I cried. 'They're building a gigantic jigsaw puzzle,' and that's what it was.

When Sohan Lal came to fetch me hours later I asked him about those teeming thousands laboring to make a road: 'Why don't they get a bulldozer?'

'Oh, no! When you have an unlimited population, you must do something to keep the people busy.'

'But it's such wasted effort. A bulldozer could build what I saw out there in a morning, if it had six good trucks bringing in the rocks and dumping them.'

'James! I'm surprised at you! If the government brought dump trucks and a bulldozer in here tomorrow morning, those men and women you saw would destroy the trucks by noon and maybe kill the drivers, too. For taking away their livelihood.'

'But if the trucks built the road, those thousands would be freed to work on projects that made more sense.'

'What projects? And how could they be sure of getting on the new work the tiny wages they earn on the road?' And then he added the comment: 'Besides, the government pays them almost nothing. They're such a bargain we can afford to use thousands.'

Simla boasted two famous features that perplexed me, considering its altitude and coldness in winter: a wealth of lovely bamboo groves and a great number of monkeys of a special breed adapted to cold weather and called Simlas. They were a naughty crowd, and as I walked alone among the bamboos and greeted them, the chattering beasts kept me company, with some old fellows growing quite bold and rebuking me for not having brought them something to eat. They would run at me, stop short and thrust out their lower jaw as if daring me to strike them, and if I did raise my hand, they became even bolder and came quite close, still jutting out their pugnacious jaws.

On this day I ignored them because I wanted to reflect on what I had seen that morning, those automatons building that road, and slowly a thought began to form in my mind: One of the most expensive commodities a nation can have is a cheap labor force. From this a host of consequences leaped forth as inevitable.

—If you get labor for almost nothing, you have no incentive to buy expensive tools and the quality of your product will lag behind that of nations who do use the best tools on the market.

—If you keep your labor occupied on menial tasks that are best suited for machines, your work force never develops those skills that would earn you more income.

—If you employ ten to do the work of one, none of the ten will work to maximum efficiency because each will realize that what he or she does isn't significant.

—If you don't pay your labor good wages, how can they ever afford to buy what you make? You limit your potential market by 50 percent at least, and if every employer in the region pays the same low wages, your market can vanish altogether.

—A nation's wealth is generated when the money from wages is quickly spread around because this causes more goods to be produced, and real wealth consists in the making and interchange of goods.

And then I made the discovery: 'Ricardo was wrong. There is no fixed quantum of money in the world, or in any nation. The rich man doesn't suffer deprivation when labor gets a bigger share, for that larger amount means a bigger total for him.

My final conviction was this: 'Labor should get the highest wage possible and then be taxed heavily to pay for the hospitals, museums, libraries, schools, roads and all the other things that make human life safer, better and more enjoyable.'

One of the truly enlightening days I've had in my life came at the end of World War II when I worked in Japan and saw a country that had been almost totally destroyed. Taken to one of the few surviving steel plants, I expected the manager, a bright fellow trained in Sweden, to tell me how gratified he was that his plant had escaped the American bombers. Not at all! As we stood watching hundreds of his capable workmen with long tongs working in intense heat to guide the emerging ribbon of red-hot steel to the area where it would be cut into usable portions, he said: 'We're in desperate trouble here. All our competitors had their old plants destroyed by your bombs. Now they'll rebuild using the latest heavy machinery from Sweden and Canada. Rationalize. No more of this hand-labor nonsense,' and he pointed to his men lifting the steel. 'If we let those others get a head start with everything new, we may never catch up.' He shook his head sadly and said: 'Much better if your planes had bombed this plant. Then we'd have to start from the beginning with fresh concepts.'

'But,' I asked him, 'haven't you enjoyed a great advantage by having your plant in operation now when they don't have theirs? Not having to rebuild, haven't you saved a great deal of money?' And he replied: 'For the present, yes, but when I travel through Tokyo and see the opposition building their new plants, I am terrified.'

His statement was phenomenally on target: 'It is often more sensible to scrap old ways even at great expense so that you start afresh with new procedures; if you cling tenaciously to the old, you will become as outmoded as the decrepit plant you're nursing along.'

I am ashamed to confess that I witnessed an economic miracle in Japan but failed at the time to appreciate its significance. When I landed there after the war, taxicabs were Rube Goldberg affairs at which we Americans laughed: crude, beat-up bundles of junk carrying a load of charcoal in the back and a small round stove in which to burn it so that the gases would propel the taxi. Later there were the famous sixty-yen cabs (basic fare sixteen cents), which were no bigger than a child's pram. Made by Toyota, they were called Toyopets and were both dangerous and ridiculous.

But as soon as practicable after the war Toyota produced a car—mostly tin, it seemed—that did provide space and run smoothly, but had someone told me then: 'Jim, in a few years these Toyotas are going to drive Detroit right into the ground,' I would have had him certified as a nut. I failed to anticipate the economic miracle that the Japanese automobile industry was about to create. I had not fully realized that hard work, inventive genius and skilled management could produce reliable products that all the world would want to purchase. But I am also famous among my friends as the man who confidently predicted that pizza would never gain a foothold in America: 'Too much dough, not enough goodies on it, and who in his right mind would go for anchovies?'

Ideas! Ideas! They are the fuel that keeps a brain functioning at a high level, and fortunately one does not have to invent one's own; choice ideas from the past are easily available in any good library or university or on the job, if one looks. Ideas have been the joy of my life and in my ninth decade I am still striving to understand those that lie beyond my grasp while finding great comfort in those I do understand.

I never saw the potency of an idea better exemplified than in a medical situation I observed in World War II when I landed on a tropical island infested with malaria and dengue. At first the index per thousand of infection by these disabling and sometimes deadly diseases was 1500.00, meaning that everyone could expect one and a half attacks, a fearful cost, which could have rendered our occupation of that island and other critical ones untenable. But in years past, medical researchers had studied malaria and dengue and found the answer to this ancient scourge, and one of these geniuses came to our island to supervise the miraculous eradication of the diseases: 'A team of twenty men will use flamethrowers to burn off the surface of all the water ditches in the area. A team of a hundred will check every square inch of our occupied area, turn over dishes, cans, sagging tarpaulins, so that there is no stagnant water standing anywhere.' When the island commander asked: 'And what will that accomplish?' he received an amazing answer: 'It will kill all the mosquito eggs, and since we know adults can't fly more than fifty yards, in a very short time every mosquito in your area will be dead. No more malaria. No more dengue,' and before the year was out our index was down to 0.003, or three cases per thousand, and we believed that those were men who had wandered into areas that had not been cleansed. The fortuitous fact that in peacetime some bright person had gathered what seemed like useless information about mosquito behavior, conducting the kind of study glib newspapers like to ridicule, helped significantly to win the war.

In accumulating new ideas there was also a strong emotional component. Of all the poetry I have memorized and lived with during my life, none has lived longer in my thinking than a four-line jingle I came upon in 1927 at the end of my sophomore year in college. It was written in 1915 by a woman poet, Sarah Cleghorn, when people were developing social consciences:

> The golf links lie so near the mill
> That almost every day
> The laboring children can look out
> And watch the men at play.

Whenever my moral fervor about decent wages for decent work flagged, I recited those lines, and they reminded me of the childhood that I will describe later. But since I cannot help editing almost every printed word I see, in time the last two lines became:

> The children sweating at the looms
> Can see the men at play.

I was astonished just now when, in looking up the original, I found that I had long lost Miss Cleghorn's words. Hers are better, but mine tug more at my heart.

This ends my report on my years of travel and reflection. The experience left me with two critical ideas: that all men are brothers and engaged in the same struggle to understand the complexities of life; and that society prospers when its workmen receive proper wages so that goods can be more vigorously exchanged, thus generating more wealth. My third idea would come later, and it would have nothing to do with travel or philosophy or politics.

VIII

Writing

HAD I BEEN a devout man, I would surely have interpreted my experience on the Tontouta airstrip as a theophany.

In the latter days of World War II I flew back to my headquarters in French New Caledonia in the southwestern Pacific after exciting duty in the Fiji Islands and a tumultuous exploration of Bora Bora. I had been so inspired by my adventures and so eager to get back to my typewriter to report upon them that my senses were very alert. As our plane approached big Tontouta Air Base for a sunset landing, the sky darkened ominously and I had a premonition that this landing was going to be somewhat more dangerous than normal.

My fears were realized when, just as we approached the long strip enclosed at the far end by a range of low mountains, we lost visibility. I remember saying to myself: 'He'd better go up and around for another shot!' and to my relief he did just that. The plane dipped its left wing, the engines roared, the nose went high in the air, and we shot upward through the menacing clouds, took a wide sweep to the left to avoid the mountains and went back out to sea to make a second attempt, hoping that in the meantime the clouds would have dissipated.

While we were executing these routine maneuvers for avoiding a hazardous landing, twilight had darkened, and as we made our approach in minimum visibility my nerves tensed, my muscles tightened. No go! Visibility nil! Again the roar of the engines, the sickening swing to the left with the wing dipping almost vertically, and the swerving away from the mountains ahead. Then back out to sea and another wide swing over waves barely visible below for a third approach.

I cannot now recall whether Tontouta had night-landing radar at that time—probably not, but if it did it was undoubtedly insufficient. During the third approach I was extremely tense but not panicked because I had flown thousands of dangerous miles in small planes in the Pacific and had learned to trust Navy pilots. I remember telling myself: It's got to be this time or we don't make it, and I did not care to speculate on whether we would have enough fuel to carry us back to Fiji or north to Espiritu Santo.

With skill, nerve and determination our pilot brought his heavy plane into perfect alignment with the barely visible runway and eased it down in a flawless landing. We applauded, but he gave no sign of acknowledgment, because he, better than we, appreciated what a near thing it had been.

That night I had no appetite, for the tenseness in my stomach banished any interest in food, but neither was I ready for bed. In what was to become the turning point of my life, I left the transient quarters where travelers like me stayed until they could get back to their home base, and unaware of where I was wandering, I found myself back on the long, dark airstrip with the mountains at the far end visible whenever the low, scudding clouds separated momentarily to reveal them.

For some hours I walked back and forth on that Tontouta strip without any purpose other than to calm my nerves, but as I did so I began to think about my future life and to face certain problems: What do I want to do with the remainder of my life? What do I stand for? What do I hope to accomplish with the years that will be allowed me? Do I really want to go back to what I was doing before? I spent at least two hours kicking these ideas about.

At this critical point I was by no means alone in this forthright evaluation of myself and my life goals; thousands of men I knew in the South Pacific were asking themselves identical questions on the lonely islands and during the long night watches on ships or airfields. An astonishing number would decide: I will not be satisfied just to plod along in what I was doing. I'm a better man than that. I can do better. And they resolved when they returned home to become ministers, or go back to law school, or run for public office, or strike out on their own in some daring venture, or become college professors, or work in hospitals. On those remote islands lives changed, visions enlarged, directions shifted dramatically, and it is to the eternal credit of those leaders then running our nation that they anticipated such frames of mind and provided financial assistance after the war to the young men who were determined to alter their lives for the better.

As one who has earnestly contemplated American history and the various acts of Congress, I have concluded that in two instances Congress has indeed helped to improve the quality of our national life. Interestingly but not surprisingly, each was passed during a war, as if the legislators as well as young soldiers and sailors were eager to brighten the future, and each act helped redirect lives.

In 1862, during the darkest days of the Civil War, Congress passed a pair of interrelated bills that I think of as one: the Homestead Act, which gave free land to settlers in the West, and the Morrill Act, authorizing the establishment of land-grant colleges in which tuition would be either minimal or free. These were acts of genius, for they ensured a free, active society in which citizens of good purpose could receive both land for homes and education to strengthen themselves and their nation.

The second laudable act of Congress was passed during World War II. What would become known as the G.I. Bill promised all men and women who had served in the war funds toward the completion of their education after the war ended. Millions of young people availed themselves of this opportunity, and I judge it to have been one of the best expenditures of public money made in my lifetime, for it helped an entire generation of bright young people improve themselves and make an effort to accomplish something meaningful. The burst of achievements in all fields that the United States saw in the decades following the end of World War II stemmed in large part from the flood of energy released by the G.I. Bill.

So I was not alone, there on the Tontouta airstrip that night, in deciding that I was ready for something better than I had been able to accomplish previously. But in another way I was unique, for I had never been ambitious in the usual sense of that word. I had not dreamed, as a boy, of becoming this or that; I had never aspired to wealth or acclaim; and the best description I ever heard of myself was one given by a college classmate: 'Jim wanders down the road picking his nose and looking for the stars.'

Therefore, my evaluations that night did not resemble those of other men who had a clearer vision of themselves. I did not aspire to be a clergyman, although I believe I would have made a good one, nor did I want to go into a different type of business, for I was happy as an editor at the fine Macmillan publishing company. I had not the kind of profound belief in my own destiny that would have propelled me into politics or public service, and I could see in myself no dormant talent that was waiting to spring into life if I gave it encouragement. Since I had already attended half a dozen of the finest educational institutions in the world I did not feel the need to go to yet another school.

As I walked in the darkness I concluded that I was not dissatisfied with my employment; I was dissatisfied with myself. And I am embarrassed at the decision I reached that night, because when it is verbalized without the qualifications I gave it as soon as I uttered it, the impression it leaves is almost ludicrous. But as the stars came out and I could see the low mountains I had escaped, I swore: 'I'm going to live the rest of my life as if I were a great man.' And despite the terrible braggadocio of those words, I understood precisely what I meant: 'I'm going to erase envy and cheap thoughts. I'm going to concentrate my life on the biggest ideals and ideas I can handle. I'm going to associate myself with people who know more than I do. I'm going to tackle objectives of moment.'

On and on I went, laying out the things I would and would not do, but always I came back to one overriding resolve: I will constantly support the things I believe in. And in the nearly fifty years since that night, I have steadfastly borne testimony to all my deeply held beliefs.

Before the night was out I modified my initial conviction; I would not act as if I were a great man, for that was too pompous; but I would act as if I knew what greatness was, and I have so ordered my life.

Was this powerful experience on the dark airstrip a theophany in the literal sense of the word, an appearance of God to a human being? As I said earlier, had I been devoutly religious I could have avowed that it was, and I might even have claimed that voices spoke to me in the hallowed darkness after the miracle of our safe landing. But that was not the case. I heard no voices other than the inward ones that warned me that I had come to the end of the line in the direction I had been heading and that I sorely required a new path. I had observed that certain men and women lived as if they had shorn away the inconsequentials and reserved their energies for serious matters, and I decided to pattern my life after theirs.

Lest the reader suspect that I am overdramatizing the perils of that difficult airstrip, let me report that some weeks later my successor in my work at Navy headquarters in Noumea wangled an aircraft for unauthorized use and, coming back to Tontouta after a jolly escapade, flew smack into the hills I had eluded earlier, killing himself and all my former staff.

How did I behave after my soul-searching experience? In no visible way differently from before. I returned to my home base on Espiritu Santo, resumed control of a vast warehouse filled with papers needed to prosecute the air war against the Japanese, and tried to continue to treat my six enlisted men with special consideration, especially Jim, the shoemaker from Tennessee, and Garcia, the wild-eyed poet from Texas. I flew to all corners of the Pacific carrying my precious wares; and I approached my fortieth birthday without having accomplished anything special.

There was one minor change. As I rode about my own island and the forty-eight others I serviced using the travel orders Bill Collins had provided, I began to listen with attention as men told stories at night in the various Hotels de Gink in which transients lived when on travel orders. I sought out men who'd had unusual experiences or more likely had usual ones that they understood with unusual clarity, and from this mélange of information and observation I acquired a good perception of what the great Pacific adventure meant in human terms. Clearly, almost clinically, I concluded that if you ordered all the young men of a generation to climb Mount Everest, you would expect the climb to have a major significance in their lives. And while they were climbing the damned mountain they would bitch like hell and condemn the assignment, but years later, as they looked back, they'd see it as the supreme adventure it was and they'd want to read about it to reexperience it.

These thoughts led to a clear-cut conviction: Years from now the men who complain most loudly out here will want to explain to others what it was like. I'm sure of it, so I'm going to write down as simply and honestly as I can what it was really like. And then I reassured myself: No one knows the Pacific better than I do; no one can tell the story more accurately. This was not a boast; it was true and relevant to the task I planned to set myself.

Loving movies as I do, and never having come upon one that was so bad I walked out before I saw how it ended, I enjoyed going to see the show each night at seven, when we sat on coconut logs under the stars to see Betty Grable and Ann Sothern and Rita Hayworth and Dick Powell and John Payne go through their paces. I found entertaining even the dreadful Republic Pictures productions shot on a shoestring in the back lots.

But at nine-thirty each night I would repair to my darkened Quonset hut, light a smelly lantern, which helped keep away the mosquitoes, and sit at my typewriter, pecking out with two fingers the stories I had accumulated as I traveled the Pacific. Sitting there in the darkness, illuminated only by the flickering lamplight—the electricity was cut off in the big sheds—I visualized the aviation scenes in which I had participated, the landing beaches I'd seen, the remote outposts, the exquisite islands with bending palms, and especially the valiant people I'd known: the French planters, the Australian coast watchers, the Navy nurses, the Tonkinese laborers, the ordinary sailors and soldiers who were doing the work, and the primitive natives to whose jungle fastnesses I had traveled.

Rigorously I adhered to my commitment: to report the South Pacific as it actually was. By nature I stayed away from heroics and I was certainly not addicted to bombast; I had seen warfare but I shied away from talking much about it, and I had none of the excessive romanticism that had colored the works of my predecessors in writing about the Pacific: Pierre Loti, Robert Louis Stevenson, James Norman Hall and especially the very popular Frederick O'Brien, author of *White Shadows in the South Seas.* In familiarity with the various islands I probably exceeded them all, but in narrative skill I was no doubt inferior.

What I did was what I would do in all my later books: create an ambience that would both entertain and instruct the reader, invent characters who were as real as I could make them, and give them only such heroics as I myself had experienced or found credible. I felt then, as I feel now, nearly half a century later, that if I could follow my plan I would fulfill my aim of refreshing the wartime memories of my colleagues in years ahead. For whom did I write as I sat night after night fighting the mosquitoes with those little bombs of insecticide the Navy gave us and pecking out my stories on the typewriter? Not the general public, whom I did not care to impress; not the custodians of literature, about whom I knew little; and certainly not posterity, a concept that simply never entered my mind. I wrote primarily for myself, to record the reality of World War II, and for the young men and women who had lived it.

I concluded after six or seven chapters that my work was achieving more or less what I desired, but I had no assurance that it was and certainly I never cried at the end of a long night—at three or four in the morning because I rewrote a great deal—'Hey, this is pretty good!'

Since I was figuratively as well as actually working in the dark I decided to seek other opinions, but to whom could I turn?

In the huge building next to mine there was a young enlisted man with a sardonic nature, a fellow drafted into the Navy much against his will, who spent his time collecting cowries, those beautifully formed little shells of lovely colors. He stuffed them with a mixture of cotton and aviation glue and strung them together on strands of silver wire to make delicate necklaces, which other sailors bought for fifteen dollars a strand to send home to their wives and girlfriends. His name was Fred, and if he is still living I hope he will get in touch with me, for I owe him much and would like to repay the courtesy he extended to me.

I could see from watching the lines of sailors who came to his building next to mine that since he was raking in a fortune with his necklaces he must be a rather sharp item. I was about to approach him about reading one of my chapters when he surprised me by saying one morning as we opened our Quonsets: 'Lieutenant Michener, when I'm working at night making my necklaces I see that you're over there working at something. What's *your* racket?' and when I told him that I was trying to write an account of what war was like in the South Pacific he said: 'I'd like to see how you find it.' Within a minute I had handed him a chapter, then suffered agonies wondering if I had done the right thing.

The next morning he appeared in my building with the chapter: 'This isn't at all bad' was all he said, and later as I fed him one chapter after another he repeated his comment: 'Not bad, not bad at all.' He never spoke about story line or character development or style or even the general coherence of the material, but morning after morning he told me: 'Not bad,' and once he said about a battle scene: 'You know what you're doing.'

His support was invaluable, for only he knew what I was trying to do there in the dark while he was making his necklaces. I never bought any and he never tried to sell me one, but had he ever asked I believe I would have inspected the necklace, admired it, and said as I handed it back: 'Not bad, not bad at all.'

He never wrote to me after the book, which was called *Tales of the South Pacific,* was published. I'm sure he felt no need to, for when I needed his assistance most he had generously given it. I cannot express how much I valued his support, for writing in an empty shed darkened with mighty shadows and infested with mosquitoes is a task that cries out for moral support, and he provided it.

.   .   .

Thus I started my writing career, and it is important to know certain aspects of my previous life to appreciate the rather unusual kind of writer I became. Three aspects of my upbringing shaped my writing: both as a boy and as a young man I read prodigiously; I had a very wide and vivid experience in dealing with the stark realities of American life; and I had served an intense apprenticeship as a New York editor in one of America's then strongest publishing houses. The last experience more than any other formed my attitudes toward the profession of writer.

Because of my experiences at Macmillan I have never called myself an author; I am a writer, and I am proud that writing is one of the great occupations in any society. Authors seemed to me to be pompous poseurs who published with the London branch of our firm and who came across the Atlantic now and then to display their grandeur before the American peasants; writers were people like Theodore Dreiser and Sinclair Lewis and Willa Cather who stayed home and wrote books. Authors were also men of the last century with three names, such as James Russell Lowell, Henry Wadsworth Longfellow, John Greenleaf Whittier and Oliver Wendell Holmes, who had long beards and who appeared in American classrooms as plaster busts; writers were unpleasant people like Melville, Whitman and Upton Sinclair. I was a writer.

Macmillan in those days had three employees who had an enormous effect on my attitudes toward publishing. Harold Latham, the senior editor, was an aloof scholar with a keen eye for the best-seller, who never married and who made Macmillan his bride and heir. He was formidable, not only for his gargantuan size. Although Macmillan published the book I was working on in the South Pacific, Latham never once spoke to me, for I was an editor who worked on textbooks while he shepherded real authors. He was invaluable to Macmillan, and I had great regard for him, because he was the editor who found *Gone With the Wind* and *Forever Amber,* two books on whose profits we lived while I worked for the company, and his other judgments were equally sound. He was a powerful man who made me allergic to editors in chief and trade publishers in general. I would never be really close to any editor or publisher: respect them I did; honor them I did for the good services they provided; but they were not my brothers, they were men destined to work with authors, not mere writers.

In those years Macmillan also had one of the most engaging editors I have ever known, a very tall fellow named Jim Putnam who dressed impeccably, spoke with an English accent and was the prototype of the New York editor. Serene, charismatic and never pompous, Jim Putnam charmed everyone he met, especially me, and I have only the warmest memories of him, not as an editor but as a gentleman. Of all the trade-book editors at Macmillan, he was the only one who ever condescended to speak to us textbook slaves on the second floor, even though it was we who earned the company most of its normal profits. I appreciated his courtesies and studied with care his modus operandi.

His principal assignment, so far as I could see, was to appear at work dressed in a fine English suit with homburg in position and to catch a taxi to one or another of the piers in midtown Manhattan where the great liners docked in the early morning after crossing the Atlantic. There he would board the vessel before disembarkation began, seek out the cabin of some author from the London branch of our firm, and escort him or her to the building on Fifth Avenue occupied by the New York Macmillan, a much grander place than what our English cousins occupied in London.

Jim would escort his author through the great main doors and up to the directors' room on the second floor, and I would watch the procession pass my rather grubby office: Jim resplendent in the lead, the self-satisfied author in tow, and the three other trade editors who were to get a free meal that day bringing up the rear. In the boardroom would be waiting a handful of executives, and later there would be a literary luncheon with perhaps one or two New York critics in attendance.

Next day Jim would escort the visiting luminary to Grand Central Station, where he or she would board the *Twentieth-Century Limited* to Chicago, whence the author would branch out to a handful of American colleges and universities for literary visits. There the guest would pontificate on almost any subject then current, give interviews, and hasten back to London, where he would deliver a second series of lectures and interviews on the barbarity of life in America, the pitiful condition of our educational system, and the general boorishness of the population. It all seemed to me a very silly business.

Here I must digress to report on one of my own experiences on the publicity tour. After I had become moderately well known as a beginning writer of some promise, I was invited to lecture at the University of Cincinnati, now headed by my old Swarthmore dean, Raymond Walter. I was met at the train by two fine-looking men, the head of the English department and his assistant. They were so unbelievably kind to me at lunch, so attentive to every word I had to say that I thought: Maybe there's something to this writing business after all, and I began to fancy myself as eligible for promotion to author. However, no sooner did the pair deliver me to the lecture hall than they disappeared.

I thought this so strange that when another pair of professors from the English department appeared at the close of my lecture to hurry me to the evening train that would speed me on my way to my next university assignment, I asked about it and the younger man explained: 'President Walter gave us an order. Whatever department invites a speaker must provide two members to meet the train, take the speaker to lunch, and deliver him or her sober to the lecture platform.' When I raised my eyebrows, the other man added: 'We had a succession of four speakers arrive here dead drunk, and Dorothy Thompson was the worst of the lot. We'll have no more of that. If they're drunk when they get off the train, we sober them up. If they're already sober, we keep them that way. But after we fellows on the second team put you on that train, you're on your own. Now it becomes the problem of the chaps at the next stop.'

They mentioned the names of the three male authors who had disgraced themselves, and distinguished they were, but I have forgotten their names; however, it was the scandalous behavior of Miss Thompson that had prompted the edict. Shortly before he died, Truman Capote went to the University of Maryland to deliver a speech, roared onto the stage completely besotted, fell down, and lay there unable to rise. Later I was told by a professor from the school that a rule similar to Cincinnati's was instituted thereafter.

My hero Jim Putnam came to a sad end, at least as far as Macmillan was concerned. At a literary cocktail party he ran into a beguiling Russian adventurer and would-be scientist named Immanuel Velikovsky, whose manuscript entitled *Worlds in Collision* offered a thrilling account of how extraterrestrial bodies at a time not far distant had collided with the earth, causing many of the phenomena that more conventional scientists ascribed to less spectacular causes. Jim persuaded Macmillan to publish the book, which became a red-hot bestseller and a major topic of conversation across the United States. It was a feather in Jim's cap and we were glad for him.

But then the community of scientific scholars descended on Macmillan in outrage, with professors who should have had better sense threatening never again to purchase a Macmillan book if we continued to publish and circulate this infamous trash. I was one of Jim's defenders, proclaiming loudly that 'freedom of speech demands that we stick to our guns and allow Velikovsky to have his say,' but I had scarcely uttered the words when editors from the college department, source of much of our profits, pointed out that if professors of science in the American universities were to boycott our textbooks, the consequences could be disastrous, and much debate was held within the company.

The professors were adamant, and some who had previously pontificated on freedom of speech as a cornerstone of American democracy, now reiterated that if Macmillan continued to distribute the Velikovsky book, Macmillan was dead. As an underling in the high school division I was not privy to the decision-making, but I well remember the solemn spring evening when a young woman who worked in the college department informed a group of us who had gathered for an evening meal that our friend Jim Putnam had been thrown to the wolves: 'Yep, fired to satisfy the scientists, and we agreed to give the book to another publisher, something never before heard of in American publishing, a bestseller and all. The scientists are finally satisfied and have promised they'll continue to use Macmillan texts.' And I never saw Jim Putnam again.

While at Macmillan I was myself involved in two cases of censorship and witness to a third, each involving references to religion. In one of the textbooks I had edited I had allowed the author to state what I believed was a historical fact about Mary Baker Eddy and her Christian Science Church. The book had no sooner been published than I was visited by two distinguished-looking gentlemen who explained that their headquarters in Boston seriously objected to what we had printed. When I tried to defend myself I learned that through the years the mother church in Boston had devised a most carefully worded statement about Mary Baker Eddy, each phrase of which had been vetted by experts so that there could be no possible taint of charlatanism, false evangelism or claims for messianism. And I learned further that no one like me, outside the Church, could possibly guess what would be offensive or contrary to official doctrine. In other words, the mother church had determined what could or could not be said about Mary Baker Eddy and nothing more or less would be permitted in print. I did not ask what the penalties would be if we did not remove from all future printings the offending passage and substitute accepted doctrine; I didn't have to.

In my second case I was visited by two lawyers from Utah who looked so much like the men from Boston that I cannot now differentiate the four. Their mission was the same. In a book about the western expansion in the United States, I had once more stumbled into an area where accepted doctrine had been laid down, this time by the Mormon Church, and anyone who did not tailor his textbook material precisely to the wishes of that august body was in serious trouble, for not only would his books never be used in Utah but legal suits might ensue. There had been, I knew well from ample documentation, a horrible affair in which settlers moving west had somehow infuriated the Mormon leadership and been annihilated by what seemed certain to have been Mormon gunmen, but it had been decreed that no mention of this affair could ever appear in print. I would later learn that if a public or university library purchased any book that dealt with this incident, mysteriously the book disappeared immediately. The Mormon visitors who came to my office were two of the gentlest complainants I would ever meet during my tenure as an editor, but it was clear that under their dark blue suits they wore armor of steel and if I refused to comply with their wishes they would prove to be fierce adversaries. I did not test them.

The third case interested me immensely, for it centered not on faulty doctrine or on matters I had not fully understood but on a single word. One of our college texts had used the unfortunate phrase 'typical jesuitical cunning,' and the full force of the Catholic educational apparatus in New York and other states fell upon us with the stated—not implied— threat that if we did not remove that phrase from the specific book in hand and, as company policy, ban the pejorative use of the word 'jesuitical,' the Catholic institutions would have to boycott not only all our textbooks, but also our other books. There was much discussion about this word in the corridors at Macmillan, and about freedom of speech, but in the end the phrase was dropped and I became so indoctrinated that I find it difficult to use it even today. I notice, however, that the new *Random House Dictionary* contains as definition (2) *using oversubtle reasoning; crafty; sly; intriguing.* Well, maybe Random can get away with it. Macmillan couldn't.

The most fascinating instance of censorship involved not religion but the entire state of Texas. As one of my editorial jobs I worked on a history of the United States written by Edna McGuire, one of the most polished writers we had, and I, proud of the assignment, was determined to do my best. But we faced a problem, and it was grave. Texas was one of the few states that required every school in the state to use the same texts, and since the state was so big, publishers battled furiously to win what was termed 'a Texas adoption,' for this meant immense sales and profits. The competition was brutal, and whenever we lost out to some other house we charged that they had used beautiful saleswomen to influence the selection in some highly improper ways. We swore that Macmillan never used this tactic, but once when I was in Texas helping to supervise the final stages of the contest in which my McGuire history was the leading contender, I saw with some relief that our women consultants were at least as good-looking as the opposition's and some in my judgment a lot more so.

Then our field operatives reported a perilous rumor: 'Opposition teams are spreading the story that Edna McGuire is a Catholic!' and in the Baptist Texas of those days, that would have killed our book if we hadn't immediately signed up a gentlemanly elder statesman from West Texas to pose as her coauthor. While I edited his supposed contribution to the book, which was actually written by Miss McGuire, I learned a great deal about Texas.

Our field men, all Texans, who would have to sell the book to local authorities, understandably felt that they had the right to caution us, within reason, regarding what went into the text, and I became their contact in the New York editorial offices: 'Jim, if we don't have adequate coverage of three men, we might as well not offer our book. Sam Houston, Stephen Austin, and Davy Crockett. Picture of each, as big as possible. Full biographies. Glowing accounts of their heroism.'

'But this is a national history for sale in all parts of the country, not a history of Texas.'

'Trick is to write it as a history of Texas and make it look national.'

But as soon as we tried this, we ran into all sorts of problems: 'Jim! What in hell are you doing to us—writing about the "Civil War." It can only be called the "War Between the States," because we weren't rebels. We were sovereign states, our own republic was fighting your republic.'

'Was Texas on the side of the South?'

'Oh my God! You're not ready for this job.'

The real problem came when I felt that we must have a portrait of Abraham Lincoln in the book. When the Texas men saw that I had introduced a handsome, full-page likeness of our greatest president, they exploded: 'You're losing us the adoption right there,' and they explained that in the Texas of that day there was no greater villain than Abe Lincoln: 'An enemy of the nation at large. Especially of Texas. It would be better if you could get away without mentioning him at all, and if you have to have a picture, let it be itty-bitty.'

When the book, properly sanitized for Texas readers, was published, I wondered what understanding schoolchildren in Vermont would have of American history from reading our text: 'Texas ran the nation and New England trailed along.' But that didn't really matter, because the Texas commissioners chose our book, so our company sold a great many volumes in Texas and very few in Vermont.

The third person who had a great impact on me during my formative period at Macmillan was a delightful, hardworking young woman whose name was Betty. She was almost identical with the scores of imaginative young women who serve as publicists for the major publishers. They all seem to me to be good-looking, in their twenties or thirties,

bright college graduates with a love of books and a Machiavellian clever-
ness. Their employers tell them: 'We can give you only a limited budget,
so get our books as much free publicity as you can.'

The young women are geniuses at networking in that they get to know
everyone in the newspapers, in radio, and in later years, television. They
know which literary clubs will be wanting what kinds of authors, and
what bookstores in what cities can be trusted to put on respectable
autographing parties. And if they like a beginning author and see a
reasonable hope that he or she might become a long-term serious figure
in their company's catalog, they can create miracles. They are some of
the brightest, most charming figures in publishing, and I have fallen in
love with about eight of them, but their names I cannot remember, nor,
I suspect, did they always remember mine. But I salute them, for they
were very good to me, bringing me in many ingenious ways to the
attention of the book industry.

But as I watched with awe and admiration their machinations, I could
not help seeing how unproductive much of their work proved to be. The
cocktail party to which no one came, the radio appearance at which the
questioner had not read the book, the newspaper interview with the
journalist who could not hide his or her contempt for both the book and
its author, the frantic casting about for anyone who would say a good
word about the book. And yet, when everything clicked, the publicist
could work wonders as she orchestrated a new talent's emergence on the
literary scene.

Nothing illustrated this better than the brilliant manner in which Bel
Kaufman's *Up the Down Staircase* was mothered into stardom. I had
never heard of either the author or her book, but as I was riding into
Doylestown one day I heard her on the car radio, and her voice was so
appealing, her wit so engaging and her common sense so refreshing that
I cried: 'I must get hold of that book!' Apparently thousands of others
were similarly affected, for a book that might have died unknown and
unmourned became a huge success, mainly, I believe, because of the
adroit manner in which the Prentice-Hall publicity people engineered
its progress. Of course, the book itself was delightfully written and the
author was unusually witty, but radio appearances had a good deal to
do with its success.

The publisher's agents had much to do with my good fortune, too,
and on three occasions when I was autographing my later books police
had to be called to keep crowds in line: in Washington and Denver and
in Centreville, Maryland. But the party I remember most vividly and
painfully was for an early novel that was held at Burdine's grand new

store at a shopping center in Miami, Florida. The store people had more than fulfilled their obligations: they had a big sign proclaiming the event, pitchers of orange juice, trays of cookies and attractive salespeople to keep the expected crowds in line. They failed in only one respect: there were no crowds. In fact, during the first awful hour, there was not even a crowd of one, and in the second painful hour only two. At one point I heard the frantic manager yelling at his staff: 'For Christ's sake, get some of the salesgirls to walk through and at least say hello.' He then must have given someone cash, for I heard him say: 'Take this and buy one of the damned things.'

At Burdine's big new store that sunny spring day I sold one book, ate a lot of cookies and drank four glasses of orange juice.

As a result of having seen at Macmillan the workings of the literary publicity racket, I developed an aversion to the whole procedure and was always loath to lend either my name or my presence to the system. And I would retain that cautious reluctance throughout my writing career. Autographing tours are brutally exhausting; travel by car from one overnight stop to the next is depressing; endless interviews are numbing; and the entire rigmarole is distasteful. I did as little of it as I could decently get by with.

But I must not take a superior attitude. Any young man or woman aspring to be a professional writer faces a horrendously difficult task in which the chances for acceptance are something like a thousand to one against. Anything honorable that the young writer can do to gain the serious attention of readers is justifiable, and I have repeatedly said that if I were starting over with no track record and no reputation, I would be on the road three nights a week, and I would go wherever and do whatever my publisher's publicist advised. I am forever indebted to those guardian angels who helped me get started, and I am always delighted when I see them ministering to the needs of some beginning writer.

My attitude toward the necessity of publicity appearances in the writing profession is best exemplified by a telephone conversation I had a few years ago with Bob Bernstein, the then president of Random House, the company that publishes my books:

PRESIDENT: Jim, I know you've fulfilled your promise to us and done the New York scene, but would you please consider visiting Washington for an autographing?

J.A.M.: You know our deal. I'll do one city, as much as you care to load on. But no more.

PRESIDENT: I understand.

PRESIDENT (two days later): Jim, I don't want to put the arm on you. You've been decent about these things. But could you, as a courtesy to me personally, drop by Washington for that autographing?

J.A.M.: The answer's still no. I've fulfilled my obligation and that's it.

PRESIDENT: I understand.

PRESIDENT (two days later): Jim, I don't think I've explained this to you properly. This guy in Washington has the authority to order thirty-six thousand copies of your book, in one order, if he takes a liking to you and the book.

J.A.M.: (after three seconds' thought): I'll be there.

The point of these memories about my introduction to publishing at Macmillan is that because of my inside experiences in the industry I saw the writer's life from a perspective that few of my fellow writers could have had. Since I knew how advertising budgets were apportioned, I never once asked about the advertising of my books, nor did I ever keep watch to see what was being done. Because I saw what futile things cocktail parties were for most writers, I never sought any. I preferred to write good manuscripts, turn them over to a professional publisher and allow him to publish, distribute and sell them as he deemed best. I still feel that way; it has been a tactic that has served me admirably and brought me great satisfaction and ease of mind.

There were two other valuable benefits resulting from my years at Macmillan. I, better than almost any other contemporary writer I know, understand what a book is. I learned how it is made, printed, stored, delivered, accounted for, advertised, remaindered. I came to understand the work of the man with the slide rule—now replaced by a computer—who mercilessly calculated the final days of a book. 'Look,' one of these men once told me, pointing to his figures. 'We have a thousand copies of this title left over and are selling them at the rate of ten copies a year. If you add up the cost of warehousing, keeping the title in the catalog and shipping out the few copies we do sell, you can easily see that it will be cheaper for us to give away the remainder.'

I then watched the adroit ways in which he disposed of those costly, useless books. First he tried to sell them at fifty cents each to the remainder bookshops that sold them for $1.50, and if they refused to buy he unloaded them at a quarter each, to be retailed at ninety-nine cents each. The ultimate indignity was to sell them for ten cents apiece to the man who used a steel press to cut out the center of each book, glue the pages together and put on a new paper cover with the inviting title

'Good Reading for a Cold Winter's Evening'; he sold them for $4.50 each. When the purchaser opened his book he found nestled inside a small bottle of gin. Watching the operation, I hoped that none of my books would fall so low.

Another important learning experience at Macmillan involved the costing out of the books I myself had edited. On the left-hand side of the publishing order, which had to be signed by the president before a penny could be spent, would be my estimate of the inescapable fixed costs of getting the manuscript ready for printing and publishing. Here were the editorial costs, the research costs, the payments to illustrators, cartographers, experts and readers, the costs of typesetting and making the plates plus a dozen other fixed items the amateur might not anticipate. These were the great immutables that had to be amortized by income from future cash sales.

On the right-hand side appeared the standard costs incurred whenever an edition, new or supplementary, was actually printed. Here we listed the printer's fees, the cost of paper, transportation from the printing plant, storage in the warehouse, keeping the book in the catalog and fliers, and, sometimes the heaviest manufacturing cost of all, binding the book in hardcovers with colorful wraparound jackets. These figures added to an imposing total, but at the bottom came the crusher: 'Add 35 percent for overhead.' This covered the costs of keeping the big offices opened, lit and heated, of paying editors, of paying salesmen, of paying for the entire apparatus of publishing.

I became almost a wizard at keeping the left-hand and right-hand costs at a minimum, only to have that dreadful 35 percent overhead kill me at the end. The art of publishing is to keep the inevitable costs of the left-hand side so low that the profit per copy on the right-hand side will be large enough to amortize the fixed costs if a reasonable number of copies are sold. Thus if the fixed costs of a proposed book are going to be $41,000 and the profit per copy is $0.52, obviously the book would have to sell 78,846 copies to break even. But remember that with each copy sold, the book contributed that 35 percent of the company's share of its purchase price to the general overhead of the firm,* so that the company might well decide to publish the book even though a final sale of 78,000 was unreasonable. Profit would still be made on the contribution to overhead.

*Understand that the publisher has only 50 percent of list price to play around with. If a book is listed at $20.00, it sells to the bookseller at a 50 percent discount, leaving the publisher with only $5.00 to cover all his costs, including the royalties to the author, which will fluctuate between 10 and 15 percent of list per copy.

There was one more factor an editor like me could play around with. We might *print* 78,000 copies, but allot funds to bind only a portion of that number. The overage would be kept in the warehouse as stored sheets whose additional cost for printing had been minimal; if the book caught on, these sheets could be rushed to the bindery and trucked out to the stores. If the book died young, the extra sheets could be pulped with little loss.

From these multiple experiences, plus my passion for books when I was a child and my admiration for the beautiful books published in England in the late nineteenth century, I acquired an abiding respect for the concept of a book as one of the finest symbols of our civilization. I saw it as a timeless pledge to the future. I wanted any book for which I had responsibility to look right, to be well printed and properly bound, to feel good to the hand and inviting to the eye. I would spend great effort to help select the proper type for a given book, the right margins, the proper spacing of paragraphs, anything at all to make it attractive. With me the making of a book was an act of dedication, and I had this devotion before I ever dreamed that I would myself be writing books.

As publisher and writer I have placed on the shelves of the world millions of books, and each has gone forth as an act of faith, the best I could make it at the time, both in content and appearance. I was asked recently: 'Do you want to be viewed as an author of novels or of nonfiction?' and I replied: 'I write books.'

Back in the Pacific, when my first manuscript was finished, at four one morning in the Quonset, I wrapped it carefully in waterproof fabric and prepared to send it off by military mail to some publisher in New York. I was in a quandary because Macmillan had an ironclad rule about not publishing works by its employees. Once, when an employee sought to publish a book in-house, the company had found that too many conflicts of interest arose. Who should edit the book? What grade of paper should be used? Into which publishing season should it fall? How much money should be allocated to its publicity? Where should it appear in the catalog? The house risked great resentment if it did not give the book all the attention the author/employee desired or the animosity of other employees if they believed it received too much attention.

My own company being forbidden territory, I decided on Knopf, a company whose books I had read with admiration. But as I was addressing the parcel it occurred to me that I was at that moment technically not a Macmillan employee, and since I believed that my company was one of the best in the business, I mailed it there under a nom de plume and with a contrived return address to which the response could be sent. Under those devious conditions it was accepted, but I was told that when the editor in chief, the redoubtable Mr. Latham, learned of my deception, he was displeased.

The manuscript fell into the hands of a most engaging Englishman, Cecil Scott, who had it edited and ready to go by the time I returned from the Pacific in February of 1946. Scott was a soft-spoken, enthusiastic man reared and educated in England. He was surprised to learn at our first meeting that I was a chap from upstairs, but he took great pains to show me how to make the manuscript better and cleaner; his standards would not allow G.I. talk, and when I insisted he invented workable substitutes. Every suggestion he made helped me improve the book, and he became in all senses of the word its sponsor.

Any young person who aspires to be a professional writer should inspect a Macmillan first printing of my first book, *Tales of the South Pacific*, because it was one of the ugliest books published that year or in any other year. Wartime restrictions concerning paper required the use of the tag-end lot of a bizarre paper that was extremely thin and had two radically different surfaces front and back, as well as a dirty brownish coloring. I saw the paper for the first time when a finished copy of the book was handed to me, and the comparison between that volume and my ideal of a book was devastating.

As an editor I had always attended to margins and visually beautiful openings for chapters. My own book had almost no margins and the chapter containing the story that would gain fame around the world started four lines from the bottom on the left-hand page in order to save paper. Other stories started in the middle of the page, and it was so obvious that Macmillan had printed the book on the cheap that Scott apologized when he handed me my copy: 'I did the best I could.' It was an ugly, monstrous book, a disgrace to a self respecting company and a humiliation to its author.*

Throughout the remainder of this narrative I shall refer repeatedly to the good luck that has followed my writing life, as it did my earlier years, and no instance was more dramatic that the one I am about to cite, even though its enormous significance will not become apparent till the end of this chapter.

Publication of my book was scheduled for the end of 1946, but in

*In its present Macmillan printing the peculiar pagination is retained, as is the color of the inside cover, one of the ugliest puces ever used on a book, but the quality of the paper and the binding have been improved. Considering the honorable life this mistreated book has had, I have grown to love its ungainly appearance and would not change it.

mid-September an editor at *The Saturday Evening Post* in Philadelphia heard an enthusiastic report about some of its stories and invited me to come down to his offices and discuss publication in his magazine. I went, was charmed by the man, and sold him two stories, but since they could not possibly appear in the *Post* until early 1947, publication of the Macmillan book had to be postponed from late 1946 to early 1947. I am forever grateful to Harold Latham that he agreed to the disruption of his orderly schedule, even though as Cecil Scott pointed out: 'If the *Post* publishes before the book publication, the author gets the entire fee, after publication we get half.'

The *Post* did a first-class job of presenting my two stories; the pages were handsome, the illustrations good, and the whole effect was pleasing. I was proud when I walked to work those weeks to see copies of my issue boldly featured on all the newsstands, and I remember that a casual incident during that wintry spell first awakened me to the fact that I might one day become a real, working writer. It was dusk and I was returning from my editorial work when I saw a discarded copy of a three-week-old *Post* lying in a snowy gutter. Without thinking, I cried: 'Hey! That's an important magazine! It contains my story!' and I stooped down to rescue the periodical. But when I saw how muddy and torn it was I drew back and kicked it farther into the gutter as I reflected upon the painfully short life of a magazine story: Magazines are ephemeral, books are forever, and if you can get your book on the shelves it will have a fighting chance to find its own life.

I have counseled hundreds of would-be writers to follow a simple rule: 'Stop daydreaming about the big money, the Hollywood contract, the glittering literary scene, the advertisements. Your job is to write the most honest book you're capable of writing, persuade someone to publish it at whatever terms are obtainable, and get that book on the library shelves. Let it find its own level while you go immediately to work on the next one. Rack your brains on how to make this one even better. All else is irrelevant.'

My own first book appeared to have slim chances. It was published in silence, reviewed by only a few journals and sold to a small number of people. It enjoyed a faltering life of about five weeks, but in that brief period it proved that a book does not have to garner a huge audience to succeed ultimately. If it falls into the hands of even a few appreciative readers it can survive, as my book did when it attracted the attention of four readers, whose reactions changed the direction of my life. They were a lineal descendant of the Marquis de Lafayette, the dean of New York literary agents, the spunky daughter of an American president, and a handsome Hollywood actor.

The Lafayette descendant was Jacques Chambrun, a debonair Manhattanite who operated a literary agency that served some notable men of letters, including Somerset Maugham. Chambrun had wit, charm, literary knowledge and a keen sense of what was happening in New York. My book had been out only a few days when I received from him a remarkable letter on stationery embossed with a coat of arms. It said in brief that he had heard such scintillating accounts of my talent that he had run right out to Brentano's to fetch a copy of my book and it had more than borne out the truth of the rumors. From his long experience in dealing with great authors like Somerset Maugham he could recognize talent when he saw it and felt sure that I was destined to follow in the distinguished footsteps of . . . and here he named four other important writers, all of whom he represented. He wanted to meet me immediately—say, that afternoon—and sign me to a long-term exclusive contract, which was certain to earn both of us a great deal of money.

Walking on air to think that I would that afternoon join the immortals, I reported to my office at Macmillan with an elation that did not subside until my encounter with Cecil Scott. Summoning me to his office, Scott told me that he was most pleased with the way my book had been received, modest though the trumpet blasts had been: 'It's being noticed by the people who count, and for that very reason I feel I must warn you about a very real danger. There's a man who listens assiduously to book gossip, then traps beginning authors before they get their eyes fully open. He writes very flattering letters, and has you signed to a long-term contract before you're aware of what's happening.'

'Jacques Chambrun?' I asked, and he moaned: 'Oh, my dear fellow! He's got to you already?' and when I showed him my letter he growled: 'That swine.'

He then told me a harrowing tale of literary life in New York: 'Chambrun reads every review, and ten minutes later, if the review is at all favorable, he dashes off a letter like this, and he traps quite a few unsuspecting naïfs. Were you intending to see him?'

'I was.'

'Thank God I caught you.'

'What's he do?'

'He keeps all the money you earn from your writing.'

'What do you mean, he keeps it?'

'Agents' rules are that the magazine or publisher has to deliver all moneys to the agent, not the writer, so that the agent can be sure of getting his ten percent. An honest agent then sends you your ninety percent, but Chambrun is a common thief. He keeps the whole hundred percent and gives you a score of reasons why you'll be getting some of it next month.'

'Don't people sue him?'

'They do, but he has a dozen dodges.'

'He says he's the agent for Somerset Maugham.'

'He is, and Maugham thinks highly of him. Says so if asked.'

'How can the publishers tolerate such a man? Why don't you do something about him?'

'He does bring us clients. He never steals from us. I clear my conscience by warning my writers.'

All Scott said about Chambrun was true. Maugham adored him, and those authors with important reputations received their proper funds on time. But novices waited for years and in many cases forever, the wily Chambrun having perfected many explanations for not paying them, and to everyone's consternation his explanations held up in court. Had I gone uptown to that meeting I would have signed my death warrant as a self-supporting writer, and I shall be forever indebted to Cecil Scott for having saved me from a disastrous situation.

Two weeks later I showed Cecil a very different kind of letter. It came from the dean of America's literary agents and personal representative of what admirers said was close to a hundred of New York's and Hollywood's brightest talents. When Cecil saw the letterhead, he whistled, for this new man dealt only with the best. The letter was much like Chambrun's, but more subdued, in the manner of a gentleman discussing a mutual interest with another gentleman, and reading it made me feel good right down to my toes, which were tingling.

The letter said that the writer had a full stable of authors but was always on the lookout for young men and women with obvious talent. He believed that if we met quietly and developed an understanding between us I would want to sign with him, and he would be eager to have me do so. Scott said it was as reassuring a letter as he had ever seen a young writer receive and urged me to call immediately, which I did from his office.

The meeting was one of the most enjoyable I would ever have with a stranger. The master agent was a big, quiet-spoken man who had mastered the exacting art of keeping high-strung writers and dramatists happy and productive. He explained that he could not perform miracles: 'I can't turn a poor writer into a good one, and I can't suddenly rejuvenate a writer who's lost his touch. But what I can do is orchestrate a productive career and protect you in all your business relationships.'

When I nodded enthusiastically he warned: 'But I can do this only

if you produce, only if you like to work and work well—toward a
purpose—and if you care about your reputation and want to enhance
it.' He was a knowledgeable expert who had seen all the triumphs and
pitfalls to which writers were susceptible. I suspect that it was my naive
enthusiasm that later made him suspect that I might not turn out as he
had originally anticipated. If he had any suspicions that day he kept
them masked, and we signed an exclusive contract; as I left he walked
me to the door, his arm about my shoulder as he said: 'You have a
tremendous future, Michener, if you can learn to tell a story.'

My experience with this man was unalloyed pleasure, the eager
learner listening to the tested professional. Our work together centered on what Hollywood had already termed 'a colossal search for
talent with a colossal reward.' The year before, one of the motion
picture companies had conducted a nationwide search for a new
novel with a fresh approach and had offered a prize of a huge
amount of money to the winner. After much hoopla, the name of the
lucky author had been announced: Ross Lockridge, a young fellow
from Indiana who had written a masterly novel, *Raintree County*. It
had received unbelievable encomiums, been reprinted in part in *Life*
and sold enormously before being turned into a movie starring Elizabeth Taylor and Montgomery Clift.

My new agent believed that my second novel, *The Fires of Spring*,
then in manuscript form, had an excellent chance of copping the second
$100,000 prize if I could revise it along lines he suggested. Under his
patient tutelage I worked from four in the morning till eight, week after
week, while putting in a full nine-to-five day at Macmillan. After work
I hied myself to the Twenty-third Street Y.M.C.A., where I served as
setter for the volleyball team that won championships, then to bed at
nine-thirty and up again at four and back to the typewriter. It was a
regimen on which I thrived, and I was glad to hear that most serious
writers do their first three novels at either four in the morning or eleven
at night while holding down a full-time job. I was proved to be in that
tradition.

After completing a prodigious amount of work, I handed the manuscript over to my agent, who had it copied and sent along to Hollywood,
where the selection committee promised to announce its decision
promptly. I spent weeks of anxiety, awaiting the communication that
would remake my life, and one Monday morning in spring a uniformed
messenger came to my door at West Twelfth Street near the Hudson
with what I thought was the news I awaited. It was a special delivery
letter, and in my excitement to hear Hollywood's verdict I failed to

notice that it did not come from California. In my nightshirt I tore open
the envelope and read one of the most crushing letters I would ever
receive. In fact, it was so devastating that once I read it I tore it up in
a fit of rage. Even today, forty years later, I can accurately summarize
the words that were burned into my soul.

The letter was from my agent and began with not 'Dear Jim' but
'Dear Mr. Michener,' and informed me not that I had won the prize,
nor even that I was still in competition, but that my agent had reached
the regrettable conclusion that I had no future as a writer. Therefore he
was terminating our contract and would be returning my manuscript
under separate cover, for he doubted it would ever be publishable. He
gave as his reason for his drastic action the fact that I did not seem to
welcome constructive criticism, that my revisions had in no way improved the manuscript, and that I showed no promise whatever of
developing into a writer whose works would find favor with the public.
In short, he was dropping me because there was no chance of my ever
attaining commercial success and that consequently I had no place in
his stable.

I was shattered by this professional estimate of my abilities and by the
impersonal manner in which it was delivered, but I remember clearly
that I was not angry with the agent, who had always treated me fairly.
As I showered, shaved and dressed for Monday's work I looked in the
mirror and said without emotion: 'I guess he knows what he's doing.'
I was aware that I must have disappointed him grievously because I
knew that initially he had liked me and had hoped that I would succeed
as a writer. I acknowledged also as I left my room that he had been
accurate and just in his principal criticisms. I did not accept advice from
others graciously, and especially not when it touched on writing; I was
determined to do things my way and accept the consequences. Gradually I had seen that I did not fit the pattern of the kind of client the agent
had in mind; I would always be an uncut diamond rather than a polished
gem and it was futile to think that I would ever change. And I certainly
did not wish to challenge his main accusation that I lacked popular
appeal because I did not see myself as ever attaining much commercial
success. I was not concerned with 'the well-crafted English novel,' nor
had I any aspiration to the literary life that accompanied such writing.
My heroes were Balzac, Dreiser, Stendhal and a handful of lesser-known
Europeans, such as the Pole Wladyslaw Reymont and the Dutchman
Douwes Dekker.

I walked to work that Monday morning bathed as it were in a mixture
of depression and good spirits. I was depressed by the letter that appar-

ently ended my writing career and certainly terminated my attempt to write a follow-up to my first lucky shot; I was a one-book man and that one had accomplished little. But, on the positive side, I was vibrantly alive. I had just passed my forty-first birthday in excellent health. I'd had an exciting weekend playing volleyball against a Harlem team composed of black railway porters who, as one of my teammates wailed after three straight losses, 'can leap in the air higher than anyone else and stay there longer.' My own comment had been: 'They had me picking volleyballs out of my teeth all night long.' But it had been robust fun and in the second game we had almost won, losing by only 15–13. Furthermore, I was finished with my Navy service and, best of all, I had published a book, modest though it was, and none of my friends could make that boast.

It was about six long blocks from my quarters on West Twelfth to my office on Tenth Street and Fifth Avenue, and by the time I reached there I was in an up mood: 'Forget the agent and his letter. I have other work to do,' and I actually ran up the broad stairs to my editorial office. There I bumped into my boss, Phil Knowlton, the demon geographer from Madison, Wisconsin, who was certainly not in a gay mood: he had lost in his daily commuter-train bridge game and was about to upbraid me for an accumulation of errors in my work.

It was a testy morning, with Knowlton lambasting me for a wide variety of offenses. He was a classicist who took editing seriously, and his lecture focused on my letters of rejection sent to educators who had submitted manuscripts that were palpably unpublishable: 'I don't want to see any cheap humor in these letters, no Mencken touches, no clever lines. Because on the day that this man receives your letter in the morning mail rejecting the manuscript that is as dear to him as his life's blood, he will be visited by a Macmillan salesman in the afternoon endeavoring to sell him some of our books. Small chance, if your letter has abused his ego.'

And he showed me a handful of *his* rejection letters. They gave the impression that he had been practically in tears when he wrote them. Never did *he* reject this wonderful manuscript; he had fought for it right to the very highest levels, but always despite his pleas some other agency had turned thumbs down—'the men upstairs' or 'the editorial board' or 'the experts in the field' or even 'my purblind associates.' By the time I had finished reading the examples of his painful rejections I felt that I was in the presence of a man who was all heart, who actually bled when he had to say no.

Phil was never a vengeful man; I once termed him a 'lovable teddy-bear of a growler,' which was an accurate description of a man who at times did growl but who bore no grudges. We took lunch together at the famous Salmagundi Club patronized by artists whose works adorned the walls, and there we played the traditional dice game of Horse, at which he beat me, and then returned to his office, where he resumed his bashing: 'Michener, I've told you a score of times, the word *data* is plural,' and he banged his desk: '*Data are insufficient. Data do not support. We are still seeking those data that will support....*' He asked me when I would ever learn, and I said I thought he had made his point, but he would later trap me again with that ridiculous usage. To me the items were singular, and each was data, despite what he said. I doubt that I have ever used *datum* in my life, and I don't find anyone else using it, either.

He then passed on to one of my letters that really grieved him. I had described a scholar who was working on one of our books as 'the famous geographer Professor Blank,' and he stormed: 'You use words cavalierly. Famous geographer indeed! I know every major geographer in the United States and I never heard of your Professor Blank. If I don't know him, he's not even well-known, let alone famous.'

'What can I say to make him feel good? He's sure to see my letter, you know, and I want to keep him happy.'

Knowlton leaned back, reflected on what he recognized as a real problem: 'Well, you could say *well-regarded,* although I don't know anyone who regards him either well or poorly. Or you might use *notable,* I'd accept that. How about *highly respected?*'

Before I could respond, there came a great knocking at the door. It was then thrust open by Cecil Scott, who shouted the amazing news: 'Jim, you've won the Pulitzer Prize!'

Soon Knowlton's office was filled with people and the phone was ringing, for the Pulitzer board had astounded the nation by awarding the coveted prize for 1947 fiction not to a novel, as required by the deed of grant, and certainly not to a work whose locale was the United States, as was also required, but to a loosely strung together collection of stories about remote areas and even more remote people like cannibalistic savages and Tonkinese indentured servants.

For about fifteen minutes there was bedlam in Phil's office, with radio stations calling for interviews and literary editors of newspapers and wire services phoning for statements. It was both exhilarating and tremendously bewildering; in those first moments I had no conception of either what it meant then or what it would mean in the future. I was allowed no time to speculate because as soon as the office cleared, Phil resumed his critical review of my work: 'You must always remember that we're a publishing company and that if we don't maintain strict standards in our letters to the public, who will?' With that he ignored the Pulitzer completely and launched into a tirade against one of his bêtes noires: 'You simply must stop using the word *lady* the way you do. Right here you say, "She is one of our best lady writers." Don't do that! Don't ever do that! The word has degenerated. It's degrading to call a woman a lady. The only proper use of that phrase is in comic phrases like *a lady wrestler* or pejorative ones like *a lady of the night.* Words get used up, Michener, or quarantined, and *lady* has lost its traditional connotations. Use it only for comic relief and then most carefully, and for the love of God, never, never use the old phrase *"She was a perfect lady."* Informed readers will laugh at you.'

That wild and wonderful day—fired at dawn, elevated at sunset— ended with Phil taking me to the WOR radio station, where I had my first-ever literary interview: 'Why do you suppose the Pulitzer committee chose your unusual book?' to which I could only respond: 'I really don't know. It's sort of miraculous.'

It was far more miraculous than I could have known, for years later at a gala dinner in Washington, a newsman interested in books whispered: 'You know that woman over there? She's the one who got you your Pulitzer Prize. Said she'd like to meet you.'

In this way I met the redoubtable Alice Roosevelt Longworth, daughter of Teddy, and now the delightful doyenne of Washington political society. When she saw the newsman approaching with me at his side she cried: 'You must be Michener. Come sit with me,' and when I did she said with obvious pleasure: 'Well, you've certainly done well with that prize we gave you.' Then she told me how that exciting affair back in 1948 had chanced to happen: 'My dear and trusted friend Arthur Krock of the *Times* was chairman of either the entire Pulitzer committee or the literary wing, and I always followed closely the deliberations, for this was a prize not to be wasted. When I heard the name of the book they were planning to designate I protested: "That's a nothing work. No vitality!" and Arthur asked: "Do you know something better?" and I snapped: "I certainly do," and insisted that all the members of the committee read your little book, which I considered very good indeed. When they finished, they agreed with me, and you received the prize, most deservedly, I must say.' Grasping my two hands, she said: 'I'm proud of the fact, Michener, that you didn't let us down. It was daring of Krock and his team to give you that award, but that's how awards should be given. To people at the start of their careers, not at the end.

But it takes courage to do that. How can we be sure who will be a producer and who not? Thank you for legitimizing our gamble.'

I said earlier that moving the publication of my book from 1946 to 1947 was of crucial importance to my career as a writer, and this was the reason: The Pulitzer is awarded each spring to the book judged best from the preceding calendar year, and had mine been published as planned there was no chance it could have won, because in the 1946 judging it would have been in competition with Robert Penn Warren's superb *All the King's Men,* which swept the field. And had it been delayed into the 1948 voting it would have missed again, for that was the year of James Gould Cozzens's magisterial *Guard of Honor.* Accidentally my book stumbled into the 1947 judging, the only year in which it had a chance of winning, and it found that haven by pure luck.

This is an appropriate point at which to consider the role of luck in the development of a professional career. I have had such good fortune in mine that it's frightening, and this good fortune reaches back to my earliest childhood, for if it was sad in many respects it was also illuminated by flashes of purest luck. Suppose I had not received the wonderful gift of carbon paper that enabled me to visualize the printing and dissemination of ideas? Suppose our small town had not opened the library when it did, so that I could grab the books I needed? And suppose my first novel had been published in 1946 as scheduled, rather than in 1947, when Alice Longworth would have a chance to serve as my guardian angel? And suppose in my three airplane accidents there had not been such capable pilots at the controls and trained rescuers near at hand?

Luck plays such an overpowering role in some lives that the thoughtful person must ask: 'Why have I been cursed with bad luck while another is blessed with so much good luck?' Believe me, the fortunate person who receives the favorable breaks also wonders about his favored situation. In my case I have no explanation. I was hardworking; I had a tough character; I was a good student; and I acknowledged the leadership of my superiors. But no amount of hard work or high standard of behavior could have brought the many good things that happened to me; pure chance dictated most of them. The only generalization I can offer is that in an irrational world if a prudent course has been followed, you make yourself eligible to capitalize on luck if it happens to strike. If you have not made yourself eligible, you may never be aware that luck is at hand. By all this I mean: learn typing, master math, learn to draft a convincing letter, broaden the mind, and do not evade challenges. Making oneself eligible to seize the breaks if and when they come is the only sensible strategy I know. Be prepared to make full use of any stroke of luck, and even if it never comes, the preparation in itself will be a worthy effort.

Long before the Pulitzer Prize was awarded I donated to the library at the University of Pennsylvania a unique book, the only one of its kind in existence, a trial printing of *Tales of the South Pacific* bearing the copyright and publishing date of 1946. Had it appeared publicly with that date, all would have been lost, for it would have been eclipsed by *All the King's Men*. Appearing in 1947 made all the difference. If Penn, which I once attended, still has that precious copy, I hope the relevant passages of this chapter will be copied and attached to the book, for it played a vital role in my life.

James Gould Cozzens was a grouchy, impossible-to-love man who lived not far from me on the other side of the Delaware River. He kept to himself, seemed to hate everyone and despised other writers. His masterwork, *The Just and the Unjust,* whose setting is the Doylestown Court House, is an intricate account of how rural justice is administered, wonderfully told with vivid characters, and I was not alone in believing that if Cozzens could continue such work he would be sure to win the Nobel Prize.

We met often in various corners of Doylestown, and especially in the courthouse, where he liked to listen in on trials and pick up ideas for his writing, but he affected not to see me, or to know me if he did see me. We never spoke as far as I can remember, but once when his drinking friend Bob Brugger tried to introduce us, he did grunt. This did not disturb me; I dismissed his coolness as his style, and in several interviews with Philadelphia newspapers I pointed out that one of the truly fine writers of our time lived just a few miles down the road. One writer asked me three times: 'What name did you say?' And when his article appeared it said that 'Michener has a high regard for the writing of James Gould's cousin, who lives across the river in Lambertville,' and I thought: What the hell. Let Cozzens fight his own battles. After that I referred to him less frequently.

To complete the Pulitzer story, two mornings after the announcement my bell rang again and it was another special delivery from my former agent. This time he extended warm congratulations and with marked generosity expressed a hope that if I did continue my writing I might meet with further success, but he did not indicate in any way that he had changed his earlier opinion that as a possible author I was a dead duck.

. . .

The fourth person who played a major role in the early days of my writing career was Kenneth McKenna, the former Hollywood actor and the sophisticated head of the literary department at Metro-Goldwyn-Mayer in charge of acquiring plays and novels for the studio. He was a handsome young man with a gift for words who was more than capable as an actor, but he found greater pleasure in uncovering good screenplay material. He told me later that even a cursory reading of my book had alerted him to its dramatic possibilities, which I certainly had not detected, and he strongly recommended that Metro buy it. But the big brass looked at the book, which was physically ugly, saw it only as a collection of loosely bound yarns and told McKenna: 'No dramatic possibilities whatever. No story line,' and he had to admit that for the movies that assessment was valid.

But he had a half-brother in the New York theater, the gifted stage designer Jo Mielziner, who had already dressed such hits as *Winterset, A Streetcar Named Desire,* and *Death of a Salesman.* He was a formidable artist. One night he told me: 'My brother in Hollywood phoned me and said: "Jo, grab a copy of this book *Tales of the South Pacific* by some G.I. named Michener. It has wonderful possibilities. The studio turned thumbs down, but I believe it would work on Broadway." I followed his advice, read your book and saw immediately what he meant.'

'What did you do next?'

'I took it to Dick Rodgers and told him it was a natural for him and Oscar and I'd volunteer to do the sets.'

When Rodgers read the book he phoned Oscar Hammerstein, who fell in love with the wild and colorful stories. There then ensued an amusing contretemps during which Hammerstein launched a series of frantic telephone calls trying to locate me so that a deal could be made for my book. He failed to reach me, which was remarkable, for I had then moved to Harvey Avenue in Doylestown and he lived on a farm at the east end of that town, less than a mile away. We had never met, two fellows from the same town who now needed each other.

In the meantime he and Rodgers had allied themselves with two other outstanding talents, Josh Logan, the director, and Leland Hayward, the charismatic producer, and on a snowy afternoon in March 1948 Hayward tracked me down in my office at Macmillan with a secret proposition: 'I think your book has dramatic possibilities, and I want to purchase all theatrical rights. Five hundred dollars, and you keep it all.'

Since I needed the money, the offer was tempting, but my rough childhood and jobs I had held in my teens that involved large sums had taught me a good deal about financing, and after a few minutes' reflection I told Hayward: 'I would always want to take risks with anything I did. Never an outright sale. Only royalties.'

'You're a smart fellow, Michener. You'll hear from us.' I have not told this story before, and in later years when Hayward and I became friends we never referred to the fact that he had tried to slip behind his partners' backs and pick up all the rights to what turned out to be a bonanza.

Rodgers and Hammerstein treated me better. In exploratory sessions with them they kept telling me how marvelous my book was, partly I think to keep up their own courage, but after they had buttered me up in ways I positively enjoyed, their longtime and shrewd financial manager would take me aside and poor-mouth me: 'You know, Michener, your book has no story line. It has no dramatic impact. We couldn't possibly pay you what we did Lynn Riggs for his *Green Grow the Lilacs,* which *Oklahoma!* was based on. That was a real play. It had structure.'

The comparison between Riggs and Michener was significant, for I had learned that Riggs had received a royalty of 1.5 percent, whereas I was being offered only 1 percent. Lest this figure seem appallingly low, I should mention that the ordinary musical budgeted only 10 percent of gross for original source, theatrical book, lyrics and music combined. Thus my 1 percent of gross was really 10 percent of the total artistic budget and on a hit show that could amount to real income. Of course, Riggs's 1.5 percent on a smash hit like *Oklahoma!* was a fortune, and continues to this day. I accepted my 1 percent and never had regrets.

It was a privilege to watch Rodgers and Hammerstein work. Dick, the music master, was the genius in things pertaining to what happened on the stage; he had an uncanny sense of what would work, what was needed to lift a scene or when to either cut it sharply or kill it altogether. He was deathly afraid of having the show run too long: 'Curtain down at eleven-ten so they can catch the trains home, you have a hit. Curtain down at eleven-twenty, they miss their trains, a flop.'

He did not bother much with me in our discussions, because he felt the book was Oscar's responsibility. At one three-hour session he asked me only one question: 'Jim, do I have to use wailing guitars and ukuleles?' I replied: 'Only musical instrument I ever heard the natives play was two clubs beating hell out of a gasoline drum.'

'Thanks,' he said with a deep breath, 'I hate guitars.'

I sat with him and Oscar at another session in Josh Logan's New York apartment when Hammerstein said: 'We lack one essential. A song that will convey the mood of the South Pacific. Something to go with Michener's inspired place name, Bali Ha'i.' I can vouch for the fact that the next minute Rodgers was at the piano—others who were present, including Mary Martin, witnessed this feat—and with two fingers picked out notes that would correspond to the pronunciation of the words Bali Ha'i, and within ten minutes he had the song in hand. Later I asked Hammerstein: 'Was that an act? To impress Mary and Josh and me? Had he already done the song?' and he laughed: 'I've seen Richard do that a dozen times. I sweat over my words, he lifts his music from the air.'

Hammerstein was the worrier, the man who had a burning desire to move his audience deeply. He slaved to find the right words, the right symbolisms and he was a jealous guardian of his lyrics. Once when I wanted to quote something of his in an article I was writing, he refused permission: 'Jim, if you quote four lines, that's half the song. Would you allow me to quote half of one of your books?'

Midway through the writing of the play, Oscar lost his nerve—he could not see how to bind the strands together and for the first time I heard the complaint that I would subsequently hear from everyone in the theater or movies or television who had to grapple with one of my books: 'You have some wonderful stuff here, Michener, but there's no dramatic story line a man can hang on to.' Artists in other fields who must work with one of my books earn their pay, and my gratitude; the difficulties they face explain why so many of my major works have never been transferred into another medium.

In the case of *South Pacific* the savior was Josh Logan, that ebullient manipulator of mood and movement. He rushed down to Doylestown and assured Hammerstein: 'This can be licked. We can hammer this into shape,' and together they did, with Logan ultimately receiving co-credit for the book of the play and a Pulitzer Prize.

What they devised was a spirited musical drama about a contingent of American sailors and Seabees waiting on a South Sea island for a major battle against Japanese forces. The play focused on two love stories, that of a Navy nurse with a French planter and that of a Navy lieutenant with a Tonkinese girl. The action was rowdy, romantic and tragic, and it won instant public approval.

I played no role in the adaptation, except for writing, at Logan's request, some narrative accounts of how the rowdy comedian Luther Billis might operate as a wheeler-dealer, and as an afterthought I suggested that he would probably run a laundry of some kind, and maybe have a shower. Who invented the delightful character of Captain Brack-

ett to represent Navy brass, the agent who holds the narrative together
I do not know, but that move was one of genius and the name invented
sounded exactly right; it exuded discipline and responsibility.

I did not then, nor ever in the dozen or so subsequent instances when
writing of mine was adapted to the stage or the screen, participate in the
creative work. Since I love the theater, have a passion for movies, and
enjoy good television, I would relish working in those fields but, alas,
I lack the dramatic touch.

I was called out to Hollywood just once, early in my writing career,
to work on the script for a South Seas epic and accomplished nothing.
I did, however, work with an amazing Hungarian writer who pointed
scornfully at the sign then prominent in the Paramount offices: 'In
these difficult times it is no longer sufficient to be Hungarian. Now
you must also work.' He assured me that any good Hungarian writer
could have saved the recent disaster *The Spirit of St. Louis,* the movie
about Lindbergh, which was probably the dullest ever made. I told
him: 'Not even you could have saved that one,' and he said brightly:
'In my version Lindbergh doesn't get to Paris. His plane runs out of
fuel in southern France and he bails out into the garden of a nunnery.
The abbess is Deborah Kerr and we have a whole new show!' His
imagination knew no constraints. Once when we were discussing a
movie version of *Hamlet* he seriously asked: 'But what if she isn't
Hamlet's mother? Suppose she's his aunt and he falls in love with her.
What do we have then?'

He was a joy to work with, a wily fellow who knew how to protect
himself when corporate battles were raging, and one day he told me:
'They don't know it, and they refuse to pay me what I'm worth, but the
writer provides the heart and soul of any motion picture. Never allow
directors and actors to push you around.' On his office wall he had
posted a large sign: 'Never forget it was an actor who murdered Lincoln.'

Six weeks of working with him satisfied me that I lacked the Hollywood touch and I never tried again. I have left the dramatizing of my
works to others, and they have served me exceptionally well, starting
with Rodgers and Hammerstein. At one point when I'd had nine movies
made from my books I told an interviewer: 'Three hits, three so-so, three
disappointments, that's batting .333 and if a man can keep that up he
can stay in the big leagues.' I have never resented a penny paid to others
for the work they did on my stories, for they knew the secrets required
for transmuting words into images and I didn't. In *South Pacific* the
conversion was miraculous.

. . .

When it became obvious that Rodgers and Hammerstein had on their hands one of the blockbusters of all time, rumors circulated that they had shortchanged me in allowing only 1 percent—a charge I never made, not even privately, because it had never occurred to me that my ugly duckling of a book would ever have a life in the theater—and Walter Winchell the columnist let it be known that he was going to blow the whistle. He phoned me to tell me so, but I begged him not to muddy the waters of what promised to be one of the most triumphant Broadway openings seen up to that time, and he promised he'd hold off for a couple of days.

That night after a full dress rehearsal Oscar Hammerstein called me to say: 'Jim, we've got a hit on our hands. We can't adjust your percentage, but we do want you to invest in the show. It'll be a sure thing. Five thousand dollars.'

'I don't have one thousand.'

'We will lend you the money—tonight. You can pay it back when the first profits come in.'

Tears came to my eyes, and I think Oscar knew it, for he waited for me to say: 'That's wonderfully generous . . . one Doylestown kid to another.' He kept his word. He lent me the money to buy shares that would have otherwise accrued to him and Rodgers, and my financial rewards were not trivial.

Winchell was faithful to his word,* and the opening night was explosively wonderful, with the audience remaining in the aisles to cheer again and again. In the years that followed I received, from my royalties and the share of the show that Oscar gave me, the funds, though never excessive, that enabled me to become a full-time professional writer.

One summer when I was preparing to sing in *South Pacific* at the Lambertville Music Circus—I had the role of the Greek professor, much augmented in my behalf—I visited Hammerstein, then dying of cancer, to tell him about how the show was progressing. He wished me well in my performance, expressing regret that he would not be able to travel the four miles to see me: 'I'm sure you'll take it seriously, Jim. Don't burlesque it,' and I said: 'I take everything seriously.' Then we chuckled over a preposterous incident at the time of the original production: On the morning after the tryout in New Haven some agitated New

---

*When the show opened he was ecstatic, and coined the phrase that remained the catchword during its run: *South Terrific*.

Englanders had accosted me at the train station and warned: 'Your play will fail if you keep in that song about racial prejudice. It's ugly, it's untimely and it's not what patrons want to hear when they go to a musical. Please beg Rodgers and Hammerstein to take it out.' I had reported their suggestion to Oscar and he laughed: 'That's what the play is about!' I thanked him for the decision.

"You've Got to be Carefully Taught" made the show memorable,' Hammerstein said. 'Everyone wrote about it and forgot the love duets.'

I was swept by emotion, seeing this man who had so loved life lying stricken. For some minutes we recalled the joys of working with Mary Martin and Ezio Pinza and Josh and Leland and that wonderful cast, and I said: 'Those days and nights were golden.'

IX

Intellectual Equipment

*T*HE BELATED and modest success of my first book, *Tales of the South Pacific,* encouraged me to consider whether I might be able with continued good luck to become a full-fledged writer. I naturally spent several months taking a hard look at myself—my personality, my intellectual equipment and my attitude toward art—and I realized that my thoughts the very first time I ever considered that I might have writing ability were somewhat shameful. In fact, they were ridiculous.

In 1942, just before leaving Macmillan to head for the South Pacific, I had occasion to check the batch of five minor English novels we were importing that season to complete our list. Each year when our editors in New York could not find enough satisfactory American novels to meet our quota, we traditionally looked to our London house and picked up four or five that had already been published there. This was both legitimate and sensible, for the manuscripts had already been vetted by Macmillan's first-class London editors and all we had to do was give the published English books to some young assistant just in from Vassar or Smith to search out and change English spellings to American: *favourite* to *favorite, aluminium* to *aluminum* and so on.

As I read these books, three by male authors, two by female, I made a discovery that suddenly struck me: 'Hey! I can write better than any of these clowns!' The judgment was hardly literary; it was simply a gut reaction from a hardworking editor who had helped revise textbooks on a variety of subjects in order to make them understandable; it had nothing to do with the books' content or narrative flow. But it was an honest reaction and it was relevant.

In ways that mattered but I could not pinpoint, I felt I really could write better than those five, and that evaluation lingered with me long after it first came to me. It was the experience at Tontouta that revived it, tempting me to consider myself at least eligible to think of writing. But after *Tales of the South Pacific* I needed a more sophisticated assessment of myself, and in an orderly way I began to marshal the pros and cons of a writing career for it is no light matter when one is past forty to consider quitting a salaried job to plunge into the wilderness of free-lance writing.

On the day I started my self-examination I asked myself these questions: 'Am I interested in people? Do ideas excite me? Am I knowledgeable enough about novels to write one?' I'm sure there were other questions, but I forget them now.

My earliest memories involve being one among many other children, so I did not grow up with a self-centered view of myself, and because of my early jobs I knew a great deal about life. I had knocked about America as a lad, seen Europe in my college years and had been in the Pacific as an adult. But most important, I had always loved people, their histories, the preposterous things they did and said, and I especially relished their stories about themselves. I was so eager to collect information about everyone I met that I was practically a voyeur, and always it was their accounts that mattered, not mine, for I was a listener, not a talker. If the writing of fiction was the reporting of how human beings behaved, I was surely eligible, for I liked not only their stories, I liked them.

As for ideas on which to base my writing, I was interested in everything—I was a kind of intellectual vacuum cleaner that picked up not only the oddest collection of facts imaginable but also solid material on the basic concerns of life. In college I'd had three majors, English, history and philosophy, and done well in each, but it was after college that I really educated myself with travel, studies in art, speculations on the nature of government, and participation in the business world. I had as broad a knowledge as anyone I knew, but about its depth I often had doubts, for I was constantly meeting men and women my age who were true scholars in some one discipline at which they far surpassed me. But as a teller of tales, an organizer of material, I needed only to incorporate certain ideas into my stories.

It was only when I reached the question about whether I had enough brains to be a writer that I felt I could give an unqualified yes for an answer, for through the years I had received several scholarly assessments of my intelligence. The first was in elementary school; a teacher took me aside and said: 'We're not supposed to tell you this, James, but your ratings on the intelligence tests you took last month were very high. You can do anything you set your mind to, so keep working as you've been doing.'

Later there was further proof of my aptitude. At Swarthmore College, I was among the students chosen on the basis of superior performance to participate in an experimental system in which we attended no classes in the last two years but had seminars and tutorials. I participated in no study group that contained more than five fellow students, and since the seminars lasted two and a half hours, each member could be sure that he or she would be called on and subjected to inspection not only by the professor but also by his or her peers.

At the end of those exciting two years we were examined for our final degrees not by our own Swarthmore professors but by a battery of experts from outside who had never seen us before. I would be tested by a visitor from Oxford, a philosopher from Harvard, an Elizabethan expert from Penn and the head of the English department at Princeton, and I would spend mornings and afternoons for a week writing the most demanding papers for them to examine, after which I would sit before the four to answer orally whatever questions they threw at me in order to refine their judgments about my ability and the thoroughness of my preparation.

In such an examination period both the student and his professors were being assessed. As the week progressed, with my finding the papers assigned by the outsiders almost ideally suited to whatever expertise I had developed, it became generally known that I was doing exceptionally well. As I said to Professor Manning, who had conducted the history seminars: 'They're asking everything we studied.' He and I were a team.

My orals came on a Saturday afternoon in June and a fair number of students filed into the hall to see how I conducted myself. Fortunately, in philosophy, history and English I was again questioned about only those matters on which I was well prepared, so I was able to achieve high marks. But toward the end of the exam the English professor from Princeton said: 'Now, Mr. Michener, my last question will have no bearing on our assessment of your work. Purely a personal interest of mine. But at the heart of the written exam I sent over here for you students was that list of ten unidentified quotations from the great works of English literature from which you were to choose two on which you would write what I merely described as glosses, expecting you to know what that meant. Your handling of that part was, well, exceptional, and I wondered if you had by luck stumbled upon the very two on which you had prepared yourself. Could you possibly have done equally well on any of the others?' He passed me my copy of his exam, and I saw the passage from *Othello* in which Iago reveals the depths of his depravity:

> Not poppy, nor mandragora,
> Nor all the drowsy syrups of the world,
> Shall ever medicine thee to that sweet sleep
> Which thou ow'dst yesterday. . . .

Curiously enough, I could quote this entire passage in English and also in French, Spanish and German translations. Early in my years at Swarthmore I had purchased at considerable expense Furness's extraordinary Variorium edition of *Othello,* in which he quoted the stunning passage as it had appeared in some two dozen foreign languages, and I had memorized three of them. I then offered the learned guesses made by others as to how Shakespeare had come by his knowledge of narcotics, and pointed out that since he had also used *mandragora* in *Antony and Cleopatra* he obviously liked the word, probably because of its euphonious sound. In my closing I said: 'Theories aside, the lasting value of these lines is their majestic poetry. These are words that sing.'

The Princeton man said: 'You've handled that quotation rather well. Could you do as well with the six others?' and when I looked again at the list I replied: 'Four of them, perhaps,' and he nodded. At this the students in the audience and some of the professors, all of whom wished me well, applauded, because at Swarthmore the college cheered academics as well as athletes.

When the results were posted, I saw that I had been awarded highest honors, Swarthmore's equivalent of summa cum laude, and one of my professors told me: 'Yours is the highest grade anyone ever attained in English and history so far as our records go.' But recently when I looked at the examinations now being given seniors at my college I saw that the level of scholarship had been raised so dramatically that I doubted I could even pass, let alone take honors.

Another demonstration of acquired knowledge was a dramatic one.

When I was a graduate student at Harvard a useful educational tool was introduced nationwide, a battery of some seven comprehensive and penetrating tests, each two or three hours long, which would reveal not only how much intellectual power the young people had who were presuming to take advanced degrees like the M.A. and Ph.D. but also how well the various colleges and universities were doing their job.

I was then in Harvard's School of Education and the faculty feared this examination because it might prove true the charge made by professors in the more prestigious schools like law and medicine that only men and women of 'inferior intelligence' go into education. Since the test was being administered in several hundred of our best institutions, the norms would have validity. If I remember correctly, our knowledge in seven subjects was tested: three sciences, two liberal arts and two general fields, perhaps vocabulary and miscellaneous knowledge. It was an exhausting investigation, and I, like my professors, nervously awaited the results. When they arrived there was both disappointment and rejoicing.

I was disgusted to learn that I was below the national average in chemistry; I was in the 45th percentile, which meant 55 percent of the students had done better than I. I was pleased, however, that I had been well above average in all else. What startled everyone, including me, was that I stood very near the top percentile in three of the other subjects; in my best two—general arts and literature, I believe, or it might have been history—my marks were so far above the top of the scale that no numbers were available for comparisons.

I was told that in total score I had either led the field at Harvard and nationally or been close to it, and that night a proud faculty group— Dean Homes, Franny Spalding, in administration, and Howard Wilson, in social studies—took me out to a celebratory dinner at which for the first time I tasted Chinese sweet-and-sour shrimp, a dish I never eat these days without recalling that triumphant night.

With three such demonstrations of my ability and the almost unbroken chain of A's in my various courses, I could have been forgiven had I become convinced that I was brilliant, but I did not, because I felt intuitively that my intelligence was of a special kind—acquisitive rather than speculative. I was obviously a man born to excel in formal examinations once I understood the parameters of the requirements, but I doubted that I had those ultimate intellectual gifts that marked the truly exceptional mind.

I discovered at an early age that I saw spatial relationships differently from other children, so that geometry and geography meant far more to me than to them. I would think that I know, eighteen hours out of every twenty-four, where north is and where the stars are in the sky. I check the newspapers at the first of every month to be sure where the planets will be, and I am uneasy whenever I am on a piece of land until I know its exact size in relation to the United States. When I am situated in any town for a length of time, I find an atlas and determine its latitude and longitude so that I can type out the names of the dozen or so settlements around the world at my latitude, and with the same longitude. Then I know whom I am like in other nations and I feel reassured.

Numbers were always of great importance to me, and I remember vividly a disappointing day in fourth grade when our teacher, Miss Ward, explained the magic of cancellation when I wasn't listening. She then placed on the board an exercise like:

$$\frac{491}{5634} \times 5634$$

and asked me to give the answer. Not having paid attention, I was unable to do so and sat dumbfounded when Eggs Hayman and Jimmy Groff rattled off the answer: 491. Because I knew I was better at figures than they, I remained after school to ask Miss Ward how they had been able to give such quick answers when the numbers were so large, and when she explained the trick she added: 'So you must not only know numbers, you must also pay attention.'

In my adult life I have proved time and again that I can keep more or less in mind details in some five hundred books on the topics to which I have dedicated myself. I take no notes but do list on the inside back cover of certain books page numbers to which I know I will want to refer, later followed by one word to indicate subject matter, but even without this aid I can and do go quickly to the right book and to the correct page, more or less, for the data I need. When I fail, I fail completely and can think of no clue that would lead me to the page I want; this would mean I had not implanted it firmly enough in my mind. I am not talking theoretically. I have done this at least a dozen times with my long novels, keeping a hundred characters in mind, controlling a tangle of different story lines, and remembering many individualized locations. I doubt that I am remarkable in possessing such a skill. I suspect that many clergymen can do the same with the Bible and it's obvious that some lawyers can maintain control over a huge volume of case law just as scientists can master a jungle of relevant experimentation in their fields. But I have done it in a score of different fields: astrophysics, geography, ancient religions, art, politics, contemporary revolutionary movements and popular music.

In the week prior to my finishing a long novel I am qualified to take a job teaching a postgraduate seminar on the subject because my knowledge then is quite extensive, especially regarding the specialized literature in the field, but if today you were to ask me to give you the names of three reliable books on the Polynesian background of Hawaiian history you would find me a blank. I am constantly embarrassed by my enthusiastic readers who question me about one or another of my old books, which I wrote twenty years ago; they've read it last week and know much more about it than I.

It was obvious that I had a fairly competent brain, but what its exact quality or special capacity was I did not know until in wartime I took a test of fiendish ingenuity. It had been constructed by the military to fill a specific need: 'We are desperately in need of cryptographers to break enemy codes and protect our own. Only men and women with special skills are fitted for this work. We know they're out there in society or in uniform.'

After intensive work a small team of geniuses came up with a wholly new kind of test, which they administered to hundreds of men and women in uniform who were known by their associates or their test scores to be unusually capable. Sent forth by the Navy, I reported for the investigation. The officer in charge said: 'This test has been devised to separate you into three groups. It has what we call "precise discriminatory capacity," which means that many of you will score five, many sixty-five, and a very few, ninety-five. What it tests for is your raw intelligence, not what you learned in chemistry class or in job training or later study. It tests the ability of your brain, unclothed as it were, to tackle abstruse problems and function with great rapidity. In this test time is vital and, again, the test is discriminatory. Some of you will complete it in an hour and a half, some in fifty minutes, and the few we are seeking in thirty.'

That was pretty heady stuff and seeing that we were apprehensive, he smiled warmly and assured us: 'How you perform on this test has absolutely no bearing on your general intelligence or your ability to do your present job. You cannot fail it, in the ordinary sense. We already know you're bright. What we now want to know is: "Have you the special skills required for cryptography?" '

It was a horrendous test, and although I handled fairly well and rapidly any questions posed in verbal form, there were others that totally mystified me and made me waste a good deal of time. When I saw some in my group galloping through the pages and others gnawing their fingers I surmised, correctly, that I was going to be in the middle group that scored sixty-five.

One question will indicate the discriminatory nature of the test: 'There are three sets of sequential numbers and in each set the sum equals the product. Find them.' You either knew what *sequential* meant (7, 8, 9) and *sum* (add) and *product* (multiply) or you had no chance even to attempt the problem. Those who were destined to score down in the fives took one look at the arcane stuff and fled. We in the sixty-fives slogged through a laborious equation and belatedly reached the proper solution +1, +2, +3 and −3, −2, and −1 and the surprising −1, 0, +1. But the geniuses who were destined to be cryptographers studied the problem for a moment, saw immediately that if the numbers were not extremely low, the products would become unmanageable, and by a process called iteration found the answer. Iteration is how a slow-minded man finds the square root of 19: '4 is too low, 5 too high, so I'm looking for something in the middle, say around 4.5' and by this process of trial and error he ultimately reaches 4.3588 if he wants to carry it out to four decimals, if not, roughly 4.4. The mathematical genius can perform iteration almost instantaneously.

In dealing with the above question as stated, such men quickly found the +1, +2, +3, and because they thought in both positive and negative numbers, the second series came almost immediately. The third series, centering on zero, gave even some of these superbrains trouble, but since they had been told there were three sets, they discovered by a process of elimination that it had to involve zero. I required perhaps five minutes to set up and factor my equation; the geniuses deduced their solution in an equal number of seconds.

When the test ended, there were, as the administrator had predicted, quite a few with scores down in the five range, and they were some of the best officers we had. There were many like me in the sixty range but almost none in the high seventies or eighties; you got either sixty-five or ninety-five and there were several who got the latter.

I was disturbed by one who did, a friend named Saul Dreditch whom I knew to be not nearly as intelligent as I was; he knew no music, had read little, showed no interest in current affairs, and could not converse easily with an elevated vocabulary. Yet he came away with the highest mark, a ninety-seven. It baffled me.

There was one set of questions on which the examiners obviously doted because they appeared in various forms, and I had been quite unable to handle any of them, while Dreditch had obviously solved them not only accurately but swiftly. They consisted of careful line drawings of a pyramid or similar structure composed of many individual building blocks, all of the same size. They were drawn with one edge of the structure showing, so that the viewer saw Face A and Face B, but not

Faces C and D, which were hidden. The question always was: 'What is the minimum number of unseen blocks required to keep this structure standing?' I was completely baffled by such a question. How could I peek around the limits of the drawing and see what stood behind? When I asked Dreditch how he solved such questions, he said: 'Couldn't you *see* that it had to be three or six or whatever the case was?' No, I could not see around corners, but he could, and instantly.

I came upon Dreditch several times during the war. He was one of the cryptographers for Admiral Halsey, and men on the staff told me he was a genius: 'Nimitz in Honolulu sends us an important message in code. It arrives garbled. Either their sending machine or our receiving has acted up, or maybe the sending operator has been careless. We hand the garble to Dreditch and alert Honolulu to send again, but in the meantime, seconds count, and if he can unravel the mystery we'll be prepared to go into action that much sooner. I've seen him do it a dozen times. He sits over his coding machine, both hands extended like a pianist about to start playing. Hands in the air, never touching the keys, and he plays "What if?" What if the fellow had forgotten to turn this switch? What if his left-hand fingers were too far to the left? He plays a hundred possibilities in the air, and quite often he hits exactly the mistake the sender has made. He decodes the message, passes it along to Halsey, and we're already taking the proper steps by the time the resubmission arrives from Honolulu. Of course, we have to wait for it. We can't go ahead on Dreditch's guesswork, but with him it isn't guessing.'

As a result of that remarkable test, which identified men with the kind of raw intelligence required for cryptography, Saul Dreditch was identified as having a special brain power far excelling mine, and with it he helped win the war. With my more ordinary power I contributed little.

It was obvious from the various tests that I had a brain but not one qualified for abstract analysis. What was it good for? After continued reflection I realized that I had what was essentially a Germanic type of intellect, the kind whose owner plods along year after year until he comes up with, say, a new theory of who wrote the first five books of the Old Testament. I was tenacious in acquiring detailed knowledge. I positively loved the game of ideas, and had the patience to spend long hours day after day playing it.

What I did not have was the scintillating type of intellect so often found in Frenchmen, Irishmen and Indian savants from the subcontinent. Their flashes of intellectual brilliance and the wit of their conversation delight me, and I envy the grace with which they marshal words and illuminate ideas. I found I was more of a pachyderm than a hummingbird, and for that reason I especially prize those things I cannot do—I leave the fiery statement, the incandescent revelation to others, not because I want to but because I have to. Convinced though I was that I would never have a flashy intellect, I knew with equal certainty that I possessed a sturdy one well qualified to grapple with the kinds of books I would want to write.

Raw brainpower is one thing; mastery of skills and techniques is another, and here my training had been exceptional. My early wide reading in the classics and in those precious Haldeman-Julius *Blue Books* had imbued me with a love for the flow of words, and my teaching of grammar at The Hill and George School had been invaluable.

At college I had learned to write substantial term papers, and here I must tell young would-be writers that effective learning, especially in the writing trade, often starts with hard work done in college. Professors do not aid their better students when they do not demand thoughtful term papers, and any course in history, English or philosophy that does not require extensive writing is fraudulent because a major aspect of the discipline is being left out.

I had three distinguished professors: in philosophy the great Brand Blanshard, in literature the noted expert Robert Spiller, and in history the irrepressible Freddie Manning, married to the daughter of the former president William Howard Taft. Both Blanshard and Spiller taught me much about writing, but it was Manning, in his two seminars on English history, who really taught me what a research paper ought to be. I'd written a forty-page paper dealing with the Great Reform Act of 1832 and in it I'd made Lord Brougham, a chameleon politician of the period, my hero, and when the class ended Professor Manning asked me to remain and said: 'Michener, that was first-rate. You could be a writer. Two criticisms. A bit too long, and you were quite misled when you had that rather pathetic bit about your hero Brougham being "kicked into oblivion on the woolsack." You misinterpret the values in English political life. When he "took the woolsack," as they say, meaning that he sat on the time-honored bale of wool on which all Lord Chancellors sit when they preside as the realm's chief justice, as a reminder that a nation's wealth comes from the land, he ascended to a major position in British politics. You must attend to detail, and dig for it if necessary.'

I had not appreciated that, but it was what he said next that lingers:

'Two years ago when my wife and I accompanied Chief Justice Taft on a tour of England the leaders of that nation were eager to meet him, not because he had been president, but because he was our Chief Justice. To them that meant something.' Why do I treasure that memory? Because it suddenly brought everything I had written into focus. Brougham was a real man who had held a real job, sitting on a woolsack. Howard Taft was a living American politician who'd had two contrasting jobs, and there was a practical possibility that I might one day meet him. History past and present became very real that day, and all because I had written a long paper into which I had plowed everything I knew and exposed all the emotions I had felt about my noble villains and worthy heroes. That paper was an augury.

No writer ever knows enough words but he doesn't have to try to use all that he does know. Tests would show that I had an enormous vocabulary and through the years it must have grown, but I have never had a desire to display it in the way that John Updike or William Buckley or William Safire do to such lovely and often surprising effect. They use words with spectacular results; I try, not always successfully, to follow the pattern of Ernest Hemingway who achieved a striking style with short familiar words. I want to avoid calling attention to mine, judging them to be most effective as ancillaries to a sentence with a strong syntax.

My approach has been more like that of Somerset Maugham, who late in life confessed that when he first thought of becoming a writer he started a small notebook in which he jotted down words that seemed unusually beautiful or exotic, such as *chalcedony*, for as a novice he believed that good writing consisted of liberally sprinkling his text with such words. But years later, when he was a successful writer, he chanced to review his list and found that he had never used even one of his beautiful collection. Good writing, for most of us, consists of trying to use ordinary words to achieve extraordinary results.

I struggle to find the right word and keep always at hand the largest dictionary my workspace can hold, and I do believe I consult it at least six or seven times each working day, for English is a language that can never be mastered.* I also keep at hand for daily reference a copy of

---

*Even though I have studied English for decades I am constantly surprised to find that words long familiar carry definitions I have not known: *panoply* meaning *a full set of armor, calendar* meaning *a printed index to a jumbled group of related manuscripts or papers.*

Rodale's *Synonym Finder,* incontestably the best thesaurus ever published; its scope is enormous, its organization superb. I have never known a professional writer clever enough to use the old Roget's *Thesaurus,* its arrangement of synonyms and antonyms being too difficult for easy reference, and I have never understood why some books waste half their space on antonyms, for I cannot remember ever having used that service. Much as I treasure Rodale, I have never used it to ferret out a dazzling new word for inserting in my manuscript purely for effect. I have always used it to remind me of some word I know but cannot recall.

As a child I was fascinated by words. One summer during my stay at George Murray's summer camp along the Delaware, I looked at the railroad sign at the end of the bridge leading from Pennsylvania to New Jersey, BYRAM, and was struck by a thought: 'If the man who named this spot had had a daughter Mary, she could have spelled her name either forward or backward!' (Mary Byram) The concept was so amazing to me that when I returned to school I boasted of my discovery, but Mary Armstrong, the brightest in our class, said in her superior way: 'That's called a palindrome and the two famous ones are "Able was I ere I saw Elba," and even more amazing, "A man, a plan, a canal. Panama!"'

Later, during the yearly lecture on health and the terrible dangers of cigarettes and alcohol I was fixated by the word the nervous lecturer wrote on the blackboard: 'A good way to refuse alcohol when your friends offer it is to say, without boasting: "I'm abstemious," ' and while he explained the meaning of that word, I saw that if you made that noun into an adverb you'd have a word that contained all the vowels, and in order. Again I trumpeted my discovery and again Mary Armstrong, after brow-knit study said: '*Facetiously* is the same, and one letter shorter.' Mary was a bright girl.

However I stumped her with a famous riddle: 'There are only four words in the English language that end in *dous.* Horrendous, stupendous, tremendous. What's the fourth?' Weeks passed, with her begging for the solution, which I finally delivered, rather condescendingly I admit: 'Hazardous.' She was both pleased and irritated that the word was so different from the other three. Months later this persistent girl marched to my desk and slapped down a small piece of paper on which a solitary word had been written: 'jeopardous.'

I rejoice in the wonderful flexibility of English and read at least one book a year on the history of our language, being especially interested in the years after the birth of Christ when English was in its formative stage. I once compared the standard dictionaries of four or five of the major contemporary literary languages and found that whereas the dictionary sponsored by the Spanish academy was limited to some sixty thousand words and the French to not more than twice that many, majestic, slap-happy English, a conglomeration of everything, offered some five hundred and fifty thousand, and in the years when Charles de Gaulle was trying to expel English words from the French, English was welcoming new words from all other languages in the world, including French. For years I maintained a notebook listing some eighty different languages and for each I wrote six words which that tongue had contributed to English, such as *dinghy* from Hindi, *cannibal* from Carib, *safari* from Swahili, *trek* from Afrikaans, and *wok* from Chinese.

The richness of English makes it possible for one writing in this language to choose for almost any thought he wishes to convey either a longish Latinate word, such as *precipitous* or a short, crisp one of Anglo-Saxon origin, such as *steep,* and a felicitous style often depends upon a judicious blending of the two.

Because I was classically trained, I tend to write my first draft with a Latinate vocabulary, preferring words of three and sometimes four syllables that sound comfortable to my ear, but this tempts me into long sentences and rolling, run-on thoughts. Editing consists of junking the high-sounding beauties in favor of short words of solid Anglo-Saxon origin. But I find that when I do my final polishing to make the sentences really sing, I occasionally go back to some Latinate word that summarizes the situation precisely and exquisitely.

English has been one of the continuing joys of my life, and I am proud that I have been allowed to publish in it; I could have been happy in no other language, even though I respect the elegance of French, the power of German and the soft loveliness of Spanish.

The English sentence can be a structure of great beauty and variety, and the writer must use it with precision to convey his or her thoughts, images and emotions. Effective sentences can be as short and blunt as Hemingway's in 'The Killers', which broke upon us with such revolutionary force when I was a student, or as seemingly endless as William Faulkner's in his Southern tales, which were greeted with indifference at first and later won such acclaim. In my own writing I have preferred the simpler sentence because my aim has always been absolute clarity. I tend to think linearly, with a strong start, a clean, sharp active verb and a reasonable conclusion, but my editing reveals a generic weakness:

I tend to use too many declarative sentences joined by *and.* To correct this, I often make the opening clause subordinate or dependent so that I can finish with a strong independent clause.

The second editorial change in my first versions is to remove useless or ineffective words at the end of sentences. I have never mastered the art, in original composition, of the longish preliminary build-up and the short, effective ending after the verb, but in revision I often achieve good results by simply chopping off and substituting pronouns for phrases. Speaking of pronouns, I am not always secure in remembering which nouns at the beginning of a sentence were the antecedents of the pronouns at the end, but if I don't catch the error either my secretary or my editor does.

The would-be sentence with no verb I abhor but sometimes find no good substitute; the run-on sentence, which loses all form and force, I try to avoid, but even so my editors have always wanted to break my worst offenses into two or even three shorter sentences, and I bow to their superior taste. Having wrestled all my life with the English sentence, I realize that I have not conquered it; but I believe I have wrestled it to an honorable draw. And sometimes I have used it to my advantage, as if I, not it, were in command.

My principal instrument of expression and one with which I feel easiest is the paragraph, which I strive to use with variation and effectiveness. I have repeatedly told younger writers: 'I do believe that the only skill I have as a writer is in creating an effective paragraph. When I sit before my typewriter, one of my constant concerns is: How is this paragraph progressing? Too long? Too short? Enough variation in the sentences? and until I feel at ease with it, the paragraph cannot be considered finished. In every manuscript I write I cross out dozens of defective paragraphs that do not meet the test.

I do not know any exercises that will teach the would-be writer to improve his technique in building paragraphs. An alternate reading of the very short ones in Hemingway with the very long and effective ones in *The New Yorker* essays would be a good start, but I cannot mimic either of those exemplars; my paragraphs fall in the middle and sometimes I am exceedingly pleased with one that finally succeeds.

Concerning punctuation, I, like many writers of my generation, was influenced by an acerbic and fearfully sexist article that appeared in a major magazine many decades ago. It bore a revealing title, *Feminine Punctuation,* and lampooned the tendency of writers who wrote cheap romances to overuse exclamation points, dashes, parentheses, ellipsis points, italic, boldface and other devices to achieve broad humor and coy effects. Sometimes, in an effort to convey a sense of irony they even used the exclamation point inside parentheses: (!). The critic said that such usage marked a mind both inferior and juvenile, and he recommended that writers, especially masculine ones who wanted to be taken seriously, avoid them. Every device he ridiculed exists because through the centuries it has been needed, even by writers of acute sensitivity; it is the abuse that is to be condemned, for a long manuscript filled with improper or jejeune punctuation irritates, but, like pepper or cinnamon, when used properly it can add both accent and style.

I try to restrict exclamation points to passages of dialogue. Some sentences cry out for a word in italics when it requires emphasis. I use dashes, perhaps too often, and ellipsis points to indicate a time lapse or a long pause. I do not use a comma before the last word in a series unless clarity requires it, and I adore the semicolon, which I use perhaps too much.

As for spelling, I keep constantly at hand a small dictionary that gives no meanings but spellings of twenty-five thousand words, and if I could find one that had thirty-five thousand words I would buy it, for about half the words I look up are missing, especially those with hyphens. I am a poor speller and suppose that I have looked five hundred times through the years for the plural of *hero,* the differences between *flaunt* and *flout, gantlet* and *gauntlet* and the spelling of *minuscule.* I am delighted to learn that recent word processors incorporate a program that automatically checks spelling, but it does me no good. I am an old-fashioned two-finger typist who won't give up his manual typewriter, but my secretary, who is a wizard on the word processor, uses it to check my spellings for me.

Throughout my writing career I have tried to use effective words that are not too arcane in sentences that are not too long to achieve paragraphs that produce a narrative that will constantly lure the reader from one page to the next.

When I assessed myself in 1947 I concluded that I had at my disposal a fairly solid understanding of the English language and the nature of books, but not even the winning of the Pulitzer convinced me that I would be able to develop a good narrative style, and having been dismissed by my agent for lacking one, it is understandable that initially I was apprehensive about a career as a writer.

If I wanted to write long, intricate books, which I did, it was obligatory that I develop a style suitable to that task, and I discovered that to a surprising degree such a style depended on the judicious linkage of paragraphs, so that the reader was invited to follow from one to another. This required the use of connectives at the start of the new paragraph to mark a transition. Authors of the past century were aware of this necessity, of course, but their best devices were so overused by poor writers that they became trite. Few today would use *Little did I realize that when I visited Sir Charles,* or the cliché of the Western film in this century: *Meanwhile, back at the ranch . . .*

Good transitions are best achieved when they do not depend solely upon a felicitous connecting word at the beginning of a new paragraph, but provide hints at the close of the old paragraph and others at the start of the new. I have often been reminded of how closely I organize my text when I try to break into the middle of one of my pages to make a correction. Taking out even one sentence often destroys the entire linkage, and to restore it I find myself required to redo both paragraphs, for my transitions have been too solidly constructed to permit easy disruption.

I once said: 'I may not be the world's greatest writer, but I'm certainly one of the great rewriters,' my years as an editor at Macmillan having taught me how much hard work writing requires. To see one of my manuscripts in its third version is to see pieces of paper that have been scribbled upon, cut and pasted and endlessly revised. When the book finally appears it often reads so smoothly that others have been led into believing that the result was easily achieved; only my manuscripts, each filed away for inspection in some accessible library,* will show how diligently I worked to attain this ever-advancing narrative flow. It did not come automatically. I hear occasionally of writers who can sit down, type out a chapter and send it to the printer with only a corrected spelling here and there, but when I read their finished publications I do not envy the result. However, I do grant that John O'Hara used to deliver to Random House manuscripts that required almost no editing except marking for the printer, and his excellent short stories were among the best. Most of us have to work hard for optimum results.

I suppose my attitude toward the creative process is much like that of Alexandre Dumas *père* when he was approached by a young aspirant who boasted that he was going to write a novel much better than either

---

*Early manuscripts, The Library of Congress; *Centennial,* University of Northern Colorado; *Chesapeake,* Public Library, Easton, Maryland; *The Covenant,* Swarthmore College; *Texas,* University of Texas; *Alaska,* University of Alaska; *Journey, Caribbean,* University of Miami. I have not yet decided where to place *Space, Poland, Six Days in Havana, The World Is My Home, Mexico* and *Workbook.*

The Three Musketeers or *The Count of Monte Cristo.* 'Have you an attractive setting?' the veteran writer asked politely, and the young man replied: 'The greatest! Ominous islands. Gleaming castles. Wooded glens with gracious mansions.'

'Have you interesting characters?'

'Kings and beautiful princesses and dubious cardinals.'

'But have you a logical plot to tie this together?'

'A most ingenious one. Twists and turns that will bewilder and delight.'

Said Dumas: 'Young man, you're in excellent shape. Now all you need are two hundred thousand words, and they'd better be the right ones.'

I came to the crucial question: Did I know enough about the novel as an art form to attempt writing one? Three facts were involved. First, in my favor, my knowledge of the literature was prodigious, as the Graduate Record Examination had shown. At about the age of twenty-four I believe I had read most of the good novels ever written, especially the ones by European writers whom few Americans read: for example, Pérez Galdós, Goncharov, Manzini, Nexø, Lagerlöf, Reymont, Couperus. I had also read Lady Murasaki, of Japan.

On the other hand, the second salient fact is that because my college was notoriously Anglophile, and also because I was overseas during much of my learning period, I had completely missed the works of three American giants, Scott Fitzgerald, William Faulkner and Thomas Wolfe, so that they could exert no influence upon me, and this was a loss. Also, for the same reasons I had pretty well missed writers like Susan Glaspell and Edith Wharton, so my literary education, though broad, was lopsided.

Third, and now we come to a more serious defect, I had never had a systematic course on the writing of fiction and had thus missed the philosophical discussions that centered on the works of Henry James, E. M. Forster, André Gide and other distinguished writers. I never attended to James's dicta concerning the point of view from which the tale is told, nor did I appreciate the extent to which the psychological insights into character can deepen a novel's meaning. Curiously, I never studied the way in which a gifted novelist like Flaubert can gather together a group of characters within a limited compass and give the entire novel a sense of the universal. And I missed entirely the scintillating word play of writers like Aldous Huxley. I would never write like that distinguished group, nor would I ever want to.

Still, my knowledge of the novel was sufficient so that I could find models among its practitioners: men like Henry Fielding, Alain René Lesage, Eugène Sue and William Thackeray; or the panoramic novels of Tolstoy and Sigrid Undset; or heavy novels like Dreiser's *American Tragedy* or Arnold Bennett's powerful *Old Wives' Tale*. In other words, I liked my novels big and rugged and extensive, but I was always aware that in making such a choice I was turning my back on a style of writing that critics had usually described as superior. I much preferred Victor Hugo to Jane Austen and so, I found, did many readers, and to label Charles Dickens inferior, as critics then did, was in my opinion laughable.

It was reassuring to know that I probably had certain writing skills, but it was equally important to identify those other important skills I did not have. My negative conclusions were specific and firm. From having read extensively the best writers the world had produced, I had observed that they had certain strengths that I could never match, and it was important for me to dispose quickly of any ambitions in those areas.

I am not trained in psychology and have little skill or interest in dealing with the psychological structure and problems of my characters, and none whatever in chasing them down the aberrational byways that other writers exploit with such riveting results. I tend to accept characters more or less at face value, preferring to have them reveal themselves in their own way. This technique has produced some wonderful characters for me, but if the reader wants involved psychological analyses he should look elsewhere.

I have tried to create men and women who capture the imagination and hold it, and whenever my wife tells me that some critic has abused me for my cardboard characters, I think of Nellie Forbush and Emile de Becque, who enchanted the world, and of Elly Zahm, about whose death from snakebite so many have written to me in protest. If these characters are cardboard, I imagine a lot of writers would like to know where I get my supply of that commodity.

I have studied the problem of dialects, and have often been tempted to try using them, but when I review the record I find that generally books which were first hailed as marvels of narratives in dialect have very short lives. However, sometimes when reading Thomas Hardy I come upon a rural word thrown in with an effect so dazzling that I wish I could emulate him; and from time to time I reread the exploits of Hyman Kaplan to remind myself of the delectable humor a lively dialect can achieve. I must leave such gems to others, for I have no talent in that direction.

I have little interest and not much skill in plotting; when I have done it well it hasn't added much to my books. I respect the intricate plotting John le Carré devises in his fine espionage books, but I do not envy it, and more often I find excessive plotting like Hardy's tedious. I have been criticized for my deficiency, and several critics and readers have complained that my books tend to fall apart in their last chapters. I do not think so. I see a narrative as an endless web moving back and forth that the writer, like a Norn, severs at some arbitrary point to end his book. I am aware that a writer skilled in plotting could wrap things up in much neater packages than I do, but in writing, as in personal dress, I have never been much involved with neatness.

I have been deficient also in the use of symbolism, which others use to such mystical effect. But I confess that when I read their books I find myself muttering: 'This is getting to be quite precious,' and I recall the sardonic statement once made by an older writer: 'Symbolism is what goes over big among juniors in Yale's course on creative writing.' Even more cynical was Moss Hart's crack about Broadway: 'Allegory is what closes Friday night.' I wish I had the deft touch that symbolism requires, but I don't. I agree that certain subjects profit from its use because it can lift the story to a higher level, but I have seen so much bad writing in this vein that I prefer to leave it to others. I rely upon the marshaling of carefully chosen facts to produce the mythic effect, and if anyone can read my *Poland* without realizing that the subject and its people have heroic and mythic dimensions, I fear there is nothing I could add to make it more clear.

In writing I prefer the understatement but am aware that I frequently fail to make my point with the average reader. Thousands of people read *Hawaii* without recognizing it as a strong statement on race relations, and this same failure to understand has happened with several of my other books, notably *The Source* and *The Covenant,* so I am no longer surprised when readers fail to grasp what I have been trying for hundreds of pages to say. Despite such failure, I refuse to beat drums or clothe either myself or my characters in cheap glory to make an obvious statement, and if I am often misunderstood, that is the penalty I must pay for my kind of writing.

If there were so many things I could not do, what could I do rather better than average? I could tell a story, and sometimes we forget what a powerful gift that is. I am sure that at the dawn of civilization when hunters went out to kill a mammoth on which their clan would have to live for the next six months, some man, not necessarily one of the shrewdest when it came to tracking the beast or bravest when the animal was cornered, returned at night to sit by the campfire and relate the incidents of that day. He told of the bird that guided his hunt; he told of the heroic resolution of the prey, noble and defensive with skills not encountered before; he identified the men who led the assault and the one on whom all depended when it seemed that the mammoth would escape; and this fireside narrator lent that day a glory that it could never otherwise have gained.

This facility to tell a rousing, meaningful story is a cultural commodity whose value will never deteriorate. I cannot foresee what form the book, which has been so precious to me, will take in the next century; perhaps its form will be lost in electronics with libraries becoming centers for films and disks. But I am positive that regardless of how the narrative is circulated, the men or women who can create it will continue to be invaluable. Societies require accounts that record experience, lampoons that ridicule pompous and empty-headed leaders, ballads that sing of youthful love, and the interpretation of those values held dear by the human community. The art of the storyteller is historically precious and I am proud to have pursued it.

My preceptors were not the poets and romancers of medieval France; they were the virile dreamers who created the sagas of Norway or the Eddas of Iceland. I felt totally alienated from Jane Austen but close to Alain René Lesage, no affinity with Henry James but a great deal with Miguel Cervantes, none with Scott Fitzgerald but much with Mark Twain. I was a storyteller and did my best to add a few links to the chain that reaches back to the cavemen. I had enormous respect for those artists I did not follow, but I did not want them as my teachers.

I seem also to have had some talent in creating the ambiance in which my stories would be narrated—the look of the land, the feel of the season, the pressure of the atmosphere, the sweep of the ocean, the endlessness of the desert. I have not been afraid of using conventional description and introducing even longer segments of it than most writers do. But I have tried not to allow it to slow down the narrative; I have been careful to maintain what I deem to be the proper balance by cutting descriptive passages rather than adding to them. I have felt that a man or a society can be fully understood or appreciated only when seen as part of a natural setting, whether it be a large American city, a small Boer town in South Africa or a dust-bowl farm in Nebraska.

I have also been keenly attentive to how my characters earn their living. They work at specific jobs, earn specific amounts, face specific

problems and reach specific solutions. I have found it irritating, especially in many European novels, that not one of the characters about
whom I am reading has ever done a day's work; we should at least see
how they manipulate those who do. I am obviously not a writer of
proletarian literature, but I certainly have proletarian instincts and I like
to observe the rise and fall of personal ambitions or the success or failure
of dynasties. I want my characters to be involved in the hunt, in the
reaping, in the marketplace and in the boardroom. While doing my
research on *Texas* I knew with varying degrees of intimacy seven mul-
timillionaires, vivid men, the wheeler-dealers of that vast state, and with
several I was invited to watch the intimate unfoldings of their business
ventures. In later years, when oil and real estate plummeted, I watched
all seven slide into bankruptcy, four in only their peripheral holdings,
three completely, and to watch such a collapse of a friend's empire is
sobering.

I have wanted to know how my characters reacted to religion and
have done rather more writing about this than other writers, gently and
often indirectly. My entire Israeli novel, *The Source,* is based on that
theme, as well as much of the South African one and large passages in
both *Hawaii* and *Centennial.* What few remember is that in *Space,* long
before the misbehaviors of our television evangelists gained publicity, I
anticipated their problems and unsavory deeds in the character of Dr.
Strabismus. Although I was approached numerous times in recent years
to move to Ireland and write about that tormented land, I refrained
because I did not know enough about the roots of the religious tensions,
but I think I do understand Islam and am regretful that I was unable
to write an extended book about it. In the earliest days of my studies
I decided that if I did tackle that subject, I would not be a partisan of
the Shiites.

I have had solid instruction on the problems of race relations, having
lived in a wide variety of societies and with men and women of every
kind of racial background. From childhood I have been congenial with
all groups and have tried my best to empathize with them. I have had
close friends in all parts of the world, and it astounds some Americans
when I say that I have at least seven or eight times lived for fairly long
periods with people who spoke not a word of English and I not a word
of their languages. I recall that once I shared a cab near Warsaw with
a businessman from Boston and we had a lively conversation with the
driver, who spoke no English. Although we understood no Polish, we
somehow learned that he had two children, owned his own cab, liked
Chopin, did not like the Russians, and had relatives in Chicago.

This affection for people of all races has dictated much of my behavior. When I brought my new wife home to my aunts in Bucks County, not a center of ecumenism, they were not surprised that she was Japanese, for they knew I had been working in Japan, but they were appalled that she was a Democrat. When Mari asked: 'Aunt Laura, have you ever known any Democrats?' she replied: 'Yes, I think there was a family that lived out on the edge of town, but they were not very nice people.'

If I have had any obsession as a writer, it has been with the condition of women in American life and elsewhere. I have found all societies, all religions fearfully unfair to women and, whenever possible, have done my best to redress the imbalances. When a young woman came to our town to work as a lawyer—and I wonder where she received *that* advice—I was one of the first to employ her. I had a woman agent, a woman accountant, a woman office manager and for more than thirty years a woman copy editor at Random House who has kept my manuscripts free from anachronisms, solecisms and misspellings.

I have done my best to introduce women into all my stories, sometimes revising entire chapters to maintain a balance. This effort is partly the result of my having read perhaps a dozen books on South Africa before first going there and having found that although the Dutch settled there in the 1650s, women and children were not mentioned in any of the books, not in any way at all, much before the 1820s. The reader would have thought that the heroic Dutchmen who had settled that marvelous land had all been the products of spontaneous generation. They had no mothers, no sisters, nor any childhood, either; in adult male majesty they ruled the land.

My experience in Yucatán while working on *Caribbean* reinforced my antipathy to the downgrading of women. I was working with a premier Mayan scholar who was shocked when I told him that my plans for the Mayan chapter involved a mother taking her son on a pilgrimage to three of the holy shrines popular with people seeking divine guidance. He said this was quite impossible, that women would never have been allowed to make such a journey and that as a matter of fact, women played no role in Mayan society whatever. He said: 'Look at the frescoes depicting Mayan life, acres of them. You don't see women. They played no role in Mayan life and for you to suggest that your mother would be allowed to take her son to a place like Palenque—'

I said: 'In my book that woman will go both to Chichén Itzá and Palenque,' and he said: 'If she does, you'll be a laughingstock.' She went and I was.

I have been unable to understand such subordination of women, just as I have been unable to understand why Judaism denigrates women so sorely, why the Catholic Church has kept them as second-class citizens, why the Mormons are so reluctant to admit women to positions of leadership, why Quakerism separated the sexes in their meetings, and especially why Islam treats them so abominably. I once spent extended periods in Afghanistan, in every part of the country, and although I was entertained lavishly, I was never allowed to see a woman; always they were hidden under chadors that covered them from crown to ankle.

I am incapable of understanding why the United States has not adopted the Equal Rights Amendment, but a friend explained: 'The mood of the mullah exists here, too, in all our religions: women are evil, not to be trusted, always to be governed by their men.'

The problem of the emancipation of women has been a particularly difficult one for me to grapple with because the English language is horribly sexist. All things virtuous are masculine, evil and corrupt things feminine; positive aspects are usually masculine; negative feminine. I do not sit at my typewriter one day of my life without confronting this problem of the inadequacy of our language in dealing with equality between the sexes; I must make a score of decisions each day as to how to express an ordinary thought, and I can find no solution. I am a prisoner within the prejudices of my own tongue.

I hope the reader has noticed that I try to vary the impersonal pronouns *he* and *she,* sometimes saying *he and she,* less often *she and he* but only because it is less euphonious, quite often merely *she* to indicate both sexes, and none of the solutions are any good. *He/she,* which some advocate, is worse, and abominations like *sher's* should not even be discussed. Try to correct this sentence by substituting *he or she* locutions for the five masculine terms involved: 'If a *man* wants to protect *his* reputation, *he* must *himself* rebut any scandal that touches *him.*' Listen to the hopeless jumble when I decide to fight sexism: 'If a *man or woman* wants to protect *his or her* reputation, *he or she* must *himself or herself* rebut any scandal that touches *him or her.*' Would anyone seriously propose that such sentences be written?

I wish we might launch a movement to make the pronouns *they, them* and *their* acceptable usage after the dual locutions: 'If a *man or woman* wants to protect *their* reputation, *they* must *themselves* rebut any scandal that touches *them.*' The more I read that final sentence the more I like it, because the only canon it offends is old-fashioned pickiness. I hope that writers braver than I will insist upon using this alternative or something similar. It is needed.

·   ·   ·

Two problems confront writers every day they sit down to work on their novels. First: any book that is explicitly *about* a subject is bound to be a bad one, for then it becomes a tract. Good books can be faithful to a central idea, but they must tell the story through the beliefs and actions of their characters. The second writing problem is one I am always aware of but am never able to handle with complete satisfaction. Narration consists in knowing how to alternate effectively two types of writing that I have defined as *carry* and *scene*. Carry is the less exciting but often more cerebral segment in which the author conveys such diverse information as what has been happening previously, or what his characters strive for in their lives, or what the condition of the nation is, or where the police are concentrating their efforts. Done well, it can be marvelously rewarding, and the carry segments of *War and Peace* are among the best ever written. Carry segments do not usually contain dialogue, and even if they do, it is brief. Scene, on the other hand, consists of characters observed in personal contact with other characters, as in a Jane Austen tea party, or a Raymond Chandler holdup or a Stendhal argument among a group of soldiers. In such scenes dialogue becomes preeminent, and when handled with skill it creates tension, reveals hitherto hidden character and advances the plot. Casual readers consider this their favorite part of any book and often skip the carry sections in their desire to rush ahead to the next scene, but in doing so they miss some of the best parts of the book, the writer's observations.

I believe that intuitively most writers favor one type of narration over the other. Doctorow wrote an entire novel without using dialogue—a tour de force. Dickens used scene as well as anyone who ever wrote. Faulkner was superb in some of his carry, Hemingway in his scene. I have done some quite good material in carry, but editing for me often involves recasting that material into scene, at which I am not particularly gifted.

Sometime in the late 1950s an idea struck me that no one else either before or since has brought up; it is quite precious to me, and I have been willing to gamble my professional life upon it.

Because I had worked overseas so much, I had never had an unbroken span of time in which to acquaint myself with television, which meant that when I did have a chance to view it seriously, it was already a mature art form. As I sat night after night staring at the tube and reveling in the variety of material it brought even then, I discovered that television existed within a cruel time constraint. Programs had to start rigorously on the hour or half hour; to accommodate advertising they had to be broken into short segments and when time was allocated to these interruptions, the typical hour program was allowed only forty-eight minutes.

I also saw that the staple fictional fare of magazines like *The Saturday Evening Post*—the serial mysteries, serial Westerns and episodic humorous material, such as the black comedy of Octavius Roy Cohen and the crafty tales of Clarence Budington Kelland—was doomed. Television would provide such entertainment in even more accessible form. I grieved to see the magazines that had helped me get started perish, while those that did survive bought no fiction at all: I heard critics sound their doleful warnings: 'Television makes reading obsolete. Books in general will fade, and the novel will absolutely vanish.'

Then, one evening after I had been well indoctrinated into the mystery and magic of the tube, I had a vision as clear as if the words *'mene, mene, tekel, upharsin'* had been written on my wall: 'When people tire of the forty-eight-minute television novel, they will yearn for a substantial book within whose covers they can live imaginatively for weeks. The eighteenth-century discursive-type novel will enjoy a vigorous rebirth, because readers will demand it.'

I never deviated from that judgment, but I must clarify one point. I did not write my long novels because I knew there would be a market for them; my mind does not work that way—I have never been geared to the marketplace. What my discovery meant was that I was free to write the kinds of books I had had in mind since that night on Tontouta: long, solid accounts of people and places in interesting corners of the world. If I could write those books with skill, I was confident that readers would support them. Subsequent events proved I was right.

I decided early on to choose as my subject the entire earth, all terrains, all peoples, all animals, and in my major works I have hewn fairly closely to that aim. I love the earth, cherish its ambiguities and do what I can to help protect it. I have climbed the great mountains, probed the deserts and explored all the oceans. To know this earth as I have known it is to know a grandeur that is inexhaustible, and it has always been my desire to communicate that sense to others.

Since I had traveled most of the world, I had the entire canvas to choose from in my writing, but I found myself focusing constantly upon those areas that I foresaw as emerging into international importance: Afghanistan, about to be embroiled in a terrible war with Soviet Russia; Hawaii, about to blend its rich social fabric into the mainland tapestry

as a new state; Poland, that battleground of history about to explode in
a variety of wildly different directions; South Africa, whose future
seemed to be so violent and so dark; Israel, the cradle and the chosen
land of three of the world's major religions; and Alaska, where continents and ideologies meet and clash.

Because I wrote about each of these areas well before they erupted
into major headlines, I was sometimes praised for having uncanny pre-
science, but that was not true; what I had was a strong grounding in
geography, totally self-taught but very pragmatic. The other day a group
of students asked me: 'If you're interested in the entire world, how do
you decide what to write about next?' and I replied: 'Painfully.'

I always carry in the back of my mind six or seven ideas that I am
sure will be powerful subjects for books, but upon closer inspection I
find that only two or three are really viable. It requires at least three
years to write a major book, and the risk is ever present that midway
through the task the writer will lose interest and thus lose his entire
book. Therefore, I have rarely chosen a subject about which I have not
speculated for some dozen years, nor a locale in which I have not lived
as an ordinary citizen.*

Notes among my papers will show that I frequently contemplated a
possible subject for up to twenty years before feeling competent to tackle
it, and I still carry after four or five decades appealing and cogent themes
that I ought to have attempted but didn't. Five of the subjects to which
I applied a good deal of preliminary investigation or even considerable
composition form an interesting group of lost opportunities: a novel on
the siege of Leningrad on which I had made a substantial beginning; a
novel on Mexico, two thirds done, whose manuscript I lost; and three
others that I planned in considerable detail but never started. I should
have halted all other work and moved to South America and tried to
unravel its mysteries; with *Iberia,* my book on Spanish culture, already
finished I would have had a head start, and the kind of book I would
have written ought certainly to be done. I was on the verge of starting
a novel that would have covered the entire Arab world, which I knew
at first hand. I may be the only American writer who has lived in all
corners of that fascinating area—from Indonesia and Malaya on the
east to Spain on the west—save only Saudi Arabia, which would not

---

*Even though I made four extensive visits to South Africa when writing *The
Covenant,* I chose not to take extended residence because of the stern laws governing
writers; I was sure they would not enforce them against me but they might against
someone who worked with me. And although I visited Poland nearly a dozen times
for extended stays, it was never practical to live there.

let me in. In recent stormy decades such a book would have been invaluable. And I always wanted to write a short, poetic novel about Turkey, which I once knew well and which sometimes seems to have more beautiful buildings of the Greek classical period than Greece itself. Of course, one can do only so much, but those failures rankle and it irritates me beyond telling to realize that I shall never attempt them.

When I first read, as an impressionable young man, the Java novel *Max Havelaar,* by Eduard Douwes Dekker, I was astounded by the freedom with which he incorporated in his novel material of the most revolutionary character: price lists, data on the cultivation of sugarcane, long disquistions on life in Indonesia and political analyses. It was as untidy a narrative as I had ever seen, but I quickly saw that he was using this chaotic material to create an ambience that was overpowering, and I reached a conclusion from which I have never retreated: 'A novel is a receptacle into which the writer throws everything he believes to be relevant, but the reader will be enticed only if the matter is thrown with skill and artistry.' I saw that he had written a novel that was technically miserable, but emotionally a masterpiece. In the fifty years since I formed that judgment I have never met one other person outside Holland who has read the book, but not long ago I saw the majestic motion picture made in the Netherlands that was based on it and learned that sensitive critics throughout Europe consider *Max Havelaar* one of the master novels.*

Like Douwes Dekker, I have been willing to write about anything that absorbed my interest, believing that what captivated me would entrance readers. Thus I have written about dinosaurs and bears and geese, the movements of continents, the growing of glaciers and the slide of earthquakes beneath the sea.

Confident that I had discovered and defined the type of writing I was qualified to do, I started writing a long novel that would test my theories, and as the pages of the future *Hawaii* accumulated on my desk, making a pile so tall that it frightened me, I often wondered: Who will take the time to read about coral building islands and workmen irrigating sugarcane? But before I could panic, an inner confidence asserted itself: If I'm interested in such things, my readers will be too, and I

---

*Curiously, I had the same experience with another European novel that meant a great deal to me, Martin Andersen Nexø's splendid *Pelle the Conqueror.* In my years of travel I never met one person who had read this great Danish novel and I began to wonder if I had overestimated its worth. Then, as I was writing these notes, a motion picture based on the adventures of Pelle's rather worthless father impressed the world and I could say: 'I knew it all along, a fine book.'

plowed ahead, not shortening a single chapter and certainly not elimi-
nating any. It was a major gamble, and when it succeeded beyond
anyone's prediction, I judged that my convictions had been justified.

When I turned to the question of how to write, what first came to
mind was that glorious *Adoration of the Magi* which Benozzo Gozzoli
had done in the chapel of the Palazzo Medici in Florence. It was evident
that he saw the art of narration in the same perspective that I did: as
a glorious procession of people and sites and the wonders of nature. I
would use words to paint vast murals, and, like his work in the palazzo,
I would break my narrative into splendid panels, leaving it to the reader,
as he did to the viewer, to bind the whole together.

In looking for subject matter I went back to Thomas Mann's *Budden-
brooks,* in which he invoked memories of a great German family striving
and thriving through the generations, and illuminating its part of the
world while doing so. I would see subject matter as continuous through
the centuries and the people who live in a given place as being closely
interrelated with those who came both before and after them.

Of profound importance in the way I would plan my books would be
Beethoven's Fourth Piano Concerto, with its very slow and measured
beginning before the piano takes over and the drama begins. I deduced
that an artist who has a sure idea of where he is heading can not only
afford to delay his opening statement but also derive much profit from
doing so. I therefore decided quite consciously to start my long novels
with spacious preambles in order to establish the setting for the emotional coloration I hoped to achieve in the body of the book. Thus it was
not uncommon for me to utilize scores of pages for the geological
background, the physical appearance and the animal life of the area I
wanted to write about before I introduced my first human beings. I
believe that had I not known Beethoven so intimately—the fire of those
opening statements in the Fifth Symphony and the Emperor Concerto
as opposed to the more restrained beginnings of the two Fourths, symphony and concerto—I might never have discovered the virtue of the
understated first chapter. I have said, not lightly but with a light phrase:
'I use those long, dull openings to weed out the ribbon clerks.' The
words come from poker, in which an old-timer raises the ante spectacularly to scare away those who are timorous or not really engaged in the
game. My openings scare away readers who are not prepared for a
narrative of long duration, and I often think: 'I probably couldn't have
held their interest anyway,' because I know that many readers who
begin my books are not able to finish them.

Suppose that in 1962 someone had assembled the fifteen brightest men and women in the publishing industry—editors, booksellers, critics, university experts, and enthusiastic readers—and had given them this commission: 'Tell us what kind of novel the American public is yearning for, one that will command attention for at least a full year.' Would that group, after mature deliberation, have conceivably reported: 'The public is thirsting for three books: an archaeologist digging in a small hill in Israel, a rabbit on a journey north from London, and a moody mystery about a Scottish monk in a medieval Italian monastery'?

I think not. Yet when I wrote *The Source* on the first subject, it was received with enthusiasm by the public.* And a few years later *Watership Down,* a book about a rabbit, had the same reception. And some years after that it was Umberto Eco's *The Name of the Rose,* which dealt with crime in a medieval church. The difference between fiction and nonfiction is that the latter often results from shrewd suggestions made by thoughtful editors. The best novels result from the often preposterous imaginations of men and women who have a flair for telling stories; clever analyses and business projections rarely play any meaningful role in their success.

As for the future of the fictitious narrative known as the novel, I am often asked, more times than you would think: 'Do you believe the novel is dead?' and I reply with a smile: 'Do you think I'm the one you should ask?'

---

*Publishers at that time had a degrading rite in which the author of a book was required to stand before the company's assembled salesmen to defend it. When I presented *The Source* as well as I could, which apparently was not reassuring, the senior salesman, who was accustomed to establishing the pattern of his fellows' reaction to a new book, said in a tone of self-pity: 'Let's face it, men, what we have here is another book of short stories,' and everyone groaned, for they knew that collections of such stories, often a sop to the vanity of an established writer, could rarely be given away. I swore then that I would never again try to defend any of my books to salesmen, even though Random House's were among the shrewdest judges of books in America, nor have I.

X

Trios

*T*WO FACTS about my writing career must be understood. First, I have always remained out of the literary mainstream, and have been satisfied to have it so. Indeed, it was an act of conscious policy on my part, because I knew what I wanted to accomplish and, in general how best to accomplish it. I am not a worthy prototype for young writers to follow, and I certainly do not recommend either my behavior or my writing to them. I am a loner to an extent that would frighten most men, and I have hewn to a straight line of my own devising, a form of behavior that entails harsh penalties but that also makes one eligible for great rewards.

The second significant characteristic is that, because of my apprenticeship at Macmillan, which gave me knowledge about publishing and the life of a writer, I chose not to become involved in the literary scene on a social level. It did not appeal to me; it did not seem rewarding; it was distracting rather than productive and, most important, because of my personality and attitudes I would not have been very good at being part of it. I have thus remained off by myself, and it may seem shocking that at age eighty-five I have known almost no other writers, American or foreign, even casually.

I had thirty-second introductions to Gore Vidal, E. L. Doctorow and Robert Ludlum. I once met James Clavell for twenty seconds in an Amsterdam restaurant, Yukio Mishima for half that time as I left a Tokyo geisha house as he was entering, and Evelyn Waugh for half *that* time in an Istanbul restaurant, where he looked up without taking my outstretched hand and said: 'I do not care to have Americans who have read my books interrupting my meal.' On the other hand, when I met his brother Alec Waugh in Honolulu we spent many fine days together, and when he handed me a copy of his *Island in the Sun* he said warmly: 'Really, Michener, with your love of islands you should visit the Caribbean one day.' It was the first time I had heard that suggestion and I would take it up years later.

When I was introduced to William Faulkner in the editorial offices of Random House he grunted, and one wintry afternoon at Toots Shor's in New York Ernest Hemingway nodded in my direction a couple of times as I spent several hours listening to his fascinating monologues. I had one delightful lunch with John O'Hara and a fine evening in Rome with Tennessee Williams, who awed me. I have been on brief television shows with Norman Mailer and Allen Drury, and I once met Herman Wouk for two minutes at a Leonard Lyons party. That's the extent of my literary life, except that once I drove a far distance in Iceland to meet with Halldór Laxness, the Nobel Prize winner from that island whose work I had held in high regard long before he won the prize.

Even at mighty Random House with its multiple subdivisions I have known only three of the editors, my own two—Albert Erskine and Kate Medina—and Jason Epstein, one of the adventurous literary editors. One day I came into the office I customarily used when working on galleys to find it occupied by a handsome black woman, and when I retreated to ask: 'Who's that?' I was told: 'Toni Morrison. She edits for us and writes books for Knopf,' but I doubt if she even saw me. I know no editors at other houses, no agents other than my own Owen Laster at the William Morris Agency, no critics except the delightful John Barkham, who has served American writing so long and with such distinction, and certainly no headwaiters at the restaurants frequented by literary coteries. I have also remained aloof from university circles, for I do not give readings from my work in progress, nor do I lecture. John Barth did introduce me one night at a reading in Baltimore, but that's about the extent of my wild life at the heart of the American literary scene. I have paid a penalty for this aloofness and would not recommend it for other writers. I have not played the role in American letters to which I was entitled and my voice has not been amplified through committees and agencies. I occupy no salaried position in the literary life of our universities, and one of the saddest aspects of my writing is that I have never come upon any young person of obvious talent whom I might have helped along to a professional career. I have been bombarded with manuscripts and visits but have failed to identify young writers with high potential whom I could have introduced to publishing circles in New York. An exception to this mournful generalization could have been a shy, modest young man whom I met during the American occupation of Japan. His name was Oliver Statler, a minor functionary on General MacArthur's huge staff. Living in Japan, he had developed a consuming love for that country and wanted to write about it, and I could have been of help, but by the time he got to me he had already written his *Japanese Inn*, which became a minor classic, so he needed no assistance.

My experience with Oliver Statler shows that if the young man or woman has a reliable talent he or she requires no boost from others. I remember an afternoon when a group of would-be writers from a Philadelphia university visited my hilltop home to discuss writing; they were an able group and I felt sympathy for them but not much assurance that any of them would become writers. However, as they started down the hill I heard one fellow growl: 'He was courteous and all that, but he certainly didn't show me much.' That one, I thought, had a chance to become a writer, because unless a young person feels intuitively that he is at least as good as some who have gone before, he has small chance of excelling them.

I am not speaking of arrogance, which is not a bad characteristic for a young person to have when trying to launch a life in the arts, but the honest kind of self-evaluation that I exercised when I concluded that I could write better than the authors of five novels Macmillan was importing that year from London. Without a solid self-confidence to sustain them, I do not see how young people will have the courage and determination to undergo the disappointments of an apprenticeship in any of the arts or the will to protect themselves if they do succeed in becoming professionals. My self-removal from the literary scene is best understood as such an act of self-preservation.

The reader must not conclude that I was a recluse. Far from it. I have always engaged in a rich social life with business leaders, politicians, the owners and coaches of professional sports and, in my frequent trips abroad, with political leaders of many countries. I have often been at the center of current events if not of the writing profession, and in retrospect it was a good decision that led to this self-imposed exile from the literary milieu. I like being off by myself and doing things in my independent way.

But even in my isolation I maintained a keen interest in the literary experience of our nation and read avidly both *Publishers Weekly* and the Monday edition of *The New York Times* with its reports on developments in publishing and writing. Like a starry-eyed enthusiast in some small obscure town, I followed the news about writers, their successes and failures, and read a large number of literary biographies and autobiographies. When it was announced that some writer was going to appear on television, I scheduled my day to watch, and can still remember one interview with S. J. Perelman, which highlighted his unique talent, but I profited more from the thoughtful programs on Faulkner, Hemingway, Dreiser, Lewis, Fitzgerald, Cather, Wharton and Kerouac. Of course, I had already read biographies of most of the great Europeans and often wished that there could have been one of Lady Murasaki, the eleventh-century novelist who wrote the masterpiece *Genji Monogatari*. From such reading and watching I evolved both an understanding of the life of the writer and my personalized attitude toward the profession.

In this chapter I shall pay tribute to six young men of about my age whose experiences were influential in forming my attitudes toward what a writer is and how he ought to behave. The lives of the first group of three ended in shattering, premature tragedy, which terrified me. The second group became adornments of our profession, often with a jocund touch that I envied. Finally I shall pay my awed respect to three women writers who have been just as gifted as the men, and a lot more stable.

The tragic deaths of my first three fellow writers helped frame my attitudes toward literature, sudden wealth and self-preservation. Assessing the way those lives had ended, I determined to set for myself orbits totally different from theirs.

It is therefore important to appreciate that I was extremely fortunate in escaping sudden early fame. Since celebrity did not burst upon me in one mighty flash, blinding and disorienting me as it did those other three, I did not have to adjust to it, or change my life patterns, or resist those temptations that a sudden flood of money can bring to a young man. Here, timetables become important, for I was inordinately fortunate that the good things that did happen to me were spaced out, so that I had ample time to adjust to each in turn, with the effects of one lucky break having diminished before another occurred. The three men I speak of, less fortunate, were so overwhelmed by their success that they destroyed themselves.

In late 1946 I was prepared to place my first book, *Tales of the South Pacific,* before the public, but as I have explained, a lucky sale of two stories to the *Saturday Evening Post* delayed publication into the less competitive year of 1947, so that in the spring of 1948 it was eligible to compete for the Pulitzer Prize. But this meant that much more than a full year had elapsed between publication and prize, and in that span the book, which had never enjoyed even a modest success commercially or critically—of the nine major reviewing media, eight did not even mention it, let alone review it—had expired and been forgotten.

The courage of the Pulitzer committee in awarding their prize to me was not applauded, major voices complained that my book was not a novel, it did not conform to the award's stated and implied conditions, and was surpassed in merit by half a dozen other novels that did conform. Contrary to awards in the past, this one did not spur any interest in the book; sales of the hardcover edition did not suddenly leap from nothing to high respectability as a result of the prize, as had often happened with earlier winners. This lack of sales was caused by a stroke of bad luck: in the month the prize was announced a paperback reprint appeared on newsstands, brutally abbreviated and for sale at twenty-five cents.

Another year of sharp deflation of ego passed so that when the wonderful musical *South Pacific* opened in 1949 the existence of the book was known by few and remarked upon by none. Indeed, several important reviewers, wondering from what magic seed this flower had evolved, bought copies of the paperback edition, which, to save space, had not reprinted the two stories on which the play had principally been based, and wrote that since Rodgers and Hammerstein had such meager material to work with, they were to be doubly praised for having invented such a heart-warming story line on which to build their play. I cannot recall that any reviewer gave me any praise, and it was generally believed that R&H had found lying in the gutter a sow's ear and had converted it into a silk purse. As I joked at a literary soiree held a few days after the opening, paraphrasing Lord Byron's comment following the publication of *Childe Harold's Pilgrimage:* 'I went to bed an unknown and woke to find Ezio Pinza famous.'

I was more fortunate than I can tell in having all these red-letter events occur so comfortably spaced over four calendar years, 1946–1949. I did not have to adjust to sharp swings of public attitude, nor decide how to handle an unexpected bonanza,* nor fend off a chain of pressing invitations.

---

*On the day my first royalty check arrived I sent a letter to Sylvia Porter, whom I had met while we were both having lunch at Sardi's: 'Dear Sylvia, it looks as if

I started slowly in the writing profession, maintained a low profile, and permitted nothing to divert me from the job at hand—to make myself into a good writer. In those sober years, when I worked so diligently at four o'clock in the morning, I was following the careers of those three ill-fated young men more or less my age, and what I saw horrified me. In each case the young writer's life intertwined with mine and left scars.

At this point the reader should lay aside this book and check out of the library a copy of an excellent book about the problems of young American writers, John Leggett's *Ross and Tom*. But since the book may not be easily available, I will summarize the parts relevant to what I wish to say.

Leggett was a New York boy with considerable writing talent. After an education at Andover and Yale, he became a naval officer in the Pacific. Upon demobilization he tried his hand at writing and submitted his first novel to Houghton Mifflin, the distinguished publisher based in Boston; the editors dismayed him by rejecting his novel, then showed their confidence in his other talents by offering him a job as one of their editors.

When he reported to work in 1954 at the age of thirty-three, he found the offices of the company still shell-shocked by the tragedies that had overtaken two of their most spectacularly promising young authors within one year, 1948–49. As Leggett began to probe the causes of the two deaths, so similar that all America commented on the almost simultaneous loss of two exceptional talents, he became obsessed with the question that had disturbed me when I was in college pondering the death of Thomas Chatterton: 'What diabolical force killed these young men?'

They were so similar, Ross Lockridge and Tom Heggen, each talented, inordinately handsome and attractive to women, Midwestern in origin and acutely aware of American values, and each achieving staggering fame with his first book. They were paradigms of the triumphs and tragedies of the American literary scene.

I will be receiving a weekly check for some years ahead. What should I do with my money?' She replied: 'Dear Jim, I am far too clever to try to handle my own money myself. I allow a man at Merrill Lynch to do it for me, and here's his name.' John Sullivan accepted every spare dollar I received and protected it so that I would have something to fall back on if my later books failed.

Ross was from an upper-middle-class Indiana family with cultural pretensions and minor accomplishments. He looked much like Tyrone Power, with copious jet-black hair, flawless white teeth, straight lean body, dark eyes and a radiant smile. He had graduated from a good school in Bloomington, Indiana, and done unusually well at the university in that town. A year of study in France converted a country boy into a sophisticate, and graduate study at Harvard edged him close to being a serious scholar. He then taught five grinding years at Simmons College in Boston, earning a meager salary. He married a high school sweetheart—she was also his college sweetheart—of considerable beauty and charm and even more strength of character, and with her would have four children, which posed serious financial problems because of his limited income. But he was a loving and caring father, and handled his family obligations responsibly. He was a quiet young man, but also one seething with ambition.

At a surprisingly early age, at a time when I had never even remotely considered being a writer or much of anything else relating to a career, he had visualized himself writing a great American novel, and as he daydreamed it underwent a subtle transformation into *the* great American novel. From that moment he channeled all his considerable talent and above-average mental and physical energy into first outlining and then drafting a massive novel, which would ultimately run to more than one thousand book pages.

The writing did not go easily, what with living in cramped quarters, with noisy children underfoot, and travels back and forth between Boston and Bloomington.

But after seven painful years of writing, he had a massive manuscript that was as good as he had hoped it would be; it was indubitably a fine novel. The trouble was, he was now totally convinced that it was a great one, and all the really dreadful things that he was now about to do stemmed from his firm belief that he was the greatest writer in English since Shakespeare.

He had a cousin living in Indiana, the writer Mary Jane Ward, whose recently published autobiographical novel, *The Snake Pit,* had been a sensational success. Focused on Miss Ward's mental breakdown, it was a harrowing account of life in a mental institution. She knew Bennett Cerf, the publisher at Random House, and said she was sure she could get Ross a hearing at that house, but through another writing friend he found entree to the staid old firm of Houghton Mifflin and he elected to take his book to them.

At this point in my narrative John Leggett's book becomes important.

I had long been profoundly interested in Lockridge—we were roughly of the same generation (I was born in 1907, he in 1914) and had had our first books published almost simultaneously—so when Leggett's book appeared I hurried out to buy one of the first copies. As I read I was appalled and at times disgusted by Lockridge's attitudes toward being a writer and publishing a book; they were completely different from mine. I told an interviewer at the time: 'If you want to get a clear picture of me, buy a copy of Leggett's book, start on page 86 when Ross Lockridge delivers the manuscript of *Raintree County* to Houghton Mifflin, and whenever he does something totally outrageous, jot in the margin in pencil "−180°," which will mean that I would have done it in a manner as far from that as possible.' Obviously, Leggett's portrait of a frenetic young man with barely a grain of common sense, humility or restraint activated nerve ends throughout my body, and especially my brain. That was in 1974, when Lockridge was already dead and I was in midflight in my own career.

Two years ago, in 1989, in preparing these notes I reread the whole Leggett book, which was an astonishing experience, for as a much older man who has seen a great deal of writing, publishing and attendant follies, I had a clearer understanding of the preposterous moves Lockridge was making, as if he was determined to destroy himself. And as I read page after page about his outlandish behavior and about his near insanity and, finally, suicide, I was sick with anger at such a great loss—tears filled my eyes, and I sat quite numb. Here is what he did.

When Houghton Mifflin accepted his manuscript, with enthusiasm, he proceeded to lecture them interminably on how to handle this great treasure. Finding himself in the hands of Paul Brooks, one of America's ablest editors of that period, he abused Brooks, questioned his judgment, and gave him insulting advice on how to do his job. He stormed through the ranks at Houghton Mifflin, advising everyone how to handle his immortal manuscript, which he described as perhaps the most important the firm had ever received.

Then he launched a manic campaign to make *Life* magazine run not only a segment of the novel but also a pictorial essay about him at his home in Indiana. He succeeded in persuading *Life* to run an excerpt in its issue of August 18, 1947, handsomely illustrated and with the editorial note that here was one of the finest American novels in many years. So his novel enjoyed a magnificent send-off.

Next he concentrated on the Book-of-the-Month Club, instructing Houghton in the steps it must take to make the club select *Raintree* as a major selection. He found time to advise Houghton's publicity department almost daily on how it could best handle his novel, ignoring the fact that the company would also be publishing quite a few other good books, each deserving attention.

He pointed out to anyone who would listen that *Raintree* was better than James Joyce's *Ulysses,* and in his later evaluations he considered it equal to Shakespeare. His behavior toward Hollywood was grotesque. When MGM acquired film rights to the book, Lockridge sent Louis B. Mayer an insulting letter in which he told the veteran filmmaker that his pictures were much inferior to those made in Europe but that if he made *Raintree* properly he had a chance to recover his reputation. It would be, he assured Mayer, a much better film than *Gone With the Wind.* He was not happy with the reported casting of *Raintree,* and since he knew his book better than anyone else, he intimated that he would be prepared, if called, to hurry to Hollywood to take over. The flood of Hollywood money seemed to unhinge his mind, for he launched a series of disgraceful attacks accusing his editor, Brooks, who had served him well and honestly, of financial misconduct.

What made me feel compassion for this arrogant, self-centered writer was the pathetic way in which he inflated both the value of his book and its importance to him. In any decade a score of good novels come along, but only rarely do they modify a life significantly. Nobody gave Ross the caution that my mentor Hugh MacNair Kahler gave me: 'Remember, Jim. Writing a book or a dozen books doesn't remake you or create miracles. Next morning, when you wake up, you're the same horse's ass you were yesterday. Writing is a job. Do it well, it's a great life. Mess around, its disappointments will kill you.'

Lockridge had allowed his book to become so all-important that when it passed out of his hands at publication, its disappearance threatened his life. No one warned him that the job of the writer is to ignore the book that's been done and buckle down to the next one. Quickly he fell into a profound depression from which he feared there was no chance of rescue, and then into a bleak despair far more intense than his earlier euphoria. Fumbling about pitifully, wondering whether he could ever reorganize his life for the long years ahead, he could devise no answers, no reassurances. On a calm Saturday afternoon in March 1948 he listened by radio to the finals of the Indiana high school basketball championships, drove into his garage, closed all the doors, left the motor running and at the age of thirty-four slipped painlessly into the lasting peace he had not known since those days eight years before when he had started writing the novel that would ultimately destroy him. Lockridge had taken his book too seriously. It was good, but it was just a book, and today nobody reads it and the movie made from it creaks when it is given a slot on *The Late Show*. But I respected both the book and the movie, so if a writer like Ross finds even one faithful reader after forty-four years, perhaps he does gain the immortality he so eagerly sought.

Lockridge's life could have been construed as an object lesson to beginning writers: 'Study everything he did, then do the opposite.' In an oblique way his catastrophic life had a slight connection to my own labors. While *Raintree County* was being written, Metro-Goldwyn-Mayer in Hollywood announced that a prize would be awarded to some outstanding unpublished American novel that could be converted into a major motion picture. The prize—$100,000, plus bonuses—could total a staggering $250,000. Lockridge won it primarily because *Raintree County* was far superior to the competition. It was this vast sum of money, incredibly greater in value in those days, that started his plunge toward disaster. It happened that the literary agency in New York that was masterminding the contest for MGM was the one that had taken me on as a client, in hopes, I believe, that I might be the following year's winner of the prize. At any rate I was intensively groomed for the competition, with considerable guidance from the agency. I suspect that it was my inability to revise my manuscript for my second novel to make it attractive to the Hollywood people that made my agent send me that devastating letter I received on the morning I was awarded the Pulitzer Prize. Ross won the Hollywood prize but not the Pulitzer; my reward was the reverse, and how fortunate I was.

Tom Heggen was utterly unlike Ross Lockridge. I first heard of him one Monday morning when my boss at Macmillan came in wreathed in smiles: 'Michener! You've got to read this book I bought. It's about your part of the world, and it's the funniest thing to come along since Mark Twain.' Before I was halfway through *Mister Roberts* I agreed, but the further I read, the more I noticed the structural similarities between Heggen's book and mine. Both depicted a draftee's life in the Navy. Both used the South Pacific as their locale. Both consisted of a group of loosely integrated short stories. Both focused on the dull routine of daily life rather than on battle heroics. And a real coincidence: both had as their central character a tall, loose-jointed, easygoing courageous junior officer who fled the safety of rear-line duty to find death at the distant front where battles raged, and in each instance the hero's death was not actually seen but reported by letter or official report back to the station he quit. Strangest of all, although I could not have foreseen it that day, the theatrical genius Josh Logan would take each book in turn, Heggen's first, then mine, and whip the stories into dramatic shape to produce two of the greatest smash hits of that period: *Mister Roberts* and *South Pacific.*

As with Ross Lockridge, whose life has meant so much to me, I never met Tom Heggen or even saw him from a distance, which is all right, for I doubt that either Ross or Tom would have found me interesting and I would have been terrified by their moves toward self-destruction. But since Heggen and I followed such strikingly parallel paths with our books my interest in him was of a special kind. All I knew about him, however, was that at the time his book was bought he either was or had recently been an editor at *Reader's Digest,* which I consider a very lucky break for a young man who wanted to write, because I have heard that salaries there were monumental.

When I turned to the second half of Leggett's revealing book, I was rewarded by finding my first full account of Heggen's life. Leggett had accumulated through much legwork and many interviews a good deal of information about Heggen's growing up and difficult behavior as a youth. Born to a middle-class Norwegian family in Fort Dodge, Iowa, not far from the Minnesota border, he was a congenital rebel, a disturber of the peace and later on a hard-drinking rowdy. Whereas Lockridge was a conservative type who dressed carefully and seemed a typical member of the Midwestern bourgeoisie, Tom dressed abominably and sometimes outrageously, and his principal characteristic was an uncontrollable tendency toward making trouble. Wherever he went or in whatever setting he was placed he violently opposed the establishment and invented ingenious pranks to create disturbances.

The Great Depression forced his family to move far south to Oklahoma City, where he enrolled in the city university, a strict Methodist institution that tolerated his antics only briefly. Expelled at eighteen, he switched to Oklahoma A&M at Stillwater, learned little, raised hell and fell in love with a quiet, lovely girl named Carol Lynn Gilmer, who must have sensed that she could have only a tempestuous relationship with Heggen, for she tried her best not to fall in love with him but did.

When his family, discouraged by their failure to accomplish much in Oklahoma, decided to try their luck in Minnesota, Tom enrolled in the university there and, in its lively, free-wheeling intellectual life, came into his own. Forming a turbulent lifelong friendship with the campus wit and scourge, Max Shulman, he became a near-professional writer on the college paper and a hell-raiser par excellence.

Upon graduating from college he persuaded Carol Lynn to marry him, and while he served in the South Pacific in the old Navy buckets he would make famous, she joined the Red Cross. She trailed her husband through the Pacific islands, hoping to join him, but she never did, and after the war they reunited tentatively. He was unable to bridge the gap of those lost war years, and their marriage was in deep trouble.

Now Leggett tells swiftly of Tom's disastrous years at the *Reader's Digest,* the last place in America he should have gone with his contempt for sober authority; the publication of his novel; the total failure of his attempt to draft, with Max Shulman as coauthor, a stage play based on *Mister Roberts;* and finally, Josh Logan's three-month collaboration with Heggen, which results in the faultlessly carpentered stage play.

When the curtain fell on opening night, Tom Heggen, at twenty-seven, was at the apex of fame and on his way to becoming a millionaire. Few young men at that age would know the accolades, the fawning and the invitations to do the sorts of challenging things he was offered, but there was gall in the honey: almost every review said that Josh Logan had taken a trivial book and hammered it into one of America's brightest comedies, and several magazines used photographs of him, not Heggen, to represent the play.

The descent from Parnassus was swift and terrible. It began the day after the play opened to raves, and Leggett reveals the curious nature of the trouble:

> Later that same day, February 19, Tom got around to the rest of the paper and found on the page following the *Mister Roberts* review a news story about Joshua Logan's future plans. He had proposed to Richard Rodgers and Oscar Hammerstein that they write the score, book and lyrics for a musical version of James Michener's *Tales of the South Pacific.* Leland Hayward was to produce and Logan would direct the play for presentation next season.
>
> While Tom knew that Logan had been probing Michener's book, as he had *Mister Roberts,* for a dramatic line, he had no idea he was so far along with it, nor that he was to be firmly excluded. This was especially painful since he believed Logan's interest in the Michener book owed much to *Mister Roberts,* that in Heggen's Elysium Logan had first seen the dramatic possibilities within the Northerner's dream of paradise.

Tom tortured himself rereading the article. Calta, the *Times'* theater man, was equally surprised by the suddenness of Logan's decision, for the director had only just confided he had no immediate plans. Tom wondered if the announcement could be a reproof and public humiliation for him.

So a bleak sky encroached on his day of triumph. With every critic in town pillaging the dictionary for superlatives to bestow on his play, Tom was indifferent to their praise. Worse, with his masochistic nerve laid bare, last night's raves now seemed patronizing.

The reviewers seemed to agree that his own contribution was the lesser, a springboard for the Logan acrobatics. In the *Times,* Brooks Atkinson observed that the play had been cast with so much relish and directed so spontaneously that it gave the impression of not having been written at all, but improvised on the stage during rehearsals, 'under Mr. Logan's idiomatic direction.'

In the *News,* John Chapman wrote that since he [Logan] was one of the very best directors in the American theater and knew just what sort of material a director needed, every line of the dramatization bore the "signature of Mr. Logan."

The *Time* magazine review was dominated by the photograph of a quizzical, wrinkle-browed Logan. It was framed by comment that as a story and a show, *Mister Roberts* was not much and was not meant to be, but as a human picture it was magnificent, due largely to coauthor Logan's brilliantly telling direction.

Time summed up the collaboration: 'Author Heggen brought his successful short novel to Logan last August after deciding he didn't like his own stage version. For three months they hacked away at it together. Says Logan: "Nothing could stop it. It got up on its two feet and walked by itself." More accurately, 6 ft.- 2 in., 200 pound Josh Logan got the play into shape. . . .'

Logan, wholly immersed now in *South Pacific,* tried to interest Tom in it, persuaded him to read the script and offer suggestions. When he returned it, Tom pointed out a line, 'Hey, fellah,' and said it struck him as a sentimental and unlikely way for one sailor to hail another, and that ended it. Tom was not a part of *South Pacific* and he wanted none of its scraps. He never went to a rehearsal and just being around the *South Pacific* people was torture to him. At times he thought he would choke on his jealousy.

He could not help feeling that *South Pacific* was the bastard child of *Mister Roberts,* that the Pacific was *his* ocean and they had snatched it away without so much as a thank you.

And then began the downward slide: after the divorce from Carol Lynn, casual affairs with a succession of women, a fugitive trip to France on a tramp steamer in an attempt to recapture the ecstasy he had once discovered on old ships—a photographer was sent along in hopes of a magazine story, but the surly crew would have none of that nonsense—and finally the collapse of everything and a tail-between-the-legs retreat back to America.

Now, stuck away in actor Alan Campbell's apartment while the owner is in Hollywood, he gains release only in solitary drinking and rebuffs any friends who try to help. At the age of twenty-nine he finds himself completely alone, for he has suffered two ego-shattering blows from girlfriends, each of whom he vaguely wanted to marry. An American girl, finding it impossible to lure Tom into any kind of social life, goes alone to a literary cocktail party given by Jim Putnam of Macmillan in honor of Arthur Koestler just in from London, takes one look at the newcomer and waltzes off with him, abandoning Heggen forever. Even more shattering, Leueen MacGrath, the Irish actress he had courted, informs him over the phone that she is marrying the famous dramatist George Kaufman, author of innumerable hits, who is sixty years old.

Tom, at twenty-nine, finds himself completely isolated in the empty apartment, and there in shadows he stares into the future and cannot tolerate what he sees: his talent frozen, his mind a blank, his hopes destroyed, his friends alienated. Tom goes to the bathroom, arranges his pills so they will be handy, draws a hot bath, slips in and invites the soothing water to bring him peace. The coroner's report was concise: 'Submersion in fresh water in bathtub. Probable suicide, Contributory cause, overdose of barbiturates. . . .'

Almost immediately after the unprecedented success of *South Pacific,* with Logan garnering a Pulitzer Prize for his share in writing it, a short article appeared in one of the New York papers to the effect that Mr.

Logan was now turning his attention to his next work, which could very well be a Broadway adaptation of Barnaby Conrad's *Matador*. On reading this startling news I felt a spasm of great pain flash across my chest. *South Pacific* was the biggest thing on Broadway, the most monumental success in years, and how could one of its creators turn his back on it and go gallivanting after some chimera about a bullfighter in Spain? Logan had an obligation to *South Pacific* and, by extension, to me, and the thought that he was not only leaving it but the country was devastating. I could hardly credit this dismaying news, and without knowing it at the time my reactions were an exact duplicate of Tom Heggen's when he learned that Logan was deserting him for me.

I spent several days in unhappy confusion—much shallower, of course, than the anguish that assailed Heggen, but as I wandered about the streets of New York after work or trailed aimlessly into the Y for volleyball, I was rescued by my old and trusted friend John Milton, whose final lines to his great poem *Lycidas* I recalled:

> At last he rose, and twitch'd his mantle blue;
> To-morrow to fresh woods, and pastures new.

From my first reading I had made the last line one of the guiding points of my life: 'Well, that's over. Let's get on with the job.' It is, I think, one of the profoundest of guidelines, the one that keeps us from festering in our defeats or becoming hubristic in our victories. Neither Lockridge nor Heggen was able to slam his book shut and walk away from his tremendous success. In their inability to turn resolutely to fresh woods and pastures new they condemned themselves to tortures unimaginable to one who has never experienced them, and although most writers escape the full torment that these two brought upon themselves, even the finest have felt twinges of self-doubt: What if I can't produce another good one?

As I traced the careers of Ross and Tom I became aware that in the first days of their success they were spending their royalties so wildly that soon they would be faced with the problem of what they had to do next to keep the money flowing. One successful book rarely ensures a life of ease; the customary requirement is a series of books, and even they provide only a reasonable degree of security. Nor can the young writer believe the speed with which he can dissipate that first flood of income. When he starts a new day he asks: 'Now what?' and at midnight the sweating begins, with the idea of suicide creeping in as a solution.

In striving to understand these lives, one must consider the two men's experience with fame, which they were granted so abundantly and suddenly, and which Lockridge pursued so shamelessly. Neither handled it well, Lockridge becoming vainglorious, Heggen obstreperous. It turned out to be fleeting. The new *Webster's Biographical Dictionary,* doesn't even list Lockridge, who considered himself superior to Joyce. And of course, it doesn't mention Heggen either.

Both Heggen and Lockridge were dead by the time the editors of Time-Life invited me to one of their glamorous lunches at which a dozen and a half senior editors sat about the table to get to know and interrogate some figure who had lately come into the public eye. Sitting rather stiffly, eating little, as was my custom at such affairs, and answering questions politely and briefly, I made a poor impression. One editor asked bluntly: 'Mr. Michener, how do you think the great success of *South Pacific* will affect you personally?' and I remember well my response, for it would come back to me repeatedly in later years: 'I hope not at all. I certainly do not want to become involved in the hysterical world of Josh Logan, Richard Rodgers, Oscar Hammerstein and, especially, Leland Hayward, all of whom I admire and to whom I am deeply indebted. And I shall remain off to the side by myself because I believe that to do otherwise would destroy me.'

My little speech caused a couple of gasps, and before nightfall they had obviously been communicated to the men I had referred to, because in succeeding days each in his own way challenged me about it. I made my apologies and said that I hoped we would remain friends, which in fact we did. Logan would later prove himself a resolute friend in certain difficult litigations we were involved in as partners; Hammerstein was a neighbor and friend; Rodgers before his death wanted to start a new venture with me; and Leland Hayward once engaged me daily over a period of three weeks when he was in his seventies and agog with a wonderful concept for a new musical on which we could collaborate. But in the vital years of my writing career, the ones when survival itself was at stake, I consciously refrained from the errors that had destroyed Lockridge and Heggen.

I am sorry that John Leggett did not add a third portrait to his study of young writers, because I wish I knew more about the life and death of John Horne Burns, who was to play a major role in my life and still does. In the years that I prowled the literary-club circuit as a public speaker while striving to accumulate enough money to make a stab at being a full-time professional writer, I offered the committees that hired me a choice of three topics. *The South Pacific* was the most popular;

Our Young American Writers was the one I enjoyed most; and neither the title nor the subject matter of the third can I remember.

In the lecture on the literary scene I reviewed the work of some half dozen writers but with special emphasis on two who had captured my imagination and for whom I had great hopes. I sold a lot of books for these two young men. The first had attended Princeton University and was either contemplating or beginning a career in the Presbyterian ministry in which he would later excel. Frederick Buechner had a style of great elegance, so highly polished that he reminded me of Wharton at her best. He liked long sentences dealing with, for example, the sensibilities of urbane parents who sent their sons to places like Princeton, and I used to read aloud with great effect several passages from his novel *A Long Day's Dying,* in which single sentences ran on for half a page. At the end of each segment I would tell my audience: 'I could not in a hundred years write like Mr. Buechner, nor would I want to, but I esteem him as one of the best young writers today and feel sure he will maintain that reputation in the decades ahead.'*

In order to provide contrast, I next read hilarious passages from Frederick Wakeman's delightful *Shore Leave,* which told of rowdy Air Force pilots in the Pacific War, and *The Hucksters,* which lampooned the advertising business and was soon to be made into an extremely popular movie with a glittering all-star cast, headed by Clark Gable. This part of the lecture was quite popular, and as the tour progressed I started playing all the roles in Wakeman's lively tales, using such dialects as I could muster.

But the highlight of my performance came when I spoke with serious affection of what I reported as the best novel to come out of the war so far. It was *The Gallery,* by John Horne Burns, and it told in unusually sophisticated style of American G.I.'s on duty in and near the famous domed shopping gallerias of Naples. Here people of great diversity meet, know one another casually, drift on, some to their homes, some to their encampments, some to their deaths. One of the most attractive features of the novel is the arbitrary insertion at the end of each chapter or isolated story of a section called 'Promenade', in which Burns keeps us moving through his galleria, seeing the sights, smelling the aromas, sensing the cross currents. In my talks whenever I read one or two of these remarkably poetic passages, the audience applauded with tremendous enthusiasm.

In the late fall of 1947, when I was giving my first series of lectures,

---

*He has. From his industrious pen has continued to flow a unique mix of intelligent novels and masterfully argued religious essays. His reputation is solid.

the public was not yet prepared for someone like me, a stranger in the community, to discuss the undercurrent of homosexuality in Burns's novel, so I avoided that aspect, feeling that it would probably alienate readers who would otherwise enjoy the book. Nor did I care to say that I liked the book because of its daring subject matter, finding it an American equivalent of E. M. Forster and André Gide. When I sat around at night with booklovers who knew the works of these two fine writers, I would often bring up Burns as an American writer who stood a chance, judging from his *Gallery,* of one day reaching their stature. 'It's about time,' I would say.

Whenever during the tour someone asked me to predict who among my young lions might win the 1948 Pulitzer for literature I invariably responded: 'John Horne Burns. He's clearly the best of the lot,' but I sometimes wondered if the judges would ignore the brilliance of his writing because of the delicacy of his theme.

During the period when I gave this lecture in all parts of the country I had not met Burns and knew nothing of his appearance or background, but I did come upon either a newspaper clipping or an ad for his book that showed a handsome, somewhat feisty-looking face some years younger than mine and with the half-sneer of the detached and amused observer. There was also a brief text saying that he had gained high marks in literature at Harvard and had taught for five years at Loomis Chafee. He had seen military service in Italy, but beyond that I knew nothing, nor would I ever know. However, my agent, Helen Strauss, forwarded a letter Burns had sent me, thanking me for the good things I had been saying about him. The letter came from New York.

I closed my lecture with an enthusiastic account of how young Gore Vidal had utilized his enforced service in the dismal Aleutians as a basis for his very good novel *Williwaw,* which demonstrated, I said rather sententiously, 'how a man sentenced to a bleak, stormswept island in wartime can convert that experience into a strong creative statement.' I hoped that the audience would make the connection to the case of a somewhat older man who had been sentenced to lonely islands in the South Pacific and had also used them to advantage.

When the time approached for announcing the 1948 Pulitzers, I must confess that I was not even aware that they were being awarded, but friends later told me that it was generally thought, especially by those who took literature seriously, that John Horne Burns was sure to win with his *The Gallery.* When the prize did not go to him, he was, I am told, almost savagely disappointed, and from the moment of the announcement he conceived a blazing hatred of me, feeling with justification that I had robbed him of a prize that was rightfully his, an opinion in which I have always concurred.

Shortly thereafter *Life* magazine conceived the idea of gathering together at one spot some twenty young writers who had done books about the war, and the editors asked me to write a longish essay about the group, making distinctions and allotting kudos. The project was under the editorial supervision of Josh Logan's sister Mary Lee Weatherbee, a woman of shrewd judgment, and when I submitted my copy, prior to the photography session, she said: 'You've left out the one we at *Life* considered the best prospect of the bunch, Saul Bellow and his *Dangling Man.*' When I said: 'I haven't read it,' she said: 'You should.'

She also explained with some firmness that one paragraph would have to come out: 'That one where you praise Pearl Buck, about her having won the Nobel Prize and being an object lesson to younger writers who want to write strong novels.'

'But all I said was true. You can check it.'

'True, but not advisable. Henry Luce has given us strict orders. We must never say anything favorable about Pearl Buck. Some fight his parents and hers had when they were missionaries in China.' She dropped her voice: 'He also thinks she's a Communist.'

Under pressure from the *Life* people, who apologized for their employer's monomania, I had to remove Miss Buck's name from my essay, even though she and I were personal friends. I felt I should inform her of what I had been forced to do and she laughed: 'Old enmities die hard. Mr. Luce's power to evict me from his empire satisfies some ancient missionary grudge,' and she forgave me.

The twenty-odd writers were assembled one day in a New York armory and arranged on a platform with three levels so that everyone's face could be seen, and some two dozen shots were taken with a big camera under half a dozen lights. Alas, my story never ran in *Life,* I received a small kill fee for my efforts, and the photograph was never printed. It must still be in the files at *Life,* or in some photographer's attic, and if it could now be published as a 'Where Are They Now?' reminiscence, with text to indicate what each accomplished since the shot was taken, it would be a fine piece of Americana. My essay, which may or may not have been perceptive, is not recoverable, unless *Life* still has a copy forty years later.

The reason why I have spent so much time on the photograph is that when it was about to be taken Logan's sister tried to introduce me to Burns, who refused to take my hand and stalked away, even though he had told me he was indebted to me for having spoken of him so widely and sold so many of his books; the corrosive sense of unfairness over the Pulitzer obscured that debt. And as Mary and I stood on the sidewalk waiting for a cab, she said by way of explanation for Burns's rudeness: 'He's quite a faggot, you know,' and when we turned he was standing less than a foot behind us, his face an ashen gray.

Less than a week later, Norman Cousins, editor of the prestigious *Saturday Review,* phoned with deep regrets: 'Michener, we have bad news. We had plans to run your picture on the cover next week. But the review of your new book, *The Fires of Spring,* just came in, and frankly, it's devastating. John Horne Burns wrote it, and there is no way we could soften it, because not a single paragraph is even slightly favorable. We'd look crazy with a glowing blurb on the cover and his review inside. So we have to knock you off. I'm sorry.'

I remember my reply: 'That's bad news, Mr. Cousins. But now I've got to get back to work on my next one, and let's hope it's better.' I had sworn that I would never be elated by praise or downcast by a drubbing, and this was the first test case. True to my word, I went back to my typewriter, for I still had much to say about my world.

When Burns's review of *The Fires of Spring* appeared, it was as if vitriol had been mixed with the ink. But the attack had almost no effect upon me, nor upon the book, for it sold about as well as might have been expected—not heavily—and it lived on to become the book of mine about which more people write to me than any other.

But what Burns did to me seemed like a kindness compared with what the older and established critics did to *his* second novel. Never in my memory had they come so close to total annihilation of an author's work. His *Lucifer with a Book* was a savage, kinky, vengeful account of a sadistic boys' private school, and the book was so avant-garde and focused on sex, sometimes of an exhibitionistic character, that the critics found the work revolting. At least one major newspaper lambasted not only Burns but also the publisher who had had the temerity to offer the book, claiming that in doing so the company had grievously offended public morals. I read it and found it a logical extension of themes and directions toward which Burns had been moving in his first book, and I was outraged that a critic and a newspaper would use their power to abuse a writer for serious work that would have been accepted without a murmur in France, Germany or Sweden. (Now the book would occasion nary a ripple.)

I wrote to the editor of the book section protesting such a blatant attempt at censorship, but the letter was not published, nor, as far as I know, did any other writers spring to Burns's defense, leaving his public reputation somewhat tarnished.

For some time I lost sight of Burns, but having met him only that brief time during the photographing session I doubt that I would have recognized him had I passed him on the street. Then I heard that after the blistering reviews his book had received, he left the country and was traveling around Europe. I heard rumors that he had dropped down to North Africa and then, some years later, that he was trying to write at a village hideout in France. Since I myself was traveling extensively in these years, I lost track of where he actually was, but I heard that his writing was not going well, and then that he had died, but where, or how, or in what circumstance I never really knew. Rumors were plentiful and they centered upon whether or not he had committed suicide, or if as one cynic phrased it: 'He had encouraged suicide to happen,' which was the same suggestion that had been made regarding Tom Heggen's death. Finally a semiauthoritative statement appeared in print: 'John Horne Burns, American novelist, died of a cerebral hemorrhage at Leghorn, Italy, at the age of thirty-six.' Whatever the cause of death, this luminous talent was gone.

Then I began to appreciate the great loss I had suffered, for men often thrive when they have competitors against whom to test themselves, and had Burns lived I am sure he and I would have competed, honorably and vigorously, throughout our lives, each checking what the other was doing, meeting now and then as adversaries and in time as friends, each going his unique way, each presenting a mirror-image of the other. He would have been one of the notable esthetes, I a stolid representative of the stable middle class; he a writer of traceries and shadowy intimations, I of conflicts in blazing sunlight; he the head of a coterie and immensely popular in universities, where his acerbic wit would be appreciated and encouraged, I off by myself plugging away at my own goals. Side by side we would have marched through the decades, and tears fill my eyes when I think of the enormous loss I and the world suffered with his death. My alter ego had vanished in the mists of sunset. I think of John Horne Burns every week of my life.

Lockridge, Heggen and Burns were my tragic trio, the ones who were so important in the first years of my writing, but there was another trio that was at times hilarious and a proper counterweight to tragedy. Their importance in any evaluation of American writing in this period lay in the masterly way they handled publicity, converting themselves into public figures and enhancing their relative importance a hundredfold. I envy them their performances, because they were the Andy Warhols of the writing profession.

Norman Mailer, Gore Vidal and Truman Capote have been of great importance to me because they performed in public in ways that I could not. To understand exactly what I mean by this, you must accompany me to MacArthur's occupied Japan in the years 1947–1957, when a group of average military American men and their wives attained enormous social power and lived in fine expropriated homes. To prove to the cultured Japanese leaders that not all Americans were boors, they began to invite to their parties a capable piano player, who offered light classical music as well as a French expatriate master of woodblock prints who had lived in Japan for many years and was known for his flamboyant art and shocking personal appearance. Paul Jacolet was a portly sybarite who kept his face covered with the white rice-powder makeup used by kabuki actors. He favored outrageous costumes, sometimes ornate Japanese kimonos such as women might wear, at other times wildly colored velvet jackets in bright green or purple, with skintight trousers of some clashing color, and bright red shoes of fantastic design. He had a mincing walk, but one look at his amazing dress and face and you knew he was an artist. He made himself a fixture at the American military parties I attended; few remembered his name—he was known simply as 'the artist.'

Jacolet was invaluable because he represented in this austere military society the other world of which the generals and colonels could never be a part but which, because they were men of good sense, they knew they ought to honor. Every society needs artists to remind itself of the finer things of life, and two aspects of this problem have fascinated me: when American businessmen and political leaders visit Europe with their wives, even though they have never attended to the arts at home, they feel obligated to visit the haunts of Balzac, Dickens, Tolstoy and Beethoven because they recognize intuitively that those were the men of their day who really mattered; and although most of us know Vincent van Gogh in Arles and Paul Gauguin in Tahiti as if they were neighbors, somewhat disreputable but endlessly fascinating, none of us can name two French generals or department store owners of that period. I take enormous pride in considering myself an artist, one of the necessaries.

In the United States in my generation it has been Mailer, Vidal and Capote who have played the very important role of symbolizing the writing artist for the public. Who automatically visualizes Saul Bellow or John Updike as an 'artist' or a 'novelist?' They seem more like university professors or stockbrokers, but neither Norman Mailer nor Truman Capote could be mistaken for such. They behaved like outrageous Pucks, who entertained us with their antics. They were also outspoken critics and sly commentators, but in that role they have been excelled by Gore Vidal, whose patrician sneer and acerbic wit have been a tonic. I have met scores of people who have read none or few of his books who treasure his appearances on television: 'He is such a breath of fresh air.' And his comments on politics have been invaluable.

I used to think that the Norman Mailer of *The Naked and the Dead,* published when he was twenty-five, was merely a sensationally successful one-book author, and his first books thereafter seemed to prove that. But he revealed himself as a protean man with the widest possible interests and the skill to tackle them all, from pertinent comments on politics to a biography of Marilyn Monroe. As if that were not enough, he lived a daring, exhibitionistic life fraught with scandal. A graduate of Harvard, he was indubitably an artist, and with his mop of unruly hair and and his outrageous behavior, he conformed to the general public's impression of what an artist should look like. He has been invaluable to American life because he is an authentic American voice.

Gore Vidal, who wrote *Williwaw* at only nineteen, was another whose early book could well have been his last, but instead he wrote a series of books that varied in subject matter from the critical days of early Christianity to the dramatic eras of American history to outrageous sexual games. I envy him two novels on whose subjects I also did a great deal of work: *Julian,* which deals with the apostate who tried to turn back Christianity in ancient Antiochea, and *1876,* which covers the amazing incident in American history that year when the Republican Rutherford B. Hayes stole the presidential election from the Democrat Samuel J. Tilden. Vidal knows how to make the most of his material, whatever the source, and I would have been proud to have written either of these books I've cited. I am especially impressed by his ability to engage in politics, for his periodic excursions into that field can be both entertaining and instructive. Himself a candidate for Congress at one time, and the descendant of important national figures, he has a wide range of information, a delicious smattering of prejudice and a ready tongue, and that mix makes for lively results. He has been an important participant in national debates, and a refreshing one.

Truman Capote was a raffish fellow who devoted his life to self-promotion, but since he had a firm base of elegant writing, it was not mere exhibitionism. His first book, *Other Voices, Other Rooms,* published when he was twenty-four and accompanied by that famous photograph of him stretched out on a chaise longue, catapulted him to both literary and social fame, and he remained a major celebrity until his untimely death. With an engaging lisp, a high-pitched voice, a languid manner and a coruscating wit, he became the darling of the television talk shows. He was incomparably the writer turned public performer, the American Jean Cocteau, but, unlike mere poseurs, he was always able to back up his public performances with his fine writing. In his tour de force *In Cold Blood,* Capote stunned me with his ability to remove himself almost completely from the narration so that the reportage became totally impersonal. That a man who flaunted his personality could have been so self-effacing was amazing.

I knew Capote slightly and once had an amusing contretemps involving him. When his *Breakfast at Tiffany's* became famous because of the movie made with Audrey Hepburn, a New York woman with a name much like the heroine's, Holly Golightly, started a lawsuit against Truman for invasion of privacy. As it happened, I had been dating the specific girl on whom Truman had based his character and I wrote Bennett Cerf a long letter informing him that I would be willing to testify in Truman's behalf in his defense against the New York claimant, because I personally knew the young woman on whom the tale was really based. When Bennett got my letter he called me and shouted over the telephone: 'For Christ's sake, Jim, tear up all copies of your letter. Truman's afraid that your girl is going to sue him, too.' The suit was either dropped or adjudicated and Truman heard no more threats from either girl.

One afternoon as I was leaving Random House after reviewing the copy-edited manuscript of one of my novels, I passed the newsstand in the lobby and stopped short with a gasp—there on the front page of a newspaper was a raffish picture of Truman Capote leering from beneath the brim of his rakish Borsalino. Below were just four lines of type:

> I am a drunkard
> I am a dope addict
> I am a homosexual
> I am a genius

Truman, I thought, had carried his campaign perhaps a little too far, and then I thought ruefully that whereas the public would probably applaud Capote for his frankness, it had castigated John Horne Burns for having dared to do in 1949 a hundredth of what Capote was doing in 1979.

American letters would have been a drab affair without the three men I have discussed, because they did what other more reticent writers could not do—they reminded the public that artists are a different breed, that they need breathing room, that sometimes they are not bound by normal rules of behavior.

I am always interested in why young people become writers, and from talking with many I have concluded that most do not want to *be* writers working eight and ten hours a day and accomplishing little; they want to *have been* writers, garnering the rewards of having completed a successful manuscript and seeing it become a best-seller. They aspire to the rewards of writing but not to the travail.

And then there are those who want to write mainly for the gratification of being published. One of these was a Denver dentist named Dr. Deppard, who received from a grateful patient a bequest of $4,800. Dr. Deppard came to me as a longtime friend and shyly announced that he had always wanted to write a book, and had indeed started one. It dealt with the relationships between a dentist and his patients and was, he assured me, both heartwarming and filled with useful information presented in swiftly moving episodes built around interesting characters. He was sure that millions would be eager to buy his book, and I noticed that he was already thinking commercially, for he said *buy,* not *read.*

When Dr. Deppard showed me his manuscript, three pages sufficed to prove that it was totally hopeless, but I had a deal with my book editor at Random House and my agent that I would refer to them all such manuscripts. In due course my editor wrote back to the dentist advising him 'that at this particular time Random House could express no interest in the manuscript. . . .

Dr. Deppard was a determined man, and I provided him with the addresses of other New York publishers, all of whom replied as Random House had. After about the sixth rejection he came to me despondent, asking me what to do next, and it was apparent that he would never accept the fact that his manuscript was unpublishable. When I said there was nothing more I could do, he glared at me and said: 'I thought you were my friend.'

A few weeks later there arrived in Denver one of the memorable figures in American publishing, J. Pitt Barclay, owner and chief executive officer of Vanitatis Press, located at a Madison Avenue address in New York. Placing a small advertisement in the local papers to alert the would-be writers of Denver that he was in town and would be pleased to meet anyone with a publishable manuscript, he waited in his suite at the Brown Palace Hotel. One of the first in line was Dr. Deppard, who unfortunately began his interview with these bell-ringing words: 'A dear patient died some months ago leaving me a totally unexpected bequest of forty-eight hundred dollars, and I said to myself: "Deppard, this is a chance to write that great book you've always had in mind," and I wondered if you would be interested—'

'Sounds just like the kind of book we've been looking for,' Barclay said, 'the sort of thing a health-conscious public will be avid to grab and recommend to their friends.' He said that he would take the manuscript back to the home office, where he would ask one of America's foremost experts on the salability of books, his senior editor F.X. Grimble, to take a look at it and give his honest opinion. Within a surprisingly few days Dr. Deppard received one of the epistolary masterpieces of our time, which he promptly showed me. As I read it I thought: No wonder Deppard's excited:

> Dear Dr. Deppard,
>
> Last night as I was leaving our office in midtown New York, I was stopped by our senior editor, F.X. Grimble, who ran up to me breathless to say: 'J.P., at last we have a book we can run with. This manuscript you handed me from the dentist in Denver has everything, and I mean everything, that we've been looking for. Please get it for us and allow us to make a splash.'
>
> Now if I have learned anything about publishing in my thirty-three years at the head of a major firm, it is to listen to F.X. when he gets really excited about a project. Never does he fail me, so I took the manuscript home with me, and that was one of the biggest mistakes I ever made, for I had intended to sit in my easy chair by the smoldering fire, drink mulled cider and read Joseph Conrad's *Victory,* but I never saw a word of Conrad that night, because I opened your manuscript first, and toward four in the morning when the fire had guttered low and the mulled cider was drained, I turned over the last page and said: 'F.X. was right, this is truly a book we could run with.'

There were five more paragraphs of the most seductive writing I had read in many years, all the intimations that J.Pitt Barclay and F.X. Grimble were hovering on the edge of publishing history if they could but land this manuscript. And Barclay made a most enticing offer:

> Dr. Deppard, F.X. and I assembled all our manufacturing experts this morning and they told me they thought it would be

possible for us to publish your fine manuscript if you could help us with the cost of the paper, a mere $4,800, a sum which we feel sure you will earn back many times over.

The letter's one-line closing was calculated to make Dr. Deppard's heart pound: 'I cannot guarantee you either fortune or fleeting fame, but I can promise you something infinitely more valuable: Immortality.'

Confident that Vanitatis had a live prospect on the hook, J.P. began tightening his net with a trick that had often proved effective; he included in the letter as if by accident, the carbon of a report from an Eleanore, obviously in the publicity department, and marked F.Y.E.O. (for your eyes only) CONFIDENTIAL. It listed some twenty of the best-known publications in the country to which advance copies would be airmailed, a dozen television stations from which she and the author would choose for personal appearances, and the seven big-market cities to which they would want to send the author, 'but only to the best radio shows and the biggest stores.' Eleanore's report ended: 'Please, J.P., get this book for us. We've been hungry for something we could really get our teeth into.'

As soon as Deppard received this letter he xeroxed it and sent a copy off to each of the legitimate publishers to whom he had sent the manuscript earlier and who had all rejected it with form letters: 'See,' he said. 'It's like I told you. This is a wonderful book. Its possibilities are endless, just like he says. Do you want to reconsider?' No one did, but my editor, Albert Erskine, told me rather brusquely 'The hell of Barclay's Vanitatis operation is that when these pitiful characters receive his letter, they always double back on us for a second opinion and we have to answer their letters.' He did not implore me to stop pestering him with such submissions, but on my own I decided to quit.

For his $4,800—today it would be more like $8,500—Dr. Deppard did receive six copies of a properly but cheaply printed book with a jacket bearing his photograph. Vanitatis did arrange for him to appear on one local television show, and an interesting release was sent to the Denver papers and to several others in the vicinity, only one of which used it. Nobody reviewed the book, but such details were irrelevant, because three hours after receiving his copies Dr. Deppard was in my apartment purple with rage: 'Look at what they've done!' and with trembling hands he showed me how Vanitatis, seeing that the book was using more paper than the $4,800 budget covered, had solved the problem rather neatly: they had dropped the four middle chapters.

Since Dr. Deppard made his call of protest on my phone I was able to hear how J. Pitt Barclay weasled out of this one, and he was more than equal to the unpleasant task: 'But Dr. Deppard, don't you see our strategy? If you detected the absence of those pages, so will the readers, and they'll be hungry for the second volume of your memoirs. Mistake? Far from it. The best brains in our office planned that strategy and F.X. Grimble tells me that stores are already making inquiries.' Some months later the disgraceful affair had a brazen ending which, strangely enough, left no bad taste in Dr. Deppard's mouth, for it was accompanied by another masterly letter from J. Pitt:

> This morning when F.X. Grimble walked into my office, his smile missing and his eyes downcast, I knew that his news was not going to be pleasant. But I was astounded by what he had to tell me. Because of the airline strike which paralyzed our part of the country for two weeks and the deplorable drop in the market just as your book appeared, the sales of your fine book have been disappointing.

Six other ingenious explanations were given, including the fact that both *The New York Times* and *The Washington Post* found their book columns full that week and could not find room for the enthusiastic reviews that had been written. The letter concluded with the paragraph:

> So we find ourselves with some two thousand of your fine books on our hands and F.X. simply refuses to discard them. 'I put my life's blood in that book,' he told me, 'and I think it ought to have a chance to live.' Our editorial board has decided that we will take our losses and offer the books to you for $1.50 each and we will pay the freight to Denver.

So Dr. Deppard had to pay for the publication of his book and then pay again to recover the copies that rightfully should have been his, but he did not feel aggrieved by the experience. The original $4,800 had been an unexpected gift, and the money he paid for the unsold copies—so far as I could learn, not one had been sold—was not wasted, for he had published a book, he now had a rather good-looking gift that he could hand to his patients, he had been on television and the pile of books he kept stored in his basement did carry on their back covers a rather fine portrait of himself.

.   .   .

I do not wish to push an elitist agenda, but I was struck as I reviewed the young men with whom I was concerned in those early postwar years by how many of them had intimate contact with the best and most expensive Eastern preparatory schools and the great universities. Buechner attended Lawrenceville, graduated from Harvard, and headed the religion department at Phillips Exeter. Burns attended Phillips Exeter, graduated from Harvard and taught at Loomis. Vidal attended Phillips Exeter, which seems to have been a training ground for writers. Mailer attended Harvard. Leggett himself attended Phillips, Andover and Yale, while I taught at The Hill and both of us attended Harvard as graduate students and taught there. Apparently would-be writers are helped by a rigorous education, whether absorbing or imparting it. I am mindful that excellent writers like William Faulkner, Ernest Hemingway, John O'Hara, John Cheever, Gore Vidal and Truman Capote attended no college, so I cannot argue that such an education is a sine qua non for a writer, but for some of us it does make the difference.

At the time I began studying contemporary writers I was unaware that I was concentrating solely on young men, for in those days I was dealing in my lectures with men writing about war. Later I realized how macho I had been and how sexist in my literary choices. I therefore took a summer off to read only books by the emerging women writers, and only then did I appreciate how blinkered my eyes had been.

This delinquency surprised me, because women writers had played a major role in my intellectual life. Lady Murasaki, Selma Lagerlöf and Sigrid Undset had introduced me to foreign-language worlds, and I considered George Eliot's *Middlemarch* and Emily Brontë's *Wuthering Heights* among our finest novels. Belatedly I discovered Edith Wharton's short stories and had been enchanted by Carson McCullers's *The Member of the Wedding,* and in Scotland I had enjoyed two exquisitely crafted minor novels then widely read but now forgotten, Margaret Kennedy's *The Constant Nymph* and Mary Webb's *Precious Bane.* Now I would catch up with the American women. Once more I settled upon three as my group of women writers, as if the concept of a trio had some mystical significance. Because I had focused on British writers I had missed three fine Americans (Fitzgerald, Faulkner, Wolfe), but had been transfixed by the tragedies of three American contemporaries (Lockridge, Heggen, Burns) and entertained by the public antics of another American trio (Mailer, Vidal, Capote). It was to be expected that I would begin my investigation with three women.

The first who commanded my attention was Sylvia Plath, who had been recommended to me many times, but whose *Bell Jar* I had not found the time to read. As I read it I could see that it was beautifully written, sensitive and allusive, but also so innately feminine that I could not imagine having written a word of it myself. I was disgusted by the callous way in which the author lampooned the woman writer who had provided her with scholarship funds and disliked her treatment of her mother. When I finished I felt that I had been in the presence of someone living on the edge and was not surprised that she committed suicide while still a young woman.

The second book I picked up in my foray into women's writing was another winner: Toni Morrison's *Tar Baby,* which alternates vibrant dialogue and philosophical essays in a masterly way. It seemed to me that if she maintained the course she had obviously set for herself, she was bound to become the preeminent black writer of our time.

The final member of my distinguished trio was a woman I was already aware of, because Joyce Carol Oates had a splendid reputation, but I had not yet read one of her books. Now, as I dug into them, I found them completely to my taste, fine-grained, firmly set in a lower-middle-class milieu, and populated with strong characters about whom I cared. She reminded me of an American Zola, and I could see that her talent was so securely rooted that she was at the opposite end of the spectrum from Sylvia Plath. She injected into her writing a kind of liquid granite, and I could see that she had ahead of her a long and increasingly strong career. I had no feeling that I was reading an essentially feminine writer; she was just a fine, solid storyteller.

In my reading that summer I encountered several other books I would recommend to anyone wanting to catch up with our women writers. Anne Rice's *Interview with the Vampire* is an inventive tale about two New Orleans male vampires who seek a woman partner and get by mistake a fourteen-year-old girl who proves a terror. It's a masterpiece in its genre. Joan Didion's *Play It As It Lays* impressed me with its excellent use of language, and I could see why her reputation had blossomed. Judith Rossner's explosive *Looking for Mr. Goodbar* blew my mind with its sexual explicitness and taught me how far from my early training in literature we had come.

I wanted to finish my survey with the work of someone in my own generation, and I did so with a selection of short stories by Eudora Welty, in whose work I found the repose amid storms that I admire. She accomplishes so much with so little, sets her stage with such precision and moves her Southern players on it with effortless ease. She is an artist, the doyenne of her group, and she must be amused and sometimes startled by what those who trail behind her are doing.

I will probably not find time for another vacation seminar in women's writing for some years, but when I do I suppose that I will again be startled by what moves and advances have been made during my absence.

If I have not played the public role that Mailer and my other heroes have, I have not gone entirely unnoticed, and on three occasions I have been honored publicly. When I was working on my novel dealing with Chesapeake Bay, a body of water I loved and of which I was created an admiral by the State of Maryland, I was invited to serve as grand marshal of the yearly Crisfield Crab Festival, which did honor to one of the bay's major industries, crabbing. Crisfield is a small waterfront town on the more impoverished eastern shore of the bay, but during its festival it puts on a major show, with the grand marshal required to test personally the two dozen finalists in the competition to see who could devise the tastiest dish using crabmeat, one of the world's most delectable foods.

Crabmeat can be baked in a casserole, deep-fried in cakes of delectable quality, mixed with green peppers and tomatoes and other tasty ingredients, or prepared in a luscious salad with one of half a dozen different dressings. Crab may be very close to what the gods eat if they have diligent fishermen up there, and I was chosen to judge this important contest for a curious reason.

When I took up residence on the Eastern Shore, I did not care to explain that I was thinking of writing a book, so I let it be noised abroad that I had come down to run a test: 'Who prepares the very best crabcakes on the Shore?' This was one of the smartest ploys I ever devised, for in the succeeding years housewives from all over, and restaurants too, asked me to judge their product and I rated each on a scale of 1 to 10 and became known as a very harsh judge, for after a while I was capable of telling an inept housewife: 'Sorry, but this one cannot possibly go higher than 2.9.' I always used decimals. But occasionally I would go into raptures, rise and kiss the cook and proclaim: 'Madam, this one rates at least an 8.7 and if you want to lie to your neighbors and say I gave you an 8.9, be my guest.'

There was a couple in Oxford, Bob and Mary Inglis, who gathered their own crabs and used the flaky meat in the best results I would ever taste, a soufflé at 9.6 and a set of impeccable cakes at 9.5. When someone asked me why, if I praised them so highly, I did not award 9.9 at least, I replied: 'I suspect there's someone up in heaven who is the master cook of them all, and I don't want to use up my numbers.'

Even today, in restaurants I frequently order crabcakes, seeking to remind myself of the ambrosial food I'd had on the Shore, and have been so disappointed that I almost gag. Not long ago, in an expensive restaurant where the cakes would register not more than 2.1 by Crisfield standards but cost fifteen dollars, I blurted out as I pushed the plate away: 'That son-of-a-bitch ought to be shot!' and patrons looked up in surprise, as did my wife, who explained to the others: 'My husband takes his crabcakes seriously, and the cook who made these things really should be shot.'

So I was a reasonable candidate for the job as grand marshal and ultimate authority on crabmeat delicacies, but as the parade was about to start, well-meaning friends came up to my car and whispered: 'Now, if they start throwing eggs and tomatoes, it's not you they're trying to get. It's the mayor. We're trying to impeach him, and he sees this as a chance to ride in the parade with you as protection. He doubts that people will want to mess you up.'

It was one of the chilliest parades I have seen, and certainly the ugliest I have ever been in personally. We rode through Crisfield in dead silence, and no matter where I looked, left or right, I was greeted with stony and hate-filled stares. No hand-clapping, not even any hisses, only those baleful stares. But the unpleasantness of the morning was forgotten in the joy of the noontime testing. I moved enthusiastically past all the entries, tasting each liberally, and awarded several marks above 8.5, several at 8.8 and 8.9 and two in the low 9's. It was a day of honor I often recall, depressing in the morning, elating in the afternoon, and brimming with contentment as I rode homeward.

Another honor bestowed on me turned out to be a somewhat dubious blessing. It happened rather suddenly. A meeting of one of my commissions in Washington was terminated ahead of time because someone from the White House wanted to talk with me: 'Michener, could you leave for Japan tomorrow night?'

'Wife also?'

'Of course. We want you to serve as President Ford's personal representative and honorary ambassador to the international Festival of Oceans being held in Okinawa.'

'That would be a distinct honor.'

At the airport my wife and I were met by Clifford Forster, a most personable young man in his late thirties and a diplomatic courier for the State Department: 'I'll be accompanying you to Okinawa. I suppose you know what this is all about?'

'I know nothing, except that the White House assured me my commission would be aboard the plane.'

'It is,' he said, tapping his courier's bag. 'The brouhaha has been most embarrassing. We had one of the top senators prepared to undertake the job you're taking, but the social staff at the White House pulled a real boo-boo. He was chosen for the job because of his great interest in Japan, but when the guest list for last night's gala dinner at the White House for the Emperor and Empress of Japan was published, his name wasn't on it. . . .'

'We went,' Mari said, 'and you're right, your man wasn't there.'

'So the senator became furious and yelled: "If you don't want me at your dinner, you don't want me in Okinawa." Damn lucky you were available.'

We had a great flight to Anchorage, where we laid over for a day so that I could rest and enjoy the mountain scenery, then we enjoyed flying over the Aleutians, which I scouted against the possibility I might one day want to write about them, and on to a stopover in Tokyo, where a group of rather burly American men, in their forties and all dressed in blue suits, came aboard and sat where they could watch me.

Only then did Mr. Forster reveal the facts: 'The men in the back there are United States Secret Service agents, called in from all parts of the Pacific. Intelligence, both Japanese and American, have heard that Communists might try to assassinate you. It would be very embarrassing to everybody to have it happen out here while the Emperor was in Washington. It would make Hirohito and Ford lose face.' Mari said it would make me lose quite a bit more than face.

'That's what I'm here to prevent,' he said and with that he handed me my commission. I was asked by the president to represent him in all ways, to be courteous as always to the Japanese officials, and to make America's presence at the fair as normal and uneventful as I could. When I landed I was greeted by the permanent ambassador to the fair, William Lane, the urbane publisher and editor of *Sunset Magazine*.

We dined with the Lanes, a congenial couple, and when we retired to our room we found that we had been given a suite, with the outside room occupied by three very big and strong men. When I asked what they were doing they said: 'We sleep here. Some of us will be with you all the way.' It was a tense three days, not made easier by being told that when the crown prince had been in Okinawa some time before, the would-be murderers had shot at *him* but had missed.

The fair, which displayed the Japanese at their best and where my wife spoke to the officials in their language, much to their delight, is memorable especially for what served as pillars to the main entrance: two immense cylindrical fish tanks, at least a full story high. Inside the one to the right was a dazzling school of thousands of small, bright blue fish, in the one to the left an equal number of brilliant red fish. I can still see them, those giant columns of shimmering color; they were worth the trip.

With that track record for near-disastrous public appearances, one might think that I would shy away from such affairs, and I do; each of the first two had been forced upon me in a fashion I could not reject, and now a third came my way, the most glamorous of all. Since I had always been an avid sports fan, had written a full-length book about games, had started Indianapolis-style races at Pocono in Pennsylvania and thrown out the baseball at a World Series game, it was not illogical that when I was working in Miami I should be asked to serve as grand marshal of the Orange Bowl parade and the subsequent New Year's Day game. I was the more inclined to accept because the two contending teams, Nebraska and Miami, in the past had each given me doctorates and were in a sense my alma maters.

The story is brief and pathetic. As in all I do, I like to report to an assignment at least a half hour before the event starts. When I reached the staging area for the eighty-odd floats, I was so early that they put me in a hospitality trailer, where I sat beside Susan Ruttan, one of the major characters in the television show *L.A. Law.* I had a most delightful conversation with her about the theater, and the time passed pleasantly.

Apparently, the people running the show forgot where they had put me, so when the time came for my big moment and the immense float on which I was to ride started out, they could not find me. The float left the staging area and covered the first half of the parade with no one in the high seat of honor.

Belatedly, someone recalled seeing me headed toward a corner of the lot, and after banging on all doors, they found me still chatting with Miss Ruttan, but it was obviously too late. We were about a quarter of a mile from where the empty float would, in four minutes, pass the television cameras, but a policeman shouted: 'I think we can make it by the back road.' I was thrown into the sidecar of a police motorcycle and we began a mad dash through alleyways and crowded feeder lanes, reaching the still-moving float one minute before camera time.

A cherry-picker crane was waiting to hoist me into my elevated chair, and an NBC technician climbed aboard to hook up my television microphone. When, at the last second, delightful Sandy Duncan, hostess of the parade, cried enthusiastically to the nation: 'And here he comes, the grand marshal of our parade,' all that the cameras caught was the rump of the NBC man as he bent over to affix my mike.

'Isn't this a grand parade, Mr. Michener?' Sandy asked, and my reply came loud and clear: 'Gggrrrmmmfff' as the technician's posterior blanked out both my face and my voice.

I decided that I was not available for any more public honors. However, just as I started work on these notes I was informed that my home county, historic Bucks in Pennsylvania, was proposing an action that so delighted me that I could not withhold support. The old jail on Ashland Street opposite the wonderful Mercer Museum featuring the Tools of Nation Makers was about to be converted into an art museum, with a big new public library to be erected close at hand. The museum was already named after Henry Mercer, our town's leading and some say only intellectual; the library was to be named after Pearl Buck, our Nobel Prize winner and humanitarian; and the jail was to be renamed the Michener Art Museum. I had hitherto resisted having buildings named after me, but this gracious invitation I could not turn down, because I delighted in the irony that when I was a troublesome boy in town many had predicted that I would sooner or later wind up in that very jail, and here I was eighty years later doing exactly that.

I would like to be remembered in my hometown as a man who helped convert a jail into an art museum.

XI

Best-seller

WHEN ANYONE refers to me as a 'best-selling author' I wince because I do not like either of those two words applied to me. The first, of course, has a specific denotation: a book that sells over a hundred thousand copies in hardcover, or the number could even be as low as fifty thousand, or thirty. If that happens to one of an author's books it's noteworthy but possibly accidental; if it occurs repeatedly, he or she is a best-seller. But the word has come to be pejorative, implying that the author is interested only in big sales and making money; what is worse, it suggests that the books she or he writes are junk; such implications are not fair, but they are understandable and inescapable.

I do not like the second word either and have always tried to avoid thinking of myself as an author, because as I have mentioned earlier, I was taught as a child that authors were pompous American men of the last century who wore beards and had three-barreled names, such as Henry Wadsworth Longfellow and Oliver Wendell Holmes. I wanted to be a writer, like Thomas Hardy, Charles Dickens, Gustave Flaubert and Leo Tolstoy, and I have tried always to describe myself with that honorable word. When people ask me what I do, I reply: 'I write books.'

Given such an attitude, how did I develop into a best-seller? I think it was because I was driven by the passion to produce good books within the great tradition that I had discovered when working with those admirable works published in London during the latter years of the last century, and fortunately I wrote some that were widely accepted. Always I was guided by a simple credo: 'Writing is never completed till it's published.' Obviously the three key terms require explanation.

I use *writing* as a convenient shorthand for the entire world of literary expression: poems, opera librettos, novels, dramas, essays, biographies.

The most difficult term to explain is *completed*. I have always believed the artistic experience to be a kind of moral and aesthetic contract between the creator and the audience, and the more deeply I probe this relationship, the more convinced I am of its correctness. One starts a novel with the implicit understanding that the end product is a book that another person can acquire, hold, read and enjoy. If the second half of this contract is not fulfilled, the totality of this operation is negated.

By *published* I not only mean the issuing of the printed version of a manuscript but also mean the *circulation of the manuscript among one's peers,* and I would accept the loosest possible interpretation of that phrase, including the sharing of one's work with a close circle of discerning friends, as in the case of Emily Dickinson. Here was a poet who wrote many marvelous poems but refused to publish them in book form during her lifetime. In fact, out of 1,775, only seven saw publication in any form, and those only in a small-town newspaper of limited circulation. But she did attain another form of publication by circulating some of her work among friends or counselors whose opinions she cherished. Inordinately shy, she nevertheless fell in love several times, usually with some married man, and wrote nearly two thousand letters as elegant as her poems. She remains one of the world's major artists most difficult to categorize, but within the broad scope of my definition she published quite widely, if only among those she felt worthy of her efforts and likely to understand them. For her the concept *peer* seems to have been paramount.

To repeat, writing is never completed until it's published, and I wish to make a blunt statement: Something written in a so-called ivory tower for oneself alone, to be shared with no one else, is not completed writing, and those who believe that it is are deluding themselves, because the implied contract with the reader has not been fulfilled. Ivory-tower writing might be useful as therapy or helpful if it is an exercise to develop skill before real writing is attempted, but as an end in itself it is without value, and it invites the outside observer to conclude that the writer has been afraid to test his work in the real world.

Having said that as harshly as I can, let me quickly add that when

I use the word *publish* in relation to a written manuscript, I am not only willing but eager to define the word as broadly as possible. Reading the work aloud to three maiden aunts is publishing; taking the manuscript to a home for elderly people and allowing it to be passed around is publishing; reading it to the members of a creative writing class is publishing; allowing a local free newspaper to print it without pay is publishing; allowing it to be abbreviated on a calendar is publishing; and even paying as Dr. Deppard did for a vanity press to print it is publishing. Any honorable and legal device whereby the writer can communicate his work to others is just as much publishing as having it brought out in a fine hardcover form by Knopf.

I have no hierarchy of value in which only publication in certain accepted forms is admissible; the task is to transform one's writing from an exclusive possession into an exchange among one's fellows; but I do have this advice: if you achieve printed reproduction of your manuscript, deposit copies in your local library and your county historical society. In my work I have used with excellent results historical books published under the most bizarre circumstances, and I do not mean *good* historical books and certainly not *fine-looking;* I mean some of the craziest-looking books you have ever seen, invaluable because of their authenticity and the obvious love that moved someone to create them two hundred years ago. Dr. Deppard's book may be invaluable someday sixty years from now when someone like me is trying to comprehend what Denver dentistry was like in the 1980s, or how a Rocky Mountain dentist earned his living in those years. Such filing is also publishing— for future circulation.

I am not so indifferent to public reaction as to argue that even the most trivial form of publication is equivalent to the most impressive; there are gradations of quality, and to appreciate this fact let us consider a talented musician who has composed an opera. He has available to him several kinds and levels of publication. He can circulate his libretto and score to his friends who can read music and visualize stage production, and they can assure him that his work has first-rate qualities. Friends can arrange a run-through with him at the piano with a few selected singers sketching out the arias, and additional vitality is pumped into the score. Or an orchestra can arrange a concertized version with six strong voices and a full orchestral score but no scenery or action, and from this the knowing listener can form a fairly accurate opinion of the work. But none of these commendable substitutes can replace a full-blown performance by a major opera company with a complete cast, excellent staging and a seventy-piece orchestra led by a conductor experienced in opera. All previous alternatives are justifiable, but the full, professional performance before an audience is the desired end product when one says: 'X has composed an opera.'

When I hear: 'X has written a novel' I wish it well and hope that if it contains sufficient intellectual content and is arranged in a form that pleases the reader, it will likely be accepted by a commercial publisher, who will help it find a place on the shelves of public and private libraries. I am grateful that I have been able to publish some thirty books that more or less agree with the preceding description. But I am certain that had I not won the favor of a publisher, I would have continued writing, and I am sure I would have had enough faith in what I was attempting that if someone unexpectedly willed me $4,800 I might very well have published with J. Pitt Barclay's Vanitatis Press, because I am so convinced that publishing is the end goal of writing that I would accept it in almost any form.

I should now like to trace the events, whereby my desire to write good books that people would like to read led to my becoming a best-selling writer. I started, as mentioned before, with an extremely lucky Pulitzer Prize, but in one sense it did me damage, because people in the world of books who were either surprised or irritated by my winning were lying in wait for my second effort, *The Fires of Spring,* and chortled when it appeared: 'Michener has demonstrated yet again that acceptable first novels are usually followed by unacceptable second ones.' My agent rejected it because he deemed it disappointing, and so did George Brett, the president of Macmillan, while John Horne Burns gave it an annihilating review. Some of this adverse reception was justified, for it was the kind of book with which beginning writers customarily start their careers, a novel about growing up and about learning to write; it was the book I should have written first, and to have it appear ex post facto, as it were, apparently struck the wrong note.

The salient fact about my writing career is that I have been able to keep it remarkably viable during the fifth through the ninth decade of my life, and I hope it will continue to be so in the 1990s. Not many accomplish this, and in my case the explanation has been, I think, that I have remained alert to all that has been happening about me; I have tried to stay in contact with young people; I have tried always to be active; and, above all, I have had a burning desire to maintain a productive creative life, always looking ahead to new challenges, never back to old victories, which seem inconsequential when reviewed from today's vantage point. I was willing to write *The Fires of Spring* out of order because I felt that it was a book that had to be written even though I was in my forties and it was the kind of book normally written when one is in one's twenties or thirties. I have never regretted that decision, because through the years it has probably brought me more mail from readers than any other book I've written, having caught the imagination of young people who were pondering the direction their lives should take. I doubt that I have ever had a letter about it from a reader past the age of thirty-five, except to recall that it had a life-changing effect when he or she read the book as a teenager.

As soon as it became apparent that I could earn a modest living writing, I decided to write in a variety of different fields. As explained earlier, I had an abiding love of art, so I wrote five books on Japanese art. In every instance the publisher to whom I took my manuscript had doubts about its ultimate success, but I barreled ahead, sometimes putting up my own money to ensure publication. I was gratified to see those books gain wide acceptance, some going into reprintings and several into foreign languages. Today first editions have become quite valuable.

I wrote also about a handful of other subjects that interested me, and I believe that this scattering of attention helped keep my mind sharp. It is not easy to keep a literary career productive over a prolonged period; most fall short, and I believe it is often not a case of losing health or brainpower but of losing momentum. I did not jump about in my writing either by accident or lack of direction; I did it intentionally to keep my brain active and my imagination engaged. For that reason when I bought records of classical music, to which I am still passionately devoted, I also bought two of the most modern compositions, just to see what my contemporaries were attempting, and when I collected art it tended to be the most recent done, for the same reason.

I had great excitement in writing one of the crucial books of my career, *The Bridges at Toko-Ri,* because I wanted to see if I had the discipline and talent to write what is known as 'the well-crafted English novel.' When I was at Macmillan I had scorned those five books imported from London that had made me think that I might do well as a writer. I warmly remember the writing of that short novel partly because of the adventures I undertook to make myself competent: duty on an aircraft carrier, checking out the newer jet bombers, long hours in briefing rooms before and after bombing runs on enemy targets deep behind the lines in Korea. When an oversolicitious public relations officer warned the admiral: 'The adverse publicity would be damaging if Michener was lost on one of these raids,' he growled: 'He said he wanted to be one of us. If he's game, I'm game.'

It is something to crawl out of bed at 3:00 A.M., report to the briefing room to check the latest photographs of the target areas and the locations of enemy antiaircraft, then to climb into the rear seat of a dive bomber—it seems so damned far behind the pilot, so out of touch with him or anything else—and to be handed a box of Kleenex by an enlisted man who will have to care for the plane when it returns: 'Kleenex, Mr. Michener. Them as throws up, cleans up.' Since I would fly scores of missions, mostly noncombatant but in turbulent weather, I usually got airsick, so I did a lot of cleaning up.

Then, strapped in with restraints holding back the shoulders and stomach, to wheel out onto the catapult in blackness, to wait nervously for the signal, the flashlight sign from the deck officer to activate the catapult and that sudden, unbelievable jerk forward, eight or nine G's— measures of gravity—which thrust the entire belly backward against the backbone, the fantastic leap forward, up to ninety miles an hour within the short length of the carrier, the takeoff and that perilous drop, more terrifying to witness from the bridge than to experience in the plane itself, because as the heavy bomber leaves the end of the runway it automatically drops, down, down, down toward the clutching waves until it seems to crash into them and sink, except that at the last minute the engines whine, the nose lifts up, and the plane miraculously gains altitude and is seen from the bridge to have completed a good takeoff. Of course, sometimes after leaving the forward lip of the ship the heavy plane does not recover and gain altitude; it keeps going straight down. Then sirens blast, deckhands run, helicopters take to the air, and all is chaos as brave men strive to rescue the pilot. On one ship I worked, a daring, bald-headed pilot named Paul Grey had ditched like that three times in icy water where survival time was calculated at seven minutes; you fished him out in seven minutes or counted him dead. I was so impressed with this cool hero who was still willing to fly again and take me along if I cared to go, that I wrote one of my best war stories about him, giving it free to the Navy for the widest possible distribution. I called it 'The Bald Eagle of the Essex,' and in it suggested that anyone like Grey who had gone down three times had done his duty and ought to be given a desk job. Headquarters in Washington agreed with me, and Grey flew no more night missions over Korea. When writers like me or journalists with a good reputation, such as Keyes Beech, Homer Bigart or Maggie Higgins, wish to work with troops in a battle zone, all the men are eager to have them go out with them on their missions in hopes that they will report honestly to the folks back home what life at the front is like, and also mention the unit's name and perhaps even the individual men themselves. The result is one that few civilians appreciate: media people sometimes see far more actual warfare than the average man in uniform, because in a sense they seek it out, or it seeks them out, and they cannot wait for mere chance to dictate what they will run into. They look for trouble. During World War II I flew more missions than most, always as a hitchhiking passenger, and in Korea I saw many more actions, on the ground and aloft, than would have been expected in ordinary circumstances.

Lest I sound as if I had been exceptionally brave, I must emphasize that there is a vast difference between a media person and the average G.I. Whenever I grew exhausted or scared I could, of course, go back to safety, whereas the soldier in the dugout had to stay there and take it. One snowy day in Korea I drove right up to the front with a daring Marine general, who led me on foot to a forward gun position. He asked: 'Want to lob one into their camp on that hillside?' Eager for any experience, I stepped forward, pulled the lanyard and sent a huge shell heading for the Communist position. As soon as I had done this, the general and I leaped in his jeep and hightailed it to the rear, leaving the Marines in the forward position to defend themselves against the retaliatory barrage released by the enemy. I have been forever ashamed of that performance, to have caused incoming fire that I could escape but the Marines could not.

Now I was in the backseat of a Douglas dive bomber on a dawn mission to strike the target I would later change a bit and describe as the bridges at Toko-Ri. This morning we would see the bridges only from a distance, because we were diverted by the accidental discovery of a very long Communist supply train containing forty or fifty boxcars trying to sneak into the safety of a tunnel before full daylight. In sickening dives, which left me hawking, our bomber struck at the engine pulling the load, and, after three or four tries, knocked it off the tracks. Then, in runs down the length of the train, we tried to damage the individual boxcars, but I could see that we accomplished little. Another carrier plane, however, came in from a better angle and wreaked havoc.

Substitute mission completed, and with the sun high and a feeling of elation in our plane that I could detect on the intercom, we headed home, and now came one of the unequaled thrills of aviation. Our heavy plane, fairly but not perfectly responsive to the pilot's wishes, comes out of the clouds at high altitude, sees the aircraft carrier below, which looks hellishly small, loses altitude, makes a beautiful, controlled 180-degree turn, and from an aft position moves toward the carrier as slowly as possible. In the last vital moments a man strapped into position at the rear of the carrier makes an informed guess: 'Looks like he can make it!' The great carrier steadies for just a moment, the plane adjusts to achieve a perfect heading, and forward motion is slowed to a minimum. 'Good! We're down!' But at that moment the man at the rear of the carrier is totally in charge, and he sees something he doesn't like, some error in either the approaching airplane or the position of the carrier that could prove fatal, and here comes the wave-off. Go round again, and when the power is poured on the plane rises rapidly to attempt another approach. This time ship and plane synchronize their movements, and the mighty plane dives at the moving deck, slows unbelievably and glides gently onto the landing area. A scream of brakes as the grabbing wire of the cable engages the landing hook dangling from the bottom of the plane, and a stoppage so swift and violent that if you are not strapped in you go headfirst right out of the plane. All that tremendous power that catapulted you into the air two hours ago is now exercised to strip the bomber of forward movement; it is a halt so total that it makes your teeth rattle.

In those days of research for *Toko-Ri* I would participate in catapult takeoffs and cable-grabbing landings many times. I never knew which was worse, the sudden leap forward to get us aloft or that instantaneous stop when we came back down, but I cherish those experiences as among the most exciting I've ever had. When the time came to write the novel, I knew what would be happening in the airplanes and how the pilots would be reacting. I strove to capture each violent action and its significance.

When *The Bridges at Toko-Ri* appeared complete in one issue of *Life,* a woman reviewer wrote: '*Life* magazine says it commissioned a major novel from Mr. Michener, first time this had happened. The question is: "Did they get one?" ' Her opinion was that they did not, but the novel achieved a noble record and lasting approval from men who fly. A recent summary by an exceptional group of critics of all motion pictures ever made about the Navy—and there have been some stunners, including *Mister Roberts* and *The Caine Mutiny*—judged that *Toko-Ri* had probably been the most honest and the truest.

But the significance of *Toko-Ri* to me was not that a meaningful story had been brought to life but that I had tried to write with complete control a short novel that observed both the Aristotelian unities and the principles of the well-made English novel. It looked as if I might in time be able to master the intricacies of that demanding form. I thought that I might learn to produce one such acceptable novel every two or three years for the rest of my life, and in later decades I would often wonder if I might not have enjoyed more critical approval had I pursued that program.

But there was no chance I could work in that vein. The tight scope of *Toko-Ri,* which required close attention to the novel's structure, gave me no satisfaction. I imagined an entirely different kind of book on which to focus, and when the time came to launch the prodigious research effort that would lead to the writing of *Hawaii,* I was emotionally prepared to attempt something almost epic in range.

At this crucial moment of my life—as I turned my back upon more established modes of writing to attempt books as massive as *Hawaii* and *The Source*—I awakened to a distressing fact: that I knew as much as one can of the publisher's point of view, the editor's and the reader's, but I knew little about the intellectual problems that confronted the writer.

Fortunately, at this juncture, I stumbled upon three books that answered my need. The first was about the art of writing. By the greatest good luck I overheard a knowledgeable friend say: 'If one has only Auerbach, one has all the instruction needed about the narrative form.' Never having heard of this writer, I hurried to the library and learned that Erich Auerbach (1892–1957) was a German librarian who during World War II found himself marooned in Istanbul with nothing to do; relying only on his prodigious memory, he wrote an extensive treatise titled *Mimesis,* about the art of using words to imitate or indicate human character and behavior. More simply, mimesis meant storytelling. Starting with Homer and moving in an orderly way to Virginia Woolf, Auerbach selected some two dozen prime examples from the world's best storytellers—Dante, Boccaccio, Rabelais, Shakespeare, Cervantes, Stendhal—and elucidated the devices they used to achieve their wonderful results. Since it was a summation and dissection of the art I proposed following, I devoured the book, and I have returned to it repeatedly.

The second book, called *I Wanted to Write,* was written by Kenneth Roberts (1895–1957), the sensationally popular historical novelist of the thirties, forties and fifties and a renowned conservative. In 451 ridiculous pages he lays bare his innermost thoughts about his experiences and beliefs. He explained how he progressed from being a writer of humor at Cornell University, a bits-and-pieces expert on a Boston newspaper and a struggling underpaid beginner, to becoming a virtual mainstay of *The Saturday Evening Post* and a frequent contributor to the book clubs and Hollywood. When he finally reaches stardom he begins vilifying some of his employers, ridiculing his colleagues, revealing his envy of others who enjoy greater popularity at the moment, and demonstrating in exquisite detail the ups and downs of the writing trade. A sample of his complaints: 'Can't find [my] *Arundel* on any list of bestsellers, but can find Zane Grey's *Fighting Caravans,* an unspeakably terrible piece of tripe; while the non-fiction list is led (for the fortieth consecutive week) by Chic Sale's *The Specialist.* Fearfully depressed that *Arundel* should sell only a few hundred, while the most ephemeral drivel is bought by the hundreds of thousands. . . .

'Nowhere in [Thornton Wilder's] *The Bridge of San Luis Rey** have I ever been able to find anything remotely suggesting the wholesome atmosphere of American life, or of Peruvian either.' In another passage he points out that in 1938 a poll of America's most powerful critics predicted by an overwhelming plurality that his *Northwest Passage* would surely win that year's Pulitzer Prize. Instead, John P. Marquand's *The Late George Apley* took it.

One passage was both startling and personally reassuring. When I recently said that before I released a manuscript to the publisher I had read it word for word at least twenty-five times, this occasioned hoots of disbelief, but Roberts says: 'I have no record of the number of times the book *Arundel* was read in longhand manuscript, revision, typescript revision, galley proof revision, page proof revision and then again for the revised edition. Certainly it was read more than ninety times.' He is speaking, of course, of his own readings, and we can probably accept his report, because he kept meticulous records of everything, including a record to the odd dollar of the income from each of his books; in one amazing sequence of ten full pages he lists more than eight hundred letters he wrote in the year 1935 while engaged in twelve-hour days working on *Northwest Passage.* I commend *I Wanted to Write,* for I know of nothing that competes with it as a detailed portrait of a writer at work. If an aspirant hopes to produce books like the best of Roberts's output, he must expect to match the kind of work Roberts did.

The third book, *Writing—From Idea to Printed Page* (1949), was compiled by faculty members of the University of Missouri's well-regarded school of journalism in conjunction with the editors of *The Saturday Evening Post.* In a big format it reproduces photographically the actual typed pages of the author's original notes and trial runs, the first typescript, the publisher's editing and the many revisions.

The virtue of this book, which I recommend to the beginning writer, is that it demonstrates with inescapable clarity the amount of hard work, revising and honing required of any writer who aspires to be a professional. Pristine pages fresh from the typewriter are hacked to bits by

---

*It had just won the Pulitzer Prize for 1928. Roberts, frantically jealous, would never win one, despite his thunderous approval by the public. This oversight seems preposterous when one compares his work with some of the books that were honored.

either the author or the editor, false starts are killed, descriptions are sharpened and story flow is improved.

Of course, the book is more or less a manual, light-years removed from Auerbach's cerebral analyses, but it does have considerable practical value. Auerbach gave me dreams of grandeur; Roberts showed me that tough, ordinary men wrote books; and the Missouri essays dragged me back to the desk. I would have been an infinitely poorer writer had I missed any one of these remarkable books. My autobiography as a writer can end at this point, for the rest concerns my adaptation of these three lessons.

To illustrate the practical aspects of publishing one's writing, I am inserting here facsimiles of four different versions of the opening page of one of my novels, accompanied by brief notes of explanation.

EDITING A PAGE OF COPY

A. Carbon copy of page 1 of the novel *Caribbean* as it came from the typewriter. Typed with two fingers by me on an old-fashioned, elite Royal. This copy, made to protect against loss of the manuscript, is filed untouched and forgotten, but it does represent my original thinking as to what I sought to accomplish. Words underlined later indicate those that will survive until the final printed version. Note the incorrect plural Mayas and Yucatan with no accent.

B. This shows what I send to my secretary for word-processing, after three careful revisions of the original copy of page A. If you could see the paper on which this has been typed you would note that two different kinds have been used and pasted together, indicating where original copy was thrown away and new substituted. The amount of editing is standard for a third version, and I liked my new opening sentence, but alas, it would not survive.

C. This is what a first-rate professional editor in a major publishing house in New York does with a pristine page of copy, which the writer has already edited heavily. In this case it was Kate Medina, a senior editor at Random House. Apparently she is a tiger on word placement and the shortening of long sentences. However, the six additional emendations within circles are proposed improvements in *her* editing made by her editorial assistant. Of course, I have to approve each proposed change and most often do.

D. Final version as retyped by Bert Krantz, brilliant copy editor, who monitors style. She has worked with me for decades, saving me from horrendous gaffes. After the manuscript went to the printer I underlined here and on page A all words that survived from the original version into the final. How limited in number they were!

Chapter I. People of the Sunset

This is the biography of <u>one of the world's most alluring</u>
<u>bodies of water.</u> The Caribbean is a <u>gem among</u> the <u>oceans</u>, a
land-locked sea of distinctive ~~beauty~~ charac~~t~~er and rare beauty,
but to appreciate its unique charm one must keep in mind its
definition and its limitations.

It is ~~bounded on the north by a trio of/important islands:~~ large and
~~from east to west Puertox Rico, Hispaniola and Cuba. On the east~~
~~it is defined~~

It is <u>bounded on the north</u> and east by islands, <u>on the south</u>
<u>and west by continental land masses</u>. It thus partakes of both
island and mainland characteristics and it would be an error to
think of it as comprising only islands, even though they are the
aspect that has given the sea its fame.

It is boubded on the north-by a <u>trio</u> of <u>large</u> and <u>important</u>
islands, <u>Puerto Rico</u> to the east, <u>Hispaniola</u> in the middle, <u>and</u>
<u>great Cuba</u> to ~~the~~ the west. <u>On the east</u> it is defined by that
a collection of
<u>heavenly</u> chain of <u>small islands</u> set like/artistically placed
jewels among <u>blue waves, Antigyas, Martinique, Barbados and</u>
<u>Trinidad among them</u>. <u>The southern shore</u> contains the continental
the
republics of <u>Venezuela and Colombia</u> and ~~much of~~ Central American
<u>nation of Panama</u>. <u>The western shore is often overlooked, but it</u>
both
contains/the exciting republics of Central America and the
<u>wonderful, mysterious peninsula of Yucatan, where the ancient</u>
<u>Mayas flourished</u>.

<u>The Caribbean does not</u> involve either the Bahama Islands or
<u>Florida</u> but does contain near its center an island which at

B.

A HEDGE OF CROTON
~~A THE RUBBER BALL OF~~
CHILDREN

Chapter I. ~~People of the Sunset~~

The hero of this book is the Caribbean Sea,

This is the biography of one of the world's most alluring

bodies of water. It ~~The Caribbean~~ is a gem among the oceans, a

land-locked sea of distinctive ~~beauty~~ character and rare beauty,

but to appreciate its unique charm one must keep in mind its

definition and ~~its~~ limitations.

~~It is bounded on the north by a trio of/important islands,~~
large and

~~from east to west Puertox Rico, Hispaniola and Cuba. On the east~~

~~it is defined~~

It is bounded on the north and east by islands, on the south
DISPLAYS
and west by continental land masses. It thus ~~partakes of~~ both

island and mainland characteristics and it would be an error to

think of it as comprising only islands, even though they are the
FOR WHICH IT IS NOTED.
aspect ~~that has given the sea its fame.~~
THE NORTHERN BOUNDARY ~~IS MARKED BY~~ IS FORMED BY A
~~It is boubded on the north by a~~ trio of large and important

islands, Puerto Rico to the east, Hispaniola in the middle, ~~and~~

great Cuba to ~~xtwx~~ the west. On the east it is defined by that
a collection of
heavenly chain of small islands set like/artistically placed
UA
jewels among blue waves, Antigyas, Martinique, Barbados and
IS FORMED BY
Trinidad among them. The southern shore ~~contains~~ the continental
the
republics ~~of~~ Venezuela and Colombia and ~~much of~~ Central American

nation of Panama. The western shore is often overlooked, but it
both
contains/the exciting republics of Central America and the

wonderful, mysterious peninsula of Yucatan, where the ancient

Mayas flourished.

The Caribbean does not involve either the Bahama Islands or

Florida but does contain near its center an island which at

Chapter I. A Hedge of Croton

ℓ3   The chief character in this narrative is (the Caribbean Sea,)
ℓ4 one of the world's most alluring bodies of water. ~~It is a gem~~
     the   *it is a rare gem, defined by lovely*
? *among* oceans, ~~a land-girt sea of distinctive character and rare~~
     islands that (encircle) *it like tiny jewels to*
ℓ6 ~~beauty, but to appreciate its unique charm one must keep in mind~~
                                              USE
ℓ7 ~~its definitions and limitations.~~
                                    Although bounded
ℓ8   ~~It is bounded on the north and east~~, by islands, on the south
                                    it is, nevertheless,
ℓ9 and west by (continental) land masses., ~~it thus displays both~~
     best known for its islands
     ~~island and mainland characteristics and it would be an error to~~
     ~~think of it as comprising only islands, even though they are the~~
     ~~aspect by which it is best known.~~

       The northern boundary is formed by a ~~trio of~~ large and
            trio:
     important ~~islands~~, Puerto Rico ~~to the east~~, Hispaniola (Haiti and
                          and
     the Dominican Republic) ~~in the middle~~, great Cuba ~~to the west.~~
     The eastern boundary
ℓ16 ~~On the east it~~ is defined by that heavenly chain ~~of small islands~~
                                        so   *the* *FIX*
ℓ17 ~~set like a collection of~~ artistically placed ~~jewels among blue~~
     waves, Antigua, Guadeloupe, Martinique, All Saints, Trinidad and
                                STES — NEEDED.
?   remote Barbados ~~among these.~~ The southern shore is formed by the
     (continental) republics of Venezuela and Colombia and the Central
     American nation of Panama. The western shore is often over-
name? looked, but it contains both the exciting republics of Central
     America and the wonderful mysterious peninsula of Yucatan where
     the ancient Maya flourished.

       The Caribbean, nearly nineteen hundred miles wide from
     Barbados to Yucatan, does not include either the Bahama Islands

Jim

Just about everyone I know has been to one of the
Caribbean islands at least once ‑ but not me. So
I decided I'd better take a good look at your map
and familiarize myself with the place I'm going to
be living in for the next months.

This retyped first page makes it all just a little
clearer to me. Are changes okay with you? (Bert

I-1

CHAPTER I.   A HEDGE OF CROTON

*THE IS MUCH
BETTER.*

The chief character in this narrative is the Caribbean Sea,

*BERT!
... ...
MAYBE
BETTER
COMMAS
??
DASHES USED
AT BOTTOM
OF PAGE.
NEEDED
THERE.*

one of the world's most alluring bodies of water — a rare

gem among the oceans defined by the islands that form a

chain of lovely jewels to the north and east. Although

bounded on the south and west by continental land masses,

it is (these) islands that give the Caribbean its unique

charm. On the north lies the large and important trio:

Puerto Rico, Hispaniola (Haiti and the Dominican Rep-

ublic) and great Cuba. On the east are those heavenly

small islands that so artistically dot the blue waves:

Antigua, Guadeloupe, Martinique, All Saints, Trinidad

and remote Barbados among them. The southern shore is

formed by the South American countries of Venezuela and

Colombia and the central American nation of Panama. The

western shore is often overlooked, but it contains both

the exciting republics of Central America--Costa Rica,

Nicaragua and Honduras--and the wonderful, mysterious

peninsula of Yucatán where the ancient Maya flourished.

The Caribbean, nearly nineteen hundred miles wide

from Barbados to Yucatán, does not include either the

When I was able to complete *Hawaii* pretty much as planned, the book was well received by readers and I had made a cautious start on producing a series of rather long books that attracted many who were interested in exploring various parts of the world. As each book in succession found a niche that it could occupy with dignity, I gained additional courage to attack the next major assignment to which history, not my own imagination, dictated that I pay attention. The Holy Land, South Africa, Poland and the exploration of the moon! Had any writer ever faced more glorious and challenging subject matter on which to test his abilities?

Those three decades from *Hawaii* in 1959 through *Caribbean* in 1989 were a thrilling time for me because not only was I constantly learning about the peoples of the world but I also had the privilege of communicating to a large number of intelligent readers my interpretation of the past and present of those peoples' lives. My attitude was invariable: I believed in the brotherhood of man, the merit of an honest life, the right of everyone to a job and a decent standard of living, and the virtue of striving to keep society peaceful and stable. My books would promote those values, and with each successive novel I would affirm them more vigorously. When I started writing, I would have been arrogant to assume that I would be able to write even one book with the breadth of *The Source* or *Centennial;* to have been allowed to write a dozen such books seems miraculous.

There has always been considerable interest in how, having just finished a book, I select the subject matter for the next. I have in this respect what seems to me an ordinary approach; numerous writers of all types face and solve this problem pretty much as I do, so there is a certain universality to my method.

My mind is unbelievably prolific in generating ideas for stories and books; wherever I go I see possibilities for a dramatic development or a situation that could be explored. I am sure many other writers have the same experience. Where do these ideas originate? From the workings of a fertile brain, from listening to the conversation of interesting human beings, and from speculating on the state of society. And some are of such force that they seem to insist on being put to use in the writer's work.

Do I ever, at the end of a big demanding task, decide to stop writing for a while and lie fallow? Never. I am exactly like Anthony Trollope, who said that if he finished writing a novel in the morning, he started the next that afternoon. The need to write is so pressing for me and the act itself so delectable an experience that with little pause I move eagerly to the next assignment; the ideas are impatient to leap from the prison of my mind. But writing a long book will require at least three years' work, so I must be careful to choose a subject that will sustain my enthusiasm over an extended period. Flashy ideas need not apply.

Do I ever start a project and find myself forced to abandon it? Yes. This has happened at least twice: I planned for a major novel on the siege of Leningrad, on which I did a great deal of work but had to halt because of poor health, and what seemed at first a viable idea for a little novel about a professor turned out to be too precious to retain my interest. Fortunately, at the time of terminating each of these projects I had just enough income from *South Pacific* to enable me to jettison the effort, even though I had invested much time and money on it, and never did I regret the decision.

At what point in the writing of a novel is it safe to start thinking about the next? At no point. It is perilous to think about anything of moment while still engaged in the creation of a given work, and I have rigorously tried to avoid this pitfall. Of course, when the first task is essentially completed or nearly so, it is to be expected that one's mind will begin to speculate on what might come next, especially if, as in my case, this will necessitate a physical move to a new site. However, when I submit a finished manuscript, as good in content, organization and style as I can make it, my New York publisher will still require about fourteen months of hard work before the finished book appears. One does not waste such a span of time, so there is a gradual phasing out of the old project while the next is slowly introduced, and not infrequently I have been well into the new before the old appears as a published book.

Except for a few full-length books written rather speedily on some major events, such as the Hungarian revolution or the bloody tragedy at Kent State, I have almost never dealt with a subject that I had not been brooding about for years or even decades, so that I usually start my work from a fairly high and solid plateau of knowledge. My notebooks show that I have not infrequently contemplated a subject in one decade before coming to grips with it in another, and the time has not been wasted because my understanding has had the chance to mature and the subject has been illuminated in ways not previously apparent.

But one day, at the conclusion of such introspection and evaluation, I decide that of three or four potential subjects I will focus my attention on the one that seems most viable at that time. I roll a sheet of paper into my machine, and below the date I type a brief statement of what my thinking was in selecting that subject, and I outline in chapter headings the entire book as I perceive it at that moment. Never do I get all the subheads right; never do I get more than one wrong. This then becomes my guide for the next three years, and with surprising accuracy I foresee at the time of making the decision the whole grand design and the interrelationship of the parts.

Having made the big decision, I never look back or spend time regretting that I didn't choose one of the other alternative subjects, but obviously I keep the rejected ones in my mental file against the possibility of returning to them later. My immediate task is to make myself as competent as possible within the broad field I have selected, and about which I have been fairly well informed for some years. While I am still trying to decide which subject to choose, my reading in all the competing fields is quite extensive, but I do not take notes or try to remember specifics. Later, when I am hard at work on my chosen subject, I will experience considerable irritation: 'I remember reading that, but in what book? What did it actually say?' I cannot remember and am powerless to recall which specific book had the data I seek. The second type of reading comes after I have decided firmly upon the subject, and now it becomes so fiercely pinpointed that I will remember with clarity almost everything I read, in which book an important idea occurs, about where in the book, and whether it is on a verso or a recto page—this last is helpful because I can quickly scan the book looking at only half the pages to find the sought-for entry.

Obviously, in doing research I cannot read all of every important book, but I have made myself adept at reading indexes, a skill I recommend to would-be writers; I see in the indexes reminders of topics in which I am interested, but, of equal value, I see notations about ramifications that had not occurred to me.

When my general reading has been more or less completed, I explore in great detail four or five ideas central to the subject and, using studies of all kinds, I give myself what amounts to an intensive seminar-level course in each. When writing about the Chesapeake, for example, I focused on shipbuilding, merchant dealings with England, slavery in a border state, the history of a typical small-town church and the building of railroads. The virtue of such study, especially if there is a time span covering several centuries, is that it fixes in the mind an appreciation of what was happening in various fields of endeavor in different periods.

None of my patient work in these chosen areas has been unprofitable, but I have never utilized all the subjects I studied in such depth. When planning *Centennial* I was certain that I would concentrate on railroad

building because it was significant, but when I began to write I don't
believe I mentioned that subject even once. Was the study wasted? Not
at all, because it helped me keep in mind what other industries were
experiencing. I must confess that had I done not five such studies but
twenty I would have been better prepared, but as with all problems
relating to writing, there is a rule of reason where the expenditure of
time is concerned. A self-supporting writer can do five such studies; he
simply hasn't the time to do twenty.

Here I must pay homage to the historians on whom writers like me
base so much of their writing. The difference between a historian and
someone like me is that the former must pay close attention to a host
of important and sometimes difficult themes, whereas I can evade the
difficult problems; however, I try never to abuse fact or invent situations
contrary to known conditions. The historian's task is many times more
difficult than mine, and I know it.

My debt to geographers is equally significant, because invariably the
first book I read when starting my intensive work is the most advanced
geography of the region I can find, and I especially seek one that
explores ecological aspects and not merely the statistics. I concentrate
on the geographical setting because I want to know the natural constraints my characters must deal with, the availability of resources, the
climate and the temperature extremes, the susceptibility to disasters like
prolonged droughts, sea-based hurricanes, land-based tornadoes, the
growing seasons and even those minor signals that alert the knowing to
the potential problems of the area, such as an abundance of pollen in
the air and the possibility of a delayed spring causing famine by hamper-
ing the growth of vegetables and grain.

I am a man bound to the earth and I am keenly aware of its potential
for either enhancing or diminishing human happiness. I am always
aware of the solstices and equinoxes, and although I do not celebrate
holidays with any enthusiasm, finding them commercially offensive, I do
always honor three days in the calendar: December 21, as the shortest
day in the northern hemisphere; June 21, as the longest; and April 23,
Shakespeare's birthday—I use him as surrogate for all the Beethovens,
Titians and Balzacs of the world to whom I owe so much.

The birds and animals that we share the earth with have always been
of intense interest to me. The Canada geese in Maryland were one of
the most appealing inhabitants of that choice countryside; my wife and
I formed a close friendship with a pair of herons who fished the swampy
area in our backyard, and we threw out bits of fish for the wonderful
osprey that took up residence atop a pole at the end of our dock; they

had been near extinction from DDT before outraged nature lovers took steps to rescue them, and we were privileged to see them slowly multiplying near our salty river.

I knew buffalo in Wyoming and sable antelope on private ranches in Texas. For six happy years we had a seven-foot black snake who lived under our house in Pennsylvania. He used to scare visitors when they found him sunning himself on the walk leading to our house, but he became accustomed to us, at least to me, and would stay in shadows as I talked with him. One day a visiting professor from Penn State who arrived in my absence was startled by him, took him to be a deadly copperhead and, grabbing a nearby hoe, hacked him to death, showing us with pride what he had done to save us. Often when I pass that fatal spot I grieve for my dead friend.

I have never claimed that I had any special skill in talking with animals or making them my friends, but I did fraternize with a hyena at a game park in Tanzania. Hyenas are one of the ugliest breeds on earth, big misshapen creatures with heads and bodies that seem deformed. When converted by affection into pets, they are among the best—rough, rowdy wrestlers, playful snappers with jaws that can break branches. The African hyena I knew was highly addicted to beer. Known as Joseph, he would range the camp and the attached motel cadging the last half bottle of beer at each table, taking it in his powerful jaws and chug-a-lugging like a veteran. He would get visibly drunk, and when in the late afternoon he felt exceptionally woozy he would bid us farewell, lurching from one to the other of us as if to say 'Thanks for the beer,' and then lumber off to find a place to snooze in one of the guest cabins. We would know which one he chose when the guests returned from seeing the wonders of the Serengeti and started screaming in terror because they had found Joseph completely passed out on a bed. He and I were strong friends, so I was moved by a letter I later received from Tanzania: 'I'm sure you remember Joseph. Time came when we had to dispose of him, and were fortunate to find him a home in a fine zoo in Edinburgh. When any one of us goes through that city we stop off to see him, and he remembers our smell and after a long visit we cry and he cries and it is all terribly sad. We may stop going because the Edinburgh people tell us that for days after we leave he sits and mopes.'

I have tried to write with authenticity and affection of the animals with whom I have shared my world, and I have sometimes been abused for falling into the 'pathetic fallacy' of attributing to animals mental and sentimental reactions of which only human beings are capable. Realists assert that this is evidence of an intellectual slovenliness that any thoughtful writer should avoid, but I wonder how one would observe that stricture and still try to convey Joseph's staggering roll as he lurched among us to thank us for his beer.

I am equally attached to plant life, and consider my deep involvement with trees one of the richest parts of my life. By planting thousands of trees, I have helped convert hillsides in Pennsylvania and flatlands in Maryland into lovely wooded areas, and my intimate association with a cacao plantation on a remote South Pacific island, where cacao trees were interplanted with coconut palms was one of the chief reasons why I could write about that part of the world as I did.

Once after I had been rescued following the crash of my airplane in the middle of the Pacific I said when asked if I had been frightened: 'No. I expected to be saved. I've spoken well of this ocean in my books and expected courtesy in return.'

One final word about the selection of subject matter. I have never written any book on whose subject I was a preeminent scholar. There have always been a score of experts far better qualified than I to write the book in question, and I have been much abused by such people for trespassing on their turf. There were in Jerusalem a hundred scholars better qualified than I to write *The Source,* in Hawaii, Poland, Alaska and the Caribbean, a score much more knowledgeable about the respective areas. On the subject of Japanese prints there were many who could have done a more scholarly job, and in Texas I suppose that conservatively there must have been two or three hundred, because down there everyone is a historian. But if I have never been the top man, I was the one who knew how to tell a story, to organize experience, and to be dogged enough to spend three years of intense work on the subject. In other words, I was a committed writer and they weren't, and that makes an infinity of difference.

When I am about to start a major project, I am much like a zen master in Japan who is about to serve a ritual tea. I wash my face, cleanse my mind, eat sparingly, exercise every evening by taking long walks, go to bed early and rise at seven to go to my typewriter. I do this seven days a week for the two years during which I am doing the actual writing, and I am loath to permit interruptions. In the morning I do not welcome either visitors or phone calls because writing is hard, exhausting work, and at twelve-thirty when I stop, I am usually sweaty. I customarily wear loose Bermuda shorts, very loose T-shirt or loose sport shirt, loose socks and floppy sandals, and I have grown to feel wonderfully at ease in that uniform; it restricts me at no point and leaves my arms and hands free to move easily. I also wear reading glasses with thick lenses, and I work with such intensity that sometimes when I pause to look out the window the world is a blur because my focus has been at such close range for so long.

Almost every day of my life, working or not, I listen to music, never while I am at the typewriter but when I am filing, or checking some old book or just wasting time. With the advent of compact disks I am prone to place some time-tested favorite on the machine—Schubert's Octet or Bartók's Concerto for Orchestra or Mahler's First or Beethoven's 'Emperor' or Palestrina's *Missa Papae Marcelli* or some Chopin waltzes— and play it maybe fifteen or twenty successive times from day to day because I know I will enjoy it and I am too lazy to keep changing disks and running the risk of getting something I do not like as much.

Many of my days are spent in research and even more in rewriting passages that are already fairly good, or drafting whole new versions of a chapter I didn't particularly like the first time around. When I am working well, I can produce perhaps five typed pages a day, rarely more and often less, but the fine-tuning aspect of writing—editing, revising, selecting the correct word—require just about the same amount of time as the original composition, which means that I produce about two pages of finished text a day, and I have never devised any way to accelerate that process.

For me, writing the original draft is murderously difficult, and I often spend more than a day striving to unravel a difficult passage requiring less than a page; but rewriting, when I know that the book will be completed and published, gives me joy, because I feel that everything I am doing is making the manuscript significantly better. And reworking a passage in galley when I really nail down a thought that has previously been fugitive is one of the most pleasurable exercises in which I can engage. If writing is hard labor, it can also be great fun.

Do I ever have writer's block? Professional writers cannot afford to indulge themselves in that dramatic experience so beloved by writers who write about writers, and especially by those who make motion pictures about them. Of course one sometimes hits a blank day or a frightening one when ominous questions flood the mind, but one does not surrender to them. In my case I turn to some later part of the manuscript that I feel will pose no problems and seek refuge in it, and the robust ease with which I sail through it restores my confidence.

However, I must with a wince confess that afterward, when I reach that part of the manuscript, I find that I cannot use the passage—that is, I cannot incorporate it into the narrative where it belongs because it fails for a subtle reason that other writers will recognize: the flow of the part done out of turn is wrong; its tone is not right; words have the wrong intonations and characters do not reflect the modifications of intervening chapters. But the work has not been done in vain, because it contains many parts that can be salvaged, and it probably does indicate the general direction in which the plotting and character behavior should go, so I quite happily sit down and rewrite the whole thing. By seeking to escape a blockage by writing an easier part, I saved no time; in fact, I wasted a good deal, but I did get back on track, and that's what's important.

I have always tried to do my work on an old-fashioned heavy manual typewriter with elite type that enables me to get the maximum number of words to the line and lines to the page. In an age of miracle electronic typewriters and word processors it is becoming difficult to find the old machines—in all of Alaska none could be located and I was forced to use a pica, which evoked profanity—and in both Texas and Florida serious searches had to be made. One dealer told me: 'Five years from now you won't be able to find one, elite or pica,' so I treat the ones I have with care.

One of my peculiarities illustrates how writers develop fixations. In revising a manuscript I have a horror of altering the original pagination. I have that sequence of pages and their contents engraved in my mind; to disturb it would be destructive. Therefore I protect rigorously each page as it stands, and if I must insert new material or delete old I do so within that page. This means that some pages are twice the normal length, others only half. When I complete my corrections—and often my corrections of my corrections—many pages are a jumble, but they still stand in their original order so that I can be sure of where topics will appear in the manuscript.

Curiously, I have never used markings to indicate transpositions or insertions of passages. I insist on seeing each item in its proper place on the page. I cut and paste, so that an old-fashioned paste pot is a mainstay in my writing routine. (Recently it has become a much-diluted self-dispensing flask of Elmer's Glue-All.)

Of course, as soon as I finish editing a chapter I turn it over to my secretary, and from then on we do all editing on the floppy disk. If I were in my youth and wanted to become a writer, I would take off a summer and make myself proficient on the typewriter keyboard—a skill I do not have and whose absence I mourn—so that I could shift easily to a word processor. Without that ability young people will find no opportunity to work in the writing professions, and the time may not be far off when writers will submit two copies of a manuscript to a publishing house, one a printout on paper, the other a floppy disk on which the publisher can do the editing and which he can deliver by telephone connection to the company that will set the manuscript in the preferred typeface and print the book.*

When I have done all I can to make the manuscript readable and meaningful, I employ at my expense the most learned man or woman available with special knowledge of the subject to read the entire manuscript to detect gross error, ridiculous misinterpretations or failure to note recent developments. Such peer review is invaluable, and I have frequently been saved by a judicious question such as: 'Do you really want that sentence to read as if Canada were west of Alaska?' For vetting several of my books I have sought different specialists for each chapter, rather than one overall expert, and with the South African novel I had at one time chapters being read on four different continents: Africa, Europe, Australia and North America.

A feature of writing that the layman may not appreciate is that leading scholars are eager to help writers avoid error because they have acquired enormous respect for the field of their expertise and do not care to see it burlesqued or misrepresented. One of the major rewards of my writing life has been my affiliation with men and women of learning; to read their thoughtful comments is a privilege. Equally gratifying, however, is the fact that I receive about a dozen inquiries a year from all over the world from scholars asking me to clarify points on which I have special knowledge or unique experiences. These are letters I answer in considerable detail, for those of us who cherish ideas are part of a brotherhood.

When I have digested the criticisms of the experts and made the revisions that will bring my manuscript nearer to the truth, I ship it off to Random House, where for most of my career a brilliant Southern gentleman, a traditional classical scholar, would study the work for three or four months, spotting errors and detecting weaknesses in a story line or characterization. Albert Erskine worked with such a distinguished parade of authors that no new one could bring him problems

*Shortly after writing this paragraph, I did submit to a publisher in another country the entire manuscript of a novel on a floppy disk. The future had caught up with me.

he had not already encountered: William Faulkner, John O'Hara, Robert Penn Warren, Ralph Ellison. He worked with me for some thirty-five years and gave me constant good advice.

When dealing with a long manuscript of mine, he would send me, over the course of six or seven months, twenty or thirty long letters of inquiry, each of which I had to answer in detail, often with substantial redrafting of individual passages and always with scores of responses to his questions about individual words that came close but missed, or sentences that were not clear. His famous Erskine's First Law has helped innumerable writers: 'If you try three times to fix a paragraph and it still creaks, kill it.' I have had only good results from that dictum.

When, after long effort, the manuscript satisfied Erskine's requirements, he would pass it along to a remarkable woman, Bert Krantz, four feet eleven, who has a magical touch with English. She was the final arbiter on matters of style, and the casual reader would not believe how often in the writing of a manuscript one has the choice of two perfectly good options: *fulfill* or *fulfil; dishabille* or *deshabille; paillasse* or *palliase.* More serious is the inclination of the average writer, and I am one, to repeat words in a manuscript, or to use them improperly, e.g., *presently* to mean *now* instead of the correct *in the near future;* and a hundred other tricky questions of taste and judgment. Bert's responsibility was to make a Random House book look like one and not some grab bag. She was brilliant in her ability to spot improprieties and adamant in her determination to correct them. She was one of the most valuable of the editors and I would not have been happy about sending any of my manuscripts to the printer before her sharp eyes had vetted it.

When she and Erskine had done their jobs, the company lawyers would check to see if anything I had written was actionable at law, and in recent years, with our society's becoming more litigious, printed statements that used to slip by are now pounced upon, to the surprise of and financial damage to the writer. There are many things a writer may not say, and it is the task of the lawyers to identify them and sound warnings.

When the printer finally sends back galleys, one set goes to an outside proofreader skilled in nitpicking—three I have worked with were incredible—who read the narrative with an eye as impartial as if it were the Bronx telephone directory he or she were reading and it is unbelievable what they come up with. By this time, if you have been keeping count, the manuscript has been read by me, by my skilled secretary, by anyone who works with me in my office, by the paid expert, by Erskine, by Krantz and by the lawyers. One would think that no error could exist, but this outside proofreader will find a score of things he or she does not approve, or old errors that have slipped past everyone. These brilliant wordsmiths work free-lance, this week for one publisher, next week for another, and when I submit a manuscript I always hope that Random will line up one of the truly great ones. I am obligated to these lifesavers, none of whom I have ever met.

I am aware that most publishers could not afford to spend the time on each manuscript that Random does on mine, and that most writers would not want them to, but when one looks at the results of this hard work in my case, it seems the effort was worthwhile. If my books have received wide acceptance and a certain longevity, it is due in part to the care with which they have been written and published, and half the credit goes to the publisher. I did bristle, however, when a sharp woman writer from *The New York Times* asked me: 'Is it true, what I've heard, that when you turn in a manuscript to Random, they hand it over to a roomful of their experts who rewrite it and make it publishable?' Whoever told her that had confused traditional editorial care with company-sponsored ghostwriting. I write every word of my books and sometimes they're the wrong words; it's the editors' job to point that out.

When the book finally appears, almost without exception on the first day I look at it, I find two misspelled words. So much for infinite attention paid by infinitely careful editors. Worse are the one or two errors of fact that seem to be inescapable. In *Centennial* five readers who know English history well did not catch me having Winston Churchill's father, Randolph, wooing an American heiress long after he had married her, and in the late pages of the book I called my Mexican hero *Triunfador* Marquez when it had been well established earlier that he was *Tranquilino* Marquez. Such errors are mine. They have been at a minimum, I am glad to say, but each is woefully embarrassing.

After years of diligent apprenticeship and assistance from a strong publisher, my books reached that enviable status which almost guaranteed they would leap onto the best-seller lists on publishing day, and sometimes well before, remaining there a gratifyingly long time. As mentioned before, I have never spoken of myself as a 'best-selling author' and am amused when others refer to me as a 'commercial writer.' My books have certainly been commercial, despite what my first agent predicted, but not because that was my aim. I have written difficult books on difficult subjects, and the reader has to have a certain degree of willpower to get through to the final pages; the commercial success has been a fortunate accident, and I believe that a writer is better off with some success than without it.

I have affection for a different phrase and am always pleased when it is used in relation to one of my books: 'a minor classic.' This is a book of limited sale that is promoted quietly by word of mouth.

Zen and the Art of Motorcycle Maintenance, by the German mystic Robert M. Pirsig, is such a book. Upon publication it achieved little notice, but so many devotees cherished its pertinence to their emotional problems that they formed a subterranean cult which forced the book upon the attention of others. Oliver Statler's *Japanese Inn* was a similar case, an essay so charmingly presented that if anyone took the trouble to look into it, he or she was captivated and told others about it. A small nothing of a book, *Wings at My Window,* by Ada Clapham Govan, an amateur ornithologist, enjoyed enormous popularity among bird-watchers, and even professional scientists have admitted that they acquired their first interest in ornithology from reading this cheerful, informal book. Some years ago another curious but lovable book was promoted by its devotees to the rank of minor classic: *84 Charing Cross Road,* by Helene Hanff, acquired such a cult following that it was later presented as a poetic motion picture, which gained a whole new group of supporters.

I have written three books that could possibly be considered for this honor because they conform to the definition of having been read not by the general public but by 'everyone who ought to have read them.' The first is *The Floating World,* my loving account of how Japanese prints were made and introduced to the Western world. I am amazed that I had the brashness to attempt such a book when I knew no Japanese nor any of the great traditions of the art. Today I would not have that courage, but I'm glad I did when I was younger.

My book on athletics, *Sports in America,* received little notice and few sales, but it became a source of great interest among university sports directors, coaches, newspaper sports writers and those civilians concerned about the destiny of sport in a society that seems not to know how to handle it and its manifold problems, some of them extremely ugly. I spent a long time on that essay with little expectation of success and am increasingly glad I did, because to find even one class in a university's athletic department using it as a provocative text is ample reward.

But a book of mine that best fits the definition of minor classic is

Caravans, which again created little stir when published, but which fell into the hands of almost everyone who had an interest in obscure Afghanistan and the curious things that happen there. Wherever I go in the world I meet people who tell me that they would never have gone to Afghanistan had they not stumbled upon my book, or that when they were there, someone had a dog-eared copy that was passed from hand to hand because, better than anything else available, it introduced them to Afghan mysteries. It is a book of which I am quite proud, even though its sales would excite little envy.

A fourth book in no way qualifies for consideration as a minor classic. *The Bridge at Andau,* depicting the Hungarian revolution of 1956, recounts my adventures, often behind Russian lines, in rescuing Hungarian refugees from Communist terror. With the help of a wonderful Catholic priest, I became a specialist in getting Jewish rabbis to change their identity: to shave off their beards, learn how to answer a few questions and pass themselves off as devout Catholics, a deception made necessary by the fact that the United States accepted so few Jews while admitting a large number of Catholics. Since the Catholics were clearly not going to fill their quota, the priest and I made temporary conversions on the spot. I was also the principal expert in teaching Jews how to become Presbyterians, for their quota also had vacancies. Today, wherever I go to whatever corner of the world, someone comes knocking on my hotel door to remind me how I had helped him or his mother or his sister cross that rickety bridge at Andau and to find later refuge in America or Venezuela or Australia.

The most memorable plan for a rescue we effected that cold winter was made right in the heart of Vienna in the hotel Bristol, which was the base for Russian spies, Polish émigrés, American Red Cross workers, future senator Claiborne Pell and American journalists. I had organized a supersecret courier service that operated not at the big crossing from Hungary to Austria at Nickelsdorf or the little one at Andau, but at the way station near Sopron. There, for a hefty number of dollars that others like me collected and doled out, heroic Hungarian refugees would undertake to filter back into Budapest and rescue some family member left behind when others had fled to safety in Austria. It was risky business and costly, but it saved enough lives to warrant keeping it going.

One afternoon a remarkable man from Hollywood flew in from Amsterdam: Tors Istvan—known in America as Ivan Tors—the ingenious fellow who had pioneered underwater photography and produced a sensationally popular television show, *Flipper,* about dolphins. Tors demanded to see me and wanted to know about the rescue chain we had established. The fee was to be five hundred dollars, and the object was to bring Tors's mother the long distance to Sopron and out to safety in Vienna and then to America. Being both a Hungarian and a Hollywood producer, he questioned the reliability of everyone, including me, and at the end of his interrogations he was not satisfied. Grabbing the phone, he told the Austrian operator: 'Get me Budapest,' and I gasped because Russian tanks were parading that city even as he spoke. In a surprisingly few minutes he got Budapest and shouted into the phone in Hungarian, which he later translated for me: 'Momma! This is Istvan. Yes, things are pretty good in Hollywood. I'm in Vienna. Momma, I'm sending a young man in with five hundred dollars to bring you out to safety. I've told him to meet you at . . .'—he gave a full address—'and you come along with him. He's an honest man, I think, and I'll wait here for you.' He gave us the money for the courier, I drove down to Sopron and saw the young fellow disappear over the border toward Budapest. Because I was then diverted to a more serious problem, I never learned the outcome of this brazen strategy of calling directly to the capital of an occupied nation and arranging over an open phone for a criminally illegal act.

My attention had been diverted to a wretched situation. My colleague on my sorties behind Russian lines was a fabulously daring American photographer, Dickie Chapelle, whose willingness to test the Russian occupation forces made me look like a milquetoast. About thirty-five and the veteran of many escapades, she had come to Vienna as a stringer for Time-Life, but when they saw the crazy adventures into which she was throwing herself they more or less cut her loose, and when I allowed her to hitchhike a ride with me during the long trip to the Hungarian border I was able to bring her daring excesses down to a manageable level.

We would have an early evening meal in Vienna, leave the city about nine-thirty and reach Andau well before midnight. There we would scout the bridge to see how many Russian guards were on duty, then slip over the border and try to make contact with the incoming refugees from Budapest, ninety-odd miles to the east. I have since suspected that the Russians were not unhappy to see these dissidents leaving the country, for they certainly could have stopped them had they wished, but, timing our work carefully, Dickie and I could collect the refugees—parents, children and a few hangers-on—and wait till the Russians were occupied elsewhere, and then run them swiftly to safety. At about four in the morning, when the stream of Hungarians slowed, we would drive

back to Vienna, where my wife would be waiting with hot chocolate and
cold beer.

It was an arduous regimen, and Dickie and I rescued hundreds, but
she became so daring, so contemptuous of the Russians that she terrified
me, and I begged her to be cautious. When I learned that she insisted
on going behind Russian lines without me I warned: 'Dickie, you know
you're not immortal. You go banging around deep into Hungary on
your own, and carrying all that photo equipment, they're bound to grab
you and charge you with espionage.'

Dickie was the bravest person I would ever know, man or woman.
She had served in battle with the Marines, had parachuted with invasion
forces, had tramped Cuba's revolutionary fronts, and had sought danger
wherever it might be found. One colleague in Vienna, watching her
operate when I wasn't with her, said: 'She's a one-woman attempt to
prove she's as good as a man.' I think that was the secret: Dickie
Chapelle was a dedicated feminist far ahead of her time, and one of the
finest.

Busy with my heavy workload of rescuing people at night and teaching them to be Catholics and Presbyterians through the day, I am
ashamed to say that I forgot her, but my wife, fortunately, did not, and
when two days passed without anyone's hearing from her, Mari grew
nervous and started making inquiries. Yes, Dickie was gone. Two newsmen had seen her heading into Russian territory but had not seen her
return, and with that ominous news my wife swung into action.

It is painful to report that none of all our friends and agencies in
Vienna but only Mari bird-dogged this thorny situation. Time-Life authorities pointed out, quite accurately, 'Chapelle wasn't actually an
employee, you know,' and washed their hands of her. Officers from the
embassy said that 'everyone knew she was hotheaded and would sooner
or later get into trouble.' But Mari struggled on, fighting red tape all the
way and finally receiving word, from what quarter I never knew, that
Dickie had been captured by Russian troops far behind the front and
was now in solitary confinement in a Budapest jail, where she would
remain for a very long time.

Again most people in Vienna dismissed the case, but Mari did not,
and as I watched her tireless efforts, badgering this official and that, I
thought: 'If I ever disappear I want her on my case.' Because of her
insistence, and undoubtedly with pressure from others more highly
placed, the Russians belatedly allowed Dickie to regain her freedom.
Feeling responsible for her, Mari and I invited her to recuperate at our
home in Bucks County, and there I loaned her my office and typewriter
so that she could write her story and sell it to the *Reader's Digest.*

That started her on the upward swing of her career: more work with the Marines, more battlefronts in Africa and elsewhere, more parachute drops, and finally, as we had all anticipated, a backward step into a Communist land mine in Vietnam and instant death.

It is from such tangled incidents and experiences that writers accumulate material they use in their books, and the searching, the listening, the comforting are incessant.

I have been speaking only of my small books, those that were never important except to readers who took special interest in the particular subjects I was dealing with. I now come to what probably seems the more important period of my writing life. As mentioned before, the advent of television convinced me that readers would be hungry for longer books of substance, and with this conclusion firmly in mind I launched a number of big novels that would lift me from the ranks of proficient but struggling writers to the level enjoyed by a relative few who are able to earn a comfortable living from their writing. It is always sobering to reflect on the plight of many fine writers who have not been able to support themselves by writing alone but have had to rely on other sources for their major income: Herman Melville was a minor clerk in the New York Customs House, Thornton Wilder a schoolteacher, Robert Penn Warren a college professor; and any number of excellent poets held jobs that were irrelevant and draining. To think of them is to remind oneself of how capriciously and unfairly the rewards from writing are distributed.

In selecting themes for my big books, I have had but one goal: to write a book that I myself would like to read, and to do it on a topic that will have more than passing interest. I have tended toward heavy, comprehensive subjects because I want the reader to spend time on ideas and concepts that matter, and I have been willing to fill my pages with a wealth of data in order to give the reader the pleasure of becoming more knowledgeable.

Having these somewhat lofty aims, I have been able to ignore the lurid themes that are popularly supposed to guarantee best-sellerdom. I have refused to deal in extreme violence, exhibitionistic sex, pornography, kinky psychological aberrations used only for shock effect, or sadism. I felt that such writing was beneath my dignity and not necessary to attract the readers I sought. I was convinced they would be interested in the aspirations and defeats of ordinary people, in the exploration of ideas, in the depiction of far regions, and in the time-honored themes of good storytelling: the maturation of a human mind, the challenges of young adulthood, the struggle for existence, the accumulation of years with dignity or despair, and the mystery of death. I would seek to deal with all human passions: my characters would fall in love, have babies, engage in adultery, experience betrayal by others and face grave moral choices. They would know warfare and economic depression and great victories, all the emotional traps that engulf real people; only a rare few would be heroes or heroines and none would be faultless.

I have endeavored to center my writing upon ordinary but memorable characters whose lives shed a kind of radiance, whose behavior, good or bad, illuminated what I was striving to impart, and whose noble, craven, godlike or hellish deportment stood surrogate for the behavior of human beings the reader has known. I have tried every device I know to breathe life into my characters, for there is little in fiction more rewarding than to see real people interact on a page. How the writer achieves such a result remains a mystery, but sometimes it happens, and when it does, it is a wonderful thing.

A writer who has become relatively well known is asked to participate in many ventures, none stranger than one that overtook me during the famous bullfights in Pamplona. One evening while many of us lounged at Bar Choko three bright young women from Australia came to my table: 'Mr. Michener, we hear that after this you're heading for Tangiers. There's an English girl there who's near death from drugs and abuse. Would you look her up and try to get her back to her parents in England?'

When I reached Tangiers she was already dead, and I helped ship her corpse back to England, after which I plunged into the heavy drug scene in Marrakech. The resulting book, *The Drifters,* irritated many of my readers, who felt it too sharp a deviation from my usual work, and infuriated others who objected to any adverse comment on drugs, but in the years that followed, no matter where I appeared in public, at the end of my talk I would be approached by anguished parents—judges and their wives, college professors, lawyers, clergymen, ordinary housewives—who would take me aside and ask what they should do about a lost son or daughter. Invariably I said: 'From my experience, eighty-five per cent of these young people will come back into orbit, and maybe as much stronger persons than when they left.'

'The other fifteen percent?'

'They're dead ducks.' I used that ugly, ungracious phrase time and again, hoping to shock these good people into the realization that their children might truly be lost, either to death or to permanent disorientation. But always I ended with: 'Eighty-five safe, fifteen lost, those are not bad odds. They justify hope.'

I had hit upon a subject of tremendous meaning to thousands of parents, and the book had a more significant reception in countries like Germany, Sweden and Holland than in the United States, for the phenomenon of wandering youth was more prevalent in those countries. It was, I judge in retrospect, one of the most valuable books I would write, for it provided illumination and hope to many.

Quietly, almost without my being aware that it was happening, sales of my big novels increased to the point at which I was tarnished with the epithet 'best-selling author,' a characterization that, as I've said, I deplored, since I thought of myself merely belonging to the long tradition of hardworking writers. Obviously I faced a dilemma: I was highly pleased to have won so many readers, and I was not unhappy with the added income this meant, but I did resent the implication that I wrote only for popularity and money.

Part of my discomfort stemmed from a bizarre experience in a unique secondhand bookstore located far out in the country near Cape Canaveral in Florida, where I was working on space-flight problems while a member of the NASA board. Needing used copies of out-of-date *World Almanac*s, I had been directed to this surprising shop: 'He has two of everything. What a jumble.'

Upon entering the cluttered shop, I saw thousands of books scattered about in what seemed like chaotic profusion, but the owner knew exactly what he had, for when I asked for copies of the *Almanac* he said without hesitation: 'Over there,' and on a rickety shelf I found three I could use. When it came time to pay he asked what I did, and I said I worked at Canaveral—or Kennedy, as the government wanted it to be called—and he supposed that I was an engineer.

'Not that sharp. I'm a writer,' I said, and when he saw from my credit card who I was he said brightly: 'I always have a couple of your books lying around. They go out pretty fast,' and I saw on another shelf that he had four used copies of my novels. What really mattered was not the satisfaction of knowing that my books were still circulating, but that next to my shelf stood a large bookcase, and to appreciate the situation the reader must visualize its dimensions. Perhaps eight feet tall, it reached almost to the ceiling, and consisted of eight big shelves exactly six and a half feet wide. Each inch of that massive affair was jammed tight with small paperbacks whose spines were visible, and what a lively, colorful array they made.

'Now, what is that?' I asked, and the manager said proudly: 'That's our Barbara Cartland bookcase.' I asked: 'Who's she?' and his jaw dropped.

'You never heard of Barbara Cartland, the most popular writer in the world?' When I said I had not, he laughed: 'You'd better learn right now,' and he turned me loose on this huge collection of paperbacks, and after I had pulled down some dozen or so it became clear that Miss Cartland, whoever she was, wielded an ingenious pen, for I believe I checked into two shelves of her books before I came to a repetitious title. It seemed from the gaudy covers that she wrote mostly about beautiful young girls, often in chiffon, who were involved with handsome men, some of dubious character.

'Who is this woman?' I asked and he told me: 'An Englishwoman, who has some tenuous relationship to noble families, publishes four or five novels a year, and has the most devoted readership in the world. Women don't read her books, they devour them.' Shortly after he said this an elderly woman, the kind Norman Rockwell might have used as a grandmother for a Thanksgiving Day cover, came into the store with a shopping bag containing five Barbara Cartland novels, and it soon became clear that by returning these for credit and paying an additional ten cents a copy she was eligible to select five new Cartland novels. Depositing her old ones, she headed directly to the Cartland case, where she rather quickly picked her five replacements, judging their merit by the liveliness of the covers.

When she returned to the checkout desk she asked the manager: 'Have I read these before?' and he deftly separated her selections into two piles: 'These three are new, I think, but you've already read these two,' and he fetched her two substitutes, which he assured her she would enjoy. When the phrase *best-selling author* is bandied about, I think not of myself but of Barbara Cartland, and much as I admire the lady, judging from what I've read of her bold public performances as a grande dame, I do not want to be put alongside her in the same category.

And yet, if the public makes an author a best-seller how can he or she escape pejorative classification? For when someone says 'Jones is a best-selling author,' what he really means is 'Jones is *only* a best-seller' with all the condescension that implies. Balzac was and is a best-seller, as were Dickens, Camus, Hemingway and Pearl Buck, but so are Harold Bell Wright and Barbara Cartland. Certainly in my day I have been one, and that inevitably raises two questions that writers do not like to talk about in public, even though they do a great deal of talking about them in private: 'What did you do with all your royalty income?' and 'How do you see yourself as a writer?' Like others, I shall duck those impertinent questions now, but I shall answer them frankly in the last two chapters.

Now, however, I should like to answer a grab bag of queries that are asked repeatedly: 'Which of your books gave you the most pleasure in the writing?' *The Source* was the biggest challenge, for it dealt with immortal themes and required research in three languages I did not read: Hebrew, Russian, German. Whenever I think of that book, I give a little prayer of thanks that I did it when I did, for now I would be too old to tackle the tremendous amount of work it required.

'In which foreign country did you most enjoy working?' I think that any young man who experienced Afghanistan in the days that I have described earlier, when life was so extremely rugged and pre-biblical, will recall it as having been an apex of his adventuring life.

'What city was the most satisfying to work in?' Incomparably Denver, my base while writing *Centennial,* because within half an hour's drive to the east I was in the great flatlands, which excited me so much and which I used to advantage; within the same time span to the west I was in the high foothills of the Rockies and some minutes later in the highest plateaus. Also, my workroom was ten minutes from a notable library, unexcelled in its collection of materials on the American West, and fifteen minutes from a huge international airport. But this mountain paradise has a crippling drawback: an intolerable smog that makes Los Angeles look as if its belching tail pipes weren't even trying. Were it not for the smog, I would live in Denver, because it is also the substitute capital of the United States with so many important government offices hiding there that exceptionally bright personnel abound.

'How big a research staff do you employ on a full-time basis?' One: me. On two occasions, the book on sports and *Centennial,* I had the part-time help of two different bright young men, but they were assigned me by others who owed me courtesies that could not be discharged by cash payments, and I must stress that they were finders and judges of data, not writers of prose. When such helpers bring the research material to my attention, I still do all the reading, evaluating and writing. In most instances I have not even had the help of book-finders, but when I did, their assistance was appreciated. I have also been fortunate in finding in every writing task I have ever undertaken secretaries who have been wizards on the typewriter, and more recently, on the word processor. As every writer knows, without such help in moving a large manuscript forward, writing would be almost impossible.

One secretary stands out. In Israel I had the help of a woman who took her Jewish religion seriously, and once when I had Jehovah striking down one of my characters for what she deemed an inadequate reason, she wrote on the margin of my manuscript: 'I don't think this was very nice of God,' and she refused to type the passage. I, who believed that Jehovah could be pretty arbitrary at times, had to write the passage out by hand and staple it to the manuscript, but I was afraid to let her see what I had done.

'Which of your books is your favorite?' Always the next one. I hope that this time I will be able to hold all the threads together, that the characters will evoke a sense of reality, that what I've written will elucidate the theme, that an occasional paragraph will sing, that I can, in a phrase I learned in England, 'bring it off.' This, I believe, is the constant ambition of the writer and his constant prayer; it is certainly mine, and the apprehension we experience about failing, especially when we are in the midst of a struggle, is far more terrifying and common than the casual observer would suspect. Does any artist other than a writer of a massive book know this anxiety, that all the energy of three years' unremitting toil might be wasted? The writer of a lyric ode does not spend three years on the poem; the painter of a normal-sized canvas does not begin to invest the time and energy that a novelist does, nor suffer the heavy consequences if he fails. I suppose the writer of a play shares an equal uncertainty, and perhaps a greater, for he must find financial backing, a theater, a composer if it is a musical, a director, a producer, a set of stars, and a play-doctor if it runs half an hour too long. I deem the playwright's job the most complex, the novelist's the most lonely and perilous, and the poet's the most hopeless under present conditions in that he can scarcely find a traditional publisher to even look at his work.

So although I have written many books that have met with a lucky reception, I still experience the most nagging fears when I am in the middle of a major project: 'Who will read so many pages about finding a gold mine, even supposing I can get it finished to my own taste?' The echoes of terror are always there, and if the public has made my books best-sellers, I have often sweated in clammy silence to bring the books to where the public could find them.

If I have refused to make subject-matter concessions to my readers in order to court acceptance, I have certainly made great efforts to make my books physically pleasing to the eye and comfortable to the hand. I revere fine books—I do not mean expensive ones—and take pride when I have helped my publisher produce a respectable one: firm boards on the cover, appropriate typeface of adequate size, good opaque paper, proper spacing on the page to allow the eye to take in a complete line without battling gutters, excellent maps when required and a general look of fine craftsmanship. I have sometimes been apologetic when seeing for the first time the smallness of the type that has had to be used because of the length of my books and have resolved to keep subsequent ones shorter so that a more comfortable type size can be used. In other words, I have a passion for making books that are aesthetically pleasing, and one or two that have been published in Asia have been gems in that respect, and all original editions published in America have been presentable. Expensive special editions have sometimes been quite handsome, and most reprints have been acceptable, but a few have been so unprofessional as to shame me.

In dealing with the physical aspects of my books I pay most of my attention to the interior—typefaces and paper—but in later years I came to respect the importance of outer appearances. To me titles have never had great importance, and I have not paid much attention to mine. I submit seven or eight possible choices, any one of which would satisfy me, and allow Random House to make the final selection; occasionally they have suggested one which had not occurred to me but which I came to prefer. I have had no aptitude for devising great titles like *Gone With the Wind* or *A Streetcar Named Desire* and have concluded that a fine title is whatever appears on the cover of a fine book. However, I remember a frolic perpetrated by a group of idle writers, some seven or eight, who agreed that each would write one chapter of a wild, sexy adventure novel to see if they could get such a mishmash published. The project would have failed had they not come up with one of the most titillating titles of recent decades, *Naked Came the Stranger,* which propelled their book right onto the lists.

I'm afraid I did not understand the importance of a colorful jacket for a hardcover book, or a lurid one for a paperback, until a memorable experience in London provided some instruction. During an unexpected layover in that city my British hardcover publisher insisted that I drive out to the countryside to visit the paperback publisher who'd had rather good luck with a whole string of my books. I saw no reason to do this, but my publisher said: 'They've been awfully good to you, Jim, and it would be a courtesy—to let them know you appreciate their help.'

Out we went into the gracious environs of London, and as I entered the publishing establishment I was led directly to a smallish but not tiny room I shall never forget, for its four walls were covered with bookracks for the display of all the various reprintings of my novels. Let's say there were ten versions each of fifteen different books, all of the same size. In the case of each title, copies were arranged in chronological order, the earliest printing to the left, the latest—often the preceding month's—to the right, all in full color. After a gasp at seeing so many bright and dancing jackets I noticed the essential fact about this display: invariably, each succeeding jacket showed an attractive girl wearing less and less clothing until I wondered what they might have in store for three or four reissues down the line.

'What we do,' one of the managers explained, 'is track bookstall sales attentively, and when it becomes apparent that one of your titles is beginning to lag, we hurry up and give it a new jacket, and your words gain a whole new life.' I believe there had been some fifteen reprintings of *Tales of the South Pacific,* or it might have been *Hawaii,* and the resulting display was awesome, but there were one or two other books whose contents did not deal with luscious beauties in dishabille, but on the covers they pirouetted wearing little.

At lunch I met the staff artist responsible for the covers and he told me: 'You assure me an almost permanent job. I've never read any of your books, but editors point out the good parts and I do the rest.' He calculated that he might have done nearly a hundred covers for my books. I was definitely not pleased with so much nudity but was powerless to make any effective protest. However, there was some consolation when, later that day in an airport lounge, I saw a display of Thomas Hardy reprints and noticed that the heroine—it could have been Eustacia Vye or the D'Urberville girl—was also rather scantily clad.

I had my most instructive visit with a foreign publisher during a stopover in Istanbul when a charming Turkish gentleman visited my hotel, having read in the papers that I was in town. He had with him five or six of my books, which he had pirated with no payment to me, for Turkey does not abide by international copyright law, and after proudly spreading them before me he asked with almost fatherly interest: 'Which of your books would you like me to take next?' I picked up one with an especially lurid jacket and asked him to explain the shocking artwork, and he said: 'We've never had in Turkey a really good lesbian novel, so I thought that if we would revise your story a little . . .' He lifted the book and offered it to me with two hands as if it were a jewel.

Finally, is it useful for the author's photograph to be on the back cover of the jacket? Not for me, since I simply do not look like an author or anything else distinctive. I leave the choice of poses to New York and sometimes gasp when I see the result: 'My God! do I look like that?' However, if the writer is a handsome young man with a strong jaw or a beautiful young woman with a provocative smile, the back-cover shot can be a powerful sales aid, especially in first-time appearances. There is apparently a brisk market in the photographs of young writers, because an enterprising company has recently uncovered a very old negative taken of me in 1946 and has been printing up a fine glossy that sells for something like three dollars. It must be doing well, because I keep receiving copies through the mail for me to autograph, and I inscribe them with my birth date, 3 February, and the current year—say, 1991— with the caption 'Portrait of the writer on his eighty-fourth birthday' and let others decipher that mystery.

It should be clear that whereas the external aspects of a book may have helped some photogenic authors who had dreamed up brilliant titles, my titles, covers and portraits accounted for little of my good fortune. As it should be with books, it was the contents, verbal and intellectual, that made the difference, but having said that, I am again powerless to specify what it has been that has attracted and retained readers. Let me describe what it is I do, and invite the reader to reach his or her conclusion.

I have worked diligently to achieve a flowing narrative style so that the reader who persists to the bottom of page one will find herself or himself invited to proceed to page two; the same applies to chapters. I have inclined toward a classic style of presentation and have hoped that the book would hang together as a whole and evoke a sense of leading to a satisfying conclusion. These are modest stylistic aims but are difficult to achieve.

Critics have learned to be suspicious of best-sellers, and rightly so. I doubt that any critic in the world has seriously reviewed each of Barbara Cartland's fifty latest novels; they discovered early on that they didn't have to. In somewhat the same way, some critics have not felt it necessary to keep on reviewing the books of any writer who has turned out a series of popular successes, such as I have. I am sure I've suffered from this easy dismissal.

However, I would like to refer to public response to four different books. When *Hawaii* appeared, readers on the islands went into a fury, local newspapers gave full pages to outraged letters vilifying me, angry discussion was rampant, and one paper carried a full-column editorial advising me to get out of Hawaii and stay out. The condemnation, however, was not so severe as that suffered by Robert Louis Stevenson when he left the islands three quarters of a century earlier. He had so offended missionary families by praising Father Damien, the Catholic priest who had served the lepers on Molokai, that the editor of one of the papers hoped that the ship carrying Stevenson away would sink. But the warmth with which my novel was received elsewhere and the fact that it brought thousands of visitors to Hawaii softened animosities, and as the years passed the locals realized that my book was one of the good things that had happened to the islands. Now a friendly editor printed an entirely different column that said in effect: 'Come on home, Jim. All is forgiven.'* The most amazing result of the book's publication however, is the problem it caused for the islands' major church. So many vacationers from the mainland, having read it and recalling that the protagonist, Abner Hale, was a clergyman, pestered the custodians of the church to find out where he was buried. The inquiries became so intrusive that the church had to publish a small handbill, in good taste and exuding patience, reminding the visitors that Reverend Hale was only an imaginary person. An official told me: 'They read it and say: "Very interesting. But where is he buried?" We may stop trying to convince them.'

Iberia, my book on Spain, was the first of three of my works that were officially banned by the nations about which they were written; the Franco government objected to things I had said about the all-important Guardia Civil and the quasi-religious secret fraternity Opus Dei. The case with Poland was much the same, for my novel of that name was banned by the Communist rulers, who felt that my comments on their master, the Soviet Union, were unacceptable. But the most instructive was the problem with South Africa over *The Covenant,* which was banned by government censors, who castigated it for its 'errors and distortions.'

Interestingly, in the first two cases, Spain and Poland, the governments found that the books they had banned were appearing in the luggage of most visitors to their country and many travelers said they had come to the country primarily because they had read the book. So in time each ban was quietly lifted and the governments even invited me to come visit and receive honors because my books had created so much international goodwill.

The South African matter was more difficult, but also more amusing,

*But a major bookstore sponsored in part by a leading intellectual agency of the islands refuses to carry *Hawaii* on the grounds that it is of no merit, despite the fact that visitors ask for it constantly.

for after having blasted my book and threatening police action against anyone bringing it into the country—this done to appease the hard right-wingers—the government unobtrusively lifted the ban with no public notice on these stated grounds: 'Mr. Michener's book is so poorly written that it does not merit banning. Nobody would bother to buy it or read it.' At the time this was said, scores of citizens inside the country were writing to me, saying how much they treasured the book because it spoke truthfully of a land they knew and loved. Strangers from foreign lands arriving at the big airport at Johannesburg carry the book with them, and write me a letter confirming or rejecting things I've said, and government inspectors know this. I expect that before I die I will be invited back to South Africa by persons aware of the wide readership the book has had and the good it has done, and if health permits, I will go.

But the incident that best illustrates the first reactions and later reassessments regarding best-sellers occurred with the publication of *Texas,* when three of the major opinion makers in the state simply tore the book apart with a viciousness I had never before experienced. They resorted to personal attacks, distortions of their own history and comments that had little to do with books or the exchange of ideas. I did not, in obedience to my long-established custom, read any of these character assassinations, but my wife and friends did, and they insisted upon sharing their outrage with me. I found nothing to complain of, because I remembered the admonition of my old mentor Hugh Kahler: 'If you spend 1322 pages saying what you think of Texas, they have a right to spend six pages saying what they think of you.'

Offsetting these public blasts were the hundreds of letters that came pouring in, mostly from Texans, assuring me that my novel was one of the finest depictions of their state ever published, and in subsequent years that chorus has continued until I had the quiet satisfaction of knowing that 1.3 million copies were in circulation and being avidly read. Under such circumstances it requires no courage for a writer to absorb initial attacks without complaint.

I must clarify one bittersweet aspect of my career. I have always been fiercely determined never to promote myself, or speak well of myself to others, or in any manner to inflate or excite public opinion in my behalf. A score of media people, after interviewing me, have said: 'Mr. Michener has only a modest opinion of himself and acknowledges that he is not a very good writer.' These have not been preposterous conclusions, for whenever I have been asked point-blank what I think of myself, I have shrugged, smiled and allowed the questioner to form his own opinion, and if forcibly pinned down for a statement, I have said: 'I know a score of writers as good as I am—I was the lucky one.' I cannot recall a single instance in my life when I have said that I deserved a higher assessment than the questioner was willing to grant. The most I have said has been: '*Toko-Ri* is a good short novel,' or '*The Source* was a massive effort,' or '*Iberia* may be around for a long time, not because it's particularly well written, but because it deals with one of the world's most exuberant civilizations.'

Newspaper and television people have described me as 'more like a small-town businessman or diffident professor in some minor college than an author,' or said: 'He shied away from any discussion of his merit, as if he knew his success was not warranted.' They mistook my courtesy to them for indifference, my refusal to blow my own horn for a lack of critical insight, but if they were misguided, the fault was mine, not theirs. My job has been to write books, not defend them.

XII

Health

ONCE WHEN I was knocking about Egypt I came upon an unusually gifted fortune-teller named the Princess, who startled people who ventured into her bar with the accuracy of her comment. She was a Gypsy-like woman in her late forties, very quick of mind and sharp of eye. Using an ordinary deck of cards, she asked her subject to cut them twice so that she would have no control of what they were about to reveal, and then dealt them out into six vertical columns of eight cards, placed so that every card was totally visible.

This meant that forty-eight cards were exposed and four were left over, and part of her skill was showing how she identified and used both groups. Before starting to lay out the forty-eight she told her eager subject: 'Since I want this to be your fortune, not mine, you are to stop me four times as I work, and we'll set the next card aside, face down like this, and at the end they will disclose the heart of your fortune.' Then she smiled warmly: 'Besides, that will make the other cards fall as you want them, not in the order I might want.' She said this with such a display of heartfelt honesty, as if duplicity were farthest from her mind, that she convinced her listener that this was going to be the most scientifically accurate and morally honest fortune he or she would ever be told.

She then launched into amazing revelations about the subject's past, present and future, and sometimes as I watched she would make a statement whose accuracy staggered her listener. One night when she was telling the fortune of an English sailor whose ship had either just passed through the Suez Canal or was about to, she said: 'Last week you had a marvelous adventure, young man. In Lourenço Marques you fell in love with a beautiful Portuguese girl, for whom you bought a fine gift. One of the best things you've ever done.'

'My God!' the sailor gasped. 'Who told you?' and with a smile that would melt an iceberg, she said softly: 'You did. The way you came to my table. You either found money you didn't expect or love. Lucky you,' and he paid her double for her happy insight.

After I had watched her for some evenings, she saw that I was more than passively interested in her skill, and my answers to her questions satisfied her that I too had concerns about her art and under my insistent questioning she revealed her remarkable system for fortune-telling.

'You can see that I have the subject cut the cards so that it'll be his fortune, not mine, and that I then arrange them—or rather he arranges them through his cutting—in six columns. These stand left to right, for Head, Heart, Home, Health, Wealth and Travel. The top rows in each column summarize the past, the bottom the future, and the group through the middle— part top, part bottom—the present. The four left over at the end, as you've heard me say, they're the heart of the affair.'

'But how does the fortune reveal itself?' and she explained: 'Certain obvious facts. Ace, King, Queen are favorable, Ace representing raw power, King masculine traits, Queen feminine. Anyone could deduce that. The two is bad luck, but the threes, though also negative, aren't merely bad, they're evil. The Jack really is a knave, but the tens are like a mother's love, great, solid and dependable.' She had comparable evaluations of the six less spectacular cards.

She then turned to the suits: 'Spades are power. Hearts are love. Diamonds are wealth. Clubs are the great contradictions of life, the complexities. Three of Clubs is one of the most powerful in the deck, ten of Hearts the most reassuring. I love that card and am always happy when it turns up in the right place.'

Tapping her table, she said: 'So there are your forty-eight cards in the order you determined, and here are the four secret ones,' and with that she began to run down each of the six visible columns, but not in order: 'Never allow the subject to see which column you're looking at when you say something. And of course, he's not like you. He doesn't know what the six rows stand for.'

With that, never allowing me to detect where she was looking, she began to tell my fortune, dealing majestically with past and present, with future aspirations and making unbelievably close guesses about many aspects of my life on which no one in that bar or in Egypt could have instructed her. Toward the close of a remarkable exhibition of insight, shrewd guessing and plain common sense, she pointed to the last vertical column, the one to the extreme right: 'As I told you, this reveals your Travel, past and future, but that includes more than just taking a plane trip or a hiking vacation. It means also your spiritual and occupational journey through life. It's a most significant column.' She then tapped the four additional cards, neatly stacked face down: 'They unravel the secrets of your most intimate wish. Make it, but don't tell me what it is. I mustn't be influenced one way or another,' and when I made a wish concerning a writing matter that I hoped would be settled in my favor, she turned over the cards, one by one and with extreme care to ensure that they preserved the order in which I had selected them. They were the Seven of Diamonds, the Jack of Hearts, the Nine of Hearts and the Three of Clubs. As soon as she saw them she grasped my left arm and said: 'My friend! Whatever it was you wished, cast it from your mind. For if it were to come true, it would devastate you—destroy you. Look at those terrible cards.' She did not explain where the terror resided, but I remembered what she had said about the Three of Clubs and any Jack, but she surprised me by saying as she gathered up the cards of my fortune: 'She would drag you through hell if you ran down that alley.' My wish had nothing to do with women, only a publishing problem, and I was about to tell her that whereas the main fortune was surprisingly apt, that revealed by the four cards had been totally irrelevant when I remembered that I had thought vaguely of a business association with a professional woman in New York and that if she did things her way I would be in trouble.

In later sessions my guide revealed some of her rules: 'Never burlesque the cards. Tell the subject whatever the cards indicate, no matter how ridiculous it may seem to you. Use any secret information your subject reveals, but don't try to base your fortune on being clever. Stick with the cards. They'll do your work for you. Remember that all human beings are vitally concerned with your six headings. "Am I bright enough to master the new job?" "Will she really love me?" "Is my home safe?" "Am I about to die?" "How in the world can I gain more money?" and for some curious reason I've never understood: "Will I be able to take a trip to get out of this damned place?" Provide guidance on those topics and you'll be a great fortune-teller.'

'I have no ambitions in that line,' I said, and she placed her hands on mine: 'Oh, yes, you do. I've never had a stranger sit in that chair who showed such interest. You could take my place at this table tomorrow and tell fortunes almost as well as I do.'

'How can you say that?'

She surprised me by saying: 'Because natural-born writers have to have the interest and insights that I do; if you didn't, you'd never be able to write much that's good.'

'How do you know I'm a writer?' I asked, and she said: 'With your degree of interest you're either a detective or an accountant chasing thieves or a writer.'

She then told me one of the great secrets of her profession: 'Never, never say anything as foolish as "You're going on a trip." You can't gain points that way. Always be specific and say, for example, "You're leaving for Cyprus on Thursday." '

I gasped: 'Why Cyprus?' for that was where I was going, and on Thursday.

'From things you've hinted I judged you were interested in the Bible and that you might be working in Jerusalem. Just a guess.'

'But why did you say Cyprus?'

She smiled: 'Because I know that with the Arabs and Jews mad at each other, you can't fly direct from Cairo to Jerusalem. You have to go through Cyprus. And Thursday? The Egyptian government doesn't give unlimited visas, and you've been here quite a while. Time to get out.'

When I had digested that, she said: 'Always remember how surprised the English sailor was that night when I told him about the Portuguese beauty in Lourenço Marques. Simple. If he was from a ship he was certain to be headed through the Suez Canal, going either back home or out to India or Australia. Why should I waste points saying: "You're going on a visit?" Of course he is, so pick something reasonable. He may stop over at Malta, or go on to New Zealand. Why not take a real guess at Mozambique, and if you do, go all the way and pick a specific city. Lourenço Marques is such a lovely pair of words. Use it. And there are always girls, of that you can be sure.'

Some years later my home district in Pennsylvania decided to launch an arts festival to run a weekend each summer, and under the enthusiastic guidance of my friend Bill Vitarelli it became an outstanding success, raising large sums of money for local charities. All citizens were urged to contribute some skill to the affair, and someone who had heard me speak about my experiences with the Egyptian Princess proposed that I tell fortunes at the festival. So a tent was procured and set up near the center of the grounds and in it I sat with my deck of cards and an outrageous hat and scarf that might, if the viewer were charitable, be considered Egyptian. Billed as 'Mitch the Witch' I followed my tutor's instructions to the extent that I remembered them. I asked the subject to cut the cards and to stop me four times as I spread them. The six columns were observed, with no spectator ever informed as to what the headings were, and with a certain confidence in my system of good Ten of Hearts, wretched Three of Clubs, I began to tell some of the wildest fortunes ever heard in rural Pennsylvania, featuring sex, criminal behavior, theft of documents and eloping wives.

Such fortune-telling became a sensation, and by sheer accident I hit just enough truths or near-truths to cause neighbors to tell others of the remarkable record I was compiling as a man who could really foresee past and future. It was then that I uncovered the real secret that the Princess had kept from me. In the course of telling a fortune the seer makes about forty-five separate statements, and at least thirty-five will be totally wide of the mark, but if he or she succeeds in the remaining ten to hit even one right on the nose, that is what is remembered, and the subject leaves the tent asking his friends: 'How could he have known that I bought stock in a dairy company?' It was a string of those lucky hits that established my reputation and began to attract clients from considerable distances.

In the process I discovered that one of the profound secrets of fortune-telling is that subjects want to believe what they are being told and will sometimes go to extreme lengths to make the prophecies come true. My reputation was sizably enhanced in the case of Mr. Kenderdine, whose Travel column showed much activity in the immediate future. Obedient to the counsel given me by the Princess I did not tell him: 'It looks as if you will be taking a trip one of these days.' Instead, I said: 'I see that you're heading for Omaha next Tuesday, and I'm glad to say that your business interest there will work out in your favor.'

The impact on Mr. Kenderdine was astonishing. He looked at me, shook his head in disbelief and walked off without telling me in what way I had struck home, but later I heard from many neighbors: 'That fortune you told Kenderdine. He did leave home Tuesday as you said. He did go to Omaha and things did work out favorably.' It seemed to me that such a threefold verification defied the laws of probability, and when I checked into what had actually happened I learned that his company had indeed sent Kenderdine west on business but to Kansas City, not Omaha. However, when he completed his work there he went, of his own accord, to Omaha, where he unexpectedly engineered a deal of some importance to his company, and when he returned home he told everyone: 'That fellow Michener is unbelievable,' and my reputation grew.

After I witnessed this phenomenon of the self-fulfilling prophecy several times, it occurred to me that the readers of serious fiction are much like a fortune-teller's clients: they are disposed to believe what has been thrown at them and unless the writer betrays them grievously, they willingly, and at times eagerly, go along with him. His task, of course, is to construct his narrative so that they can believe and to avoid with the most intense care any statement or situation that will awaken them to the fact that this is only fiction.

Never in my fortune-telling did I break one of the Princess's basic rules: 'Don't burlesque the system.' I told my subjects only what the cards revealed, which meant that I followed those cards wherever they led, and this faithfulness produced some of my most startling hits. One day at the festival there came into my tent a most beautiful young lady, obviously proud of her appearance and attended by three or four young men of about her age. She had come, they told me as I started to lay out her cards, from Somerville, a suburban town of some importance across the Delaware River in New Jersey.

She was one of those appealing subjects who seriously wanted her fortune told and leaned forward to hear every word. I instinctively liked her, not only for her beauty but also for her obvious intelligence, and I rather outdid myself in the completeness of my report. Her Head column proved that she was of more than average intelligence and that her ventures were sure to succeed for that reason. Her Home situation was good, and both her Health and Wealth seemed far above average. She had several interesting trips ahead, but when I reached her Heart column I saw fearful confusion, and when I studied more closely I saw that what had at first appeared like favorable signs in the Health column were actually signs of violent disorder that coincided at every level with equal disruptions in the Heart line. I cannot now remember what it was specifically that alerted me to a grave problem, but I certainly remember what I told her, for this became a subject of much conversation in the weeks that followed: 'Young lady! I see a most serious confusion in your love life. You are being pulled in contrary directions, and have been for some time, and unless you decide which of these fine-looking young men you really prefer, you're going to find yourself in serious trouble. And what gives me most concern is that this confusion in problems of the Heart seems to affect adversely your general Health, or well-being.'

The tent was silent. The young lady stared at me, then averted her eyes, and her male companions looked away. Rarely had I ever told a fortune that elicited such a downcast reaction, and as the young people filed out I felt that in some unknown way I had offended them all, but later one of the men came back privately to inform me that the subject I had taken to be a beautiful young lady was actually a professional transvestite who appeared in nightclubs and whose emotional life was, as I had detected, in chaos.

My fortune-telling, which was beginning to earn large sums for our festival, came to a bad ending. It was my custom, and that of many clairvoyants, I suspect, to draw back from reading the more disastrous combinations of cards, especially those that predicted impending death. I was not averse to telling a subject: 'You would be well advised to have that operation within the next two months. Do not delay,' and one of my loveliest experiences in what was becoming almost a trade came when I told a woman of ninety-one whose grandchildren had brought her into the tent: 'Madam, you will live to be ninety-seven,' because years later those grandchildren told me in a letter: 'One of the best deeds you ever did, Mr. Michener, was to tell our grandmother: "You'll live to be ninety-seven, so get yourself a new set of teeth and some pretty dresses." We'd been unable to get her to spend a penny on herself, because she kept telling us: "I won't be here long enough to enjoy it." You changed her entire outlook and she did get new teeth that gave her comfort and three new dresses, which she loved. She died at ninety-six, a dear and contented grandmother.'

The bad ending came abruptly. When a woman in her fifties sat across from me, I saw something I had never seen before: at the bottom of her Health line were the two and three of Clubs, at the bottom of Travel the two and three of Spades, the worst configuration possible. Before saying anything else, I told her with some force: 'Madam, you and your husband are driving to Iowa next weekend. I implore you, don't go.' She gasped, but decided to ignore my comment. She returned the next year to ask: 'Mr. Michener, do you remember me? Last year you warned me not to take a trip to Iowa, but we went, and the first night out our car was hit by a truck and my husband was killed.'

This, and other extraordinary coincidences that resulted from sheer guessing, began to make me think that what I was doing was irresponsible; it had become far more serious than just a silly game, and I realized that I had better quit the nonsense, because even if I refused to take it seriously, others did.

I was not allowed to quit entirely, for sometimes at parties my wife would casually tell of my exploits as Mitch the Witch and guests would importune me for an illustration of the system; I would be almost forced to spread the cards and run through my nonsense. At one such party in Hawaii the guest of honor was the famous industrialist who had taken up residence on Oahu, Henry J. Kaiser. As soon as he heard about my skill he revealed himself as a devotee of the art and insisted that I tell his fortune. When the cards were spread I saw an interesting configuration, and the first words I told him were: 'By next weekend you will have to arrange a loan of four and a half million dollars or you're going to be in serious trouble.' He gasped, and I was never to know how close I had come to the truth, but it was obviously what Navy people call 'a near-miss,' which sometimes does almost as much damage as a direct hit.

That night Kaiser adopted me as his local seer, and sometimes came to my apartment for readings, always calling on me at any social gathering for a quick look at the cards. He had at that time almost adopted a charismatic full-blooded Hawaiian tenor named Alfred Apaka, whose melodious records of island songs enjoyed a wide sale both in the islands and on the mainland. He had given Apaka, who sang with great success in Kaiser's big tourist hotel, a white Continental convertible, and sometimes the two men would arrive at my place so that Henry J. could have his cards read. One afternoon there was such a heavy concentration of bad news in the Health column that death was clearly indicated. This was not improbable, since Henry J. was in his mid-seventies and somewhat overweight, but I had an invariable rule: 'No matter what the cards say, never tell anyone he or she is about to die.' It was easy to pass this part of the fortune in silence, because I saw in related columns that it was not Kaiser himself who was doomed but one of his friends. It is to be expected that if a man is advanced in years he will have a few acquaintances older than himself, so with the constraint lifted, I said: 'Henry J., one of the friends you've cherished in the past is going to die and you will mourn his loss.'

A few days later, Alfred Apaka, a young fellow in full possession of his unusual powers, dropped dead and I told no more fortunes.

. . .

I have gone into this fortune-telling episode more fully than might have been expected because I wanted to make several points. Fortune-telling as the Princess taught me to practice it bore a striking resemblance to storytelling. In both activities one used observation, shrewd guesswork and the proper selection of emotion-laden words to create empathy. One also performed best if one relished the jovian exercise of moving mortals here and there on the chessboard.

There the similarity between my fortune-telling and my fiction ends. Never once, not even when I was reaping great acclaim as a seer, did I believe a word of what I told my subjects, nor did the Princess. We each had an animal type of cunning, seeing things that others missed. We had an overdeveloped sense of humor, and we loved the world's wild contradictions. In traveling about in various lands we had acquired an intense love of storytelling. But each of us acknowledged that what we did was nothing but delightful trickery.

Whenever others who believed in a world of spirits, gnomes and Tarot cards tried to enlist me in their crusades, and this happened often, I demurred. I was frequently invited or badgered to confess that I had supernatural powers, or was in touch with spirits, or had at some point been inducted into the world of black magic, but I was never remotely inclined to accept such nonsense and quickly dropped my involvement when others began to take fortune-telling more seriously than I did. I had no powers of spiritualism whatever. Tarot, I Ching and astrology disgust me, and I think that newspapers that publish daily horoscopes are enemies of sanity. When people ask 'What sign are you?' I cringe.

Because my mother must have had inadequate nutrition during her pregnancy with me, I was born with deficient bone structure, especially in my rib sections, and low levels of calcium in my teeth which made them weak. I also had severe astigmatism, which required frequent changes in the prescription of my glasses, once I began to wear them.

Otherwise I was gifted with a remarkably durable body that was able to withstand considerable punishment. Twice I walked completely across Scotland in two unbroken days, the first time covering nonstop a stretch of some sixty miles from St. Andrews toward Oban. I made similar tough journeys in Afghanistan and when hitchhiking across the United States. Three times I drove alone practically nonstop from New York to San Francisco, pausing alongside the road when I grew tired to sleep in the car. I was never a weakling.

Through a series of the most fortunate accidents I never smoked or drank, or ate harmful foods or experimented with drugs, so that my body husbanded whatever strength its genes entitled it to. It was mostly luck that determined these patterns, for without a father or a surrogate father in my home I might have fallen into bad habits. Fortunately, when I started hanging around Frank Mitch's enticing pool hall at an early age, two townsmen who frequented the place, Henry Ullman and Russell Gulick, took me aside and said: 'Jim, you're not the type of kid who ought to be here. You're better than this. Don't come here anymore, and don't fool around with cigarettes,' and I obeyed.

Shortly thereafter I fell into the hands of an excellent basketball coach, Allan Gardy, who had jumped center for Lehigh University. He was one of those foursquare men to whom everything was either good or bad, and he not only knew the difference but was also eager to tell others. Smoking was bad. Alcohol was bad. Fatty foods were bad. Girls were bad. Democrats were bad. The good things were manliness and basketball, and he offered instruction in each. Once on the night before a big game Coach Gardy peered in the window of a hot-dog stand that had introduced a new-style dog called the Texas Weiner at ten cents rather than the usual five. It was bigger, fatter and topped by a generous helping of chili swimming in heavy golden grease, and I had decided to try one.

Coach Gardy merely looked at me, his face full of disgust, and he passed beyond the window, leaving me to gag on the chili dog in my mouth. When I see my friends dying prematurely of emphysema, cancer, complications from obesity and alcoholism, I reflect on the great good my early instructors did me when they steered me away from destructive habits.

I was always careful to keep my body strong and healthy. I engaged furiously in games, became something of a minor star in high school sports, played semi-pro basketball for a while and on a championship volleyball team in New York gyms. In later years I played a tremendous amount of tennis, continuing the game well into my seventies. Above all, I walked, covering many miles each week no matter where or how I lived, and I neither stopped nor slowed down when I came into my mid-eighties. I have said with accuracy: 'Whenever my writing goes poorly, it's because I haven't walked enough at sunset,' because it is on those quiet rambles that I have not only cleared my mind and relaxed my muscles, but also contemplated the structure of what I wanted to write the next morning. The hundreds of characters whose lives I have reported lived those lives with me from seven to eight on summer and winter evenings.

I passed the first five decades of my life without physical incident except for a badly broken nose sustained on three different occasions when I was speaking when I should have been listening. A main difference between boys and girls is that no matter how tough a fellow may be, he is dead certain to meet, sooner or later, some other lad who is bigger and tougher, and in such humbling situations noses get broken. All my adult life I have had a difficult problem with breathing through my once-shattered nose, but I have also learned to live with my fellow men in relative harmony.

I also broke my right elbow in schoolboy roughhousing, and this had a curious effect on my athletic aspirations. Badly set by an inept doctor, it left me unable to use my right arm in a normal way and thus terminated my career as a pitcher in baseball. But it gave me a monolithic arm as rigid as an oak tree, and if I have never been able to scratch my right ear with that arm or develop a good forehand in tennis, I was able to shoot a basketball with great accuracy, no matter how many opponents slammed into my right, shooting arm, and because of its extraordinary strength I had a powerful backhand in tennis and an equally powerful shot to the undefended back corner of the opponent's court in volleyball.

I was fifty-three when I first met the famous heart doctor Paul Dudley White, who was then in his energetic late seventies. We were in Leningrad attending a meeting of Soviet and American private citizens and during a break he told me of how the American military at the close of World War II had handed him an extraordinary commission: 'They told me to assemble a team of heart specialists and go to the great air bases in Alaska, where young colonels who had served in the war were reporting for duty, doing a good job and then going out on the ski slopes and dropping dead. Terrible attrition of first-class men in their forties and fifties.'

Seeing that I had more than the usual interest in the subject, since I was the same age as some of the stricken colonels, he explained: 'We never found the exact cause, and we won't till sometime in the next century when computers can make sense of the reams of statistics we're gathering.'

'What did you find?'

'We found without question that seven factors—ultimately they may turn out to be seventeen—seem to produce killing heart attacks. The first four you can control. High blood pressure, elevated level of cholesterol, gross obesity and smoking. The last three are inherited characteristics, and you're stuck with them. Diabetes, a family history of father

or older brother dying prematurely of a heart attack, your somatotype.'
When I asked what that meant he said: 'It means body build. Bones,
muscle, chest structure, the whole mix. Three distinct types have been
identified. Ectomorph, the long, lean stringbean type like John Kenneth
Galbraith sitting over there on the other side of the table. They never
get heart attacks, or hardly ever. The round, pudgy type, endomorphs,
like Pierre Salinger. He's not a pound overweight. God meant him to
be that way, and his kind doesn't often suffer a heart attack.'

'What's the third type?'

He pointed directly at me: 'Mesomorphs like you. Heavy chest structure, arms attached somewhat like an ape, forward leaning as you walk,
big-boned, a throwback to primitive man. Most superior athletes are
mesomorphs, many powerful political leaders. Tense men who pay the
price with sudden heart attacks.'

I remember questioning him in greater detail because we had spoken
casually about the possibility of my working with him to write about this
fascinating subject, and at the conclusion of our meeting there in Leningrad I asked directly: 'Well, if I don't smoke or have diabetes and am
not overweight, and have a moderate cholesterol index and an extremely
low blood pressure, am I relatively safe?'

'With clear cause and effect not yet known, we can never give assurance,' he said. 'How about your father and brothers?'

'I've never known who my father was.'

'You could be at risk, and we know that you're an almost prototype
mesomorph.'

So I left him feeling somewhat vulnerable. Later I discovered that I
had not told him the complete truth about diabetes, not because I was
trying to hide something but because I was ignorant of the facts.

One afternoon when I was in my mid-forties I played in a vigorous
basketball game at the YMCA in Honolulu, and later, when I was about
to enter the shower room, I gave my left big toe a tremendous bang on
the raised doorsill. I thought I had broken the toe, and during the flight
back to New York the next night the pain became so unbearable that
the airline radioed ahead for an early morning ambulance to meet me
at the airport in San Francisco.

Suffering from the worst pain I had ever had, I was whisked to a local
hospital, where a clever doctor asked only four questions: 'Where were
you when you broke your toe?' At the Y. 'What time was it when you
broke it?' About five-thirty in the afternoon. 'Did you go out for dinner
that night?' Yes. 'How far did you walk to the restaurant?' About five
blocks.

The informed reader already knows the solution to this mystery, but I didn't. The doctor smiled at me reassuringly and said: 'I have good news and bad. The good is that your toe is not broken. The bad is that you have gout and you will have it for the rest of your life.'

He proceeded to give me a crash course on this dreadful disease about which those not afflicted have made many unfeeling jokes. 'It comes from an oversupply of uric acid crystals that your urine cannot dispose of. It's exacerbated by consuming rich food, heavy wines and champagne. Attacks come two or three times a year, and their severity can be lessened by not eating liver, brains, kidneys, heavy gravies or lima beans and by forgoing red wine and champagne. You can also help yourself by drinking lots of mineral water, which flushes away some of the uric acid.'

'About the pain right now. No cure?'

'Yes, I'm giving you these little white pills. Colchicine. You take one every half hour with plenty of water until you vomit. Then stop.'

The pain on my flight to New York was almost more than I could bear, and the colchicine treatment kept me close to violent nausea the whole way. In later days I consulted with other specialists and heard only confirmation of what the San Francisco doctor had said: 'It's a lifetime affliction. The pain is often unbearable. Make a little tent over your toe so that the bedcovers can't touch it. And take what comfort you can from the known fact that gout is the disease of geniuses.' One of the doctors read from a paper the names of great men who had suffered from the ailment. Statistically, at least, there did seem to be an affiliation between high-strung brilliant men and the disease, but since I was markedly low-strung and not close to the genius class, I found little comfort in that.

It is difficult to describe the awful pain of gout. Each of the periodic attacks continues in flaming flushes for four or five days, during which the sufferer is assailed by horrible thoughts of amputation, shooting off the inflamed toe and suicide.

Apart from the folklore concerning gout, the doctors also told me certain substantive facts: 'The villain in the foods that induce gout seems to be a complex compound called purine, found in concentrated form in surprising things like lima beans, anchovies and champagne. There's a simple blood test that warns about high levels of purines, and that's a signal to watch your diet. Incidentally, you ought to find a copy of the eleventh edition of the *Encyclopaedia Britannica*. It contains an entertaining essay on gout.'

When I consulted the remarkable essay, I learned about the famous men who had suffered from the disease, and it was an impressive roster, but it gave me scant comfort.

After my introduction to this disease I had four violent attacks in two years and thought that the rest of my life was going to be recurring hell, and I found what comfort I could in tactics devised by gout sufferers through the centuries: a stool to keep the toe elevated so that the throbbing diminished, drinking gallons of water to flush out the purines, and cutting away most of the front part of a shoe so that I could hobble about. And I did sleep at night with that little tent over my toe because I learned the truth of a famous description of gout: 'Even the fall of a silken handkerchief on a gouty toe produces pain unbearable.'

I had at this time a housekeeper who had a marvelous empathy for people in trouble, and it pained her to see me suffering. Calling upon old country remedies, she did what she could to help, and then told me one day: 'You know, I have a sister who knows someone who can cure gout.'

I visualized a witch with blood of newt and hair of newborn calf and told her: 'No, my doctor has it under control.'

'It doesn't look like much control to me,' she said as she huffed off, and some days later when the pain was at its maximum, she repeated sternly: 'I have a sister who can help you,' and in my despair I cried: 'All right! Call your sister!' That night an unusually beautiful young woman in her twenties came to my bedside and said: 'I work as a nurse for a famous doctor in Philadelphia, and his team has produced a cure for the gout.'

When I appeared before this miracle worker he said: 'We've developed within the past two years a drug that specifically cures gout. Work was done in Sweden by some clever men who hooked radio isotopes to the purines of lima beans and took x-ray photographs as they worked their way through the body. They found that gout is caused by the malfunctioning of a tiny gland others had overlooked and when our completely new medicine is taken, that gland is encouraged to perform its normal function.' He then handed me a small vial of pills and a prescription that would get me more at any pharmacy. The pills were called Benemid and the instructions were simple: 'One a day for the rest of your life. About every seven years a residue of purines will build up, and you'll have a mild attack, which you can handle with colchicine.'

Breathing free and smiling at the wonder-working sister of my housekeeper, I had one nagging question: 'All the books say that gout is caused by riotous living, rich food and excessive drinking of champagne. I've always lived on a simple Pennsylvania Dutch diet and I've never touched alcohol.'

He broke into a laugh: 'Throughout history the legend has persisted that gout is the disease of profligates. But all that time doctors knew that exactly half their patients were as abstemious as you say you are. We've never really accounted for this contradiction, we just called cases like yours "poor-man's gout" '

His predictions that day were completely accurate. One Benemid a day, no more gout, no necessity to restrict my diet and yes, every seven years or so I have a real toe-grabber, which I can handle by taking a minute white colchicine every half hour until I vomit. I usually start throwing up at pill nine, and thank my patron saints that my house-keeper had a sister who worked for a bright doctor who set me free from a terrible affliction.

One September afternoon in 1965 I finished a fine three-set doubles match with my longtime tennis partner, Mary Place, a wizard with the drop shot, went home, did a little work on a novel on the siege of Leningrad and went to bed. At four in the morning I was stricken with such a violent case of what I thought was indigestion that I telephoned a doctor, who said: 'Take bicarbonate of soda and call me in the morning.' I took the bicarbonate and I remember going into the bathroom shortly thereafter and seeing a ghostly figure staring back at me from the mirror. Feeling that I was about to faint, I said to myself: 'Come on, kid, pull yourself together. Not now. Not now,' and I made it back to bed. But the presence of a doctor was imperative, and when one arrived at a quarter to six he took one look, felt my pulse and called the ambulance.

'Heart attack,' he said. 'They often come in these early morning hours.'

When they studied the cardiograms, the hospital experts said it was a major myocardial infarction, meaning that the supply of blood to a portion of the heart had been cut off by a blockage of some kind in the blood vessels feeding the heart. Most men who suffer such attacks prior to the age of fifty die of them and those past fifty who do not get to a hospital immediately die, too, but the doctors said that in my case, although I was in my late fifties, an unusually strong physical condition and the fact that I had continued to exercise long past the time when most men quit had enabled me to absorb the effects of the massive attack.

This chapter is not intended to be an account of a heart attack; it is meant to offer an explanation of how health problems affect a writer, and this part of the story is quickly told. At the Doylestown Hospital in which my aunt Hannah had sometimes worked, skilled local doctors did what was necessary, and in their decisions they were assisted by Paul Dudley White, who flew down from Massachusetts as soon as he heard of my attack. When he came into my hospital room, it was as if we were resuming our conversation in Leningrad: 'Well, now you know how chances work out. Not a single warning indicator. But I'm sure that a man with a structure as tough as yours is going to survive.'

Those were words I had wanted to hear, and he told me: 'Jim, if you survived the first three hours, your chances are great for surviving the first five days. And if you survive them . . .' His voice trailed off. It was to be a step at a time. Then he said: 'In the old days we'd have made a basket case out of men like you. In bed most of the time. Never climb a stair. No big meals. Avoid sex. Become a vegetable out on the front porch. No more. When you get out of this bed, and I'm sure you will, I want you to do everything you ever did before. In moderation. But as returning strength permits, try everything. Because if you do drop dead, you were probably going to do so anyway.' He was not going to baby me and I was not going to baby myself.

Under his benign care and aided always by the good local men, I would recover, and travel several times around the world, play vigorous tennis again, write eight of my best long books, and serve the nation in a wide variety of fields. I would also refrain from ever losing my temper violently, or forging ahead when I suddenly felt tired, eating eggs of any kind, or whole milk or large amounts of cheese. And each day whenever possible I would take an afternoon nap and get to bed by eleven at night. It was a rigorous regime, which I followed to the letter and which has brought me both productivity and happiness.

But there was one moment in my recovery that terrified me, and still does. When I returned from the hospital after six weeks of relative immobility, I was careful to get back into my normal routine in easy steps, and on a day when I felt that I had regained my strength and my control I went into my study and picked up the pages of the Russian novel I had been working on before I was struck down. To my horror I could not focus on the material, nor could I recall where I had stopped in the narrative and certainly not where I had intended to go. Desperately I tried to make sense of the material, speaking to myself as I had that crucial night in the bathroom: 'Come on, kid, don't lose it here.' But the pep talk was to no avail. Some major change had taken place in my life and I left the study distraught.

For more than a week I lived in fear that I might never be able to regain intellectual control over my writing. When I regained some confidence I returned to my study only to find myself as blocked as before. The Leningrad novel on which I had done so much work was lost forever. Regretfully, but without self-pity, I closed the notebooks on which I had been working, put aside forever the chapters I had finished on the Leningrad book. Afraid that I might never write again, I applied myself to a slow, steady course of rehabilitation consisting of long walks with my dogs, care of the trees I had planted on the hill and a quiet resumption of social meetings with my supportive friends. One day I even guardedly tried some tennis with Mary Place, who must have known how important the effort was to me, even though I accomplished little. One of my doctors, hearing of this improvement, asked if I would help with one of his patients. 'Talk to him,' they begged, 'and tell him what Dr. White told you,' and I went to the hospital to meet with the patient.

He was, I recall, a graduate of Cornell and a ski enthusiast. Many years younger than I, he had suffered a major heart attack at a time in his life when I knew it to be extremely dangerous. Sitting in his hospital room, I said: 'Dr. White, the one who saved Eisenhower, told me that at the ages twenty to thirty, a heart attack is almost invariably fatal because the shock is too great for the heart to absorb. Thirty to forty it's usually deadly. Forty to fifty the odds are about sixty-five to thirty-five that it will be fatal. My age group, fifty to sixty, the odds favor recovery. And sixty to eighty, many men have heart attacks and don't even know it. Recovery time for them is about the same as with a bad cold.'

The Cornell man was not impressed with anything I had said, but he did ask casually: 'Why the difference in ages?' and I said: 'Because as you grow older the heart has experienced a lot of knocks and set up alternative feed lines against the day when something even harder comes along.'

'Did you have a bad one?'

'One of the worst, they tell me.'

'And have you recovered?'

'No. But I'm moving in that direction. If you take it easy, like the doctors say, I'm sure you'll make it, too.'

'I'll be back on the ski slopes within a month,' he said arrogantly, not even bidding me farewell and certainly not thanking me for my efforts in trying to help. He did go back to the ski slopes within the month and he did drop dead.

.   .   .

When the shock of not having been able to resume the work on the Russian novel and my fears of never being able to work again had been brought under control, I decided that the time had come for me to test the strength of my new heart and my reconstructed mind. I had always wanted to write about my deep affection for Spain and my appreciation of the slow, stately experiences I'd had there, and it occurred to me that I could work nowhere better in a test of my capacity than in the splendid country whose history and mores I had come to know so well.

As a young man, as I have said, I had traveled for a while with a group of bullfighters—one of whom was Domingo Ortega, who later became famous—and now I wanted to see Spain again, to run with the bulls at Pamplona and to make the traditional journey to Santiago de Compostela, the ancient holy site in the northwest corner of the country. I felt that if I could do those things comfortably, I could work my way back into a writing career. My return to Spain was a spiritual and physical pilgrimage of the utmost importance.

I was accompanied during parts of the extended journey by three delightful companions of former days: Robert Vavra, the distinguished nature photographer who would ultimately illustrate my report with his pictures; John Fulton, an American bullfighter who had taken his *alternativa* (bullfighting doctorate) in Seville; and Kenneth Vanderford, the bearded petroleum expert who looked exactly like Hemingway. We traveled everywhere and renewed acquaintances with men and women we had known years before. We went to Pamplona for the running of the bulls, and I recall a brush with death that I had miraculously survived. It was the result of an act of plain foolishness on my part. Because of my love of Spain and my acquaintance with bullfighters there and in Mexico, I had become an aficionado of Pamplona's famous festival in honor of San Fermín, a saint who had performed some holy act now forgotten. His day chances to be a remarkably lucky one, the seventh day of the seventh month—July 7—and this became the occasion of a grand eight-day festival in which at seven each morning, wild bulls are coursed through the narrow streets and alleys from the corrals at one end of town to the bullring more than a mile away. Brave young men run a few inches ahead of them. Ernest Hemingway's *The Sun Also Rises,* and especially the motion picture made from it with Tyrone Power, Ava Gardner and Errol Flynn, featured the festival in a manner that caught the fancy of millions, who dreamed of running with the bulls of Pamplona.

In my late sixties I had decided it was time for me not to watch but to run; I ran, it is true, but only briefly, for when the bulls bore down on me I would duck into the doorway of a hospital and stand there as the seven bulls went roaring past. Even watching from the safety of my doorway it was a thrilling experience, those great, deadly animals practically stepping on my toes as they flashed past.

The area just in front of where I stood is confined on the left by a long, unbroken high stone wall, and here the very bravest men run or congregate, because about every fourth year some errant bull, leaving the others, runs his left horn along that wall—*limpiando la muralla,* washing the wall it is called—and knocks men down, causing wounds and contusions. On the first three mornings of the festival that year I had comfortably made it to my safety spot as the bulls thundered past, but on the fourth morning one of the bulls washed the wall, became disoriented, veered across the narrow lane and killed a man not six yards from me. He then turned wildly and killed a second man, who fell at my feet. Now totally confused, he hesitated for a terrifying moment, his horns six inches from my chest, and then he snorted and galloped after his mates.

Three or four Pamplona photographers who were patrolling that spot happened to photograph the bull just as it approached me; they did not catch him at the point when he was closest to me but they did get stunning photographs of a confused bull facing a man who is standing very still. When we were in Pamplona years later and admiring Spaniards brought me their copies of *Esquire* with the series of photographs, I could not believe that it was I in that doorway or that the bull had spared me and trotted peacefully on.

I took the pilgrims' route to Santiago de Compostela, where I spent more than a week studying the great sculptures that grace the porch of the twelfth-century cathedral, and then in a surge of reassurance started to write the book of mine that will probably live the longest, *Iberia,* a testament to a land I loved and to my own regeneration. The book will live not because it's especially well written nor because I wrote it, but rather because it deals with a country that will always be of interest to Americans and Europeans from cold climates. *Iberia* is my letter of gratitude to my notable forebears: George Borrow, who wrote *The Bible in Spain,* one of the noblest of all travel books; Prosper Mérimée, who after the briefest of visits wrote his novella *Carmen,* and Georges Bizet, who set the tale to imperishable music; and Miguel Unamuno, the philosopher who wrote of Spain's attitude toward the world.

Iberia played a focal role not only in my rehabilitation as a writer but also in my introduction to the mysterious relationship between writer and reader. The book became widely used throughout the United States as a collateral text in the teaching of the Spanish language and culture, and in due course I began to receive a large amount of mail from readers who had either studied the book or taken it with them during a trip to Spain. So consistently were three episodes referred to that one might have thought they had been printed in red.

The first was an account of how English marmalade was made from Valencia oranges, a fascinating tale but in no way exceptionally told. The second was the amusing story of a Texas traveler eating potted pheasant that hadn't been well cooked—a mere bit of trivia, really. And the third was an account of arriving at dusk at a small Romanesque church in the tiny mountaintop village of Cebrero on the way to Compostela. I had taken some care in revising and polishing these paragraphs, but I never felt that I had accomplished anything special. Yet these were the segments of the book that readers referred to again and again, both in writing and verbally when I chanced to meet them.

The author is never a good judge of what he deemed inconsequential will be cherished by others, nor what successful passage he slaved over will be ignored. No better illustration of this can be found than in *The Source.* The novel contains one of the best bits of writing I've been able to do, the account of the impact of King Herod upon the Jews. It is an original and well-crafted book, but in all the years it has been in circulation not one reader has ever written or told me personally that he or she found the tale rewarding on a serious level.

But at the same time my readers were ignoring the fine story, they were settling like honey bees on a rose on a purely accidental thing I had more or less thrown into the book. Needing the name for a young Jewish woman involved in the story of King David, I vaguely recalled a biblical passage about the Brook Kerith, and I remember that even upon first reading I liked that name and thought it exceptionally attractive, although I had no concept of where the brook was nor of its significance.

Decades after first seeing it, the name came back to me and I christened my character with it, without giving much thought to the selection. But as soon as the novel appeared I began getting letters of inquiry about that lovely name, how I had come upon it and what its meaning was. Usually the writers said: 'We are naming our new daughter Kerith, and when she grows older we want to share your explanation with her.' In fact, I received so many such inquiries that I had to draft a form reply that went out to the parents of scores of little Keriths.

In the letter I said: 'Years ago somewhere in the New Testament I came upon the phrase "the Brook of Kerith" and obviously it stuck in my mind, for I went back to it when I needed a resonant name for my character. So your daughter is named after a beautiful flowing brook in the Holy Land.'

But my memory was poor and each word of my explanation was wrong. Nowhere in the Bible does the phrase 'the Brook Kerith' appear. However, the phrase 'the Brook Cherith' does appear twice in I Kings 17, verses 3 and 5, but obviously it is in the Old Testament, not the New; it was where the Prophet Elijah was fed by ravens during a time of drought, and it could hardly have been what I described as 'a beautiful flowing brook,' because the Bible says specifically: 'And it came to pass after a while that the brook dried up, because there had been no rain in the land.'

Embarrassed that I had misled my correspondents, I began to cast about as to how I had come upon that phrase I cherished, but to no avail. Finally, however, someone to whom I told the story informed me that the highly regarded Irish novelist George Moore, whose novel *Esther Waters* I had read with relish, had written a later novel, *The Brook Kerith,* dealing with the times of Jesus. I had looked into it after having liked *Esther Waters* so much; *Kerith* did not hold me, so I did not finish it. I then learned that Moore had stumbled upon the passage in Kings about the Brook Cherith, had liked the sound of the words and changed the *ch* to *k,* and so mysterious is the power of words that I have often wondered: would either Moore or I have lingered over this dried-up little rivulet had it been called *Cherith Brook* or even *Cherith Stream?* I doubt it. Half the charm of the name comes from the inversion of words and the other half from the unusual spelling; obviously Moore did not like Cherith, but spelled with a *K* it had caught both his imagination and mine.

I trust that any of the Keriths frolicking about as a result of my novel will paste this correction to the erroneous letters I sent to their mothers and fathers.*

When I recovered from the heart attack, I recovered completely, and with *Iberia* safely behind me as proof that I could work again, I launched into a concentrated regimen of travel, research and writing that resulted in many books. In my later years, because of accidents in

*In 1991 I received three letters from the 1966 crop of Keriths, women now in their twenties, asking me about the derivation of their name. And each year I hear from some family that is naming their newborn Kerith and seeks information.

the publishing business over which I had no control, my books sometimes appeared rather rapidly, but they were not written in haste.

A series of bucolic experiences formed my attitude toward what was
prolific and what was not. In 1976, when I moved to the Chesapeake Bay
area to attempt a major writing effort about that splendid body of water
and its surrounding villages, I had the good luck to rent a waterfront
cottage. I remember it with special affection because our backyard
contained a semistagnant pond occupied by two huge herons, Victor and
Victoria, whom we tamed as they prowled our waters seeking fish. They
were awkward but noble birds and we grew to love them as congenial
neighbors.

The front of the cottage was patrolled by the landlady's Irish hunting
dog, a rowdy beast named Brandy, who learned early on that at dusk
I could be counted on for a long walk through the woods. An amber-
colored beauty, she galloped at breakneck speed two hundred yards
ahead, then doubled back even faster to check up on my progress, then
would be off again. I used to become more tired from watching her than
from my own exertions.

During our walks I came upon an abandoned farm, which had behind
its crumbling fence a very old apple tree that reminded me of the one
that had been so important to me when I was a lad. I would consider
the large amount of work I was doing as an elderly man and contemplate
the charge of being overly prolific that was sometimes thrown at me. But
then the tiny library in which I was writing my novel about the Chesapeake provided a definition of what that word really meant. The room
I was in was lined with bookcases whose shelves were filled with complete sets of works by the great nineteenth-century novelists: Dickens,
Thackeray, Kingsley and, most formidably, Sir Walter Scott. Leaning
back from my typewriter and contemplating the massive array of
volumes made me cry: 'Get back to work, Buster. By those standards
up there you're positively delinquent.'

Anyone who cares about books and who strives to assess modern
trends ought to spend a morning in that little library. He or she will not
only experience a claustrophobic shock from being hemmed in by so
much literature but will also receive a refreshing reminder that the great
writers of the past were preeminently writers; they wrote books, enormous quantities of them, and their tireless efforts have enriched us.

But it was a small book on the shelves by a writer of no consequence
that provided the most help in defining 'prolific,' for it contained in
the rear pages an advertisement from the solid old London house of
A. & C. Black, proud holders of copyright on the still-popular novels

of Sir Walter Scott. Black boasted they could supply readers with six different sets of the complete Scott novels at 1915 prices, when the shilling was worth twenty-five American cents:

New Popular Edition	25 Vols.	6d [sixpence] each
The Portrait Edition	25 Vols.	1/- [one shilling] each
The Victoria Edition	25 Vols.	1/6d each
Two Shilling Edition	25 Vols.	2/- each
The Standard Edition	25 Vols.	2/6d each
The Dryburgh Edition	25 Vols.	3/6d each

That's a hundred and fifty different very long volumes kept in print* at prices that were substantial in those days, and there appears to have been a good sale for all of them. They must have made a brave display on a bookseller's shelves, and that's my definition of 'prolific.'

What makes my own output during these years of intense effort noteworthy was the fact that the books were produced while I suffered from an incessant, crippling pain. My left hip, probably as a result of my long hikes when I was young or my tennis on cement courts at an older age, had deteriorated so badly that the ball at the top of my thighbone and the eroded socket in my torso ground against each other without any protective lubrication. This grating of bone on bone produced not only an awkward stiffness when I walked but also an almost unbearable pain whenever I had to stand still. After as little as two minutes' standing erect, I simply had to move about, or preferably, find some place to sit. Miraculously, even two minutes off my feet alleviated the pain, but as soon as I stood again, it returned in redoubled intensity. Life with such constant pain was not pleasant, and trying to write under such circumstances required willpower. But I take the writing of books with deadly seriousness. It is a noble profession that seeks to both enlighten and entertain.

Now comes the part not easy to explain. When I started asking others about my defective hip, I rather quickly learned about the historic experiments of a Lord Charnley of London, who had cut into the hip of his first patients willing to act as guinea pigs, sawn off the top of the femur, replaced the ball with a steel one whose shaft was rammed down the center of the big leg bone. The deteriorated socket was also reamed

---

*Probably Black had only one, or at most two, different sets of printed sheets of the novels. They could slap on six differently priced bindings, adding a portrait of the author in one, illustrations in another.

out and replaced by a metal cup into which the new ball would snugly fit. *Voilà!* The patient had a new hip, which not only functioned perfectly but, what was equally important, without pain. It was a miracle operation and it performed miracle cures.

Why, if I was in such debilitating pain, did I not hasten to Lord Charnley and get myself a new hip? The answer is complex, and casts a considerable light on how I visualize the role and responsibilities of a writer.

I first heard of the Charnley operation when I was doing research in southern Spain on bullfighting and the production of sherry. Near Puerto de Santa María a congenial Englishman named John Culverwell had a *rancho,* on which he produced a fine brand of honey that he sold under the lovely trade name of Oropéndola (Golden Oriole). His petite English wife, Cecilia, had long suffered from the kind of worn-out hip that afflicted me and had been one of the first of Lord Charnley's patients. The operation had been a great success, but, as so often happens, the patient did not recover well. When I saw her she could not manipulate her new hip and the pain had simply shifted to new locations.

In my interrogations about this phenomen I conducted interviews with twelve friends who'd had the operation, and eight gave enthusiastic reports: 'The operation was a great success,' but there were another four like Cecilia Culverwell, who had dismal negative reports: 'It has never really worked.'

The chances, apparently, were two-thirds successful, one-third not, and since I had always been ready to accept such odds in whatever I did, why did I not go ahead with the operation? Well, among the eight friends whose operations had been a technical success were four who had suffered the most grievous kinds of unexpected side effects. One developed a horrendous thrombosis in the affected leg and nearly died. Another suffered a pitiful mental derangement. Another underwent a lingering attack of phlebitis, which incapacitated him. And the fourth simply deteriorated.

This meant that of my dozen friends four had failed to get relief in their hips, four had lost the capacity to work at a productive level, and four had had a total success. For a person like me who required maximum control over his mental processes, the odds seemed to be two-thirds negative, one-third positive, and those were odds I did not care to risk.

My thinking was clearly stated: 'I have a lot of books I still want to write, and I must not take unjustified risks that might render me unable to write them. I'm not required to say whether I'm a good writer or not. What I've proved I can do is an immense amount of demanding research and then whip it into such compelling shape that readers in many countries want to share my thoughts with me. I'm not willing to sacrifice that skill before I'm finished, and certainly not merely because it would relieve me of a little pain. Right now the odds against me are too great. Maybe later we'll do it, when the doctors have worked out procedures that produce better odds.'

On those firm principles, never diluted, I rejected the hip operation and proceeded to the task of writing the series of novels that would be accepted in many countries. But as a prudent man I consulted year after year with the best orthopedic surgeons in the world who always x-rayed my hip and kept me informed on the degree of its deterioration. They were a wonderful group of men, studious, informed and helpful. They all said the same thing: 'If I were you I'd have the operation right now. But if you can stand the pain you can afford to wait, because this operation works very well with people in their seventies and eighties.' None pressed me to have the operation and all said: 'Some morning you'll try to get out of bed, and your wife will call me and say: "Jim thinks you'd better do it now." ' One doctor said after looking at the x-rays: 'Good God! Are you walking around with that? I'd have had that fixed years ago.' But while I delayed, brilliant experimenters were coming forward with new improved techniques that necessitated less cutting and with extraordinary new metals for the replacement devices and new plastics with which to hold them in place. The odds I would face when I did have the operation had moved strongly in my favor, not the original two to one against, but something like ninety-eight to two in favor.

Because of this planned postponement, I wrote my major books while attacked by constant pain. On rising in the morning it would nag at me. Whenever I moved about the house pain would accompany me, and if I went out at night there it would be waiting in the street or in the assembly hall. Although it did not increase noticeably week to week, it never diminished. The problem became acute at dusk, when I took my walks, for I was never willing to surrender them; I needed the exercise and the spiritual replenishment that came with a romp with the dogs and the changing views of nature.

Sometimes when I left the house with my cane I would think during the first minutes: I can't go on with this. It's just too damned painful. But as I swung into the rhythm of the walk through the woods around the Chesapeake, or the roadways of Cape Canaveral when working on the space age, or the ranches of Texas or the mountain-rimmed streets of Sitka, Alaska, the grating bones would temporarily adjust to one another and I would return home actually delighted with how relatively painless the last portion of the hour-long walk had been. But an hour later the pain would recur.

I have been told that I have an unusually high tolerance for pain, meaning that it has to be fairly strong before I start to complain, and from a variety of experiences I judge this to be the case. Whatever the facts, I continued to work under the conditions I have described, and I would do so again rather than run the risk of a phlebotomy or a diminution of my intellectual capacities.

In 1985 I was confronted with a much more serious problem. Because the fine treatment that had more or less cured me after my heart attack had run its course, I found myself in an ambulance headed for a hospital in Austin, Texas, where a cursory examination showed that I had a dangerous blockage in five of the major coronary vessels that help the heart to function. At a bedside conference at five in the afternoon, I asked some questions.

'Is there any known fact in my case that might make a coronary bypass unusually dangerous?' There was none.

'How many of these operations have you men done before?' The team of four had considerable experience.

'How many bypasses do you estimate will be necessary?' They thought three.

'Is that standard?' Yes.

'Then let's go for it.' They did. They made not three but five eliminations of clogged veins, substituting fresh veins from my left leg, the one with the bad hip, and everything worked perfectly.

On the third day after the quintuple bypass I proved to be so unexpectedly healthy at age seventy-eight that I was encouraged to take a few steps in the hall, accompanied by a nurse, and as I did so I found myself facing a black man in his late thirties. With a big smile he asked me how I was doing and I was rather pleased with myself to be able to say: 'Just fine.' When the nurse and I returned to my room she asked: 'Didn't you recognize who he was?' and when I said no, she explained: 'That's the fellow who had the complete heart transplant. First time ever in this hospital. Twelve hours on the table and he's almost as good as ever.'

The black man and I became fast friends, working out together on the clever machines in rehabilitation, and he became the principal reason why I was never allowed to feel sorry for myself with my trivial little quintuple.

. . .

From the day I finished my first book, *Tales of the South Pacific,* I had always aspired to write a strong novel about Alaska. This stemmed from hearing my Macmillan senior editor, Philip Knowlton, recount his experiences in Alaska in the rough old days. Often in those and subsequent years I toyed with the idea of heading for the far north to tackle Alaska, but always refrained because I felt that at forty I was much too old to brave the horrendous low temperatures that Knowlton had spoken of. One phrase alone intimidated me: 'Jim, it got so cold and still at Fairbanks where I was that on a clear morning you could see the steam rising from the outhouses twenty miles away.' I was not ready for such cold, and since I would never write about any place I had not known intimately, I decided regretfully that my Alaska book would never be written, much to Knowlton's disgust.

But many readers, including officials in Alaska, kept sending me letters: 'You did good work for the South Pacific. You're obligated to cover the north,' and although I never changed my basic decision to avoid involvement in those Arctic lands, I did, when occasion presented an opportunity, route my journeys through Alaska so that I could familiarize myself with what has always been an exciting area for me. For example, when I was offered a fee to give the mid-year graduation address at the University of Alaska in Fairbanks during the middle of winter, I surprised the authorities by saying that I would do it for free if they could arrange a side trip for me to the newly developed oil field at Prudhoe Bay on the edge of the Arctic Ocean. They did, and in this exciting way I caught my first glimpse of that frozen sea; indeed, I walked out about a mile on it to see if one could spot from that distance the difference between land and sea, and I could not.

Equally rewarding was a hunting trip I took to Kodiak Island with my old friend from Korea, Admiral Perry, in search of grizzly bear, and I especially treasured the times my airplane on the way to my work in Japan landed at the incredible windswept base at Shemya Island at the far end of the Aleutians. Once during an enforced layover there, with fog so dense that one could not see most of the huts built at least partially underground, I gained a vivid insight into what warfare had been like in nearby Kiska and Attu, held by the Japanese.

But despite my growing knowledge about Alaska, I still considered myself too old at sixty to face the rigors of minus 52 degrees during an endless night. But as I approached eighty with a cleaned-out heart and a left leg that wasn't any worse than it had been for many years, I decided that if a man had always wanted to do something since age thirty-one and he was now close to eighty, it was time to get started. Once that decision was reached, I never reconsidered. Dispatching my energetic wife to find us a place to work, I remained in Texas to finish some writing I had started there and listened attentively when she called from Sitka to inform me: 'There's a wonderful log cabin on the campus of a small college here. Just right for us,' and promptly thereafter I was in Alaska launching what would turn out to be an entirely new life.

Ignoring all disabilities, I leaped into a travel program that would take me to almost every distinct region of the vast new state. To test myself I began with the toughest of all, the lands north of the Arctic Circle on the shortest day of the year, December 21, when the temperature was 52 below zero and the summer-resort hotel at Fort Yukon had only a meager supply of canned goods left over from September. It wasn't bad—the only part I disliked was the constant putting on and taking off of the five layers of clothing that such cold required, but when the temperature rose to minus 22 it was so congenial I went about in only a heavy shirt.

I loved Alaska: the terrifying solitude of the empty north, the lonely salmon fisheries of the farthest south, the gold fields on the Canadian border and above all that dramatic chain of little Aleutian islands reaching out toward Russian Siberia. Once when I was visiting Little Diomede, less than two miles from Russia's Big Diomede, I became so preoccupied with talking about books to the inhabitants and signing the surprising number of mine that they had imported for the long winter nights that I reached the shore to see, with horror, that my cruise ship had already sailed, with no other likely to come by for months. Fortunately some quick-witted Eskimos saw my quandary, revved up the outboard on their sealskin umiak and set out to overtake the departing liner. Someone on board spotted our little craft and asked the captain to slow down. I slipped the boatman ten dollars and was safely back aboard.

On that cruise we landed on eight different Aleutian islands, and on each I covered the last fifty yards wading through the surf. I flew to the most remote outposts, including a helicopter landing at the forlorn spot on the edge of Arctic seas where round-the-world aviator Wiley Post and his passenger, Will Rogers, had fatally crashed in 1935. I paused to collect seashore stones to outline his monument, as I had done with the lonely memorials of James Cook on a remote beach in Hawaii, Robert Louis Stevenson in Samoa, Pierre Loti in Tahiti, Ernie Pyle on the tiny island of Ie-jima near Okinawa. On other journeys and in other ways I had saluted the graves of Chopin in Paris, Henry Fielding in Lisbon, and Wladyslaw Reymont in Warsaw. I feel a strong affinity with men and women who have excited my imagination and always seek to pay them honor.

The move to Alaska was one of the most sensible I ever made, because it finally discharged an obligation to myself that I had ignored for many decades, but in my long walks around Sitka at night, including climbs up the hill from which Aleksandr Baranov had surveyed his domain when serving as governor of Russian Alaska, I began to experience so much additional pain from my hip that one night I had great difficulty in reaching my log cabin on Jefferson Davis Avenue, and when I finally limped into the room where my wife was waiting, I said simply: 'This is too much. Let's call the doctor.'

Once the decision was made to have the operation I made intensive inquiries and learned that since the early days when I had found that eight of my twelve friends had had negative results, procedures had improved radically. One expert told me: 'We've developed an entirely new approach. We don't make the steel inserts highly polished like before and then fasten them to the interior of the bone with a glue which, though powerful, does deteriorate in ten or eleven years. Now we make the steel as rough as possible, crisscrossed with reticulations, drive it home with no glue whatever, and invite the bone itself to grow into the interstices, locking everything together, forever.'

An impartial referee from a major center in Boston told me: 'The no-glue process seems to work well and promise an indefinite life. But we have no extended track record on it. We know that the present method of epoxy-fixed smooth steel works, but the hardened glue does ultimately begin to fragment and require replacement. We're advising: "If you're under age fifty, by all means try the new system and gamble on a lifelong solution. If you're over seventy-five, by all means use the old method, because you might get fifteen years of good use, and who cares after that?" When I asked about the fellow between fifty and seventy-five, he said: 'You toss a coin.'

When it came time to select the specific doctor to do the job, I was given more reassuring news by his nurse: 'Our man is remarkable. He's learned to cut your entire hip apart without damaging muscle. You won't believe how quickly you'll be out of bed, and when you get home you'll walk without crutches—all you'll need is a four-legged walker.'

I had the operation in Miami, where flat land and kindly temperatures would encourage me to walk long, easy miles in rehabilitation. I chose the old-style, smooth steel insert and lots of epoxy, and the second night after the operation I was taking cautious steps to the commode in my bedroom with the assistance of my wonderful four-legged helper. The male nurse said: 'Mr. Michener, you have no idea how people suddenly get up and walk when they see me coming with my bedpan.'

An unexpected bonus from the hip operation was the beautiful Haitian nurse who helped me recover. She was a splendid example of those numerous young Caribbean women who come to the United States and help us keep our hospitals open. As I lay immobilized I was planning a novel about the Caribbean, and she served as a prototype for the most engaging heroine in the book, Thérèse, the Haitian graduate of Radcliffe, who dominates the final chapter.

When I left the hospital after ten days, riding home in a car I could have driven myself, I quickly resumed my long walks on level ground as planned, but lengthened them to a mile each night. As I was correcting this manuscript I calculated that at least five nights a week for four years would be more than a thousand nights, a thousand miles. Yes, on my new painless hip I've walked that much and I suppose I shall maintain that pace for as long as I am able, for my writing does not go well when I am totally sedentary.

I have belabored this matter of health because I wanted to encourage others who suffer disabilities to keep striving for a productive life. I felt that if they knew I had written most of my long, demanding and essentially optimistic novels while suffering intense pain they would realize that it can be done. I do not consider my behavior unique because I know of many men and women nagged by physical impediments who succeed in forging ahead.

How long can a healthy person continue working in the arts? Titian and Verdi were both active until eighty-eight, and Hokusai said when approaching ninety that if he could only live a little longer he might really learn how to draw. I have no aspirations of such a long working life, but I often reflect that had I lived two hundred years ago I would probably have died in my forties. When someone asked the other day if I had any more books I'd like to write, I replied: 'About thirty. But if it takes three years to write one of the long ones, that would advance me to the age of a hundred and seventy, and history is not replete with examples of men or women who have continued writing to that age.'

Many years ago a well-intentioned friend asked my wife: 'Why doesn't your husband retire?' When Mari asked: 'Why should he?' the friend said: 'Because then he could travel and meet interesting people,' and Mari whispered to me: 'We mustn't tell her that's what you've been doing for half a century.'

Of course one's health is a limiting factor, and if one receives a genetic inheritance that is heavily flawed, creative work can become impossible. I believe I have accepted the body I was given, protected it sensibly and worked with it about as well as could have been expected, but I have never pampered it.

My life-style and intense work habits have put me at risk, especially in the degree of nervous tension they might inflict. But instead of trying to avoid tension, I have sought it out because through the years I learned that if I started my morning's work in a lackadaisical mood nothing I wrote was worth a damn; it was only when I tensed myself for the day's task that things went well. If I have paid heavily for this self-imposed risk it is an option I would repeat three times over if I had three lives to live.

The other day I heard the distinguished political adviser Clark Clifford, who must himself be over eighty, say: 'If you're past eighty and you wake up in the morning with no pain anywhere, it means you're already dead.' And it occurred to me that the appropriate heading for this chapter might well have been 'Slouching Toward Euthanasia.' I have strong feelings on that subject; having watched several close friends die anguished and prolonged deaths, I have given strict instructions: 'I am in favor of allowing totally helpless and lost persons, including me, to seek the help of friends in ending their meaningless misery. But I do not want on my board of review any book critics, people to whom I owe debts, or conservative Republicans.'

XIII

Wealth

*H*AVING BEEN unusually frank about the fourth column of my fortune-telling system, Health, I shall try to be equally so with the more sensitive column Wealth. Memoirists usually avoid this delicate subject, but because of my good luck I have so often been accused of writing for money that I simply must clarify the record. My atypical background dictated that money—or the lack of it—would frequently be the bones and marrow of my existence, and although I seem never to have handled it well I have at least tried to be sensible in the way I have used it.

First let us establish the intellectual basis for my attitude toward money. In my youth I had the good luck to become acquainted with the work of an English novelist well known at the time but whose reputation has somewhat withered. George Gissing, born in 1857, was a young man of considerable talent who wrote half a dozen books of high caliber; they were a little advanced for me, but I plowed through two of them. I read somewhere that he died prematurely in 1903 at the age of forty-six as a result of extreme privation, due to his never having been able to earn a decent living. In his best-known book, *New Grub Street*, which dealt with London's literary world, he spoke of the humiliating lives men lived when they had writing talent but achieved only limited or no financial success, and somewhere he uttered a cry from the heart to the effect that every writer would be better off if he could but have an assured income of a few hundred pounds a year. His story played an important role in my life.

While steaming to Alaska on the cruise ship *Royal Princess,* Captain John Young invited me to dine at his table. At dinner another guest at the table asked him: 'Where are you from, Captain?' When he said: 'Bristol, England,' a surge of memories flooded my mind and I blurted out: 'St. Mary Redcliffe.'

The captain stared at me and asked: 'How do you know that church?' and I referred to the incident that had made it famous in English literature: 'That's where the chest of manuscripts was found.' He said: 'It was, indeed.' Someone at the table asked what we were talking about and I answered: 'Chatterton,' and the captain said: 'Yes. He is the ghost of St. Mary Redcliffe.'

Now our table was really curious, and when questions were asked, Captain Young pointed to me and I said that like many others of my generation I had long been under the spell of the doomed English poet Thomas Chatterton, who was born in 1752 and had a tempestuous life of eighteen years; I went on to explain: 'When Thomas Chatterton was just a boy in Bristol he became infatuated with the Middle Ages and while rummaging through the long-forgotten rooms of St. Mary Redcliffe, the main church of his city, he came upon an old chest containing very ancient parchment documents. On the spot he conceived one of the most famous—or infamous, if you wish—literary forgeries in history. Using the old paper and what he conceived to be old-style ink, he created an imaginary fifteenth-century monk named Thomas Rowley and wrote several poems that he attributed to him.'

'Did he get away with the fraud?' a listener asked and I pointed to Captain Young to finish the story: 'He was most precocious, had written first-class religious poems at ten. His Rowley poems were very good— excellent, in fact—but when experts began to examine them they quickly saw that whereas the paper was authentic, the ink, capitalization, spelling and general style were suspect and the deception was easily unmasked. But in Bristol he remains a hero.'

Our listeners wanted to know how the affair ended and I happened to know, for a very good reason which I would reveal later: 'Putting aside the forgeries, which had brought him fame, he went to London to be a poet in his own right. He had success but no money. Living in a garret, he wrote frantically but could find no publisher, no purchasers. Alone with no friends and no food, this young genius took arsenic and died.'

Captain Young broke the silence by asking: 'How do you know so much about Bristol and Chatterton?' and I replied honestly but with some embarrassment: 'When I was eighteen, his age when he died, I came upon the story of his life in the library stacks at Swarthmore College and was so deeply moved that I ignored all my studies and began to write a play about him in blank verse. I found an etching of St. Mary Redcliffe as it had been at that time and I imagined every stone, every cranny in the old building. I can still see my Chatterton with the brassbound trunk.'

'What happened to your play?' someone asked and I said: 'I learned that I wasn't quite ready for such a task,' and laughed, 'My second attempt to be a writer and my second failure.' When someone wanted to know what the first attempt had been, I said: 'When I was about eight I was desolated to find that the honorable Trojans had lost their war to the dishonorable Greeks, and I became so outraged at the unfairness that I took two notebooks and rewrote the entire ending of the *Iliad,* giving what-for to Achilles and his bully boys. But I wasn't ready for that job, either.'

Gissing's *New Grub Street* poses the question with harrowing realism: How can the serious artist earn enough money to live? I would suggest that all graduate schools of writing recommend this worthy novel to their would-be authors. It is obligatory that beginners know what can happen to men like Chatterton and Gissing when they earn nothing; my knowledge of what transpired* in their tragic lives colored the rest of my life because it reinforced what I already knew. As a baby I lived in a family of women where money, or the lack of it, was a daily problem. My mother, Mrs. Mabel Michener, of Doylestown, Pennsylvania, made

---

*When a friend sought a blurb for his novel, I wanted to contribute a touch of class and wrote: 'This fine novel explains what transpires on a hot Saturday afternoon.' His editor replied: 'I fear you do not know the meaning of that word,' and when I checked, I didn't. *Transpire* and *perspire* are cousins. On that hot Saturday a man who sweated through his pores *perspired.* If the moisture seeped through his skin he *transpired,* hence the second meaning *to leak out later:* 'In the next week it transpired that she had stolen the $5,000.' However, a big new dictionary that came out shortly thereafter listed this third erroneous meaning "to occur, to happen" with the note: 'As used by J.A. Michener' and when the next big dictionary appeared, my usage was listed in first place, but with a long note to the effect that purists still avoided it. Since I am the patron saint of the new definition, I try to flaunt the word at least once in each of my books.

her living by taking in orphaned children, for which the social services of the time paid her a pittance, and doing other families' laundry, for which she received even less. The family I was reared in usually had four or five and sometimes as many as six other children. Food was not plentiful. In some years even Christmas was a bleak affair, but there was abundant love, and although as a reasonably intelligent child I was aware that other children received many things denied us, I never brooded over the fact that we were deprived.

The chief characteristic of my childhood, and later too, was constant moving from one low-rent house to another, and I can recall with infinite and exact detail each of eight different houses we occupied on seven different streets. I remember moving at night to escape some problem or another, and at midday with someone yelling at us, and at all other hours of the day. We did not improve our lot with each move, but we didn't diminish it either. We moved laterally, you might say, and someone researching that period on his own has recently come forward with an explanation that, hearing it as I did in my eightieth year, seems reasonable: 'A man who owned a lot of houses allowed your mother to shift from one to another in order to clean them up and make them presentable to would-be renters. For doing this, she got to live in the various houses without paying rent.'

I know a lot about the laundry business because it was my job to visit the neighbors who used my mother as their laundrywoman and pick up the bundles of dirty clothes. I was also intimately acquainted with the man who came to Doylestown on the trolley car from Philadelphia bringing with him cloth sacks filled with unfinished shirts, with small bundles of buttons tied to the side. My mother finished sewing the shirts and then attached the buttons, but she often ended up with a few more buttons than needed, and these she kept in a quart jar with a green lid. The earliest memory I have of games is playing with those buttons, which I arranged in a hundred different patterns. I have often thought that my love of geometry and maps stems from those games with vari-colored buttons, for they introduced me to an appreciation of spatial relationships. To me, even today, a jarful of mixed buttons is a symbol of home.

The point is that from as far back as I can remember I knew that a lack of money was a terrible affliction and one from which some families never recovered. We had none, never a spare nickel that I can remember, but I have related how Uncle Arthur who had a job did bring us that Victrola and the Red Seal records, so there were days of celebration and nights of music that I have never forgotten.

However, the normal childhood presents did not come our way, and it is important in view of later developments to understand what I did not have. I never had a wagon, or a pair of roller skates, or a baseball glove, or a tennis racket, or a radio, or a bicycle, or a pair of ice skates. I never had more than one good suit, and it had to last years, or more than one pair of shoes, and I can reconstruct as if it were yesterday my reaction to this deprivation. I listened to my mother explain why others could have these things but I could not, and with an act of will as powerful as a steel bear trap snapping shut I simply closed my mind to them. I never longed for a bicycle, because bicycles did not exist. I never regretted my lack of roller skates, because there was no sensible reason why I should ever have had a pair. I wiped the slate completely clean, leaving myself about as unacquisitive a child as one could imagine, and later, when other boys tried so hard to get hold of automobiles, I avoided the problem completely, because since such vehicles did not exist, I had no longing to have one. Even today I am bored by Olympic ice-skating because eighty years ago I satisfied myself that there were no skates.

Obviously I did myself psychic damage by adopting this evasion but just as obviously I learned to live with whatever dislocation it caused, and this will be important when the subject of real money comes up, for I would be just as rigorous in dealing with it as I was in dealing with bicycles. I have never in my life applied for a job, never asked for a raise, never worried about comparative salaries or purchase prices for my work or royalties paid for my books as compared to those paid for someone's else. I have been able to banish such subjects from my mind, but I have never been indifferent to just rewards for work I've done. I demand them, but allow others to make the determinations as to how much and when I should receive them, and whenever I have accidentally acquired money that came to me in some process that I did not respect or did not initiate, I have given it away before nightfall. Again, I have probably paid a high psychological price for this attitude, but to lament it is to ignore the more important fact that I never had any other option. Once one determinedly establishes a mindset that automatically eliminates unpalatable facts, it will continue to operate regardless of time or tide, and such damage as it may commit is offset by the ease of mind that one enjoys.

If I failed to receive the customary presents of childhood, I received almost by accident certain others that provided wondrous compensation. One bleak Christmas a gentle-hearted woman who barely knew me summoned me to her home to give me the only present she could afford, a slim cardboard box with a flap lid containing a sheaf of used carbon paper. She showed me how to use this magical stuff, and I spent all that Christmas enraptured with the idea that a person could write a sentence and have it duplicated endlessly. That seemed so amazing that I am still delighted when I open one of those slim boxes with flap tops and see the glistening black carbon with which I can do so much good or so much damage.

At a surprisingly early age I received another present whose value was incalculable. Two delightful, soft-spoken sisters, the Misses Price, opened a small library in our town, and it is a matter of record that the two children who first applied for cards were Margaret Mead and me. We used to meet occasionally as we came in to take out our next armful of books, and I remember the elder Miss Price saying one day: 'Goodness, Margaret and James, I believe you've read all the children's books we have. If you wish, you can start on the other shelves,' and in that way both Margaret and I were reading advanced adult books before we were eleven. No bicycle, but all the great books of the world! What an uneven exchange, what a benefaction to a boy with no money!

The second unexpected gift came somewhat indirectly. A slick salesman in Detroit, where my aunt Laura taught school, conned her into buying a complete bound set of Balzac's novels in translation. I suppose she had been assured that reading them would make her a cultured woman and possibly enhance her chances for a promotion in the Detroit school system. If that was the pitch, it worked, because she rather quickly became principal of a school. But to me the important part of the story was that she boxed up the forty-odd handsome volumes and shipped them to our house, so that before I was twelve I had read *Le Père Goriot, La Cousine Bette* and all the novels involving Rastignac, whose journey from the provinces to Paris set me to imagining an American Rastignac, me, hiking off to New York. No skates or bicycle but the complete *La Comédie Humaine*! The Muse Thalia herself must have arranged that exchange.

Since my mother worked so unceasingly, it was natural that I would want to help, and at the age of nine I took my first odd job. Those were the days when chestnut trees flourished in America before the remorseless blight killed them all, and as children we knew where in the woods all those beautiful trees were. They were tall and branchy and laden with those prickly golden burrs inside which lay the kernels of sweet, nutty goodness. We used clubs to knock them out of the trees. I gathered them to peddle through the neighborhood, and these chestnuts were so rich and mealy when boiled that I had no trouble selling them. Almost every household to which I went was so eager to buy that during the season I made a substantial and steady amount of money.

My first regular job came at what must have been age eleven. I rose at six each summer morning, walked the two miles out to the Burpee Seed Farm west of town and labored—and I do mean labored—from seven in the morning till five in the afternoon, six days a week, for seven and a half cents an hour in the hot sun cultivating phlox, a miserable flower of varied colors whose seeds were apparently sought after by amateur gardeners. I have sown phlox, thinned phlox, hoed phlox, gathered phlox and heavens knows what else, and if my birthday were tomorrow and someone were to give me a bouquet of the horrid flowers, I would punch him in the nose. Ten hours a day times the meager pay made seventy-five cents a day times six days a week yielded the very real sum of $4.50 a week, and since we worked at our phlox some fourteen weeks, it can be seen that I earned a real salary—$63.00—all of which I gave to my mother, who was generous in giving back small sums for things I needed.

At a very early age I was apprenticed to a plumber who kept his gloomy shop in the cellar of Barrett's Hardware. I worked there for real wages all one summer, and it began to look as if I might quit school and become a plumber, because I showed aptitude for the work. I was especially good at using a long-handled wrench to bend water pipe to the needed angle, but the thing I remember most about the job was that our noon break for a paper-bag lunch ended when the one-o'clock trolley car to Philadelphia came down the hill past our workshop, and I can still rattle off the schedule of that trolley which ran at thirty-six-minute intervals starting before dawn and ending at one in the morning: 1:00, 1:36, 2:12, 2:48, 3:24, 4:00. It seemed quite wonderful to me that after five trolleys had passed, the sequence of minutes repeated, and any one of the numbers remains a very real thing to me. It was the 8:12 and could be nothing else.

My apprenticeship to the plumber ended dramatically. When Uncle Arthur came home for one of his regular visits and learned that I might quit school in favor of plumbing, he put his massive foot down and insisted that I quit the job instantly: 'James, you were not intended to be a plumber.' That was all he said, but he said it repeatedly, the last time with tears in his eyes. In later years when plumbers were doing exceptionally well and as an underpaid teacher I wasn't, I often wished that he had left things alone.

I have only the warmest memories of being a paper carrier. From the seventh grade through the twelfth, I rose at four, had a quick breakfast and hurried down to the newspaper stand run by Kenneth Rufe to which he brought in his small truck the Philadelphia morning papers that had been delivered to the Reading railroad station at the southern end of town. The five of us boys would sort the papers into the proper piles, jam them into the canvas shoulder bags he provided, and go through the sleeping town to place them on the front doorsteps so they would be available to the citizens at breakfast. Since at one time or another I served each of the five routes, I came to know the occupants of every house in town—yes, every family name in every house—and I can still remember the residents of certain entire streets that I had served the longest. My paper routes gave me an insight into the complexity of life in a small town that not many boys acquired: I knew who had committed suicide; who had eloped; whose business was in trouble; where the mortgage was about to be foreclosed; and where the attractive girls lived, but that last was inconsequential because I considered all girls attractive.

In those years Philadelphia had six outstanding newspapers, five in the morning and the great *Philadelphia Bulletin* in the evening. I lived with those papers, and still remember the keen joy I found in the musical criticism of Samuel Laciar in the *Ledger;* in fact, I rather fancied myself as a typical reader of the *Ledger,* which was favored by bankers and judges, and would have been appalled had anyone predicted that when I grew up I would prefer the *Record,* that radical rag whose editors seemed always to be in trouble.

On Saturdays, I worked for Nick Power, the charismatic manager of our local Strand Theater, delivering handbills advertising forthcoming motion picture attractions, and I remember with warmest affection lounging in the upstairs office when work was done and reading the lurid promotional material that arrived two weeks before the films themselves came up on the train. It was then that I gained my first insights into the motion picture industry in which I would in later years participate substantially, and I judged it then and forever after from the exhibitor's point of view. I sympathized with one distraught theater owner who'd had bad luck with a chain of historical dramas that no one really wished to see. In despair he wrote to his central distributor: 'Don't send me no more of them pitchers where the hero writes with a feather.'

I did not get paid for distributing the handbills; instead I was allowed to see movies free, and it was from that beginning that I acquired my passionate devotion to them. My knowledge of movies at times has been almost encyclopedic, but what I remember most fondly were the improbable Saturday afternoon serials. I discovered that the secret of a good serial was to present in the first of the fifteen episodes a hero so gallant, a heroine so vulnerable and a villain so dastardly that the children would keep coming back through the next fourteen episodes to see how the good characters survived and I recall most vividly one opening episode that demonstrated the formula for drama.

The director, wanting us to understand that the black-suited villain was really a villain, showed him performing three vicious acts: he kicked his dog, he struck his mother, and looking for a piece of paper on which to write a ransom note, he tore a page out of the Bible. Oftentimes the writer, also, cannot anticipate which of his signals is going to be picked up by the reader, and while three such deplorable acts may seem excessive, sometimes a little repetition is justified to assist those who are a bit slow to catch on.

The other day I recalled with extraordinary clarity a sermon that I must have heard when I was nine or ten, because I was old enough to understand and savor every word in the text on which the sermon was based. On a wintry day I was the only child who accompanied my mother to the Presbyterian church—which we attended because Doyleston at that time had no meeting that we could go to as Quakers—when the Reverend Steckel was giving either a pre- or post-Christmas homily. He began in an unusual way, not by reading the text from the Bible but with a short preamble: 'We've had a tragic death in our Congregation, a young boy cut down in the morning of his life, and I do not want this grievous incident to pass unnoticed or to have its meaning lost as we resume our holidays. I am therefore taking my text from the very end of the Christmas story as told by Saint Luke, Chapter 2, Verse 19,' and with a consoling voice I can still hear, he read: 'But Mary kept these things, and pondered them in her heart.'

He then proceeded to say how the birth of Jesus had been of the greatest significance to Joseph, and the shepherds, and the three kings from the Orient, and especially to King Herod, who was so afraid of what the child might signify that he would order him slain, but Jesus was of special concern to Mary, who said nothing but who listened to all the rumors about what might happen to her child and kept them to herself. Steckel said that the women of Doylestown were like Mary. They wondered constantly about what might happen to their sons, but kept their secrets and their fears and their hopes to themselves: 'Like Mary, they pondered these things in their hearts.'

He said a good deal more that sad morning, and I cannot now recall how he developed his main points, but his message seemed to have been composed for me alone. It was a revelation of the relationship between mothers and sons and a challenge to me personally to make something of myself in order to put my mother's fears at ease. It was probably the most meaningful sermon I would ever hear.

My next job was one that put to the test the resolutions I made at the conclusion of Reverend Steckel's sermon. It was an experience straight out of Charles Dickens. In our town there was a lawyer who represented the trolley-car company whose one o'clock special had summoned me back to work in the plumbing shop. Someone had told him that I was a good worker and the son of a worthy widow, so he asked me if I would like to have a job at the company's famous entertainment park, Willow Grove. In those years, throughout the nation, many traction companies, as they were called, purchased large acreages some distance from the center of their city and built amusement parks featuring wild rides, carousels and hot-dog stands. The main purpose, obviously, was to lure city dwellers to spend the fare out to the park and back, but Willow Grove was special in that it provided not only cheap rides and food but also four free concerts a day in a fine bandstand by a lake. To the podium came the great names of American popular music at the time: the suave Victor Herbert, the bumptious Giuseppe Creatore and the imperial John Philip Sousa, plus classical musicians of high merit like Wassili Leps, who appeared between the popular heroes to play Beethoven, Johann Strauss and Lehár.

Elsewhere I have told of my adventures in this scintillating arena and of my youthful friendship with Herbert, Sousa and the musicians from the Philadelphia Orchestra who played there to pick up summer income. My concern now is with finances. My introduction to the underworld structure of this great amusement park, thought by many to be the finest and best run in America, was an eye-opening experience for a boy of fourteen, which is what I was when I reported for work as a cashier for one of the rides.

The system was simple. Park management paid mature men who specialized in the work fifteen dollars a week to serve as cashiers on amusements that took in thousands of dollars a day with the implicit understanding that these men would be permitted to steal as much as possible from the unsuspecting public. If a woman put down a two-dollar bill, then in heavy circulation, the cashier quickly handed her change for one and rushed her along before she realized what had happened. A skilled cashier at a busy ride could pick up forty or fifty dollars a day in what was known as 'honest stealing'—that is, from the public—and a good deal more in 'dishonest stealing' from the company. The really fine cashiers, those upon whom the park depended, stole only from the public. What the other more unscrupulous cashiers did was appalling. They resold tickets supplied them furtively by the men who collected them; they finagled the receipts from the turnstiles; they charged double and treble what they were supposed to and pocketed the difference; and in ways that only the most ingenious thieves could invent, they stole from everybody. For those rewarding and criminal opportunities, mature men would ride miles each day for an official salary of $2.14 and go home at night with as much as a hundred dollars.

I was afraid to steal from the company, but by the end of my first summer I was one of the more adept shortchange artists, so skillful that I felt confident of taking something from one person in four who bought tickets from me. But during my second year, when I was fifteen, I had a midnight experience that led to making me more cautious in my business dealings. As I was leaving the park a man loomed out of the shadows—one of the ticket takers at the ride I was then serving. He had in his hand a wad of the numbered tickets I had sold that day and he had collected, and his proposition was simple: 'You substitute one of these from time to time tomorrow, and the numbers won't show on the amount you have to account for. At the end of the day you'll have a nice surplus, and we'll split, fifty-fifty.' The tickets he slipped me represented sales of close to fifty dollars, and if the plan worked, we'd each get twenty-five. The next day the plan did work, and that midnight we split the take.

But about this time the park, in order to keep what it recognized as considerable theft under control, arrested one of the men who stole the most blatantly, and the resulting publicity scared the other cashiers. When I asked why this had not been done before, one of the old-timers explained: 'No park can tolerate bad publicity. If they had a lot of such arrests and it got into the paper, people might stop coming and they'd lose a lot more than they lose to us. We have a free ride if we don't get greedy. Max got greedy and they had to stop him.'

There were no more substitutions of used tickets at midnight, and when my supplier asked why, I said I was scared, and I was so young that he did not try to change my mind. Then an amazing thing happened whose import I did not understand at the time: one morning I was asked to go to the office where we got our tickets and our bag of money for change, and a gray-haired man asked me if I would like to be a relief cashier: 'You wouldn't have any specific booth, you'd serve wherever a man was absent that day and take over any of the spots when the regular cashier needed time off for supper.' When I said that this sounded great, he added: 'And we'd want you to let us know about any suspicious situations, where men are selling tickets twice or fiddling with the turnstiles.' In this bizarre manner I became a kind of private detective.

Why had I been offered the job? From time to time the head office painstakingly checked the proper serial number of the ticket that opened that day's sale for a given ride or stand, then riffled through the tickets presumably sold during the day to see if any old ones were being substituted. They had spotted the fact that I had for some days been selling old tickets—not so many as to be a serious offense—and that I had definitely stopped after the arrest of the other cashier. I was, indeed, precisely the kind of young man they wanted, one who had been through the mill, knew the tricks and had, of his own volition, turned honest.

The famous old war-horses among the cashiers, the ones given the big rides where the flow of money could be tremendous, ate from paper bags and did not leave their booths for supper because they did not want to risk anyone's fouling their system, so I never got to see their operation. But one day one of the very biggest rides had no cashier; he was in the hospital with an ulcer of some kind, and I was given his booth. Just before noon break when I counted up the money I had and compared it with the number on the turnstile counter telling me how much I should have, I found myself with an overage of more than a hundred dollars, which meant that something was terribly wrong, so I followed the strategy of the old-timers and did not leave my booth for my evening meal, and by ten o'clock that night, at the height of the busy period, I had accumulated a small fortune.

Then I figured what had happened. A turnstile consists of a vertical pole to which are attached at the top six metal arms so spaced in a circle; that only one customer at a time, having paid his fare, can squeeze through. Invisible to the customer and at the bottom of the revolving pole, is a small wheel containing six projections or cogs. As the arm above rotates, indicating that the customer has paid his fifteen cents, one of the moving cogs activates a counting device that registers that payment. At the close of day the cashier notes the number on the counting device, subtracts from it the number at the start of day, multiplies the difference by fifteen cents and that's what he gives the company. Anything over belongs to him, but anything under he must pay out of his own pocket. His task is to see that there is always an overage.

The turnstile on my ride contained, when it left the factory, the regular six projecting cogs, but my absent cashier had filed one of them off, thus enabling him to keep one out of every six fares and clearing a 16 percent profit on each day's take. How long this scam had been in operation I could not tell, but during that spell he must have made a fortune. On this day I stood to make well over a hundred and fifty dollars.

At about eleven that night a breathless messenger from the hospital rushed up to my booth and whispered: 'He'll be back tomorrow. He says "Keep it all and tell nobody." I kept half and told everybody, so that when he reported for work next morning he was quietly told that his services were no longer required.

I worked at Willow Grove for many summers, even into my college years, serving the park well as a relatively honest cashier, and I left with insights into the workings of at least a part of our financial system: the agreed-upon ignoring of unsavory situations, the insidious preying upon the public, the efforts of good men to keep the operations reasonably clean, and the pressures upon the individuals ensnared by their own greed in the various traps. I did not leave the Park a hardened cynic; the lovely music I heard four times a day would not have allowed that, nor had I let my experiences there color my attitude toward either business or personal involvement.

I had one other job as a young man before I entered serious adult employment, and from it I also learned a great deal. While a college student I gave a public political speech that pleased a listener so much that he came forward at the end of the evening and said: 'Impressive. You have the kind of mind I'm looking for,' and he offered me a job, which lasted four years and could have continued permanently had I not been drawn away to other interests.

My employer was Frank Scheibley, exuberant owner of the highly regarded Strath Haven Inn in my college town of Swarthmore. He offered me a job that included being a nightwatchman of the lead hotel in his chain, and since it was a completely wooden and rambling affair, I was obliged to make an hourly round of all the hallways and crannies, carrying with me a time clock, which I punched with keys hanging from critical points to prove I had been there to check for fire. In the morning the clerk would verify my tape to ensure that I had been at each of the twenty or thirty spots at the proper times and certify my fidelity to the insurance company.

My other duties included operating the switchboard through the night when I wasn't on my rounds and attending to any emergencies. It was a peaceful job and I often dozed at the switchboard, but what fascinated me about it, in addition to the chance to study the human beings who staggered in late, was the business that Uncle Frank (as he insisted that I call him—he wanted to adopt me but I did not allow that) specialized in. He had made such a pronounced success of Strath Haven

that he went around to other regional hotels and told their board owners: 'Look, your place is a mess. In four or five years you'll be out of
business. Tell you what I'll do, I'll come in here with my team and turn
this place completely around, save your investment and earn you a
bundle.' He wanted no fee, just 15 or 20 percent of the stock, and when
the deal was struck he never failed to fulfill his promise. He was a wizard
at rejuvenating run-down hotels and made himself a modest fortune.

I helped in various of his adventures, working in this hotel or that,
and I saw that he had half a hundred rules for running a good establishment, the most interesting to me being this: 'When you are about to
serve a meal, and the customers have ordered, whisk the menus away
immediately so the women don't change their minds.' He was a fanatic
about cleanliness, and he also trained his desk people to lean forward
to greet guests as if impatient to help them. From Uncle Frank I learned
that businesses can go extremely sour through mismanagement and
even lose their entire investment, but that they can be resuscitated by
some miracle worker who returns to basics. Uncle Frank was basic.

So from the age of nine through twenty-two I was never without a
paying job of some kind, and I worked interminable hours while at the
same time pursuing a rigorous education in which I consistently got top
marks, engaging in vigorous athletics in which I helped win championships, and keeping up a wide-ranging reading program. I was not an idle
boy.

My next confrontations with the inescapable problem of making a living
came in rapid sequence, and I shall dispose of them briefly, but this will
not mean that they were less consequential than my earlier experiences;
they shocked me profoundly and crystallized my attitudes.

In 1929 I graduated from college in that rosy June when the prosperity
of the world, and especially the United States, seemed unlimited. But
in October of that same year the fairy-tale castles collapsed and many
of my classmates, from one of the finest colleges in the country, were
unable to find jobs and remained desperately unemployed, some of them
for years. I escaped the trauma because before the crash came I had
landed a fine job teaching at The Hill, in Pottstown, Pennsylvania, a
private school for the sons of well-to-do parents where, as is so often the
case with energetic beginning teachers, I learned far more than I taught.
At the very depth of the depression, when jobs simply could not be had,
I was given an opportunity to travel to Europe and astonished everyone
by announcing that I was resigning to study abroad for a couple of years.

Older teachers warned: 'You're making the biggest mistake of your life, quitting a good job in the midst of a depression. You may never find another,' but I refused to listen, and on the munificent Swarthmore College scholarship of six hundred dollars plus my savings from The Hill I would spend two wonderful years doing graduate work at the University of St. Andrews in Scotland and traveling to all parts of the Mediterranean and the Baltic on tramp steamers. This bold move, the surrender of a secure, well-paying job in order to roam, was both the beginning of my broader education and one of the wisest choices I ever made.

I once spent six weeks in Italy subsisting on cheap pasta dishes, fresh peaches and milk, and the tramp steamers carried me to worlds I would never otherwise have known; my salary was one shilling for ten weeks and required me to do odd jobs about the ship. But since I was given free time at each port we touched I judged the pay to have been more than fair.

When I returned to America I was offered a job at the excellent experimental Quaker-run George School near Philadelphia, for a salary of $1,200, and there I met three of the finest young teachers I would ever know—Rees Frescoln, Bill Vitarelli, Jack Talbot—each of whom received $500 a year and was glad to get it. I remember one especially cold morning in January when I was walking along a one-mile stretch of country road to my classes and thinking of the advertisement I had seen that morning. It showed a blissfully happy married couple in their fifties and was entitled: 'How We Retired to Happiness on $2,500 a Year.' I can recall every word I said to myself as I trudged along: Boy, wouldn't it be great if a man could have $3,600 a year, guaranteed for the rest of his life—my goodness, he could do everything. The famous Polish transatlantic ship *Batory* was then carrying students to Europe for $50, and for many years my ideal of ultimate riches continued to be $3,600 a year.

When my professors at Ohio State University, where I was doing graduate work, heard that I was leaving my secure job at George School for a teaching assignment at the fine experimental College of Education at Greeley, in eastern Colorado, they warned: 'You'd be making the biggest mistake in your life. The sands of the desert are white with the bones of promising young men who moved west and perished trying to fight their way back east.' For me the opposite proved true. Any young fellow of ability who worked in a state like Colorado enjoyed an enormous advantage, for when prestigious national committees were formed, participants from the East Coast were more or less automatically selected, the good men from the Mississippi Valley were quickly identified, as were the men from the Pacific Coast. That left a great gaping hole in the west, and someone would remember: 'Hey, there's a bright kid out in Greeley.' You didn't have to be good; you simply had to be there, and when the White House wanted to convene a small group to talk about problems in education I and four others enjoyed a long dinner with Franklin and Eleanor Roosevelt. From Greeley I was also appointed to one significant national position after another and was invited back to Harvard as a visiting assistant professor. So much for white bones in the desert.

But the part of my Colorado experience relevant to this chapter was a shattering one. As an administrator of the career procedures of would-be teachers, I became a minor official in the college's branch of the National Youth Administration headed by a great-hearted professor of sociology, Hal Blue. Congress, in an admirable attempt to keep promising students in college and knowing that their skills would be needed in the years ahead, paid young people thirty-five dollars a month for some service so they could continue their studies, and it became my duty to help select the worthy students and see to it that they received their funds and spent them properly.

It was a painful task, heartbreaking really, for to deny a student an NYA grant might mean the termination of his education, and I became known as a soft touch, for when some especially bright young woman or man failed to qualify for one reason or another, I gave her or him a temporary scholarship out of my own funds until the student could clear up discrepancies and qualify properly.

But two of the students I was monitoring, one man and one woman who did not know each other, seemed to be doing so poorly in their studies that with Professor Blue's approval I had to call them in with every intention of removing them from the list of grantees. However, when I had them before me and had outlined my proof of their inadequacies—missed classes, poor work turned in late and the like— the young woman began to cry convulsively, and when I had quietened her, she revealed that of the thirty-five dollars a month I had been giving her, she had been sending half to her family out in the drylands because they had absolutely nothing else to live on. She had been starving herself to feed them.

When I turned to the young man, he placed before me proof that he had been sending to his parents twenty dollars of his allowance, and when I began to question other students I found that these two examples, while in no way typical, were not unique. To have gone through the Great American Depression in a dust-bowl state like Colorado was to have lived in hell.

A few years ago, when I stopped by Greeley to watch a television show being made from *Centennial,* a group of adults who had been my students in those terrible years asked if they could come to see me, and in the group were the wonderful Kagoharas, the Japanese children who had conducted themselves so admirably in those difficult years, maintaining their courage, and their ebullient spirits. I remembered them with affection, the whole troop, and then one of the girls began to speak: 'Mr. Michener, did you ever realize why we thought so highly of you in those days?'

'You were good students. You made it easy to like you.'

'But do you remember the time you drove us to Denver in your car? To see the museum? And you gave us each a dime?'

'I remember the trip but not the dimes.'

'In all the years we were with you, when you and Miss Selberg kept us going, each of us was given by our father five cents a semester to do with as we wished. We used to lie awake at night, wondering what to do with our nickels and we never spent them foolishly. And then in one swoop, you gave each of us a full dime. We have never forgotten and we came here today to thank you.'

I think the reader can now deduce what my attitudes toward money would be when at age fifty, I began to earn substantial sums as a writer, whether I was fully entitled to them or not. But it may be helpful to recapitulate those points that seem significant.

Money had been terribly important in my childhood and its absence meant real deprivation, but at a very early age I eliminated it as a dominant factor in my thinking and refused to allow it to tyrannize over me. From the age of eleven I had steady work in a wide variety of occupations in which I learned the day-to-day significance of money, but I held it in such contempt that twice I felt free to quit good jobs and go off exploring, and never did I allow financial considerations to dictate career choices, nor did I ever seek a job, promotion in the one I had, or a salary increase. My attitude toward money was bizarre and contradictory.

But when I stopped looking at myself to study others, I saw a world in which money was of terrifying importance, its lack sometimes leading to disaster or suicide. It could also color personal relationships, as when acquaintances would ask, sometimes in print: 'Why has he been so lucky and not I? Especially when I'm twice as talented?' and for that unfair situation there can be no explanation.

On the morning after the announcement of my Pulitzer Prize I was allowed a peep into one of the great secrets of publishing. My boss, Phil Knowlton, did not come to work that morning; perhaps the celebration, during which he told me about Alaska, had made him ill. In his absence it fell to me as his assistant to note and verify the Macmillan royalty statements that would soon be mailed to all our authors, a precaution intended to forestall either preposterous over- or under-payment, and this proved a sobering experience to a beginning writer.

Running down the list I would come upon one famous name after another in British and American literature, for Macmillan had a noble group of writers, and see to my dismay that the yearly royalties were minuscule—John Masefield, $289.63—and others of equal repute at figures like $111.57 and $988.94.

But then I stumbled upon a name I had never heard of—Michael O'Toole, $89,468.52—and I was so startled that I called Miss Habekorst, Mr. Knowlton's longtime secretary, and she explained that O'Toole was one of the authors of our famous *Beginning Chemistry,* by Dorsett, O'Toole and Ginsburg, and when I checked the earnings of the other two men, I found that Dorsett, long dead, was still pulling down a hefty $20,000 for his estate and that young Isadore Ginsburg was getting $48,000. Upon asking around I learned this was a college text of splendid reputation written in the closing years of the last century by Brantley Dorsett, professor at Yale. When both he and his text began to run out of steam, Macmillan presented him with an ultimatum: 'To keep your book alive you simply must bring in a younger author who teaches beginning chemistry in some big university,' and they made a persuasive case. But when Mrs. Dorsett learned that the man nominated to update the sacred text was an Irishman named O'Toole who was professor in a minor school like Indiana University, she exploded at the indignity, whereupon a brutally tough Macmillan editor warned the Dorsetts: 'Revise with O'Toole or your book goes out of print.'

Of course, some years later, when Dr. and Mrs. O'Toole were informed by that same editor that his famous beginning chemistry, Dorsett and O'Toole, must now add the name Ginsburg or go out of print, they complained with Indiana pride: 'But not someone from one of those big amorphous New York Jewish schools,' and the editor repeated what he had told old Dorsett years before: 'We go where the big freshman classes are. Dorsett's dead and you no longer teach. It'll have to be Ginsburg,' and in this way the famous old book gained renewed life and continued its huge sales to freshman chemists, even though the original version was now well over fifty years old and its original author long dead.

From checking those lists that day I learned that Charles Duckworth, who wrote a sensitive novel about a young lawyer in Louisville, was likely to earn $1,109.93, while both Lemnitzer and Riley, who had the hot new text for *Beginning Psychology,* would each earn well above $60,000. The number of writers whose names I knew who earned less than a thousand dollars that year was appalling, and my own book, which appeared for the first time on this list, earned so little that I am ashamed to report it. When I finished checking the list I was a rather shaken man, but I realized that it was salutary for me to know the gruesome facts.

We have now reached the point where my professional career as a writer began—rather humbly, I must say. I had published a fairly good book, *Tales of the South Pacific,* but except for the Pulitzer Prize it had accomplished little beyond a couple of good reviews—few of the major journals noticed it—and it had certainly not brought me any financial returns worth mentioning. About this time the Authors League in New York launched a comprehensive study of what professional writers really earn, and the results were depressing, something like two thousand dollars a year on average, and the Macmillan list of royalties for serious writers confirmed the study.

On the other hand, if the average book earned little, it could lead to a better reputation for the writer, promotion in his or her profession and, surprisingly often, to income from other sources that had not been anticipated. For example, after the moderately good reception of my novel I was approached by the leading speakers' agent, a wonderful genius named Colston Leigh, who signed me to a long-term contract as one of his lecturers, and I proved, for reasons neither he nor I understood, to be fairly popular on his circuit. One day he gave me a fascinating insight on the lecture business: 'Always remember the case of John Doe. It will teach you a lot. The real money to be made in this business is with the Jewish women's clubs. They pay and they're wonderful to work with, but to succeed with them you must have topics that will interest them. Now I'm sure you know Doe. Wrote one book that had modest success, *Israel in Jeopardy.* But as a lecturer he's sensational. Darling of all the clubs and I help him make a damned good living. Had only two subjects. Most good speakers have four. His were "New Hope in Israel" and "Thunder Out of Africa." Great successes both of them, but pretty soon, what with all his traveling, he had used them up. Clubs wanted something new so he offered "Thunder Out of Israel" and "New Hope in Africa." Total bust. Now he's back to the original names and he's on top again.'

Since I was vaguely toying with the idea of quitting my job at Macmillan and trying to be a full-time writer, I worked hard for Leigh. His rules were simple: 'There are two choices, but you must decide on one at the beginning of each season and stay with it for that entire season. We split the fee fifty-fifty and I pay for all travel and hotels. Or we split seventy-thirty and you pay all expenses.' The problem was that if you chose the fifty-fifty deal he billed you into five successive nights in Buffalo, paid only one fare, and made a fortune. So next year you chose seventy-thirty, and you were one night in Buffalo, the next in Ames, Iowa, and right after that in Dallas, Texas. It was a horrible way to earn a living, which is why, after having left his stable, I never again gave speeches willingly, and if I was muscled into doing so, I gave away the fee before nightfall, usually to some black church. In obedience to that law, I've disbursed quite a few thousands.

However, if I were again a beginning author I would be on the road three or four nights a week, because it does put one in personal touch with people who cherish books and it is an honorable way to get started.

In my fourth year with Leigh I decided to leave the lecture circuit; the work was much too hard, what with my full-time editorial job at Macmillan, plus the fact that I happened to hear during layovers those two masters of the art of speaking, Bennett Cerf and John Mason Brown, and I realized that I could never equal them. But when I tried to quit, Leigh informed me that I was under contract and must perform as he wished. We fell into a deplorable dispute which was mostly my fault, but he proved intransigent, so I developed a ploy that drove him crazy. I would drive to the next afternoon engagement he had lined up for me, scout out the building to satisfy myself that I could make it from my parked car to the stage so as to arrive at precisely two-thirty, and then read a book sitting in the car while people ran back and forth to see if I had arrived and called New York to find out what the matter was. At the appointed moment I would eagerly walk onstage and try to give the best lecture the group had ever heard.

It was a mean trick and one I am not proud of now, but it began to work, because it left Leigh in a real bind. His clients vehemently protested my split-second timing for my arrival but they also reported that I gave one of the best talks they'd ever had and could they sign me up for next year, even if the fee had to be raised?

Things between Leigh and me deteriorated badly, and at one point he threatened me with a lawsuit unless I paid him the full commission on what he would have earned on the speeches I would have given. Unable to devise an escape, I paid and stewed as to how I could get out of this fearful bind. The moment of decision came at a night meeting in Seattle, where the audience was delighted to see me, but the program was somewhat delayed by a long speech from the chairman who was trying to prove that neither he, nor his daughter, nor his wife had stolen the club's two thousand dollars. At one point he asked rhetorically, pointing directly at me: 'Do I look like a man who would steal two thousand dollars?' and I had to admit to the audience that he did not. He looked like an accountant, which he turned out to be. But then he roared: 'Stand up, Betsy,' and again he appealed to me: 'Does my daughter look like a girl who would steal two thousand dollars?' and now I had a very different problem, because little Betsy not only looked like a bimbo who might steal the two grand, but who probably had. When he appealed to me, I begged the question.

The problem of the missing money having been more or less settled, the distraught chairman proceeded to introduce me, and apparently his club had had an unbroken series of fine speakers—the hall was crowded and the fee was maximum—because he said in sonorous tones: 'To this hallowed platform, which has been graced by William Jennings Bryan and Clarence Darrow and Herbert Hoover and Amelia Earhart, tonight we bring you—' Then he looked at me in abject horror because he had not the slightest idea who I was. He recovered fast, and in a shout of triumph he cried: '—their worthy successor!'

That night I decided to end this foolishness, and when I returned to New York I stormed into Leigh's office prepared to deliver a well-rehearsed ultimatum. 'You have me, sir. I admit that for another year and a half I'm obligated to perform as you direct. the contract says so, as you claimed. But the contract, of which I have a copy here, does not say that I have to wear shoes when I speak, and it doesn't stipulate that I cannot wear a bearskin coat, and it certainly doesn't say that I have to put in the tooth that is missing from the front of my smile.'

Seeing the grim look on my face, he stopped me before I got well started. He leaned forward on his desk as if to grab something with which to beat me over the head and shouted: 'Get out of here!' When I stomped from his office, a free man, I tried but failed to slam the door hard enough to break the glass.

I have never been proud of that performance, but neither have I regretted taking strong steps to terminate my bondage. After we'd both cooled down I remained business friends with Leigh, and on at least a dozen occasions when foreign authors or old friends found they needed the services of a speakers' bureau, I have recommended him: 'He's the best in the business.' And on about the same number of occasions he has asked if I would like to come back to work with him: 'With your ability to give a good speech and your favorable reputation with the clubs, I can get tremendous fees.' I have declined. On my very last public speech for him—in Denver, I think it was—I did have a brief moment of regret. In the front row sat two fine-looking women who listened to every word I said, nodding in approval at the points I was trying to make, and I caught myself thinking during the questioning: It's been rugged, but there have been moments of real meaning like this, when you bring important ideas to people who really want to learn. Besides, people in a hundred towns now know that I write books, so maybe it hasn't been so bad. When the lecture ended, the two women were first among those who swarmed onto the platform. Their question was: 'Mr. Michener, we've been wondering all through your talk. Where did you buy that handsome suit?' And that was my farewell to the podium.

At about this time I said farewell to another old pattern of life. The head of Macmillan was in many ways a testy man. George P. Brett, Jr., was the son of that powerful man who had converted the insignificant New York agency of the traditional and very powerful London firm into an outfit bigger than the home office. Young Mr. Brett, as his son was called, had hired me personally after a nationwide search for an editor 'who doesn't have to be good, he has to be thirty-five' to fill a managerial gap in the company hierarchy. Three names surfaced repeatedly, and I was third in line, but the first landed an important teaching job, the second became president of something, and I was left. In my hiring interview Mr. Brett had said repeatedly: 'Remember, Michener, we are not an eleemosynary institution. We publish books to make money,' but then he added: 'And the only way I know how to do that is to publish the best books possible.'

In the subsequent eight years he had never spoken to me directly, for he did not suffer either fools or underlings gladly. In some ways Macmillan was unbelievable: there were two entrances to the handsome gray building on Fifth Avenue at Tenth, and only the upper echelon was allowed to enter by the imposing big door; lesser employees, and they were legion, entered by the small side door and punched a time clock. The unforgettable day sometimes came when an older editor, never Mr. Brett himself, would take a newcomer by the shoulder in a manly way and utter the precious words: 'We've been watching you, Michener, and you seem to be one of us. You can use the big door.'

On a memorable night, the second time in my life that Mr. Brett spoke to me, we ate alone in the dark-paneled board room with the great forebears of the company looking down on us, and as our meal ended Mr. Brett surprised me by placing on the table before me, the manuscript of my second book, *The Fires of Spring,* and said: 'Michener, I have bad news. We've decided not to publish this.' Before I could speak he added: 'My wife read it and did not like it at all.'

I did not know how to respond to this second devastating attack on my ability—New York's leading literary agent, had fired me, and now George P. Brett, the president of Macmillan, was doing the same. I was stricken.

But that was not the end of our session, not by a long shot, because he now became avuncular, and, with the offending manuscript out of the way, said: 'Michener, I've been watching you, listening to reports, studying the sales records of the books you've edited, and I'm convinced you have a brilliant future as a publisher. I want you to start immediately working closely with me with an eye to your becoming in due course the president of our company.'

I was so astounded that I could say little. This followed the pattern of every good thing that had happened to me since childhood. Kenneth Rufe has sought me out as one of his paperboys. The Willow Grove lawyer had come to me with his offer of a job. A wonderful teacher had submitted my name to Swarthmore for my scholarship. John Lester had come to the college to offer me a job at The Hill, and the same kind of thing had happened at George School, the Colorado school and Harvard. I had received my job at Macmillan without ever having known that I was in contention, and now a chance at the presidency—'No promises, you understand'—had arrived like a bombshell. My attitude of being uncompetitive and simply trying to do as good a job as possible had again paid off, and I left Mr. Brett that night with his words ringing in my ears: 'Michener, you really have no future as a writer but a tremendous one as a publisher.'

I have often wondered how my life might have turned out had not a totally unexpected phonc call reached me the next morning when I was bleary-eyed after a night spent pondering the unexpected proposal from Mr. Brett. The call came from a man with a most persuasive voice who said: 'Is this Mr. Michener, the writer fellow?' When I said yes, the man introduced himself and said: 'I come to New York regularly—from Philadelphia—and have been wanting to meet you for some time. Could we have lunch tomorrow?' and I said yes. In this unusual way I met a much older man who would, by his wisdom, shrewdness and knowledge of publishing, modify and in a sense determine my behavior as a writer. Hugh MacNair Kahler had been a sensationally successful author of commercial short stories but had retired from that profession to serve out his days as fiction editor of *The Ladies Home Journal,* then one of America's most prestigious monthlies.

When I met him he was a tall, fine-looking elder statesman, dignified in the aloof way one might expect of a Princeton graduate. But he also had a warm smile and a manner that enabled him to reach out and put at ease anyone with whom he was talking. In our first minutes together I thought: This man wants to like me and I shall do everything I can to make that easy for him, because I certainly want to like him.

'Let me explain first who I am,' he said. 'I was one of the best writers in my field. Set an all-time record. Sold one hundred and twenty-three short stories in a row to the finest magazines. *Saturday Evening Post, Women's Home Companion, Collier's,* all of them. Once I got started, never one rejection. I knew what American readers wanted and, equally important, what the editors wanted. Formula writing? Maybe, but also some very attractive stories.

'But that's enough about me. I've sought you out, Michener, because I've read two of your stories, also your book on the war, and I can see that you have the golden touch that makes a man or a woman a teller of stories.'

In succeeding weeks he came often from his editorial offices in Philadelphia to New York in search of stories for his magazine, and during those visits he sought me out, counseling me on how to become a tough, disciplined professional. Once when I said airily: 'I don't believe I'd want to join a writers' union,' he exploded: 'Damn it, son, you stand to make a fortune with your pen. Well, it's the lucky ones like you who must pay dues to the writers' groups to support those who can't afford it. You must do everything in your power to strengthen the writing profession. You join the Author's League tomorrow.' And when I said offhandedly I didn't think I'd need an agent, he used the same argument about responsibility to the profession: 'I'll find you an agent tomorrow. The money she makes from you will enable her to help other writers who bring in no income now, but may bring in a lot later—if they survive.'

It was a spring day, I remember, when Kahler took me to lunch at a fancy restaurant and introduced me to Maryland crabcakes, a bottle of Châteauneuf-du-Pape and a moral dilemma: 'Michener, time to make up your mind. Bruce and Beatrice Gould, my bosses at the magazine and two of the best editors in the business, want to hire you. They've been reading your stuff, too, and listening to my reports as to what kind of person you are. They want to offer you an immense fee if you will read six issues of their magazine and type out a report on every item of fiction, stating whether had you been fiction editor you would have bought it for the magazine.'

Without telling me the fee the Goulds had in mind, he handed me six issues of the *Journal,* and I retired to my room and over a period of two weeks typed out some of the most detailed editorial comments the Goulds had ever received. On Kahler's next visit he took me to lunch again, this time Dover sole *bonne femme,* and exciting news: 'Michener, everyone at the *Journal* wants you, especially the Goulds,' and he mentioned a salary several times what I was then getting. But before I could express my gratitude and astonishment he added: 'No one was more eager to have you join us than me. I made them jack up the proposed salary so you'd be more likely to accept. You and I could be a great team.' Then he cleared his voice and said with unusual firmness: 'But I advise you not to take our job. More than ever I'm convinced you're destined to be a writer. Don't be an editor, be a writer.'

Bewildered as to what I should do, I made a phone call to the Century Club and asked to speak to John Mason Brown. When he came to the phone, I asked if I could come to see him.'

'And who are you?'

'An admirer. With a most difficult problem.'

'Well, now . . .'

'I'm a friend of Harold Latham,' I explained, using the word *friend* rather loosely to cover my relationship to the austere, reserved chief editor of Macmillan.

'Well then, come along.'

When I reached the club I spotted immediately the dean of critics, the urbane, gentle man beloved by women's clubs. I spoke first: 'Mr. Brown, several people have told me that in your lecture this year you've been referring to my book as if it had some merit—'

_ 'The title of your book?'

'Tales of the South Pacific.'

'Michener! Indeed I have been using your book, and with considerable applause from the audiences, I must say.'

Feeling that the ice had been broken, I said: 'Do you think I could risk it, to chuck my job at Macmillan and try to become a professional writer?'

He was aghast at the impropriety of such a question, especially since we had never spoken before and he knew nothing of me. But he was, as those who remember him will testify, one of the kindest, most sensible men of his generation, and in the next hour he asked me every question whose answer might cast light on my decision: Did I have an agent? Had I saved my money? Did I know any editors of magazines? Did I have in my mind a rich backlog of ideas? Was I able to stick to a job after starting energetically? Was I really determined to become a writer? And the one he considered most important: 'Tell me honestly, Michener, can you survive financially and emotionally if things don't work out during the first three years?'

When I said yes, he shook my hand and said: 'If I were you, I'd risk it.' The next day with my manuscript of *The Fires of Spring* under my arm I boarded a bus, rode up Fifth Avenue and walked unannounced into the offices of Random House. I asked one of the editors, Saxe Commins, if he would like to publish the book that Macmillan had turned down, and after reading the manuscript he said 'Yes.'*

By that act I made myself a writer.

The agent that my godfather Kahler picked out for me was one of the best, the inspired Helen Strauss, who would handle my business affairs for many years, and now she performed her first bold act in my behalf: 'Jim, I think you're ready to go up to Pleasantville to meet Dewitt Wallace, publisher of *Reader's Digest*,' and she led me on that excursion which so many young writers took to their advantage. The company offices so resembled the buildings of some time-honored New England college that I felt I was being led to registration by a caring aunt, and this impression deepened when I met Mr. Wallace, who seemed like a reticent dean of admissions.

At lunch in the corporate dining room, a quiet, relaxed affair, he introduced me to his senior editors: 'This is the young man whose work we've been following so closely. No question but that he is destined to be one of our writers.' When the junior editors nodded, which they were prone to do when he spoke, he turned to me: 'We want to find a place for you on our writing staff.'† He made then, and a dozen times subse-

---

*In this way Random House, without having spent a dime for a phone call or a dollar for lunch, acquired me as one of its writers. One day, before his retirement, the longtime president, Bob Bernstein, stopped me and said: 'I just heard how you got here, Michener. I figure we owe you that first bus fare,' and he handed me a nickel, conveniently forgetting that from the lower end of Fifth Avenue I would have used the more elegant bus line reserved for that flashy boulevard, for which the fare was ten cents.

†Thus within a brief time after publishing some stories and a book, I was approached by two major agents—one a charlatan, the other a genius—and two major magazines. This experience was not unique. Many beginning writers are approached

quently, some of the most generous offers a writer could have received, but I always told him honestly that I felt I would be able to write more effectively as a free lance. After he'd finally given up on having me as a staff writer he made a suggestion that through the years was the kind of bulwark few writers have ever had: 'Jim, you and Mari are like my children. The only Democrats Lila and I know. I want you to go wherever in world you care to, write about anything that excites you, and Lila and I will pay all your expenses for as long as we live. Your only obligation will be to allow us first refusal of anything you write, and if we take it, we pay you regular rates for it, just as if you were a stranger.'

I never availed myself of that amazing offer, but there it remained, my security in years when I produced little or received little for what I did produce. Later, when it was apparent to the Wallaces that I was not going to join their family, they made a further gesture. Summoning my wife and me once more to High Winds, he said: 'All the good that has happened to us has come because people like you know how to write. We pay you well, none better, but that doesn't begin to cover what you've done for us. We want you to help us give away our money to projects that are worthy,' and for many years, though I brought the *Digest* no profits, I helped disburse the profits that others had earned for them.

By this circuitous route of turning down dazzling job offers from three of America's finest publishers—Macmillan, Curtis, the Digest—because I felt I had a chance of becoming a writer, I set forth on the perilous road of the free lance. Of ten who attempt this venture, nine fail, because to succeed one requires equal parts of talent, ideas, fortitude and luck. I was aware at the time I made this daring choice that I had just turned down three splendid salaries, each higher than the one before, so as I started my work it could not be said that I was doing it for money.

Then a quiet miracle happened. Because I was able to touch on some nerve in the reading public, my books were accepted widely, and in all countries, so that without my ever being aware of exactly how it had

---

by New York scouts, always on the prowl seeking promising young talent. In Matthew Brucolli's instructive *Conversations with Writers,* both William Price Fox and Wallace Makefield, distinguished teachers of writing, relate stories much like mine, of having published something and then being invited to write a great deal more. That is the goal for which a young, would-be writer is entitled to shoot.

happened I was catapulted into the high finance aspects of publishing.

It has always seemed to me that the general public, and even many informed people in the book trade itself, fail to appreciate the magnitude of what it means financially to be the author of a fantastically successful book.

Let us follow the experiences of an imaginary writer, Tim Jones, from a little town in Kansas, who has written four rather good novels that he couldn't sell, then two that were published by Galaxy Hall in New York and received good notices but no sales. His editor has been convinced since reading his first short stories in the little magazines, which pay nothing but do showcase beginners, that he has a real talent. Somewhat against the advice of older editors in her firm, she has insisted that Jones, despite his early failures, get one final advance: 'One of these times he's bound to break through.'

As soon as she finishes reading the word-processed pages of his new work she knows that Tim has made the big leap. Ignited by her enthusiasm, which fellow editors endorse after quick scanning of the manuscript, she rushes copies of the work to magazine editors, book clubs, readers for motion-picture companies, paperback houses and representatives of European publishers. And this is what can happen to a good book supported by an editor who launches it with expertise:

Grudging advance two years ago	$ 10,000
Royalty of 10 % on first 5,000 copies, 12.5 % on the next 5,000 copies, then 15 % of $17.50-per-copy price on first printing of 180,000 copies	465,938
Later rush printing of 490,000 copies	1,286,250
Author's share of advances from foreign publishers	185,000
Book-of-the-Month Club main selection—author's share	110,000
Prepublication to magazines and newspapers	20,000
Sales to motion pictures with small royalty on later profits	900,000
Results of auctions among competing paperback houses, advances against later royalties, half-share of $800,000	400,000

Royalties from third Galaxy Hall printing of 350,000 additional copies	918,750
Later royalties on extra European printings	169,650
Unexpected collateral income, various sources such as newspaper articles on book, speeches, commercial	52,000
	$ 4,507,588

So Tim Jones, after a protracted apprenticeship, finds himself with a best-seller and an income of more than $4.5 million, from which he must pay his agent the standard 10 percent, leaving him an astonishing $4,056,829, a good deal of which he will hand over to the Internal Revenue Service, as he should. Each of the individual items listed above has been equaled or surpassed by some book in recent years, but it would be misleading to suggest that Tim's hypothetical bonanza has often been reached. Some books have come close, but not many and none of mine.

The first thing to say about such figures is that they are indecent, not because they are out of line with what a good baseball player or a popular singing star makes, for they are not, but because when a few lucky writers receive such outlandish rewards, they deprive a host of worthy writers from earning the more modest sums to which they are entitled, and which would enable them to earn a decent living. Today's boom-or-bust rule in publishing—spectacular rewards for a few, niggardly returns for the many, including some of our finest writers—must prove deleterious to the normal growth of American culture and personally destructive to aspiring writers, who otherwise might constitute the next generation of distinguished literary figures. Things are badly out of balance.

I have realized for two decades that I am one of the worst offenders, for I have enjoyed an almost unbroken series of best-sellers, some of them on the list for months and even years, and although most have fallen far below Tim's dazzling figures, I have obviously earned substantial sums and have had to grapple with the propriety of accepting them.

From what I have said about my background and my painfully acquired attitudes toward money, it should be obvious that I would handle these unexpected and unsought sums in ways peculiar to my upbringing and my personal habits. The following facts are relevant:

I have never been obsessed with money, nor sought it avidly.

About half the books I've written have not been best-sellers, nor were they intended to be. They have dealt with restricted or even arcane subjects that could never conceivably have gained popular acceptance, and several of them were so clearly noncommercial that I had to help pay production costs.

I have never once in my entire publishing life discussed royalty rates or size of the first printing or advertising budget. Nor have I ever sought cocktail parties for the press or other such amenities; I have been honored at many when others insisted and have sometimes appreciated them but have more often been ill at ease or embarrassed.

A typical business phone call from my agent Owen Laster concerning financial details lasts about three minutes at most: 'Jim, Random insists they can't go any higher, considering the increased cost of paper and the length of your manuscript,' to which I say 'O.K.'

Year in, year out I receive directly or from my agent about four major inquiries a week about writing projects, some gratifying beyond any dreams I might have had as a boy, and always I say: 'Sounds good. You handle it.'

Now I am not so naive as to think that negotiations are as simple as I try to keep them at my end. I know that Laster works diligently and imaginatively to protect my interests, and hence his own. If it takes me only minutes to accept arrangements he has made in principle with Random, I remember that in some intricate cases it has taken him and Random more than a year to hammer out details regarding new adjuncts to publishing like audio books or cable television. I have proceeded with very large contracts after only a telephone handshake, and never have I goaded Owen or expressed dismay when he later found himself in a stalemate. Often a final contract, not necessarily from Random, will run to fifteen pages, and I can never recall having read one, not even from Random, from start to finish, nor have I bothered to take note of the provisions. Almost never have I known what I was being paid and a week after filing the papers I could not possibly recall what the terms were.

Some two dozen times in my life other people working with me—publishers, producers, Hollywood—have had to go to Owen and ask him, because of adverse business conditions, to beg me to accept a cut in my royalty, and in every instance I have listened, never interrupted, and said: 'Sounds reasonable.' Never once has any such caller said that in consequence of success beyond expectations someone wanted to increase my share; always it has been a reduction, and I have always consented.

I have not been indifferent to balances, but when income tax or other legal situations require accounting, I leave this to others, scan their figures and generally forget them. I have from time to time known vaguely what the rough balances were, but only because others required the estimates. The real figures I have never known.

During the past fifteen years or so I have never been in a bank except to affix my signature to a legal paper that required notarizing. My wife cares for our accounts and provides me with an allowance. Only rarely do I carry a wallet, and when I do carry a credit card I use it only in emergencies.

Like many men who were scarred by childhood poverty or the Great Depression, I have always lived as if bad times were sure to recur, and for years I expected that one day I would be applying for a job at this year's reincarnation of the Federal Writers' Project, writing the new version of those great state guides. As a Quaker, I live simply, spend little and often chide my wife for her reluctance to give away things we don't need, such as property we don't use, but she acquired from her Japanese-American parents a strongly rural attitude toward real estate and cannot bring herself to give away any land that she cherishes. This embarrasses me, but I am powerless to alter mindsets that began in her cradle, and in other details of our married life her stubborn approach has aided our family immensely.

If I disdained money, how did so much of it come into my possession? As a writer I enjoyed two accidental advantages, for I published my books at the precise time when Americans were beginning to look outward at the entire world rather than inward at themselves. They were spiritually and intellectually ready and even eager to read the exploring kinds of books I wanted to write. And with the intrusion of a largely banal television many were prepared to seek refuge in long books. Had I come along fifty years earlier, when America was isolationist, I doubt if anyone would have bothered much with my writing.

I now see that the harsh years of childhood and my premature introduction to the financial problems of adult life, especially at the Willow Grove amusement park, produced gaps in my life and perhaps even psychological imbalances, as a result of which I have never handled money well. It isn't that I have abused it or allowed it to abuse me; I have been contemptuous of it. If it could do the damage it did to my mother and me when I was a child, and if it achieved so relatively little in the development of my playmates who had plenty, it could be dismissed, and I did just that. It is important to note that I never adopted as my basic reaction the biblical creed that it was more difficult for a wealthy man to enter heaven than for a camel to pass through the eye of a needle. I never objected to someone else's having money, and I do honestly believe that never in any period in my life has envy of other people's affluence played even a minor role.

. . .

In some respects turning my back on money left me quite limited and it certainly made me unprepared for the life I would lead as a result of my good fortune. My wife says: 'You live as if prices are what they were in 1934,' and she is right. I remember when Frescoln, Talbott, Vitarelli and I used to drive into Philadelphia in Rees's car and have a robust Italian five-course lunch for thirty-five cents—antipasto, soup, pasta, meat dish, dessert—with a twenty-cent tip from all of us. That remains, unfortunately, my concept of just about where prices ought to be, and when my wife buys me a pair of ordinary garters, the kind that used to cost $.50, and now costs $14.50, I feel that the world is going insane. Then she points out that the novel that sold then for $1.50 now sells for $22.75, but I do some quick calculation and tell her: 'The garters have still increased at twice the rate of the books,' but she either does not believe my figures or is simply unimpressed.

My life as a writer with considerable wealth is the exact reverse of George Gissing's mournful protagonists who sweated away their lives on Grub Street with no money. In each case there was a dislocation from normal living experiences, but for anyone to claim, as some do, that the damage from having too much is comparable to that from having too little is nonsense, pure and simple nonsense. When I look at the scores of writers whose lives would be enriched if not actually ennobled by the small assured yearly stipend that Gissing once dreamed of, I conclude that their collective deprivation is vastly greater and more lamentable than the damage done to the occasional American writer who is knocked loose from his aesthetic or moral underpinnings by accidental wealth.

I must now cite several personal experiences that have taught me the relationship between the artist and money. One morning Bennett Cerf called me from his office at Random House about a woman I'll call Madame Xenia: 'Jim, we have a problem. Madame Xenia is in my office,' and I visualized the intense wife of the amiable artist—writer, musician, painter, poet?—whom I knew only slightly. 'She's distraught and says it's so unfair for you to be so well paid for your books while her husband has to struggle to survive. She says she and her husband are going to commit suicide unless you give them five hundred dollars right now. And they'll leave letters blaming you and Random House.'

I shivered, because whereas a threat of suicide from an ordinary citizen can sometimes be taken casually, when high-strung Madame Xenia and her delicately balanced husband made the threat it had to be taken seriously. Then I could hear Bennett's wise, consoling voice:

'Madame, relax. Your husband will be attended to. Jim Michener has said he'll give you two hundred and fifty and so will I.' And the scandal was averted.

On three other occasions artists from a variety of fields have told me they would have to commit suicide if I did not assist them, immediately, and a score have come simply to plead for even fifty dollars to tide them over, and more often their need has been in the thousands. Invariably I have given assistance because I remembered what need is, but it seems strange that never has one of these borrowers repaid the loan, even though in some cases they have had subsequent successes.

I do not take it kindly when well-meaning acquaintances lecture me about money and the artist, pontificating that the true artist never worries about money because it is unimportant. It is damned important and can be, as in the case of Chatterton, Gissing and Madame Xenia, a matter or life and death.

From the things I've said one might conclude that I think Tim Jones with his fantastic income from one lucky book is grossly overpaid, but do not jump to that conclusion. My thinking on this matter divides into two categories, the economic and the moral. Economically I have been strongly influenced by a study made some years ago by the economists of the Brookings Institution, who investigated from a hard-nosed business point of view the notorious salaries then being paid superstar athletes like the basketball wizard Kareem Abdul Jabbar or the latest hotshot baseball pitcher. Relying not on biased opinion but only on certified box-office statistics, they proved that not only did superstars earn back every dollar they were paid, but owners would still have had a bargain if they paid their superstars twice or three times what they were already paying. Their presence in a game or a season brought into the club coffers many times what they were being paid.

The same is true in publishing. Let's look at the figures cited earlier regarding the runaway best-seller by Tim Jones. His publisher, Galaxy Hall, sold out three huge printings of his book for a gratifying total of 920,000 copies at a list price of $17.50 each, but since the publisher allows the retail bookstore a discount of about 40 percent, Galaxy Hall keeps only 60 percent of the income, in this case an enormous $9,660,-000 of which Tim receives $2,415,000. He falls into the same category as Kareem: theoretically he could be paid double whatever royalty he did receive. The so-called superstars of writing are not overpaid; they are underpaid.

Of course, it isn't quite that simple. It is to everyone's benefit—writer, publisher, reader, the nation—that Galaxy Hall not only remain in business but remain strong. The large sums earned from best-sellers must help to finance the publication of those fine books that cannot be expected to turn a profit, or even, in many cases, break even. I have been a positive boon to beginning writers, because the rewards I did not get, and to which I admit I was not entitled in the long run, have been invested by Random House in the careers of younger writers who were battling to establish themselves. This is the way it should be and I do not want any more from Random, providing they are applying my surplus to young writers who have a greater need.

But with the recent changes in publishing the proper balance between paying popular writers at traditional levels and investing the excess profits from their books in younger writers has been imperiled. Speaking still from the economic point of view, I fear that publishers are not protecting their own long-range interests by focusing so much on popular writers of today while ignoring the development of good young writers for tomorrow.

Priorities are out of balance and I do not know how they should be corrected. I do not think that one can ask a successful writer to refrain from publishing his or her next book so that space will be made for a more deserving younger writer. Nor can we ask the bookstores or book clubs to place an embargo on the work of writers they know their subscribers want to read. In healthy economic enterprises the operations of the marketplace serve to make adjustments and should probably be allowed to do so in publishing, too.

I must make an important point. In none of my reflections on writing do I ever waste time on the pornographic work that sells well, the acknowledged trash or even the nonbook, for I believe that serious writers are not in competition with them. It is improbable that Thomas Berger or Robert Coover could ever have sold a book to the audience of such books even if the junk had not been available.

In such matters I am guided by a telling experience I had in 1929, when I was just becoming aware of contemporary American writing; prior to that I had concentrated on authors like Balzac, Dickens and Flaubert, but now a publishing sensation burst upon the American scene, a book by a veteran vaudeville comedian with a magical feel for the hilarious statement. Chic Sale's *The Specialist* offered the rib-tickling, mock-serious reminiscences of an imaginary carpenter somewhere in the Deep South who had spent his life in rural areas digging and then building outdoor privies. Through the years he had accumulated a wealth of practical wisdom about his trade, summarized in his recurring dictum: 'Dig 'em deep and dig 'em wide.'

Like thousands of others that year, I chuckled over his salty advice, and just when, two thirds of the way through the masterpiece I said to myself: 'Well, he can't work this vein any longer,' he launched into a high-level philosophical discussion as to whether you should cut into the door of your finished outhouse a star or a crescent moon, and his justifications for first one, then the other were humor of the most uproarious kind. The book was a tremendous success.

Did *The Specialist* in any way affect or diminish the chances of serious writers working at the same time? Hemingway was first publishing his stories then, Edith Wharton and Susan Glaspell were at the apex of their careers, and Scott Fitzgerald and Theodore Dreiser were working away. I doubt they gave even a passing thought to the fact that Chic Sale was outselling all of them, just as today I doubt that Saul Bellow or Joyce Carol Oates bewails the fact that the latest steamy novel of sex and mayhem outsells their more serious work.* Books like *The Specialist* are irrelevant and we must expect that many times in each century some book of no value will sweep the nation, with no deleterious conse-quences. Such books do not even detract from the sale of good books, because the two markets are not the same; they do not seem to help other writers but they do help bookstores, and thus indirectly help writers.

But wait! I must not say anything that might be considered as deni-grating Chic Sale because he achieved something I never will. The latest edition of the Random House Dictionary contains this entry:

> Chic Sale, *Facetious.* an outside privy. [from the pen name of Charles Partlow (1885–1936), American actor and author of *The Specialst* (1929), a humorous treatise on outhouse construction]

He entered the English language as a proper noun while his peers Edith Wharton and Theodore Dreiser did not.

Far more serious than competition from bad or worthless books is the changing structure of American publishing, in which conglomerates with no history of interest in books and certainly no experience in the patient cultivation of young authors, sweep in, gobble up a publishing company with historic antecedents and change the pattern of publishing

---

*But on p. 371 we have seen Kenneth Roberts bewailing the fact that *The Special-ist* has led the best-seller list for forty consecutive weeks, while his fine competing novel gets nowhere.

completely. The new owners, concerned only with the bottom line of financial success, mess around with their toy for a while, force old ownership to make all kinds of wrong moves, and far too often find that the 8 percent they can earn on capital investment in publishing is distressingly lower than the 35 percent they can make on some other arm of their diversified business. In disappointment and sometimes disgust they scour the marketplace to unload what they now recognize to have been a bad gamble. The original fine house, much weakened, staggers into the network of some other corporate owner no better qualified to direct a publishing firm than the first.

I had two chilling experiences with this denigration of a once noble profession. When Bennett Cerf and his longtime partner, Donald Klopfer, two gentleman publishers of fine character, felt for inheritance reasons they must take Random House public by selling to a corporation, I demurred about being handled in the future by a conglomerate with no interest in books. 'What happens to me,' I asked, 'if the wife of the president doesn't like my next manuscript?' and Bennett said reassuringly: 'No need to worry, she likes *your* books.' Years later, when Random was dumped by that same conglomerate and was being peddled around the country like a used carpet, a buyer was rumored to have been found at last, one abysmally unqualified to direct a publishing house, and I geared up to start a movement among my fellow writers to leave Random House if the sale went through, and it became obvious to the would-be buyer that a publishing house without its writers was not going to be attractive. When a new group of young men, the Newhouse brothers, with a family history of being interested in magazines and books, stepped in to buy, I and others breathed easy again.

An inescapable consequence of such sale and resale of the great American houses is that less emphasis is being placed on books and more on profits. This is fine for writers like me with proven track records; if we wished to forget all past principles we could toss our services into grandiose bidding wars and earn even more than we do today, to the destruction of everyone, especially ourselves. From that day I rode up Fifth Avenue to find a home for my second book I have never spoken to another publisher, nor would I so long as my fellowship with Random House remained congenial. It would be unthinkable,* and

---

*Lippincott's of Philadelphia did ask permission in a friendly way to publish a small treatise of mine dealing primarily with Philadelphia and I gladly agreed, for I doubted that Random would want it. For Macmillan I wrote a long evaluation of Margaret Mitchell's *Gone With the Wind* on the occasion of an anniversary edition and not long ago Scribner's asked me to write a foreword for a long-forgotten

I have never envied other authors who have skipped from one publisher to another, for I have not seen that it profited them much. I'm told they sometimes get a big initial advance for switching, but in subsequent years their careers have not advanced; more often they have deteriorated because of the jumping around.

If well-established writers profit from the big sums being pumped into publishing by the new corporate owners, who loses? Everyone else, I fear, but especially the beginning writers on whom the hardboiled new managers cannot afford to waste their time. Most of the houses today cannot even bother to read unsolicited manuscripts—and my Pulitzer Prize–winning first novel was so submitted under a nom de plume— because they spend their time trying to lure some established writer who is deemed about ready to break into 'the big time.' It is easier and cheaper to buy a writer than to develop one. I often wonder what such houses and editors are thinking about, because each year established writers like Toni Morrison are a year older and Saul Bellow gets longer in the tooth. They can't be around forever. If our new system is not geared to help young writers through the painful and nonproductive developing years, from what other source can the new Norman Mailers and Gore Vidals come?

Friends warned me that my indifference to business details might one day lead to trouble, and they were right; disaster did strike and it was largely my fault. A group of men with whom I had the closest association in a television project conceived the idea of putting together some scripts we had been working on, unsuccessfully as it turned out, and publishing them as a book. They asked permission to refer to my name, since I had been associated with the filming, and I consented, for the films had been narrated but not written by me.

Grabbing this approval and leaping into action, they put together a mishmash of stuff, not one word written by me except for excerpts from some things I had published long ago for which they had acquire permission from the publisher. With the aid of skilled editors they produced a manuscript that read as if I had written it. Then, to make it even more inviting, they composed a foreword with which I had nothing to do and, by a ruse, obtained a signature of mine, which they reproduced in facsimile and attached to the spurious foreword. They issued the book

---

manuscript by Hemingway that they wished to bring out, and I was proud to comply. And I have published small books with others.

to a public that had been deceived at every point, dressing it in a gaudy cover to make it more inviting. I overheard them boasting: 'The agent says anything by Michener is bound to be a best-seller. Our royalties will be in boxcar numbers, real boxcars.'

When I first caught sight of the book, *James A. Michener's U.S.A.,* I was aghast. It was fake from start to finish, a complete deception and in parts a forgery, a triumph of editorial legerdemain and the most cynical merchandising, but I was powerless to halt it without going to court and creating a public scandal. That I refused to do, for I had been taught to avoid the courts, but I was delighted when the book proved to be a disaster. I was even more pleased to learn that the huge edition that had been printed in expectation of an easy kill had remained largely unsold.

In the years that followed I have often heard of the ingenious tricks used by the publisher to unload his thousands of unsold copies, and though I have been disgusted by the devices and have tried fruitlessly to stop them, I have been amazed at their inventiveness. About once a month some reader asks me to autograph this disgraceful job and I usually refuse, but if the person says: 'I have all your other books and wanted to have everything you've written,' I sign it 'Not by James A. Michener' and then explain the fraud. One woman spoke for all when she said: 'Well, that does make it a collector's item,' and this happens just often enough to keep me mindful of my shame.

I have had only one redeeming moment in connection with this episode. One afternoon while autographing books at a bookstore in Washington, an interesting-looking man in his late forties appeared in line with no book to sign, but he did carry a handsome wood-and-leather box about the size of a book. When he reached the desk where I sat he said: 'I have something special to show you, Mr. Michener. My company provides expensive gifts for big corporations to purchase as Christmas presents for their best customers to whom it would be undignified to give a turkey. I've bought up a lot of your books and had these beautiful cases made. Of course, the box costs many times what we have to pay for the book, but when they're put together, they make an impressive gift, don't you think?'

They did, and when I handed the sample back I said: 'It's more appropriate than you might think. In a sense you're still giving them a turkey.' Later, the proprietor of the bookstore explained, in answer to my questions: 'There's a dozen ways of getting rid of unsold books that look fairly good in their colored jackets. That boxing business was one of the best.'

'How much does the publisher get per copy in a deal like that?'

'Worst case I ever heard of was nineteen cents a copy. A good-looking book like yours could fetch as much as eighty-nine.' Cocking his head, he asked: 'Why are you still smiling?' and I replied: 'Because I feel wonderful.'

I realize that much of what I've been saying in the preceding pages must seem like crocodile tears: 'He accepts the royalties, laments their inequity, but does nothing to correct the situation.' I have often heard this charge and must now rebut it, my behavior in the case of our art collections being typical.

When it became apparent that I was going to receive substantial sums from my writing, my wife and I reached the decision: Since we earn our income from the arts, each April, after we've paid our taxes, we will plow whatever is left back into the arts. Choosing first the exotic and relatively little-known field of Japanese prints, I studied that subject, made myself a fourth-rate expert, consulted with the great scholars and museum curators and published five books on it. Only when I felt I knew a little something did we begin to collect some six thousand of the finest prints in the low-priced days before the rest of the world began to prize them. Never intending to keep such treasures to ourselves, we placed them on permanent loan with the Academy of Art in Honolulu, where the public could enjoy them.

Aware that we could never collect real Titians and Rembrandts, we decided to focus on American paintings done during my lifetime, from 1907 on. Starting methodically, as before, I carefully analyzed some sixty scholarly works on the subject, after which I understood American painting in this century about as well as an amateur could. Specifically I knew which painters the experts considered the worthy masters but also, more important, which appealed to me personally. Aided by my wife, who has an affinity for the most advanced artists of the modern schools, we quietly spent our yearly royalties until we had some four hundred major canvases, not the ultraexpensive ones like those of Jackson Pollock and Willem de Kooning, but fine works by most of their distinguished contemporaries. Again, since we had not assembled these paintings for ourselves alone, we placed them on extended loan at the University of Texas in Austin, where art students could use them.

What happened next astounded us. Because we had striven always to acquire the best, we were vaguely aware that we had some rather fine works, but for many years we paid little attention to market prices. But in the mid-1980s we began to hear of explosions in the market. The essays I had written about Japanese prints had helped spur such a tremendous interest in them that single prints for which we had paid perhaps five hundred dollars were now selling to Japanese businessmen, who were coming late into the market in an effort to recover national treasures, for two hundred thousand, while a complete set of some famous series by either Hokusai or Hiroshige might go for a million. Less spectacular but equally amazing, the worth of our American paintings had also escalated wildly while we were not looking, so that what we had accumulated as an intellectual and artistic exercise had been transmuted into a small fortune. And that posed a problem, for we had certainly never collected art in order to make a profit, nor, with my attitude toward money, could we accept a reward we had not earned.

After a brief review of the alternatives we decided that the only responsible course was to give the art to the public, which had in a sense paid for it through the purchase of my books. The Japanese prints would go to Hawaii, about which I had written a book, the American art to Texas, the subject of another book.

I have no excessive hang-ups about the money I've earned, no sense of guilt. I earn every dollar I receive, refuse to do any writing for free, and advise all young writers who consult with me: 'Safeguard your financial safety.' I do not mean 'Write for money,' an attempt that is usually self-defeating, but I do mean that the would-be writer must be self-protective, and many will recall my asking them: 'Now, what are you going to do about money? Will your parents assist if things go poorly the first years? Will your wife (or husband) be willing to take a job?' Life taught me the preeminence of survival, and I am eternally grateful that good fortune enabled me to escape the misery of George Gissing's doomed characters.

But I do also have that strong liberal conscience that makes me morally ill at ease with recent national policies that shower rich men with tax advantages while depriving the poor of necessities. I know that I am not entitled to windfalls that reach me in this immoral way and feel that I must dispose of them lest they contaminate me. Driven by this curious mix of pragmatism and idealism, I consulted the two saints whose precepts guided my life: Paul, who preached, 'Keep it pure. Keep it clean,' and James, who argued: 'It isn't what you say, it's what you do.' Obedient to their counsel, I made the following decisions, supported always by my wife, who shared my attitudes:

Because young American writers encounter new difficulties these days in launching their careers, we have given all the royalties from seven of my novels to the graduate writing schools of three different universities to provide fellowships for would-be writers.

Because American poets have a difficult time getting a hearing, we gave the royalties from another book to programs that would help them get published here and in Europe.

Because we would not want to take royalties out of a foreign country in which we had worked extensively, we gave all the royalties from books published in Canada and Poland to programs in those nations for the support of young writers.

Because we want to encourage bright young people to enter publishing, we gave the royalties of another book for graduate internships at a university press where the recipients concentrate on the various skills required in bookmaking.

Because we are mindful of the contributions made by our colleagues at the localities related to our books, we have funded scholarships for the children of war correspondents and space experts.

And because we hear constantly of older writers who have fallen on difficult times, we have allocated the royalties from another book to a society whose generous members care personally for such writers.

Thus we share our royalties with young writers to help them get started and with older ones to help them end their lives with dignity.

Some years ago when President Reagan and his wife wanted to honor citizens who had given private support to the arts and letters in America, their inquiries led to me. I knew nothing of how I was chosen, but when the group gathered in the White House—corporate givers mostly—the president's staff revealed that their research showed that my wife and I had given to various projects relating to writing a total of eight million dollars. Since then we have divested ourselves of our art windfalls, and that sum has grown considerably. It must be obvious that when I die the legally required half of what's left will go to my wife and the balance to colleges and universities. Of course, when she dies, her share will be distributed in comparable fashion, but which institutions will benefit she will not tell me.

By what seems a series of fortunate accidents I shall have earned a deal of money from writing and will have given it all away. With my background I could not have done otherwise.

XIV

Meanings

A YOUNG MAN who has lived his life without a birth certificate, for the reason that no one seems to know where or when or to whom he was born, as was my case, gets along perfectly well as long as he stays in his home village and tries to do nothing of importance. Of course he runs into embarrassments, as when the stern principal of his school demands proof of his eligibility to enroll and grumbles when such proof is not forthcoming. Sometimes at children's games or parties there is an awkward moment when birthdays or birthplaces are asked and eyes turn toward the boy who shrugs his shoulders and says: 'I don't know.'

Of course, throughout the village it becomes generally known that such a boy has no antecedents, and speculation provides a score of answers as to who his parents might have been, but little harm is done by the guesswork. However, the boy is certainly set apart and he knows it, as do his fellow students in Sunday school and the larger public school. But, speaking from experience, I know that whereas the psychological scarring can be profound, modifying every act the boy will ever engage in, it is not crippling, for he begins to build defenses against his impediment, and whereas the scars will be with him wherever he goes and in whatever he tries to do, he does learn to live with them.

But as he leaves boyhood a network of interlocking entrapments face him, and the ones that produce inescapable difficulties are those enforced by society. If the Army drafts a young fellow to go overseas to fight for his country, the big brass is glad to get him as he is, birth certificate or no. But if the tests that all recruits take reveal him to be unusually capable in fields needed by the Army, he will be thrown into training to become an officer, and when on being ordered to produce his birth certificate he replies: 'I have none,' the entire Army goes into spasm, for it fears that the man whom they have nominated to be one of their future officers might be an enemy in disguise: 'Get us a birth certificate or else!' And then the trouble begins.

Or, should he wish to travel abroad to enlarge his view of the world or to train himself to be more useful to society, he must again prove who he is and what his lineage, lest he again be a spy traveling abroad for some nefarious purpose.

Twice, first when I wanted to continue my education in Europe, second when the Navy wanted to make me an officer, I had to prove to the government that I had been born, and preferably in the United States, but I had no birth certificate.

In such circumstances it is common for the applicant to hire a lawyer who will interrogate neighbors to establish the earliest possible date at which the child was known to have been in the community. On both occasions I employed, with the full assistance of my mother, the Doylestown lawyer John D. James, who compiled impressive testimony by Presbyterian Sunday school teachers, public school teachers and others that proved I had lived in that town since the age of two. No reliable evidence put me there any sooner, but it was generally believed that I had been born in New York and had arrived in town when I was about two weeks old.

No parentage could be established, but testimony was clear that from a very early age I had lived in the household of Mabel Michener. However, the government required a specific statement of parentage, and for reasons I have never known, lawyer James concocted one of the craziest stories ever filed and one that was bound to unravel when anyone inspected it even casually. Witnesses under James's direction swore that I was the son of Edwin Michener and his lawfully wedded wife, Mabel Michener, and was born on 3 February 1907, although it was well known that Edwin had died five years before. I suppose that copies of this document can be found in either Navy or State Department files; all I know is that I was issued a passport under that spurious arrangement and all subsequent legal documents state the same.

Lawyer James, for whom I once worked as a boy tending his lawn, and who could personally certify me back to age two, told me: 'Prior to that we can find no paper trail whatever. Therefore we could not tell the government what everyone believes to be true, that Mrs. Michener obtained you as she did all the other abandoned babies she took in when no parents could be found. So far as we know, you were an orphan and it seemed most practical to make you Edwin Michener's son, even though there is that discrepancy in dates. We had to say something, and we believed that the papers you now have will get you by, probably forever.' They have.

Mrs. Michener, into whose hands I fell one way or another, was one of those great women who serve in silence but leave behind a legacy that glows forever. The oldest of six children of a Pennsylvania farmer whose Haddock ancestors came from England and a mother whose Turner antecedents were from the Protestant section of Northern Ireland, she inherited in her teens the task of playing mother to her five younger siblings—three boys, two girls—and she did such a superlative job that the four who lived into maturity, though impoverished, did so with dignity. But Mabel spent both her youth and her chance for an education in caring for others, and after her husband died young, leaving her with a son, Robert, she continued her role as a universal mother by taking in a dozen or so abandoned children, for whose care she was paid a meager sum by a local charity organization.

It seems of utmost importance to me, as I look back upon those formative days, to remember that I grew up surrounded by noisy, loving, rambunctious children who played with me, knocked me about, tussled with me in the mud, and kept me from ever thinking myself as grand or favored or especially bright or entitled to privilege, or as anything but one of a mob. I was constantly reminded that I was a member of a social organization—a troubled, robust, loving extended family—which explains why, as an adult, I have repeatedly said that one of the lasting goals of my life has been to keep vital the social organisms of our nation: churches, newspapers, political parties, colleges, families. I have made great sacrifices to enhance such social groups and deem such service to be the best contribution I have made.

I have said earlier that working at a very early age in a variety of businesses taught me much about American ways of making money, and I've told about how delivering papers at four in the morning introduced me to the intricacies of small-town life, but more important, I think, was the fact that growing up in a nest of foster children plunged me at an extremely early age into some of the more tragic situations that confront helpless people. And that awareness which never leaves a person and colors all that he or she does in later life can be of enormous value, as it was to writers like Charles Dickens, Maxim Gorky and Richard Wright. It influenced all I would write.

I caught on fairly quickly to the fact that about half the children my mother shepherded reached her through big-city social agencies that helped young women in their late teens and early twenties who were in trouble, and although I was too young or too slow to decipher what that trouble might be, it was clear that copious tears were involved when the young women visited the children in whom they took a special interest, and I began to piece together odd bits of information.

We had at one time an adorable little Jewish boy with whom I fell in love, Harry Litwack, whose young mother, always referred to as Mrs. Litwack, was even more appealing than her son. When she took Harry in her arms on Sunday afternoons, she became radiant, and because she knew I helped care for him as a kind of big brother—I could have been no more than five at the time—she always brought me some small gift, and since it was usually edible, my affection for her increased.

There was no attempt to hide the fact that Harry was her son, but why they did not live together I could not fathom. However, starting on Wednesday one week, everyone in our crowded house was given repeated orders: 'We must all see that Harry looks his best on Sunday,' and I had the special task of seeing that his nose, which was often runny, was kept clean. At lunch on Sunday our house was extremely tense, as if a fire threatened or some other disaster loomed, and I remember my mother warning me: 'Keep his nose clean.'

At her regular Sunday time, about two, Mrs. Litwack appeared on our porch bringing with her an extremely nervous young man about her own age whom she introduced as Mr. Solomon, at which my mother stepped forward holding baby Harry by his little hand and engineering things so that the child moved toward Mr. Solomon, whom he had never seen before.

There was a long moment when nothing happened, but then my mother gently pushed the child forward, and again, for a most painful interval nothing happened, but then Mr. Solomon came alive, lost his nervousness, stooped down and took the boy in his arms, bringing him up level to his face and giving him a kiss. Then, pushing Harry away to study his joyous features, he embraced him again and said to all of us: 'He's a wonderful boy!'

Late that afternoon when it came time for Mrs. Litwack and Mr. Solomon to depart, they took Harry with them, and I never saw him again, but that night, after we had all gone to bed, I went back to the kitchen for some reason and there sat my mother, rocking back and forth with a hand to her mouth and tears in her eyes. She thanked me for having taken such pains to ensure that Harry looked his best when Mr. Solomon arrived, and some weeks later we received a wedding picture of Mrs. Litwack and Mr. Solomon holding Harry between them, and I can still see them after almost eighty years, but what I remember most is how Mr. Solomon stooped to take Harry in his arms.

I could recount a score of such stories—Paul, Dorothy, Virginia, Eleanor, David, Edward—but they seem to blend into a vague blur of troubled parents, lively children and the abiding love my mother showered on everyone. I was in no way precocious and some of the most poignant stories I probably missed. Two years ago the delightful tomboy Mildred, whom I had especially liked, drove quite a distance to see me after seven decades. She was a matron now with a husband who had obviously loved her for many years: 'I wanted to share something with you, Jimmy. You were always so good to me. My mother came from southern Jersey, daughter of a minister who would not let her marry the young man she loved. When she got pregnant her father, an unforgiving man, sent her away till I was born, then hustled me off to Mrs. Michener's.'

'What happened to your mother?'

'Since my grandfather was a minister, he was powerful in the community, and he had her committed to an insane asylum in another town, unbeknownst to me, until he died. When I married they told me about her, still in the asylum, and asked if I wanted to see her, but Eddie and I talked it over and we said "No." It was too long ago, and besides, someone told us after all those long years in the madhouse she had become pretty much a loony herself. Mrs. Michener was my real mother.'

I was surrounded by such stories, but in many ways the most dramatic was my own. To understand it you must know what an impressive and far-reaching family the Bucks County Micheners of Pennsylvania are. At one of the yearly summer gatherings of the clan, to which Micheners come from hundreds and even thousands of miles, for they are a proud, ancient breed, I met a man who told their story:

'A lot of us made up a kitty, quite a few dollars, and had Anna Shaddinger, the schoolteacher in Doylestown—she's a Michener through her mother's line—pursue her studies of just who the Micheners were in history. She put together a marvelous book proving that everyone in the United States bearing the name is related to everyone else. And she can tell you how.

'So when the book came out it told the truth. The first Micheners came here to Bucks County in the 1680s as indentured servants with William Penn. Boy, when our people saw those words *indentured servants* they exploded, me among them. Saying something like that in a book we had paid for.

'So in the second edition it appeared the original Micheners had been "sturdy English yeomen" but that still didn't satisfy us, so in the third edition they became "trusted friends and advisers of William Penn" and I understand that in the next edition William Penn is going to come over with us.'

Much of what he said was teasing, but one thing was clear—those early Micheners had a propensity for bearing male twins who took to farming, and soon the rural areas were filled with people of their name, and the rumor is correct: every known Michener in the United States is the cousin of every other, and the year I won the Pulitzer Prize and was expected to be guest of honor at the big picnic I was totally upstaged by Roland Michener, governor-general of Canada, and another pair who had come all the way from Ceylon or some such place.

In one edition Anna Shaddinger had said somewhat petulantly that she had been able to place every Michener in the grand hierarchy except one family in the Detroit area, and she would appreciate information about them. In a later edition came the somewhat acerbic note that the Detroit affair had been clarified: a Polish family had immigrated into Hamtramck with a name like Miczelowski and had anglicized it to Michener.

In my day Micheners simply abounded and at one time there were half a dozen James Micheners in our vicinity with several of them having the middle initial of 'A.' Down the years I've known quite a few James A.'s; one of the best was a Marine colonel in Virginia whose handwriting was exactly like mine; one of the most lively an imaginative young man who, like me, attended Swarthmore. He kept me hopping for a while, and once when I returned to visit Hawaii the police were waiting on behalf of local citizens who had paid large advance fees to a James A. Michener of Swarthmore who had advertised that he was leading a group of tourists through the islands of the South Pacific.

Several energetic young men using my name have swept through the countries of Asia that I used to frequent, buying jewels and other valuables and assuring the sellers that their checks were obviously good, but the James A. that I will remember the longest and with the deepest affection was a man of that name who, against all odds of probability, came to live a short distance from me in our small village of Pipersville. The confusion this caused was so great that after trying in vain to sort things out, the local Sears, Roebuck store asked one of us to give back our credit card because they were incapable of keeping our accounts straight. After an amiable consultation that gave me an opportunity to meet this most congenial fellow, we agreed that he needed his card more than I did mine, and Sears lost a good customer.

Problems of an amusing nature proliferated that centered on the fact that I had an unlisted telephone number while he did not, and when people in various parts of the country tried to get Jim Michener in Pipersville, Pennsylvania, they had no difficulty in completing the call. In fact, the other James A. received so many calls that he became a kind of additional secretary for me, and in time he became so familiar with the kinds of calls he might expect and so knowledgeable about my movements that he helped me considerably by handling inconsequential calls himself, then telephoning me in the evening with any he thought might require my attention.

I stopped by his house once to apologize for the inconvenience I was causing him, but he brushed that aside: 'It's fun to get calls from all parts of the country and even sometimes from foreign newspapers. I never know what's going to happen when the phone rings.' I offered to remunerate him for his time but he said: 'No, it's a pleasure except for nights like Christmas Eve and New Year's Eve.'

I asked him what happened then and he said: 'It's that Catholic priest up in Scranton who talks for a long time.' As soon as he said this I could remember the dear fellow, a jovial faced Irishman who had served with me in the South Pacific as Navy chaplain and to whom I used to turn over my hard-core discipline cases.

I recalled the time when, as island censor, I was faced with the problem of Lombardelli Kutz from a small town in Arkansas. He was totally incorrigible and though almost illiterate he was able to write short letters to his wife, one girl in a town nearby and a third girl not far off, all of whom had become pregnant. As censor I had to clear all letters from the war zone but was under strict orders not to concern myself with morals, but when in one mail Lombardelli, a Neanderthal type, sent out four semiliterate letters threatening to murder his three girlfriends if they did not straighten themselves out, I had to intervene because now potential crime was involved.

Plopping Lombardelli beside me in my jeep, I took him first to the base legal officer, who warned him that sending threats like that through the mail was a criminal act for which he could get years in jail. But the young fellow seemed not to comprehend, so the lawyer suggested that I take him to see the base chaplain. I told Lombardelli to wait in my jeep while I went ahead to instruct the chaplain about my problem boy. He read the letters, peeked out his door to see the fellow sprawled in the jeep and returned to ask: 'So what?'

'Well, what are you going to do about him?'

'Nothing.'

'Look, he's threatening murder. We've got to do something.'

'Lieutenant Michener, in this job you learn that with some men there's nothing you can do. He wouldn't understand if I tried, so I'm not going to waste my time on him. There is nothing to be done but pray that when he gets home he doesn't carry out his threats.'

This attitude was so alien to my Quaker-Presbyterian upbringing that I could not comprehend it. With us, if you had the bad luck to come upon someone like Lombardelli you became agitated and beat your brains and prayed a lot in an effort to save him. But the good chaplain, having seen many such men, realized that there was nothing that he could do and the less time he wasted on this hopeless case, the more he would have for people who could be helped.

I became quite attached to the chaplain; out of gratitude for the common sense he taught me I arranged for him to get from the submarine base his share of torpedo juice, the ultra-high-proof pure alcohol used to propel torpedoes on their deadly runs. I often thought that this very expensive and closely guarded fuel did far more damage to our American troops than it ever did to the Japanese enemy, but my chaplain did like his nip now and then, so now I was not surprised when my Pipersville James A. told me: 'Apparently this priest goes to the local bar on big nights and toward midnight he must shout: "Do I know Jim Michener? Get me Jim Michener in Pipersville!" and when he gets me he reminds me of the great times he and I had together on Espiritu Santo, and then he introduces me to all the fellows in the bar. His calls go on for maybe forty minutes, but I don't mind because they are festive and he never realizes that he isn't talking to you.' When I asked: 'How do you handle him?' he said: 'Oh, I grunt just enough to keep him going.'

The Micheners were a constantly surprising lot, and although I was not a Michener, a fact that was widely known, I attended their yearly picnics with relish; I was happy with them and appreciated the warm courtesies they extended me.

It had not always been that way. In those early years when my mother was struggling to feed and shelter her brood in the strange houses into which we moved with such frequency, we were sometimes visited by two tall, austere women in their fifties who were known to us as the Michener aunts—sisters or cousins of the deceased Edwin Michener to whom Mabel had been married. Edwin and Mabel's son Robert, older than I, was a thoroughly likable lad; in fact, I tried to model myself after him, for he was a good athlete, and it was to see him that the Michener aunts came to our home. They brought with them little paper bags of goodies, and with stern looks intended to dismiss the rest of us hangers-on, they gave the candy only to Robert.

They were especially hard on me, and I realized even at that early age that they resented the fact that I bore the name Michener, and on not one but many occasions they pointed out to me as they gave Robert his little treats: 'You're not a Michener. You don't deserve any.' And some of the things they said when neither Robert nor Mabel was around were painful to me. They were harsh, unlovely creatures, two characters from a Grimm's fairy tale or like Frank Baum's Wicked Witch of the West. They despised all the children my mother had taken into her home, judging this to be an occupation unworthy of the widow of their sainted brother, but the others, so far as I knew, did not receive the constant hammering I did.

They were among the ugliest memories of my childhood, the first time I had encountered real hate, and I have often wondered what lasting effect they had on me. At the time when the aunts were persecuting me, my response was neither anger nor fear, though I was furious that Robert received candy and I didn't. They certainly did not dampen my enthusiasm for life, for I was incurably ebullient, nor did they sour me on Micheners, for the others I have known have all been as warm and friendly as the James A. of Pipersville. I believe I did not allow them to do any damage beyond what harsh words could do, but perhaps I am not the one to judge. Certainly, something in those early years made me more reserved and introspective than the normal boy, and some alteration occurred that would make me more withdrawn in later years. Perhaps it is best said that a dark cloud had passed my way, of which I was aware, and that it threw harsh shadows on a palette that had hitherto been mostly a bright gold. At least the Michener aunts served a constructive purpose in that they taught me the journey through life was not going to be easy.

Sadly, the aunts must have turned Robert against me because, some years later, when he went to California to marry a fine Doylestown girl who had moved there, I wrote to him the kind of letters a thirteen-year-old would write to an older brother whom he idolized, but he refused to answer. After being thrice rebuffed, I wrote no more, and during the remaining sixty-odd years of his life we exchanged not one word or visit.

Some unknown Michener, and it may have been two different people, one male, one female, although I have always thought of the person as a man some years older than myself, played a significant role in my life when I became a writer and began to attract local attention. The day after my name first appeared in a Philadelphia newspaper he mailed me a letter from that city:

> Dear Mr. 'Michener'????
>
> You don't know who I am but I sure know who you are. You aren't a Michener and never were. You're a fraud to go around using that good name and you ought to be ashamed of yourself. Sooner or later the truth will be made public and you will stand disgraced in the eyes of all good people. Why don't you operate under your own name, which I am sure is something like Ginsburg or Cohen.
>
> I'll be watching you,
A real Michener

From that day he hit me with a barrage of letters, always writing after I had accomplished something, no matter how trivial. His letters were not illiterate, and in a curious way they extended the animosity the Michener aunts had exuded, for he too was infuriated by my presence in the family. I could not conceivably have posed any threat to him, and nothing that I did defiled his precious Michener name—quite the contrary—but any positive behavior of mine caused him to vent his spleen. Repeatedly he advised me to resume my proper name, which he again assumed was something like Berkowitz, Liebowitz or Hoffberg, and why didn't I sink back into obscurity so that I could not offend good people.

But it was when I won the Pulitzer that he really exploded. His letter this time exceeded any that had gone before, and I am sorry I did not keep it, although it may still be hidden somewhere in my papers. He started with the old accusation that I was not a real Michener and gave great offense to those who were. Then he advanced to splenetic sentences like: 'I would think you would be ashamed to show your face in public,' and 'we will smoke you out,' and 'It's disgraceful to pose as someone you aren't.' He denigrated the award I had won and supposed that the judges were Jewish, and then he closed with a sentence whose counter-parts I have heard all my life, in one form or another—not directed at me but at others with whom I identify—'Who in hell do you think you are, trying to be better than you are?'

The last seven words of that cry are burned into my soul because one meets them everywhere. Jesse Jackson runs for president, and who the hell does he think he is, trying to be better than he is? In South Africa any black who aspires to a decent job is excoriated for trying to be better than he is. English literature is replete with ridicule of persons of lower class who by dress or speech are trying to imitate people who are better than themselves. In my novel *Texas* I tell of rednecks who gunned down freed slaves who by merely walking on sidewalks were trying to be better than they were entitled to be, and of a choleric white judge who shot a black lawyer dead for presuming in court to be better than he was. In Miami newly arrived Cubans are scorned for putting on airs, and in many other cities immigrants from all nations are censured for trying to be better than their station in life would warrant.

One of the most terrible things I have seen in my life was a gang of white hoodlums in a small Western town who drove their car close to the sidewalk on Sunday morning, reaching out with a tar brush to smear the freshly pressed clothes of black women going to church. When I reprimanded them, the local police being unwilling to do so, the young punks snarled: 'Where in hell do those niggers get the nerve, trying to be better than they are?'

I have spent my life trying to be better than I was, and am brother to all who have the same aspirations.

The valuable thing about those Philadelphia letters was that they reached my desk on mornings when I might have been tempted to think that some good thing I had accomplished was more important than it really was. Awards, doctorates, public notices, small victories in politics, all were chipped down into proper perspective by the next monitoring letter: 'We know what a fake you are, and pretty soon the whole world will find you out.'

Sensible ancient emperors, who might be tempted to consider them-selves immortal, kept near them human skulls to remind themselves that they, like everyone else, must die someday. *Memento mori,* a reminder of death, was what such a useful object was called, and for me my friend's letters served roughly the same purpose: no matter what I did he reminded me that I was a fraud. His attacks reached a frenzy when I ran for Congress in 1962, for then he bombarded me weekly and sometimes daily with postcards onto which he pasted bits from newspapers that vilified Democrats and on which he wrote or printed harsh statements about my right to run for anything. He was especially bitter about the fact that I had a Japanese-American wife and asked scornfully at least once a week: 'What's the matter with you, trying to slip a Jap spy into our national capital?' Only then did I wish I had his address, for I would have enjoyed reminding him that there were already in Congress several congressmen and senators of Oriental ancestry, a fact he seemed not to know. But night after night when I returned home dead tired from campaigning, awaiting me would be his latest bit of savagery.

In 1976 the papers carried a notice that President Ford had elected to give me the highest civilian award this nation has to offer, and the final letter from my mentor was a scorcher: 'Still using a name that isn't yours. Still a fraud. Still trying to be better than you are.' He was right on all his accusations. He must have died shortly thereafter because his letters ceased, and I missed them, for they had been therapeutic.

I was nineteen years old before I knew for certain anything substantial about my background. Prior to that time I had stumbled along happily knowing only in a vague way that I was not like other boys my age; I supposed that the scowling Michener aunts knew what they were talking about when they snarled that I was not a member of their family, but I was not unhappy about that, because they offered little inducement for me to want to join them. I never really knew who I was, and neither my mother nor Uncle Arthur ever told me, even supposing they knew. But as thousands of adopted children or those of uncertain birth invariably learn, some well-intentioned adult can always be counted on to break the secret, and usually at some moment when it is least appropriate.

In my case it was a beautiful girl from a Michener family in another town, about my age and a frequenter of the big Michener reunions. With the kindliest intentions she told me one Thursday night: 'You know, of course, that you aren't one of us, and that the woman you call your mother really isn't your mother.' She then gave me the first of about twenty variations of who I really was—I would hear every possible version in the decades that followed and still do—and then she waltzed along to talk with others.

My world was shattered and there was no one with whom I could talk. Assumptions with which I had been content and which had kept me happy were proved to be insecure, and that Friday was one of the worst days I would ever encounter. I cut my college classes, walked about in a daze and could come to no conclusions about anything. I had, of course, known from my treatment at the hands of my Michnener aunts that I was not a member of their family, and I had certainly had it drummed into me that I was not like my brother Robert, but I had carelessly supposed that although I was much like the many children who came and went in our household, I was somehow different. But if I was not a duplicate of Harry Litwack, who was I? And what was my relationship to Mrs. Michener? Such questions could not have struck me at a worse time because for some months I had been pondering the moral nature of mankind in the universe,* specifically the question of whether God did or did not exist; and on the less important but more immediate level I felt I must resign from my college fraternity because I found myself opposed to what it stood for.

I wrestled with these three questions all Friday and found no answers, nor could I think of anyone to whom I might appeal for help, but on that tempestuous weekend I slowly managed to resolve the problems. On the basic question of who I was I decided that I would never know the answer, that a hailstorm of solutions would probably be thrown at me, and that I would never be clever enough to sort truth from legend. As calmly as if I were a practiced surgeon performing a major operation, I cut that part of life out of my existence, then and forever. I did not know who I was, nor did I care, and what was more important, I would never again bother myself about it. I would not daydream, I would not construct what-ifs, and I would find contentment in myself as I was at any given moment; I would have no envy for anyone else's position, no shame for my own. From that moment of decision I never wavered or looked back. I knew who I was, a young man of nineteen with certain proved abilities and known weaknesses ready for the long haul of years that lay ahead.

Two later evaluations of that period must be inserted here. When Alex Haley's excellent novelized account of his African forebears, *Roots,* swept the country in 1976, it launched a nationwide frenzy in which adults who had been adopted in childhood started digging in genealogies and a great deal of nonsense was written about the necessity for every human being to know his or her real roots. Laws were passed giving such people the right to inspect their previously locked adoption papers

---

*At this time I had no birth certificate, nor did I get the fabricated one till I was twenty-four and required a passport. This spurious one was confirmed by the government when I was thirty-five and the U.S. Navy wanted to commission me as an officer. It is understandable that at nineteen I would be confused.

to enable them to search for their birth parents, especially their mothers. Having solved this problem for myself years before, I was amused at much of the nonsense being peddled by both professional and amateur psychologists. From what they were preaching one would have thought that it was impossible to lead an acceptable life if one didn't know every detail of one's origins, and women who had been adopted were particularly susceptible to this hysteria.

Much harm was done, for although I am aware that in a few cases out of a million someone might want to know his or her family background because of possible predisposition to genetically inherited diseases whose lifesaving cure might be started if knowledge came early enough, for the average person such knowledge, especially if acquired in a way to cause pain to oneself or others, is of little practical or emotional value. I must know of at least a hundred men with uncertain parentage who achieved both personal and professional success in a competitive world, and two of my heroes, Ramsay MacDonald, who became prime minister of Great Britain, and Alexander Hamilton, one of the architects of the American system of government, were such men.

I have been consulted by many people asking my advice on these matters and it has been short, firm and consistent: 'If you think that such knowledge will do you any good, or if you think you might have fun trying to track down elusive facts, by all means have a go at it. But if you think the discovery of such knowledge will in any significant way improve your life, don't waste your time. The morning after you find what you seek, you'll be the same confused, reasonably competent bloke you are today, and not a thing will be changed.' With men I often end my statement a bit more roughly: 'You'll be the same miserable jerk you are today,' and we laugh at ourselves. The older I get the more secure I feel in giving such advice.

I have been accosted even more frequently by married couples who are thinking of adopting children and who seek counsel on whether to tell their children right from the start that they are adopted. Now, there is no flippancy in my response, for on this subject I am really one of the best-informed men in the world.* It has been my experience that there

*When Pearl Buck, Oscar Hammerstein and I lived as close neighbors in Bucks County we were appalled at the number of Asian-American orphans who were judged by the then experts on the subject to be unadoptable. Under Pearl Buck's inspired leadership we established a home for such children, plus Asian-African orphans and found ordinary homes for every child that came into our hands, and in doing so we had to counsel almost daily on the best procedure for informing children of their early histories. I was particularly involved in that aspect of our operation.

is no good way to handle the problem. Whatever is done will probably turn out to be wrong, or at least will create certain unpleasant problems. If you tell the child as soon after birth as possible, it sometimes disturbs him a great deal at the very time when he most needs the reassurance of a normal background; and if you defer telling him you can be sure that sooner or later some well-meaning person will reveal the secret to him, and usually at the moment that will be the most psychologically damaging. Of one thing you can be certain: ultimately the child will find out and, even with the most stable child, such a discovery can be painfully disorienting. But if he or she is reasonably stable to begin with, recovery can be swift and complete. I know of no good way to handle this problem, and have seen even the best-prepared procedures go awry, but I have seen only occasional long-term damage.

At the end of my tortured weekend wrestling with the problem of my heritage I moved on to the greater question of religious proof, which had been worrying me for some time. Because we had no Meeting in our area, I was a Quaker reared in strict Presbyterianism, a form of religion I found congenial and about which I would do a great deal of study and some writing in my lifetime. But I had never been interested in theological aspects of the religion; I was what might be called a religious sociologist: I respected the actions taken by Christians. I was confused about both the nature of God and the question of whether he did or did not exist, and that weekend as I roamed about the Swarthmore campus I decided that if I was never going to solve a relatively simple problem like my parentage, I was certainly not competent to solve the infinitely greater problems relating to the existence of God. With a mind as clear as it would ever be, I decided: 'I will never know about God and I shall never bother my head again about it.'

I decided further that I would live my life henceforth as if Deuteronomy and the New Testament had laid down the best patterns for human life. I would be a practicing Christian, would support churches, would aid Christian endeavors of all kinds, would be impartial toward the various denominations, and would conduct my life so that I need rarely be ashamed of my behavior. Never in the years since, in moments of either elevation or despair, have I deviated from that simple conclusion, and I would think it highly unlikely that on my deathbed I would suddenly cry: 'I have seen the light!' and announce that I was joining this or that specific church, for I see the light almost every morning when I awake and look out upon my world.

I am quick to admit that the creed I follow, which is a kind of liberal humanism in the vein of Thomas More, Thomas Jefferson and John Dewey, would be ill suited to many and probably not satisfactory for a community whose members require structure, priests of one sort or another and meeting places for worship and socializing, but for me it has been most satisfying and reassuring. When I taught in Colorado during the depression, teaching positions with an assured income were at a premium, and rural schoolboards took almost fiendish pleasure in interrogating would-be teachers about all aspects of their behavior: Did the young woman date during week nights? Did the young man smoke? And especially: Are you religious and if so, what do you follow? I had a sardonic head principal who devised an effective answer to that last question: 'I am a Home Baptist.' I am a Home Quaker.

The last moral crisis I grappled with on that difficult weekend was more agonizing than either of the other two but in retrospect seems almost comic; it was preposterous that I should have allowed it to torment me as it did. From what I have revealed so far about myself it should be clear that I was somewhat different from the average young college student, immeasurably more insecure and naive than many, but at the same time tougher and more worldly wise than most. I was not, and I was aware of this when I allowed it to happen, qualified to be the the typical fraternity member, but on arriving at Swarthmore I had accepted an invitation from the brain-trust fraternity on campus, Phi Delta Theta, with whose serious and capable members I felt congenial. But even a brief acquaintance with fraternity life proved that I had made a grievous mistake. If the fraternity would be able to do very little for an uncut diamond like me, I could do even less for it, so in decency I resigned.

I did not know it, but those were the years when a strong antifraternity sentiment was beginning to develop in various corners of the nation, and the older men who supervised fraternity affairs nationally felt that they must nip any incipient negative movement in the bud. Such was the mission of a Mr. Maxwell who arrived on campus to talk things over with me. He was in his late forties, a handsome man in a handsome three-piece suit and a handsome pair of shoes. He was suave, understanding, sympathetic and forthright: 'Mr. Michener, we simply cannot afford to lose a man of your caliber. Winner of an important scholarship. Very high marks. Fine, clean-cut appearance.' I had never before thought of myself in those terms. 'Now let me broach a ticklish subject. If your problem is money, if you cannot afford fraternity life, I have some influential friends to whom the fate of a young man like you is important. They'll lend you the money, no interest, and you pay them back after you graduate and we have found you a good job.'

For two long days Mr. Maxwell hammered at me, never raising his voice, always playing the role of a friendly adviser, which in fact he was, but I remained adamant, and then at the close of the second day he moved the discussion to a level of great significance. We were having an iced Coca-Cola in the corner of the local drugstore—no alcohol was allowed anywhere at Swarthmore College or in the town nearby—and he asked in a fatherly way: 'How old are you, Michener?' When I said 'Nineteen,' he snapped his fingers and said: 'Dash it. I have a lovely daughter, almost your age,' and he produced a photograph, which he allowed to rest on the table between us. Then he continued: 'Now, a young fellow with your background and brains, you're certain to do very well in American life because we need men like you. And in due course you'll want to get married, and it could be that you'll meet Patricia and fall in love, and, like any decent, self-respecting young man, you'll come to my office and say: "Mr. Maxwell, I would like permission to marry your daughter," and after the usual questions back and forth I'll ask: "And what fraternity were you in in college?" and if you say, "Mr. Maxwell, I wasn't in any fraternity," do you think for one minute I'd let you marry my daughter?'

The question hung in the air like an unexploded bomb suspended by a parachute. It opened vistas I had never considered before, and when Mr. Maxwell returned to his hotel room for a night's sleep before leaving in the morning he said: 'Think about that, Michener, and tomorrow at breakfast tell me you've changed your mind.'

I spent a horrible night. Pressures were crowding in on me from too many directions and with too many ramifications, but this time as I again wandered the campus I could see the delectable Patricia's photograph resting on the soda-fountain table, and I could visualize the rejection when I asked her father for his permission to marry her, and I could see myself roaming the world, unable to find anyone to marry me because I was not a fraternity man. The prospect was bleak, but just as I was about to conclude that I was damaging myself for life, I saw not Patricia Maxwell but her father, that handsome man, so polished, so sure of himself and I could hear his reassuring words: 'I have some influential friends to whom the fate of a young man like you . . .' I could see him dining with those friends for discussions of great importance, and it suddenly occurred to me: 'Hey! It wouldn't make the least bit of difference if I did belong to a fraternity. He would *never* allow me to marry Patricia!' and suddenly things began to fall into place: my parentage, God, the fraternity and, at the center of it all, me.

Next morning, feeling as certain of my judgment as I ever would in my life, I called Mr. Maxwell at the Strath Haven because I could not trust myself to confront so persuasive a man face to face, and told him: 'Mr. Maxwell, you've been so understanding and helpful. A perfect gentleman. But I've got to go ahead. I'm resigning.'

'Son,' he said without losing his temper, 'I'm sorry for you. You're making a mistake you'll regret for the rest of your life.' And I never saw him again.

The college subject matter that fascinated me the most was a query posed in biology when the professor asked almost casually: 'Which factor influences human behavior most strongly, heredity or environment?' Since this ancient riddle was offered toward the end of class, he had only a few minutes to discuss it, and after briefly summarizing the current thinking, he said: 'With our present knowledge, no conclusion can be reached.'

With me this brief introduction to the subject touched a vital nerve. I saw that a young man who comes from a historically important family is inclined to accept the opinion of a proud woman who told Winston Churchill: 'I think breeding is the most important thing in life,' to which he replied: 'It is fun, but one can have other interests, too.' Such young men tend to choose their wives from families of equally illustrious background, so that the superior breeding can continue.

But when a young man has no secure knowledge of his genetic inheritance he is prone to think that everything good that happens to him is the result of his upbringing and the strength of character he is resolutely developing. I obviously fell into this second category, and it led me into investigations that would never end. I noted every scientific study that strengthened the environmental hypothesis, and I could see in the lives of those about me ample evidence that those boys and girls who studied, went to Sunday school and learned to utilize public schools, libraries, churches and Boy Scouts were the ones who prospered. Heredity had very little to do with it, so far as my inquiries went, and I was pleased to know this, because it meant that my clever use of environmental opportunities would ensure me ultimate success.

I had been engaged in this speculation for only a brief spell after graduation when I began to hear from learned friends of a brilliant Russian scientist, Trofim Lysenko, who was accumulating old evidence and producing new data that quite blasted the Mendelian theories of genetic control of plant destiny. He substituted the Communist doctrine that a plant's environment, properly controlled to produce benevolent results, became a far more powerful developmental factor than its inherited capacity. Furthermore, and this was stunning news, Lysenko seemed to be proving that the favorable behavior patterns that were induced in the present generation would be inherited in the next and future generations. In other words, the inherent nature of a plant or a human being could be altered, if properly acted upon by a benevolent environment; this meant that salutary change could be transmitted to future human generations until it became embedded as part of the genetic structure of the plant or human. Thus the entire future history of a plant or of a human society could be modified if one applied the right pressures now. It was a theory most reassuring to a new society like the Soviet Union that wanted to break with the past or someone like me who had no idea of what his past was. So, like Stalin, I embraced it enthusiastically, for it solved a lot of problems and gave great hope for the future.

But as the decades passed I began to hear most distressing reports from Russia and the international scientific community about Lysenko. When he succeeded in persuading Stalin to make Lysenkoism the official state policy, he installed himself as a virtual czar in control of agriculture and associated fields, and from this position dictated how crops should be grown and that scientists who opposed his doctrine be removed from office. When I first heard stories of these excesses I blithely attributed them to partisans of old ways of doing things.

But evidence that discredited Lysenko began to mount. His plan for growing wheat in new ways was such a disaster that famine became a real threat. It was proved that many of the so-called experiments on which Lysenkoism was based never took place; they were total frauds. And refugee scientists he had persecuted told of others less fortunate whom he had sent to Siberia and their death. The world community of scientists raised an uproar, ridiculing his concept of new forms of plant life on demand, and heaped mockery on Russian science. So ended one of the most bizarre episodes of scientific perversion.

I now realized that my assumption that environment accounted for perhaps as much as 85 percent of human development was ridiculous, and after carefully restudying the evidence I summarized my new conclusions in this way: The genetic factor does impose definite limits as to what can be altered by the environment; I'd say the balance is about sixty-five environment, thirty-five heredity, because I still insist that what a man becomes is largely due to what he determines he shall become. Now, at the close of a life of speculation, I conclude that I have always, for personal, not scientific, reasons, underestimated the significance of the genetic factor. The fierce discipline I have imposed on

myself, the endless hours of work, the obsessive attention to the project
at hand, have probably been superfluous. I really didn't need to work
as hard as I have.

It now seems likely that I started with a fairly stalwart genetic background; certainly my longevity and the fortunate retention of my mental
circuits would point to a strong initial endowment. I suppose also that
my ability to withstand hard psychological and physical shocks stems
not from determination but rather from a nervous system with quick
recuperative powers, and as my doctors and dentists have pointed out,
I can bear a lot before I call for help.

I conclude that my genetic inheritance was so favorable that it provided a sturdy base on which my acquired characteristics could thrive.
But then the question arises: From where did that genetic inheritance
come? and I am left as much in the dark as when I started. If my good
fortune in life has been due more to my grandparents than to my own
dogged willpower, who were those grandparents?

The reader already knows that during that vital weekend when I was
nineteen I reached two conclusions: I would never know what my
parentage was, and I would not speculate idly upon it. I have never
deviated from those decisions and have had a remarkably placid emotional life as a result. But others have spent a good deal of time prodding
into the record, of which there is almost none, and trying to judge the
validity of rumors, of which there is an abundance. One reporter who
spent time and ingenuity on the matter called me after his work was
done and told me breathlessly: 'Jim, I've found out who your parents
really were. Do you want to know?' and he must have been bewildered
when I said: 'Not really.'

Despite my strong intention to keep myself isolated from this fruitless
speculation, hints of some dozen or so radically different answers to the
question have surfaced; I have not attempted to catalog them. They run
the gamut, and had I been disposed to join the *Roots* hysteria of some
years back, I would have had many titillating alleyways to explore, but
I was far past that point in my life.

But I was not immune to shock, and in 1987, as I was celebrating my
eightieth birthday, a dear friend from school days, Helen Gallagher, one
of the finest girl athletes I had ever known, sent me a letter that was quite
startling. She said that as a girl seventy years ago she had overheard a
kitchen conversation in which the mother of one of her girlfriends was
telling another woman how disgraceful it was that Mr. Blank, one of
Doylestown's most upright and respected leaders, refused to help in any
way the widow Mabel Michener and her son James, when everyone

knew that he, Mr. Blank, was the father of the boy. The letter had such a stamp of honesty about it, the kind that might have been written by a character in Hawthorne or Dickens, that I could not dismiss it.

I had known Mr. Blank well, had even had business dealings with him and had liked him. He was proper, staid, a respected voice in the business community and a veritable pillar of the Presbyterian church. When having my hair cut at Nelson's Barber Shop I had always faced that handsome row of shaving mugs that the leading men of our town kept there on display, the name of each owner outlined in gold, and Mr. Blank's was the finest of the lot, as befitted his high station. Now, as I twisted Helen's letter in my hand I could easily visualize him, the kind of small-town businessman that Theodore Dreiser might have described as conducting his affairs in Chicago, or Samuel Butler might have shown on his way to important business in London.

What I have to say next summarizes an important aspect of my life. From what I have written earlier it should not surprise anyone when I claim that that revelation—and it has by no means been proved—had little effect on me. If Mr. Blank had been my father, so be it. He'd given me a sturdy body and a clear mind, and a boy can wish for little more; I am being completely honest when I say that so far as I personally am concerned I bear him not the slightest grudge. But when I think of my mother slaving as she did, toiling at the most menial jobs, unable to give her children the things she knew they needed, I find it incomprehensible that a man of means and position who was in major part responsible for her condition should have refused to help. If indeed he stood close at hand and did nothing to help her, then I can only echo St. Paul as he cried in Corinthians when wishing to utter a crushing condemnation: 'Let him be Anathema,' to which I add my own: 'Let him rot in the lowest level of hell.'

It was fortunate, if he was my father, that I never knew it, because my free and wild upbringing had given me a surprisingly rugged character, and had I known that he was treating Mrs. Michener in the way some said he did, I would surely have killed him.

Why, if I had such a potentially violent nature and such a motley background, did I escape a life of rebellion and perhaps even crime? Various factors civilized me. Among them were the three women who raised me who were paragons and together compensated for the lack of any man in my life.

Aunt Laura was a magnificent teacher in the tempestuous Detroit school system, a champion of uneducated blacks who were flocking to that industrial town. Gallant, pugnacious where human rights were concerned, and militantly active into her eighties as a strict disciplinarian, she was beloved wherever she taught and recognized as a great woman.

Aunt Hannah was a shy, retiring woman who served a huge area of Bucks County as the public nurse. Tireless, she was available to all at all hours of the night and pushed her beat-up Ford down back roads to the lonely farmhouses. She was an angel of both mercy and common sense, and doctors treasured her because she seemed to save the lives of more babies and elders than they did.

Mabel Michener was, of course, the most important of the trio. As a young woman at the death of her mother she had surrendered her own life to the rearing and educating of five siblings. She was the Mother Earth of fable, and with no assistance other than what her younger sisters could provide, she brought love and stability to the children who fell under her care and continued doing this into her seventies.

I was raised in an atmosphere of love, responsibility and service, but what I remember most is the constant laughter in my home. We laughed at our own follies, chuckled at the foolishness of others, mocked the nonsense of our elected officials, and relished the jokes that circulated in our small town. Despite the anguish we suffered at times, we did not live tragic lives; laughter, not tears, surrounded me.

I remember one Christmas Day when our doorbell rang incessantly: grateful villagers bringing presents to Aunt Hannah, who had nursed them back to health, and older children returning to thank Mabel for having given them a loving home when no other homes were available. I vowed that day to live my life the way the three sisters had lived theirs, not that of others in town whose selfishness appalled me, and each Christmas throughout the remainder of my life I would renew that pledge.

But a growing boy needs contact with men, or even better, with a man, and Doylestown almost magically provided such a one in the person of George Murray, a placid, uneducated, unmarried man in his late forties who worked as a roofer, earning a modest salary, which he spent on the underprivileged boys of our community. He personally ran the local branch of Boys' Brigade, a group once strong nationally but now in retreat before the much more alluring and socially acceptable Boy Scouts. This Brigade was a paramilitary outfit with wooden guns, bugles, uniforms and marching formations. It was affiliated in each community with some Protestant church, in our case the Presbyterian, but boys of all denominations were welcomed.

Murray rented a kind of gymnasium where Friday-night drills were held and where during the rest of the week his boys played basketball. It was there I honed the skills that would serve me well in later years, but what we enjoyed most was the summer camp he ran on the banks of the Delaware River some miles to the east. There we whipped ourselves into condition, playing rugged games, canoeing up and down the river and, best of all, riding the coal barges that brought anthracite out of the Pennsylvania mining regions to markets in Philadelphia. Heavily laden, they drifted down a beautiful canal running beside the river and were hauled back north by mules that trod the towpath. It was on those barges that I acquired my love for water travel.

Murray amused us by his Sunday sermons in which he frequently said: 'In the Bible Jesus says . . .' What caused merriment was that he pronounced *says* as *saze* and other words in equally curious ways. (As I type this I wonder for the first time why *says* should not be pronounced to rhyme with *ways* and *days.*)

In his quiet, almost Christ-like insistence on boys living a good life, Murray saved many of us, especially those without fathers, but just as I left his care, the Boy Scout movement moved into our community with explosive force. All the better families who had ignored the lowly Brigade now placed their sons in the Scouts and provided huge endowments, while Murray with his roofer's pittance was forgotten.

But today, three quarters of a century later, scores of aging men in my hometown still meet each spring to pay tribute to this man who, by the force of his quiet character, rescued so many of them. In most years my peripatetic life prevents me from attending these reunions, but I send in my dues, because the debt I owe that good man can never be discharged.

The third factor in disciplining my rebellious and contentious nature was the bigger boys I kept running into. They were tougher than I, quicker on their feet, and abler with their fists. After absorbing fearful punishment, I concluded that since I had not the equipment to be a bully boy, I would accomplish more with mouth shut than open.

The consequence was that at thirteen and fourteen, when I was about to begin that life of impetuous travel on the road and the near-criminal activities at the amusement park, I could not think of myself as the cockiest kid on the block; instead I carried with me the memory of a meaningful home, a fatherly roofer who had taught me what 'Jesus saze.'

.   .   .

Having escaped the personal degradation or even criminality that could have been the consequences of my deprived childhood, I have been driven in later years to reflect on the plight of the average black boy in modern American society. Raised with no man in the family, often unable to determine who his father is, rejected by white society, demeaned by almost every agency of government and cheated by his teachers, who routinely pass him along instead of trying to teach him, he is the outcast of our society, doomed from birth.

I have, understandably, compared his lot with my own and tried to explain why I, as a fatherless boy in a household headed by an unmarried woman, could make my way in American life while the black boy of comparable character and skills cannot. The answer seems simple. All the black boy needs is a mother like Mrs. Michener, who has the moral support of her brothers and the assistance of her sisters, all of whom have good jobs; the support of her church; the moral support of his entire community; the counsel of older men who tell him: 'Get out of this pool room and stay out!'; the ennobling aid of an inspired friend to the young like George Murray; instruction from dedicated teachers who insist that he learn; and a fees-paid scholarship to a great college like Swarthmore.

The unceasing support that I encountered is not available to the black boy, and the mistreatment he suffers is one of our national disgraces, which, if continued, will do irreparable damage to the country itself. The tragedy gnaws at me, for whereas I had the Boys' Brigade, the black boy has a gang. I had Coach Grady, who preached: 'Don't eat greasy foods'; he has the man in the corner saying: 'Here, kid. Try this new one, crack.' And while my opportunity of going to college was backed by that good night job at the hotel, he can find no work of any kind that can support him.

I am appalled at the difference, at the waste of human talent. Of course, every boy is better off if he grows up in a family where a wage-earner father is present, but if that is not possible, society ought to help mothers provide constructive alternatives. The black boy faces mainly destructive options, and my heart grieves for him.

Now, toward the end of a long and lively run, how do I see myself as a man and a writer? I see myself as a standard American with a usable I.Q. and a strong education drilled into me by dedicated professors. Throughout my life I have been able to work more diligently than most and to keep my wits about me. I was deficient in the standard manifestations of ambition and once said, accurately: 'I've been content if I could reach Friday in one piece. And I never start worrying again till Monday.' I do not think of myself as a romantic dreamer; my life has been too hard for that indulgence. But when I have suffered my physical setbacks I have muttered a saying I heard once but whose source I have not been able to identify: 'I will lay me down and bleed awhile, then rise and fight again.' I have been persistent.

But I have never set goals for myself save one: I insist on being a reliable citizen who works to help society hold itself together.

Viewing myself as a writer, let me first comment briefly and in good humor about how critics see me. Academic critics dismiss me completely because, like Beckmesser in *Die Meistersinger,* they have fairly rigid rules as to what constitutes literature and it does not include what I write. I am sorry, because I think they are wrong, and so do many readers.

Literary critics have a difficult time with me. They sometimes condemn me for writing for money, but as I demonstrated in the preceding section, that is patently absurd. Others say that I direct my writing only to middle-brow or even lower tastes, but two recent studies have disproved that. In the first, a national magazine interrogated a large sampling of the well-educated mature men who run the nation's largest industries as to their reading habits, and while many said honestly that they were too busy to read anything but reports relating to their jobs, many others said they knew they ought to keep reading and when they found time they habitually read a book by Michener because they knew it would be readable and reward them with knowledge of value. The second inquiry was directed to the young military men in training to be fighter pilots and they said: 'Only Saint-Exupéry and Michener. Those two knew what flying was,' and I thought: If a writer can keep the old lions and the young tigers with him, he must know something about narration.

Other critics intimate that no one should bother with my books because they are not written in approved styles, but the books continue to live and not only at home. The Englishman in charge of Britain's excellent program by which the government collects data on reading tastes in public libraries throughout the nation and then pays cash awards to the authors of the books taken out most frequently did me the honor of sending me a report of what the British system would have paid me had they paid similar fees to foreign authors (which they should not). My books stood close to the top of the list for foreign authors and quite high even among local writers. The same would be true, I judge,

for certain of my books, not all of them by any means, in countries like
the Netherlands and Germany.

Typical criticism of my work was well voiced recently by Chauncey
Mabe, books columnist of the Fort Lauderdale, Florida, *News Sun-
Sentinel:*

> Sometime in the late 60's or early 70's James Michener ceased
> to be a serious writer, at least in the literary sense and became
> something else—an industry, his typewriter a factory upon
> which, with two fingers pecking, he took history and processed
> it into best-selling novels that could also be used as door-stops
> and further processed into movies or, better yet, TV miniseries.

The rest of the review was well phrased, witty and laced with legitimate
content, but in the covering letter Mabe illustrated the ambivalence that
some critics feel about me: 'While I do not think you are a great writer,
I see you as a great American whose ideals and whose life provide one
of the few examples worthy of admiration in our troubled age.'

Christopher Lehmann-Haupt, of *The New York Times,* makes somewhat the same point as Mabe in his review: 'Rice Krispies happens to
be one of my favorite junk foods, just as I regard Michener as superior
among junk writers.' That is a clever juxtaposition of ideas, to which I
take no offense, for it is an honest opinion amusingly delivered, but I
suspect that some of my readers will be surprised to learn that the books
that have meant so much to them are only junk.

A writer is well advised never to respond to negative criticism, a tenet
that was hammered into me by prudent editors and publicists when I
worked at Macmillan and by several grizzled veterans of the writing
wars when I joined their ranks. The rules were laid down by my trusted
mentor Kahler: 'The Old and New Testaments regarding criticism:
"Never complain. Never explain. Never disdain." To complain makes
you look petty and juvenile. Make sure that your publisher sends you
a check for whatever you've honestly earned, and keep your mouth shut.
Put your full attention on the next job, because to complain is fruitless.
And don't try to explain. If you've spent three hundred pages putting
your thoughts down and haven't succeeded, what makes you think you
can clarify them in a one-page letter? Anyway, the editor will cut you
to a quarter page. And as for disdaining your critics, remember, never
make a joke at their expense. They're probably brighter than you, have
thought more deeply about literature, and could probably write a
damned sight better than you if they put their minds to it. If you fight

with such a talented man you will lose. Besides being superior to you in every way, he will have that big, forty-eight-page newspaper in which to blast you for the next six months.'

I read far more criticism than the average citizen: what movies are best, what shows to go to, what music is worth buying in compact disk, what restaurants are worth the effort of getting a table. I prize the opinions of critics and am guided by their recommendations, but I never, never read criticisms of my own work. I summarize the problem this way: 'Critics are invaluable in advising me how to spend my money. They are not qualified to tell me how to spend my talent.'

At one period in my life numerous critics, when writing of other writers, were fond of comparing them with me, and always the other fellow came off best: 'He is a lot better storyteller than Michener,' or 'His novel moves more honestly than a Michener.' For a while I kept a list of such comparisons because I wanted to know what happened to all those people who were so much better than me,* but it came to naught because most of them were never heard from again, and those that were had only feeble lasting power.

Obedient to Rule Three of the professional writer's code, I have never tried to rebut any critic, and in general I had no cause to, because so many greeted my books with an enthusiasm that enabled publishers to garner as many encomiums as they had space for in their paperback editions and no critic, so far as I can remember, ever treated me unfairly. I know that those who did not like what I had written, or the style I used, usually had ample quotations to back their judgments, but, to repeat a solemn fact, for the past eighteen or twenty years I have refused to read even one review of anything I have written. (The Mabe review arrived in a personal letter and I had to read the first paragraph to know what it was about.) I find praise distasteful, harsh criticism irrelevant; I am not saying that I ignore criticism or denigrate it—I just don't read it. My wife does and chortles over good notices, moans over bad ones, but down the long years of any productive life what critics say has only limited relevance to a career, because it will all be reevaluated some decades hence.

It would ill behoove me to speak poorly of critics, since two played major roles in my writing life. When my first book was published, Orville Prescott of *The New York Times* wrote a glowing comment, one

---

*I know that the proper pronoun in this usage is *than I was,* but like many other contemporary writers I find that cumbersome. We use *me* in conversation in our books, and I am testing it in nonconversational situations.

of his most enthusiastic, in which he predicted that I was a writer from whom more might be heard; and John Mason Brown, that gallant, polished master of the lecture circuit, spent an entire season reading excerpts from my first book, thus bringing me to the attention of thousands of people who were interested in books and bought them. My debt to those two experts is incalculable, and in their lifetimes I told them so.

Critics have problems, too, and here are examples to illustrate the point. When *The Drifters* was published, one man of considerable erudition wrote: 'Mr. Michener absentmindedly shifts the point of view in his narration in each of his first three chapters, forgetting that many of his readers will remember Henry James' dictum that a consistent point of view is everything.' He was correct in his facts; my point of view did shift in a most un-Jamesian riot, but what he did not know was that over a period of some months the publisher and I had studied the problem in prolonged discussions to see if my daring plan would work: to have the narrator slowly reveal himself after two episodes in which he was only peripherally involved. I liked the idea, one of my editors did not, and obviously the critic didn't either, and maybe he was right. But to assume that it was through careless oversight was quite wrong. The presence of superior knowledge in the critic's mind had tempted him, not the writer, into error.

Another critic who got himself into trouble because he knew too much rather than too little was the one who included in his review of *Caravans* the observation: 'Apparently Mr. Michener never looked at a map of Afghanistan, for if he had he would have seen that it has no seacoast and therefore no navy. So there could be no naval attaché in the American Embassy and his story falls apart.' What this able gentleman could not know was that the appearance of the naval attaché was the result of two weeks of difficult discussion back and forth which was resolved only by the brilliant suggestion of a high-priced libel lawyer. This was what happened. In the novel I experimented with having my faintly unpleasant embassy officer hold five or six different offices, but the real ones were too libelous and the imaginary ones too clearly fake; it was then that the lawyer said: 'Let me see the map,' and we were saved by giving Afghanistan not only a navy but also a naval attaché who was free to behave as I wished. The critic was right to condemn me for an error, but he should at the same time have commended the lawyer for having helped us avoid a lawsuit.

The problem of libel is one that faces all writers, and it can best be illustrated by what happened in my novel *Space* when it was imperative that I have the fictional junior senator of some state play the role that a real senior senator in a real state had played. Good idea, but when you're working in a known time period when there was a known junior senator from that state holding the office, and you have your man acting up, the real senator can rightly claim that whatever you say about your fictional character has to represent him; his claim for damages would be valid on the face of it, and lawyers know this. So they advise writers to create a fictional state—in *Space* I chose the State of Franklin— which gave me an imaginary junior senator who could misbehave as either he or the author wished. A lot of lawsuits are avoided by such a device.

Sometimes critics are devastatingly right. In *The Bridges at Toko-Ri* I have my hero flying a jet fighter and creating a wash with his propeller. One critic, a pilot himself, wrote: 'Miraculous! I wish Mr. Michener had explained how he did it.' I spent one afternoon trying to devise an answer but gave up; jet fighters don't have propellers. But if I feel honor-bound never to quarrel with a critic, my wife is not so constrained, and if anyone bad-mouths one of my books she makes a little wax effigy of him and attacks it with red-hot needles. I can tell you that certain critics are walking about in far more peril than they realize.*

I sometimes wonder when I read what even knowledgeable people say about writers and writing if they have any conception of what the life of a writer is like, especially if his or her books achieve wide circulation in many languages. What they don't know might include: a visit to the dentist when people from six surrounding offices come with their books to be signed; the letters that arrive daily thanking you for books that changed the letter-writers' lives; the startling experience of walking to the rear of an airplane to exercise your bad legs and finding six or seven people reading your novels, and often ones published a quarter of a century ago; the warming contact with people who love books and who are endeavoring to entice their children to read, too, by testing them with one of yours; and the knock on the door from a group of neighbors: 'We heard you were in town. We have almost all your books—would you please sign them?'

I know of no finer portrait of a writer than one offered some years ago by a young black aspirant from one of the small Caribbean islands:

*If I never read criticism, how did I learn about the three just cited? My publisher asked me how I had made such embarrassing errors.

'When I finally reached New York City my heart expanded and in sheer joy I cried: "To think that I am in the same town with James Baldwin and that when I turn the next corner I might meet him." '

Sometimes we catch a better portrait of a writer when we see him obliquely, as through the letters from strangers who seek contact with him. Critics have sometimes made jokes about the length of my books, as if that were a detriment, but every month throughout the year I receive letters complaining that the novels were too short; they wanted more, and I have supposed that this was because I had been so patient in building the locations of my stories and so studious in peopling them with characters who mattered that the readers were loath to bid both place and people farewell. This has been borne out by the surprising number who have said the same thing, year after year: 'When I realized that the book was coming to an end, I was so sorry to leave it that I began to ration myself, only so many pages a day, and it was painful to see those pages stop.'

I receive about fifty letters a year begging me to write about the correspondent's home state or country on the theory: 'If you make rural Nebraska come alive so beautifully in *Centennial,* think what you could do with Minnesota!' All corners of the nation have been represented in these suggestions but none with the frequency with which the citizens of California press their claims, and I more than most know that I would have found excellent material in that majestic land, but I have not had the courage to tell the writers that years ago I intended moving to California, but my wife refused to accompany me back to a state which she too loves but which had treated her so savagely in 1941 during World War II: 'Soldiers came to the little store my mother ran south of Los Angeles and said: "All Japanese are traitors! Lock them up!" and our property was taken from us without compensation. We were thrown into the horse stables at Santa Anita racetrack, and then into concentration camps, American style. I have no hostility toward California—it's a wonderful state—but I could not bear to go back to where we were treated so unfairly.'

I have constantly received suggestions that I work in some foreign land that merits attention, and certain foreign governments have invited me, sometimes with tempting inducements, to work in their countries. Every suggestion has been intellectually defensible in that I had already done much work in that particular area. The rationale has been: 'If you could make Poland so interesting with so little to work upon, think what you could do for us!' But the most telling invitation came from a Turkish diplomat who visited me when I was working in Israel. He said: 'It is quite painful, Mr. Michener, to be a Turkish intellectual and realize that when you go to Paris to address an international group and stand before the audience, not one person in that well-educated group has ever read any book about Turkey except *The Forty Days of Musa Dagh.* Come and do for us what you did for Israel.'

The correspondence that has meant most to me has been with great scholars in various countries who write to me about something I have said regarding their fields, and often they tell me further things I did not know when I wrote but should have. They form a network of active minds throughout the world, and when, as sometimes happens, they point to errors in what I have said or important aspects that I have overlooked, I feel ashamed at having let them down.

In 1968 I was in Venezuela as a cultural ambassador to the university in Caracas, but the Communist student body threatened to shoot me if I stepped on campus, so I was whisked far west to Maracaibo to address students there. My speech, which I had carefully prepared, was to have been delivered at eleven in the morning, but at ten the local Communists burned down the assembly hall, and for the rest of that eventful day my wife and I were spirited about the city from one safe hiding place to another. When night fell we were hustled to a forbidding dock on the shore of Lake Maracaibo, where a small boat waited to ferry us to the eastern shore. It was a dramatic ride—when the moon appeared we could see above us, rising from the middle of the lake, the derricks of great oil wells.

When the radio told of my seeking refuge at the headquarters of an oil-drilling company, in succeeding days some hundred people streamed in from as far as a hundred miles away with copies of my books to ask for autographs. Most, of course, were American oilfield workers stationed in remote areas where books were essential for sanity, and mine were there perhaps because they were so long and gave such good return for their cost. But a surprising number were Venezuelans who had bought the books because their North American co-workers had recommended them as a good way to learn English, others were ordinary citizens of half a dozen different nationalities, and as in all countries wherever I go, a few were Hungarians whom I had led to safety across the bridge at Andau. Every person whose book I signed in that informal literary festival had a special story, and taken together they explained something about books that even professionals connected with the industry forget: books are bridges between people, and when the author is respected as someone who has made a valued contribution to one's life, a journey of a hundred miles from a jungle station in Venezuela to an oil field near Maracaibo is not considered excessive. It took me a long time to sign those books, because I wanted to hear the story of everyone who stood before my writing desk.

More dramatic in some ways was the day in Sheridan, Wyoming, when at ten in the morning I learned that a plane I had expected would not arrive and that I would have to stay where I was. The town librarian, hearing of my plight, asked whether I would meet that evening with a few local people who liked books, and when I agreed, she got on the telephone and radio to alert people in distant towns that I would be in her library that night at seven. Free from responsibilities till then, I spent the afternoon visiting the Little Bighorn to see where General Custer had led his cavalry into disaster, and when we returned after sunset we found the library absolutely jammed with families that had driven tremendous distances in response to the radio messages in their little towns announcing the improvised meeting. Carloads of enthusiasts had driven down from Billings, 128 miles away; others had come two by two from remote settlements; and a surprising number had brought their children to share in an experience that would not often be repeated. It was an amazing audience, because anyone who was present was there because he or she liked books, and as always at such occasions we talked not only about my books but about books in general: Which is most important, characters, theme or plot? How difficult would it be for a young person in Billings to find a New York publisher? Does a writer have to have a big staff to do research? Is there still a market for children's books? Do you go to Hollywood when they make a picture from one of your stories? Is the writer obligated to provide a psychological profile of each character? The meeting lasted two hours, and for an excited few it could have continued till dawn.

There remains a major mystery about my selection of subjects. Why, if I had such a deprived childhood, and such a dramatic adolescence, with hitchhiking trips up and down the continent and work in the amusement park, followed by the grave dislocation about my parentage, my adventures with radical ideas in Europe and then two painful divorces, why have I not treated that darker kind of material in my novels and how can I possibly be what so many have called me, the incorrigible optimist?

There are two answers to the question. First, looking at the way in which good luck seemed determined to seek me out, with one scholarship after another, a series of good jobs plus a Pulitzer for my first book and a subsequent glorious Broadway musical, and with one best-seller after another, who should be optimistic if not I? Second, if I survived three major airplane crashes, revolutions and several major health problems, why would I not conclude that I was being kept alive in order to tackle some challenging job?

When I was fifteen, hiking westward from Detroit with thirty-five cents in my pockets and a thousand miles from home, I was convinced that I would complete my journey safely, for I was as optimistic then with untested life before me as I was at sixty with so many challenges behind me. It seems that I was born to smile at the world, and such men do not write tragedies.

I have consistently dealt with several themes: Man as a six-decade actor in the unbroken chain of human experiences. Man as a resident of a physical world that he shares with all other living creatures and forms. Man as an economic being who is forced to earn a living. Man as a brother to all other men. Man as a questioning human being who strives to understand his relationship to an unknown spiritual world. And man as an arrogant tyrant who loves to victimize the helpless. This somewhat restricted focus has meant that I have never dealt with nor desired to deal with some of the great themes that have been the mainstays of other writers: Man as an essentially tragic figure. Man as the victim of hubris. Man in violent personal and social revolution against his society. Man as a vulnerable figure losing control over his mental and emotional powers. And man as totally confused in his relations to the opposite sex. If I were a young writer today starting over, I would focus my attention on the changing relationships between the sexes; despite my age I am fascinated by this and the other subjects but do not feel myself qualified to write about them.

If I have consciously cut myself off from many of the most rewarding literary subjects and forms, what accounts for the fact that my books remain so vigorously in print so long after original publication? It stems, I suppose, from my ability to take an ordinary subject—the most ordinary in the world like a dust storm or a wild bird defending its young on the tundra—and give it a vivid reality that engages the reader's interest. I can take the most insignificant piece of land and people it with ordinary citizens undergoing ordinary experiences and command attention. I can tell the story of a mound of dirt in Israel and illuminate an entire religion. And I can go to the very depths of the Pacific and explain how tiny corals can build great islands and even greater volcanoes and make readers who originally had no conceivable interest in such arcane material send me hundreds of letters telling me that this was one of the most moving bits of writing they had ever read. In short, I can take ordinary things and ordinary people and make them extraordinary, and I have proved it repeatedly.

Not long ago a scholar who was primarily interested in current events said in introducing me: 'There are many areas in the world of riveting interest. Afghanistan stands at the center of world attention. So does Poland, with its remarkable semirevolution. The Near East is always in ferment, and South Africa has yet to find a resolution to its problems. We are reassured by Japan's spectacular recovery from her misguided war and Spain's return from dictatorship. The tragedy in space commands our attention. Amazing things are happening in Hungary. Michener wrote full-length books about all of these areas long before they emerged into headlines.' I was not clairvoyant; I was merely a man whose education and background had alerted him to history's inevitables. In every case cited by the scholar I had gone to the areas long in advance of their explosion into headlines, and I did so because I knew they must sooner or later merit world attention. I did the same when I perceived that Hawaii must soon become a state, when I guessed that Spain was about to escape from its long imprisonment under dictatorship, and that Russia and the United States must meet in friendship in the Arctic while Cuba and our nation must do the same in the Caribbean. I gambled long years of my life in my belief that sensible readers would want to know about these peoples, cultures and problems. Was the commitment worth the effort?

As I entered my seventies and began to speculate on whether I had succeeded or failed, an event occurred that threw some light on the matter. On a day of blizzards in January 1977 President Ford, upon advice of his counselors, invited me to the White House, where he awarded me our nation's highest civilian honor, the Medal of Freedom, in recognition of various civic contributions.

A few evenings later my wife and I dined with the British ambassador, who excited Mari by saying: 'What happened in the White House the other day is your American equivalent to our Queen's honors list announced each New Year's. In our country it would mean that your husband is now Sir James and you are Lady Mari.' While she was preening in her new title another Englishman really stunned her: 'In such lists, now and then, the Queen may spot a knight to whom she will give the next higher rank, and several times it has fallen to artist types like Laurence, Lord Olivier or Alfred, Lord Tennyson. One of your men heard that your husband stood high on the list, so if you wish you can make believe he's now James, Lord Michener.'

'And what would my title be?' Mari asked, and he replied: 'Still Lady Mari. With women that covers everything from the wife of a knight to a baron,' and she said: 'Discrimination at its worst,' and I thought: 'Dreams of glory.'

I have always wanted the areas, nations and states about which I have written to receive my books dispassionately and to acknowledge that I had written with fairness if not total accuracy, but that has rarely happened. Hungary, Spain and South Africa banned my books; Indonesian and Afghan officials threatened to beat me up if I ever again set foot in their territories; Israel, Hawaii and Texas abused my work. But I was especially grieved when Poland, a land in which I had toiled with diligence and affection, not only banned my novel but also let it be known that I would not be allowed back in the country. I must admit, however, that my castigation of Communist rule in Poland did give its leaders ample cause to reject me. But in late 1988, when the spirit of *glasnost* was emanating from the Soviet Union, I received cryptic word that I would be granted a visa if I wished to return to renew my acquaintance with the brave members of the writers' union I had known in the old days.

Eager to see a land I loved, I slipped into Warsaw, and on my second night in the city it was arranged that I would meet the writers. It was a snowy, sleety night, the kind I remembered well as we drove to the meeting hall, but as we approached it I thought: Mistake. This has got to be Warsaw Castle. But before I could ask what was happening I was whisked inside, down corridors and into a meeting room.

It was not the writers' union hall. It was the grand ballroom of the castle, a great gold-and-silver reception hall filled with flowers and some five hundred leading Polish artists and government officials. Before I could catch my breath, Mieczyslaw Rakowski, the prime minister of the country, with the prior approval of General Jaruzelski, the Communist dictator who had banned the book, came forward, embraced me and pinned on my chest the highest medal that Poland can award a citizen. Later I was told: 'We still don't like certain passages in your book, but we realize that people throughout the world are reading about our nation in a way they never did before. You have proved you were an honest friend.'

Writers should write what they feel has to be written and trust that with the passing years those who did not like the book originally will see that *sub specie aeternitatis* it was a truthful effort. Writers can afford to wait. I treasure my Polish medal.

. . .

In the summer of 1989, when this manuscript was completed, I had an experience that demonstrated how groups of citizens will sometimes react to writing that has treated them with respect. On the sailing ship *Wind Song* I visited the remote Marquesas Islands, haunt of Melville and Gauguin, and the captain, without telling me, wired ahead to inform the people of Bora Bora that at sunrise on the morrow he would bring me to visit them.

Eager to see again the island on which I'd had such dreamlike experiences during World War II, I was on deck in predawn darkness to see the magnificent volcano rise from the waves. When we slipped into the flawless lagoon I was astounded to see a flotilla of eleven ancient canoes approaching us, each with flowers, fruit and musicians and manned by half-naked warriors in traditional costume as in the old days.

Then from the very large lead canoe, which contained a dozen men and an empty throne came via the megaphone the deep-throated announcement: 'James Michener! Come home to your island!' Sailors led me down an improvised gangway and into the ceremonial canoe, where I was placed upon the throne, my wife beside me. Flowered leis were heaped around my neck till I could scarcely see, music played, men cheered, and in this stately manner I approached the island on which I had worked so intimately with the Polynesians I had grown to love.

Waiting on shore were hundreds of people, a band, dancers, a score of flower women laden with leis, and many of the people I had known in the war days, older now but still stately in bearing.

All that day, as I moved about the island from one celebration to the next, islanders came to tell me: 'You were good to us in uniform but even better in your books. You wrote of us as we are, and the entire island wants to celebrate your return.'

Alas, I could not determine where our vast naval establishment had been; the buildings had vanished, tropical plants had taken over. However I did meet several Bora Borans in their mid-forties who let me know that their fathers had been American sailors, but I could not detect the Caucasian strain in their appearance. I also met two vahines, now in their late sixties, who had attended with me those numerous showings of *Flying Down to Rio*, and one showed me where the huge movie theater had been. I remembered her and her sailor, but not the theater's location.

Much later, when I had returned to the States, friends on the island sent me a copy of an article celebrating that day of remembrance: 'He was greeted by a magnificent escort of authentic pirogues, double pirogues, pirogues under sail, and simple pirogues, all decorated with the crowns, flowers and fruits of our island. The people of Bora Bora accorded him a reception traditionally reserved for a head of state.' They did so because in war I had treated their island with dignity, in peace I had written of it with affection, and it was appropriate that when I entered the lagoon that morning the man with the megaphone should have welcomed me home.

I would hope there might be other spots, widely scattered, to which I could return to similar receptions.

How would I like to be remembered? Because I am not a true Michener, I have no desire to have that name affixed to anything, and I have frequently perplexed well-wishers by sticking to this resolve. But when friends wanted to name fine libraries after me I had to consent, because such institutions are a noble symbol of the writer's trade and I feel honored by the association. The same has happened with art museums, and one of the acts about which I am proudest is that I helped transform our old jail in Doylestown into a center for the arts. I am more pleased, however, that three great universities now have training programs for young writers that I either started or assisted in starting and I find quiet pleasure in knowing that three hotels in which I spent many fruitful hours now have rooms bearing my name: Aggie Grey's in Samoa; historic Raffles in Singapore; and the one judged by many to be the best in the world, the Oriental in Bangkok. In the next century young travelers who aspire to be writers will hear someone explain: 'Years ago an American much like you who occupied this room fell in love with our land and heard the stories he later put into a book,'* and that might give them encouragement.

But mostly I would want to be remembered by that row of solid books that rest on library shelves throughout the world.

During my years as a writer I have never once defended either myself or my books when criticism was lodged against me. But I would like to say now that I am enormously proud of that long shelf of books that bear my name, and consider myself one of the ablest storytellers of my

*The Oriental has a cluster of elegant suites honoring writers who worked there, the three others: Joseph Conrad, Somerset Maugham, Noël Coward.

generation. Unobtrusively I have lived by my own rules, obedient to my own purposes. I have written a series of books which, without bizarre excesses, wild sex or savage violence, have captured the minds and loyalties of many readers who have found them richly rewarding. Within the guidelines I developed for myself and with an unruffled equanimity, I have dedicated myself to the task of writing books the way I want them to be; the miracle is that in all countries readers have ringingly endorsed what I have produced. The explanation must be that they trusted me to write of important matters in a manner that promised both delight and instruction. The director of one of the world's premier libraries said the other day: 'You've been educator to the world.'

I have been more: a working resident of that world, one who has labored to describe it with understanding and affection and share it with others. With my pen I have engraved warrants of citizenship in the most remote corners, for truly the world has been my home.

Index

At several points in this account Mr. Michener has referred to the existence of documentation 'among my papers.' Just as he was beginning his writing career the Library of Congress invited him to deposit with it his papers, and since 1946 he has placed there all business records of an active career, these to be made available at his death.

The more interesting portion is a running account providing an intimate view of how one writer reacted to current matters from 1946 onward. These papers will become available twenty-five years after his death.

A virtue of this record is that entries have been bundled up and mailed off to the Library at frequent intervals, so that editing, polishing comments for effect, or second guessing become impossible. At last count several score such packages have been deposited.

THE EDITORS